P9-DFM-815

SCRIBNER'S POPULAR RELIGIOUS SERIES

VOLUMES NOW READY

St. Paul's Conception of Christianity. By Prof. A. B. Bruce, D.D.

The Place of Christ in Modern Theology. By Prof. Rev. A. M. Fairbairn, M.A., D.D.

The Beginnings of Christianity. By Prof. George P. Fisher, D.D.

The Unity of the Book of Genesis. By Prof. William H. Green, D.D., LL.D.

The Life of Martin Luther. By Julius Kostlin.

What is the Bible? By Prof. George T. Ladd, D.D.

The Problem of the Old Testament. By Prof. James Orr, D.D.

The Theory of Preaching. By Prof. Austin Phelps, D.D.

The Evidence of Christian Experience. By Prof. Louis F. Stearns, D.D.

The Pauline Theology. By Prof. George B. Stevens, Ph.D., D.D.

Price 90 *cents each net. Postage* 10 *cents per copy additional.*

THE BROSS PRIZE . . . 1905

THE PROBLEM OF THE OLD TESTAMENT

CONSIDERED WITH REFERENCE TO RECENT CRITICISM

BY

JAMES ORR, D.D.

PROFESSOR OF APOLOGETICS AND SYSTEMATIC THEOLOGY
UNITED FREE CHURCH COLLEGE, GLASGOW

" Nubecula est, quae cito evanescet."

221·6^{c. 2}

OR

8302

Copy 2

CHARLES SCRIBNER'S SONS
NEW YORK 1911

TO

THE PRESIDENT, TRUSTEES, AND FACULTY

OF

LAKE FOREST COLLEGE

This Volume is Gratefully Dedicated

BY

THE AUTHOR

THE BROSS FOUNDATION

In 1879, the late William Bross of Chicago, lieutenant-governor of Illinois in 1866–1870, desiring to make some memorial of his son, Nathaniel Bross, who had died in 1856, entered into an agreement with the "Trustees of Lake Forest University," whereby there was finally transferred to the said Trustees the sum of Forty Thousand Dollars, the income of which was to accumulate in perpetuity for successive periods of ten years, at compound interest, the accumulations of one decade to be spent in the following decade, for the purpose of stimulating the production of the best books or treatises "*on the connection, relation, and mutual bearing of any practical science, or history of our race, or the facts in any department of knowledge, with and upon the Christian Religion.*"

In his deed of gift the founder had in view "*the religion of the Bible, composed of the Old and New Testaments of our Lord and Saviour, Jesus Christ, as commonly received in the Presbyterian and other evangelical churches.*" His object was "*to call out the best efforts of the highest talent and the ripest scholarship of the world, to illustrate from science, or any department of knowledge, and to demonstrate, the divine origin and authority of the Christian Scriptures; and, further, to show how both Science and Revelation coincide, and to prove the existence, the providence, or any or all of the attributes of the one living and true God, infinite, eternal, and unchangeable in His being, wisdom, power, holiness, justice, goodness and truth.*"

At the close of the Trust Agreement, the donor expressed the hope that, by means of this fund, the various authors might, "*every ten years, post up the science of the world and show how it illustrates the truth of the Bible, and the existence of God,*" and that thereby "*the gospel of our blessed Saviour, Jesus Christ, and the glories of His sacrifice and plan of salvation,*" might be preached "*to the end of time.*"

The books or treatises procured by either of the methods described below are to be published as volumes of what is to be known as "The Bross Library."

The gift thus contemplated in the original agreement of 1879 was finally consummated in 1890. The first decade of the accumulations of interest having closed in 1900, the Trustees of the Bross Fund began at that time the administration of this important trust.

The Trust Agreement prescribes two methods by which the production of books of the above-mentioned character is to be stimulated: —

A. The Trustees of the Bross Fund are empowered to select able scholars, from time to time, to prepare books, upon some theme within the terms of the Trust Agreement, that would "illustrate" or "demonstrate" the Christian Religion, or *any* phase of it, to the times in which we live.

Ordinarily, the authors of these books are requested to deliver the substance of such books in the form of lectures before Lake Forest College, and any of the general public who may desire to attend them, such courses to be known as The Bross Lectures.

In pursuance of the first method, two writers have already been specially appointed: —

(1) The Reverend President Francis Landey Patton, D.D., LL.D., of the Princeton Theological Seminary, whose lectures on "Obligatory Morality," delivered in Lake Forest in May, 1903, are being revised and enlarged by the author and will be published in due time by the Trustees of the Bross Fund;

(2) The Reverend Professor Marcus Dods, D.D., of New College, Edinburgh, whose lectures on "The Bible: Its Origin and Nature," delivered in May, 1904, have already been published as a volume of the Bross Library.

B. The second method for securing books for the Bross Library is as follows : —

One or more premiums or prizes are to be offered during each decade, the competition for which was to be thrown open to " *the scientific men, the Christian philosophers and historians of all nations.*"

Accordingly, in 1902, a prize of Six Thousand Dollars ($6,000) was offered for the best book fulfilling any of the purposes described in the foregoing extracts from the Trust Agreement, the manuscripts to be presented on or before June 1, 1905.

The following were appointed a Committee of Judges to make the award : the Reverend George Trumbull Ladd, D.D., LL.D., Professor of Moral Philosophy, Yale University; Alexander Thomas Ormond, Ph.D., LL.D., Professor of Philosophy, Princeton University, and the Reverend George Frederick Wright, D.D., LL.D., Professor of the Harmony of Science and Revelation, Oberlin College.

The authorship of the various essays was not known to the judges until after the award was made, the undersigned having been the custodian of the sealed envelopes containing the names of the writers of the respective manuscripts.

The Committee of Judges has unanimously awarded the Bross Prize of 1905 to the essay entitled " The Problem of the Old Testament," which is now issued as Volume III of the Bross Library.

The next Bross prize will be offered about 1915, and will be announced in due time by the Trustees of the Bross Fund.

The Trust Agreement requires that once in every thirty or fifty years (according as the Trustees of the fund may decide at the time) the entire sum of simple interest accumulated during the previous decade is to be offered as a single premium or prize for a competition similar to the one which has just been completed.

RICHARD D. HARLAN,

President of Lake Forest College.

LAKE FOREST, ILLINOIS,
NOVEMBER, 1905.

PREFACE

THE thanks of the author are due, in the first place, to the Trustees of Lake Forest College, and to the adjudicators acting on their behalf, who, in their generosity, have awarded to this book the munificent prize at their disposal from the Bross Fund. It is right, however, to say, that, although the present volume has been so fortunate as to obtain the Bross Prize, it was not for the Bross Prize, or with thought or knowledge of the same, that the book was written. But for a long-standing promise to the English publishers, it is doubtful if it ever would have been written at all. The book was sent to press in the beginning of this year, and the delay in its publication has been due principally to the afterthought of submitting it in proof to the judgment of the Bross Prize arbiters. The author is deeply sensible of the courtesy of the publishers in so readily meeting his wishes in this matter at inconvenience to themselves.

The book in one sense is not new, but represents, as will probably be evident from its perusal, the gathering up of thought, reading, and formation of opinion on its subject, going as far back as the days of the old Colenso and Samuel Davidson controversies, and of the appearance of Graf's work in 1866, when the author's interest in these

xiii

questions was first thoroughly aroused—an interest which
has never since flagged.   Much water had flowed under
the bridge in the interval, and the author entered on the
task of putting his book into shape with many misgivings.
Still, now that the work is done, and apart altogether from
the material reward which has so unexpectedly come to
him, he does not regret having undertaken it. The time
is past when the discussion of Old Testament questions
can be left wholly to professional experts, who represent
one, but only one, of the many points of view necessary to
be taken into account in considering this subject.   The
conclusions of the critics, of whom personally the author
would speak only with respect, force themselves on everyone's attention, and it is a matter, no longer of choice, but
of necessity, to pay regard to their opinions.   Especially
for one engaged in the teaching of theology, in whatever
department, it is absolutely indispensable to possess some
acquaintance with the methods and results of Old Testament study, and to try to come to some understanding with
himself in regard to the theories of Old Testament religion
and literature which he finds prevailing around him.   The
judgment of such an one may not be of the highest value;
but, if it is his own, and has been reached at the cost of
prolonged thought and study, the expression of it, and the
exhibition of the grounds on which it rests, may not be
without help to others working their way through similar
perplexities.

The standpoint of the present book can be readily
understood from a survey of the Table of Contents, or from
reading the sketch of its scope at the close of the first
chapter.   Those who expect to find in it a wholesale
denunciation of critics and of everything that savours of

criticism will be disappointed. The author is not of the opinion that much good is accomplished by the violent and indiscriminating assaults on the critics sometimes indulged in by very excellent men. The case which the critics present must be met in a calm, temperate, and scholarly way, if it is to be dealt with to the satisfaction of thoughtful Christian people. On the other hand, those who come to the book expecting to find in it agreement with the methods and results of the reigning critical schools will probably be not less disappointed. The author has here no option. With the best will in the world to accept whatever new light criticism may have to throw on the structure and meaning of the Old Testament, he has to confess that his study of the critical developments—now for over thirty years—has increasingly convinced him that, while Biblical students are indebted to the critics, and to Old Testament science generally, for valuable help, the Graf-Wellhausen hypothesis now in the ascendant is, neither in its methods nor in its results, entitled to the unqualified confidence often claimed for it. He is persuaded, on the contrary, that it rests on erroneous fundamental principles, is eaten through with subjectivity, and must, if carried out to its logical issues — to which, happily, very many do not carry it — prove subversive of our Christian faith, and of such belief in, and use of, the Bible as alone can meet the needs of the living Church. Only, if this is to be shown, it must, as far as one's knowledge enables him to do it, be done thoroughly, and with due regard for all really critically-ascertained facts.

Being designed specially for an English-reading public, the book is purposely cast in a form as little technical as the nature of the subject permits. Hebrew words and minute philological discussions are, as a rule, avoided, and where English translations of foreign books exist, references are usually made to these. The customary form of the divine name, " Jehovah," is retained ; but in quotations authors have been allowed to use their own various spellings of the name. If, throughout, a seemingly disproportionate space is given to German writers, this is simply due to the fact that at least nine-tenths of the " Higher-Critical " theories now in vogue had their origin and elaboration in Germany, and in Britain and America are largely of the nature of importations. One early learns that, if these theories are to be dealt with satisfactorily, it can only be by going at first hand to the sources—tapping the stream, as it were, at the fountain-head. At the same time the Indexes will show that representative writers of English-speaking countries, of different schools, have by no means been overlooked.

In so immense a field, it is hardly necessary to say that no attempt whatever is made at a complete or exhaustive treatment of Old Testament questions. That would have been impossible in the space, even had the author possessed the knowledge or ability qualifying him to undertake it. Some aspects of the Old Testament—the Wisdom Literature, for example—have had to be left altogether untouched. The idea has been, as far as practicable, to concentrate attention on really crucial points, and to make these the pivots on which the discussion of other questions turns (see Appendix to first chapter). In handling so large a mass of material, and copying and re-copying so many references, it is inevitable that, with the utmost care, slips and mistakes should occur. The author can only hope that these will not prove in any case to be of such magnitude as seriously to affect the main argument.

Since the book went to press in the spring, no small amount of literature has appeared to which it would be interesting to refer. Allusion may here only be made to the appearance of a valuable work by Professor W. Lotz, of Erlangen, entitled *Das Alte Testament und die Wissenschaft*, with which, in parts, the treatment in these pages may be compared. It would be endless to specify articles and pamphlets. Professor James Robertson, of Glasgow, has contributed to the May and June numbers of the periodical *Good Words* two interesting papers on "The Beginnings of Hebrew History and Religion"; and Professor R. D. Wilson, of Princeton, has completed in July and October his valuable articles on "Royal Titles" in the *Princeton Theological Review*. The October article is specially devoted to the statements of Dr. Driver on the use of royal titles in the books of Ezra and Nehemiah. Three papers by Professors Driver and Kirkpatrick on *The Higher Criticism* have been published, aiming at the removal of misconceptions. In his *Biblische Theologie des Alten Testaments* Stade has re-stated his views on the religion of Israel in more systematic form.

With these remarks, the book must be left to its own mission. The author entertains no over-sanguine expectations as to its effect on general conviction, but he is not without hope that it may at least rouse to reflection some who have given too easy an assent to current theories, simply because they are the theories of the hour. He has no wish to be ultra-dogmatic on any point. Time may not justify all his conclusions; but he has the strong persuasion that, when the day for summing-up comes—if

b

ever such **arrives**—the positions into which men's minds will be disposed to settle will be found much nearer those advocated in these pages than they will be to those of the advanced Wellhausen school. The future will show.

The volume, it will be observed, has been amply fitted with Tables of Contents, Indexes, and cross-references in footnotes. These should make the task of consulting its pages comparatively easy, and should lighten somewhat the impression of abstruseness created by certain of its chapters. The author's thanks are specially due to the Rev. J. M. Wilson, B.D., Highbury, London, and to George Hunter, Esq., Glasgow, for valuable aid in the correction of the proofs.

GLASGOW, *October* 1905.

CONTENTS

CHAPTER I

INTRODUCTORY: THE PROBLEM STATED.—Pp. 1-24.

What is the Old Testament?
Problem of the Old Testament: relation to criticism.

CONTENTS

Illustration by contrast : "book-religions."
No unity in ethnic Scriptures (Koran, etc.).
The Bible has an organic character.
Marked by plan, purpose, progress.
Unity grows out of religion and history.

II. FULFILMENT OF THE OLD TESTAMENT IN THE NEW.
The Bible in two divisions.
The second the counterpart and completion of the first.
The "Servant" of Isa. liii.: fulfilment in Christ.
Religion of Israel a religion of hope.
Anticipation of better economy.
The Messianic idea.
New Testament realises hopes and promises of the Old.
This relation inward and vital.

III. TELEOLOGICAL CHARACTER OF THE *HISTORY*.
History dominated by idea of purpose.
Sketch of development—primitive and patriarchal history.
Mosaic and later history.
History viewed retrogressively.
Uniqueness of this.

IV. UNIQUE IDEAS OF THE *RELIGION*.
The uniqueness generally acknowledged.
  1. *Negative* side—absence of features found in other religions
     Magic, nature-superstitions, etc.
  2. *Positive* side—fundamental ideas of Israel's religion.
     (1) Monotheism of religion.
         Peculiar to Israel.
         Opposite tendency in other religions.
         Underlies the *whole* of Old Testament.
     (2) Developing purpose of grace.
         Sin and grace in Scripture.
         The Bible a "history of redemption."
         Found in no other religion.
     (3) Indissoluble relation between religion and morality.
         General relations of religion and morality.
         Religion of Israel *dominated* by this idea.
         God as the Holy One.
         Union of religion and morality in psalms and prophets.
         Such a religion not man-originated.

V. CLAIM TO AN ORIGIN IN REVELATION.
Modern substitution of psychology for revelation.
Biblical point of view—"Thus saith Jehovah."
Revelation of God in act and word.
The Israelite conscious of being possessor and guardian of a special
  revelation.

CHAPTER III

THE OLD TESTAMENT AS AFFECTED BY CRITICISM—I. THE HISTORY : ARGUMENT FROM CRITICAL PREMISES. — *Pp.* 53–81.

CHAPTER IV

CONTENTS

CHAPTER V

CHAPTER VI

**THE OLD TESTAMENT AS AFFECTED BY CRITICISM—II. RE-
LIGION AND INSTITUTIONS: ARK, TABERNACLE, PRIEST-
HOOD, ETC.—*Pp.* 149–190.**

CONTENTS

CHAPTER IX

DIFFICULTIES AND PERPLEXITIES OF THE CRITICAL HYPOTHESIS: THE PRIESTLY WRITING.
I. THE CODE.—*Pp.* 285–329.

CHAPTER X

DIFFICULTIES AND PERPLEXITIES OF THE CRITICAL HYPO-
THESIS: THE PRIESTLY WRITING. II. THE DOCUMENT.—
Pp. 331-377.

CHAPTER XI

ARCHÆOLOGY AND THE OLD TESTAMENT.—*Pp.* 393–430.

PART II

THE PREDICTIVE ELEMENT IN PROPHECY

d

CONTENTS

NOTES TO CHAPTERS

——◆——

CHAPTER I

Introductory: The Problem Stated

"I have been obliged to bestow the greatest amount of labour on a hitherto entirely unworked field, the investigation of the inner constitution of the separate books of the Old Testament by the aid of the Higher Criticism (a new name to no Humanist)."—EICHHORN.

"It is true that the present destructive proceedings in the department of Old Testament criticism, which demand the construction of a new edifice, are quite fitted to confuse consciences and to entangle a weak faith in all kinds of temptation. If, however, we keep fast hold in this labyrinth of the one truth, *Christus vere resurrexit*, we have in our hands Ariadne's thread to lead us out of it."—DELITZSCH.

Wellhausen "has identified himself with that 'so-called criticism' (Ewald's phraseology) which has 'given up Moses and so much that is excellent besides,' and which leads on directly to the contemptuous rejection of the Old Testament, if not also of the New (again, Ewald's phraseology)."—CHEYNE.

"Erroneous criticism cannot be corrected by dogmatic theology, but only by a better, more searching, and less prejudiced criticism."—OTTLEY.

CHAPTER I

INTRODUCTORY: THE PROBLEM STATED

WHEN we speak of a problem of the Old Testament, what
do we mean? What is the problem, and how does it arise?
A consideration of these questions will form a suitable
introduction to the subsequent discussions.

It can hardly be necessary for us, in opening our inquiry,
to define what is meant by the Old Testament, though on
this point also, as between Protestants and Roman Catholics,
a few questions might arise. By the term is here understood, in brief, that collection of Scriptures which now
forms the first part of our ordinary Bibles,[1]—which the Jews
technically divided into "the law, the prophets, and the
(holy) writings,"[2]—which our Lord and His apostles spoke
of as "the Scriptures,"[3] "the Holy Scriptures,"[4] "the oracles
of God,"[5] "the sacred writings,"[6] and uniformly treated as the
"God-inspired"[7] and authoritative record of God's revelations
to, and dealings with, His ancient people.[8] This yields a
first regulative position in our study. It may be laid down
as axiomatic that, whatever they may be for others, these
ancient Scriptures can never have less value for the Christian Church than they had for the Church's Master—Christ

---

[1] This excludes the Apocrypha. On the name itself Bishop Westcott
says: "The establishment of Christianity gave at once a distinct unity to
the former dispensation, and thus St. Paul could speak of the Jewish
Scriptures by the name which they have always retained since, as the 'Old
Testament' or 'Covenant' (2 Cor. iii. 14). . . . At the close of the second
century the terms 'Old' and 'New Testament' were already in common
use."—*The Bible in the Church*, p. 5.

[2] Cf. Luke xxiv. 44: "In the law of Moses, and the prophets, and
the psalms."

[3] Matt. xxi. 42; Luke xxiv. 27.   [4] Rom. i. 2.

[5] Rom. iii. 2.   [6] 2 Tim. iii. 15.

[7] 2 Tim. iii. 16. Cf. 2 Pet. i. 21.

[8] Matt. v. 18; xv. 3, 6; xxii. 29, 31, 32; Luke xxiv. 27; John x. 35,
etc. See Note A on the Jewish Canon.

3

Himself.   Believing scholars of all standpoints may be trusted to agree in this.[1]

But what is meant by the problem of the Old Testament? Naturally there are many problems, but our title indicates that the problem we have now in view is that which arises peculiarly from the course of recent criticism.   That problem will be found large and complex enough to occupy us in this volume, and, as going to the root of a believing attitude to the Scriptures of the Old Covenant, will probably be allowed to be, for the present moment, the fundamental and essential one.   In this chapter we shall seek to convey as clear an idea as we can of where we conceive the *crux* of this Old Testament problem to lie, and shall indicate generally the lines to be followed in the handling of it.

I. THE PROBLEM TWOFOLD: RELIGIOUS AND LITERARY

The problem of the Old Testament, then, as it presses on the Church from various sides at the present hour, may be said to be twofold.   First, and most fundamentally, the question raised by it is—How are we to conceive of the *religion* which the Old Testament embodies, and presents to us in its successive stages, as respects its nature and origin? Is it a natural product of the development of the human spirit, as scholars of the distinctively "modern" way of thinking—Kuenen, Wellhausen, Stade, and the like [2]— allege; or is it something more—a result of special, super-natural revelation to Israel, such as other nations did not possess?   Then second, How are we to conceive of the *literature* itself, or of the books which make up the Old Testament, as respects their age, origin, mode of composition, trustworthiness, and, generally, their connection with the religion of which they are the monuments?

At first sight it might seem as if the second of these questions had no necessary relation to the first.   Nothing, it may be plausibly argued, depends, for the decision of the supernatural origin of the religion, on whether the

---

[1] Professor G. A. Smith says: "The Bible of the Jews in our Lord's time was practically our Old Testament.   For us its supreme sanction is that which it derived from Christ Himself. . . . What was indispensable to the Redeemer must always be indispensable to the redeemed."—*Modern Criticism*, p. 11.

[2] See below, pp. 12 ff.

Pentateuch, as we have it, is from the pen of Moses, or is
made up of three or four documents, put together at a late
date; or at what period the Levitical law was finally
codified; or whether the Book of Isaiah is the work of one,
or two, or of ten authors; or whether the Psalms are
pre-exilic, or post-exilic, in origin. Yet, as will be seen more
fully later,[1] the dependence of the literary criticism on the
religious theory is really very close. For, if it be true,
as every fair mind must admit, that there are many
scholars who succeed, to their own satisfaction, in combining the acceptance of the main results of the critical
hypothesis of the Old Testament, even in its advanced form,
with firm belief in the reality of supernatural revelation
in Israel, and in the culmination of that revelation in
Christ; it is equally true that, in the case of others, and
these pre-eminently, in Dr. Cheyne's phrase, "The Founders
of Criticism," the decisions arrived at on purely literary
questions,—the date of a psalm, e.g., the genuineness of a
passage, or the integrity of a book,—are largely controlled
by the view taken of the origin and course of development
of the religion; and, with a different theory on these
subjects, the judgments passed on the age, relations, and
historical value, of particular writings, would be different
also. This dependence of many of the conclusions of
criticism—by no means, of course, all—on the religious and
historical standpoint is practically admitted by Wellhausen,
when he declares that "it is only within the region of
religious antiquities and dominant religious ideas — the
region which Vatke in his *Biblische Theologie* had occupied
in its full breadth, and where the real battle first kindled—
that the controversy can be brought to a definite issue."[2]

It is the perception of this fact and of its results which
affords the explanation of the very genuine disquiet and
perplexity which undeniably exist in large sections of the
Church as to the tendency and outcome of recent develop-

[1] See below, pp. 16 ff.
[2] *Hist. of Israel*, p. 12. On Vatke, see below, p. 13. Graf also, the
pioneer of the new movement (see below, pp. 199 ff.), in his chief work, lays
stress on the fact that Pentateuch criticism was bound to remain "unclear,
uncertain, and wavering," till it grasped the fact of the post-exilian origin
of the Levitical legislation. To attempt to decide its problems on mere
literary grounds was to move in a "vicious circle."—*Geschicht. Bücher*,
pp. 2, 3.

ments in Old Testament criticism. From the popular point of view—the light in which the matter presents itself to the average Christian mind — the problem of the Old Testament is simply one of how we are to regard the Bible. It is not merely, as the instinct of the humblest is quick enough to perceive, the dates and authorship of books that are in dispute in these critical theories : it is the whole question of the value of the Bible as an inspired and authoritative record of God's historical revelation to mankind. Has God spoken, and does this book convey to us His sure word for our salvation and guidance ? Have the Scriptures of the Old Testament any longer the value for us which they had for Christ and His disciples ? Or are we to concede to the writers of the school above mentioned, that, as the result of the critical discussions of the past century, the historical foundations of Old Testament revelation have in the main been subverted ? Must man's changing and erring thoughts about God henceforth take the place of God's words to man ? Are the erewhile "lively oracles" of God simply the fragmentary remains of a literature to which no special quality of divineness attaches, and is the supposed history of revelation largely a piecing together of the myths, legends, and free inventions of an age whose circle of ideas the modern spirit has outgrown ? These and like questions, that extensive body of opinion which arrogates to itself the title "modern" would answer with an unhesitating "Yes"; it need not occasion surprise if the great mass of believing opinion in the Church, on the other hand, meets such a challenge with an emphatic "No."

It is to be admitted that the position of those who, at the present time, occupy a believing standpoint, yet are strongly repelled by the rationalism which seems to them to inhere in much of the prevailing criticism, is one of peculiar difficulty. On the one hand, they feel keenly the seriousness of the issues by which they are confronted. They seem to themselves to be called to give up, not only those ideas of the Bible in which they have been nurtured, and with which their tenderest associations are entwined, but the view of the Bible that appears to them to arise from an impartial study of its contents and claims. They see the disintegrating processes which have wrought such havoc, as they regard it, with the Old Testament, extended to the New, and with like results.[1] On the other hand, they are met by the assertion that practically all competent scholarship—believing and unbelieving alike—is agreed in the acceptance of those critical conclusions about the Old Testament which so greatly disturb them. What, in the "storm and stress" of this conflict and confusion of opinion, are those who hold fast by the Bible as the Word of Life for their souls to do? General assurances, such as are sometimes given, that, when they have parted with the greater part of what they have been accustomed to regard as the historical substance of revelation, they will find the Bible a diviner book to them than ever, do not yield the desired comfort. Is it to be wondered at if, in their perplexity and resentment, many who feel thus should round on "Higher Criticism" itself, and uncompromisingly denounce it as the prolific parent of all the mischief—an invention of the Evil One for the destruction of the unwary?

Nevertheless, this attitude of unreasoning denunciation of what is called "Higher Criticism" is also manifestly an extreme; and the problem we have to deal with, if it is to be profitably discussed, requires a clearer discrimination of issues. In particular, it cannot too early be recognised that this is not, at bottom, a question simply, as is too commonly assumed, between "Higher Critics" and "Non-Higher Critics." Questions of criticism, indeed, enter deeply—far more deeply, to our thinking, than many are disposed to allow—into the dispute; but it is only to confuse the issue, and is a gratuitous weakening of the believing case, not to recognise that the real cleft goes much deeper—viz., into a radical contrariety of view as to the natural or supernatural origin of the religion of Israel, and that on this fundamental issue those whom we call "critics" are themselves sharply divided, and found ranged in opposing camps. There are, one must own, few outstanding scholars at the present day on the Continent or in Britain—in America it is somewhat different—

---

[1] As examples reference may be made to the articles of Schmiedel in the *Encyc. Biblica*, and to such works, among many others, as O. Holtzmann's *Life of Jesus*, and Wernle's *Beginnings of Christianity*, recently translated. Cf. below, p. 478.

who do not in greater or less degree accept conclusions
regarding the Old Testament of the kind ordinarily de-
nominated critical;[1] yet among the foremost are many whom
no one who understands their work would dream of classing
as other than believing, and defenders of revealed religion.
Such, among Continental scholars, recent or living, are
Delitzsch, Riehm, Dillmann, König, Kittel, Köhler, Strack,
Oettli, Westphal, Orelli; in Britain, Dr. Driver, the late
Dr. A. B. Davidson, Professor G. A. Smith, and many
others: all more or less "critics," but all convinced upholders
of supernatural revelation. This is not a reason for unquestioning acceptance of their opinions; as critics it will
be found that they are far enough from agreeing among
themselves. But the attitude to criticism of so large a
body of believing scholars may at least suggest to those
disposed to form hasty judgments that there is here a very
real problem to be solved; that the case is more complex
than perhaps they had imagined; that there are real
phenomena in the literary structure of the Old Testament,
for the explanation of which, in the judgment of many
able minds, the traditional view is not adequate, and for
which they seem to themselves to find a more satisfactory
solution in some form or other of the critical hypothesis.[2]

[1] This is true even of so cautious a scholar as Professor James
Robertson, of Glasgow, whose works, in a conservative spirit, have done
such excellent service. It is Dillmann, himself a pronounced critic, but
decided in his opposition to what he calls the "Hegel-Vatke" view of
religious development, who speaks of Professor Robertson's *Early Religion
of Israel* as "hitting the nail on the head" (*Alttest. Theol.* p. 59).
Yet, as will appear, the views of Professor Robertson, and those, say, of
Dr. Driver, on such subjects as the Mosaic authorship of the Pentateuch, the
gradual growth of legislation, the origin of Deuteronomy, etc., are not *in
principle* so far apart as might appear, though Professor Robertson's results
are somewhat more positive, and the *accent* falls differently. Cf. *Early
Religion*, pp. 332 ff., 382, 420-27.

[2] An interesting example of how the leading results of criticism may be
accepted by a devout and intensely evangelical mind is furnished by the
Rev. G. H. C. Macgregor, a favourite teacher of the "Keswick" school.
See his tribute to Professor W. R. Smith in the *Biography* by his cousin
(p. 100), and the frequent references to critical positions in his *Messages
of the Old Testament*, with Preface by Rev. F. B. Meyer. It is significant
also that the productions of critical writers of believing tendency, such as
König and Kittel, are now being translated and reproduced in conservative
quarters, in refutation of the theories of the more rationalistic school.
Cf. below, pp. 79, etc., on Kittel's pamphlet, *Babylonian Excavations and
Early Bible History*, published, with Preface by Dr. Wace, by the London
Society for Promoting Christian Knowledge.

The truth is, and the fact has to be faced, that no cne who studies the Old Testament in the light of modern knowledge can help being, to some extent, a "Higher Critic," nor is it desirable he should. The name has unfortunately come to be associated all but exclusively with a method yielding a certain class of results; but it has no necessary connection with these results. "Higher Criticism," rightly understood, is simply the careful scrutiny, on the principles which it is customary to apply to all literature, of the actual phenomena of the Bible, with a view to deduce from these such conclusions as may be warranted regarding the age, authorship, mode of composition, sources, etc., of the different books; and everyone who engages in such inquiries, with whatever aim, is a "Higher Critic," and cannot help himself. The peculiar distribution of the names of God in Genesis, *e.g.*, is a fact to be recognised, whatever account may be given of it,[1] and the collation and sifting of evidence, with a view to the obtaining of a satisfactory explanation, is, so far, a critical process. There is nothing in such scholarly examination of the Bible, even though the result be to present some things in a new light, which need alarm anyone. As the world of nature presents a different aspect to the man of science, still more to the metaphysician, from that which it does to the common view of sense, yet is the *same* world; so the Bible may present a somewhat different aspect to the eye of the trained critical scholar, yet is the *same* Bible, for edification, devotion, and instruction in the way of righteousness.

That we may discharge our debt to criticism, even of the rationalistic sort, once for all, let us acknowledge that, with all its attendant evils, its course has been productive, under the providence of God, of many benefits, which in large measure counterbalance, if they do not outweigh, these evils. Some of the positive advances in its course it will be our business to notice hereafter.[2] It is assuredly not for nothing that, for more than a century, the light of the best European scholarship has been keenly directed on every page, verse, line, and even word, of the sacred record. Many of the leaders of criticism, however defective in their apprehension of the full truth of revelation, have been

---

[1] See below, p. 196.   [2] See below, Chap. VII. pp. 196 ff.

men of fine literary gifts, wide culture, acute critical faculty,
and genuine appreciation of the nobler elements in the
religious and ethical teaching of the prophets; and the
result of their labours, as everyone must own, has been,
in modern times, a wonderful freshening of interest in
the historical, poetical, and prophetical parts of the Old
Testament, and an immensely better understanding of its
textual meaning and historical setting. What student
of Old Testament history or prophecy, *e.g.*, would willingly
part with the aid afforded by the works of Ewald?[1] What
most rabid opponent of criticism is not ready to own his
indebtedness, on the linguistic side, to that dry old
rationalist, Gesenius? There is a yet greater gain. It
is not too much to say that one direct result of the application of the strictest historical and critical methods to the
Old Testament has been to bring out, as never before, the
absolutely unique and marvellous character of the religion
of Israel.[2] With the best will in the world to explain the
religious development of Israel out of natural factors, the
efforts of the critics have resulted, in the view of many
of themselves, in a magnificent demonstration of the
immense, and, on natural principles, inexplicable difference
between the religion of this obscure people and every
other.[3] Some may regard this as a small result; to us
it presents itself as something for which to be devoutly
grateful.

II. THE FUNDAMENTAL ISSUE: ATTITUDE TO THE SUPERNATURAL

Still the deep cleft remains between what we have
called the believing and the unbelieving views of the Old
Testament,—between the view which admits, and the view
which denies, the properly supernatural element in the
history and religion of Israel,—and it is not in our power,

[1] "From another side," wrote Principal John Cairns, "a great scholar
like Ewald redressed the unfairness of Schleiermacher to the Old Testament,
and, with many and great drawbacks of his own, asserted in his own way
the historical greatness and necessity of the Bible revelation."—*Unbelief
in the Eighteenth Century*, p. 230.

[2] See next chapter.

[3] This is the argument pursued, on critical lines, in Lecture IV., on
"The Proof of a Divine Revelation in the Old Testament," of Professor
G. A. Smith's *Modern Criticism*, etc.

neither is it our wish, to minimise it. We must now approach the subject more closely, and endeavour to fix with greater precision where the dividing-line between the two views lies.

In certain external respects, as in temple, priesthood, sacrifices, the religion of Israel necessarily presents a resemblance to other religions. To the eye of the outward observer, it is simply one of the great historical religions. If at the same time it presents differences, this does not of itself establish more than a relative distinction between it and others. Every religion has not only a certain resemblance to every other, arising from the fact that it *is* a religion, but has, moreover, a definite character or physiognomy of its own, resulting from the different genius of the people, from the individuality of its founder, or from the circumstances of its history. If now, however, we go further, and affirm that, in the midst of all resemblances, this religion of Israel presents features which not only differentiate it from every other, but differentiate it *in such a way* as to compel us to ascribe to it an origin in special, supernatural revelation, we obviously take a new step, which we must be prepared to justify by the most cogent reasons. It will not be enough to show that the religion of Israel is a *better* religion than others—or even taking into account its fulfilment in Christianity, that it is the *most perfect* of existing religions : for conceivably it might be that, yet have essentially no higher origin than they ; just as one people may be endowed with the artistic, or philosophic, or scientific genius beyond others, — the Greeks, for instance, among ancient peoples, in art and philosophy,—without its being necessary to postulate for this a supernatural cause. Most critics, even of the rationalistic order, will admit that Israel had a genius for religion, and was the classical people of religion in antiquity ; will not hesitate to speak also of its providential mission to humanity, even as Greece and Rome had their vocations to mankind. It is a proposition different in kind when the origin of the religion of Israel is sought in a special, continuous, authoritative revelation, such as other peoples did not possess. Here we touch a real contrast, and, with reservation of a certain ambiguity in the word " revelation," [1] obtain a clear issue.

[1] See below, pp. 19 ff.

For now the fact becomes apparent,—there is, indeed, not the least attempt to disguise it,—that, to a large and influential school of critical inquirers—those, moreover, who have had most to do with the shaping of the current critical theories—this question of a supernatural origin for the religion of Israel is already foreclosed; is ruled out at the start as *a priori* inadmissible. The issue could not be better stated than it is by the Dutch scholar Kuenen in the opening chapter of his work, *The Religion of Israel.* The chapter is entitled " Our Standpoint," and in it the principle is expressly laid down that no distinction can be admitted in respect of origin between the religion of Israel and other religions. " For us," he says, " the Israelitish religion is one of those religions; nothing less, but also nothing more." [1] This is, in the style of assumption too usual in the school, declared to be " the view taken by modern theological science." [2] " No one," he says, " can expect or require us to support in this place by a complete demonstration the right of the modern as opposed to the ecclesiastical view." [3] It is an " ecclesiastical " view, it appears, to assume that any supernatural factor is involved in the history or religion of Israel: the " modern " view rejects this. If any ambiguity could attach to these statements, it would be removed by his further explanations, which, in so many words, exclude the idea that the Jewish and Christian religions are derived from " special divine revelation," or are " supernatural " in their origin.[4] He puts the matter with equal frankness in his work on *Prophets and Prophecy.* " Prophecy is," he tells us, " according to this new view, a phenomenon, yet one of the most important and remarkable phenomena, in the history of religion, but just on that account a human phenomenon,

---

[1] *Religion of Israel,* i. p. 5.   [2] *Ibid.* p. 6.
[3] *Ibid.* p. 7.
[4] *Ibid.* pp. 5, 6. In a Life of Kuenen in the *Jewish Quarterly Review,* vol. iv., by Mr. Wicksteed, the Dutch "modern" movement, of which Kuenen was a principal leader, is thus described. "It was an attempt of singular boldness and vigour to shake the traditions of Christian piety free from every trace of supernaturalism and implied exclusiveness. . . . It involved the absolute surrender of the orthodox dogmatics ; of the authority of the Scriptures ; of the divine character of the Church as an external institution ; and of course it based the claims of Jesus of Nazareth to our affection and gratitude solely upon what history could show that He, as a man, had been, and had done for men " (p. 596).

proceeding from Israel, directed to Israel."[1] And later: "So soon as we derive a separate part of Israel's religious life directly from God, and allow the supernatural or immediate revelation to intervene in even one single point, so long also our view of the whole continues to be incorrect. . . . It is the supposition of a natural development alone which accounts for all the phenomena."[2] Quite similar to the standpoint here avowed by Kuenen is that of a wide circle of leading scholars — of Duhm, Wellhausen, Stade, Smend, Gunkel, and a multitude more in the front ranks of the modern critical movement. We noted above Wellhausen's declaration of his identity in standpoint with Vatke — Vatke being a thorough-going Hegelian rationalist in the first half of last century. Shortly after in his book we have the express acknowledgment: "My inquiry comes nearer to that of Vatke, from whom indeed I gratefully acknowledge myself to have learned best and most."[3]

This, then, quite unambiguously stated, is the issue to which the religion of Israel—and with it Christianity, for in this connection the two very much stand or fall together— is brought at the present day. Yet the contrast drawn by Kuenen in the above passage between the "modern" and the "ecclesiastical" view, which he announces as the ruling principle of his treatment, is, it need hardly be said, a flagrant *petitio principii*.[4] To assume beforehand, in an inquiry which turns on this very point, that the religion of Israel presents no features but such as are explicable out of natural causes,—that no higher factors are needed to account for it,—is to prejudge the whole question; while to assume this to be the only view held by "modern" scholars—in other words, to exclude from this category men of the distinction of those formerly enumerated, who, with

[1] *Prophets and Prophecy in Israel*, p. 4.
[2] *Ibid.* p. 585. Dr. John Muir, at whose instance the work was undertaken, contributed an Introduction to the English translation. In the course of this he thus states Dr. Kuenen's position: "Israelitish prophecy was not a supernatural phenomenon, derived from divine inspiration; but was a result of the high moral and religious character attained by the prophets whose writings have been transmitted to us" (p. xxxvii). From a published letter of Kuenen's we learn the interesting fact, otherwise attested to us, that Dr. Muir subsequently changed his opinions, and recalled from circulation the volume he had been instrumental in producing.
[3] *Hist. of Israel*, p. 13.
[4] Cf. the remarks of Ladd, *Doct. of Sac. Scripture*, i. p. 371.

their critical views, take strong ground on the subject of revelation—is to contradict fact, and degrade the term "modern" to the designation of a clique. If, on impartial consideration, it can be shown that the religion of Israel admits of explanation on purely natural principles, then the historian will be justified in his verdict that it stands, in this respect, on the same footing as other religions. If, on the other hand, fair investigation brings out a different result,—if it demonstrates that this religion has features which place it in a different category from all others, and compel us to postulate for it a different and higher origin,[1]— then that fact must be frankly recognised as part of the scientific result, and the nature and extent of this higher element must be made the subject of inquiry. It will not do to override the facts—if facts they are—by *a priori* dogmatic assumptions on the one side any more than on the other. Thus far we agree with Kuenen, that we must *begin* by treating the religion of Israel exactly as we would treat any other religion. Whatever our personal convictions—and of these, of course, we cannot divest ourselves—we must, in conducting our argument, place ourselves in as absolutely neutral an attitude of mind as we can. We must try to see the facts exactly as they are If differences emerge, let them be noted. If the facts are such as to compel us to assume a special origin for this religion, let that come to light in the course of the inquiry. Let us frankly admit also that it is no slight, recondite, contestable, or inferential differences, but only broad, obvious, cumulative, indubitable grounds, which will suffice as basis of a claim to such special origin. If such do not exist, we concede that candour will compel us to fall back on the naturalistic hypothesis.

It is perfectly true that it is impossible in any inquiry to dispense with guiding principles of investigation, and with presuppositions of some kind, and there is no criticism on earth that does so—certainly not that of Kuenen and Wellhausen. Only these should not be allowed to warp or distort the facts, or be applied to support a preconceived conclusion. The scientist also finds it incumbent on him to "anticipate nature" with his interrogations and tentative hypotheses, which, however, have to be brought to the test

[1] This is the argument in Chap. II.

of experimental verification. We find no fault with these writers, if they are persuaded that their view of Israel's religion is the true one, for endeavouring, with all the skill at their command, to show that it is so. It is even well that such experiments should be made. The case, in short, is one of competing interpretations of the Old Testament, and, assuming Israel's religion to be divine, the effect of the most searching application of critical tests can only be to bring out this divineness into stronger relief. No Christian, therefore, who has confidence that God, who spoke to the fathers by the prophets, has in these last days spoken to us by His Son,[1] need shrink from any trial to which criticism exposes the Bible. It is the Nemesis of a wrong starting-point in every department of inquiry that those who adopt it find themselves plunged, as they proceed, into ever-deepening error and confusion; while a right guiding-idea as infallibly conducts to a view marked by simplicity and truth. If Kuenen and those who think with him are right in their first principles, they will find their theory work out easily and naturally in its application to the phenomena of Scripture:[2] if they are wrong, their hypothesis will inevitably break down under its own weight, as did that of Baur in the sphere of the New Testament half a century ago. The ultimate test in either case is fitness to meet the facts. It has already been pointed out that the result of a searching inquiry has been to produce in many minds the conviction that Israel's religion can *not* be explained on mere natural principles.

III. THE LITERARY PROBLEM: ITS DEPENDENCE ON THE RELIGIOUS

Thus much on the more fundamental part of our problem; it remains to be asked how far the conclusions reached on this point affect the questions raised, in the field of literary discussion, on the age, authorship, structure,

---

[1] Heb. i. 1.

[2] This is their own claim. Professor W. R. Smith, *e.g.*, in his Preface to Wellhausen, says: "In the course of the argument it appears that the plain, natural sense of the old history has constantly been distorted by the false presuppositions with which we have been accustomed to approach it."—Pref. to *Hist. of Israel*, p. viii. The implication is that Wellhausen's view gives the "plain, natural sense."

and historical value of the Old Testament *books*—especially
of the Pentateuch, or "five books" traditionally attributed
to Moses. What is the interest of Christian faith in these
discussions, or has it any? Abstractly considered, of
course, as already said,[1] questions of age, authorship, and
historical genesis are, in comparison with those we have
now been considering, of secondary importance. The later
age, or composite structure, of a book is no necessary
disproof of its truth. Freeman's *History of the Norman
Conquest, e.g.*, though written in the nineteenth century,
does not give us a less just or vivid idea of the series of
events to which it relates, than the contemporary monkish
chronicles, etc., on which it is based. The age, authorship,
and simple or composite character of a book are matters
for investigation, to be determined solely by evidence, and
it is justly claimed that criticism, in its investigation of
such subjects, must be untrammelled : that faith cannot
be bound up with results of purely literary judgments.
It will be urged, further, that, as we have admitted, the
denial of the supernatural in the Old Testament history
or religion in no way necessarily follows from any theory
of the dates or relations of documents. All this is true;
still the matter is not quite so simple as this rather
superficial way of presenting the case would picture it.
There *is*, as was before hinted, a very close connection
between critical premises and critical results, and it is
necessary in the present discussion that this connection
should be kept carefully in view.

It has already been explained that it is no part of the
design of these pages to cast discredit on the function of
criticism as such. It is not even contended that the critical
theories at present in vogue are constructed wholly in the
interest of rationalism : far from that. If they were, we
may be sure that so many believing men would not be
found accepting or advocating them. To account for such
acceptance we must assume that they are felt by candid
minds to answer in some degree to real facts, to rest on a
basis of real evidence, to afford an explanation of real
phenomena, to possess a plausibility and reasonableness
which constrain a genuine assent.[2] On the other hand, it
can as little be doubted that the critical hypothesis, in the

---

[1] See above, p. 5. [2] See below, Chap. VII. pp. 195–6.

form into which it has gradually crystallised, shows, in many of its features, a marked dependence on rationalistic presuppositions. There is no gainsaying the fact that, historically, it was in rationalistic workshops, mainly, that the critical theory was elaborated, and that, from this circumstance, a certain rationalistic impress was stamped upon it from the first.[1] From Eichhorn and those who followed him—Von Bohlen, Vatke, De Wette, and the rest—the critical treatment of the Pentateuch received a "set" in the direction of naturalism which it has to some extent retained ever since. Most of all is it true of the type of theory which is at present the dominant one—the theory which, to indicate the line of its origin, we might describe as the Vatke-Graf-Kuenen-Wellhausen-Stade one—that it is rationalistic in its basis, and in every fibre of its construction. Yet it is this theory which, chiefly through the brilliant advocacy of Wellhausen, has for the time won an all but universal recognition in critical circles on the Continent and in English-speaking countries. Its arguments are adopted, its conclusions endorsed, its watchwords repeated, with almost monotonous fidelity of iteration, by a majority of scholars of all classes—in Churches and out of Churches, High Church, Broad Church, and Low Church, sceptical and believing. This says much for the plausibility of the theory, but it suggests also a grave problem. The critical hypothesis must, of course, be considered on its merits; but is there not, on the face of it, a supreme improbability that a theory evolved under the conditions we have described should be, in that form, a theory adequate to Christian faith, or with which Christian faith can ultimately be content? Is it such a theory as Christian faith would ever have evolved from its own presuppositions? Can it ever be purged of its rationalistic leaven, and adapted to the use of the Christian Churches, without a complete re-casting on

---

[1] The statement of the late Dr. Green may need qualification as respects later scholars, but is in the main true of the originators of the critical movement: "The development of critical hypotheses inimical to the genuineness and the truth of the books of the Bible has from the beginning been in the hands of those who were antagonistic to supernatural religion; whose interest in the Bible was purely literary, and who refused to recognise its claims as an immediate and authoritative revelation from God."—*Higher Criticism*, p. 177. Cf. Dr. Cheyne on the indebtedness of the German critical movement to English Deism (*Founders of Criticism*, pp. 1, 2). See also below, p. 58.

principles which are the direct antitheses of those which
obtain in the schools in which it originated? We take
leave to doubt it. Christian scholars are no doubt entirely
serious in their acceptance of its conclusions, but there
must grow up, we are persuaded—if there is not already
growing up—a perception of the incompatibility of their
belief, as Christians, in a historical revelation, culminating
in the Incarnation,[1] with a set of results wrought out on
the basis of a purely naturalistic view of Israel's history
and religion—which, in fact, as will be discovered, reduces
the bulk of that history to ruins![2]

Criticism, it is granted, must be untrammelled; also, the
results complained of do not *necessarily* follow from the
reigning critical hypothesis. This last remark we must admit
to be true, for part of our own argument in a future chapter
is built upon it.[3] Still it cannot well be denied that, if all
the results do not necessarily follow from the theory, a
good many of them do very easily and naturally follow;
that the way is logically open for them, as it would not be
on another theory; and that the reason why the stronger
conclusion is not drawn often is simply that the believing
critics are less logical than their fellows. A theory may
not always be *followed* to its conclusions, where these,
nevertheless, very logically *follow*. It could not be otherwise, when regard is had to the presuppositions under the
influence of which the theory was formed. Everything, as
Rothe said, can be laid hold of by two handles; and where the
case is one, as before remarked, of competing interpretations
of the same facts, while it is true as ever that both will not
be found equally suitable to the facts, and that no ingenuity
can make them so, the room left for the play of subjective considerations is still very large. In this connection, questions
of age and authorship are far from being always of secondary
moment. The true inwardness of many of these will appear
after in the course of our discussion. It will be forced
upon us when we observe how frequently the dating does
not arise from purely literary considerations, but is determined by critical assumptions, or by congruity with an
a priori scheme of development, and when we see the *use*
to which the dating is put, viz., to lower the dates of other

---

[1] See Ottley below, p. 22.   [2] Cf. Chap. III. pp. 56 ff.
[3] Chap. III.

writings, or subvert the credibility of the history.[1] The
late date of the documents composing the Pentateuch, *e.g.*,
may be employed to support the contention that the narrative of the Pentateuchal books is wholly, or in great part,
legendary ; the post-exilian date of the Levitical laws may
be used to destroy the connection of the laws with Moses ;
the low date assigned to the psalms may be really a corollary
from a particular theory of Israel's religious development,
and may be used, in turn, to buttress that theory. In other
ways the literary criticism, not intentionally perhaps, but
really and effectively, may be put at the service of the
theory. Books may be divided up, or texts manipulated
and struck out, till the writing is made to speak the language
which the critic desires. The hyper-analysis of documents
may result in the dissipation of everything of grandeur,
not to say of consistency and truthfulness, in a narrative.
Whether this is an over-colouring of the character of the
critical procedure, in the hands of many of its representatives,
will be better judged of in the sequel.

IV. Attitude of Criticism to " Revelation "

A little may be said before closing this chapter on a line
of remark sometimes met with, to the effect that the
contrast we have sought to indicate between the believing
and the " modern " ways of regarding the Old Testament is,
after all, less important than it seems. Partly, it may be
urged, we have unduly narrowed the scope of the words
" revelation " and " supernatural " ; partly, we have not done
justice to the high views of God and of His providential
government which even rationalistic critics allow that the
prophets of Israel ultimately attained. Professor W. R.
Smith, in his lectures on *The Prophets of Israel*, may be taken
as representing this latter standpoint. Referring to that
" large and thoughtful school of theologians " which yet
" refuses to believe that God's dealings with Israel in the
times before Christ can be distinguished under the special
name of revelation from His providential guidance of
other nations," he observes that " in one point of view
this departure from the usual doctrine of Christians is
perhaps less fundamental than it seems at first sight to be."

[1] See Appendix to Chap. X. pp. 378-9.

He goes on : "For, as a matter of fact, it is not and cannot
be denied that the prophets found for themselves and their
nation a knowledge of God, and not a mere speculative
knowledge, but a practical fellowship of faith with Him,
which the seekers after truth among the Gentiles never
attained to."[1] The idea seems to be that, these high views
of God and of religion in the prophets being acknowledged
to be there, it is not necessary to burden the argument with
too curious questions as to how they got to be there,—
whether by supernatural revelation, or in the way in which
spiritual truth is grasped by thinkers of other nations.
Enough that we now have them.

This appears to us, however, to be very fallacious
reasoning; the more that Professor Smith admits that behind
"there appears to lie a substantial and practical difference
of view between the common faith of the Churches and the
views of the modern school,"[2] and proceeds to give very
cogent reasons for assuming a more direct and special revelation.[3] Not only, on the view described, is the prophet's
own consciousness of the source of his message denied, and
the higher character of his knowledge of God left without
adequate explanation; but the results in the two cases are
not the same. The ideas of the prophets on God, on the
naturalistic hypothesis, cannot be allowed, at best, to rise
higher than man is capable of attaining by the reflection of
his own mind on his natural and providential environment,
i.e., to certain general truths about God's existence, unity,
ethical character, and universal providence. Even this, it
might be shown, assumes much more than the premises of
the system will warrant, and, like the "natural religion" of the
eighteenth century Deism, implies an unacknowledged debt
to revelation. In any case it does not yield an authoritative
revelation of God's purpose, and saving will for man, derived
immediately from Himself: it lacks, even in what it does
yield, in certitude; and in both respects falls short of what
is demanded by the full Christian faith. It is further
apparent that on such a view justice cannot be done to the
earlier stages of the religion of Israel. The temptation of
the critic who proceeds on these lines—if, indeed, he has
any alternative—is to lower the character of the religion to
suit the conditions of its hypothetical development; to give

[1] *Prophets of Israel*, p. 9.   [2] *Ibid.* p. 10.   [3] *Ibid.* pp. 11, 12.

a mean view of its origin and early manifestations; and to contend against the recognition of a divine redemptive purpose manifesting itself from the first in its history.

With respect to the usage of the words "revelation" and "supernatural," we have gladly acknowledged that there are few scholars of the present day—among serious investigators probably none—who would deny that Israel had a unique vocation, or would refuse to recognise, in some degree, a "providential guidance" in its history. Thus Duhm makes the quite general statement that, objectively regarded, there is no alternative to "the necessity of accepting a providential guidance in the actual stages of the development of religion."[1]   Most, however, in recent years go further, and freely use the word "revelation" to express the peculiarity of Israel's religion.   Thus Gunkel, one of the most radical of critics, says: "The conviction remains irrefragable that, in the course of the Israelitish religion, the power of the living God reveals itself";[2] and elsewhere: "Israel is, and remains, the people of revelation."[3]   When the matter is inquired into, however, it is found that the term "revelation" is here used in a sense which does not in reality cover more than Kuenen's "natural development," or Duhm's "providential guidance."   That which, on the human side, is natural psychological development, is, on the divine side, interpreted as God's revelation of Himself to man.[4]

Whichever formula is employed, the advocates of this type of theory find themselves in an obvious difficulty. God's "guidance" is recognised, but the guidance is of so faulty a character that it results in a set of ideas as to a *super*natural government of the world, and *super*natural dealings of God with Israel, wholly alien to the actual state of the facts as the critics represent it.   If "revelation" is affirmed, the revelation is held to be compatible with an abundance of error and illusion, and results, again, on the part of the prophets, in a total misreading of the past history of the nation, and in views of God, His purpose, and living relations with men, which, if true, would cut the

[1] *Theol. d. Propheten*, p. 89.
[2] *Schöpfung und Chaos*, p. 118.
[3] *Israel und Babylonien*, pp. 37–38.
[4] Gunkel says: "The history of revelation transacts itself among men according to the same psychological laws as every other human event."—*Ibid.* p. 37.   Cf. the whole passage, pp. 34–38.

ground from under the rationalistic theory. The elements, in either case, which the critics permit themselves to extract from the prophetic teaching do not, as said, rise above a vague theism, and the announcement of an ethical ideal. "Revelation," in the specific, supernatural sense, is not, and cannot be, admitted on this view, either in the process or in the goal. Not in the process, for there is nothing there, confessedly, transcending natural conditions; and not in the goal, for Jesus, with all these writers, while reverenced as the highest type—for us the pattern—of spiritual religion, is nothing more : [1] least of all is He the Son of God incarnate. Our distinction between natural and supernatural in the history of Israel, therefore, remains. Even with regard to those—and they are many—who do in some form admit "supernatural" revelation, it cannot be too constantly borne in mind that it is not any and every kind of admission of the supernatural which satisfies the Christian demand. It is Christ Himself in the full revelation of His glory as the only-begotten Son who is the touchstone and measure of the supernatural for faith; and only that view of revelation in Israel is adequate which finds its necessary culmination in His Person and redemption.[2]

It is now proper that a sketch should be given of the general course to be followed in the discussions in the succeeding chapters.

First, a brief preliminary survey will be taken of the witness which the Old Testament itself bears, in its structure, and in the uniqueness of its history and religion, to its own authority and inspiration as the record of God's revelation to His ancient people (Chap. II.). Thus far critical questions are held over.

[1] See on Kuenen above, p. 12.

[2] Ottley says: "If Jesus Christ were merely the last and most eminent of a line of prophets, there would be more to be said for that familiar type of criticism which represents Israel's religious development as a purely natural phenomenon, having its starting-point and controlling principle not in any intervention of a gracious and loving God, not in any supernatural revelation imparted to elect souls at different epochs in Israel's history, but in fetishism, or totemism, or polytheism, whence by a slow process of purely natural evolution it passed to its final stage in ethical monotheism."—*Aspects of O.T.*, p. 13. Ottley, in this work, with his belief in the Incarnation and in miracle, admits too much not to admit more. His positive Christian beliefs fit badly into the frame of Wellhausenism.

The next four chapters will be devoted to the consideration of the question—How far is this view which the Old Testament gives of itself affected by the results of modern criticism?   At this stage the ordinary analysis of the Hexateuch (JE, D, P) [1] will be provisionally accepted, and the aim will be to show that, even on this basis, the essential outlines of the patriarchal and Mosaic history (Chaps. III., IV.), and the outstanding facts of the religion and institutions of the Old Testament (Chaps. V., VI.), are not sensibly affected,—that they are not, and cannot be, overturned.   The way being thus cleared for consideration of the critical hypothesis on its own merits, the four succeeding chapters are occupied with a somewhat careful examination of that hypothesis in its fundamental positions and several parts.   In this examination attention is concentrated on the points which are thought to be most crucial.[2]   These chapters (VII.–X.) set forth the reasons which prevent us yielding our assent to the current critical hypothesis, except under conditions which essentially transform its character and bearings.   The chapters may, if the reader likes, be viewed as setting forth our "sceptical doubts" on that hypothesis, though in many respects they are really more than doubts.   It is sought to be shown how precarious and arbitrary are many of the grounds on which the critical hypothesis rests, and how strong are the reasons for challenging its principal postulates, and some of what are regarded as its most "settled" results.   This is argued particularly in respect of :

1. The alleged distinction of the documents **J and E,** and the dates assigned to these (Chap. VII.).

2. The origin of Deuteronomy in the age of **Josiah** or Manasseh (Chap. VIII.).

3. The post-exilian origin of the so-called Priestly Code (Chaps. IX., X.).   Chap. IX. deals with the Code and Chap. X. with the document.

The question of the divine names is discussed in Chap. VII.

With respect to the Priestly writing (P), it is contended that, whilst it is distinct in stylistic character from JE, there

---

[1] For explanation of these symbols see **Chap. III. pp. 65–66, and Chap.** VII. pp. 196 ff.

[2] Cf. Appendix at end of chapter.

is no evidence of P ever having existed as an independent document; that, on the contrary, it stands in the closest relations with the other elements in the narrative, and is most appropriately regarded as (at least in Genesis) the "framework" in which the JE narrative is set, with slight working over of the latter. Reasons are given for carrying back both books and legislation to a much earlier date than the critical hypothesis allows, and for recognising in both a substantially Mosaic basis.

A glance is taken at the later historical books in an Appendix to Chap. X.

The conclusions reached in the preceding discussions receive corroboration in a chapter on the bearings of Archæology on the Old Testament (Chap. XI.).

A closing chapter deals with the age of the Psalter, the reality of predictive prophecy, and the progressiveness of divine revelation (Chap. XII.).

APPENDIX TO CHAPTER I

CRUCIAL POINTS IN THE CRITICAL THEORY

IT is interesting to note what the critics themselves regard as the crucial points in their theory. Here are a few utterances on the subject.

Westphal says: "We shall take Deuteronomy as Ariadne's thread in the labyrinth into which the historical problem of the Pentateuch introduces us."[1]

Delitzsch says: "Since then [Graf's time] the Book of Ezekiel has become the Archimedean point on which the Pentateuchal criticism has planted itself, and from which it has lifted off its hinges the history of worship and literature in Israel as hitherto accepted."[2]

Wellhausen says: "The chapters xl.–xlviii. (in Ezekiel) are the most important in his book, and have been called by J. Orth, not incorrectly, the key of the Old Testament."[3]

Smend also says: "The decisive importance of this section for the criticism of the Pentateuch was first recognised by George and Vatke. It has been rightly called the key of the Old Testament."[4]

Wellhausen in another place says: "The position of the Levites is the Achilles heel of the Priestly Code."[5]

Elsewhere he emphasises the centralisation of the cultus as containing his whole position. "I differ from Graf," he says, "chiefly in this, that I always go back to the centralisation of the cultus, and deduce from it the particular divergences. My whole position is contained in my first chapter" (on "The Place of Worship.")[6]

Kuenen also has his Achilles heel. Speaking of Graf's original division of the priestly history and legislation (see

<hr>

[1] *Sources du Pent.* ii. p. xxiv.   [2] Luthardt's *Zeitschrift*, 1880, **p. 279.**
[3] *Hist. of Israel*, p. 421.   [4] *Ezechiel*, p. 312.
[5] *Hist. of Israel*, p. 167.   [6] *Ibid.* p. 368.

below, p. 200), he says: "I saw clearly that his division
of the *Grundschrift* was the Achilles heel of his whole
hypothesis: the solution of Graf could not be the true one:
it went only half-way."[1]

In the argument in the present book special weight
will be found to be attached to the following facts:—

1. The "pre-prophetic" character of J and E, as involved
in their admitted priority to Amos and Hosea.

2. The admittedly "parallel" character of J and E, and
their marked stylistic resemblance.

3. The admitted priority of J and E, and of the "Book
of the Covenant," to Deuteronomy.

4. The admitted priority of J and E to P (in reversal
of the older view), and the fact that P is throughout
parallel to, and presupposes, JE (Wellhausen).

5. The admission by many critics (*e.g.*, Driver, Baudissin,
Ryle) of the priority of the Levitical collection known as the
"Law of Holiness" to Ezekiel.

The turning points in the discussion are those indicated
in the text:—

1. Are J and E two documents, or one?

2. The Josianic origin of Deuteronomy.

3. The post-exilian origin of the Levitical Code.

The critical positions on these three points are traversed
and the rejection of them is shown to involve as its only
tenable alternative (middle views as Nöldeke's and Dillmann's being cut out by the Wellhausen polemic) the
essential Mosaicity of the Pentateuch.

[1] *Theol. Tijdschr.* 1870, p. 418.

CHAPTER II

The Old Testament from its own Point of View

"Israel has the idea of teleology as a kind of soul."—DORNER.

"Behind it all is the mystery of race and of *selection*. It is an ultimate fact in the history and government of the world, this eminent genius of one tiny people for religion. We know no more: and, in M. Renan's own terms, the people was 'selected,' just as, in words more familiar, Israel is 'the chosen people.'"—ANDREW LANG.

"When we say that God dealt with Israel in the way of special revelation, and crowned His dealings by personally manifesting all His grace and truth in Jesus Christ the incarnate Word, we mean that the Bible contains within itself a perfect picture of God's gracious relations with man, and that we have no need to go outside the Bible history to learn anything of God and His saving will towards us,—that the whole growth of the true religion up to its perfect fulness is set before us in the record of God's dealings with Israel culminating in the manifestation of Jesus Christ."—W. R. SMITH.

"If the first three chapters of Genesis are taken out of the Bible, it is deprived of the *terminus a quo*: if the last three chapters of the Apocalypse are taken away, it is deprived of the *terminus ad quem*."—MENKEN.

CHAPTER II

THE OLD TESTAMENT FROM ITS OWN POINT OF VIEW

OUR subject of study, then, is this book of history, of laws, of prophecy, of psalms, of wisdom literature, which we call the Old Testament. Before, however, entangling ourselves in the thorny brakes into which the critical study of this older collection of Scriptures conducts us, it is desirable that we should look for a little at the book by itself, in the form in which we have it, and allow its own voice to be heard on its character and place in the economy of revelation.

There are obvious advantages in this course. No slight is intended to be cast on criticism : but it may be gravely questioned whether this constant discussion going on *about* the Bible,—this minute dissection and analysis of it, and perpetual weighing of its parts in the nice scales of a critical balance,—has not at least one harmful effect, that, viz., of coming between men and the devout, prayerful study of the Bible itself, out of which alone can grow that sense of its harmony and proportion, and experience of its saving and sanctifying power, which yield the best proof of its divine origin. The dissecting chamber is necessary ; but it is not exactly the best place for acquiring a sense of the symmetry and beauty of the living human body, or for cultivating reverence for it. It is hardly less difficult to grow into a spiritual appreciation of Scripture, when we are not permitted to make acquaintance with a Biblical book till it has first been put upon the critic's table, and there sliced, severed, and anatomised, till all the palpitating life has gone out of it, and we are left, as chief result, with dry lists of the sections, verses, or parts of verses, supposed to belong to the different narrators or editors![1] The Bible has a character and power of impression which belong to it as a living book; it is right that these should have justice done to them before the process of disintegration begins.

We would here indicate, therefore, at the outset, what precisely it is we propose to do, and what we do not propose to do, in the present chapter. We propose, then, treating the Old Testament for the time as part of the general organism of Scripture, to take the Bible just as it is,—just as it lies before us,—and to ask what kind of a book it is, what sort of an account it gives of itself, and what kind of impression of its origin and source grows out of this first-hand acquaintance with it. We shall have little or nothing to say at this stage of theories of criticism—these will come after; nothing of questions of age, authorship, or genuineness; little of theories of revelation or inspiration. There may be gain, for once, in leaving these things for a short while aside, and permitting the Bible to speak for itself—to utter its own unconstrained testimony—to produce on the mind its own immediate effect, without reference to outside controversies. The Bible may prove in this way, as it has often proved before, to be its own best witness, and it is this aspect and evidence of its divineness which, it seems to us, it is necessary at the present time, in the difficulty and uncertainty in which many are involved, most of all to emphasise.

I. THE ORGANIC UNITY OF THE BOOK

We take up the Bible, then, in the way suggested, and the first thing, we think, that must strike us in connection with it, is, that this book is, in a remarkable sense, *a unity*. From another point of view, of course, the Bible is not one book, but a collection of books : as Jerome named it, "a divine library." It comes to us "by divers portions and in divers manners."[2] The writings that compose it are spread over at least a thousand years. Yet the singular fact is that, when these writings are put together, they

---

[1] In illustration, the reader may consult, *e.g.*, the tabular summations which are the chief outcome of the (otherwise able) article on "Exodus" in Hastings' *Dict. of the Bible* (i. pp. 806 ff.). The sensation is like chewing glass.

[2] Heb. i. 1.

constitute, structurally, one book; make up a " Bible,"[1] as
we call it, with beginning, and middle, and end, which
produces on the mind a sense of harmony and completeness.

This peculiarity in the Bible, which is not essentially
affected by any results of criticism—since, indeed, the more
the critic divides and distributes his material, the outcome
in the book as we have it is only the more wonderful[2]—is
best illustrated by contrast. For Christianity is not the
only religion in the world, nor is the Bible the only
collection of sacred books in existence. There are many
Bibles of different religions. The Mohammedan has his
Koran; the Buddhist has his Canon of Sacred Scriptures;
the Zoroastrian has his Zendavesta; the Brahman has his
Vedas. On the basis of this very fact, comparative religion
groups a number of religions together as "book-religions."
These sacred books are made accessible to us by reliable
translations, and we can compare them with our own
Scriptures. But, not to speak of the enormous superiority
of the Bible to these other sacred books, even in a literary
respect,—for few, we presume, capable of judging, would
think of comparing even the noblest of the Babylonian or
Vedic hymns, or of the Zoroastrian Gathas, in power or
grandeur, with the Hebrew psalms; or would liken the
few really lofty passages on God in the Koran with the
sustained sublimity of the Hebrew prophets; or would draw
a parallel between the wild extravagances of the Buddhist
Lalita Vistara and the simplicity, beauty, and self-restraint
of the Christian Gospels,[3]—we would fix attention only on
this one point—the contrast in respect of unity. We seek
in vain in these ethnic Scriptures for anything answering to
this name. The Koran, for instance, is a miscellany of dis-
jointed pieces, out of which it is impossible to extract any
order, progress, or arrangement. The 114 Suras or chapters
of which it is composed are arranged chiefly according
to length—the longer in general preceding the shorter.[4]

[1] Originally *Biblia*, "The Books," then "in the thirteenth century, by
a happy solecism," says Westcott, "the neuter plural came to be regarded as
a feminine singular, and 'The Books' became, by common consent, 'The
Book,' in which form the word has passed into the languages of modern
Europe."—*Bible in the Church*, p. 5.
[2] See below, Chap. III.
[3] See Note A on the Bible and other Sacred Books.
[4] They were originally, as given by Mohammed, written on pieces of
stone, bone, leather, palm-leaves, or whatever material was available, and

It is not otherwise with the Zoroastrian and Buddhist Scriptures. These are equally destitute of beginning, middle, or end. They are, for the most part, collections of heterogeneous materials, loosely placed together. How different everyone must acknowledge it to be with the Bible! From Genesis to Revelation we feel that this book is in a real sense a unity. It is not a collection of fragments, but has, as we say, an organic character. It has one connected story to tell from beginning to end; we see something growing before our eyes; there is plan, purpose, progress; the end folds back on the beginning, and, when the whole is finished, we feel that here again, as in the primal creation, God has finished all His works, and, behold, they are very good. This is a very external way, it may be granted, of looking at the Bible, yet it is a very important one. It puts the Bible before us at the outset as a unique book. There is nothing exactly resembling it, or even approaching it, in all literature.[1] To find its explanation, it compels us to go behind the fragmentariness of the parts, to the underlying unity of thought and purpose in the whole. The unity of the Bible is not something factitious—*made*. It grows out of the unity of the religion and the history, and points to that as its source.

II. FULFILMENT OF THE OLD TESTAMENT IN THE NEW

To deepen our impression of this unity of the Bible, and at the same time carry us a step further into the heart of our subject, we notice again that the Bible consists of two parts—*an Old Testament and a New*,—and would observe *how the second of these parts folds back upon the first.* The Old Testament is one group of writings, mostly in Hebrew, and the New Testament is another group of writings, in Greek, with centuries between them. Yet how manifestly is the latter the counterpart and completion of the former! The argument from prophecy has often been overdriven, and may easily be run into exaggeration and triviality; but if

thrown into a chest; thence, after Mohammed's death, they were taken out and copied. Some were preserved only by memory.

[1] "No other literature is linked into one whole like this, instinct with one spirit and purpose, and, with all its variety of character and origin, moving forward to an unseen yet certain goal."—Kirkpatrick, *Divine Library of the O.T.*, p. 92.

we take the Bible's own way of putting it, "The testimony
of Jesus is the spirit of prophecy,"[1] it is difficult for any
candid mind to deny that the spirit of the Old Testament
fulfils itself in the New. This, again, is a result largely
independent of critical discussions. Take, for example, that
wonderful picture of the suffering Servant of Jehovah in the
53rd chapter of Isaiah, which the Church has always,
and rightly, regarded as Messianic.[2] Dismissing for the
moment all critical considerations as to age, authorship,
or original reference, let anyone steep his mind in the
contents of that chapter, then read what is said about Jesus
in the Gospels, and, as he stands under the shadow of the
Cross, say if there is not the most complete correspondence
between the two. In Jesus of Nazareth, alone in all history,
but in Him perfectly, has this prophecy found a fulfilment. The meekness, the pathos of undeserved suffering,
the atoning function, the final triumph, will suit no
other.[3]

The result is not different if we enlarge our view to the
consideration of the religion of Israel as a whole. The
religion of Israel has been called a religion of hope. Its
face is always to the future.[4] The system of things in the
Old Testament presents itself prevailingly as something
provisional, temporary, incomplete. There is growth in the
Old Testament—from the patriarchal stage to the Mosaic ;
from the Mosaic to the prophetic ; but it is like the plant
developing from stalk to bud, and from bud to flower, there
is a final stage yet to come—that of the ripened fruit.[5]

[1] Rev. xix. 10.

[2] Cf. Dr. A. B. Davidson, *O.T. Prophecy*, pp. 411, 427, 445. "There
is not one," he says, "of the better class of critics who does not recognise
the pertinence of the question, In whom are the features of the Servant to
be recognised ? or who does not give the same answer to the question as
the orthodox theologian" (p. 411).

[3] Bleek, quoted by Dr. Davidson, says : "What the prophet here says as
yet in general, in reference to the Servant as such, as it were *in abstracto*,
has received its complete fulfilment in the One, who was the only holy and
perfectly sinless among the human race, and therefore the only one whose
sufferings had such a character that, not being due to His own individual
transgression in any way, they can be regarded as serving for the atonement
of the sins of men."—*O.T. Prophecy*, p. 411 ; cf. Orelli, *O.T. Prophecy*,
pp. 387 ff.

[4] *E.g.*, Gen. xii. 3.

[5] Dillmann says : "This religion of the ancient people of Israel everywhere points beyond itself, exhibiting itself as a work begun, which lacks
its final perfection, and so compels us in the nature of the case to apprehend

The old covenant is to give place to a new,—a more
inward and spiritual,—when the law of God shall be written
on men's hearts;[1] the old national forms are to break up,
and Jehovah is to become the God of the whole earth;[2] in
their deepest abasement and humiliation the people of Israel
never lose the assurance that from them the light is to go
forth which shall illumine the darkness of the whole world
—that the Gentiles shall come to their light, and kings to
the brightness of their rising.[3]   These things are not to be
brought about without instrumentality, and here we find,
trait after trait, the figure of the Messiah shaping itself,—
the King who is to reign in righteousness,[4] the Immanuel-
Child, with the wondrous fourfold name, who is the
guarantee for the perpetuity of the throne and kingdom of
David,[5] the Servant of Jehovah, who is to bear the people's
sins,[6] the Branch who is to build again the temple of
Jehovah.[7]   The Spirit will be poured out upon all flesh,[8]
and the kingdom of God will come.

Now, let anyone open his New Testament, and say if
there is no counterpart to, and completion of, all this there.
Something higher, grander, diviner, no doubt, than even the
prophets could imagine; yet bringing to pass in every
essential respect all that they foretold, all that lay in the
bosom of that old covenant waiting its realisation.[9]   May
we not say that the Christian Church itself is a living proof
of the truth of these predictions?   Is it not Israel's God
we worship?   Is it not Israel's faith that beats in our
hearts?   Israel's Messiah we trust in for salvation?   Israel's
privilege to which we are admitted?   Every time we sing
these old Hebrew psalms, which are to this hour so marvellous an expression of the faith, and hope, and aspirations
of the soul seeking after God, do we not declare that we
it in relation to Christianity, as that in which essentially it is perfected."—*Alttest. Theol.* p. 8.

[1] Cf. Deut. xxx. 6 ; Jer. xxxi. 31-4 ; xxxii. 39, 40 ; Ezek. xi. 19, 20 ;
xxxvi. 26, 27.
   [2] Num. xiv. 21 ; Isa. xlv. 22, 23 ; Zeph. ii. 11 ; Hag. ii. 6, 7.
   [3] Isa. lx., etc.   [4] Isa. xxxii. 1 ; xxxiii. 15, 16.
   [5] Isa. vii. 14 ; viii. 8, 10 ; ix. 6, 7 ; cf. Mic. v. 2, 3.
   [6] Isa. liii.
   [7] Zech. iii. 8 ; vi. 12 ; cf. Isa. iv. 2 ; Jer. xxiii. 5.
   [8] Joel ii. 28, 29.   On these passages see the works on O.T. Prophecy by
Davidson, Delitzsch, Riehm, Orelli, etc., and cf. below, Chap. XII. p. 460.
   [9] Cf. the suggestive sections in Riehm's *Mess. Prophecy* (E.T. 1876),
pp. 33 ff.

belong to the same spiritual city as the men who wrote
them ?[1] When, accordingly, the New Testament gathers up
all these types and prophecies of the Old Testament, and
sees them fulfilled in Christ,[2]—calls Him, for example, the
"Lamb of God, which taketh away the sin of the world,"[3]
the "chief corner stone, elect, precious," which God has laid
in Zion,[4] identifies Him with that Servant of whom it is
declared that the Spirit of Jehovah was upon Him, to
preach good tidings to the meek, to bind up the broken-
hearted, to proclaim liberty to the captives, and the opening
of the prison to them that are bound,[5]—do we not feel that
it is justified in so doing ? When the writer of the Epistle
to the Hebrews sees all the old rites and institutions
glorified in the light of the new religion, and represents
them as types and shadows which have fulfilled their
function, and pass away now that the reality has come,[6]—do
we not recognise that he is giving us the truest *rationale* of
that old economy ? When the Book of Revelation tells of
Paradise restored, and figures the tree of life growing in the
midst,[7] do we not feel that the end of revelation, in very
truth, looks back to its beginning, and that here the ruin of
Eden is repaired, and the curse of man's first disobedience,
which "brought death into our world, and all our woe,"
finally abolished ? There is again nothing mechanical in
this relation of the Old and New Testaments. The connec
tion is vital, not external, but is on that account all the
more wonderful, and without parallel.

III. Teleological Character of the History

We have seen that this surprising unity which characterises the Bible is only to be explained by going back
to the *history* and the *religion* which the Bible makes known

---

[1] Cf. Ps. lxxxvii. (R.V.).

[2] Kuenen allows that this fulfilment was claimed by Jesus and His
disciples, and says "it is impossible for us to form too high an estimate of
the importance of the application of these passages."—*Prophets and Prophecy*,
pp. 522 ff. But he holds that the interpretation is unwarranted. Yet how
singular that these representations should admit of "being merged in one
grand figure," if nothing of the kind was intended.

[3] John i. 29.   [4] 1 Pet. ii. 6 ; cf. Isa. xxviii. 16.

[5] Isa. lxi. 1 ; cf. Luke iv. 18. It is Jesus Himself who makes this
identification.

[6] Heb. ix. 9 ; x. 1.   [7] Rev. ii. 7 ; xxii. 2.

to us, in which the real mystery or wonder lies. The Bible is a unique book, because it is the record and literature of a unique religion. We turn first to the *history*, and here are at once arrested by what may be described as its *teleological* character. "Israel," says Dorner, "has the idea of teleology as a kind of soul."[1] Its history, that is, is dominated by the idea of purpose. It is this which gives unity to the history and to the books which contain it. The purpose is not always consciously apprehended by the actors in the events; still less, as we shall see hereafter, is it something which exists only in the minds of the authors of the books, and is by them *put into* the history.[2] It lies in the facts themselves, and reveals itself with increasing clearness as the history proceeds, till at length the mystery "hid from all ages and generations"[3] is fully unveiled in Christ and His salvation. This teleological character of the history is recognised by every writer of genuine insight into the spiritual nature of Israel's religion,[4] and is allowed to stamp the religion with a uniqueness which absolutely distinguishes it from every other.

But the fact lies on the face of the history itself. This is readily seen by a glance at the development. The basis is laid in the account of the creation of the world, and of the culmination of that creation in man. From this the narrative goes on to recount man's fall, and to trace the development of the race in the lines of piety and impiety through Seth and Cain respectively, till the growing corruption of the world brings upon it the judgment of the flood. A new start is made in the covenant with Noah, from whom the repeopling of the world, and the distribution of its races, proceed. The growing spread of godlessness, and lapse of the nations into heathenism, leads to the next step in the unfolding of the divine purpose in the call of Abraham, and in the promises made to him and

[1] *Syst. of Doct.* i. p. 274.
[2] See this discussed below, Chap. III. pp. 62–64.
[3] Col. i. 26 ; cf. Eph. iii. 3, 9.
[4] Schultz, *e.g.*, in his *O.T. Theol.* p. 2, says : "We mean to describe, not various forms of religion, which have merely an external connection of place or time, but a *single* religion in the various stages of its development, which stages consequently have an organic inner connection. Hence in such a presentation each member must be properly linked to its fellow. A common ligament of living growth must bind all the parts together. The presentation must be, not merely historical, but *genetic.*"

to his seed. The promise of blessing, beginning in Eden,[1] afterwards restricted to the line of Shem,[2] is now, in the Abrahamic covenant, definitely associated with this patriarch and his posterity—not, however, in the spirit of a narrow particularism, but with a view to the ultimate blessing of mankind.[3] Already appears at this early stage of the history that law of election,—of gracious purpose working along a defined line for an ultimate larger good,—which is so marked a feature of the history throughout. The line of promise still further narrows itself—for limitation and definiteness here are essential to success—in Abraham's sons, in the election of Isaac, not Ishmael; in Isaac's sons, in the choice of Jacob, not Esau; in Jacob's sons, in the designation of Judah as the royal tribe.[4] The patriarchal age, with its renewals of the covenant, its prophetic announcements, its singular providences, its preparation in the elevation of Joseph for the descent into Egypt, ends with the removal to that country, where the people had room and opportunity to multiply, till, with change of dynasty, the fiery trial overtook them by which they were finally welded into a nation.

The Mosaic age, which succeeds the patriarchal, is closely linked with the preceding through the promises to the fathers, of which it brought the fulfilment. Allusion need only be made to the series of events which marks this beginning of Israel's national life—the birth and call of Moses, the Exodus, the covenant at Sinai, the discipline of the wilderness, the settlement in Canaan, the land before promised to Abraham. The vicissitudes and disorganisation of the time of the Judges and of Samuel lead up to the rise of the monarchy, and to the new hopes and promises attached to the line of David.[5] The rending of the kingdom, and the backslidings and often wholesale lapses into idolatry of the people, might seem to portend the ruin of these hopes, and the frustration of the divine purpose. But the singular—the unexampled—thing in the history of this people is that the purpose of God in the history is *not*

[1] Gen. iii. 15. Ottley says that this passage "strikes at the outset of redemptive history the note of promise and of hope."—*Hist. of Hebs.* p. 11. Cf. Driver, *Genesis*, pp. 49, 57.
[2] Gen. ix. 26.   [3] Gen. xii. 3; cf. xviii. 18; xxii. 18.
[4] Gen. xlix. 10. On the interpretation, cf. Driver, *Genesis*, pp. 385, 410–14; Orelli, *O.T. Prophecy*, pp. 118–23, etc.
[5] 2 Sam. vii.

defeated by outward failure; rather, it is in the **depth of** adversity and seeming defeat that it asserts itself **most** clearly, enlarges, purifies, and spiritualises itself, and **is** never, in the prophets, more confident of victory than when, to the eye of sense, the cause of the kingdom of God **a**ppears hopelessly lost.

We need not pursue this proof of a teleological character **in** the history of Israel further. The same result would be **o**btained if, starting with the completed revelation, we **l**ooked at the history retrogressively. Not only does the Gospel of the kingdom which Jesus proclaimed unfold itself from the bosom of the Jewish community, but the whole consciousness of Jesus roots itself in the older revelation,—presupposes it, moves in the circle of its ideas, claims to be the fulfilment of it. It was not the prophets only that Jesus came to fulfil, but " the law and the prophets," [1]—the whole Old Testament revelation. If we go back to the prophetic age, we find the prophets as uniformly basing their message on the covenant relation of Israel to Jehovah which the earlier history attests.[2] The national consciousness of Israel connects itself unalterably with Moses and the Exodus, and with the laws and statutes it then received from Jehovah; yet with not less distinctness it declares that the national stage in its history was not the earliest, but was preceded by the patriarchal, and by the covenants with the fathers. Israel's God was the God of Abraham, of Isaac, and of Jacob. The starting-point in its covenant history was not Moses, but Abraham.[3] There is thus displayed throughout the whole of these Old Testament Scriptures a historical continuity, a firmness and coherence of texture, a steadily evolving, and victorious, self-fulfilling purpose, which has nowhere, even in the remotest degree, its parallel in the history of religions.

IV. Unique Ideas of the Religion

Thus far we have looked at the *book* and at the *history* of Israel's religion, and have found in both a character for

[1] Matt. v. 17.
[2] *E.g.*, Amos ii. 4, 10 ; iii. 1, 2 ; Hos. viii. 1 ; xi. 1-4 ; Mic. vi. 4 ; Isa. i. 2 ; v. 1-7 ; xi. 16 ; li. 1, 2, 10 ; Jer. ii. 17, etc.
[3] Isa. xxix. 22 ; li. 1 ; Jer. xxxiii. 26 ; Ezek. xxxiii. 24 ; Mic. vii. 20. See on this below, pp. 94 ff.

which no proper parallel can be discovered elsewhere: we now advance a stage further, and inquire whether the *religion itself* does not present a similar uniqueness. Only those who have not truly entered into its spirit, or appreciated its relation to other forms of belief, will dispute the proposition that the religion of Israel is unique. It is not the fact of its uniqueness, but whether the uniqueness is of such a kind as to require us to postulate a special, supernatural cause for its explanation, which is matter of controversy. We shall see immediately what the Old Testament itself has to say on that point.

1. A unique religion will display its character equally by what it has and by what it wants. There are, on the *negative* side, many things absent in Israel's religion which we should expect to find there, if it was simply one among other religions. Resemblances, as before remarked, in outward respects, there necessarily are. In the religion of Israel we have a sanctuary, priesthood, altars, sacrifices, ritual— much more that has its counterpart in other cults. When, however, from this outward vesture of the religion, we come to its heart and essence, it is not the resemblances, but the contrasts, which impress us. We are not disposed to be stinted in our acknowledgment of the better elements in the ethnic religions; but, whatever place may be given to these, the fact remains that, in their historical forms, the higher elements are hardly visible, while the foreground is occupied by an idolatrous worship, an extravagant and often immoral mythology, customs and usages debasing to the last degree. We need only recall the spirit-worship and magic of Babylonia; the animal-worship and ancestor-worship of Egypt; the stone-worship, and tree-worship, and serpent-worship, the human sacrifices, the lustful rites, the self-immolations, which enter so deeply into most non-Biblical religions. How great the contrast when we come to the religion of Israel! We do not enter into details at present, for we shall have to return to the subject in dealing with the very different theory of the critical school, that Israel began practically on the same level, and with much the same beliefs and practices, as its heathen neighbours, and only late in its history, in the days of the prophets, attained to higher

conceptions.[1]   It will not be contended, at least, that this is
the view of things that meets us on the *face* of the religion.
Few will be bold enough to maintain that tree-worship,
stone-worship, serpent-worship, image-worship, and similar
superstitions, are conspicuous features on the Bible page.
These things, we grant, or some of them, are found in the
Bible history—in patriarchal and Mosaic times in sparse
traces ; later, in times of general declension, when the
people fell away into the idolatries and vices of the nations
around them, more abundantly; but they are no proper
part of Israel's religion, and are invariably resisted,
denounced, and condemned, as apostacy from Jehovah.
Idolatry is sternly condemned in the oldest code of laws :[2]
divination, necromancy, consulting with familiar spirits,
are prohibited;[3] the instances in which contrary practices
appear, as Rachel's teraphim,[4] Micah's images,[5] Saul's consulting of the witch of Endor,[6] etc., are sporadic and
occasional, and appear either as survivals of older superstitions, or as violations of fundamental principles of
the religion, such as are met with in every age and
country.[7]

2. We do not dwell longer on these negative features
of Israel's religion, but turn to the *positive* side, in which,
naturally, the clearest proof of its uniqueness must lie.
Here it may be sufficient to fix attention on *three great
fundamental ideas*, in which, perhaps, the contrast between
it and other forms of religion is most distinctly to be traced.

(1) We take, first, what meets us on the surface—the
monotheism of this Israelitish religion. This of itself is
much, if we think of the polytheism and idolatry which
everywhere else overspread the earth. We look to the
religions of ancient Babylonia, Assyria, and Egypt, or

---

[1] See Chaps. IV. p. 86 ; V. pp. 133 ff.   [2] Ex. xx. 4, 5 ; xxiii. 4.
[3] Deut. xviii. 9-14.
[4] Gen. xxxi. 34 (stolen from her father Laban, ver. 30).
[5] Judg. xvii.
[6] 1 Sam. xxviii. The fact that Saul had put down all witches and
wizards is proof of the law.
[7] Kuenen objects that the current conceptions of Israel's religion are
drawn, not from the facts, but from the general reviews of the Hebrew
historians.—*Nat. Religions*, etc. (Hibbert Lectures), pp. 69 ff. Professor
Robertson aptly replies that, if we turn to these reviews, "they are precisely
in the tone of the prophets Amos and Hosea, the very earliest witnesses to
whom we are allowed to appeal."—*Early Rel. of Israel*, p. 116.

to those of Israel's own kinsfolk and neighbours in and around Palestine;[1] and, while recognising higher elements in these religions, ever, however, becoming dimmer as we recede from their source, we find them, one and all, in historical times, grossly, growingly, and incurably, polytheistic and corrupt. In Judah alone was God known. In no single case, moreover, was this polytheism ever thrown off by inherent effort. Even, therefore, were the theory, favoured by modern critics, that "ethical monotheism" was only attained by Israel in the age of the great prophets, allowed to be established, the fact would still remain to be accounted for that Israel, alone of all nations, *did* attain to it, and became the teacher of the rest of the world. We do not, however, give our adherence to the view that this monotheism of the religion of Israel was a late development of the time of the prophets. As will be shown more fully in a subsequent chapter,[2] the Old Testament knows of no time when the people of Israel were without the knowledge of the one God as the Creator and providential Ruler of the whole world. Monotheism is not the doctrine of one part of the Old Testament, and not of another. Its oldest parts — those which the critics allow to be the oldest[3]—have this doctrine of the unity of God as well as the latest. In these oldest parts, we have as fundamental ideas the creation of the world by God, the unity of the human family as descended from a first pair, made by God, the destruction of the whole race by a flood on account of sin, the promises to Noah, embracing the whole earth,[4] a new descent and distribution of the race from Noah, the recognition of God by Abraham as the Judge of the whole earth,[5]—all laying the foundation for the call of Abraham, the covenants with the patriarchs, the growth of Israel into a nation, its redemption from bondage, and formation into a people for God's glory. While, therefore, it is not contended that there was no advance in the ideas of God,— no deepening, purifying, or spiritualising of these ideas, —from the days of Abraham and Moses, it may very confidently be maintained that, in the Old Testament as we

[1] As respects the Semitic peoples, cf. Professor G. A. Smith's *Modern Criticism*, pp. 111-29.
[2] Chap. V. pp. 123 ff.
[3] The J and E histories, see pp. 65-66.
[4] Gen. viii. 20, 21 : ix.
[5] Gen. xviii. 25.

have it, the unity of God is present as a basal conception
from the first.

(2) The monotheism of Israel, however, is not the whole,
is not even the main thing, in this religion. It is not so
much, after all, in its declarations of what God is in
Himself, or of the unity of God, as in what it tells us of
the relations of God to man, and of *His purposes of grace to
the world*, that the peculiarity of the religion of the Old
Testament lies.[1] No religion exalts man so high as the
religion of the Bible, in representing him as made in the
image of God, and capable of knowing, loving, and serving
God; and no religion abases man so low, in picturing the
depths of his apostacy from God, and his inability to deliver
himself from the guilt and bondage in which that apostacy
has involved him. But it is the glory of the religion of
the Bible—this in both Old Testament and New—that over
against the picture it gives of the developing sin and corruption of the race, there appears almost from its first
page the developing plan and purpose of God for man's
salvation.[2] The history of the Bible is essentially, what
Jonathan Edwards called it, "the history of redemption."
If the malady is aggravated, the remedy provided is
adequate to cope with it, even on the Bible's own showing
of its evil. In Paul's language, "Where sin abounded, grace
did abound more exceedingly."[3] This again brings us to
the idea of teleology, but now shows us more precisely in
what the teleology consists. It is the unfolding in its successive stages of God's gracious counsel for man's salvation.[4]
It is this which gives its unity to the Bible; which is the
golden thread running through history, psalm, prophecy,
Gospel, epistle, and binding all together. There is nothing,
again, which even remotely resembles this in any other
religion. The partial exception is the Zoroastrian, which,
in a dim, mythological way, has the idea of a conflict of the
good principle with the evil, and of a final triumph of the

[1] Cf. Kirkpatrick, *Divine Library*, p. 93.
[2] See below, pp. 61–62.   [3] Rom. v. 20.
[4] Cf. Ottley, *Aspects of O.T.*, pp. 55 ff. : "The Old Testament is to be
studied, in the first place, as a record of the history of redemption. It
contains the account of a continuous historical movement of which the
originating cause was the grace of God, and the aim the salvation of the
human race." On p. 93 : "In the Pentateuch and the historical books, the
two most prominent ideas are those of redemption and revelation."

good. But, apart from the fact that, as was inevitable on a dualistic basis, good and evil are in Zoroastrianism largely physical conceptions, the idea receives no development, is the subject of no history, is embodied in no plan which is historically carried out. The uniqueness of the Biblical religion appears only the more strikingly from the contrast.

(3) The aim of God's salvation, of His entire work of grace in humanity, is, that man shall be made *holy*.[1] This brings us to a third marked feature in the religion of the Old Testament, as of the Biblical religion generally—*the indissoluble relation it establishes between religion and morality*. Religions can readily be found which have no close connection with morality; we are familiar also with a morality which would fain make itself independent of religion. In few of the higher religions, however, is this relation between religion and morality altogether obscured. Throughout history there is generally some dim perception that the gods will protect and reward the good, and will not fail to punish the evil-doer. The peculiarity of the Biblical religion is that in it this idea of the connection of religion with morality is the all-dominating one. To minds awakened to the significance of the moral it may now appear self-evident that a religion has no real worth which does not ally itself with moral ends,—which, going beyond even external guardianship and sanction of duties, does not take morality up into itself as the expression of the will and character of God, and count moral obedience an essential part of His service. But it should not be forgotten that this was not always the view taken of religion, and that it is largely through the influence of the religion of the Bible, purifying and ennobling our conceptions, that we have now come to perceive even this truth as clearly as we do. Already in its first pages—before the word " holy " is yet met with—the Old Testament sets itself against sin in heart and deed.[2]   God accepts and vindicates righteous men like Abel, Enoch, and Noah; overwhelms with His judgments a world corrupted by sin; destroys wicked cities like Sodom and Gomorrah. He requires that Abraham shall walk before Him and be perfect; Abraham's assurance

[1] Cf. Dillmann, *Alttest. Theol.* p. 42.
[2] See below, pp. 114–15.

about Him is that the Judge of all the earth will do right.[1] As revelation advances, the indissolubleness of this connection of religion and morality becomes only clearer. The ethical was never so exalted; the ideals of conduct were never raised so high; religion and duty were never so completely fused together, as in the pure and sublime precepts of psalms and prophets. "He hath showed thee, O man, what is good, and what doth Jehovah require of thee, but to do justly, to love mercy, and to walk humbly with thy God."[2]   A religion of this kind, so high in its views of God, so true to the needs of man, so adequate in its provisions for man's deliverance, so holy in its spirit, so exalted in its moral demands, never emanated, we may be sure, from man's own devisings. It is too high for him; he could not attain to it. Even if he could have conceived the idea of it, he could not have translated it into fact and history as is done in the Scriptures.

V. CLAIM TO AN ORIGIN IN REVELATION

This, accordingly, is the next thing which impresses us in our study of the Old Testament,—the consciousness which everywhere pervades it that this religion, the historical stages of which it unfolds to us, is not the creation of man's own spirit, but is a product of *special divine revelation.* The tendency of the modern mind, it was before seen, is to substitute psychology for revelation. Instead of God's word to Isaiah, or John, or Paul, it gives us the thoughts of Isaiah, or John, or Paul about God. Even where the word "revelation" is used, it is with this purely psychological connotation.[3] This, however, is not the Bible's own point of view. The Bible is not primarily a record of man's thoughts about God, but a record of what God has done and revealed of Himself to man. Its basis is not, "Thus and thus thinks man," but, "Thus and thus saith Jehovah," or, "Thus and thus Jehovah has done." It records, indeed, man's thoughts about God—his prayers, struggles, hopes, meditations, aspirations—but these spring always out of what God has made known of Himself in word and deed. The Bible is not a mere revelation of

[1] Gen. xvii. 1, xviii. 25, etc.
[2] Mic. vi. 8.   [3] See above, p. 21.

abstract, or what Lessing would call "eternal," truths about God, but above all a discovery of the way in which God has revealed His loving will to man in word and deed in history. "He made known His ways unto Moses, His doings unto the children of Israel."[1] It is this, we would here observe, which makes the historical element in Scripture so indispensable and precious, and warns us against the tendency to speak slightingly of it, as if myth and legend would serve the purposes of revelation equally with fact.[2] Everyone feels that this is not the case with the history of Christ in the Gospels; but in the Old Testament also it is in great measure true that it was not from inward intuition, or reflections of their own, that prophets and psalmists, or the ordinary pious Israelite, derived their knowledge of God, and assured confidence in Him, but from what God had revealed of Himself in the past history of the people.[3] The *acts* were the source, the medium, the authorisation of the knowledge; and, if these were taken away, the knowledge would disappear with them. Accordingly, we find that, in the highest point which the saint of the Old Testament can reach in the apprehension of this revelation, he still feels that it transcends him, is infinitely above him, in a way which anything proceeding from his own thoughts could not be. Thus: "Many, O Jehovah my God, are Thy wonderful works which Thou hast done, and Thy thoughts which are to us-ward: they cannot be set in order unto Thee: if I would declare and speak of them, they are more than can be numbered."[4] Or again: "My thoughts are not your thoughts, neither are your ways My ways, saith Jehovah. For as the heavens are higher than the earth, so are My ways higher than your ways, and My thoughts than your thoughts."[5]

Here, then, we strike on another great peculiarity of Israel's consciousness — the sense, viz., that it was the

[1] Ps. ciii. 7.

[2] Thus, *e.g.*, Schultz, *O. T. Theol.* i. pp. 17-23: "In fact, legend must be regarded as fitted in a higher degree than history to be the medium of the Holy Spirit." Would Schultz apply this to the history of Jesus in the Gospels? See Note B on Mythology and History in the Old Testament.

[3] Cf. W. R. Smith, *Prophets*, pp. 10-14 ; Ladd, *Doct. of Sac. Scripture*, i. pp. 737 ff. ; Bruce, *Chief End of Revelation*, pp. 57 ff. This connecting of revelation with *acts* of God is the strong point made in Rothe's *Zur Dogmatik.*

[4] Ps. xl. 5.   [5] Isa. lv. 8, 9.

possessor and guardian of a quite peculiar revelation from God, and in this respect occupied a perfectly unique position among the nations of the earth. The answer to this, we know, is thought to be simple. It is often said by those who believe all religions to be equally a natural growth: "Every nation in the beginning of its history has its wonderful stories to tell of miracles, revelations, apparitions of the gods: all religions in this respect are much the same: the Jewish and Christian religions are just like the rest." But we would take the liberty to reply: That is not quite the case. There *is* no other nation on earth which has such a story to tell of the beginnings of its religion—even as a story, we mean—as the Israelite had to tell of his, and the Israelite was perfectly conscious of this absolutely unique character of his history. Mythologies, fables, legends of appearances of the gods there are in abundance; but no such orderly, coherent history, charged with great ideas, as that which meets us in the Bible. This consciousness of the absolutely exceptional character of the history is brought out very strikingly in one passage in the Book of Deuteronomy. Moses there speaks: "For ask now of the days that are past, which were before thee, since the day that God created man upon the earth, and from the one end of the heaven unto the other, whether there hath been any such thing as this great thing is, or hath been heard like it? Did ever people hear the voice of God speaking out of the midst of the fire, as thou hast heard, and live? Or hath God assayed to go and take Him a nation from the midst of another nation, by temptations, by signs, and by wonders, and by war, and by a mighty hand, and by a stretched-out arm, and by great terrors, according to all that Jehovah your God did for you in Egypt before your eyes? Unto thee it was shewed, that thou mightest know that Jehovah He is God: there is none else beside Him." [1] If this be true of the origin of the religion of Israel, it is still more true of the origin of Christianity; for, assuredly, no other religion is founded on such a history as that of Jesus Christ,—on the character, claims, work, life, death, and resurrection, of such a Person as Jesus Christ is,—no, not in all the world!

The truth is, it is vain to attempt to find a parallel for

[1] Deut. iv. 32-35; cf. vers. 6-8.

this wholly unique phenomenon of the religion of Israel.
Take again the two points already mentioned: the monotheism of this religion, and the indissoluble connection it
establishes between religion and morality.   It is not
uncommon to hear this monotheistic faith spoken of as if
it were a stage which, given only favourable conditions,
every nation was bound to reach in the course of its
development.[1]   Man begins, it is supposed, by worshipping
spirits, or ghosts of ancestors, or something of the kind;
then mounts to the conception of a tribal deity; then
extends the power of this deity, or blends the deity with
others, till he is viewed as the sole ruler of the world.   But,
unfortunately, the facts do not bear out this ingenious
theory.   It has frequently been pointed out that there are,
even yet, only *three* monotheistic religions in the world—
the Jewish, the Christian, and the Mohammedan, which,
in this respect, is derived from the other two.   That is to
say, all the monotheistic religion there is in the world is
derived from the religion of the Bible.   It is not meant
that, beneath and behind the polytheism of older religions,
there are not many indications of a purer monotheistic
consciousness, or that there have not often been, in individuals and schools, very remarkable approximations to the
truth about the unity, power, wisdom, goodness, and
providence of God.[2]   In that sense God has never left
Himself without witness.   But it is a well-understood truth
that philosophical speculations have never founded, or can
found, a religion; and it is simple fact of history that no
monotheistic religions—religions, that is, based on the unity
and spirituality of God as fundamental articles—have ever
arisen, except those above mentioned.

Or take the other point—the indissoluble blending of
morality and religion.   Where, again, do we find anything
corresponding to this outside the Biblical revelation?   One
of the early fathers of the Church gives us a description
of an Egyptian temple—lofty, spacious, gorgeous, inspiring
the worshipper by its grandeur with solemn awe.   You

---

[1] Kuenen, *e.g.*, says: "To what we might call the universal, or at least
the common rule, that religion begins with fetishism, then develops into
polytheism, and then, but not before, ascends to monotheism—that is to
say, if this highest stage be reached [a very important proviso]—to this rule
the Israelites are no exception."—*Rel. of Israel*, i. p. 225.

[2] See p. 128 below.

enter the precincts of the temple, but when the priest, with
grave air, draws aside the veil that hides the inner shrine,
you behold — what? A cat, a crocodile, a serpent, or
other animal, rolling on a purple couch.[1] Visit now the
temple of Jehovah at Jerusalem. Here, too, you have a
gorgeous building; here, too, a priesthood, altars, a shrine
hidden by a veil. Within the veil stands the ark of the
covenant, covered by the mercy-seat, sprinkled with blood
of atonement, and shadowed by the golden cherubim. Let
that covering be lifted, and within that ark, in the very
core and centre of Israel's religion, in its most sacred place,
you find—what? *The two tables of the moral law.* There,
in a word, is the contrast of the two religions. There is
the declaration of the truth that, before and above all
things else, Israel's is an ethical religion. For these are
" the tables of the testimony " [2]—the basis and bond of the
nation's covenant with God—and all the ritual of ceremonial
institutions is but a scaffolding to protect this ethical core
from injury, or a means of restoring the worshipper to
favour when sin has disturbed his fellowship. It will be
remembered that, when Jesus came, He did not cut Himself
off from that older revelation, but declared that on its two
commandments of love to God and love to man hung all
the law and the prophets.[3]

VI. REVELATION IN RELATION TO ITS RECORD

If we thus let the Bible—Old Testament and New—
speak for itself, and compare it part with part: still more
if we yield ourselves to its power, and strive faithfully to
follow its directions, the conviction will irresistibly grow
upon us that it is right when it claims to be based on
divine revelation. Out of that revelation, the *literature of
revelation*, which we call the Bible, grows. If this fact be
firmly apprehended, particular questions about the dates or
placing of books will not much trouble us. The revelation is
there, and no changes in the dates or placing of books—none
at least that are likely to be permanently brought out—can
do anything to alter its fundamental outlines. *If* a revelation has been given, it is surely the most natural thing in

[1] Clem. Alex. *Pæd.* iii. 2.
[2] Ex. xxxii. 15. See below, Chap. VI. pp. 152 ff.   [3] Matt. xxii. 40.

the world to expect that a record should be made or kept
of the stages of that revelation, either by its original
recipients, or by those who stood within the circle of
revelation, and possessed in an eminent degree its spirit.[1]
That such a literature exists, adequate in every respect for
making known to us the revelation, animated and penetrated by its spirit, though in varying degrees,—for the
strictest upholder of inspiration will hardly place the Books
of Chronicles on the same level with the Gospel of St. John,
—fitted as a whole infallibly to accomplish its great end of
making men wise unto salvation through faith in Jesus
Christ, and of completely furnishing the man of God unto
every good work,[2]—*that* such a literature exists, the only
ultimate proof that can be given is the existence of the
book itself; and such a book, as we have seen even from
this brief inspection of its character, we have in the Bible.
The simple fact that in this sacred volume, so marvellous
in its own structure, so harmonious and complete in the
view it gives of the dealings of God with man, so rich and
exhaustless in its spiritual content, so filled with the manifest presence and power of the Spirit of God, we have everything we need to acquaint us fully with the mind and will of
God for our salvation, and to supply us for all the ends of
our spiritual life, is sufficient evidence that the revelation
which God has given is, in every essential particular, purely
and faithfully embodied in it. No more than the revelation from which it springs, is the Bible a product of mere
human wisdom, but has God for its inspiring source!

This, as we understand it, is the Bible's own test of its
inspiration, alike in Old Testament and in New,[3] and by
it, without nearer definition, we are content, for our present
purpose, to abide. The subject is taken hold of by its
wrong end, when the test of inspiration is sought primarily

---

[1] " What would be the conceivable nature of revealed religion, without a
record of facts ? The briefest consideration convinces us, that either the
whole nature of revelation must be essentially changed, or else a record of
its historic process must somehow be preserved. To be sure, the fact of
ultimate and supreme importance is the fact of revelation itself. But the
very nature of revelation, if it is to take the form of an historic process, is
such as to demand a record of that process. The foundations of Christianity
are historically laid," etc.—Ladd, *Doct. of Sac. Script.* i. p. 737.

[2] 2 Tim. iii. 15–17.

[3] Cf., *e.g.*, Deut. xxx. 10–16 ; Josh. i. 7, 8 ; Pss. i., xix. 7–14, cxix. ;
John xiv. 26 ; xx. 31 ; Rom. xv. 4, etc.

4

in minute inerrancy in external details, as those of geography, or chronology, or of physical science. Inspiration does not create the materials of its record: it works upon them.[1] The crucial question is—Do the qualities which inspiration is expressly declared to confer on Scripture—*e.g.*, in such a classical passage as 2 Tim. iii. 15–17—really belong to it? We think it will be difficult for any candid mind to deny that they do. Who, coming to this sacred book, with a sincere desire to know God's will for the direction of his life, will say that he cannot find it? Who, desiring to be instructed in the way of salvation "through faith which is in Christ Jesus," will consult its pages, and say it is not made plain to him? Who, coming to it for equipment of his spiritual life, will say that there are still needs of that life which are left unprovided for? Who, seeking direction in the way of the life everlasting, can doubt that, if he faithfully obeys its teaching, he will reach that goal? The Scripture fulfils the ends for which it was given; no higher proof of its inspiration can be demanded.[2]

VII. Relation of the Old Testament to Christ

There is but one further remark we would make in closing this chapter. It relates to the place which Christ holds in Scripture, and ought to have in our study of every part of it. If what has been said of divine revelation is true, it follows that everything else in Scripture has its centre and point of connection in Him. If the Bible is a structure, Christ is the corner stone in that structure. All else in it is designed to lead up to Him, while in knowing Him, in learning to see in Him the image and revelation of the Father, in being drawn into sympathy with His

[1] See Note C on Inspiration and the Materials of the Record.
[2] Cf. Westcott, *Bible in the Church*, p. 14: "The Bible contains in itself the fullest witness to its divine authority. If it appears that a large collection of fragmentary records, written, with few exceptions, without any designed connection, at most distant times and under the most varied circumstances, yet combine to form a definite whole, broadly separated from other books . . . if in proportion as they are felt to be separate they are felt also to be instinct with a common spirit; then it will be readily acknowledged that, however they were united afterwards into the sacred volume, they are yet legibly stamped with the divine seal as 'inspired of God' in a sense in which no other writings are."

Spirit, in tasting the grace of His salvation,—in coming to know that in Him we possess "the true God and eternal life," [1]—we gain the key which sets all else in Scripture in its true light. Without this key we are bound to miss our way in the search for its secret. No learning, no cleverness, will enable us to find it out. In vain do we go to the Old Testament, or to any part of Scripture, for the satisfaction of a mere intellectual or literary curiosity. It was not for this it was given, but to conduct us into the presence of Him who, of God, is made unto us wisdom, and righteousness, and sanctification, and redemption.[2] What the closing verse of the 20th chapter of John's Gospel says of that book: "But these are written, that ye may believe that Jesus is the Christ, the Son of God, and that believing ye may have life through His name," [3] may with equal truth be applied to the Bible as a whole. Christ is the central sun in that firmament: only when we are brought within the range of His beams have we the light of life.

[1] 1 John v. 20.   [2] 1 Cor. i. 30.   [3] John xx. 31.

CHAPTER III

The Old Testament as affected by Criticism—
I. The History: Argument from Critical
Premises

"The Bible is through and through of historical nature and spirit."—
EWALD.

"For what is the Old Testament from the Christian point of view—
and from no other point of view can it be rightly understood—but the
record of God's gradual revelation of Himself to Israel in His purpose of
redeeming love with a view to the establishment of His universal kingdom!
The Incarnation was to be the culminating point of that revelation and
that purpose."—A. F. KIRKPATRICK.

"On the other hand, writers of the liberal school in Germany take so
completely for granted,—either on mere *critical* grounds, or because they
assume from the first the utter impossibility of miracles or supernatural
revelations,—the unhistorical character and non-Mosaic origin of the greater
portion, at least, if not the whole, of the Pentateuch, that they do not
generally take the trouble to test the credibility of the story, by entering
into such matter-of-fact inquiries as are here made the basis of the whole
argument."—COLENSO.

"We nevertheless firmly maintain that the preceding history of Israel,
from the Elohistic account of the creation to the history of Joseph, was
written in ancient pre-exilian times."—DELITZSCH.

"Kuenen's name for the book [JE] with which we are dealing, viz.,
the 'Prophetic' narrative, is scarcely happy. Some of its most remarkable
elements are, as Kuenen himself points out, pre-prophetic. . . . The two
books evidently proceeded in parallel lines of narrative, and it is often hard
—nay, impossible—to say whether a particular section of the Hexateuch
belongs to the Jahvist or the Elohist."—ADDIS.

CHAPTER III

THE OLD TESTAMENT AS AFFECTED BY CRITICISM —I. THE HISTORY: ARGUMENT FROM CRITICAL PREMISES

LONG ere this point is reached, loud protests will have been raised against the flagrantly " uncritical " character of our procedure, as shown in our ignoring of those well-established results of scholarship which have had the effect of shivering the supposed unity of the Old Testament, and of destroying the credibility of its narratives, especially of those which have had most weight attached to them in the history of revelation. We shall now do what we can to remove this reproach by proceeding to inquire how far the view of the Old Testament to which we have been led by the consideration of its own structure is overthrown or modified by the application of a really scientific criticism. Further, that no undue advantage may be taken, or cause given for complaint that the strength of the critical position is overlooked, we propose, in the first instance, as indicated in the preliminary sketch, to discuss the questions of the history, and of the religion and institutions, of Israel, on the basis of the critical theory itself, that is, with provisional assumption of the correctness of the ordinary critical analysis and dating of books. The canvassing of the critical theory on its merits will come after. But it is well at the outset to see what follows, even if the generally-accepted critical analysis, to its full extent, is admitted. In this chapter and the next we shall deal with the *history*.

It is not necessary to repeat the caution formerly given, that all critics are not offhand to be classed as of the same mind on this and other subjects. There are, as we shall constantly have occasion to see, more radical and more moderate schools of criticism. But it has also in justice

to be recognised that it is largely the methods and conclusions of the *most* radical school—the Graf-Kuenen-Well-
hausen school—which, without always the adoption of its
anti-supernaturalistic premises, have been imported into
English-speaking countries, are actively propagated under
the name "Higher Criticism," and chiefly rule the
current representations of Old Testament history and
religion.[1] The late Professor W. R. Smith already claimed
in 1885: "Almost every younger scholar of mark is on
the side of Vatke and Reuss, Lagarde and Graf, Kuenen
and Wellhausen "[2]—an ominous utterance for the Old
Testament. This is our justification, if one is needed, for
treating the radical school as representative.

I. CRITICAL ASSAULT ON OLD TESTAMENT HISTORY

We begin by looking at the general attitude of this
advanced school to the history of the Old Testament.

1. It does not put the matter too strongly, then, to say
that, to the more radical school of critics, the Old Testament
is in the main *unhistorical*. Not necessarily, of course, that
there is not in parts—some would acknowledge in considerable parts—a historical substratum. Everyone may
not go so far, at one end of the history, as Stade, who
doubts whether Israel as a people was ever in Egypt at
all;[3] or, at the other end, as Kosters, who denies the return
from the exile at Babylon under Zerubbabel.[4] But the
books as they stand are, for all that, held not to be, at
least till the days of the kings, and even then only very
partially, genuine history.

---

[1] Cf. above, pp. 12, 17. In proof we may refer generally to the Old
Testament articles in Hastings' *Dict. of Bible* (with exceptions) or Cheyne's
Encyc. Biblica; to Addis and Carpenter on the Hexateuch; to the volumes
on Joshua, etc., in "Polychrome Bible"; to those on Numbers, Judges,
Samuel, etc., in the "International Crit. Commentary"; to Professor
H. P. Smith's *O.T. History*, in the "International Theological Library,"
and many other works of the same class.

[2] Preface to Wellhausen's *Hist. of Israel* (E.T.), p. vi.

[3] *Geschichte*, i. pp. 129-30.

[4] In his *Het herstel van Israel* (1894). H. P. Smith adopts his theory,
O.T. Hist. chap. xvi. According to the latter writer, "the decree of Cyrus
is impossible," and "the theory of a return, of an interruption of the work,
of any interference by Darius, is contradicted by Haggai and Zechariah"
(p. 353). Of Ezra, if he existed, "we know nothing" (p. 396). See below,
Chap. IX. p. 295.

To illustrate: the Book of Genesis, we are told, is "a book of sacred legend, with a mythical introduction."[1] It yields us "no historical knowledge of the patriarchs, but only of the time when the stories about them arose in the Israelite people: this later age is here unconsciously projected, in its inner and outer features, into hoar antiquity, and is reflected there like a glorified mirage."[2] The "descriptions of the Exodus from Egypt, the wandering in the desert, and the conquest and partition of Canaan . . . to put it in a word, are *utterly unhistorical.*"[3] "Briefly described, then, the Book of Joshua is an historical romance. . . . We must lose much of the religious value the Book of Joshua possesses while we treat it as history, and, indeed, until we treat it as what it is—romance."[4] "The narrative gives us exactly what did not occur at the conquest."[5] The Jehovistic writer in the Hexateuch (J) "feels himself in an ideal fairy land in which no wonders are surprising."[6] The unfortunate Priestly writer (P), on the other hand, has neither historical nor literary merit, and is refused credence on all hands. Nöldeke, we are told, made an end of him "once for all"; but "Colenso is properly entitled to the credit of having first torn the web asunder."[7] His names, numbers, and precise details, which imposed even on such good critics as Bleek, Hupfeld, and Knobel, "are not drawn from contemporary records, but are the fruit solely of late Jewish fancy, a fancy which, it is well known, does not design nor sketch, but counts and constructs, and produces nothing more than barren plans."[8] In brief: "We have no really historical knowledge of a patriarchal period preceding Israel's conquest of Canaan. The individuals, Abraham,

[1] Schultz, *O.T. Theol.* i. p. 31.
[2] Wellhausen, *Hist. of Israel*, pp. 318-19.
[3] Kuenen, *Hexateuch*, p. 42 (italics his). It is of this writer's work that Professor W. R. Smith permitted himself to say: "His [Kuenen's] discussions of the more complicated questions of Pentateuch analysis are perhaps the finest things that modern criticism can show."—Preface to Wellhausen, p. viii.
[4] Professor G. B. Gray, in a review of Bennett's *Joshua* ("Polychrome Bible"), 1899.
[5] H. P. Smith, *O.T. Hist.* p. 332.
[6] F. H. Woods, art. "Hexateuch" in *Dict. of Bible*, ii. p. 372. Cf. with Dr. Driver's statement in his *Genesis*, p. xlv, quoted below, p. 105: "The patriarchal narratives are marked by great sobriety of statement and representation," etc.
[7] Wellhausen, *Hist. of Israel*, p. 347.
[8] *Ibid.* p. 348.

Isaac, and Jacob, are eponyms—personifications of clans, tribes, or ethnological groups—and they are nothing more."[1]

As respects the later books, a basis of political history is necessarily recognised, but the books as we have them are declared to be throughout unreliable and misleading. "In Judges, Samuel, and Kings," we are told, "we are not presented with tradition purely in its original condition: already it is overgrown with later accretions. . . . To vary the metaphor, the whole area of tradition has finally been uniformly covered with an alluvial deposit by which the configuration of the surface has been determined."[2] Here are a few examples. On 1 Sam. vii.: "The mere recapitulation of the contents of this narrative makes us feel at once what a pious make-up it is, and how full of inherent impossibility."[3] On 1 Sam. xix. 18–24: "We can scarcely avoid the suspicion that what we have before us here is a pious caricature; the point can be nothing but Samuel's and David's enjoyment of the disgrace of the naked king."[4] On the Deuteronomic revision of Kings: "The most unblushing example of this kind, a piece which, for historical worthlessness, may compare with Judges xix.–xxi., or 1 Sam. vii. seq., or even stands a step lower, is 1 Kings xxii."[5] On editorial additions: "These valuable notes commence even with Solomon, though here they are largely mixed with anecdotic chaff."[6] Chronicles, of course, so far as it does not embody extracts from older works, is regarded as past redemption. It is the product of a "law-crazed" fancy, which effects "a complete transformation of the original tradition."[7] "His work must not be called history."[8] In the irreverence of much of this, one is forcibly reminded of what Dr. Cheyne says of the indebtedness of the newer criticism to eighteenth century English Deism.[9] The atmosphere into which we are brought back is that of Morgan, and Bolingbroke, and Hume, and the impression produced is correspondingly painful.[10]

---

[1] H. P. Smith, *O. T. Hist.* p. 48.
[2] Wellhausen, *Hist. of Israel,* p. 228.
[3] *Ibid.* p. 248.
[4] *Ibid.* p. 268.
[5] *Ibid.* p. 285.
[6] *Ibid.* p. 286.
[7] *Ibid.* pp. 195, 224.
[8] H. P. Smith, *O. T. Hist.* p. 5.
[9] *Founders of Criticism,* pp. 1, 2.
[10] We have not taken notice of the older mythological theories, *e.g.*

2. It will not be disputed, we think, that these extracts, taken almost at random, fairly represent the views and spirit of the majority of the books and articles written from the newer critical standpoint,—certainly those of the most influential representatives of the school,—but, as already said, there are critics also of *more positive tendency,* who contest these deductions of the extremer party, and take much firmer ground on the historicity of the patriarchal and Mosaic periods. Such, *e.g.,* on the Continent, are König, Strack, Kittel, Oettli, and many more.[1] In England, Dr. Driver, in his reverence and moderation of tone, represents the mediating position of many believing scholars, though he is obviously hampered by his adherence to the Wellhausen basis. He argues for a historical " core " in the patriarchal narratives, thinks, even, that there are "reasonable grounds for concluding that the narratives are *in substance* historical"; but comes in the end to the rather lame conclusion, that " it is still, all things considered, difficult to believe that *some* foundation of actual personal history does not underlie the patriarchal narratives." [2] The main stream of the critical movement, however, is not to be held in by these feeble barriers, and continues to spread itself over the entire field of patriarchal and Mosaic history in a broad flood of scepticism.

3. What are the *grounds* on which this sweeping indictment against the Old Testament history, and specially the

those of Goldziher in his *Mythology among the Hebrews,* who takes the characters in Genesis and Judges to be sun-myths ; or of the newer extravagances of Winckler, whose theories are favourably regarded by Dr. Cheyne (*Nineteenth Century,* Dec. 1902). See Note A on Critical Extravagances.

[1] In his *Neueste Prinzipien* König combats the views of Stade, Guthe, and others, who would resolve the patriarchs into "personifications " of tribes (see below, pp. 88 ff.) ; Kittel defends the earlier history in his lecture (translated) on *The Babylonian Excavations and Early Bible History,* etc. Dillmann, in his posthumously published *Alttest. Theol.* (pp. 77–78, 82–83), says : " We have no right to explain these Genesis narratives as pure fiction, as so many now do. . . . We mistake if we do not recognise that they rest *in essentials* on sound historical recollection. . . . Even if none of their names had been handed down to us, we would require to postulate such revelation-figures as we have in Abraham and those who followed him. . . . The facts, therefore, afford rational justification for the picture of the course of events given in Genesis, at least in its main features (*im grossen und ganzen*)." Even Dillmann, however, concedes a good deal more than is necessary.

[2] *Genesis,* pp. xlv, xlvii, lvii. Canon Cheyne, on the other hand, is seriously disturbed at what he thinks to be the halting attitude and spirit of compromise in Dr. Driver's *Introduction.* He thinks " his fences are weak, and may at any moment be broken down."—*Founders of Criticism,* pp. 251 ff.

earlier part of it, is based? They are, as we shall see, various: the late date of composition, the manifest legendary character of the narratives, assumed variations and contradictions in the sources, supposed incompatibility with the rudimentary state of religious belief in early times, and the like. The historicity of the early narratives, it is held, cannot be maintained in view of the fact, which criticism is said to have established, that the Pentateuch (or with Joshua, the Hexateuch) is composed of documents of late date, based on tradition many centuries old—in the case of the Exodus at least 500 or 600 years, in the case of the patriarchs 1000 to 1300 years—which, therefore, cannot be supposed to preserve accurately the memory of such distant events.[1] Kuenen, who here may be taken as representative, gives four special reasons for rejecting the patriarchal narratives. They are: the religious ideas which are ascribed to the patriarchs, insoluble chronological difficulties, the familiar intercourse of the deity with the patriarchs ("we are not in the habit of accepting as history the legends which afford evidence of that belief"), and, "the principal cause of hesitation," the persons who appear as actors in the narratives "are all progenitors of tribes."[2] We wonder how many readers of the Bible feel these "obstacles" to be as "insurmountable" as they were to Dr. Kuenen.[3] Much of all this, in any case, as we shall soon discover, is undiluted assumption: the criticism rests on the theory, not the theory on the criticism. How obviously, e.g., does the argument from "religious ideas"[4] rest on a certain assumption as to the stage of religious knowledge of the patriarchs—an assumption which has no warrant save in the critic's own theory of the course of the development.[5]

[1] Cf. Kuenen, *Rel. of Israel*, i. pp. 16, 17; Driver, *Genesis*, p. xliii; H. P. Smith, *O.T. Hist.* i. p. 7.

[2] *Rel. of Israel*, i. pp. 108–9. Cf. below, pp. 88 ff.

[3] Cf. Ladd, *Doct. of Sacred Scripture*, i. p. 362.

[4] Dr. Driver also argues for an "idealisation" of the narratives, on the ground that "in the days of the patriarchs religion must have been in a relatively rudimentary stage" (p. lx). It is shown later (p. 115), however, that it is not the case, as Kuenen argues, that the patriarchs are represented as "not inferior to the prophets of the eighth century B.C., in pureness of religious insight and inward personal piety."

[5] Hommel says: "When we find that a whole school of evangelical theologians do not hesitate to declare that a passage was composed at a later date or interpolated, simply because they are unwilling to recognise the existence of any high moral teaching or lofty conception of the Godhead prior

Postponing meantime, however, the discussion of these objections, we propose to proceed in more constructive fashion, in setting forth, first, the grounds of our belief in the substantial trustworthiness of the Old Testament history, even under the limits prescribed by the critical hypothesis.

II. IGNORING OF TELEOLOGICAL ELEMENT IN THE HISTORY

The critical treatment breaks down the Biblical narratives, disintegrates them, causes them to crumble to pieces. But there are features in the narratives which resist this treatment, and constitute a standing protest against it. In the previous chapter we laid stress on the singular character of "teleology" in the Hebrew history. It is history dominated by the idea of purpose, and that a purpose of *grace*—of redemption. There is little, if any, recognition of this in the writers we have chiefly in view, though, to do them justice, they do not seek to get rid of the impression of the extraordinary and unique in Israel's history. Still the necessity of explaining the development out of purely natural factors causes a very different picture to be given from that which the Old Testament itself sketches.[1] One looks in vain in Kuenen, or Wellhausen, or Stade, or Gunkel, or in such an *Old Testament History* as that of Professor H. P. Smith, for any perception of the deeper ideas that lie in the Genesis narratives, or of their organic relation to the rest of Scripture. To a developing purpose of salvation they seem altogether blind. In this their criticism is already self-condemned; for what they fail to see is discerned by many others, as keenly critical as themselves. An example or two may be cited from such critical writers, if only to show that this idea of purpose is no hallucination of our own fancy, which we are seeking perversely to import into the narratives. Dr. Kautzsch, of Halle, in a lecture on *The Abiding Value of the Old Testament*, thus writes : " The abiding value of the Old Testament lies above all in this, that it guarantees to us with absolute certainty the fact and the process of a divine plan and way

to the time of the prophets of the eighth or seventh centuries B.C., then, in view of the facts adduced in the present volume, we cannot but regard their attitude as a deplorably mistaken one, and hope that it may soon become a thing of the past."—*Anc. Heb. Trad.* pp. 291-92.

[1] See below, pp. 86, 133 ff.

of salvation, which found its conclusion and fulfilment in the new covenant, in the Person and work of Jesus Christ."[1] Dillmann likewise sees in the Old Testament the development of God's redemptive "plan." "So soon," he says, "as man becomes untrue to his original idea, and, forsaking the attitude of obedience to God, begins his self-seeking way, there comes also to manifestation the saving activity of God directed to this apostacy of the creature. . . . So soon as, and so long as, sin is in the world, there is also a saving activity of God."[2] Dr. Driver says of the narrator J: "The patriarchal history is, in his hands, instinct with the consciousness of a great future: Abraham, Isaac, and Jacob are vouchsafed in succession glimpses of the divine plan."[3] Kautzsch, again, just quoted, says of his (two) J writers: "Both relate the primeval history from the standpoint of a history of redemption."[4]

To all this, so far as it is admitted, the reply which comes from the side of the criticism that seeks to get rid of the teleological element in the history is, that the Biblical representation is an unreal and artificial one: not a development in accordance with the actual history, but an *imaginary* development, the result of a reading back into the primitive legends of the ideas of the prophetic age. The appearance of development is superimposed on the historical tradition by the manner in which its materials are manipulated. Grant, it is said, the critical scheme—its analysis and partition of documents—and the illusion of teleology in the Old Testament story disappears; so far at least as any extraordinary cause is required to account for it. In the words of Professor Robertson: "What they maintain is, that the scheme of the Biblical writers is an afterthought, which, by a process of manipulation of older documents, and by a systematic representation of earlier events in the light of much later times, has been made to appear as if it were the original and genuine development."[5]

[1] *Die Bleibende Bedeutung des A. T.*, p. 28.
[2] *Alttest. Theol.* p. 411.   See whole section.
[3] *Genesis*, p. xxi ; cf. pp. lxx ff.
[4] *Lit. of O.T.*, p. 38.   See also Ottley's *Aspects of the O.T.*, pp. 56 ff.; McFadyen's *Messages of the Prophetic and Priestly Historians*, pp. 27 ff. on "The Progress of the Divine Purpose in the Book of Genesis."
[5] *Early Religion*, p. 30.   Most critics agree with the above view, so far as the reading back of prophetic ideas into the narratives is concerned.

Now we do not wish to shirk any real difficulty: we do not really feel that there is any difficulty here that needs to be shirked. We shall not even at this stage, as before said, raise any objection to the currently-accepted critical view. We are prepared to assume provisionally that, within reasonable limits, that view is correct. But we ask—Is it the case that, if the general critical hypothesis be granted, this organic unity of the history, with the remarkable teleological character which we have seen to belong to it, disappears, or is shown to be an illusion? It is there in the Old Testament as it stands:[1] can it be got rid of by any skilful dividing up, or re-dating, of documents, or supposed later touching-up, interpolation, or re-editing? We answer that question very confidently in the negative.

1. For, in the first place, this teleological character we speak of is not a thing upon the *surface* of the Biblical history,—not a thing that could be produced by any number of editorial touchings and interpolations, and ingenious piecing together of fragments,—but is ingrained into the very substance of the history, is part of its texture, is, to use the happy figure of Bushnell about the image of Christ in the Gospels, like a watermark in paper, which cannot be destroyed without destroying the paper itself. It is not the ingenuity of the writer in arranging his materials, but the facts of the history and development of the people, which work out this plan for us. It makes little difference how far we multiply the parts; the singular thing is that, when the parts are put together, this remarkable appearance of teleology should present itself. If the critic persists: "That depends on your way of arranging the materials: let me arrange them *my* way, and this appearance of development will be destroyed"; it is a fair reply to make that, if the Biblical way of arranging the materials brings out a manifest divine design, whereas his yields only confusion, this of itself is a good reason for thinking that the Biblical way is probably the right one. Take an illustration. The pieces of a child's puzzle map are put together to form, say, the map of Europe. "Oh," says a bystander, "that is because you have put the bits together in a particular way.

[1] Wellhausen himself, we shall find, allows: "There is no primitive legend, it is well known, so well-knit as the Biblical one," and he speaks of "the linked unity" of the narrative.—*Hist. of Israel*, pp. 285, 318.

Let *me* arrange them in another way, and you will have no map at all." Possibly ; but the fact that the pieces, when so put together, form the map is the best proof that this was the contriver's intention. But the map of Europe is a small matter compared with this purpose of God wrought out in the history of Israel from patriarchal times, and culminating in Christ.

2. A second reason for our answer is, that, if the plan inwrought into the history of Israel is an artificial or invented one, we *have to find the mind* capable of inventing it. If anyone can bring himself to believe that the teleology we meet with in Scripture—the divine plan of grace which forms its connecting thread—is of so simple and superficial a character that it would readily and naturally occur to any casual collector of legends, or prophetically-minded man, in the ninth or eighth century B.C., so that he could sit down and work it into a whole history, and give it an appearance of naturalness there, we can only say of such an one that he has a very large faith,—a faith nearly as great as that of the theorists who suppose that the portrait of Jesus in the Gospels was created by a Church gathered promiscuously out from Jews and Gentiles, working on the legendary reminiscences of a good and wise teacher, when the real image of Jesus had been forgotten ! The difficulty is tenfold enhanced if we accept the descriptions furnished us by the Wellhausen school of the state of prophetic orders in the age when the narratives are supposed to have originated; and further assume, with the newer critics, that the authors of these narratives were not, as formerly believed, individuals, but were "schools" of writers.[1] This is how Wellhausen speaks of the prophets before Amos: " In the time of Ahab and Jehu the *Nebiim* were a widespread body, and organised in orders of their own, but were not highly respected; the average of them were miserable fellows, who ate out of the king's hand, and were treated with disdain by members of the leading classes. Amos of Tekoa, who, it is true, belonged to a younger generation, felt it an insult to be counted one of them." [2] Truly a likely soil for the growth of such conceptions as we have in the Book of Genesis !

[1] On this, see below, pp. 206 ff.
[2] *History of Israel,* p. 293 ; cf. p. 461. See also Stade, *Geschichte,* i. pp. 476 ff.

III. Credibility of History on Premises of Critical Theory

It is possible, however, we believe, on the premises of the critical theory itself, to show that this "teleology" in the history of Israel is not an invented or manipulated thing,—an element which does not inhere naturally in the facts, but a conception unhistorically imported into them,—and to furnish strong reasons for belief in the essential trustworthiness of the narratives. This we shall now attempt to do. We confine attention to the Pentateuch, or Hexateuch, in which most will admit that the crucial part of the problem lies, and limit ourselves, at this stage, to absolutely essential outlines and most general agreements. The full discussion of particular points involved in the theory belongs to later chapters.

We take, then, the history of things that lies before us in our present Pentateuch, and ask what, on the critical theory, is the origin of this book. Setting aside Deuteronomy, commonly assumed to be a composition of the age of Josiah,[1] we have, on the currently-accepted view, three main strands of narrative in the Pentateuch, of which one—the Priestly Writing (P)—is understood, in its present form, and principal contents, to date from the time of the exile, or after. It furnishes the "framework" of the Book of Genesis,[2] and contains, in the middle books, the Levitical legislation, to which the slender thread of narrative and genealogy in the earlier part serves as introduction.[3] It is not supposed to be an independent historical source, but in its narratives —so Wellhausen thinks[4]—presupposes and runs parallel to the other and earlier history books, J and E, by that time united into one. Nothing is lost, therefore, by meanwhile leaving this P portion aside, and confining ourselves to the two older writings. The theory regarding these, in brief, is, that they were originally separate, probably independent productions, extending, with inclusion of the Book of Joshua, to the conquest of Canaan, but latterly were combined with

[1] Cf. Chap. VIII. [2] Dillmann, *Genesis*, i. p. 16. See below, pp. 215, 340 ff.
[3] See Wellhausen, *History of Israel*, p. 332, quoted below, p. 342.
[4] *Ibid.* pp. 295, 318. See below, p. 107. The P narrative up to Ex. vi. is given by Wellhausen, pp. 327–32.

5

each other into something like the form in which we now
find them in the Pentateuch. They are allowed to be works
extremely similar in character, and largely parallel in
contents;[1] but are marked, the one by the use of the
divine name Jehovah,[2] the other by the use of the divine
name Elohim (God).[3] Hence the designations J and E
applied to them respectively. One of these histories (J) is
commonly thought to have originated in the Southern
Kingdom of Judah; the other (E) in the Northern Kingdom
of Israel.[4] How far they were the fixing of mere oral
tradition, or how far they rested on older written material, is
a moot question, to which different answers are given. It is
further a point in dispute which of these assumed narratives,
J or E, is the earlier;[5] but it is agreed that, in the words
of Dr. Driver, "both belong to the golden period of Hebrew
literature."[6] The stylistic and other differences between
them are slight; whereas both present a strong contrast to
P, which is distinguished by marked peculiarities of style
and method.[7]

What are the dates of these books? On the current
view, we may say roughly, not later in their independent
form than the ninth and eighth centuries, or from 850 to
750 B.C.; in combination a century or two later. Dr.
Driver may be usefully quoted on this point. "On the
relative date of E and J," he says, "the opinions of critics
differ. Dillmann, Kittel, and Riehm assign the priority to
E, placing him 900–850 B.C., and J c. 750 (Dillmann), 830–
800 (Kittel), or c. 850 (Riehm). Wellhausen, Kuenen, and
Stade, on the other hand, assign the priority to J, placing
him 850–800 B.C., and E c. 750 B.C." In a footnote to the

---

[1] See below, pp. 218 ff.
[2] Variously spelt by the critics, in its original form, Yahweh, Yahveh,
Jahweh, Jahveh, Yahve, etc. The form "Jehovah," arising from the combination of the Hebrew consonants with the vowels of the name "Adonai"
(see below, p. 228), was first introduced by the Franciscan friar Petrus
Galatinus, in 1518 A.D. It is, therefore, quite modern.
[3] E is supposed to begin in Gen. xx.: according to some, earlier (chap. xv.).
See below, p. 217.
[4] See Chap. VII. pp. 208 ff.   [5] See Chap. VII. pp. 204 ff.
[6] *Introd.* p. 124: Wellhausen also says that JE "dates from the golden
age of Hebrew literature."—*History of Israel,* p. 9.
[7] J is described as vivid, flowing, anthropomorphic: E as slightly less
⌐, more elevated, etc. P, on the other hand, is pragmatic, formal,
precise, statistical, genealogical, juristic, and abounds in words and phrases
peculiar to himself. See below, Chap. X. pp. 330 ff.

first of these sentences, he adds: " So most previous critics, as Nöldeke (J *c.* 900), Schrader (E 975–950; J 825–800), Kayser (*c.* 800), Reuss (J 850–800 ; E 'perhaps still earlier ')." And in a second note: " H. Schultz, *O.T. Theology,* i. pp. 66 ff. (J to the reign of Solomon: E 850–800)." [1]

Accepting provisionally this account of the documents, we proceed to inquire what inferences may be deduced from it as to the trustworthiness of the history.

1. And, first, we invite the attention of the reader to the important fact, that, according to the dates given, these writings *antecede the age of written prophecy,* and embody the traditions which the Israelitish people possessed of its history *prior* to that age. We do not ask at present whether this tradition was oral, or was already in any degree written. It was there, and these writings are the literary depository of it, in somewhat the same way as the Synoptic Gospels are the records of the oral teaching about Christ in the apostolic age. It is customary to speak of J and E as the reduction to writing of the popular *legends* of the Israelites about their own past. Be it so: the essential point is that they are at least not histories invented or doctored by prophets in the interests of a later theory of the religious development. The more *naive* the consciousness they exhibit, the less can they be regarded as the products of reflective manipulation. In any case they antecede the period of written prophecy.[2] They cannot, therefore, as regards their general character, be reasonably assumed to be influenced, modified, or transformed, by the ideas of that period. Their authors—the unknown J and E —we are entitled to suppose, put faithfully down the tradition as they found it in circulation among their people. They might select according to predilection from the material furnished to them, but they did not consciously falsify or invent. It is a contradiction, in one breath to speak of these writers as giving literary form to the current

---

[1] *Introd.* p. 123.   Further dates of interest are given below, pp. 73–74.

[2] " The general conclusions," says Dr. Driver, " to which a consideration of all the facts has led critics . . . are that the two sources, J and E, date from the early centuries of the monarchy, J belonging probably to the ninth and E to the early part of the eighth century B.C. (*before* Amos or Hosea)."—*Genesis,* p. xvi.   See below, p. 97.   It will be seen after, however, that this theory has come to be greatly modified in the interests of later dating (see pp. 205 ff).

traditions of their nation, and in another to represent them
as elaborating and transforming the narratives to make
them the vehicles of the ideas of an age which, on the
hypothesis, had not yet come.

It could be wished that critical writers showed themselves a little clearer here as to the implications of their
own admissions as to the dates of these J and E narratives.
Two representations cross and mingle continually in their
pages: one, that the writers of these narratives were simple
" collectors of legends,"[1] as Grimm might collect the folk-
tales of Germany; the other, that they were consummate
literary artists, altering, embellishing, and idealising their
material at pleasure: one, that the narrators are "*pre-
prophetic*,"[2] that is, antecede the age of the great writing
prophets, when, we are told, "ethical monotheism" was
first introduced; the other, that they were *prophetic*
narrators, instinct with the prophetic spirit, dominated by
prophetic ideas, and adepts in recasting their narratives to
make them express these ideas.[3] Manifestly the critics
cannot have it both ways: on the one hand holding the low
views of Wellhausen, Kuenen, and Stade, on the state of
people and prophets in "pre-prophetic" Israel, and regarding "pure Jahvism" as the "creation" of Amos and Hosea;[4]
and on the other, picturing the ninth and eighth centuries
as already penetrated with lofty prophetic ideas, bringing to
the birth, and giving exquisite expression to, the elevated
conceptions which we find in Genesis and Exodus—writing
histories "from the standpoint of redemption." A choice
must be made, and either the books be brought down to an
age when prophetic ideas were in the ascendant, which
involves the abandonment of the given dates, or the contention be surrendered that these higher ideas first entered

[1] "The Jahvist and the Elohist," says Addis, "were historians, or
rather collectors of national myths and legends, which passed for history."
—*Hex.* p. lxvi.

[2] "Both belong," says Bennett, "to the pre-Deuteronomic, pre-prophetic
stage of the religion of Israel."—*Primer*, pp. 11, 15. Cf. Wellhausen,
Hist. of Israel, p. 32 ; Addis, p. liii ; Driver, *Genesis*, p. xlviii, etc.

[3] Thus, *e.g.*, Kautzsch, *Lit. of O.T.*, pp. 35 ff. ; McFadyen, *Messages*
etc., pp. 25, 26 ("Prophetic Documents"): Kuenen likewise uses this
designation (*Hex.* pp. 138 ff., 232 ff.), but regards J and E as undergoing
extensive changes in a later "Judæan edition" (p. 248).

[4] Or, with Duhm, Micah and Amos. "Micah and Amos," he says,
"first raised religion out of the sphere of nature into that of morality:
thence it could develop higher."—*Theol. d. Proph.* p. 103.

with Amos and Hosea. The natural course would seem to be to regard the writings as, indeed, "pre-prophetic" in the sense of anteceding written prophecy, but at the same time as faithfully recording the ancient tradition,[1] in which prophetic ideas were already present.

2. The fact thus conceded of the "pre-prophetic" character of the narratives yields several weighty results.

(1) We deduce from it, first, as just said, that the internal unity and teleological character so conspicuous in these narratives formed *an integral part of the tradition*, and was not put into it by later prophetic manipulation. It was part of the tradition as early as the ninth century, when at least one of these narratives took written shape. If here, again, anyone is content to think of what he finds in the J and E histories as answering to the idea of loose, popular legend, he must be allowed to retain his opinion, but we cannot share it. Legend does not usually assume this character of depth, coherence, developing purpose; does not embody ideas, transactions, promises, such as we find in these narratives,—the protevangelium, for instance, the call of Abraham, the covenants, the revelations at the Exodus,— containing in them the germs of a long future. If these things are there in a "pre-prophetic" narrative, they clearly formed part of the original tradition, and were not *put* there by a later prophetic hand.

(2) We deduce, next, that this tradition, at the time of its being written down by J and E, must already have assumed a *quite developed and settled form*. When we look at the range of this J and E history in the Pentateuchal books—at its rich content, at its well-developed biographies, with their wealth of characterisation, finished dialogue, connection with specified localities and situations, at its

[1] On this point of the faithful recording of the tradition, on which much hinges, we have such testimonies as the following :—
Dillmann says that E "preserves unchanged in its narrations the manner, tone, and colour of the living legendary lore of the people."— *Genesis*, p. 9.
Gunkel says: "The legends of J and E are taken over by the collectors *essentially as they found them.*"—*Genesis*, Introd. p. lvi.
Driver says: "J and E give us pictures of the traditions as they were current in the early centuries of the monarchy."—*Genesis*, p. lviii. He speaks of the indications "that these narrators were keeping themselves within the limits of a tradition which they had received, rather than freely creating ideal pictures of their own" (p. xlv).

articulated unity from beginning to close, it seems clear as
day that it is no floating, Protean legend we have to deal
with, but a legend—if the critic will have it so—already
firmly fixed in outline and in the bulk of its contents,
already clothed with flesh and blood, already as definite in
substance, if not in form, as a written narrative itself could
be. The loose way in which many speak of J and E giving
literary shape to floating, popular legends, as one might
write down countryside fairy tales, shows that they have
never clearly apprehended what kind of history this in the
JE narrative is, or what it is needful to presuppose as the
condition of such a history being there to write. If the
ideas in these writings were elaborated in any early
prophetic workshop, how profoundly spiritual, how deep-
seeing, the minds in that workshop must have been!
How explain the presence, or prevalence, of such ideas
in the age of Elijah and Elisha, on Wellhausen's theory
of the religious development and of the state of the
prophetic orders?[1]

(3) There is a yet weightier consideration—one based
directly on the critical hypothesis—which we do not see
how anyone can easily get over. It is the fact that, on this
theory, we have *not one only*, but *two* histories of early
times to reckon with. Here, as the critics tell us, are
two lengthy and practically independent[2] histories, one
emanating from the South, the other from the North, at
a time when (on the hypothesis) the kingdoms were
already divided, and separate in interests. Both cover the
same ground, and give the history of the people for the
same period. But now comes the startling thing about them,
that, while two in authorship, place of writing, and perhaps
tendency, these histories are, in nearly every other respect,
almost identical. The substance of the narrative is the
same, or varies only in trifling details. They record the
same incidents, follow nearly the same order, tell their story

---

[1] Elijah was, in Wellhausen's view, the first to grasp the idea " that
there exists over all but one Holy One and one Mighty One, who reveals
Himself not in nature, but in law and righteousness, in the world of
man."—*Hist. of Israel*, p. 462. But Elijah's idea was not generally shared.

[2] Addis says that Hupfeld made it plain "that each of these documents
had once been an independent work."—*Hex.* p. xxix. Gunkel strongly
affirms the independence of the documents (*Genesis*, p. lvii). Other critics
suppose partial dependence of one on the other. See below, p. 204.

in almost the same language.　They are parallel narratives
in the fullest sense.　The proof of this lies in the fact that,
on the critical view, these narratives have subsequently been
combined, and in the union, not only is sometimes the section
of one, sometimes the section of another, taken into the
record, but in many chapters the two narratives are blended
line by line, clause by clause, with such minuteness, somewhat after the fashion of a Harmony of the Gospels, or are
so completely fused together, that the keen-scented critics
often declare themselves baffled to separate them, and differ
widely in their attempts to do so.[1]　The reader has only
to examine the analysis offered of such chapters as Gen.
xxvii., xxviii., xxx., xxxvii., to be convinced of the truth of
what we state.

So striking a class of phenomena naturally suggests the
question whether we are really dealing with two documents
at all.[2]　Keeping, however, meanwhile to the critical
hypothesis as given, we ask—What follows from it?　Two
things very plainly.　In the *first* place, such phenomena put
an effective check on any theorist who would contend that
the J and E writers did not, as we have supposed, faithfully
reproduce the tradition, but wrought it up artistically in a
new form of their own, as Shakespeare might work up the
old stories of Macbeth or King Lear, or Tennyson the
legends of King Arthur.　If that were admissible for one
writer, it plainly would not be admissible for two, working
independently.　The fact that two writers—one Northern,
the other Southern—give the same cycle of stories in much
the same way, is proof that both are reproducing, not inventing.　But, *second,* it proves also the truth of what has
been said above of the fixed character of the tradition.
Here, *ex hypothesi,* we have two writers setting down the
traditions current in their respective localities and circles;
and these, when compared, are found to be, in the words of

[1] On the parallelism of the narratives, see below, Chap. VII. pp. 218 ff.
Wellhausen, as already noted, extends the parallelism to P ; see below, p. 107.
Testimonies as to the closeness of the resemblance, and intimate union, of
the J E narratives are found in every writer.　Dillmann says : " It is often
very difficult or impossible to make a complete separation between them,
where their narratives have been worked into each other by later editors,
and material criteria are wanting."—*Genesis,* p. 14.　Cf. Gunkel, *Genesis,*
pp. lx ff. ; and see below, pp. 219 ff.
[2] The question is discussed in Chap. VII. pp. 216 ff., and there answered
in the negative.

Klostermann, "throughout parallel."[1] The slight discrepancies that are alleged are quite outweighed by the substantial agreement. Criticism, therefore, if its division of these documents could be trusted, would furnish us with a powerful corroboration of the genuineness and fixed character of the tradition at a period not later than the ninth century B.C. It would give us two witnesses instead of one.[2]

IV. STEPPING-STONES TO EARLIER DATE OF TRADITION

The above results are obtained from the simple considerations that our assumed documents antedate the age of written prophecy, and that they are two in number. From the vantage-ground thus gained, we may now push our inquiry into the value of the Hebrew tradition a good way further back. Obviously there is need for doing this. Grant that we have a rich, and in the main coherent, tradition as a possession of the people of Israel in North and South as early as the ninth or eighth century, it will be felt that we are still a long way from the events themselves to which the tradition relates,[3] and the question may properly be asked whether an earlier date can be assigned to the tradition than that which we have yet reached? Conjecture here is of little value; but there are some very definite stepping-stones, to which we may, we think, trust ourselves with great confidence.

1. It is first to be noted that the *facts already ascertained* about the tradition *of themselves carry us a good way* beyond the dates assumed for the reduction of the tradition to writing. The point here is, that, whatever the date of authorship of the supposed documents, the tradition itself, from its fixed and settled character in both branches of the kingdom, must be much earlier. The tradition which J and E found did not come into existence in that year, or that century. It had a definite, stable form, which it

[1] *Der Pentateuch*, p. 10 ; see below, pp. 218–19, 345.
[2] Cf. Kittel, *Hist. of Hebs.* i. p. 168 ; Driver, *Genesis*, p. xliv ; Westphal, *Les Sources du Pent.* i. Pref. p. xxviii.
[3] Kuenen asks in regard to these narratives : "Do we arrive at the certainty of which we are in search with regard to Israel's former history ?" and he answers : "To begin with, we obtain nothing but the idea which was entertained of that history in the eighth [or ninth] century B.C."—*Rel. of Israel*, i. p. 103.

must have possessed for a considerable time before, and which took a much longer time to grow into its settled shape. It must have had substantially the shape in which we find it before the division of the kingdom,—only thus can we account for its being found in practically the same form in both North and South,—and for the absence of all allusions to the division.[1] This means that it was the possession of Israel in the days of Solomon and David: there is no great stretch of imagination in saying, even in the days of Samuel. If it be urged that this is incompatible with its mode of transmission by vague popular repetition, it may with great cogency be replied that the coherence, consistency, and persistence of the tradition may be itself a proof that it was *not* left to depend entirely on this mode of transmission, but already existed, in some form, in written shape, or was at least the subject of careful and continuous instruction.[2]

2. With this has to be taken into account another fact of great importance. We have hitherto, in deference to prevailing views, accepted the ninth and eighth centuries as the periods of the composition of the J and E narratives. These dates, however, it is now necessary to remind the reader, are at most the *termini ad quem* for the writing of these histories. They were not *later* than 850–750 B.C., but it does not follow that they were not much earlier. "The *terminus a quo*," says Dr. Driver, "is more difficult to fix with confidence: in fact, conclusive criteria fail us."[3] The statement that J and E originated at about the dates named has settled down into a kind of commonplace in the critical schools; yet it is far from being a secure result of criticism: we should be disposed to say it is one of the most insecure. If the reader will consult the list of dates formerly given, he will see that critics like Dillmann, Riehm, Kittel, carry back the date of E as far as 900–850 B.C.; Schrader to 975–950 B.C.; Nöldeke puts J about 900 B.C.; Schultz puts J in the reign of Solomon, etc. Writers of older standing went back still further. Bleek, *e.g.*, put the Jehovist in the

---

[1] Stade, indeed, thinks that the Jacob-Joseph legend supposes the divided kingdom (*Geschichte*, i. p. 128). This is a good specimen of the style of argument.

[2] Cf. Gen. xviii. 19; Ex. xii. 26, 27; Deut. vi. 7, 20–25; xi. 19; Ps. lxxviii. 3, 4.

[3] *Introd.* p. 123.

reign of David; Colenso, in the age of David and Solomon.[1]
But many recent writers also uphold a very early date.
König, *e.g.*, thinks that E can be placed with greatest certainty in the time of the Judges; J is put by him in the
reign of David.[2] Köhler gives similar dates: E in the time
of the Judges (*c.* 1100 B.C.) and J in the reign of David
(*c.* 1000 B.C.).[3] Klostermann, from an independent standpoint, attributes to the old Pentateuchal history a very
high antiquity, the upper limit of which cannot be
determined.[4]

If, in surprise, the reader asks on what grounds
the dates have undergone so remarkable a lowering in
the Wellhausen school, the answer is not far to seek. It
is not that any new and revolutionary discoveries have
been made as regards the language, text, or contents of
the books. The really determining factor will be found
generally to lie in *a new theory of religious development*,[5]
combined with assumptions as to the reflections of later
events (*e.g.*, the wars of Syria with Israel) in the patriarchal
stories.[6] But here again, as we shall see more fully below,
the newest school of all—that of Gunkel—comes in with
a weighty caveat. Gunkel argues strongly for the "pre-
prophetic" character of the narratives; finds the formation
of patriarchal legends concluded as far back as 1200 B.C.;
is clear that their after working-up is not later than the
early kings; rejects the mirroring of the Syrian wars,
and (with one exception due to later addition) can discover

[1] *Pent.* Pt. vi. p. 536. It is to be remembered that all these older
writers put the Elohist writer (including P) still earlier than J. Ewald,
e.g., places his "Book of Origins" under Solomon; Colenso assigns his Elohistic narrative in Genesis to the age of Saul and Samuel (*Pent.* Pt. vi.
App. p. 116).

[2] *Einleitung*, p. 205.

[3] Hauck's *Realencyc.* art. "Abraham," i. p. 102.

[4] *Pent.* pp. 77, 219-20. There have, of course, always been those also
who defended a direct Mosaic authorship.

[5] Dr. Driver says: "We can only argue upon grounds of probability
derived from our view of the progress of the art of writing, or of literary
composition, or of the rise and growth of the prophetic tone and feeling in
ancient Israel. . . . For estimating most of which, though plausible arguments, on one side or the other, may be advanced, a standard on which we
can confidently rely scarcely admits of being fixed."—*Introd.* pp. 123-24.

[6] *E.g.*, "In the story of Jacob and Laban, again, the contemporary
background shines through the patriarchal history very distinctly."—
Wellhausen, *Hist. of Israel*, p. 323; cf. Addis, *Hex.* i. p. 62; Driver, *Genesis*,
p. lix. See below, pp. 111, 209.

no indication of political conditions after 900 B.C.[1] It need not be said that if dates such as those preferred by the above-mentioned writers be admitted, the whole state of the question is revolutionised, and we are brought within measurable distance of a period from which sound tradition could easily be preserved. The argument from the firmness and consistency of the tradition acquires in that case enhanced importance.

3. The supposition is made above that the J and E histories, if the dates assigned to them by the critics are correct, were not based wholly on oral tradition, but may rest on *older written material* as well. Is this entirely conjecture? Let us see.

(1) The history of the *language* affords the best grounds for believing that the history of the people must have existed in some earlier written form. We have argued that the existence of the tradition in a fixed and settled form in the ninth and eighth centuries implies its existence at a long anterior period. But what shall we say of the works J and E themselves, and of the language in which they are written? That language belongs, as we have seen, "to the golden age of Hebrew literature."[2] It was a fully-formed literary language—a language with the finest capabilities of historical narration already developed. How did that language come into being? Whence did it derive its literary capabilities? Whence the literary art and skill to produce these books we are dealing with? These are questions which seem often strangely ignored. The language of Shakespeare was not Shakespeare's creation; neither was the language of Chaucer, Chaucer's creation. But here are two historians—according to some, "schools" of historians —expert to the highest degree in the use of the pen. The men who wrote the 24th chapter of Genesis—that "charming idyll, the captivating picture of the wooing and bringing home of Rebekah"[3]—the story of Joseph, the dramatic scenes between Moses and Pharaoh, the narrative of the crossing of the Red Sea, were authors of the first rank. How were they created? On what models did they work? **Is it not** necessary to assume earlier literature, and that,

---

[1] *Genesis*, pp. lxi, lxii. See below, pp. 111, 209.
[2] Driver, Wellhausen, see above, p. 66.
[3] Delitzsch, *Genesis*, ii. p. 104.

too, of a highly developed kind,—not songs merely, or dry court chronicles, but historical compositions,—to explain the existing productions?

(2) But here, again, it is important to note, we are not left wholly to inference or conjecture. The productions of J and E are *not*, on the current view of their dates, the earliest specimens of Hebrew literature we possess.[1] We need not go further than the pages of Dr. Kautzsch, whose devotion to criticism will not be doubted, in proof of this statement. According to this authority, the language was already highly developed, and the art of writing disseminated among the common people,[2] in the time of the Judges. The Song of Deborah in Judges v.—"a poem of priceless worth," "genuine, splendid poetry"—is ascribed by him to about 1250 B.C., and the fable of Jotham (Judg. ix. 7 ff.), the artistic finish of which, he says, is so high, and the delicate satire so great, "as again to suggest the conjecture that this form of composition must have been long and diligently cultivated, is referred to the same period."[3] Between this and the reign of David fall other pieces, as the Song of Miriam, the poetical fragments in Numbers, the address to the sun and moon in Joshua. To David's reign (1020–980 B.C.) belong the elegies of David on Saul and Abner, and to the same age, or that of Solomon, a number of other highly finished productions.[4] The speech of Solomon at the dedication of the temple, 1 Kings viii. 12 ff. (how much?) is held to be "an authentic monument

---

[1] It would scarcely be necessary to emphasise this, but for the suggestion in a remark of Wellhausen's, that in the interval between Elijah and Elisha and Amos, "a non-literary had developed into a literary age."—*Hist. of Israel*, p. 465.

[2] *Lit. of O.T.*, p. 10; cf. Judg. viii. 14 (R.V.). Many critics carry literary composition much further back. Ewald, *e.g.*, supposes Gen. xlix. 22–26 to go back to the times before Moses (written?).—*Revelation: its Nature and Record* (E.T.), p. 323. Delitzsch thinks the Song and Blessing of Moses may have been written by him.—*Genesis*, i. p. 45, etc.

[3] *Ibid.* pp. 4, 5. Kautzsch thinks it probable, however, "that we must come down to the time of David for the writing out of the products of those earlier days" (p. 10. Why?). Stade also says the Song of Deborah bears traces of having been composed under the immediate impression of the victory it records. See the remarkable list of testimonies on this point in König's art. "Judges," in *Dict. of Bible*, ii. p. 813. Professor Robertson thinks the Song "may have come down in writing from that period."—*Early Religion*, p. 79.

[4] He includes here the Blessing of Jacob, and the original form of the Balaam-Discourses.

of the reign of Solomon."[1]   Then we come to the so-called
"Hero-Stories" of the Book of Judges, and to the "Jerusalem-
Stories," the "David-Stories," and the "Saul-Stories," which
make up a large part of the Books of Samuel.   These are
placed between 933–911 B.C.—the "Saul-Stories" a few
years later.[2]   The "Jerusalem-Source" is assigned "to the
period immediately after Solomon,"[3] and is described as
"one of the most complete, truthful, and finished products of historical writing which have come down to us
from the Hebrews, and indeed from the whole ancient
world."[4]

Here then we have the language nearly in its prime
carried back to the thirteenth century B.C., with a long
cultivation necessarily preceding,—are brought, in short,
almost to the verge of the Exodus.   Are we to suppose
that all this while nothing was done to produce some
records of the people's history, of the events of the Exodus,
which admittedly so deeply moved them,[5] and, beyond that,
of the traditions of the fathers?   To us this appears so
incredible, that, even if no literature existed which seemed
to require such records for its explanation, we should be
forced to suppose that they once existed, but had unfortunately become lost.   Much more are we driven to assume
them, if regard is had to the mass of the tradition, and
to the clearness, coherence, and religious importance of its
contents, so different from what forms the staple of popular
oral legend.   It is not a conclusive answer to this to say
that we have no direct evidence of the existence of such
records.   If the essential parts of such records are incorporated in the works we have, it can readily be understood
why they should drop out of memory and use;[6] or it may
turn out in the end that the so-called J and E are
themselves such records,—that is, we may be compelled by
the internal character of the history to antedate its written

---

[1] *Lit. of O.T.*, p. 12 ; cf. p. 177.   See below, p. 102.
[2] *Ibid.* pp. 178–79.   [3] *Ibid.* p. 27.
[4] *Ibid.* p. 25.   Dr. Driver says of this narrative (2 Sam. ix.-xx.) : "The
abundance and particularity of detail show that the narrative must date
from a period very little later than that of the events related.   The style
is singularly bright, flowing, and picturesque."—*Introd.* p. 183.
[5] See below, pp. 100 ff.
[6] Thus the voluminous records which underlie the historical books
(Samuel, Kings, Chronicles, etc.) have perished : so also the early attempts
at the composition of written Gospels (Luke i. 1).

form, and to revise our conceptions of the literary capabilities of an earlier age.[1]

(3) A third consideration under this head remains. The use of earlier records in the composition of J and E is not a hypothesis opposed to critical science: it is one to which adherents of the critical school in perhaps increasing number are coming back. Not to speak of others more conservative, such writers as Delitzsch always insisted on the use of ancient material, part of it Mosaic, in the Pentateuch; but, as representing a newer position, we may instance Kittel. "Certain it is," this writer says, "that such sources, probably even in documentary form, to some extent, lay before E as well as J. . . . In many cases it seems demonstrable that E worked in accordance with sources that were ancient, and in part very ancient. And further, where this cannot now be discerned, we may accept his descriptions as resting on older material, oral or written, except where there are conclusive reasons of a special kind to the contrary."[2]

V. CORROBORATIVE EVIDENCE OF EARLY DATE OF SOURCES

There are, we would say in concluding, three things which strongly corroborate the positions we have laid down.

1. The first is the enormous increase of light which recent discovery has cast on the *very early, and indeed common, use of writing,* and *high development of literature* in the ancient East. We return to this subject in a later chapter,[3] and only here anticipate the general result. The discoveries amount to a revolution in old beliefs, and, as scholars are beginning to recognise, alter the perspective of everything that relates to arts, laws, and letters in the early parts of the Old Testament. Culture and writing are carried back in Babylonia to an almost fabulous antiquity—millenniums

---

[1] This, it will be seen after, is what we take to be the true solution. The classic period of the JE writings does not then come after, but, as seems most reasonable, lies behind the flourishing age of Kautzsch's "Jerusalem-Source." Can it be thought likely that such skill should be bestowed on the reign of David, while the whole wonderful past of the nation stood neglected?

[2] *Hist. of Hebs.* i. pp. 90, 95.

[3] Chap. XI., where details are given.

before the days of Abraham, and the age of Abraham itself
is shown by the Code of Hammurabi and the contract
tablets of the same age to have been one of highly-developed
civilisation and general enlightenment. In Egypt we find
that the hieroglyphic system was already complete by the
time of Menes, founder of the first dynasty (*c.* 4000 B.C.);
in Canaan, as the Tel el-Amarna tablets discover to us,
epistolary correspondence was freely carried on about
1400 B.C., in the Babylonian language and cuneiform
character;[1] Crete is proved to have been the abode of an
advanced culture long before the age of Moses: if Dr.
Glaser's speculations are correct,[2] the inscriptions of the
kingdom of Maon in South Arabia are possibly as old as the
Exodus. It cannot be denied that this wholly unexpected
light on the all but universal diffusion of letters in the
ancient world[3] puts the problems of the patriarchal and
Mosaic times in an entirely new setting.[4] It is no longer
sufficient to reply that a nomad people like the Hebrews
was an exception to the general rule. The nomad theory
rests on the critic's own assumptions, and is of no force
against the indications of the history itself.[5] Moses was not
a nomad, but is figured as "learned in all the wisdom of
the Egyptians."[6] Joseph and his family were not nomads,
and the position of the Hebrews in Egypt under Joseph's
régime must have been one of great honour and influence.[7]

2. The progress of discovery, again, has brought to light

[1] Dr. Sayce goes so far as to say of Canaan: "Schools and libraries, in
fact, must have existed everywhere, and the art of reading and writing must
have been as widely spread as it was in Europe before the days of the
penny post."—*Higher Crit.* p. 57 ; cf. his *Early Israel*, Introduction.

[2] Cf. Sayce, *Higher Crit.* pp. 39 ff.

[3] Sayce says: "From one end of the civilised ancient world to the
other men and women were reading and writing and corresponding with
one another ; schools abounded and great libraries were formed, in an age
which the critic only a few years ago declared was almost wholly
illiterate."—*Monument Facts*, p. 42.

[4] "According to all analogy," says Professor Kittel, "we may henceforth
expect that in the case of Biblical science also, the stakes may be pushed
further forward and the cords much further lengthened than anxious minds
were prepared for, and that, too, without leaving the ground of the
historically possible and admissible. If in the case of Hellas and the
Islands the second millennium before Christ is no longer absolutely a
terra incognita, in all probability the presumably older culture - field of
Syria and Palestine will be still less so."—*Babyl. Excavs.* pp. 17, 18.

[5] See below, pp. 104, 154.   [6] Acts vii. 22.

[7] Gen. l. 7–11.   Cf. Hommel, *Ancient Heb. Trad* p. 229.

so much *minutely confirmatory of the historical, geographical, and ethnographical data* of the early parts of the Old Testa-ment, that the assumption of early records seems indispens-able to explain how such knowledge—often antiquarian and obsolete—has been preserved. Such, *e.g.*, is the light thrown on the historical conditions in the account of the expedition of Chedorlaomer in Gen. xiv.; or on the remarkable state-ments in Gen. x. as to the origin and relations of the most ancient peoples; or on the vivid picturing of Egyptian life and customs in the history of Joseph, and in the narratives of Moses and the Exodus.[1]

3. Lastly, there is the *evidence of the Biblical narratives* themselves as to the early use of writing in Israel. Thus far we have refrained from drawing on the Biblical history, but, in an inquiry of this kind, its evidence cannot in fairness be disregarded. It is not to be thought of, that, while every scrap of testimony from profane sources is welcomed, and made the most of, the Scriptures alone are to be treated like criminal suspects, whose every word is to be doubted, unless hostile cross-examination fails to shake it, or independent confirmation of it can be produced.[2] Like other witnesses, the Biblical writers are entitled to be heard with a *prima facie* presumption of their honesty. It is the case, then, that writing and written records are frequently referred to in the Pentateuchal narratives. Not, indeed, in the patriarchal narratives — an internal mark of their truthfulness[3]—but in the age of Moses and Joshua. Re-peatedly things are said to be written, or are commanded to be written. Writing is implied in the name of the "officers" (*Shoterim* = scribes)[4] set over the Israelites in their bondage. No inconsiderable amount of written matter is directly ascribed to Moses, creating the presumption that there was more, even when the fact is not directly stated. Moses wrote "all the words of Jehovah" in the "Book of the Covenant."[5] He was commanded to write in a

[1] See below, Chap. XI. pp. 413 ff.
[2] Cf. Ladd, *Doct. of Sac. Scripture*, i. p. 345. Ladd quotes Lessing on the N.T. : "If now Livy and Dionysius and Polybius and Tacitus are treated so frankly and nobly that we do not put them to the rack for every syllable, why not also Matthew and Mark and Luke and John ?"
[3] Cf. Delitzsch, *Genesis*, i. p. 3. But see below, p. 375. The argument from silence is precarious, and Babylonian analogy would suggest that writing would be used in such a contract as that in Gen. xxiii.
[4] Ex. v. 6, 14, etc.   [5] Ex. xxiv. 4, 7.

(the) book the decree against Amalek.[1] He wrote "the goings-out" of Israel from Egypt, "according to their journeyings."[2] There was a written register of the seventy elders.[3] He wrote "the words of this law" at Moab, "in a book until they were finished,"[4] and also wrote his "Song," and "taught it to the children of Israel."[5] "All the words of this law" were to be written on stones at Mount Ebal,[6] and the Book of Joshua records that this was done.[7] Joshua assumes, in conformity with Deut. xxxi. 24–26, the existence of a "book of the law," and it is said of Joshua's own address to the people that "he wrote these words in the book of the law of God." All this, as we now know, is in keeping with the state of culture at the time,[8] and lends support to the view that much first-hand material from the Mosaic age is substantially preserved in the books which refer to this period.

The conclusion we draw from the whole discussion is, that the view is untenable which regards the Biblical history of Israel's early condition and religious development as a projection back on patriarchal times of the ideas of the prophetic age. Even accepting the critical premises—in part by help of them—we are warranted in the belief to which we were led by the consideration of the organic and purposeful character of the Old Testament narrative itself, that it is a faithful representation of the actual course of the early history of the people. This conclusion will obtain confirmation from the detailed examination which follows.

[1] Ex. xvii. 14.
[2] Num. xxxiii. 2.
[3] Num. xi. 26.
[4] Deut. xxxi. 9, 24, 26.
[5] Deut. xxxi. 19, 22.
[6] Deut. xxvii. 8.
[7] Josh. viii. 30–35. See below, p. 263.
[8] Referring to the Tel el-Amarna discoveries, Professor Robertson says : "We need no longer, therefore, wonder that among the towns taken by Joshua was one called Kirjath-Sepher, *Book-town* (Josh. xv. 15 ; Judg. i. 11), or Kirjath-Sannah [*City of Instruction*] (Josh. xv. 49) ; or that a lad caught at the roadside was able to write down the names of the chief men of Succoth in the time of the Judges (Judg. viii. 14, R.V.)."—*Early Religion*, p. 78. See further on Hebrew writing in Chap. X. below, pp. 374-5.

CHAPTER IV

The Old Testament as affected by Criticism—
I. The History: Counter=Theories Tested

"The characteristic of the Israelitish mind was an outlook into the future. . . . Was the case different with Abraham? If he was anything like that character which these early histories describe him to have been, nothing would seem more natural than that he should be made to know what the goal was to be to which his history looked. One can scarcely explain how Israel came to direct its attention to Canaan when it escaped from Egypt, unless it had some tradition of its destiny alive in it."—A. B. DAVIDSON.

"Abraham in that early dawn of history, with polytheism and idolatry all around him, saw his own creed triumphant in the world ; he predicted its triumph, and the prediction has as a matter of fact come true. It is triumphant. The creed of Abraham has become the creed of the civilised world. The patriarch's creed has been victorious over the idolatry of the human race, and grown from a deposit in the breast of one man into a universal religion."—MOZLEY.

"There are certain points which all the sources take for granted as firmly established by tradition : namely, that Moses, of the tribe of Levi, was the first to proclaim Jahweh as the God of the whole people of Israel, and as their Deliverer from the bondage of Egypt ; that at Sinai he brought about the conclusion of a 'covenant' between Jahweh and Israel ; that he at least laid the foundation of the judicial and ceremonial ordinances in Israel, and that he left behind him more or less copious notes on all this."—KAUTZSCH.

CHAPTER IV

THE OLD TESTAMENT AS AFFECTED BY CRITICISM —I. THE HISTORY: COUNTER-THEORIES TESTED

IT is necessary now to widen our argument, and look more closely at the construction of the history which the radical criticism opposes to the Biblical—to test its grounds, and weigh the force of the considerations which are thought to be fatal to the latter. This will afford us opportunity of reinforcing our previous conclusions, and will prepare the way for the discussion, in succeeding chapters, of the bearing of critical principles on religion and institutions.

I. RIVAL CONSTRUCTIONS AS DEPENDENT ON THEIR PRESUPPOSITIONS

It was pointed out in the first chapter [1] that nearly everything in the critical discussion of the history and religion of the Old Testament depends on the presuppositions with which we start. If the Old Testament is read in the light of its *own* presuppositions,—which, surely, in the first instance, is not an unfair thing to ask,—its contents present a very different aspect from what they do if read in the light of principles which contradict these presuppositions. Let one assume, and hold fast by the idea, that there has really been a great scheme of historical revelation extending through successive dispensations, and culminating in the Incarnation in Jesus Christ, and many things will appear natural and fitting as parts of such a scheme, which otherwise would be rejected as incredible, or be taken account of only to be explained away.

It need not surprise us, therefore, that, rejecting the Biblical presuppositions, the more radical criticism rejects

---
[1] See above, p. 14.

of necessity the history which depends on these, and, for the picture of the origins of Israel, and of Mosaic times, given in the Old Testament, substitutes another and very different one, evolved from its own assumptions. For it, the unhistorical character of the Biblical narratives is decided before the inquiry begins. Israel, on its view, emerges from the dim past as a loose aggregation of tribes; polytheists, or at least monolaters; not a people chosen and called of God, with the memory of a past, and the consciousness of a future, but a horde of semi-barbarians, sharing the ordinary Semitic ideas, customs, and superstitions, and indebted for what rudiments of culture they ultimately came to possess to the more advanced Canaanites. There was no revelation; everything happened by natural development. It is obvious that such a people could not have had the history which the Bible ascribes to it. With such a theory in the background of his mind, and consciously or unconsciously used as the standard of his judgments, the critic has no alternative but to regard the stories he is dealing with as a bundle of legends. The sole question he has to ask himself is, How did such legends come to be formed? What tribal reminiscences may be supposed to shimmer through them? The paradoxical thing is, when his conclusions are taken over by those who do not share his presuppositions, and receive endorsement as the results of the latest critical scholarship!

When, however, as just said, the standpoint is reversed, and we look at the matter from the Bible's own point of view, things appear very differently. Assume, for instance, what is the Bible's own assertion, that God did really call this man Abraham, and make His covenant with him, —assume that this was a grave, serious transaction, of the utmost moment to Abraham himself, to his posterity, and to mankind, and was felt to be so,—assume that it was required of him that he should diligently train his children and his household after him in the knowledge of it,[1]—then, can it be doubted that the utmost pains would be taken to preserve and transmit faithful accounts of these doings, till such time as a permanent record could be made of them; and does not the patriarchal history, with its rich

[1] Cf. Gen. xviii. 18, 19.

biographies, and impregnation with covenant-ideas, **present**
precisely the character we might expect in such a record?
Assume, again, that the Exodus really took place in some
such way as the Bible relates,—that Jehovah, the covenant-
keeping God of the fathers, really revealed Himself to
Moses, and really brought the people out of Egypt with
wonderful manifestations of His power and grace,—we have
only to ask the question, Could the people ever forget it?
to see how impossible is the supposition. We shall then
cease to wonder at the graphic narratives which have come
down to us from that soul-stirring time, and will be ready
to see in them a faithful reflection of the consciousness
of the period.

All this, naturally, is folly to the newer critical school;
for does it not imply those higher religious ideas, and that
"familiar intercourse of the Deity with the patriarchs,"[1]
which Kuenen tells us are conclusive marks of the unhistorical character of the narratives? We are not without
hope that a different impression may be produced by a
candid examination of the grounds of his objections.

The foregoing, it should be noticed, yields us the right
point of view for answering the question sometimes asked
—In what sense do we speak of "history" in these early
parts of the Bible? So far we must agree with the critics
when they remind us that the history in the Bible is
religious history—that is, not bare narratives of outward
occurrences, as an ancient chronicler, or modern newspaper
reporter, might set them down, but history written from a
religious standpoint, for purposes of edification, and reflect-
ing in its story the impression on the mind of the beholder
and on the writer, as well as the objective fact. As
respects the early periods, it follows from what has been
said, and is evident of itself, that what we have to do with
is, for the most part, not contemporary narration, but
history in the form of *carefully preserved tradition*,—not,
indeed, as the critics will have it, mere floating folk-lore,
but sacred tradition of real events and transactions in the
lives of real men, and of God's revelations and dealings
with them—tradition on which we can rely as faithfully
conveying to us the contents of God's message to them and
to ourselves — yet still *tradition*, having the rounded,

[1] *Rel. of Israel*, i. p. 108. See above, p. 60.

dramatic character which narratives naturally assume as the result of repeated telling,[1] and recorded in the form in which they finally reached the literary narrator. Such transmission may not exclude a measure of "idealisation," and reflection of later ideas and conditions; but this, we are persuaded, to a far smaller extent than many—even believing writers—suppose. The view of the history thus indicated we now proceed to vindicate.

II. THEORY THAT PATRIARCHS WERE NOT INDIVIDUALS, BUT "PERSONIFICATIONS"

An interesting light is thrown on the method of un- proved assumption and arbitrary hypothesis by which, as we think, much of the work of this newer criticism is done, in what Kuenen adduces as his "principal cause of hesita- tion" in accepting the patriarchal narratives, viz., that the actors in them "have one characteristic in common—they are all *progenitors of tribes.*" He infers from this "that the narratives in Genesis present us, not with real historical personages, but with personifications."[2] Since the days of Ewald the theory of personification has been a favourite one with critical writers, though generally there has gone with it, as in the case of Ewald himself, the recognition of a basis of real personal history in the narratives. Wellhausen, Stade, and the more thorough-going members of their school, how- ever, make no such reservations. With them all historical reality is given up,—logically enough, for, if individual progenitors of tribes are admitted *at all*, a main foundation of the theory is destroyed,—and only collective names, and reflections of tribal relations and characteristics remain.[3] Wellhausen actually thinks that Abraham was a compara-

---

[1] Dr. John Smith, in his *Integrity of Scripture*, p. 38, speaks of the Pentateuch, which he upholds as "a credible and substantially con- temporary record of a true revelation of God to Moses, and through Moses to Israel," as "incorporating the sacred family traditions of earlier revelations."

[2] *Rel. of Israel*, i. pp. 109–112.

[3] Cf. Kuenen, *ut supra*; Wellhausen, *Hist. of Israel*, pp. 318 ff. ; Stade, *Geschichte*, pp. 28 ff. ; Gunkel, *Genesis*, Introd. ; Guthe, art. "Israel," *Ency. Bib.* (also arts. on Patriarchs) ; Cornill, *Hist. of Israel* ; H. P. Smith, *O.T. Hist.* pp. 38 ff., etc. For criticism of the theory, cf. König's *Neueste Prinzipien*, pp. 35 ff. ; Köhler, art. "Abraham" in Hauck's *Realencyc.* ; Robertson's *Early Rel.* pp. 121 ff., etc.

tively late "free creation of unconscious art";[1] others can
persuade themselves that even Amos and Hosea did not
regard the patriarchs as individual persons.[2] It is well that
Kuenen should tell us that this is his strongest proof, for,
in testing his chain in its firmest link, we are better enabled
to judge of its strength as a whole.

The theory, then, is, that the patriarchs were not actual
individuals, but "personifications" of tribes. To the critic's
mind nothing could be simpler or more demonstrable. "To
the Oriental," says Professor H. P. Smith, "it is natural
to speak of the clan as an individual. . . . The common
method of our Hebrew writers was to personify clans,
tribes, nations, or geographical divisions, and treat them
as individuals."[3] No shade of doubt is held to rest on
this conclusion. "What interests us here is the fact that
the patriarchs cannot be taken as individuals. If individuals
Reuben, Gad, and Judah never existed, it is plain that
individuals Jacob, Esau, and Abraham cannot have any
more substantial reality. We have to do here with figures
of the poetic or legend-building imagination."[4] Let us
look at the reasons by which these confident assertions are
supported.

1. The theory has its starting-point in the statement
that the *names of the patriarchs* in the history are not individual, but tribal. But this, to begin with, is only partially
true. Of the majority of the progenitors of tribes (*e.g.*, Dan,
Gad, Naphtali), little is recorded save the names; of a few
(Judah, Simeon, Reuben), only special incidents; of the
three great patriarchs—Abraham, Isaac, and Jacob—on the
other hand, and of Joseph, we have full and detailed biographies. But, as has often been pointed out, neither
Abraham nor Isaac[5] gave their names to tribes; Joseph,
also, did not do so directly, but only through his sons,
Ephraim and Manasseh. Lot is not the name of any tribe,
though this "weak-kneed saint," as Wellhausen calls him,

---

[1] *Hist. of Israel*, p. 320.
[2] H. P. Smith says : "Amos and Hosea at anyrate had little idea of the
patriarchs as individual men."—*O. T. Hist*. p. 38.   So Guthe, etc.
[3] *Ibid*. pp. 38, 39.   [4] *Ibid*. p. 42.
[5] In Amos vii. 16 the designation "house of Isaac" is used, but for the
whole nation, and plainly with reference to the Biblical statements as to
the relation of Isaac to Jacob. No light is thrown from the history of the
tribes on the origin of the name.

is the father of the Moabites and Ammonites. Neither
does Esau give his personal name to his descendants, the
Edomites. Even of Jacob, whose names (Jacob, Israel)
became, quite naturally and reasonably on the Biblical view,
those of the nation, it is to be noted that he is regarded, not
as the founder of a special tribe, but as the progenitor of the
individual tribes from whose union the nation was formed.
His name and character, therefore, can hardly have been
a mere abstraction from the nation collectively. There
seems, indeed, to be now evidence that both his name, and
those of Abraham and Joseph (with Ishmael, and others)
were proper names in use in Babylonia and Palestine from
early times.[1]

Abraham, as might be expected, is a special difficulty to
the theory. He is, as Wellhausen owns, "a little difficult
to interpret."[2] We have just seen that his name is not a
designation of either tribe or nation: neither is Isaac's.
The critic is therefore driven, as above hinted, to suggest
that he is "a free creation of unconscious art";[3] later than
Isaac.[4] But then how explain these long and detailed
biographies, which bear so inimitable a stamp of reality,
yet have so little to suggest the reflection of the features
of a later age? For here again the theory is in difficulty.
"It is remarkable," confesses Wellhausen, "that the heroes
of Israelitish legend show so little taste for war, and in this
point they seem to be scarcely a true reflection of the
character of the Israelites, as known from their history. . . .
The patriarchs, Abraham, Isaac, and Jacob, are all peace-
loving shepherds, inclined to live quietly beside their tents,
anxious to steer clear of strife and clamour. . . . Brave
and manly they are not,[5] but they are good fathers of
families,"[6] etc. There are evidently knotty problems still

[1] In a list of Thothmes III. (c. 1480 B.C.) there occur the names Jacob-el
and Joseph-el (the latter doubted by some), as those of places in Central
Palestine. Much earlier, in Babylonian contract tablets (c. 2200 B.C.), are
found the names Jacob, Jacob-el, and the name Abe-ramu, similar to
Abraham. See below, Chap. XI. pp. 409–10.

[2] *Hist. of Israel*, p. 320. The idea that Abraham was the name of a
"god" has been very generally abandoned, but is now revived by Winckler;
see above, p. 59.

[3] *Ibid.*

[4] Professor Robertson pertinently remarks : "One would like to know how
much of the story of Isaac, as a popular legend, would be comprehensible
without reference to that of Abraham."—*Rel. of Israel*, p. 125.

[5] See below, p. 109.   [6] *Hist. of Israel*, pp. 320–21.

unsolved on the theory that the history is simply a form of "ethnographic genealogy."

2. A special proof of the personifying tendencies of the Hebrew writers is sought in the forms of some of the *Scripture genealogies*. These, it is pointed out, are frequently ethnographical, not individual. A familiar example is the "table of nations" in Gen. x. When, *e.g.*, one reads there: "The sons of Ham; Cush, and Mizraim, and Phut, and Canaan. . . . And Mizraim begat Ludim, and Anamim, and Lehabim, and Naphtuhim. . . . And Canaan begat Sidon his first-born, and Heth, and the Jebusite, and the Amorite, and the Girgashite,"[1] etc., everyone readily perceives, that not individual persons, but nations or tribes, are meant. The genealogies bear their ethnographic character upon their face. But all genealogies are not of this nature; and the existence of such tables no more proves that Abraham and Sarah, Isaac and Rebekah, Esau and Jacob, Joseph and his brethren, Moses and Aaron, were not real persons, than it proves, say, that Elkanah was not the father of Samuel, or Eli of Hophni and Phinehas, or Jesse of David, but that in all these cases we are dealing only with tribal abstractions. We do not suppose, *e.g.*, that when we read, "Salmon begat Boaz, and Boaz begat Obed, and Obed begat Jesse, and Jesse begat David,"[2] we have before us a scrap of "ethnographic genealogy," because elsewhere it is said that Canaan begat the Jebusite and the Amorite. When we find richly-developed biographies like those of Abraham and Jacob attached to such names as "Mizraim," or "Ludim," or "the Girgashite," it will be time to consider the analogy.[3]

3. The crowning support for the personification theory is sought by Kuenen, Stade, Guthe, and others, in *an assumed law of the growth of societies*. "New nations," Stade says, "never originate through rapid increase of a tribe; new tribes never through derivation from a family propagating itself abundantly through several generations."[4] To which König aptly replies: "Often as I have read these sweeping statements, I have always missed one trifle: I never found a proof of this thesis."[5] Such a proof, in fact, is not to be

[1] Gen. x. 6, 13, 15, 16.   [2] Ruth iv. 21, 22.
[3] See further illustration in Note A—König on the Personification Theory.
[4] *Geschichte*, i. p. 28.   Cf. Kuenen's *Rel. of Israel*, i. p. 110.
[5] *Neueste Prinzipien*, p. 36.

found; for none can be offered which does not, as in the present case, assume the thing to be proved. As a general *dictum* on the origin of society, its truth would be disputed by many far better entitled to be listened to on the subject than Stade. H. S. Maine, for instance, in his book on *Ancient Law: its Connection with the Early History of Society*, maintains the directly opposite thesis. To him the "patriarchal theory" of the origin of society is the one which best accords with all the facts. Jurisprudence, he affirms, is full of the clearest indications that society in primitive times was not a collection of individuals, but *an aggregation of families*. " The unit of an ancient Society was the Family. . . . The elementary group is the Family, connected by common subjection to the highest male ascendant. The Aggregation of Families forms the Gens or House. The Aggregation of Houses makes the Tribe. The Aggregation of Tribes constitutes the Commonwealth."[1] Allowing, however, what is probably the truth, that society does not follow everywhere the same law of growth, we are still in no way shut up to the conclusion that it was not thus that the Hebrew nation, under its peculiar conditions of call and destiny, did develop. The development from the one chosen individual into the many,[2] in fulfilment of promise, is the most natural thing imaginable, provided the nation's own account of its antecedents and mission to the world is accepted. The history here is in complete harmony with itself. From the earliest period to which we can trace back the Hebrew tribes, they are "the sons of Israel," and of what that title meant they believed themselves to have the clearest historical recollection. Why should that recollection not be trusted, and designations like "house of Jacob," "house of Isaac," "seed of Abraham," not be allowed to mean what they obviously suggest, and were always believed to mean—that the people were historically descended from these patriarchs, instead of being twisted into proofs that these progenitors of the race never existed?

The result to which we are thus far led is that the newer criticism is unsuccessful in its attempt to make out the patriarchs to be "not persons, but personifications." The

[1] *Ancient Law*, pp. 126, 128.
[2] Isa. li. 1, 2: " When he was but one, I called him, and I blessed him, and made him many."

patriarchs, in the Biblical view, are *both* persons and progenitors of tribes, and there is no necessary contradiction
between the two things. It is to be anticipated that
ancestral traits will reappear in the descendants, and it is
not inadmissible to suppose that characteristics of the
descendants, to some degree, will be found, designedly or
unconsciously, reflected in the portraiture of the progenitor
—as, for instance, in the cases of Ishmael and Esau.[1] In
this sense there may be an element of "idealisation" in the
narratives, as there is, in fact, in every good painting, or
every good biography, of a person who has become historical.
This does not detract from the fidelity of the history, but
enhances it by interpreting its inner significance, and
investing it with the charm of literary art.

III. WITNESS OF ISRAEL'S NATIONAL CONSCIOUSNESS: THE PATRIARCHS

There is another branch of the critical method on which
it is proper that something should now be said. This relates
to the point just touched on—*the testimony of the national
consciousness of Israel to its own past.*

It was seen above that exception is taken to the high
religious ideas ascribed to the patriarchs, and to the stories
of the divine communications made to them. The question
of the early religion of Israel will be investigated in next
chapter. Meanwhile it may be permitted to remark on
Kuenen's *dictum* that "at first the religion of Israel was
polytheism," that *that* can hardly be a sure result of criticism
which many of the most distinguished critics of both past
and present times energetically repudiate. Ewald was free
enough in his treatment of the history, but he had no doubt
of the existence of the patriarchs, or that they "thought and
spoke monotheistically."[2] Dillmann, and Delitzsch, and
Riehm were critics, but none of them would assent to the
propositions of the Kuenen school about the religion of
early Israel. As little would König, or Kittel, or Baethgen,
or Klostermann, or Oettli, or the late Dr. A. B. Davidson,
or many others that might be named. Dillmann may be
quoted in this connection as an example. "If anyone,"
he says, "desires to maintain that this representation rests

[1] Cf. Gen. xvi. 11, 12 ; xxvii. 40.   [2] *Hist. of Israel*, i. p. 320.

only on an idealising conception of later writers, and is not to be accepted as historical, it must be contended in opposition that not merely Genesis, but the whole Old Testament, speaks of a covenant, of a peculiar relation in which God stood with the fathers, Abraham, Isaac, and Jacob; that Moses attached himself with his work to the God of the fathers; that without this attachment his work would be incomprehensible; that, therefore, even if Genesis had said nothing on the subject, we should be compelled to postulate a certain acquaintance of these fathers with the living God, a higher faith in God."[1]

This deep consciousness which the Israelites possessed throughout their history of their origin from Abraham, Isaac, and Jacob, and of the peculiar favour of God to these fathers of their race in making His covenant with them, might be deemed an irrefragable argument for the truth of the Biblical representations. So in reality it is; but it is essential to the modern critical view that the argument should be deprived of its force, and the method by which this is sought to be accomplished is an excellent example of the arbitrariness we complain of in the critical procedure. The aim is to show that the references to the patriarchs and their doings—even to Moses—are *so late* as to deprive them of all value, and the means employed for this end is the summary excision from the text of all passages that speak to the contrary as later additions. It is a method beautiful in its simplicity, easily worked, and, when applied with sufficient courage, as it is in both history and prophets, never fails in silencing all opposing witness.[2]

1. We begin by giving two examples of the application of this method to the *prophets*. "A striking fact is," says Professor H. P. Smith, "that none of the prophets allude to Abraham till we come to Ezekiel. The weight of this in an inquiry into the historicity of the patriarchs can hardly be

---

[1] *Alttest. Theol.* p. 82; cf. pp. 414-15. Cf. Klostermann's *Geschichte des Volkes Israel*, pp. 28 ff. Klostermann rejects as an "absolutely irrational opinion" the view that the patriarchs are mythical forms, and contends that only grounds of real tradition could have led the people to see, not in Moses, who actually formed them into a nation, but in fathers, sharply distinguished from Moses, and living in quite other times and relations, the founders of their monotheistic religion.

[2] It need scarcely be said that our remarks are not intended to apply to soberly-directed attempts to correct errors or corruptions in the Hebrew text, which reliable evidence shows to be really such. See Note H to Chap. X.

over-estimated."[1] Wellhausen, who, as we saw, is disposed
to regard Abraham as "a free creation of unconscious art,"
similarly writes: "The later development of the legend
shows a manifest tendency to make Abraham the patriarch
par excellence, and cast the others into the shade. In the
earlier literature, on the other hand, Isaac is mentioned
even by Amos. Abraham first appears in Isa. xl.–lxvi."[2] The
two statements, it may be observed, are not quite in
harmony, for Ezekiel, in which the one critic allows a
reference to Abraham, is at least earlier than the date
assumed by Wellhausen for Isa. xl.–lxvi., where, on his
showing, Abraham first appears. The passage in Ezekiel
(chap. xxxiii. 24) reads: "Abraham was one, and he inherited
the land." Even on the meagre footing of these passages,
it might be urged, we would not be without important
witnesses to the singular place occupied by Abraham in the
Israelitish tradition.

But are the facts as stated? If we take the Hebrew
text as it stands, they certainly are not. We go back to
Jeremiah, and there read, chap. xxxiii. 26: "I will take of his
seed to be rulers over the seed of Abraham, Isaac, and
Jacob." We go back a stage further, to the *earlier* Isaiah,
and there read, chap. xxix. 22: "Jehovah who redeemed
Abraham." We turn to Isaiah's contemporary, Micah, and
read, chap. vii. 20: "Thou wilt perform the truth to Jacob,
and the mercy to Abraham, which Thou hast sworn to our
fathers from the days of old." Here, then, are passages
which directly contradict the categorical assertions of the
critics: how are they dealt with? In the simplest possible
fashion, by denying that they should be there. Thus, to *his*
statement that no prophet prior to Ezekiel alludes to
Abraham, Professor H. P. Smith calmly appends the footnote: "The present text shows two passages, Micah vii. 20
and Jer. xxxiii. 26, but both are confessedly (?) late additions
to the prophetic text."[3] Wellhausen is equally summary:

[1] *O.T. Hist.* p. 49; cf. p. 38.   [2] *Hist. of Israel*, p. 310.
[3] As above. The whole passage Jer. xxxiii. 14–26 is omitted in the
LXX, which otherwise takes extensive liberties with the text. But no good
ground exists for its rejection from the Hebrew text. Graf defends it, and
Ewald says: "Nothing is so perverse and groundless as to find in this
passage, or generally, in chaps. xxx.–xxxiii., additions by a later prophet."—
Die Propheten, ii. p. 268. The remaining passages are in the LXX as well
as in the Hebrew.

"Micah vii. 20," he says, "belongs to the exile, and the words 'who redeemed Abraham' in Isa. xxix. 22 are not genuine : they have no possible position in the sentence." To which it may be as summarily replied, that there is no convincing reason for changing any of the passages,—if reason at all, except in the critic's own caprice. Even Kuenen, in his *Religion of Israel*, accepts as genuine the passages to which Wellhausen takes exception.[1] Gunkel, one of the newest and most radical of critics, enters a much-needed protest against the whole system of procedure. "The author," he says, "at this point cannot conceal his conviction that the reigning school of literary criticism is all too zealous to explain as not genuine the passages which do not exactly fit in with its construction of the history, or which are hard to be understood by the modern investigator, and that a powerful reaction must follow on the period of this criticism."[2]

2. It is now to be remarked, however, that even if the critics were right in their assertion that there are no express allusions to Abraham in the prophets prior to the exile, *no such dire results* would follow for the historicity of the patriarchs as the authorities we have quoted imagine. Direct allusions in the prophets are, after all, only a fraction of the evidence, and hardly affect the force of the argument from the national recollection of Israel. In the first place, it is to be observed that where allusions to Abraham *do* occur, it is always as to a person well known, and enshrined in the highest honour in the memory of the people. It is no stranger that is being introduced to them. Israel is "the seed of Abraham My friend."[3] They are exhorted to look to Abraham their father, and to Sarah that bare them, and are reminded for their encouragement, how, when he was but one, God called him, and blessed him, and increased him.[4] He was one, and he inherited the land.[5] It is declared that God will perform the truth to Jacob, and the mercy to Abraham, which He had sworn to their fathers from the days of old.[6] But further, these patriarchs appear

---

[1] *Rel. of Israel*, i. p. 101. Another historical passage in Micah, chap. **vi. 3, 4,** declared by some to be late, is also accepted by Kuenen in this **work** (p. 113).

[2] *Genesis*, p. 113. Gunkel's own methods, as will be seen after, **are** sufficiently arbitrary.

[3] Isa. xli. 8 ; cf. lxiii. **16.**

[5] Ezek. xxxiii. 24.

[4] Isa. li. 1, 2.

[6] Mic. vii. 20.

as figures in a connected history, and whatever in the prophets implies acquaintance with *part* of that history may fairly be regarded as implying knowledge of the rest, at least in its main features. The admitted allusions to Isaac and Jacob, for instance, and to incidents in the life of the latter,[1] inferentially imply some knowledge of Abraham as well.

But this is by no means the whole. Nothing is surer in criticism, as was shown in the last chapter, than that, by the time of Amos and Hosea—*i.e.*, long before the time of the exile—written histories of the patriarchal period existed, and were in circulation, embodying the current tradition of the nation,[2] in which Abraham plays so prominent a part. "When stories were told of Isaac and Ishmael, and Lot and Esau," says Wellhausen himself, speaking of a time when, as he thinks, the stories only circulated orally, "everyone knew at once who these personages were, and how they were related to Israel, and to one another."[3] Is it credible that the same should not be true of Abraham? What stories of Isaac, or Ishmael, or Lot, could be in currency in the days of the monarchy, which did not imply a knowledge of that patriarch? Or what stories could be told of Joseph which did not bring in Jacob, and Judah, and Reuben, and Benjamin, and the patriarchs generally?[4] Then what of the Book of Deuteronomy?—a prophetic book, on the theory of the critics, yet based upon, and saturated with allusions to, this whole earlier history, including the Abrahamic covenant and promises.[5] Is not this book before Ezekiel, or Isa. xl.–lxvi., as the critics date the latter? What, in view of such facts, becomes of Professor H. P. Smith's "can hardly be over-estimated" in relation to the historicity of the

---

[1] *E.g.*, Amos vii. 9, 16 (Isaac); Hos. xii. 3–5, 12.

[2] Professor W. R. Smith says that the story of the patriarchs "is still recorded to us as it lived in the mouths of the people. . . We still read it very much as it was read or told in the house of Joseph in the days of Amos and Hosea."—*Prophets*, pp. 116, 117.

[3] *Hist. of Israel*, p. 333.

[4] Professor Bennett says: "The story of Joseph may be taken as the account of events which really happened to a historical individual, Joseph, who really existed. Such history might be supposed to be accurate in every detail by those who held the strictest theory of verbal inspiration."—*Genesis*, p. 47. But how much of the remaining history is involved in that of Joseph? If he is historical, Jacob, Judah, Reuben, etc., are no longer "personifications."

[5] Deut. i. 8, vi. 10, etc.

7

patriarchs,—because, as he alleges, nothing is heard of Abraham before Ezekiel? Does not the use of such language recoil rather on himself as showing his singular lack of perspective in dealing with the subject?

IV. Moses and the Exodus

To the testimony which the prophets and related writings bear to the period of the patriarchs falls to be added that of the later historical books, and of the psalms.[1] Here, however, we prefer to cast a glance at the *Mosaic* period, to which objections of the same kind are made, and to which the same general considerations, based on the immovable certainty of the consciousness of the nation as to its own past, apply. Attention is naturally concentrated in this connection on two things—the personality of Moses, and the great deliverance of the Exodus.

1. If there is one personage in Hebrew history about whose character and doings it might be supposed without doubt that every Israelite had some knowledge, that person is *Moses*. Yet in regard to Moses also we have occasionally the suggestion that the earlier prophets knew little or nothing about him;[2] and particularly it is argued that only in the latest period is he definitely connected with a code of laws. Thus in an authoritative work we read: " The indications of subsequent literature suggest that Moses was only gradually connected by tradition with the production of a continuous body of legislation. . . . Even to the author of Isa. lxiii. 11 Moses is the heroic leader under divine guidance to whom Israel owed its liberty rather than its laws. Malachi is the first of the prophets to refer to a Mosaic code (iv. 4)." [3]

This appears to us, in the light of admitted facts, to be remarkable reasoning. We go back again to the Book

---

[1] Pss. xlvii. 9, cv. 9, 42, etc. On the Psalms, see Chap. XII.

[2] Mic. vi. 4, with its explicit reference to Moses, Aaron, and Miriam, is declared to be an interpolation. Ghillany, an older writer, cannot find Moses named in the prophets before Malachi. Cf. König's *Hauptprobleme*, pp. 15, 16. Yet besides Mic. vi. 4, which Kuenen accepts as genuine, there is Isa. lxiii. 11, and the reference to Moses in Hos. xii. 13. Even Kautzsch, however, who, on the whole, stands up for a higher conception of Moses, arbitrarily declares the passage in Hosea to be an interpolation ("Rel. of Israel," *Dict.* p. 625).

[3] Carpenter, Oxf. *Hex.* i. p. 19.

of Deuteronomy, alleged by critics to be a work of
"prophets," which, in any case, came to light in the days
of Josiah. This book, in point of form, is a repromulgation
by Moses in the steppes of Moab of the commandments,
statutes, and judgments received by him thirty-eight years
before from God in Horeb, and by him then communicated to
the people. In it, it will hardly be denied, Moses appears
pre-eminently as the lawgiver. But the book itself, it is
now well recognised, presupposes the older code of laws
in the "Book of the Covenant" of Ex. xx.–xxiii. Moreover, not only are the laws Mosaic, but both the "Book of
the Covenant," and the "law" of Deuteronomy, are declared
to have been *written* by Moses.[1] What then does the writer
of the above-quoted passage mean by saying that "for the
pre-exilian seers there was no fixed and definite 'law'
recorded in precise and definite form"?[2] Was Deuteronomy
not a law-book? The Mosaic authorship of Deuteronomy
and of the "Book of the Covenant" may be disputed; but
can it be denied that "tradition" at any rate had by that
time come to regard Moses as a lawgiver, and in the fullest
and most "definite" way ascribed the laws of the nation
to him, or to God through him? There is the further
argument from the JE histories. Already in these histories,
which antecede the time of written prophecy, and extend,
in the view of the critics, to the conquest, there is
embodied the whole history of the Exodus, of the lawgiving
at Sinai, of the covenant, of the events of the wilderness,
of the entrance into Canaan. How then could any Israelite
or prophet of that or any subsequent time possibly be
ignorant of the *rôle* of Moses as a lawgiver? How could
the writer of Isa. lxiii. 11 be ignorant of it? It is amazing
that the critics do not see more clearly the force of their
own admissions in these matters. If Deuteronomy was
promulgated in the reign of Josiah; if the JE histories
existed a century and a half earlier; it is a strange in-
consequence to talk of the paucity of references in the
prophets before Malachi as showing that Moses was not

---

[1] Ex. xxiv. 4; Deut. xxxi. 24. See below, Chap. VIII. pp. **262 ff.**

[2] As above. Kautzsch says : "Over against this [scanty mention] must
be set the fact that, throughout the Old Testament, *all* the various legislations . . . are said to have been introduced, and in part even written
down by him."—"Rel. of Israel," *Dict.* p. 626.

connected in the Israelitish mind with the work of legislation.[1]

The basis of the argument is greatly strengthened, if, from the references to legislation, we extend our view to the related history. Here, again, it is to be remembered, the history goes in a piece. The people who knew of the Exodus, of the Red Sea deliverance, and of the wilderness journeyings, knew also of Sinai, of the covenant of their nation with God, and of the commandments and laws on which the covenant was based. It seems futile to contend, with Professor W. R. Smith, that " the early history and the prophets do not use the Sinaitic legislation as the basis of their conception of the relation of Jehovah to Israel, but habitually go back to the deliverance from Egypt, and from it pass directly to the wilderness wanderings and the conquest of Canaan." [2] The Levitical legislation, if that is meant, the history and prophets do not use,—no part of Scripture uses the Levitical law as the basis of God's relation to Israel,—but it is hard to see how anyone can imagine that either prophets or people could be familiar with the Exodus and the wilderness wanderings, and leave out of view, or be indifferent to, that which forms the kernel of the whole history,—the covenant which God made with the nation through Moses; when, as Jeremiah says, He "brought them out of the land of Egypt, from the iron furnace, saying, Obey My voice, and do them [the words of the covenant], according to all which I command you ";[3] or when, as Hosea expresses it, He espoused the nation to Himself in the wilderness, in the days of its youth.[4] Are we to suppose that the prophets (even Jeremiah) were ignorant of the recapitulation of the law of Horeb in Deuteronomy?

2. It is true, nevertheless, that the great fact in which the consciousness of Israel ever rooted itself, as that which first gave the nation its freedom, and *made* it a nation, was the *Exodus*, with which is constantly associated the deliverance at the Red Sea. It was remarked at the beginning that we have only to reflect on the nature of such an event as the

[1] The position of Moses as legislator is further discussed in Chap. VI. Cf. pp. 151 ff.

[2] *Prophets*, p. 111.   [3] Jer. xi. 4.

[4] Hos. ii. 15 ; cf. viii. 1. The passages are among those cited by Professor Smith himself. See Note B on the Covenant with Israel.

Exodus to see that, if it really happened, it could never again be forgotten by the people whose redemption it was. Some things in a nation's history may be forgotten; of others the memory is indelible. Could the English people ever forget the Normans and the Conquest; the Scottish, Bannockburn or Flodden, or the events of their Reformation; Americans, Bunker's Hill or the Declaration of Independence? Yet these are small matters compared with what the Exodus, and the events which followed it, were to the Israelites. When we turn, accordingly, to the poetical and prophetical books of the Old Testament, we find that, amidst all the vicissitudes in their fortunes, the memory of the Exodus, with its attendant circumstances, never was obliterated, but remained fresh and green in the minds of the people as long as their national life lasted. In song, and psalm, and prophecy, the echoes of this wonderful deliverance in Egypt and at the Red Sea ring down their history till its close.[1] The same difficulty meets us here, indeed, as before, that the historical and prophetical books are not allowed to be used as witnesses till they have been critically adjusted, and, in the multitude of editors and redactors among whom their contents are parcelled out, it is never hard to find a way of getting rid of an inconvenient testimony. Apart, however, from the direct narratives, which, in their freshness, force, and dramatic power, speak so unmistakably to the liveliness of the impression under which they were composed, the literature *en bloc* is a witness to the vivid recollection of the essential facts. An old monument is the Song of Miriam at the Red Sea, in Ex. xv., the genuineness of which there are no good grounds for disputing.[2] Joshua and Samuel go back on these facts in rehearsing the great deeds of God for their nation.[3]

---

[1] Cf. Ex. xv.; Josh. xxiv. 4–7; 1 Sam. xii. 6 ff.; 1 Kings viii. 16, 51–53; Pss. xliv. 1, lxxvii. 12–20, lxxviii., etc.; Amos ii. 9, 10; Hos. xi. 1; xii. 13; Isa. li. 9, 10; Jer. ii. 6, etc.; Deut. iv. 34; xvi. 3, 6, 12; xxvi. 5, etc.

[2] Dr. Driver says: "Probably the greater part of the Song is Mosaic, and the modification or expansion is limited to the closing verses; for the general style is antique, and the triumphant tone which pervades it is just such as might naturally have been inspired by the event which it celebrates."—*Introd.* p. 30.

[3] References as above. Josh. xxiv. is usually ascribed by the critics to E, with later touches. 1 Sam. xii. 6 ff. is attributed by Kautzsch to his Saul-Source in the tenth or ninth century B.C. H. P. Smith, on the other

Solomon dwells on them in his speech and prayer at the dedication of the temple.[1] They appear as the motive to obedience in the Decalogue,[2] in the discourses and legislation in the Book of Deuteronomy, and in the Levitical Code known to critics as the "Law of Holiness,"[3] assigned by very many to an early date. Amos, Hosea, Jeremiah, and the other prophets appeal to them; and they inspire many of the psalms. These recollections of the nation we can fully trust. "No nation," as Professor Kautzsch says, "ever gratuitously invented the report that it had been ignominiously enslaved by another; none ever forgot the days of its deliverance. And so through all the centuries there survived in Israel the inextinguishable recollection that it was once delivered out of Egypt, the house of bondage, by Jahweh, the God of its fathers, with a strong hand and outstretched arm; that specially at the passage of the Red Sea it experienced the mighty protection of its God."[4] This knowledge dwells, not as a vague reminiscence, but as a strong, definite, historical assurance, in the heart of the nation, and it is as inconceivable that Israel should be mistaken about it, as that a grown man should forget the scenes of his boyhood, or episodes of his early life that burned themselves into his very soul.

The confidence which the dramatic vividness and tone of reality in the Mosaic history beget in us is not dissipated by the often far-fetched criticism to which its details are subjected by writers like Colenso, in search of arithmetical and other "contradictions" and "impossibilities." This criticism will come before us for consideration after;[5] meanwhile it would be well if those who urge these objections to the

hand, holds it to be exilian. Driver, following Budde, ranks it as pre-Deuteronomic, etc. See below, p. 386.

[1] Kautzsch says that "in his speech dedicatory of the temple, 1 Kings viii. 12 ff., we have an authentic monument of the time of Solomon." He apparently attributes, however, vers. 14–43 to the "Deuteronomist" (*Lit. of O.T.*, pp. 12, 241). The LXX derives vers. 12, 13 from "the book of the Song."

[2] Ex. xx. 2; Deut. v. 6, 15.

[3] Lev. xix. 36; xxii. 33; xxiii. 43; xxv. 55, etc. On this Code see below, pp. 308 ff.

[4] *Lit. of O.T.*, p. 9; cf. his "Rel. of Israel," *Dict.* p. 631. It is the more unaccountable that, acknowledging the essential facts, Kautzsch should sit so loosely to the history as given. He rejects, *e.g.*, the upbringing of Moses at the court of Pharaoh.

[5] See below. Chap. X. pp. 362 ff.

truth of the history would reflect a little on the difficulties which, on the other side, attach to their own too hasty rejection of it.   After all, these things which the Mosaic books record were not, any more than the events in Christ's life, to which Paul appealed before Agrippa, "done in a corner."[1]   They were public events, in the fullest sense of the term.   Does it involve no strain on belief to say that an event so extraordinary as, in any case, the Exodus of Israel from Egypt must be admitted to have been,[2] happened in the full light of one of the most brilliant civilisations of the time, and yet that the people who came out, with a leader like Moses at their head, did not know, or could not remember, or could ever possibly forget, *how* it happened ? The Israelites themselves, as we have seen, did not believe they did not know.   They had but one story to give of it all down their history—the same story which, in circumstantial detail, is embodied in these old books.   If this is not how the Israelites got out of Egypt, will the critic, in turn, furnish us with some plausible explanation of how they *did* get out ?   It is here as in the discussion of the origins of Christianity.   It is not enough to discredit the Gospels and the Acts; the critic must be prepared to show how, if these are rejected, Christianity *did* originate. So, in the case of the Exodus, it is not enough to discredit the one history we have of that event; the critic has to show how, if the whole history was different from that which we possess, it came about that no echo of it was preserved in Israel, and that this lifelike, vivid, detailed narration came to take its place.   It is admitted, with few extreme exceptions, that the people of Israel were once in Egypt; that they were in bitter bondage; that Egypt at the time was ruled over by one or other of its powerful monarchs; that they came out, not by war, but peaceably; that they were at least tolerably numerous, with women, children, and cattle; that they found their way, under pursuit,—so Wellhausen allows,—across the Red Sea.   Is it unfair to ask—How did they make their way out ? Theories of course there are: ingenuity, when freed from

[1] Acts xxvi. 26.
[2] Cf. Wellhausen, *Hist. of Israel*, pp. 432–33 : "His design was aided in a wholly unlooked-for way, by a marvellous occurrence, quite beyond his control, and which no sagacity could possibly have foreseen."

the necessity of respecting facts, is equal to anything. But have they warrant, or even verisimilitude?[1] It is easy to pen sentences about an "escape" of nomadic tribes on the border, in whom the despotic policy of the Pharaoh had awakened "the innate love of freedom";[2] or to hazard the conjecture that there was a slipping away of the tribes one by one;[3] but such speculations, alongside of which the Egyptian story of an expulsion of lepers is respectable, conflict with tradition, and break on the hard facts of the situation. For the Israelites were no loose conglomeration of tribes on the border.[4] According to every testimony, they occupied a wide territory, dwelt in houses, were the victims of a systematic oppression,[5] were engaged in forced labour, were broken-spirited, under strict *surveillance* of tyrannical overseers, etc. How, in these circumstances, was furtive escape possible? Where is there analogy for such a horde of "runaway slaves" finding their way out of bondage, and defying the power of a mighty king to bring them back? It is a simple method to reject history as we have it, and evolve hypotheses, but the process is not always as satisfactory as it is simple. There is need in this case for the "strong hand" and "stretched-out arm."

V. INTERNAL CHARACTER OF NARRATIVES A GUARANTEE FOR HISTORICITY

Attention may now be given to the *internal character* of the narratives, and to the bearings of this on their credibility.

It sounds paradoxical, yet it is the case, that internal evidence of truthfulness is sometimes such as to outweigh in value even external evidence, and to support confidence in a narrative where external evidence is lacking or disputed. Had we, for instance, no external evidence for the Gospels,—did they come to us for the first time from

---

[1] See Note C on Theories of the Exodus.
[2] Thus Kuenen; cf. Colenso, *Pent.* Pt. vi. p. 600.
[3] This theory is thought to find support in indications of the presence of the tribes of Asher (W. Max Müller; cf. Hommel, *Heb. Trad.* p. 228) and Judah (Jastrow) in Palestine prior to the Exodus. The facts probably really point to an earlier date for the Exodus. Cf. below, Chap. XI. pp. 422 ff.
[4] Cf. above, p. 79.
[5] Note the recurrence of "house of bondage" in history, law, prophecy.

unknown hands,—it might still be possible to argue that
the holy and gracious Personage portrayed in them was no
invention, but a drawing from a divine Original. In like
manner it may be contended that there are internal marks
which support our confidence in the patriarchal and Mosaic
histories, apart from all reasoning as to the age of documents,
or mode of transmission of the traditions. Something has
already been said of the teleological character of the narratives; the argument may, however, now be widened to include a number of other features, hardly less remarkable. We
draw our illustrations chiefly from the patriarchal age.

1. A first question relates to the *general credibility* of
the patriarchal narratives. Discussion of alleged historical
and chronological "contradictions" can stand over; but
what of the credibility of the narratives as a whole? Here
we willingly avail ourselves of the well-weighed judgment
of a moderate critic like Dr. Driver. "The patriarchal
narratives," Dr. Driver says, "are marked by great sobriety
of statement and representation. There are no incredible
marvels, no fantastic extravagances, no surprising miracles;
the miraculous hardly extends beyond manifestations and
communications of the Deity to the earlier patriarchs, and
in the case of Joseph there are not even these:[1] the events
of his life move on by the orderly sequence of natural cause
and effect. There is also a great moderation in the claims
made on behalf of the patriarchs." He goes on to ask:
"Do the patriarchal narratives contain intrinsic historical
improbabilities? Or, in other words, is there anything
intrinsically improbable in the lives of the several patriarchs,
and the vicissitudes through which they severally pass?"
And he answers: "Though particular details in them may
be improbable (*e.g.*, Gen. xix. 31 ff. [?]),[2] and though the
representations may in parts be coloured by the religious
and other associations of the age in which they were
written, it cannot be said that the biographies of the first
three patriarchs, as told in JE, are, speaking generally,
historically improbable: the movements and personal lives
of Abraham, Isaac, and Jacob, are, taken on the whole,
credible."[3]

[1] Cf. Professor Bennett on Joseph, above, p. 97.
[2] See below, p. 115.
[3] *Genesis*, pp. xlv, xlvi. Exception is taken by Dr. Driver, however, te

The witness here borne is true. Nothing is more striking to an impartial mind than the sobriety of tone and sparingness of miracle in the Book of Genesis, where, on the legendary theory, one would expect a superabundance of marvels. To say, as is done, for instance, in the article, "Hexateuch," in Hastings' *Dictionary*, that, "in J the most wonderful phenomena appear quite natural, the writer feels himself in an ideal fairy land in which no wonders are surprising,"[1] is to convey a quite misleading impression. Apart from the theophanies to the patriarchs, and a few instances of revelations in dreams, there is but *one* recorded miracle in the whole long period from Abraham to Moses—the destruction of the cities of the plain, and even this, like the Noachian deluge, is connected with physical causes. If the birth of Isaac is reckoned another, there are two. This, as one has said,[2] is a frugal provision of signs and wonders for the first foundation of an economy by which all families of the earth were to be blessed. In this respect the patriarchal period presents a marked contrast to the period of the Exodus, which *is* distinguished by the number, frequency, and stupendous character of its miracles. All the remaining miracles of the Old Testament, in fact, are scarcely so numerous and striking as those which are crowded into this single generation. But this again is intelligible from the nature of the case. It is characteristic of the miracles of the Bible that they are never mere prodigies, or aimless displays of power, but stand in intimate connection with, and strict subordination to, the ends of revelation. It need stagger no one that the Exodus took place, and the foundations of the covenant with Israel as a nation were laid, amidst surpassing manifestations of divine power and grace, designed to produce an indelible impression on the minds of the beholders, and burn into their hearts a grateful sense of their indebtedness to Jehovah. And this end, as we saw from the history, was effectually attained.

2. As another point in the argument from internal character, which powerfully supports belief in the historicity the chronology "as it stands." A particular example from an article by Dr. Driver in the *Contemporary Review*, lvii, p. 221, is considered in Note D, on the Patriarchal Chronology.

[1] *Dict of Bible*, ii. p. 372.
[2] Birks.

of the patriarchal narratives, we may note the *unity* of the
picture of the patriarchs in the various sources. There are,
we are assured, three main strands of narrative, at least, in
Genesis,—in the case of Abraham there are *four*, for Gen.
xiv. is allowed to be a source by itself,—yet it is the same
personages, the same environment, the same doings, the
same idiosyncrasies, essentially, which we have in each.
"There is," as Wellhausen himself declares, "no primitive
legend so well-knit as the Biblical one."[1] Nor is this simply
a matter of artificial arrangement. "This connection," he
says, "is common in its main features to all the sources
alike. The Priestly Code runs, as to its historical thread,
quite parallel to the Jehovist history."[2] Again: "In the
history of the patriarchs also, the outlines of the narrative
are the same in Q [=P] and in JE. We find in both,
Abraham's immigration into Canaan with Sarah and Lot,
his separation from Lot, the birth of Ishmael by Hagar,
the appearance of God for the promise of Isaac, Isaac's
birth, the death of Sarah and Abraham, Ishmael, Isaac's
marriage with Rebekah, Jacob and Esau, Jacob's journey to
Mesopotamia, and the foundation of his family there, his
return, Esau, Joseph in Egypt, Jacob in Egypt, Jacob's
blessing on Joseph and his sons, his death and burial."[3]

Closer observation discovers that the case for unity is
even stronger than Wellhausen represents it. The sources
specified not only presuppose the same persons and the
same history, but are so interwoven as to constitute a
compact single narrative of which the several parts imply,
and depend on, each other. *E.g.*, the change of the names
of Abram and Sarai in Gen. xvii. into Abraham and Sarah
governs the rest of the story,[4] and there are continual
similar interlacings. Wellhausen, in fact, overstates the
matter when he says that all the above details are found
in each of the three sources. It is not the case, *e.g.*, that
the birth of Ishmael, or the death of Abraham, is mentioned
in JE.[5] The separation of sources only makes the problem

---

[1] *Hist. of Israel*, p. 295.
[2] *Ibid.* By "Jehovist" Wellhausen means the *combined* J and E.
[3] *Ibid.* p. 318.
[4] This is assumed to be the work of a redactor. See below, p. 220.
[5] Wellhausen points out (*Compos. d. Hex.* pp. 27, 28) that Abraham
disappears from view in Gen. xxiv., and (quite arbitrarily) conjectures that
originally ver. 67, "Isaac was comforted after his mother's death," may

harder; for the unity which exists in the book as it is disappears when its parts are sundered. Abundant illustration is given in later chapters,[1] and only an example or two need be cited here. Thus, Haran is assumed in JE as the place where Abraham received his call,[2] but, with the elimination of Gen. xi. 31, xii. 4b, 5, assigned to P, the reference to Haran in the story of Abraham's migrations disappears. So no explanation is given in J of "the land" which Abraham, chap. xii. 6, is said to have passed through: it is P, in ver. 5, who tells us it was "the land of Canaan." It has been mentioned that the death of Abraham is not recorded in JE. But, strangely enough, it is in P alone, on the current analysis, that an account is found of the deaths of *any* of the patriarchs.[3] In JE the account of Jacob's funeral is actually given before any allusion to his decease.[4] This had preceded in P. Apart, however, from such details, which might be indefinitely multiplied, the entire picture of the patriarchs, alike in their personal characters, their attitude to God, the promises made to them, and of the persons connected with them in the story, as Sarah, Lot, Hagar, Ishmael, Esau, is identical throughout, and leaves essentially the same impression on the mind in all the supposed sources. Thus, in the P narrative of Abraham's dealings with the sons of Heth in Gen. xxiii., he appears as "a mighty prince" (ver. 6); with this agrees the picture of him in chap. xiv—a separate source—as the possessor of 318 trained servants, born in his own house.

3. This leads us to remark that *the figure of Abraham* might almost be adduced as of itself a guarantee of the historicity of the narrative in which it is embodied. It is difficult, indeed, in our familiarity with the story, rightly to estimate the nobility and grandeur of the personality that here presents itself. To speak of Abraham's faith is to touch the central and most conspicuous point in his greatness; yet it must not be overlooked that this faith is only the highest expression of a largeness of soul which manifests

have read, "after his father's death." Addis actually adopts this conjecture into his *text*!

[1] Cf. Chaps. VII., X.
[2] Gen. xxiv. 4, 7, 10; cf. xxvii. 43.
[3] Gen. xxv. 7–10; xxxv. 28, 29; xlix. 28–33; l. 12, 13.
[4] Gen. l. 15.

itself in all the aspects of his character. As instances of this magnanimity, with which is joined a rare meekness, peaceableness, and unselfishness, together with a never-failing courtesy and politeness, we need only refer to his dealings with Lot about the choice of a settlement,[1] his relations with the king of Sodom and with Melchizedek,[2] and his negotiations with the sons of Heth about a burying-place for his dead.[3] But this is only one side of his character. Wellhausen was never further astray than when he spoke of this patriarch as unmanly. With his gentleness and reasonableness of disposition were united, as the rescue of Lot showed, the most conspicuous courage and decision. Abraham was no mere wealthy sheikh; no mere stay-at-home watcher by the sheepfolds. His was a strong as well as a meek nature. Sarah, his wife, though in many respects a noble woman, worthy of such a husband, is a far inferior character. She moves throughout on a lower level. Stead-fast and loyal in her affection to her lord, and moved by a true religious feeling, she has not Abraham's strength of faith, tends to be haughty, imperious, and impatient, can brook no rival, is stung by Hagar's conduct, though she was herself to blame for putting the girl in her false posi-tion, complained petulantly to Abraham, treated her maid with intolerable harshness, and finally would be content with nothing but the expulsion of Hagar and Ishmael from the household. In comparison with her, the strong, patient, much-enduring Abraham appears greater than ever.

Yet there is no attempt to picture Abraham as faultless. It is, indeed, difficult to understand how a man whose faith was uniformly so strong should so far yield to fear as twice, according to the history, to stoop to falsehood or evasion to conceal his true relation to his wife. It was not a casual lapse, but seems to have been part of a settled policy, that Abraham should pass off Sarah as his sister, when travelling in dangerous parts.[4] One can only say of it, that, by whatever excuses Abraham may have sought to justify his behaviour to himself, it was a course of conduct unworthy of him, indefensible even with such moral knowledge as he possessed, inexcusable in the eyes of God, and certain to

[1] Gen. xiii.   [2] Gen. xiv.   [3] Gen. xxiii.
[4] Gen. xx. 13.   On this incident, see below, Chap. VII. pp. 237 ff.

involve him, as it actually did, in much danger and unhappiness.

The highest point of view, however, in which to consider Abraham in these narratives is in his connection with the plan and purpose of revelation. Alike on the divine and the human sides, we are here in presence of transactions unsurpassed in the Old Testament in interest and importance. The call of Abraham—the covenant made with him —is the beginning of a new era in the religious history of mankind.[1] The faith with which Abraham responded to that call, and, in prompt and unhesitating obedience to the divine word, left home and kindred to go to a land which yet he knew not; his patient waiting, in spite of apparent natural obstacles, for the fulfilment of the promise of a son; his disinterested and lofty intercession for Sodom; above all, the great act of surrender of Isaac on the altar at Moriah, in undoubting confidence, apparently, that God was able to give his son back to him, even if from the dead,[2]— in general, his habitual enduring as seeing Him who is invisible,—all show the magnificent greatness of this man, as, to the end of time, the Father of the Faithful! It is this unique and profoundly significant character which the revolutionary criticism would dissipate into unsubstantial myth or legend. But the thing cannot be done. What legend can effect for the life of Abraham is sufficiently evidenced by the fables and stories in Jewish, Mohammedan, and Persian sources. The history of Abraham in the Bible stands, from internal evidence alone, on an entirely different footing from these. In its simple, coherent, elevated character, its organic unity with the rest of revelation, its freedom from the puerility and extravagance which mark the products of the myth-forming spirit, it approves itself as a serious record of important events, the knowledge of which had been carefully preserved—*possibly* at an early age had been written down[3]—and the essential contents of which we may safely trust.

---

[1] Cf. the fine remarks of Mozley on Abraham, *Ruling Ideas*, etc., pp. 21 ff.

[2] Heb. xi. 17-19; cf. Mozley, p. 60.

[3] Cf. Hommel, *Ancient Hebrew Tradition*, pp. 277, 296; and see below, p. 375,

VI. Fidelity of Narratives to Patriarchal Conditions

One of the most pronounced internal signatures of the truth of the patriarchal history is undoubtedly found in its primitive character, and its simplicity of ideas and worship, as compared with later stages of revelation.

1. This appears on the surface in the fact that the patriarchal history moves in *primitive conditions*, and keeps true to these throughout. The patriarchs have a character of their own, and are not modelled after the pattern of heroes, and prophets, and warriors of a later time.[1] They live their own free life under the open heaven, moving from place to place, building their altars, and calling on the name of Jehovah. Their thoughts, hopes, interests, outlook into the future, are all relatively simple. They are untroubled by the problems and mental conflicts of later times,—the problems met with in Job, for instance, or in some of the psalms,—even their temptations, as in the command to sacrifice Isaac, are those of a primitive age. It is generally agreed, therefore, that it would not be possible to assign a late date to the narratives in Genesis on the ground of that book alone.[2] Many critics, no doubt, think otherwise, and fancy they can see in the narratives in question reflections of almost the whole political history of Israel,—the revolt of Moab, the contempt for the wild Arabs on the south-west border, the subjection and revolt of Edom, the Syrian wars,[3] the prosperity and pride of the Northern Kingdom, etc.[4] But it may safely be affirmed that most of these supposed mirrorings of later conditions are imaginary. Gunkel recently has cogently argued that the narratives in Genesis —"legends" as he calls them—are far more distinguished by contrast to the later period than by resemblance. With

---

[1] Cf. Robertson, *Early Religion*, p. 126.

[2] "The Book of Genesis," says Kuenen, "may here be left out of account, since the picture it contains of the age of the patriarchs gives us no unequivocal indications of the period at which it was produced"—*Hex.* p. 42. "The question of the *dates* of the sources of which the Book of Genesis is composed," says Dr. Driver, "cannot be properly answered from a consideration of this book alone," etc.—*Genesis*, p. xv. See below, Chap. X. p. 273.

[3] See above, p. 74.

[4] A large collection of these may be seen in the Introduction to Mr. Fripp's book on *The Composition of Genesis*, written from the standpoint of Stade.

one exception, that of the revolt of Edom (regarded by him as a later addition),[1] he can find no trace of reflection of political events after 900 B.C., and the narratives themselves he takes to be much older—completed by the time of the Judges. He points out that there is no trace of the sanctuary at Jerusalem, of the kingdom of Saul, of the conflict of Saul with David, of the kingdom in its united form under David and Solomon, of the division and wars of the separate kingdoms, of the frightful Syrian wars, etc. As little, he argues, is there any trace of the later conflicts of the prophets against image-worship, Asherahs, *maççebas* (pillars), high places; the worship of the patriarchs, on the contrary, is *naïve* and free, and betrays no sense of the existence of these bitter contests.[2] Gunkel's own theory of the origin of the patriarchal stories is, we grant, as untenable as any which he criticises;[3] but he is surely right, at any rate, in his defence of their relative antiquity.

2. We observe next, in partial anticipation of subsequent discussion, that the *religious ideas*, and *forms of worship*, in the patriarchal history, are those which suit an early stage of revelation, and would not be in place later. The patriarchs worship one God—there is no trace of any other in Genesis [4]—but their worship is of the simplest order: prayer and sacrifice. There are no temples or fixed sanctuaries. The only ceremonial rite is circumcision; the one suggestion of Levitical prescriptions is in the distinction of clean and unclean animals, and this is found in J,[5] not in P. The form of revelation is not, as in the prophetic age, internal, but is predominatingly objective—by dream, vision, theophany, or through the Mal'ach, or "Angel of Jehovah." This last mode of revelation is one deserving of special attention. The doctrine of angels generally is undeveloped in these earlier books. The critics note it as a mark of P that he does not introduce angels; but even in J and E angels are brought in very sparingly. In E they are only

[1] On Edom, see below, p. 209.

[2] *Genesis*, Introd. pp. lxi–lxiii. Cf. Note E on Gunkel's Theory of Patriarchal History.

[3] It is surprising that Gunkel does not see that his argument is as cogent against the *late writing down* of the narratives in their present form (ninth and eighth centuries) as against their *composition* in or near that age. The "mirrorings" are a chief reason for the later dating.

[4] See below, p. 124.

[5] In the story of the flood, Gen. vii. 2, 8; viii. 20.

introduced twice, and then collectively—in Jacob's dream at
Bethel,[1] and again at Mahanaim, when "the angels of God"
—"God's host"[2]—met him. J mentions "angels," in
forms of men, at the destruction of Sodom.[3] The apparent
exception to this reticence, the appearances of the
"Angel of Jehovah," or "Angel of God," is really a striking
confirmation of our argument. For this form of revelation
is one almost peculiar to the earlier periods—patriarchal and
Mosaic—and stands by itself. "The Angel of Jehovah" is
not an ordinary angel, like those in the above passages, but
is a peculiar manifestation of Jehovah in the creaturely
sphere, for purposes of revelation. Jehovah's name is in
him; he is distinct from Jehovah, yet again mysteriously
identified with Him; in address his name is interchanged
with that of Jehovah; he is worshipped as Jehovah.[4] How
came so remarkable a conception to be there in this early
age, and how came it to be confined to this age? It is
certainly no creation of the prophetic mind, and can only be
explained as the tradition of a well-known form of revelation of the older time.

3. The *idea of God* Himself in these narratives is appropriate to that early age, and is readily distinguishable
from the more developed conceptions of later epochs of
revelation. Without discussing at present the divine names
as the basis of a theory of documents,[5] we can at least say
that the names of God proper to the patriarchal history—
El, Elohim, El Elyōn, El Shaddai—are those which represent God under the most general forms of His being and
manifestation, and in this respect stand in contrast with the
name Jehovah, as, in its fullest significance, the covenant-
name of the God of Israel. El, the most generic of all, is
the only name that enters into the composition of proper
names in Genesis. It corresponds with the Babylonian Ilu,
but is not ordinarily used without some predicative designation—El Elyōn (God Most High), El Olam (God Everlast-

---

[1] Gen. xxviii. 12.   [2] Gen. xxxii. 1, 2.
[3] Gen. xix. 1, 15.
[4] Cf. Gen. xvi. 7, 11, 13 ; xxi. 17 ff. ; xxii. 12, 14, 15 ; xxxi. 11–13 ; xlviii.
15, 16 ; Ex. iii. 2, 6 ; xiii. 21 ; xiv. 19, 24 ; xxiii. 20 ff., etc. On the views
taken of these appearances and their significance, see the works on O.T.
Theology of Oehler, Schultz, Dillmann, Smend, etc. (Oehler, i. pp. 183 ff.,
has good remarks) ; art. "Angel" by Dr. A. B. Davidson in *Dict. of
Bible*, etc.
[5] See below, pp. 221 ff.

8

ing), etc. Elohim, a plural form with a singular sense, is peculiar to Israel, and is likewise general in signification. It denotes God as the God of creation and providence. El Shaddai, again, marks a distinct stage in patriarchal revelation,[1] but seems still, like the two former names, to be connected with the idea of power.[2] The fuller manifestation of the divine attributes implied in, or to be historically connected with, the name Jehovah, lay yet in the future. It is true that in the sections of Genesis ascribed by criticism to J the name Jehovah is carried back into the days of the patriarchs—is put even into the mouth of Eve.[3] Even there, however, careful observation of the phenomena will suggest that while, in the view of the narrator, the name Jehovah was not unknown in earlier times, it is used by him sparingly and with discrimination in comparison with other designations—often is used simply proleptically.[4] Its absence in proper names is a testimony to this discrimination in its use.

The ideas of the divine *attributes* suggested by these names, though high, are yet in many respects undeveloped, relatively to later stages of revelation. What later Scripture means by the holiness, righteousness, wrath against sin, condescending grace, and covenant-keeping faithfulness of God, is, indeed, everywhere implied. God is the Judge of all the earth, doing right. He accepts and saves the righteous, and overwhelms a sinful world, or sinful cities, like Sodom and Gomorrah, with His judgments. Yet the terms "holy," "righteousness," "wrath," "love," are not yet found. The word "holy" first appears in connection with the revelations at the Exodus.[5] Schultz, in his *Old Testament Theology*, speaks of "the impression of the terrible God of the Semites" in earlier times, and says "the ancient Hebrews, too, tremble before a mysterious wrath of God."[6]

[1] Gen. xvii. 1 ; xliii. 14 ; xlix. 25 ; cf. Ex. vi. 3.
[2] The etymology of this, as of the other names, is uncertain, but probably the root-idea is power (God Almighty). The power denoted by El Shaddai is power exercised within the sphere of revelation, *e.g.*, in the promise of a son to Abraham. Cf. Driver on "The Names of God" in *Genesis*, pp. 402 ff. ; Ottley, *Aspects of O.T.*, pp. 181 ff. ; also Oehler, *O.T. Theol.* i. pp. 128 ff.
[3] Gen. iv. 1 (LXX, however, has "God").
[4] See Note F on the Name Jehovah in the Patriarchal Age, and Note B to Chap. V.
[5] Ex. iii. 5 ; xv. 11.　　　　　　　　　　[6] *O.T. Theol.* ii. p. 175.

He strangely forgets that, on his own hypothesis, the passages he cites in proof are all from the *very latest* parts of the Pentateuch—from P. The Book of Genesis has no mention of the "wrath," any more than of the "holiness," of God—a fact the more striking that the writers are familiar with these ideas in Exodus.[1] But the limits of the earlier revelation are in the former book carefully preserved.

4. As it is with the idea of God, so, we observe lastly, it is with the *ethical conceptions* of the patriarchs. These again, as already seen, are relatively high, yet fall short in many respects of the ethical standards of the period of the prophets. Abraham marries his half-sister; Jacob marries two sisters, Leah and Rachel; the custom is recognised of the childless wife giving a handmaid as concubine to the husband for the purpose of obtaining children by her—a custom now so singularly attested by the provisions of the Code of Hammurabi as belonging to that age.[2] The conduct of the daughters of Lot in Gen. xix. 30 ff., and that of Judah in chap. xxxviii., shock our moral sense, but are in keeping with the degrading offer made by Lot of his daughters to the men of Sodom. The patriarchs Abraham and Isaac fail in a due sense of the sin involved in their conduct about their wives. With all the religious and ethical elevation we must ascribe to the patriarchs, therefore, Kuenen is not borne out in his formerly-quoted remark that Abraham, Isaac, and Jacob are pictured as "not inferior to the prophets of the eighth century B.C., in pureness of religious insight and inward spiritual piety."[3]

When we advance to Exodus, we are conscious of a great progress. The writers are, on the theory, the same, and the history is the continuation of the preceding. Yet everything is on a changed and grander scale. The ideas are deeper; the scene is larger and more imposing; the forces at work are more titanic; the issues are more

[1] Cf. arts. "Anger" and "Love," in *Dict. of Bible.* A similar line of argument is developed in Dr. Watson's little work, *The Book Genesis a True History*, which we had not seen before writing this. Dr. Driver singularly misses the point of Dr. Watson's argument in supposing it to prove only that the narratives reached their present form before the age when Amos, Hosea, etc., "began to emphasise and develop beliefs and truths such as those referred to" (*Genesis*, p. xlviii). Dr. Watson's argument turns on the contrast of *Genesis* with *Exodus*, which was likewise prior to that age, yet has these ideas.

[2] *Code* (Johns' Edition), sects. 144–47. [3] See above, p. 60.

tremendous. The hour has come for Jehovah to fulfil His promises to the fathers. The instrument is prepared; the yoke of bondage is to be broken; the people are to be led forth to breathe the air of liberty in the desert, and, as redeemed, to make voluntary dedication of themselves to their Deliverer. With this access of religious enthusiasm, and unparalleled experience of divine grace, goes of necessity an immense uplifting both in the religious ideas and in the standard of ethical obligation. The people have now given them "statutes and judgments" which are to serve as the norm of moral conduct. The ideal set before them is nothing less than the holiness of Jehovah Himself. They are to be a "holy" people to Him,[1] and are to prove their fidelity by obedience to His voice. The scenes in this great drama are depicted with a realism and fresco-like vividness of colouring which irresistibly suggest that the narratives were written under the recent impression of the events which they record: when, at least, the vividness of that impression had not yet faded from the memory and heart of the nation. The strands of the story may be multiple,—that is yet to be inquired into,—but we cannot admit that they are diverse. Moses and Aaron are the central figures in the history, but, as in the case of the patriarchal narratives, the portraits of the two are the same in J, E, P, D alike. It is one and the same Moses, with one and the same Aaron beside him, who appears in all the so-called "sources," and mediates, under God, the freedom and covenant-organisation of the nation.

[1] Ex. xix. 6.

CHAPTER V

The Old Testament as affected by Criticism— II. Religion and Institutions: God and His Worship

"The πρῶτον ψεῦδος, historically considered, of Graf, Kuenen, and all their followers, consists in this: that they make use of the variety of material afforded them for positively constructing a history of ancient Israel, only to destroy the possibility of such a history. This they appear to do, not so much because of the discrepancies which exist in the materials, as because of their predetermination to reject as untrustworthy all the materials which partake largely of the Hebrew belief in the supernatural."—LADD.

"The view of Israel's early history, offered by any writer, will largely depend upon his thought of Israel's God."—J. E. CARPENTER.

"We must first firmly assert that, while there have been different forms of monotheism in many peoples and at various times, nevertheless Israel is and remains the classical people of monotheism; of that monotheism which we confess, or, more strictly, which is the precursor of ours; and in Israel this monotheism is of native origin: we know the history of its origin very well."—GUNKEL.

"God, in creating, theomorphises man; man, therefore, necessarily anthropomorphises God."—JACOBI.

CHAPTER V

THE OLD TESTAMENT AS AFFECTED BY CRITICISM —II. RELIGION AND INSTITUTIONS: GOD AND HIS WORSHIP.

It will be evident from the preceding discussions that the real leverage of the newer criticism is found in its theory of the religious development in ancient Israel: to this subject, therefore, special attention must now be given. It is not disputed that difficult problems have to be faced on any theory of the Israelitish religion and institutions. Questions exceedingly hard of solution arise in regard to laws, institutions, and practice, and it is the service of criticism to have set these in the clearest light. We are far from persuaded, however, that the methods which have come into vogue with the radical school hold out the promise of a satisfactory solution of these difficulties. On the contrary, these methods seem to us eaten through with an arbitrary subjectivism which vitiates their application at every point. Stade and Budde are conspicuous examples of this fault; but few of the other best-known writers of the school are far behind in their wilful setting aside, or mutilation, of the Biblical accounts, and substitution for these of an imaginary history, built up from ingenious conjectures, and brilliant combinations on the line of what the critic thinks the history *should* have been.

I. Fault of the Critical Method

It may be useful, before entering on the main discussion, to offer one or two examples of what we regard as the radical vice of the newer critical method—its continual substitution of arbitrary conjecture for the facts of the history as given.

We take the following from Budde, who prides himself—
be it said—on his *respect* for the history.[1]   After propounding
the extraordinary thesis that "the tradition claims that it
was *not* Israel's *own* God who performed these great deeds"
at the Exodus, "but a God up to that time completely
unknown to the Israelites, whose name even they then
learned for the first time"[2] (the statement that the forefathers had known Yahweh is a later "palliating addition"),[3]
he proceeds to explain how this God became transformed
into the Yahweh of a later period by the absorption of
"other gods" into Himself. "Yahweh had not expelled or
annihilated them (the Canaanitish gods), but had made them
subject; He had divested them of their personality by
absorbing them into His own person."[4]   Then, with charming frankness: "*To be sure, neither the law, nor the historical
narratives, nor the prophets, say a word of all this*, yet it can
be proved," etc.[5] Nearly anything, we imagine, could be
proved in the same manner.

Budde's respect for the history does not allow of his
agreeing with those who, "while relinquishing everything
else, have tried to save the Ten Commandments, the 'Mosaic'
moral law, for these oldest times." For, "the Ten Commandments base all their demands on the nature of the God of
Israel. If, then, they really did come from this period"—
we may ask the reader to note what, in Budde's view, is
involved in the acceptance even of the Decalogue—"it
appears that there existed, even in the earliest times, a
conception of God so sublime that hardly anything could
have remained for the prophets to do. This of itself should
suffice to show the impossibility of the Mosaic origin of the
Ten Commandments." Then, with the same engaging
frankness: "It is, therefore, in the highest degree improbable that Yahweh demanded at Sinai the exclusive
veneration of His own Godhead. *True, this is the unvarying
testimony of Old Testament tradition*. It is to this day the
generally accepted view, and is held even by advanced
specialists. But it can hardly be maintained," etc.[6]

---

[1] "Thus treated," he says, "the Biblical tradition, even of the oldest
times, has proved itself to me to be, in its main features, trustworthy—
I speak of the history of Israel as a nation, not of the stories of primeval and
patriarchal times in Genesis."—*Rel. of Israel*, **p. 3.**

[2] *Ibid.* p. 14.   [3] *Ibid.* p. 15.   [4] *Ibid.* p. 41.
[5] *Ibid.* (italics are ours).   [6] *Ibid.* p. 59.

We quote these passages because they are typical. Delitzsch has said: "If history is critically annihilated what is left but to fill the *tabula rasa* with myths?"[1] This we take, as said, to be the primary vice of the prevailing theory—*either*, the arbitrary setting aside of the Biblical narrative in favour of some novel, no doubt highly ingenious, construction of the critic's own; *or*, the persistent reading into the history, in the interest of some fancy, of a meaning which it cannot be made to bear.   A main difficulty, in fact, in the discussion, is, that, in the multitude of hypotheses, and unbounded liberty claimed by the critic to accept or reject as suits his convenience, it is impossible ever to feel that one has a sure hold on anything.   The critic should at least, one would think, abide by his own assumptions; but he is far from doing so.   How constantly, for instance, are Jephthah's words in Judg. xi. 24,[2] relied on in proof that, in the time of the Judges, Jehovah sustained the same relation to Israel as Chemosh did to Moab.   Yet this section is declared by the critics not to belong to the older stratum of the Book of Judges, but to be a late insertion of uncertain date:[3] certainly, therefore, on the theory, no real speech of Jephthah's.   Wellhausen cites it,[4] yet, as Dr. A. B. Davidson points out, "elsewhere regards the whole passage, with the allusion to Chemosh, as a later interpolation founded on Num. xxi. 29."[5]   Similarly, the statement of David in 1 Sam. xxvi. 19, that his enemies had driven him out of Jehovah's inheritance, saying, "Go, serve other gods"—continually quoted in proof that to David Jehovah was only a tribal god[6]—is, with the chapter to which it belongs, assigned by Kautzsch, with others, to a comparatively late date:[7] is valueless, therefore, as a testimony to David's own sentiments. Is it desired, again, to prove an original connection between Jehovah and Moloch?   Kuenen, to that end, accepts as "historical" the statement in Amos v. 26 that the Israelites carried about in the desert "the tabernacle of Moloch,"[8]

[1] *Genesis*, i. p. 9.   [2] See below, p. 131.
[3] Thus Kautzsch, Moore (*Judges*), Thatcher (*Judges*, "Cent. Bible"), etc.
[4] *Hist. of Israel*, p. 235.
[5] *Expositor*, 3rd Series, v. p. 49.   "This pet passage," Dr. Davidson says, "figures of course in Wellhausen, as it does everywhere else since Vatke." He refers to Wellhausen's *Bleek*, p. 195.
[6] See below, p. 132.   [7] *Lit. of O.T.*, pp. 45, 237.
[8] *Rel. of Israel*, i. p. 250.

MINNESOTA BIBLE COLLEGE
LIBRARY

though the whole history of the wanderings, which, in its
JE parts, is allowed to be *older* than Amos, is rejected by
him. A proof of the bull-worship of Jehovah from ancient
times is found by some in the story of the making of the
golden calf in Ex. xxxii.; yet the story is rejected as unhistorical.[1] Others take it as a protest *against* bull-worship : [2]
Kuenen, as will be seen below, thinks it glances at the fact
that the idolatrous priests of the Northern Kingdom claimed
descent from Aaron.[3]

To take only one other example, Professor W. R. Smith
writes thus of the sacred pillars of the patriarchs : " In the
Biblical story they appear simply as memorial pillars, without
any definite ritual significance." This, however, he goes on,
" is due to the fact that the narratives are conformed to the
standpoint of the law and of the later prophets, who look on
the ritual use of sacred pillars as idolatrous."[4] The critic
forgets, or ignores, that, on his own showing, these patriarchal
stories anteceded the age of written prophecy, and that,
according to him, in the days of Amos and Hosea, pillars
were still thought to be legitimate.[5] Where then is the
place for the conforming of the narratives to the ideas of
" later prophets " ? With the talismanic power which
such instances exemplify of getting rid of unwelcome facts,
and making a theory prove itself by employing it as a means
to break down opposing testimony, it is not difficult for
criticism to produce astonishing results.

Accepting for ourselves the historicity of the Biblical
narratives, till at least their title to our confidence is
disproved, we propose to invert the procedure of the
schools, and, instead of sacrificing the history to *a priori*
considerations, to inquire at every point whether reason
is shown for setting it aside.

[1] Most writers see some connection with the bull-worship, *e.g.*, Stade,
Geschichte, i. pp. 466–67. Addis dates the narrative later than the fall
of Samaria (722 B.C.) on the ground that only then "the old worship of
Yahweh under the form of a calf, long maintained by kings and Levitical
priests (Judg. xviii. 30), received its death-blow."—*Hex.* i. pp. 151–52. On
this see below, pp. 143 ff.

[2] Cf. Kittel, *Hist. of Hebs.* i. p. 152.

[3] *Hex.* p. 245. See below, p. 211.

[4] *Rel. of Semites*, p. 186 ; *O.T. in J. C.*, pp. 241, 354.

[5] *Ibid.* pp. 186–87 ; *Prophets of Israel*, p. 116.

II. EARLY ISRAELITISH MONOTHEISM

We begin by contrasting the Biblical and the critical views of the early Israelitish conceptions of God.

1. It was formerly shown that, in the earliest tradition we possess of Israel's beliefs, there is no trace of any conception of God but one essentially *monotheistic.* There is but one qualification, which, in justice to the facts, it is necessary to make on this statement. It is not contended that, at any period of their history, the Israelitish people as a whole rose to, or maintained themselves at, the full height of the monotheistic conception : we know they did not. To many the conception of Jehovah was no doubt simply that of their national god ; nor was it always, or perhaps even generally, clear, that some kind of inferior reality did not belong to the gods worshipped with so much pomp and ardour by the nations around them.[1] Even in apostolic and sub-apostolic times, Christian believers and Church fathers did not regard the idol-gods of the Gentiles as simple nonentities: paganism was to them a system of demon-worship.[2] Still harder would it be for Israel to rise to the height of the prophetic conception that the idols were "nothings" (*elilim*),[3] in a world where every people was polytheistic but themselves. But that the religion of Abraham, and Moses, and the other great leaders of the nation was at heart the worship of the one true God, recognised by them to be the Creator, Ruler, and Lord in providence of the whole world, we see not the smallest reason to doubt. This was the common view, prior to the advent of the Kuenen-Wellhausen school, among the critics themselves,[4] and, as the passage above cited from Budde acknowledges, is the view of leading

[1] It would be unsafe, however, to infer this from such expressions as, "Who is like Thee, O Jehovah, among the gods?" (Ex. xv. 11), for such expressions are found in prophets and psalms where the monotheistic consciousness is not doubted. See below, p. 438.

[2] 1 Cor. x. 20, 21 ; cf. Justin Martyr, *1 Apol.* 14, 54, 62, etc.

[3] Cf. Deut. xxxii. 21 ; Lev. xix. 4 ; Isa. ii. 8 ; Ps. xcvi. 4, 5, etc. In the last passage we read : Jehovah "is to be feared above all gods," but in ver. 5, "For all the gods of the peoples are nothings."

[4] So De Wette, Lengerke, Hitzig, Ewald, Bleek, Dillmann, etc. On the other hand, the views of Vatke, and of writers like Daumer, Ghillany, etc., met with little countenance. Cf. König's *Hauptprobleme,* pp. 7 ff.

Old Testament specialists still.[1] It is the view also, we are persuaded, which answers to the natural reading of the facts.

The Book of Genesis, originating, it is to be remembered, as respects at least its JE parts, in the " pre-prophetic " age, is, as before pointed out,[2] throughout a monotheistic book.[3] God is the Creator of the world and of man : destroys the whole human race by a flood; is present and active in all lands—Babylonia, Mesopotamia, Egypt; works out a gracious purpose in the lives of men. The difficulty in Genesis is not its recognition of God as supreme,—that appears in every part,—but its almost entire ignoring of what we nevertheless know to be the fact, the existence of polytheism and idolatry in tribes and nations outside the patriarchal circle. The God worshipped by the patriarchs is the *only* God whose existence, presence, and working are recognised in it. We read nothing of gods of Canaan or Egypt. Melchizedek is, like Abraham, a worshipper of El Elyŏn—"God Most High," [4] and even Abimelech and Pharaoh speak generally simply of "God." [5] The single glimpse we get to the contrary is in the "strange gods" (teraphim) which Jacob's household brought with them from Mesopotamia, and which Jacob required them to put away.[6] In Exodus and the remaining Pentateuchal books it is different. There we have a sharp contrast drawn between Jehovah and "the gods of Egypt";[7] the people are stringently forbidden to worship "other gods ";[8]

---

[1] See above, p. 120 ; and Chap. IV. p. 93.   [2] Cf. above, p. 41.

[3] This is very generally admitted of the Book of Genesis as we have it. H. P. Smith, *e.g.*, says of the early part, where anthropomorphism is most marked : "What J has preserved he was able to bring into harmony with the strictest monotheism. For the Yahweh of our account, anthropomorphic as He is, is yet the Supreme God."—*O.T. Hist.* p. 16. Cf. Wellhausen, *Hist. of Israel*, p. 304. Gunkel acknowledges this "monotheistic trend" of Genesis, and carries it back to an early date.—*Genesis*, p. xlvii ; see also his *Israel und Babylonien*, p. 29.

[4] Gen. xiv. 18–22. It is not easy to say how far polytheism had advanced in Canaan in the time of Abraham. The Tel el-Amarna tablets speak of Baalat of Gebal (frequently), Asherah, Milku (Moloch), Ammon (? Amon), Samas, Dagon, etc., but do not give much definite light.

[5] Cf. Gen. xxi. 22 ff. (in chap. xxvi. 27, 28, "Jehovah"); Gen. xli. 39, etc.

[6] Gen. xxxi. 19, 30 ; xxxv. 2, 4.

[7] Ex. xii. 12 (P); xv. 11. It will not be claimed that P, in the former passage, writes other than monotheistically.

[8] Ex. xx. 3 ; xxiii. 32.

they are enjoined to keep themselves apart from, and to root out, the idolatry of the Canaanites.[1] But Jehovah is still regarded as exalted above all these other gods in nature, dignity, and power, as the God of the whole earth —its Creator, Ruler, and Lord. He is the One who says of Himself, "All the earth is Mine."[2] Budde, we have seen, acknowledges that this is the view of God involved in the Decalogue. While, therefore, Kuenen is right when he sums up Israel's religion in the formula, "Yahweh Israel's God and Israel Yahweh's people,"[3] this does not in the least imply that Jehovah was simply to Israel a tribal or national god. He was the God of their fathers—the God of heaven and earth [4]—who of His condescending love had chosen them to be a people for Himself, with a view to the ultimate larger blessing of mankind. The keynote in these early books is precisely the same as in Amos— the alleged introducer of the "ethical monotheism": "You only have I known of all the families of the earth."[5]

What is here said of early monotheism is not contradicted by the anthropomorphisms attributed peculiarly to the J writer in the Genesis narratives. The anthropomorphisms are *naïve* and popular enough;[6] yet, beneath them, the conception of Jehovah as the Creator and Ruler of the world is never lost sight of;[7] and the sublimity of the representations of God in other parts of the J narrative —in the revelation of God's name, *e.g.*, in Ex. xxxiii. 18, 19, xxxiv. 5–8 [8]—shows clearly that no such paltry ideas of God as the critics ascribe to this writer were really his. The anthropomorphisms belong either to the older tradition the writer is dealing with, or to a vivid and personalising way of setting forth God's presence and interest in human

---

[1] Ex. xxiii. 24 ; cf. Deut. xii. 2 ff.   [2] Ex. xix. 5.
[3] *Nat. and Univ. Religions* (Hibbert Lectures), p. 105.
[4] Cf. Gen. xxiv. 3, etc.   [5] Amos iii. 2.
[6] "Jehovah *forms* men and beasts, *breathes* the breath of life into man's nostrils, *builds* a rib into a woman, *plants* a garden, *takes* a man and *puts* him into it, *brings* the beasts to the man, *walks* in the cool of the day, *speaks* (Gen. iii. 22) as though He were *jealous* of the man" (Knobel, in Dillmann).
[7] Cf. the narrative of the flood, the representations of God in Gen. xviii. 25, xxiv. 3. See H. P. Smith, quoted above.
[8] On the sole ground of this loftier character these passages are treated by certain critics as later insertions.—Cf. Oxf. *Hex.* ii. p. 134.

things,[1] such as is found in prophets and psalmists to the latest time.

2. Entirely different from this is the early Israelitish conception of God *imagined by the new critical school*. The guiding idea here is no longer "revelation," but "evolution." Man's oldest ideas of God being supposed to be his poorest, an original monotheism in this people is decisively rejected. "At first," says Kuenen, "the religion of Israel was polytheism."[2] "Monotheism," says Wellhausen, "was unknown to ancient Israel."[3] "The knowledge that there is a supreme spiritual Being, alone of His kind, Creator and Preserver of all things, is perfectly lacking to ancient Israel," is the first sentence in Stade's chapter on pre-prophetic religion in Israel.[4] If we ask what conception is to take the place of that which is discarded, we have first the general answer that "the relation in which Yahweh stands to Israel is the same as, for instance, that of Chemosh to the Moabites."[5] Beyond this, we are offered a wide choice of theories. Kautzsch, *e.g.*, can find nothing in the religion of pre-Mosaic Israel but a species of "polydemonism." "It is only in a very restricted sense," he thinks, "that we can speak of such a notion [as God] at all."[6] A connection is sought by Kuenen between Jehovah and Moloch, the fire-god, who was worshipped with human sacrifices.[7] A favourite theory at present, revived by Budde, is that Yahweh was originally the storm-god of Sinai, worshipped by the Kenites, from whom Moses borrowed the name and cult.[8] With these theories are blended by Stade and others

---

[1] Cf. Dr. A. B. Davidson, art. "God" in *Dict. of Bible*, ii. p. 198 : "The language only testifies to the warmth and intensity of feeling of the writers"; *Theol. of O.T.*, pp. 108–9. Gunkel remarks: "In the Old Testament there are occasionally strong anthropomorphisms; but they are not so gross as is usual in Babylonia; Israel never said that Jehovah eats and drinks. Such anthropomorphisms are, in the Old Testament, archaisms," etc.— *Is. und Bab.* p. 32.

[2] *Rel. of Israel*, i. p. 223. He deduces this from the later practice of idolatry.

[3] *Isr. und Jud. Geschichte* (1897), p. 30. [4] *Geschichte*, i. p. 428.

[5] Kuenen, *Rel. of Israel*, p. 224; so Wellhausen, Stade, Budde, W. R. Smith, etc.

[6] Art. "Rel. of Israel" in *Dict. of Bible* (Extra), p. 623. Kautzsch severs himself from naturalistic theories when he comes to Moses. *His* idea of God, he thinks, can only have come from special revelation (p. 625). But it was not yet a monotheism: only a "monolatry."

[7] *Rel. of Israel*, i. pp. 226–28, 240, etc. On the similar theory of Daumer, etc., cf. König, *Hauptprobleme*, pp. 7 ff.

[8] The Kenite theory, on which see below, pp. 129 ff., is advocated by Budde,

a number of other elements drawn from fetishism, animism, ancestor-worship, totemism, etc.— of which more again. What are some of the grounds of these allegations, and of the rejection of the Biblical view ?

(1) First, and perhaps deepest, of the reasons for this rejection is the *a priori* one, that such a conception of God as the Old Testament attributes to the patriarchs and to Moses was *impossible* for them at that stage of the history. It is too elevated and spiritual for their minds to have entertained. The idea of the unity of God has for its correlates the ideas of the world and of humanity, and neither of these ideas, it is asserted, was possessed by ancient Israel.[1] The idea of the world did not arise till the time of Amos, when it was introduced through the Assyrian invasions. These "introduced," says Wellhausen, "a new factor, the conception of the world—the world, of course, in the historical sense of that expression. In presence of that conception, the petty nationalities lost their centre of gravity, brute force dispelled their illusions, they flung their gods to the moles and to the bats."[2] Thus arose the universalism of the prophets : thus was brought about the transformation of Yahweh-worship from monolatry to monotheism.

This seems to us most singular reasoning; is, indeed, throughout, both as to the idea of the world, and the impossibility of framing a spiritual conception of God, again a huge *petitio principii.* Here is a people whose own traditions, with the best warrant, went back to Babylonia and Mesopotamia; who had lived for centuries in Egypt in the most brilliant period of its civilisation; a people of the age of the Tel el-Amarna tablets; who entered Canaan when it stood in connection with, and was the highway of,

---

Tiele, Stade, Cheyne, etc. It was favoured by Colenso, and some older writers. It is one of the conceits of Budde that originally the Israelites traced their descent to Cain ! Cf. Delitzsch, *Genesis*, i. p. 192.

[1] Thus Stade, Kuenen, Wellhausen, etc. On the creation of the world, Wellhausen declares that "in a youthful people such a theological abstraction is unheard of, and so with the Hebrews we find both the word and the notion only coming into use after the Babylonian exile."—*Hist. of Israel*, p. 305. "The religious notion of *humanity* underlying Gen. ix. 6 is not ancient with the Hebrews any more than with other nations."—*Ibid.* p. 312.

[2] *Ibid.* p. 473. Wellhausen fails to show what other nations flung their gods to the moles and the bats as the result of the Assyrian conquests, or even that Israel did so as the result of these conquests, or till after the exile.

all the great empires of the world; who knew something of
the vast power of the Hittites in the north; yet we are
asked to believe that it had no conception of the world, or
of anything larger than a petty state, till the days of Amos!
The JE parts of the "table of nations" alone, in Gen. x.,
cry out against such a notion. As to the spirituality of
God, how can it well be maintained, in view of the exalted
conceptions of God now proved to have existed in both
the Babylonian and the Egyptian religions in periods long
anterior to Abraham and Moses,[1] that such conceptions
were beyond the grasp of the greater spirits in these times?
The Code of Hammurabi, in the simplicity and elevation of
its idea of "God," as the One in whose name, or before
whom, oaths were to be taken,[2] is a singular example of
what thoughtful minds were capable of in the age of
Abraham. In the Mosaic religion itself we have the
powerful witness of the Decalogue. We agree with Budde
in his testimony to the spirituality of the conception of
God involved in the Ten Words,[3] but we do not, on that
account, in face of the strongest historical improbabilities,
deny these precepts to Moses. The First Commandment,
indeed, "Thou shalt have no other gods before Me," might
be interpreted in the sense of monolatry,[4] not of monotheism;
but, in its actual setting, the obvious meaning of the precept
is, that Jehovah alone is to be worshipped, because He alone
is the living and true God.[5]

[1] On the pronounced monotheistic elements in the oldest Egyptian texts,
cf. Renouf, *Hibbert Lectures*, 1879, pp. 89 ff. See also Note A, below.

[2] The formula in the Code is simply, "shall swear in the name of God,"
"shall recount before God," or the like. The language is nearly identical
with that of the Book of Genesis. The difference is, that with this high
conception of divinity, the Babylonians worshipped many special gods, while
the Hebrews were forbidden to worship any but Jehovah. See Note A on
Early Ideas of God.

[3] Wellhausen also speaks of "the actual monotheism which is undoubtedly
presupposed in the universal precepts of the Decalogue."—*Hist. of Israel*,
p. 440. We have thus the alternative of denying the Decalogue to Moses,
or of admitting that a monotheistic conception of God lay at the foundation
of the religion of Israel. See below, pp. 152 ff. Even Kuenen admits that, in
its fundamental form, the Decalogue is Mosaic.

[4] Thus Kuenen, Kautzsch, etc. The theory on which this rests, viz.,
that "monolatry," or the worship of one sole (tribal) god, was the rule
among surrounding peoples is open to the gravest doubts. Cf. Dr. A. B.
Davidson, art. "God," in *Dict. of Bible*.

[5] Cf. Dr. A. B. Davidson on this precept in *Expositor*, 3rd Series, v.
p. 44.

(2) The modern theory may be usefully tested by reference to its most prevalent recent form—the alleged *Kenite origin* of the Yahweh cult. The theory, in essence, is, as above stated, that Yahweh, whose name and worship Moses introduced into Israel, was originally the storm-god of the Kenites, believed by them to have his local seat on Mount Sinai. A connection is thought to be established by the facts that Moses was living among the Kenites, with Jethro, when Yahweh was revealed to him; that the abode of Yahweh is placed at Sinai; and that His presence there is associated with thunder, lightning, and storm. The classical passage in proof is Deborah's Song,[1] in which, according to Wellhausen, Yahweh is "summoned to come from Sinai to succour His oppressed people, and to place Himself at the head of His warriors."[2] Budde, it was seen, draws the conclusion that Yahweh was a God absolutely unknown to the Hebrews before the Exodus, and explains His intimate association with Canaan by the notion that He "absorbed" the Canaanitish deities into Himself!

The far-fetched and arbitrary character of this theory, which Budde allows to be contradictory of the uniform tradition of the Old Testament, can be judged of by the most ordinary reader. Not only does it lack real evidence, but it is directly in the teeth of the fact that the Jehovah who appeared to Moses is expressly identified in the oldest sources with the God of the fathers, and His interposition is represented as in fulfilment of His covenant promises to them.[3] This is independent of any theory we may form as to whether the sacred name was known earlier or not. In point of fact many of the critics now hold that it *was* known, if only in limited circles.[4] On the other hand, there is not the least proof, as Kittel points out, that Yahweh was the name of a Kenite deity.[5] When Moses, later, invited Hobab the Kenite, his brother-in-law, to come with the Israelites, it was that they might do *him* good, "for Jehovah hath spoken good concerning Israel," not that he, as an earlier worshipper of Yahweh, might do *them* good.[6] It is but a precarious hold which the theory finds

[1] Judg. v.   [2] *Hist. of Israel*, p. 344.
[3] Ex. ii. 23–25, iii. 13–16, etc.
[4] See Note B on the Antiquity of the Name Jehovah. Many now trace it as far back as Babylonia. See below, p. 409.
[5] *Hist. of Hebs.* i. p. 250.   [6] Num. x. 29.

9

in the Song of Deborah, especially when it is remembered that by the time of the Judges Jehovah's presence is beyond all question presupposed as in the midst of His people in Canaan.[1] How then should He require to be "summoned" from Sinai?[2] The bold, figurative language in the opening of the Song is most easily understood as a reminiscence of the manifestations of Jehovah's presence and power in the desert and at Mount Sinai, viewed as a pledge of present help.[3]

Stade has himself no little difficulty in maintaining his theory of a local and limited deity, whose seat was at Sinai. Yahweh, he allows, was "everywhere" present to His worshippers in Canaan, and could be worshipped "everywhere."[4] His presence and help are not confined to His own land: He accompanies His worshippers into foreign lands, and there guards and defends them. Thus He promises to Jacob at Bethel to be everywhere with him: He is with Joseph in Egypt, goes with Jacob down to Egypt, works miracles for Elijah at Zarephath, etc. He knows Sarah's thoughts; it is declared of Him that nothing is too hard for Him; He can help by many or by few; He destroys wicked cities; visits lands like Egypt with famine; and otherwise displays His universal might.[5] Stade speaks of these things as indications of a tendency to "break through" the old notion of God;[6] they are in reality a disproof of his theory of that notion. The Song of Deborah itself, rightly regarded, is evidence of a far higher conception of Jehovah in the time of the Judges than the modern theory will allow. How sublime the picturing of the majesty and omnipotence of God in the opening theophany; how irreconcilable with the idea of a local deity the resist-

---

[1] The whole book is evidence; but cf. Judg. i. 19, 22; or chap. xi. 11: "Jephthah uttered all his words before Jehovah in Mizpeh"; or the presence of the ark of Jehovah at Bethel and Shiloh.

[2] "The truth is," says Professor Robertson, "the Song says not a word about Jehovah being 'summoned' from Sinai on the occasion of the battle referred to."—*Early Rel.* p. 193.

[3] Cf. for parallels, Deut. xxxiii. 2; Hab. iii. 3 ff.; Pss. xviii. 7 ff., lxviii. 7 ff., etc. Kuenen himself says: "Of course, we do not deny that the pious among the Israelites, in using these expressions, were aware that they spoke in metaphors."—*Rel. of Israel*, i. p. 241.

[4] *Geschichte*, i. p. 446.

[5] *Ibid.* i. pp. 430-32. Cf. the references, Gen. xviii. 14; xxviii. 15 ff.; 1 Sam. xiv. 6; 2 Kings v. 15 ff., etc.

[6] *Ibid.* p. 430.

less presence of Jehovah in Seir, at Sinai, in Canaan;[1]
how manifest the supremacy of this God in nature and
providence, when even "the stars in their courses" fight
against His enemies;[2] how distinct the assertion of Jehovah's
righteousness;[3] how lofty and *spiritual* the closing strain—
suggestive of the Second Commandment and of Deuteronomy
—"Let them that love Him be as the sun when he goeth
forth in his might!"[4] The theory as a whole thus fails of
evidence, and we are not surprised that critics like König,
Kittel, Kautzsch, Dr. A. B. Davidson,[5] and others reject it.
The fact that Horeb is already spoken of in Ex. iii. 1 as
"the mountain of God" is a very fragile buttress: the expression is probably used proleptically.

(3) We come back, then, in support of the theory that
Jehovah was a "tribal" (or merely national) god to the
two passages which, from their perpetual recurrence, may,
without offence, be called the stock proofs of that hypothesis,
viz., the words of Jephthah in Judg. xi. 24, and those of
David in 1 Sam. xxvi. 19. But, impartially examined,
what do these passages amount to? Jephthah says to the
king of the Ammonites: "Wilt thou not possess that which
Chemosh thy god giveth thee to possess? So whomsoever
Jehovah our God hath dispossessed from before us, them
will we possess." Even accepting the interpretation put
upon the words, one may reasonably demur to the erecting
of the utterance of this rude Gileadite chieftain, in a time
of religious disorganisation, into a standard for the true
idea of God in the Mosaic religion. That must be judged
of on its own ampler evidence, apart from a passage like
this. But even on the lips of Jephthah, rude soldier though
he is, it is by no means clear that the words are intended
as more than a form of speech in accommodation to the

[1] Judg. v. 4, 5.
[2] Ver. 20. "In the Song," says Dr. A. B. Davidson, "we observe Him
regarded as ruling in heaven and on earth, commanding the stars in their
courses, and the rivers as they flow."—*O.T. Prophecy*, p. 38.
[3] Ver. 11. In Budde's view, the Yahweh of Moses had not even moral
character (*Rel. of Israel*, p. 30).
[4] Ver. 31. Dr. Davidson says here: "Had we a few more poems by
prophetic minds such as this, and not the external histories of rude soldiers,
such as unfortunately we possess alone [But see below, pp. 143, 384], we
should, I believe, be able to form a higher idea even of the religious condition
of the people under the Judges."—*Ibid.* pp. 37–38.
[5] Kautzsch speaks of it with respect, but does not accept it.—"Rel. of
Israel," *Dict.* p. 62; cf. Davidson, *Theol. of O.T.*, pp. 50–52.

Ammonite point of view. The section seems based, as
before said, on Num. xxi. 22 ff., where, it might be shown,
a sufficiently high idea of God is implied. Jehovah, in any
case, is obviously far more to Israel than Chemosh is to
Ammon; is even, in ver. 27, invoked as "the Judge" to
judge between them.[1] The second passage, in which David
says, "They have driven me out this day that I should not
cleave unto (or, have no share in) the inheritance of
Jehovah, saying, Go, serve other gods," has, to our mind,
even less probative force. Wellhausen entirely misrepre-
sents its import when he speaks of David as "compelled to
serve other gods,"[2] and Professor W. R. Smith not less when
he says that David takes it for granted that a man who is
excluded from the commonwealth of Israel "must go and
serve other gods."[3] One desiderates here some more exact
thinking. Does anyone—even Wellhausen—really suppose
that when David crossed into Philistia he ceased to worship
Jehovah, and served Dagon instead? or that Naomi
worshipped Chemosh in Moab? or that Elijah served Baal
at Zarephath? What, on this theory, would be the meaning
of Naaman's apology for "bowing down" in the house of
Rimmon?[4] We have learned from Stade himself, what all
the history teaches, that Jehovah accompanied His servants
in their wanderings: how could David imagine it would be
otherwise with him? Taking the passage most literally,
David is not speaking for himself, but declaring what *others*
say; and he uses this bold mode of speech to emphasise his
sense of the deprivation implied in being banished from
Jehovah's immediate presence, and driven into a land where
other gods are worshipped. The fact that precisely the
same expression occurs twice in an undoubtedly monotheistic book like Deuteronomy should warn us against
attaching too much weight to its presence here.[5]

[1] We may quote Dr. A. B. Davidson again: "The truth is that such
references to Chemosh and other heathen gods prove nothing, because they
would prove that even Jeremiah regarded Chemosh as a real divinity (Jer.
xlviii. 7)."—*Expositor*, 3rd Series, v. p. 49. We may compare our own way
of speaking of heathen gods. Even in the case of a monotheistic religion
like Mohammedanism, we make a distinction between the Christian's God
and Allah. Both are designations of the Supreme Being, yet the conceptions of God are so different that we hold them apart in thought, and give
them different names.
[2] *Hist. of Israel*, p. 22.   [3] *Prophets*, p. 54.   [4] 2 Kings v. 18.
[5] Deut. xxviii. 36, 64. Wellhausen cites as another proof: "When

We conclude that no good ground has been shown for the view that "ethical monotheism" was first introduced by the prophets, beginning with Amos.[1] We have found monotheism already embedded in the narratives in Genesis, which, in their J and E parts, are, on the critic's own showing, "pre-prophetic." So far from monotheism being the creation of the prophets,—with, perhaps, Elijah as precursor,—these prophets, without exception, found upon, and presuppose, an older knowledge of the true God. They bring in no new doctrine, still less dream of the evolution from a Moloch or a Kenite storm-god,—as much the product of men's fancies as Chemosh or Dagon,—of the living, holy, all-powerful, all-gracious Being to whose service the people were bound by every tie of gratitude, but from whom they had basely apostatised. They could not have understood such evolution from an unreality into a reality. They were in continuity with the past, not innovators upon it. Dillmann speaks for a large class of scholars when he says, in decisively rejecting this theory : "No prophet is conscious of proclaiming for the first time this higher divine Principle : each reproaches the people for an apostacy from a much better past and better knowledge : God has a controversy with His people."[2]

III. Early Israelitish Worship

Budde stands nearly alone in denying an ethical element in the original Mosaic conception of God; but it is hardly possible to put lower than most writers of this school do the ideas entertained by the people in the pre-prophetic age of the proper mode of representing and worshipping the deity to whom they had attached themselves. Fetishism, animism, totemism, image-worship, ancestor-worship, tree-and stone-worship, human sacrifices, etc., all play their part

Cain is driven out of the land (Canaan), he is driven from the presence of Jehovah" (Gen. iv. 14, 16). Similarly Stade : "Cain, driven out of Palestine, and pleading for the alleviation of his punishment, is made to say," etc. (i. pp. 446–47). Cain, on this view, is supposed to have had his abode in Palestine. Wonderful is the power of criticism to make the text say what it pleases—even to the turning of it into nonsense !

[1] Cf. Duhm, quoted above, p. 68.

[2] *Alttest. Theol.* p. 56. Cf. Schultz against Stade in *O.T. Theol.* i. pp. 123–24. Baethgen maintains that the religion of Israel never was polytheistic : that its strange gods were imported.—*Beiträge*, p. 289.

here. Most writers are content to explain a religion by the help of one or two such principles—by fetishism, *e.g.*, or ancestor-worship, or totemism. It is reserved for Stade, in his picture of pre-prophetic religion, to blend *all* these forms of superstition in one grand *mélange*. We shall consider this subject under the general head of worship.

The simple elements of patriarchal worship, in the Biblical view, are prayer and sacrifice. The patriarchs build their altars, and call on the name of God. After the Exodus, worship is regulated by the Mosaic constitution. The fundamental laws of the covenant forbade the worship of God by images, required the extirpation of idolatry, denounced witchcraft, and condemned the practices of the Canaanites generally.[1] In the hands of the critics this picture of Israel's history undergoes a complete transformation. It was seen before that the Biblical history, on the face of it, does not lend support to the view that tree- and stone-worship, ancestor-worship, totem-worship, teraphim-worship, human sacrifices and the like, were prominent features of the religion of the patriarchs, or of the people who came out of Egypt with Moses.[2] How then is the theory made out? In the first place, as before, by rejecting the history we have, and substituting for it a construction evolved from a general theory of the origin of religion; in the next place, by reading back the disobediences and corruptions of the later history into the original form of the religion, and fastening on stray passages and incidents an interpretation contrary to the general impression of the narrative.[3] The method can best be illustrated by observing it at work.

1. The Book of Genesis gives us a clear and intelligible account of how *places* like Bethel, Hebron, Beersheba, Shechem, came to be regarded with peculiar veneration by the Israelites. They were places hallowed by the residence and worship of their fathers, and by the revelations of God. These stories form part of the patriarchal history, and we have sought to show that there is no reason for discrediting them. The newer criticism, however, cannot accept so

[1] Ex. xx. 4, 5, 23 ; xxii. 18, 21; xxiii. 24, 32, 33.
[2] See above, pp. 39, 40.
[3] Kautzsch says he "must emphasise very strongly that in almost every instance we have here to deal with hypotheses, and not with facts."—"Rel. of Israel" *Dict.* p. 613.

simple an explanation. It rejects the history, and assumes that these places were really *old Canaanitish sanctuaries*, which the Israelites adopted on their entrance into Canaan, and afterwards glorified by weaving around them this web of patriarchal legend.[1] If we ask for proof, none is forthcoming. We are thrown back on assertion, and on the assumption of the mythical character and non-historicity of the patriarchal narratives generally.

2. Stade gives the matter a further development. There were *graves* at some of these places (Hebron, Machpelah, Shechem). What is clearer than that the real origin of the sacredness of these sanctuaries was *ancestor - worship*? "Before the altars at Hebron and Shechem were altars of Yahweh, sacrifices were offered on them to the ancestral spirits of Abraham and Joseph, and we have here a proof" —the reader will note the stringency of Stade's ideas of proof — "that we are right in our conclusion that the worship of ancestors was a usage in ancient Israel."[2] The tribal system is thought to be connected with ancestor-worship,[3] and additional proofs are found in mourning customs.[4] Other writers amplify the suggestion. "The teraphim," Budde thinks, "belong to the extensive domain of ancestor-worship, which, in many lands and continents, even in the New World, has formed the oldest verifiable foundation of religion."[5] The yearly sacrifice of David's family in Bethlehem may be presumed to have been originally offered "to a deified eponymous hero."[6] The rule is a simple one—wherever you find mention of burial-places, be sure you are on the track of worship of ancestors.[7] Addis finds Jacob in Gen. xxxv. 14 "pouring out a libation

---

[1] Wellhausen, *Hist. of Israel*, pp. 18, 30, 325, etc.; Budde, *Rel. of Israel*, p. 107, etc. *E.g.*, Jacob's vow at Bethel is supposed to be meant as a sanction of the payment of tithes to the priests of the calf-worship at that place.

[2] *Geschichte*, i. pp. 451–52.   [3] *Ibid.* p. 452.

[4] Mourning customs are supposed to have their rationale in the attempt, as Kautzsch says, "to render oneself *unrecognisable* by the spirit of the dead, and thus to escape its malign influence."—"Rel. of Israel," *Dict.* pp. 614–15. Kautzsch criticises the theory, and concludes that if ancestor-worship ever prevailed in the pre-Mosaic period, no consciousness of it survived to historical times.

[5] *Rel. of Israel*, p. 64. Max Müller subjects the theory of ancestor-worship to a historical examination in his *Anthropological Religion* (Lect. V.), and rejects it as based on totally mistaken data.

[6] *Ibid.* p. 65.   [7] *Ibid.*

to the soul of the dead."[1] And these things, in all seriousness, are regarded as "scientific" treatment of the history.

3. Was *animism*, or belief in a spiritual presence in
natural objects, a feature of the religion of ancient Israel ?
These writers have no doubt of it. Primitive peoples are
accustomed to connect the presence of the deity with wells
and trees.[2] Now there are "wells" mentioned in Genesis,
at Beersheba and elsewhere.[3] It is true that there is no
hint in the patriarchal narratives that the wells were valued
for anything but the supply of water they yielded. But
this is no obstacle to the belief that originally the wells
were thought of as dwelt in by spirits, and that this was
the real ground of the reverence paid to them.[4] So trees
were wont to be regarded as manifestations of a divine life.
And the patriarchs were fond of the shade of spreading
trees, built altars near them,[5] sometimes even planted them.
Abraham dwelt by the "oaks" or "terebinths" of Mamre ;[6]
he planted a tamarisk at Beersheba ; Deborah, Rebekah's
nurse, was buried under "the oak" at Bethel, which thenceforth was called "Allon-bacuth"—"the oak of weeping."[7]
"The famous holy tree near Shechem," says Professor W. R.
Smith, "called 'the tree of soothsayers,' in Judg. ix. 37,
and 'the tree of the revealer' in Gen. xii. 6, must have been
the seat of a Canaanite oracle."[8] Possibly ; though there is
in the statement the full measure of assumption usual in
such matters.[9] But there is nothing to connect the
patriarchs with these superstitions, or to indicate that they
thought of a god as dwelling in these trees. The Canaanite

---

[1] *Hex.* ii. p. 226. Addis takes this verse from its place, and connects it
with the death of Deborah.

[2] Cf. W. R. Smith, *Rel. of Semites*, pp. 151 ff.

[3] Gen. xvi. 7 ; xxi. 25, 30 ff.; xxiv. 16 ; xxvi. 15, 19 ff., etc.

[4] Stade, *Geschichte*, i. p. 456.

[5] Gen. xiii. 18.

[6] Gen. xiii. 18 ; xiv. 13 ; xviii. 1. The LXX has the singular, "oak."

[7] Gen. xxxv. 8. Stade would connect the very names of the trees—
Elah, Elon, Allon—with the divine name El (i. p. 455). "This attempt,"
says Professor A. B. Davidson, "may be safely neglected."—*Dict. of Bible*,
ii. p. 199.

[8] *Rel. of Semites*, p. 179.

[9] "The famous holy oak" has already a touch of such assumption. It
is assumed that the "Moreh" in Gen. xii. 6 is not, like Mamre, a proper
name (cf. Dillmann, *in loc.*), and that the identity of this tree is certain with
the "oak of Meonenim" in Judg. ix. 37. Similarly, "the palm tree"
under which Deborah sat and judged (Judg. iv. 4) is identified with "the
oak" which marked the grave of Rebekah's nurse (Gen. xxxv. 8).

Asherahs, or tree symbols of Astarte, on the other hand,—
another of the proofs,—were no doubt idolatrous; but they
were from the first, and all down the history, absolutely
condemned.[1]

4. The proofs offered of *fetishism* and of *stone-worship* in
ancient Israel are equally numerous—and equally inconclusive. Only allusion need be made here to the ark of
the covenant, which will form a subject of discussion by
itself after.[2] The history speaks of an ark, the visible
symbol of the presence of Jehovah among His people,[3] in
which were deposited the two tables of the law.[4] Jehovah
dwelt, not *in*, but above the ark, between (or upon) the
cherubim."[5] This, however, in the view of the critics, is a
mistake. Analogies are drawn from other religions to prove
that "the ark of Yahweh" was really a fetish-chest; and
the tradition that it contained tables of stone is to Stade
the "most convincing" evidence that it had in it two stones in
which Yahweh was believed to dwell.[6] The stones were probably "meteorites"—appropriate to the lightning-god.[7] " If
the divinity of Sinai resided in a rock," says Professor H. P.
Smith sagely,—"which from Arabian analogies seems very
probable,—it would be natural for the people to secure His
presence by providing such a chest in which to transport
the fetish."[8] One feels sometimes that it would require

[1] Ex. xxxiv. 13 ; cf. Deut. xvi. 21.
[2] Cf. Chap. VI. pp. 161 ff.
[3] Num. x. 33 ff.; Josh. iii. 6.
[4] Hence the name "ark of the covenant." Cf. Deut. x. 1–6, 1 Kings
viii. 9, with Ex. xxiv. 12 ff., xxv. 21. See below, p. 162.
[5] 1 Sam. iv. 4 ; 2 Sam. vi. 2. Cf. A. B. Davidson, *Theol. of O.T.*, p. 112.
Kuenen says of these passages : "We must hold that the author wrote
' the ark of Yahweh,' and ' the ark of God,' nothing more."—*Rel. of Israel*, i.
p. 259. Apart, however, from the omission of the words "of the covenant" in the LXX (Vat. Cod.) of 1 Sam. iv. 3–5, which is not decisive,
the " must " is in his own theory. See below, p. 162.
[6] *Geschichte*, i. pp. 448–49, 457. "This conception," Stade says, "is
what from the standpoint of the history of religion must be called
fetishistic" (p. 448).
[7] *Ibid.* p. 458 ; cf. Kuenen, i. p. 233. Kautzsch adopts the "meteorite"
theory.—"Rel. of Israel," *Dict.* p. 629. Bennett says: "According to
early tradition, two sacred stones were preserved in the ark." — *Genesis*,
p. 282. Tradition, however, says nothing of "two sacred stones," it speaks
only and definitely of the two tables of the law.
[8] *O.T. History*, p. 71. Professor A. R. S. Kennedy, in art. "Ark" in *Dict.
of Bible* (i. p. 150), dissociates himself from this view, "now generally
adopted," he says, "by Continental writers." On the literature, see
Kautzsch, as above.

the irony of an Elijah to deal fittingly with such hypotheses, but we are content to leave them to the reader's own reflections.

A more direct proof of stone-worship, however, is thought to be found in the setting up of sacred "pillars" or *maççebas* by the patriarchs and others—as by Jacob at Bethel,[1] by Jacob and Laban in Mount Gilead,[2] by Joshua at Shechem,[3] by Samuel at Ebenezer,[4] etc. It is true that, as Professor W. R. Smith admits, these pillars or stones are never represented in the narratives as anything but memorial pillars;[5] but it is insisted that the real idea underlying them is that God was actually present in the stone, or at least then took up His abode in it.[6] It is pointed out that, in the case of Jacob, not "the place," but the "stone" itself, is called "Bethel," in Gen. xxviii. 22,[7] and a connection is sought with the Greek word βαιτύλια, a name for sacred stones.[8] But there is not a vestige of evidence that there was ever a class of sacred stones in Israel called "Bethels,"[9] and it is surely obvious from the context that the *stone* is called "Bethel," merely as marking the site of the *place*. This ingenious hypothesis, in short, is simply a reading into the narrative of ideas which do not necessarily belong to it. "It cannot be inferred," Dillmann says justly, "from Gen. xxviii. 18, xxxv. 14, 15, xlix. 24, that the patriarchs worshipped holy stones: the stone of Jacob appears only as a symbol of a place, and monument of the experience of God's nearness; also in later times we read nothing of stone-worship among the people."[10] Neither, we may add, is there the slightest evidence that the prophets, in their later polemic against idolatrous *maççebas*, intended the least disrespect to such memorial pillars as were set up by Jacob or Joshua. In

---

[1] Gen. xxviii. 18, 22 ; xxxv. 14.
[2] Gen. xxxi. 45. Also in vers. 46–49, a heap or cairn.
[3] Josh. xxiv. 26, 27.
[4] 1 Sam. vii. 12.   [5] Cf. above, p. 122.
[6] Professor W. R. Smith distinguishes such dwelling in stones from fetishism proper (*Rel. of Semites*, p. 189).
[7] *Ibid.* p. 187.
[8] Cf. art. "Bethel" in *Dict. of Bible*, i. p. 218.
[9] As Schultz, *e.g.*, would seem to suggest, *O.T. Theol.* i. p. 207.
[10] *Alttest. Theol.* p. 90. So König in art. "Symbol" in *Dict. of Bible* (Extra), p. 170 : "The *maççeboth*, again, were not set up on their own account. They were not meant to be dwelling-places of the deity, but were symbols, expressive of gratitude for a divine revelation," etc.

Isa. **xix.** 19 it is even predicted that "in that day there shall be an altar of Jehovah in the midst of the land of Egypt, and a pillar (*maççeba*) at the border thereof to Jehovah." It is a forced explanation of such a passage to say that, in Isaiah's time, pillars were not yet regarded as unlawful.[1] Memorial pillars never were so regarded: "pillars" on the other hand, connected with idolatrous worship were already condemned in the first legislation,[2] —far older, on any showing, than Isaiah.

5. Another form of superstition with which the religion of Israel is brought into relation is *totemism,* or belief in the descent of a tribe from a sacred animal. Professor W. R. Smith found in this the key to the clan system and sacrificial customs of the Semites—the Hebrews included.[3] Support is sought for the theory in Biblical names—in the name Caleb, *e.g.,* which means a dog,[4]—and Stade urges such facts as the "horns" of the altar, and the bull-worship of the Northern Kingdom.[5] The theory has not met with general acceptance, and hardly needs here fuller discussion.[6]

6. To the long list of heathenish practices asserted to belong to the religion of ancient Israel may be added— *human sacrifice.* Human sacrifice was a feature of Moloch-worship: the Israelites were acquainted with it; in times of religious declension even caused their children to pass through the fire to Moloch.[7] If, then, as Kuenen thinks, Yahweh was originally connected with Moloch,

[1] According to Vatke, Kuenen, Duhm, etc., the abolition of *maççebas* was included in the reforms of Hezekiah. Cf. König, *Hauptprobleme,* p. 68.

[2] Ex. xxiii. 24 (images=*maççebas*); cf. Isa. xvii. 7, 8; Mic. v. 13. Hosea, in chap. iii. 4, seems to group together lawful and unlawful objects.

[3] *Rel. of Semites,* pp. 117 ff., 130, 251 ff., 424 ff.; *Kinship and Marriage,* chap. viii. ; "Animal Worship and Animal Tribes," *Jour. of Philology,* 1880.

[4] Cf. *Kinship and Marriage,* pp. 218 ff. : "The nomadic populations of Southern Palestine, which ultimately became incorporated with Judah, also present animal names, of which the most important is that of the Calebbites, or dog-tribe" (p. 219).

[5] *Geschichte,* p. 465. Stade mentions (p. 466) that W. R. Smith supposes the serpent to be the totem of the house of David.

[6] See Note C on Professor W. R. Smith's Theory of Sacrifice. Kautzsch criticises the totem-theory in "Rel. of Israel," *Dict.* p. 613. If the theory were as ingeniously applied to *British* personal (animal) names, symbols (*e.g.,* John Bull, British Lion), tavern signs (a large class), etc., it would bring out startling results.

[7] Cf. 2 Kings xvi. 3 ; xxi. 6 ; xxiii. 10 ; Jer. xxxii. 35, etc.

human sacrifice was to be expected in His service.[1] If, on the other hand, this abhorrent idea of the connection of Jehovah with Moloch is rejected, the chief basis of the theory is destroyed, and other proofs become of secondary account. No fair reader of the history of Israel can say that human sacrifice was at any time a legitimate or recognised part of the worship of the nation. Proofs drawn from Abraham's temptation (the moral of which is that such sacrifices were *not* desired by Jehovah),[2] from the destruction of the first-born,[3] Samuel's hewing of Agag in pieces before Jehovah,[4] the hanging of Saul's seven sons,[5] etc., are quite illusory, for none of the last-named cases answers properly to the idea of sacrifice. If Micah asks: "Shall I give my first-born for my transgression, the fruit of my body for the sin of my soul?"[6]—asks it only to reject the supposition—this no more proves that human sacrifice was a usual or recognised part of Jehovah's religion, than Paul's words, "If I give my body to be burned,"[7] prove that surrender to death by fire was a common form of devotion in the apostolic Church. There remains the case of Jephthah's sacrifice of his daughter in fulfilment of his rash vow.[8] The circumstances are unusual, and there is still doubt as to the manner in which Jephthah fulfilled his vow.[9] But, admitting that the maiden was actually slain as a sacrifice, and not simply devoted, we may be excused, as before, for not accepting the action of this very partially enlightened Gileadite, in a rude age, as a rule for judging of the true character of Israel's religion. How would it fare with Christianity, if it were judged by individual instances of misguided zeal, in contrariety with its own first principles, occurring, say, in the Middle Ages? We may safely apply to all human sacrifices

---

[1] Cf. *Rel. of Israel*, i. pp. 228, 237. Kuenen carries over all the things condemned by the prophets, including female prostitution, into the worship of Yahweh (cf. p. 72).

[2] Gen. xxii.

[3] Ex. xiii. 2, 11–12, etc. The redemption of the first-born is thought to have its origin in this practice. Cf. Kuenen, i. p. 290.

[4] 1 Sam. xv. 33.

[5] 2 Sam. xxi. 1–14. These are Kuenen's own instances (i. p. 287).

[6] Mic. vi. 7, 8.   [7] 1 Cor. xiii. 3.

[8] Judg. xi. 30, 31, 34–40.

[9] Cf. Sanday, *Inspiration*, p. 133; and see the full discussion in Köhler's *Bib. Geschichte*, ii. pp. 100–3.

what Jeremiah says of the sacrifices to Moloch: "Which I commanded them not, neither came it into My mind, that they should do this abomination, to cause Judah to sin."[1]

IV. IMAGE-WORSHIP IN ISRAEL

A more important question than any of the above is— Was *image-worship* an original or permissible part of Israel's religion? To most the Second Commandment would seem decisive on that point; but it is not so to the critics. The Decalogue is denied to Moses, and a principal reason for rejecting the precept prohibiting images is precisely that images are held to have been, in point of fact, worshipped.[2] That there was deplorable defection, and lapsing into idolatry, in the time of the Judges, and under the kings, no one, of course, denies; it is the assertion of the Bible itself, and the constant subject of the denunciation of the prophets. It is a different matter when it is maintained that the worship of Jehovah was originally, and all down the history, by images. The assertions of the critics here are of the most positive kind. Wellhausen says roundly: "The prohibition of images was during the older period quite unknown."[3] Professor H. P. Smith tells us that even the great prophets "no doubt conceived God as existing in human form."[4] It was not, however, in human form, but under the image of a bull, that Jehovah is supposed to have been worshipped from ancient times in Israel.[5] The support for this is chiefly drawn from the calf-worship set up by Jeroboam in Northern Israel, and confirmatory evidences are sought in the ephod of Gideon,[6] the images

---

[1] Jer. xxxii. 35. Another prophetic passage adduced by Kuenen is Hos. xiii. 2, with the reading, "Sacrificing men, they kiss the calves" (i. p. 75). Even so, the practice is only mentioned to be condemned. See Note D on Sacrifice of Children.

[2] See above, p. 120; and below, p. 153. Cf. Kittel, *Hist. of Hebs.* i. p. 248. Cf. Schultz, *O.T. Theol.* i. p. 210. Professor W. R. Smith says: "Even the principle of the Second Commandment, that Jehovah is not to be worshipped by images . . . cannot, in the light of history, be regarded as having so fundamental a place in the religion of early Israel."—*Prophets,* p. 63.

[3] *Hist. of Israel,* p. 439.

[4] *O.T. History,* p. 18. Kautzsch also thinks that the idea of Jehovah as having bodily form continued *till* the prophetic age.—"Rel. of Israel," *Dict.* p. 637. Cf. Kittel, *Hist. of Hebs.* i. pp. 248 ff.

[5] Thus generally.   [6] Judg. viii. 27.

of Micah,[1] the brazen serpent of Moses.[2] It is allowed that there was no image of Jehovah in the temple at Jerusalem;[3] but it is urged that there were other visible symbols,[4] and that images were common among the people.[5] Nothing, in our view, could be more baseless than this contention, but it will be well to look at the subject more closely.

1. We are entitled to say that the *oldest periods* of the history afford no confirmation of this theory. The worship of the patriarchs, in the Book of Genesis, was without images. The only apparent exception, as before noticed, is in the "teraphim" of Laban's family.[6] What these "teraphim" were is obscure. They are probably correctly enough described by Kuenen as "images which were revered as household gods, and consulted as to the future."[7] They were at any rate not images of Jehovah, and were put away by Jacob at Shechem as incompatible with the pure worship of God.[8] In the cases of Abraham, of Isaac, of Jacob, of Joseph, or, indeed, of any of the patriarchs, image-worship is not so much as hinted at. "The worship of God in the house of Abraham," as Dillmann says, "was imageless."[9] Baudissin, indeed, would carry back the bull-worship even to Abraham;[10] but this is baseless conjecture. Again, in Mosaic times, and in the Book of Joshua, there is no suggestion of a lawful worship of images. The only recorded instance of image-worship is in the making of the golden calf at Sinai,[11] and this is denounced and punished as a flagrant transgression, which all but cost the people their covenant privilege. The prohibitions of image-worship, and of participation in the idolatry of the Canaanites, are, on the other hand, absolute. The brazen serpent erected by Moses was not an image of Jehovah, or an image for worship at all, though it became at a later time an object of worship to the Israelites, and was in consequence destroyed by

---

[1] Judg. xvii. 3, 4 ; xviii. 14, 20, etc.   [2] Num. xxi. 8, 9.

[3] Kuenen, *Rel. of Israel*, i. pp. 80, 289.

[4] The ark is held by Kuenen, Stade, etc., to have been such a symbol. The two brazen pillars in the temple of Solomon are alleged by Professor W. R. Smith to have been "doubtless symbols of Jehovah."—*Rel. of Semites*, p. 191.

[5] Kuenen, as above, p. 80.

[6] Gen. xxxi. 19, 30–35.   [7] *Rel. of Israel*, p. 246.

[8] Gen. xxxv. 2–4.   [9] *Alttest. Theol.* p. 90.

[10] Cf. König, *Hauptprobleme*, p. 58.   [11] Ex. xxxii.

Hezekiah.[1] Neither Moses nor Joshua — none of the
leaders—showed the least tendency to image-worship. The
first notice of idolatrous practices in the wilderness journeyings is in the prophet Amos—if even there.[2]

2. When we pass to the *Book of Judges*, it is different.
We are now in a period expressly signalised as one of
declension and sinful adoption of Canaanitish idolatries.[3]
But even here we seek in vain in the greater part of the
book for evidence of an image-worship of Jehovah. The sin
for which the people are blamed is much more that of
forsaking Jehovah, and serving "the Baalim and the
Ashtaroth" (Astartes), "the Baalim and the Asheroth"
(sacred trees or poles), of their heathen neighbours,—an
undeniable violation of fundamental law, — than image-
worship of their own God.[4] One clear example of the latter
is in the case of the Ephraimite Micah, whose images were
carried off by the Danites.[5] The other case usually cited is
that of Gideon, who, after his victory over the Midianites,
made from the spoils a golden "ephod," which, it is declared,
became a "snare" to Gideon and his house.[6] On this
mistaken act of a man whose zeal had been conspicuous
against the Baal altars and the Asherahs,[7] a whole edifice of
rickety conjecture is built up. It is first assumed that
Gideon's "ephod" was an "image" of Jehovah; it is next
taken for granted that the image was in the form of a
bull;[8] lastly, it is concluded that bull-worship, or at least

[1] 2 Kings xviii. 4. Professor H. P. Smith, who sees in the brazen serpent
a survival of primitive totemism in Israel, has some characteristic remarks on
the subject. See Note E on H. P. Smith on the Brazen Serpent.

[2] Amos v. 25, 26. The interpretation of the passage is much disputed.

[3] Judg. ii. 11–14.

[4] Judg. ii. 11, 13 ; iii. 7 ; x. 6, etc. It is possible, however, to paint
even this period of backsliding and disorganisation in too dark colours. It
is, *e.g.*, an exaggeration to say with Mr. Thatcher : "There is no conception
of spiritual worship or moral duty in our book."—*Judges* ("Cent. Bible"),
Introd. p. 33. This is only true if first of all the higher elements (the repentances, etc.) are critically eliminated. The very absence of image-worship in
so large a part of the book is a disproof of the statement. The Song of
Deborah strikes a lofty, and at the end, spiritual note. Cf. above, p. 131 ;
and see the remarks of König on this point in art. "Judges," *Dict. of Bible*,
iii. p. 816 (cf. below, p. 384). Cf. also the Book of Ruth.

[5] Judg. xvii., xviii.

[6] Judg. viii. 27.   [7] Judg. vi. 28–32.

[8] Thus even Schultz, *O. T. Theol.* i. p. 149: "The molten image . . . is,
according to the analogy of other passages (Judg. xviii. 30 ; 1 Kings xii. 28
ff. ; Ex. xxxii. 4) to be thought of as the image of an ox." Cf. Kuenen,
Rel. of Israel, i. p. 236.

image-worship, was common among the people. It may be
observed that, even if it were true that Gideon made an
image for worship, these sweeping inferences would not be
justified. There would in itself be nothing more wonderful
in this heroic man falling in his latter days into the sin of
idolatry, than there is in Solomon, in his old age, building
idolatrous shrines for his wives.[1] But the inferences are
unwarranted on other grounds. What the text says is, not
that Gideon made an "image," but that he made an
"ephod"[2]—a massive and costly piece of work,[3] certainly,
and not designed for actual use, but in some way suggestive
of the high priest and his oracle. There is no indication
that he meant the ephod for worship. Least of all is there
any ground for the assertion that it was an image in the
form of a bull.[4] The ephod is expressly declared to have
become a "snare" to Gideon and his house : a condemnatory
statement not to be got rid of by the too easy hypothesis of
interpolation. There remains, therefore, as the single prop
of the theory of an image-worship of Jehovah in the time of
the Judges, the case of Micah, who made for himself "a
graven image and a molten image," a sanctuary, "an ephod
(here evidently distinguished from the images) and teraphim":[5] an undisputed instance of idolatry in the worship
of Jehovah. We willingly make a present of this weak-
minded, superstitious Ephraimite, and of the Danites who
stole his images from him, to the critics; but decline to
accept his behaviour as evidence of the fundamental law, or
better religious practice, in Israel. It is more to the point
to notice that even Micah does not appear to have had
images till his mother suggested this use of the stolen silver
to him.

3. The stronghold of the case for image-worship, how-

[1] 1 Kings xi. 4, 5.

[2] Kuenen, in a long note in his *Rel. of Israel* (i. pp. 260 ff.), "decidedly
rejects" the opinion that the ephod was an image ; but in his *Hibbert Lectures*
he accepts it (p. 82).

[3] This is shown by the amount of gold used, about 70 pounds.

[4] The idea rests, as the passage from Schultz above cited shows, on the
reading back into the time of the Judges of the calf-worship of Jeroboam. It
has no basis in the Book of Judges itself. Even so extreme a rationalist as
Dr. Oort contests this idea (cf. Kuenen, i. pp. 261–62).

[5] Judg. xvii. 3–6 ; xviii. 14, 20. Budde says of Micah's ephod, which
he takes to be "a silver, oracular image," that "unfortunately we do not
know its form."—*Rel. of Israel*, p. 80. See Note F on Dillmann on Image-
Worship.

ever, is in the *two calves of gold* which Jeroboam set up at
Bethel and Dan, after the division of the kingdom. It is
true that no hint is given that such images were known
before in Israel, unless the words, "Behold thy gods, O
Israel, which brought thee up out of the land of Egypt," be
an allusion to the golden calf of Ex. xxxii.; but it is
thought *unlikely* that Jeroboam would set up a symbol
entirely new,[1] and it is pointed out—at least alleged—that
no protest was made against the worship of the calves by
prophets like Elijah and Amos.[2] The denunciations in the
Books of Kings are regarded as representing a later point of
view. Here, again, the history which we have is thrust
aside and a new history invented which suits the critic's
theory. No ingenuity, however, can give this new theory
the semblance of probability. How strange, if this was an
old and well-known custom in Israel, that absolutely no
trace of it should be discoverable, or that it should need to
be "revived"! How remarkable that nothing of this bull-
worship should be known in Jerusalem, or in the temple,
the seat of Jehovah's worship,[3] in which there was no image,
or, apparently, in Judah generally, where it was universally
regarded as an abomination! The narrator in the Book of
Kings, who had access to old records, plainly regarded it as
something new. The judgment of the prophets, when we
turn to these, does not differ from that of the Book of
Kings. Hosea, it is generally admitted, is unsparing in his
denunciation of the calves,[4] and he was a prophet of
Northern Israel. It is held, however, that his attitude in
this respect is not that of his predecessors. "There is no
feature in Hosea's prophecy," says Professor W. R. Smith,
"which distinguishes him from earlier prophets so sharply

[1] A connection is conjecturally sought with the old sanctuary at Dan,
Judg. xviii. 29–31.

[2] Thus Wellhausen, Kuenen, Stade, W. R. Smith, and generally. The
suggestion may be made that Jeroboam got the idea from Egypt, where he
resided from the time of his revolt against Solomon till the accession of
Rehoboam (1 Kings xi. 40; xii. 1–3). Kuenen, however, rejects this, and
says: "It is much more reasonable to suppose that the ten tribes who rebelled
against Solomon's exactions, and his leanings towards foreign manners and
customs, introduced a genuinely national and ancient Israelitish worship."—
Rel. of Israel, i. p. 236.

[3] Are the "lions, *oxen*, and cherubim" that supported the "bases" in
the temple (1 Kings vii. 29) thought to be an exception? They were
certainly not objects of worship.

[4] Hos. viii. 5, 6; xiii. 2.

as his attitude to the golden calves, the local symbols of Jehovah adored in the Northern sanctuaries. Elijah and Elisha had no quarrel with the traditional[1] worship of their nation. Even Amos never speaks in condemnation of the calves."[2] This last sentence is astonishing. To the ordinary reader Amos and Hosea would seem to speak with precisely the same voice on the Northern calf-worship —Amos, if possible, with the greater vehemence of the two. "When I visit the transgressions of Israel upon him," says this prophet, "I will also visit the altars of Bethel."[3] "Come to Bethel," he exclaims, "and transgress."[4] He speaks of those "that swear by the sin of Samaria, and that swear, As thy god, O Dan, liveth."[5] Even Kuenen agrees that Amos speaks in the same way as Hosea of the calf-worship.[6]

With greater plausibility it may be maintained that there is no direct denunciation of the calf-worship by Elijah and Elisha. The argument from silence, however, is a peculiarly unsafe one here. In the only episodes in which Elijah is brought before us, he is engaged in a life-and-death struggle of another kind—the conflict between Jehovah and Baal arising from the introduction of the Tyrian Baal-worship into Samaria by Ahab and Jezebel.[7] It requires great faith to believe that a stern and zealous monotheist like Elijah could have any toleration for the calf-worship, which every other prophet of that age is represented as denouncing.[8] It is a sounder application of the argument from silence to observe that Elijah is never found as a worshipper in the neighbourhood of Bethel or Dan, and that he never drops a word indicative of recognition of that worship.[9] When he speaks despairingly of Jehovah's altars being thrown down,[10] he can hardly have included Bethel and Dan among their number, for these altars stood, and doubtless

[1] The reader will mark the *petitio* in the word "traditional." To Professor Smith also the calf-worship is as old as the days of the Judges (*Prophets*, p. 96).

[2] *Prophets*, p. 175.

[3] Amos iii. 14.　　　　　　　　[4] Amos iv. 4; cf. v. 4, 5.

[5] Amos viii. 14.

[6] *Rel. of Israel*, i. pp. 73–74. Cf. the pungent remarks of Dr. A. B. Davidson, *Bib. Essays*, pp. 91, 120–22.

[7] 1 Kings xvi. 30–34.

[8] *E.g.*, Ahijah (1 Kings xiv. 7 ff.); the prophet from Judah (chap. xiii. 2); Jehu, the son of Hanani (chap. xvi. 1, 2).

[9] Elisha was mocked at Bethel (2 Kings ii. 23).

[10] 1 Kings xix. 10.

had their crowds of worshippers. We may suppose that to him they would be practically in the category of the Baal-altars. And does his threatening to Ahab, " I will make thine house like the house of Jeroboam, the son of Nebat," [1] etc., convey no allusion to that by which peculiarly Jeroboam " made Israel to sin " ?

A dispassionate review, therefore, of this long catalogue of superstitions alleged to belong to pre-prophetic religion in Israel fails to establish the theory of the critics that any one of these formed part of the genuine religion of Israel. They show abundant defection in particular periods from the pure norm of that religion; but the evidence is overwhelming that they were foreign to the true genius of the religion, were condemned by its laws and by the prophets, and at no time received countenance from its great representatives. The ideas on which the religion rested—the unity, holiness, universal providence, and saving purpose of God—were, as before shown, entirely distinct from those of other religions. As it is with the idea of God and with the adjuncts of His worship, so, we shall next see, it is with the institutions of the religion.

[1] 1 Kings xxi. 21-24.

CHAPTER VI

The Old Testament as affected by Criticism— II. Religion and Institutions: Ark, Tabernacle, Priesthood, etc.

"I believe that, alongside of the modern representations, which resolve the founders of the Old Testament religion into flitting shadows that elude the grasp, and throw overboard the solid mass of the Pentateuchal history, like unnecessary ballast from a ship, my attempt will still meet with sympathy, to find an intelligible meaning in the narrative of the Pentateuch, and to apprehend the religion of Abraham as the preliminary stage, and the proclamation of Moses as the foundation, of the Old Testament faith, thought, and life. The Bible remains : scientific attempts to represent the Biblical history come and go."—KLOSTERMANN.

"It [German criticism] has generally been wanting in flexibility and moderation. It has insisted upon knowing everything, explaining everything, precisely determining everything. . . . Hence complicated and obscure theories, provided with odd corners in which all the details may be sheltered, and which leave the mind little opening or leisure to observe the tendency of facts and the general currents of history."—DARMESTETER (in Ottley).

"In Wellhausen's review of the history, he has much to say of the gradual rise of feasts from the presentation of first-fruits, and of their annual observance at neighbourhood sanctuaries, and the growth of larger sanctuaries towards the close of the period of the Judges. . . . But the whole thing is spun out of his own brain. It is as purely fictitious as an astronomical map would be of the other side of the moon."—W. H. GREEN.

CHAPTER VI

THE OLD TESTAMENT AS AFFECTED BY CRITICISM —II. RELIGION AND INSTITUTIONS: ARK, TABERNACLE, PRIESTHOOD, ETC.

THE subject of laws and institutions in Israel is bound up with so many intricate critical questions as to dates and succession of codes, that it may seem scarcely possible to deal with it satisfactorily till the critical questions have been, at least in some provisional way, disposed of. On the other hand, it is to be observed that the discussion of laws and institutions does not *wholly* depend on the conclusions reached on such matters, say, as the age of Deuteronomy, or date of compilation of the Priestly Code; for, conceivably, these books, in their present form, might be late, yet the laws embodied in them might be very old.[1] It will be found, in fact, that the determination of the critical questions themselves depends in no small measure on the view we are led to take of the history and nature of the institutions.[2] There is room and need, therefore, for some preliminary consideration of the latter, so far as this can be done without begging any question not yet critically dealt with.

I. GENERAL POSITION OF MOSES AS LAWGIVER

We may first advert a little further than has yet been done to the general position assigned to Moses in tradition as the *lawgiver* of Israel.[3] This is a point on which the critics can hardly avoid involving themselves in some inconsistency. On the one hand, it is necessary to exalt

---

[1] This is the position taken up by some critics, as König.
[2] See Wellhausen above, p. 5.
[3] See above, Chap. IV. pp. 98–99.

the personality and work of Moses, in order to explain how it comes about that all the legislation in the Old Testament is connected with his name;[1] on the other hand, it is necessary to minimise his influence almost to vanishing point, in order to make it credible that he really gave to Israel no laws at all—none at least of which we have any knowledge. It will be recalled how we are told that "Malachi is the first of the prophets to refer to a Mosaic code."[2] This line of reasoning, as shown before, is fatuous. The JE history, put by the critics as early as the ninth or eighth century, gives the foremost place to Moses as a law-giver. The Book of the Covenant, older than this history, and incorporated into it, is expressly ascribed to Moses as its author. The Book of Deuteronomy, again, whenever written, is evidence that Israel had but one tradition about Moses—that he gave and *wrote* laws for the nation. The force of this testimony is not in the least satisfied by sup-posing, with Wellhausen, W. R. Smith, and others, that the repute of Moses rested on such *oral* decisions as those referred to in Ex. xviii. 13–16, 26.[3] Budde will have nothing to do with this basing of the legislation of Moses on these oral *toroth* of Ex. xviii.,[4] and there is certainly something arbitrary in founding on this chapter as more historically trustworthy than its neighbours. If it is accepted, one must notice the evidence it yields of a high organisation of the people at the time of the Exodus.[5] What then are the reasons for refusing to Moses such legislation as the Old Testament ascribes to him?

1. If anything can be attributed with certainty to Moses, it surely is the *Decalogue*, which lies at the foundation of the whole covenant relation of Jehovah to Israel. Yet even this, which Delitzsch calls "the most genuine of genuine

[1] Cf. Wellhausen, *Hist. of Israel*, pp. 432 ff., 438 ff. ; Kuenen, *Rel. of Israel*, i. pp. 272 ff. The latter says : "The collections of laws were fearlessly embellished with his name, because it was known that he had laid the foundations of all legislation " (p. 279). He thinks, indeed, that "this he could do without writing down a single precept."

[2] Carpenter, as above, p. 98. "The prophets of the eighth century," says Professor W. R. Smith, "never speak of a written law of Moses."—*O.T. in J. C.*, p. 302. To show this, he has to put a non-natural sense on Hos. viii. 12 (see below, p. 325). But at least the prophets knew of the Book of the Covenant, professing to be written by Moses.

[3] Wellhausen, *Hist. of Israel*, p. 439 ; W. R. Smith, *O.T. in J. C.*, pp. 304, 339.

[4] *Rel. of Israel*, p. 33.   [5] Ex. xviii. 21, 25.

productions,"[1] it has of late become almost universally the fashion to deny to the lawgiver. But on what subjective and arbitrary grounds![2] A main reason, as we have seen, is the prohibition of images in the Second Commandment[3]— a subject already discussed.[4] Apart from this, and the too elevated idea of God in the Decalogue as a whole, two special objections may be noticed: (1) the variation in the form of the Fourth Commandment in the Deuteronomic version,[5] and (2) the alleged occurrence of a second Decalogue in Ex. xxxiv. 12–26—a notion borrowed from Goethe. The first of these objections comes badly from those who see in Deuteronomy a free prophetic composition of the age of Josiah, and, apart from the supposition of an original shorter form, seems sufficiently met by Delitzsch's remark that "the Decalogue is there freely rendered in the flow of hortatory oratory, and not literally reproduced."[6] The variation may indeed be regarded as an incidental mark of genuineness in Deuteronomy, for hardly any other than the lawgiver would be likely to allow himself this liberty of change. The second objection derives some colour from a slight ambiguity or confusion in the language of Ex. xxxiv. 27, 28; but cannot overbear the clear connection of ver. 28, "And He [Jehovah] wrote upon the tables the words of the covenant, the ten commandments [words]," with ver. 1, "I will write upon the tables the words which were upon the first tables, which thou brakest," or the plain intention of the narrative as a whole. The so-called second Decalogue of J in Ex. xxxiv. 12–26, is, in fact, pretty much, as scholars are coming to see, a figment of the critical imagination. It is only by straining that the section can be made into a Decalogue at all,[7] and, with its mixed precepts, it has no

[1] *Genesis*, i. p. 29. Smend also formerly wrote: "The Decalogue, whose Mosaic origin no one can doubt."—*Stud. u. Krit.* 1876, p. 643. Cf. in defence of the genuineness, Riehm, *Einleit.* i. p. 166 ; Kittel, *Hist. of Hebs.* i. p. 244 ff. (in shorter form).

[2] For a summary by Addis, see Note A on Objections to the Decalogue. Cf. also Wellhausen, *Hist. of Israel*, pp. 392–93, 439 ff. ; Smend, *Alttest. Religionsgeschichte*, p. 47.

[3] "There would be no valid reason," says Kautzsch, "for refusing to attribute to Moses himself a primitive, concise form of the Decalogue, were it not for the formidable difficulty presented by *the prohibition of the use of images*."—"Rel. of Israel," *Dict.* p. 633.

[4] See above, pp. 141 ff.   [5] Deut. v. 15.

[6] *Genesis*, i. p. 30.

[7] Scarcely two critics divide the precepts so as to make ten in precisely

suitability for taking the place of the historical "words" of the tables.[1]

2. If the Decalogue is allowed to be Mosaic, there is little reason for denying that the remaining laws ("judgments") of the *Book of the Covenant*, with which the "ten words" stand in so close a connection, also proceeded from Moses in *substantially* their present form.[2] The principal objection urged to this is that they imply a settled life and agriculture.[3] But, on the one hand, the laws in question are of a very primitive and simple character, probably resting on old usage;[4] and, on the other, the people were not the undisciplined horde the critics for their own purposes would make them out to be.[5] They had long had the experience of orderly and settled life, and were, moreover, on the point of entering Canaan. They were organised, and had "statutes of God" and "laws" given them in the wilderness.[6] What more likely in itself than that Moses, by divine command, should draw up for them a simple code, suited for present and prospective needs? How, indeed, could a people like Israel have been kept together, or have preserved its distinction from the Canaanites, without some such body of laws,—moral, civil, and religious,[7]—and this not simply in the form of floating

the same way, and the attempt to do so is now being pretty generally given up, even by advanced critics. Addis speaks of the division into ten as "mere guess-work." "Many critics," he says, "(*e.g.*, Wellhausen), adopting a suggestion of Goethe, have tried to disentangle ten 'words of the covenant,' answering to the Ten Words or Decalogue of the Elohist. This, however, is mere guess-work."—*Hex.* i. p. 157. Carpenter also does not favour the notion. Kittel says : "It requires the utmost arbitrariness even to find in it the number ten."—*Hist. of Hebs.* i. p. 198. Kautzsch rejects the second Decalogue.

[1] Cf. Kittel and Riehm, as above, in reply to Wellhausen.
[2] Thus Delitzsch, *Genesis*, i. p. 31.
[3] Thus Wellhausen, Kuenen, Addis, etc. Cf. Riehm in reply, i. pp. 170 ff.
[4] The Code of Hammurabi presents interesting ancient analogies. See for details art. in *Dict. of Bible* (Extra Vol.). One regrets to find Mr. Johns, in the section on comparison with Hebrew legislation, writing in the usual flippant style—"The current opinion of critics does not ascribe much of the Hebrew law to Moses. So his personality may be set aside" (p. 608).
[5] See above, pp. 79, 104.   [6] Ex. xviii. 16, 21, 25.
[7] Wellhausen himself points out that "when the Israelites settled in Palestine, they found it inhabited by a population superior to themselves both in numbers and in civilisation," yet "it never had the effect of making the Israelites Canaanites ; on the contrary, it made the Canaanites Israelites. Notwithstanding their inferiority, numerical and otherwise

oral *toroth*, but in the shape of definite, authoritative
" statutes and judgments," such as the history, the prophets,
and the psalms, uniformly assume the nation to have
possessed ?[1]   And if this was needed, can we suppose
that a man of Moses' capabilities and prescient mind would
have left the people without it ? We have several codes
of laws—" programmes "— which the critics assume to have
arisen at various junctures in the history of the nation.
But, as Dr. Robertson observes, " it is strange indeed that
critical historians should postulate the putting forth of
' legislative programmes' at various later points in Israel's
history, and should be so unwilling to admit the same for
the time of Moses."[2] We seem fully entitled, therefore,
in accordance with the whole tradition of Israel, to look
on Moses as the fountain of both civil and religious institutions to his nation, and to consider without prejudice any
statements attributing such institutions to his time. The
question of ritual laws demands separate treatment.

II. THE SACRIFICIAL SYSTEM AND RITUAL LAW

The Book of the Covenant deals mainly with civil
matters, and, except in the law of the altar,[3] and the
ordinance about the three feasts,[4] has no properly religious
enactments. This of itself creates a not unreasonable presumption that such will be found elsewhere. To most it
will appear incredible that, in settling the constitution of
Israel, Moses should not have given the people, among his
other laws, at least *some* ordinances for religious worship.
The critics, however, hold a directly contrary opinion. Not
content with denying that Moses was the author of any
ritual legislation, they go so far as to maintain that, till
the time of the exile, no sacrificial or other ritual existed
which was even *believed* to have Mosaic or divine sanction.
The prophets, it is declared, show clearly by their denunciations that they know nothing of such a divinely-ordained
ritual. " Thus it is," says Wellhausen, " that the prophets

they maintained their individuality, and that without the support of any
external organisation. Thus a certain inner unity subsisted long before
it had found any outward political expression : it goes back to the time
of Moses, who is to be regarded as its author."—*Hist. of Israel*, p. 433.
[1] See below, pp. 308, 324.   [2] *Early Religion of Israel*, p. 337.
[3] Ex. xx. 24–26.   [4] Ex. xxiii. 14–19.

are able to ask whether then Jehovah has commanded His people to tax their energies with such exertions : the fact presupposed being that no such command exists, and that no one knows anything at all about a ritual *torah*."[1] The idea of a ritual which "goes back to Moses or to Jehovah Himself"[2] is said to be foreign to them. It first came in with the Priestly Code, which is so insistent on the Mosaic origin of lawful sacrifice that it carefully avoids, in the earlier history, ever ascribing sacrifice to the patriarchs.[3] Without at this stage entering into details, which will more properly come up when discussing the Code itself, we would make on these representations the following remarks :—

1. There is, to put it mildly, some absurdity in the often-repeated statement that "the Priestly Writer *knows nothing* of sacrifice by the servants of God before Moses."[4] We might ask—How often is sacrifice mentioned altogether in the Book of Genesis ? And in how many instances does the meagre thread of narrative assigned to the Priestly Writer admit of the act of sacrifice being introduced ? But there is a more obvious answer—one of which a good deal more will be heard as we proceed. The Priestly Writer knew at least about the patriarchal sacrifices all that the J and E histories had to tell him ; for he had, on the newer theory, these histories before him, presupposes and founds upon them, if he does not actually furnish the frame in which their narratives are set.[5] He cannot, therefore, be supposed designedly to contradict them on this point of patriarchal sacrifices.[6] It is in truth no part of the theory

---

[1] *Hist. of Israel*, p. 56 ; cf. the whole section, pp. 52–59. Thus also Kuenen, *Hex.* pp. 176–77 ; W. R. Smith, *O.T. in J. C.*, pp. 293–95. "All this," says Professor Smith, "is so clear that it seems impossible to misunderstand it. Yet the position of the prophets is not only habitually explained away by those who are determined at any cost to maintain the traditional view of the Pentateuch," etc. We shall see immediately about the " explaining away."

[2] *Hist. of Israel*, p. 56.   [3] *Ibid.*

[4] Addis, *Hex.* p. li.   [5] See below, pp. 340, 360.

[6] Colenso, in combating Kuenen on this point, says : "Is it credible that he supposed the patriarchs to have offered no sacrifices *at all* before the delivery of the sacrificial laws at Sinai—more especially if he had before him the sacrifices mentioned in Gen. iv. 3, 4 ; viii. 20, 21 ; xxxi. 54 ; xlvi. 1, etc. " ; and in another connection : " It seems incredible that a later post-captivity writer, sitting down (as Kuenen supposes) with the J narrative before him, and of course known to him, and *now venerable by age*, should deliberately contradict it."—*Pent.* Pt. vi. pp. 126, 139.

of the Priestly Writer that sacrifices began with Moses.
His own legislation gives no hint that up to that time these
were unheard-of. Rather, in such phrases as, "If any man
bring an offering to Jehovah," . . . "If his offering be a
burnt offering of the herd,"[1] etc., it assumes that such
sacrifices are well-known and customary.

2. As little can it be maintained, with any show of
reason, that, up to the time of the exile, sacrifice in Israel
was simply, as Wellhausen affirms, traditional custom,
without divine sanction, or regulation of the *when*, the
where, the *by whom*, the *how*.[2] The Book of the Covenant
already makes a beginning in regulations about the altar,
and the times and manner of sacrifice—"My sacrifice";[3]
and the Book of Deuteronomy, "which still occupies the
same standpoint as JE,"[4] has abundance of prescriptions
and regulations about sacrifices—described as "all that I
command you."[5] How can it be claimed that Jeremiah,
whose mind is steeped in Deuteronomy—if he had not,
as some of these writers think, to do with its production—
is ignorant of these commands, or means to deny them, in
his impassioned protestations that it was not about burnt
offerings and sacrifices, but about obedience, that God
commanded their fathers, when He brought them out of
Egypt?[6]

3. The strong language of the prophets in *denunciation
of outward ritual*,[7] while the ethical side of religion was
neglected, admits of easy explanation: the one explanation
it will not bear, it is safe to say, is that which the critics
put upon it. This for a twofold reason. Probably, first,
not one of these prophets could form the conception of a
religion for a nation which had not its temple, priesthood,
sacrifices, and outward order of worship, or ever dreamt of
the abolition of these things; and, second, so far from regarding sacrifice as not well-pleasing to Jehovah, when the right
spirit was present, there is not one of the greater prophets
who does not include sacrifice in his own picture of the

---

[1] Lev. i. 2, 3, etc.
[2] *Hist. of Israel*, p. 54.
[3] Ex. xx. 24, 25 ; xxiii. 18, 19.
[4] Wellhausen, as above.
[5] Deut. xii. 11, etc.
[6] Jer. vii. 22, 24. Professor W. R. Smith nevertheless thinks "it is
impossible to give a flatter contradiction to the traditional theory that the
Levitical system was enacted in the wilderness."—*O.T. in J. C.*, p. 295.
[7] Amos iv. 4, 5 ; v. 21, 27 ; Isa. i. 10–15 ; Jer. vii. 22, 23, etc.

restored and perfected theocracy.[1] It is to be remembered that it is not sacrifice alone, but prayer, feast-days, Sabbaths, etc., that the prophets include in their denunciations; yet we know the importance they attached to prayer and the Sabbath in other parts of their writings.[2] In many places and ways, also, we see incidentally their recognition of the divine sanction of these outward ordinances, which, in other connections, viz., when made a substitute for heart-piety and moral conduct, they condemn. It was in vision of the temple of Jehovah that Isaiah received his call, and by the touch of a live coal from the altar that his lips were purged.[3] It is Jehovah's courts—"My courts"—that were profaned by the people's splendid but unholy worship;[4] just as in Hosea it is "the sacrifices of Mine offerings" which the people turn into "sacrifices of flesh."[5] If the 40th Psalm is relegated, as on the critical theory it must be, to post-exilian times, we read in it also: "Sacrifice and offering Thou didst not desire . . . burnt offering and sin offering hast Thou not required."[6] But who misunderstands these words?

4. Strange to say, all this, and a great deal more, is, in the end, *admitted* by the critics. Their argument means nothing, if it does not amount to a rejection by the prophets of a ritual worship of God absolutely. Yet we are told by Kuenen: "We must not assert that the prophets reject the cultus unconditionally. On the contrary, they too share the belief, for instance, that sacrifice is an essential element of true worship (Isa. lvi. 7; Zech. xiv. 16–19; Mic. iv. 1 ff.; Isa. ii. 1 ff.; xviii. 7; xix. 19 ff., etc. etc.). The context always shows that what they really protest against is the idea that it is enough to take part in the cultus," etc.[7] Only, it is argued, they did not allow this cultus to be of Mosaic or divine origin. It is precisely on this point that the proof fails. The proof was supposed to be found in the fact that the prophets condemned the cultus; now it is owned that they did not condemn it as in any sense incom-

---

[1] Cf. Isa. lvi. 6, 7; lx. 7; lxvi. 23, etc.; Jer. xvii. 24–27; xxxiii. 17–18, etc. (cf. p. 95); Ezek. xl. ff.

[2] Cf. Jer. xvii. 21–27; "As I commanded your fathers" (ver. 22), Isa. lviii. 13, 14.

[3] Isa. vi.   [4] Isa. i. 12.   [5] Hos. viii. 13.   [6] Ps. xl. 6.

[7] *Hex.* p. 176; cf. Smend, *Alttest. Religionsgeschichte*, p. 168. See also Smend's article, referred to on next page.

patible with the belief that it was a lawful and necessary part of the service of Jehovah. If, further, we ask—What *kind* of cultus was it which existed in the days of the prophets? we get a number of surprising admissions, to which it will be necessary that we return later. It was a cultus "of very old and sacred usage,"[1] and highly elaborate in character. There were "splendid sacrifices . . . presumably offered in accordance with all the rules of priestly skill."[2] We have, in fact, only to analyse the passages in the prophets to see what a highly elaborate ritual system was already in operation in their day—as elaborate, practically, as in the Levitical Code itself. It is interesting to read what one of the ablest adherents of the Graf school—Rudolf Smend—had to say on this point at an earlier stage in his development. In his work *Moses apud Prophetas*, Smend discerns what he calls "Levitismus" peering out from the pages of the oldest prophets—Amos and Hosea. He says, even: "It is sufficiently evident that the cultus of Jehovah, as it existed in the time of the earlier prophets, and doubtless long before, is by no means at variance with the character of Leviticus. Whatever judgment may be formed of the age of this book, the opinion hitherto entertained of the birth, growth, and maturity of the religion of Israel will undergo no change."[3] In a valuable article contributed to the *Studien und Kritiken* in 1876, he reiterates these views, and concludes: "Accordingly, we do not know what objection can be made to the earlier composition of Leviticus on the ground of the older prophetical writings."[4] In such statements, supported by reasons which time has done nothing to refute, we are far enough away from the theory that nothing was known of a divine sanction of ritual ordinances till after the time of the exile.

To ourselves, as before said, it appears incredible that no ordinances for religious worship should have been given to the people by Moses, in settling the constitution of

[1] Wellhausen, *Hist. of Israel*, p. 59.
[2] *Ibid.* p. 55. See below, p. 303.
[3] P. 75.
[4] *Stud. und Krit.* 1876, p. 661. This important article was written ten years after the appearance of Graf's work (see below, p. 325), in criticism of Duhm, and from the standpoint that up to that time "a stringent proof" had not been offered "either for or against" Graf's hypothesis of the age of Leviticus, and that such "was not to be looked for in the near future" (p. 644).

Israel. If such *were* given, they must, in the nature of the case, have included regulations about priesthood, sacrifice, purification, and much else.[1] This does not prove the existence of the Levitical ritual Code; but such laws, if given, must have covered a large part of the ground of that Code. It does not prove even that the laws were written, but it is highly probable that they soon were.[2] If these laws are not incorporated in our present Levitical Code, it is certain they are not to be found anywhere else. We shall be better able to judge on this point, when we have looked at some of the more special institutions of the national worship.

We proceed now, accordingly, to consider how it stands with such institutions as the *ark*, the *tabernacle*, the *priesthood*, and, in connection with these, with the *unity of worship*, made by Wellhausen, as we shall see, the turning-point of his whole discussion.[3] Graf, with his thesis of the post-exilian origin of the Levitical Code, is the pioneer here, and we are not sure that the case for the new theory, as respects the above institutions, has been more plausibly presented anywhere than it is in his pages.[4] It is not denied by the Graf school that there was an ark, a tent to cover it, and priests of some sort, from early times, but it is contended with decision that these were not, and could not have been, the ark, tabernacle, and priesthood of the Levitical Code. All we read on these subjects in the Priestly sections is "unhistorical fiction" of exilic or post-exilic origin. Rejecting hypotheses, our duty will be to turn the

---

[1] We shall see below that Dillmann, in fact, supposes Lev. xvii.–xxvi. (mainly) to be a very old, and in basis Mosaic, code, which he thinks may originally have stood after Ex. xxiv. Cf. his *Exod.–Lev.* on Ex. xxv. and Lev. xvii., and see below, pp. 328, 376.

[2] See below, p. 329. Dillmann says in the Preface to his Commentary on Exodus–Leviticus: "That the priesthood of the central sanctuary already in ancient times wrote down their laws is the most natural assumption in the world, and can be proved from A, C, D [= P, J, D]: that the laws of the priesthood and of divine service were written down, not to say made, first of all in the exile and in Babylon, where there was no service of God, is contrary to common sense."

[3] *Hist. of Israel*, p. 368. See below, pp. 173 ff.

[4] On Graf and his place in the critical development, see next chapter (pp. 199 ff.). His principal work, *Die Geschichtlichen Bücher des Alten Testaments*, was published in 186⁹. His chief predecessors were Vatke and George, but their works had produced little impression, and were regarded as conclusively refuted. Cf. Delitzsch, Luthardt's *Zeitschrift*, 1880, pp. 57 ff.

matter round about, and try to look at the facts historically
This will prepare the way for the later critical inquiry.

III. The Sacred Ark

It has been seen above what the critics think of the
original ark which they allow to have existed. It was a
sort of fetish-chest in which Jehovah, represented by two
stones, probably meteoric, was thought of as carried about;
or it was itself a fetish.[1] This may be met by observing
that, while Jehovah's presence is conceived of as connected
with the ark, the special *symbol* of His presence—the cloud,
or pillar, or glory—is always distinguished from both ark
and sanctuary: this in both JE and P sections.[2] The cloud,
or pillar of cloud and of fire, is represented as *above* the
tabernacle, or *over* the people, or as going *before* them in their
journeyings. Jehovah descends in the pillar to commune
with Moses at the tabernacle. He dwells upon or between
the cherubim.[3] His presence, therefore, it is perfectly plain,
was not identified with the ark, or with anything in it.

1. It is not denied, then, and it is a valuable admission,
that there was an ark of Jehovah in Israel from the times
of Moses. Where did it come from? The ark does not
appear to have been with the people in Egypt: we may
therefore conclude it to be a Mosaic institution. A first point
of interest relates to the *making* of the ark. The only
account we have of its construction is in the Priestly Code,
Ex. xxv. 10 ff.; xxvii. 1 ff.; outside of P the first incidental
notice is in the important passage, Num. x. 33–36, "And
the ark of the covenant went before them," etc., where,
however, its existence is firmly assumed. On the critical
side it is said—indeed, is taken for granted as one of the
things about which "no doubt" exists[4]—that originally
the JE narrative also must have had an account of the
making of the ark, now displaced by that of P.[5] Let this

[1] See above, p. 137.
[2] Cf. Ex. xxxiii. 9; xl. 34–38; Num. x. 34; xiv. 10–14; xx. 6; Deut.
xxxi. 15, etc.
[3] Ex. xxv. 22; 1 Sam. iv. 4. etc.
[4] Addis says: "He [the J writer] no doubt also mentioned here the
making of the ark, to which he refers shortly [where?] afterwards."—*Hex.*
i. p. 155.
[5] Thus practically all the critics, as Wellhausen, Kuenen, Dillmann,
Driver, Addis, Carpenter, Kennedy, etc.

11

be assumed : we discover from Deut. **x.** 1–5, which is supposed
to follow this older account, that the ark of the JE story
was an ark made "of acacia wood," and was the repository
of the two tables of the law, which agrees perfectly with
the history we have. Thus far, therefore, there is no contradiction. It remains to be seen whether any emerges in
the further notices of the nature, uses, fortunes, and
destination of the ark.

2. We pass to the *subsequent history* of the ark, and note
on this the following interesting facts. Its familiar name
is "the ark of the covenant."[1] It is connected with the
presence of Jehovah among His people.[2] It goes before, or
accompanies, the people in their journeys.[3] It is invested
with the most awful sanctity : to touch it irreverently is
death.[4] It is taken charge of, and borne, by Levitical
priests, or by Levites simply.[5] It is found, in the days of
the Judges, at Bethel, where Phinehas, the son of Eleazar,
the son of Aaron, ministers before it.[6] In Eli's days it is in
the sanctuary at Shiloh.[7] It is overshadowed by the
cherubim.[8] After its captivity among the Philistines, and
prolonged sojourn at Kirjath-jearim,[9] it is brought up by
David with the greatest solemnity and the utmost re-
joicings to Zion, and there lodged in a tent he had pitched
for it.[10] Finally, it is brought into the temple of Solomon,
when we are told it had nothing in it "save the two tables
of stone, which Moses put there at Horeb."[11] Here, as it
stands, is a very fair history of the ark from pre-exilian
sources, and it requires some ingenuity to discover wherein
the ark of these accounts differs, in structure, character,
and uses, from the ark of the law in Exodus. That ingenuity,

[1] This name occurs in Num. **x.** 33 ; xiv. 44 ; Deut. **x.** 8 ; xxxi. 9, 25, 26 ;
Josh. iii. (seven times) ; iv. 7, 9, 18 ; vi. 6, 8 ; viii. 33 ; Judg. xx. 27 ;
1 Sam. iv. 3–5 (see above, p. 137) ; 2 Sam. xv. 24 ; 1 Kings iii. 15 ; vi. 19 ;
viii. 1, 6, etc. etc. In *all the cases in the older history* the words "of the
covenant" *are simply struck out by the critics.* Cf., *e.g.*, Kuenen, *Hist. of Israel*,
i. pp. 257–58 ; or Oxford *Hex.* on Josh. iii., iv. The passages then read
"the ark of Jehovah" only. See Note at end of chapter.
[2] Num. **x.** 33, etc.
[3] Num. **x.** 33–36 ; cf. Ex. xl. 36, 37 ; Num. **ix.** 15–23 (P). On the
position of the ark, see below, pp. 168–69.
[4] 1 Sam. vi. 19 ; 2 Sam. vi. 7.
[5] Josh. iii., iv ; 2 Sam. xv. 24, 29 ; cf. Deut. xxxi. 9, 25.
[6] Judg. xx. 27, 28.
[7] 1 Sam. iii. 3.
[8] 1 Sam. iv. 4 ; 2 Sam. vi. 2.
[9] 1 Sam. vii. 1, 2.
[10] 2 Sam vi.
[11] 1 Kings viii. 1–11.

however, is not wanting. One point of alleged contradiction, viz., that in JE the ark is represented as borne at a
distance *in front of* the host, while in P it is carried, with
the tabernacle, *in the midst* of the host, is considered below
in connection with the place of the tabernacle.[1] For the rest,
the method is always at hand, and is freely resorted to, of
getting rid of inconvenient testimony by the assumption of
interpolation. This disposes, as noted above, of the words
" the covenant," and also of the mention of the " cherubim," [2]
and gets rid of the notices of " Levites " as bearing the ark, in
distinction from the priests. Thus, *e.g.*, Professor H. P. Smith,
following Wellhausen, disposes of the testimony in 2 Sam. xv.
24. That passage reads : " And lo Zadok also, and all the
Levites that were with him, bearing the ark of the covenant
of God." This will not do, so the comment is : " The present
text inserts 'and all the Levites with him.' But as the
Levites are unknown to the Books of Samuel [they had
been mentioned before in 1 Sam. vi. 15], this is obviously a
late insertion. Probably the original was ' Zadok and
Abiathar.' " [3] On this subject, it can scarcely be held to
be a contradiction that in some of the above passages it is
the " priests " who bear the ark, while the Levitical law
assigns that duty to the " Levites." The carrying of the
ark by the Levites on ordinary occasions, and as servants
of the priests,[4] does not preclude the bearing of it by priests
on special occasions, as in Josh. iii., iv. It was the priests
who were at all times primarily responsible for its right
conveyance.[5]

3. A point of some importance in its bearings on the
descriptions of the ark in the Priestly Code, which, however, we do not remember having seen adverted to, is the

[1] This, as will be seen below, is a question of some real difficulty. It is not
clear whether the ark was always, or only on special occasions, borne in front
of the host ; or whether it was not borne usually in front of the tabernacle
in midst of the host, still with the idea of leadership. In either case, as the
passages cited show, it was the movement of the ark, or of the guiding
pillar, which determined that of the camp.

[2] " It is more than probable," says Kuenen, " that the cherubim were
not mentioned by the author himself, but were inserted by a later writer."—
Rel. of Israel, i. p. 259.

[3] *Samuel* (" Internat. Crit. Com."), p. 344. In defence of these passages
(also in LXX), see Van Hoonacker, *Le Sacerdoce Lévitique*, p. 199.

[4] Num. iv. 15, etc.

[5] Num. iv. 19. In 1 Sam. iv. 4, Hophni and Phinehas (priests) are said to
be " there *with the ark* of the covenant of God " (not, apparently, its bearers).

relation of the ancient ark to that of the Solomonic temple. It is not denied, as we have seen, that there was an old Mosaic ark; but the fact is perhaps not always sufficiently attended to that, according to every testimony we have, it was this identical ark which was brought up and deposited in Solomon's splendid house. The Mosaic tabernacle, on Graf's view, is a "fiction"—a "copy" of the temple: it is the temple made "portable," and projected back into Mosaic times. But the ark, at all events, was not a new thing in the temple. It was the *old* ark that was brought into it;[1] the same old ark that can be traced back to the times of the Judges, and of Moses, and had experienced so many vicissitudes. It was an ark, therefore, which continued to exist, and whose character and structure could be verified, down to late historical times. It follows that, if the ark of the law is a "copy" of the ark of the temple, it must, in its general character, form, and structure, be pretty much a "copy," likewise, of the *real* ark of the pre-Solomonic age. Exilian priests would hardly invent an ark totally different from that which had perished within quite recent memory.

Another reflection is suggested by the pre-Solomonic history of the ark. No one disputes the sacredness of the ark in the eyes of the Israelites. It was in a sense the centre and core of their religion. They had the most undoubting belief in the manifestations of God's presence in connection with it, and in the importance of its possession, and of worship before it, as a pledge of God's favour and protection. Yet after its return from the Philistines, and the judgment at Beth-shemesh, we find this holiest of objects taken to the house of a private Israelite, Abinadab, and allowed to remain there till David's time, *i.e.*,[2] during the whole reign of Saul, guarded by this man's son; apparently, therefore, without Levitical ministration, neglected and almost forgotten by the people.[3] Then again

---

[1] 1 Kings viii. 6 ff. "The ark was guarded," says Dr. Driver, "till it was transferred by Solomon to the temple."—*Introd.* p. 138.

[2] The twenty years of 1 Sam. vii. 2 do not denote the whole duration of the ark's stay at Kirjath-jearim, but the period, apparently, till the time of Samuel's reformation.

[3] 1 Sam. vii. 1, 2. Cf. below, p. 178. The ingenious suggestion of Van Hoonacker (*Le Sacerdoce*, p. 192) that " Eleazar his son " should be "son of Eleazar " (a priest) is without sufficient warrant.

we find it raised to highest honour by David and Solomon. We ask—Would it be safe to argue from the seeming neglect, at least intermission of religious use, of this sacred object for so long a period, to the denial of its earlier high repute, and established place, in the worship of the people? Or, if so extraordinary an irregularity must be admitted in this confused time, must we not, in consistency, admit the likelihood of many more?

IV. THE TABERNACLE

An initial difficulty in the Mosaic account is the richness and splendour of the "tent of meeting," said to be reared by command of God in the wilderness. This of itself, however, is not insuperable. Neither the resources nor the skill of the people in leaving Egypt were so slender as the critics represent,[1] and the rearing of a sanctuary was an object for which they would strip themselves of their best. If the ark was as fine an object as its description implies, we should expect that the tabernacle made for its reception would have some degree of splendour as well. Much more radical is the position now taken up by the Graf-Wellhausen critics. Such a tabernacle as the Priestly Code describes, they tell us, never existed. The tent of the wilderness is a pure creation of the post-exilian imagination. In Wellhausen's language: "The temple, the focus to which the worship was concentrated, and which was not built until Solomon's time, is by this document regarded as so indispensable even for the troubled days of the wanderings before the settlement, that it is made portable, and in the form of a tabernacle set up in the very beginning of things. For the truth is, that the tabernacle is the copy, not the prototype, of the temple at Jerusalem."[2] The critical and other difficulties which inhere in such a conception are left over for the present; we look only at the facts.

1. Our starting-point here, as before, is the admission of the critics that *a tabernacle of some sort* did exist, as a

---

[1] Cf. Knobel, quoted by Dillmann, *Exod.-Lev.* pp. 268-70.

[2] *Hist. of Israel*, pp. 36-37. In these expressions about the sanctuary being "made portable," and the tabernacle being "the copy," not the prototype, of the temple, Wellhausen but repeats Graf, *Geschicht. Bücher*, pp. 53, 55, 61, etc.

covering for the ark and a place of meeting with Jehovah, at least as far back as they will allow the history to go. Graf may be quoted here, though his concessions are ampler than those which Wellhausen would be disposed to make. "The presence of the ark in the field (1 Sam. iv. 3 ff.)," he says, "presupposes also that of a tent, of however simple a character, which might serve as a protection and lodging for the ark and for the priests with the sacred utensils; and it lies likewise in the nature of the case that before this tent, where sacrifice was offered by the priests, and the will of Jehovah inquired after, meetings and deliberations of the host were also held; hence the tent was the *ohel moed* (tent of meeting)."[1]   But then, it is contended, this is not the tabernacle of the Priestly Code, and reference is made in proof to "the tent" which, in Ex. xxxiii. 7, Moses is said to have pitched (R.V. "used to pitch") "afar off" without the camp, and to have called "the tent of meeting," when as yet the tabernacle of the law was not erected. Wellhausen goes further, and will have it that the pre-Solomonic tabernacle was not a single tent at all, but a succession of changing tents, staying himself in this contention, of all authorities in the world, on the *Chronicler*,[2] whose words— "have gone from tent to tent, and from one tabernacle to another"—are made to bear a sense which that writer assuredly never dreamt of.

Now it is the case, and is an interesting fact, that after the sin of the golden calf, before the Sinaitic tabernacle was made, Moses is related to have taken—strictly, "used to take"—"the tent," and pitched it "without the camp, afar off from the camp," and to have called it "the tent of meeting."   The mention of "*the* tent" comes in quite abruptly, and may fairly suggest that we have here, as the critics say, part of an originally independent narrative—the same to which also Num. xi. 16 ff., and xii. 4 ff. (cf. Deut. xxxi. 14, 15) belong. As it stands in the context, however,

---

[1] *Geschicht. Bücher*, pp. 57–58.

[2] *Hist. of Israel*, p. 45: "The parallel passage in 1 Chron. xvii. 5 correctly interprets the sense" (cf. 2 Sam. vii. 6). How the Chronicler could be supposed to say this, in Wellhausen's sense, not only of the "tent" (*ohel*), but of the "tabernacle" (*mishkan*), is not explained. "The passage says no more," remarks Delitzsch, "than that the ark of Jehovah wandered from place to place, so that He abode in it, sometimes here and sometimes there."—Luthardt's *Zeitschrift*, 1880, p. 63.

the impression distinctly produced is, that the withdrawal of the tent or tabernacle from the camp is *penal* in character (cf. vers. 3–5: "I will not go up in the midst of thee"), and that the tabernacle itself is a provisional one, meeting a need till the permanent "tent of meeting" is got ready. The tenses, indeed, imply usage; but duration of usage is limited by the writer's thought, and need not cover more than the period of alienation, or at most the interval—the greater part of a year—till the erection of the new tabernacle.[1] The critics, however, will not admit this; and, comparing the passages above mentioned, maintain that there are the clearest points of distinction between this JE tent or tabernacle and that of the Priestly Code. The former, it is said, is always represented as pitched *without* the camp; the latter is as invariably pitched *in the midst of* the camp. The one is a place of *revelation* (Jehovah descends in the pillar *to the door* of the tabernacle); the other is a place of divine service or *worship*. The one has *Joshua* as its attendant;[2] the other is served by *priests and Levites*. On this last objection—the absence of Levites— it is enough to remark that, at the time referred to in Ex. xxxiii., Levites had not yet been appointed; the ark itself had not yet been made. The other two objections deserve more consideration. They rest on grounds which have a degree of plausibility, though closer examination, we are convinced, will bring out the essential harmony of the accounts.

2. The first question relates to the *place* of the tabernacle. Is there real contrariety here between the JE and the P accounts? When we examine the evidence for the contention that all through the wanderings, in the JE narrative, the place of the tabernacle was without the camp—"afar off"—we are struck, first, with its exceeding meagreness. It consists of the two passages in Numbers above referred to, concerning which it may be observed that, while their language, taken alone, will agree with this hypothesis, it certainly does not necessitate it. It is not

[1] Cf. Ex. xxxv. 30 ff.; xl. 1 ff.

[2] Wellhausen says: "Thus Moses has Joshua with him as his *œdituus*, who does not quit the tent of Jehovah."—*Hist. of Israel*, p. 130. Cf. Addis *in loc.*, *Hex.* i. p. 155: "The tent of meeting is outside the camp; it is not guarded by Levites, much less by the sons of Aaron, but by Joshua, the 'minister' of Moses" But see Deut. xxxi. 9, etc.

conclusive that we are told on one or two occasions that persons " went out " from the camp to the tent,[1] or that Moses "went out" from the tent to the people;[2] for the same language would be as appropriately used of going out from any particular encampment to the open space in the centre where the sanctuary stood; just as it is said of Dathan and Abiram that they "came out" and stood in the door of their own tents.[3] The question requires to be decided on broader grounds. Even in Ex. xxxiii. 7, the natural suggestion of the statement that Moses, in particular circumstances, took the tent—assumed as known—and pitched it "without the camp, afar off from the camp," would seem to be that the original and proper place of the tent was *within* the camp; and there are not wanting in the narratives indications that this was the real state of the case. Both in the JE and the P sections the region outside the camp is regarded as a region of exclusion from Jehovah's presence; it would be passing strange if His tabernacle, surmounted by the cloudy pillar, were thought of as pitched "afar off" in this region. It requires much faith, for instance, to believe that when Miriam, smitten with leprosy, was "shut up outside the camp seven days,"[4] she was nearer the tabernacle of Jehovah than the people who were within; or that, when quails were sent, the tabernacle was in such a position as to be certainly smothered by them when they fell;[5] or that, when Balaam, looking on Israel, testified, "Jehovah his God is with him, and the shout of a king is among them,"[6] the tabernacle of Jehovah was really beheld by the seer as far apart from the people. But there are other and more crucial JE passages. When, in particular, it is declared in Num. xiv. 44 that "the ark of the covenant

[1] Num. xi. 24–30 ; xii. 4, 5.

[2] Num. xi. 24. Cf. Strack's remarks on these passages in his *Commentary, in loc.*

[3] Num. xvi. 27.

[4] Num. xii. 14, 15. It should be noted that this JE narrative implies the leprosy law of Lev. xiii. (P).

[5] Num. xi. 31, 32. Van Hoonacker, in his *Le Sacerdoce Lévitique* (pp. 145–46), has an ingenious way of explaining these passages, in comparison with Ex. xxxiii. 7 (where, as he points out, "the tent" is assumed as already known), by the supposition of a series of transpositions in the narrative ; but we do not feel this to be justified or necessary.

[6] Num. xxiii. 21. Balaam, in chap. xxiv. 2, sees "Israel dwelling according to their tribes," which implies the orderly encampment of P.

of Jehovah, and Moses, departed not out of the camp," it
cannot be supposed that the ark was, before starting,
already outside of the camp—"afar off"; the words imply
as plainly as may be that its resting-place was *within* the
camp. When, again, Moses is related in Num. x. 36 to
have said at the resting of the ark, "Return, O Jehovah,
to the ten thousands of Israel,"[1] his formula has hardly
any meaning if the ark did not return from going before
the people to a resting-place within the camp. In the
same direction point such allusions as "the cloud of
Jehovah was *over* them by day, when they set forward
from the camp"[2]—"and Thy cloud *standeth over* them[3]—
allusions which those who adopt the hypothesis we are
criticising think it necessary to relegate to P or a redactor;[4]
together with instances of an immediate acting, speaking,
or calling of Jehovah from the tabernacle[5] (were Moses,
Aaron, and Miriam, *e.g.*, "afar off" when they heard Jehovah
call "suddenly" to them, as in Num. xii. 4?), or of direct
transactions with the officials of the sanctuary.[6] Taken
together, these things show that, while there may be
divergences in the mode of representation, there is no
essential disagreement in the accounts as to the *place* of
the tabernacle.

3. Neither, when we take the history as a whole, does
there appear to be any better basis for the statement that
in JE the tabernacle is a place of *revelation* only, whereas
in P it is peculiarly a place of *worship*. In P also, as in

---

[1] Cf. Dillmann and Strack, *in loc.* Professor Gray's comments on this
passage, Num. x. 33–35, are a good example of the new method. "Here,"
he says, "if we may judge from so fragmentary a record, it [the ark] is
conceived as moving of itself (!) . . . 35. Here, as in ver. 33, the ark starts
of itself, and the words that follow ['Rise up, O Jehovah,' etc.] may be
taken as addressed to it. . . . 36. Such words could be suitably addressed
to the ark returning from battle to its fixed sanctuary . . . after the
people were settled in Canaan. It is less clearly suitable to the circumstances of the march through the wilderness : the people overtake the
ark, the ark does not return to them" (?)—*Numbers* ("Inter. Crit. Com."),
p. 97. How would Dr. Gray apply his canon to Ps. cxxxii. 8 ?

[2] Num. x. 34.   [3] Num. xiv. 14.

[4] Thus Dillmann, Gray, the Oxford *Hex.*, etc. (not Addis). On the
ground that "E nowhere describes it [the pillar] as 'over' it" [the tent]—
the thing to be proved—the Oxford annotator arbitrarily makes the word
over in Num. xii. 10 bear a different sense from what it ordinarily has
in this connection. The phrase is identical with that in Ex. xl. 36 ; Num.
ix. 17 (P).

[5] *E.g.*, Num. xi. 1, 10, 16 ; xii. 4.   [6] *E.g.*, Deut. xxxi. 9, 25, 26.

JE, the tabernacle is a place of revelation; in JE, and in pre-Solomonic times, as in P, it is a place of worship, with its altars and sacred furniture, its priestly ministrants, its assemblies at the feasts, etc. Only by isolating one or two special passages, in which the aspect of revelation in JE is prominent,[1] can it be made to appear otherwise. In certain respects there is obvious resemblance from the first. In P, as well as in JE, the tabernacle is called *ohel moed* (tent of meeting):[2] in P this alternates with the name *mishkan* (dwelling). A curious fact here, and one puzzling to the critics, is that in certain sections of P (Ex. xxv.–xxvii. 19) only *mishkan* is used; in others (chaps. xxviii.–xxxi.) only *ohel moed*; in others the names intermingle.[3] In both JE and P Jehovah manifests His presence in a cloud of fire;[4] the fact that in JE the cloud is spoken of as a "pillar" is no contradiction. If in JE Jehovah descends in the pillar to the *door* of the tabernacle to speak with Moses, this mode of communication is also recognised in P ("At the door of the tent of meeting . . . where I will speak with you," Ex. xxix. 42, 43);[5] elsewhere Jehovah speaks from between the cherubim.[6] The tabernacle in both JE and P contains the ark of the covenant; a Levitical priesthood in its service is implied in the JE notices in Joshua,[7] and in Deuteronomy.[8] A tabernacle existed, and was set up in Shiloh, in Joshua's time, as Josh. xviii. 1, ascribed to P,[9] declares: this reappears under the name "the house of God" in Shiloh, in Judg. xviii. 31.[10] In this connection it should not be

---

[1] Num. xi., xii.; Deut. xxxi. 14, 15. These are the only passages after Ex. xxxiii. 7–11: a narrow basis for an induction.

[2] In JE, *e.g.*, in Num. xi. 16; xii. 4; Deut. xxxi. 14.

[3] Cf. Oxford *Hex.* ii. p. 120. In consistency different authors ought to be assumed.

[4] Numbers and Deut. for JE; in P, Ex. xl. 34–38; Num. ix. 15–23, etc. It should be noted that in the narrative of the dedication of the temple in 1 Kings viii., vers. 10, 11 are modelled directly on the *P passage*, Ex. xl. 34–35.

[5] Cf. Oxford *Hex.* ii. p. 120.   [6] Ex. xxv. 22; Num. vii. 89.

[7] Josh. iii.–vi.   [8] Deut. x. 6, 8; xxxi. 9, 25, 26.

[9] On the critical analysis here, cf. Van Hoonacker, *Le Sacerdoce*, p. 177.

[10] Cf. Judg. xix. 18, "to the house of Jehovah," where, however, the LXX has "my (the man's own) house" (R.V. marg.). The "house of God" in Judg. xx. 26 is more correctly "Bethel," where either the tabernacle was for a time (cf. chap. ii. 1, in LXX), or where the ark was temporarily taken for the war.

overlooked that the Book of the Covenant (JE) already provides for offerings being brought to "the house of Jehovah thy God."[1] At the sanctuary at Shiloh an annual feast, described as "a (or the) feast of Jehovah,"[2] is held, which is most naturally identified with one of the three prescribed feasts[3] (cf. 1 Sam. i. 3). The notices of the ark,[4] again, and the custom of "inquiring of Jehovah,"[5] attest the existence of a stated priesthood, of sacrifices—the offering of "burnt offerings and peace offerings before Jehovah"[6]—and of the priestly ephod. In face of all this, Wellhausen's assertion that in the Book of Judges "there is no mention of the tabernacle . . . it is only in preparation, it has not yet appeared,"[7] can only excite astonishment.

When we pass to the Books of Samuel, we get fresh and valuable light on the tabernacle, and its place in the religion of Israel. At the end of the period of the Judges, it is still at Shiloh, with Eli, of the house of Aaron, as its principal priest. It bears the old name—"the tent of meeting"—to which no suspicion need attach;[8] contains the ark with its cherubim;[9] is the centre of worship for "all Israel";[10] in its furniture and ritual suggests the prescriptions of the Levitical Code. "The lamp of God" burns, as directed, all night;[11] from the later incidental mention of the shewbread, and of the regulations connected with it, at Nob,[12] we may infer the presence of the table

[1] Ex. xxiii. 19. It is one of the astounding statements in Wellhausen that "house of God" always means "house of an image."—*Hist. of Israel*, p. 130.

[2] Judg. xxi. 19.

[3] According to Bertheau, the word *hag* is almost without exception used of the three great feasts.—*Exeg. Handb.* p. 278.

[4] Judg. xx. 27, 28.

[5] Judg. i. 1 ; xx. 18, 23, 28.

[6] Judg. xx. 26.

[7] *Hist. of Israel*. Graf also says that there is no mention of "a sacred tent" in the time of the Judges, but remarks that this is not to be wondered at, as the ark of the covenant is also not mentioned (p. 58). The critics in both cases reach their results by rejecting what does not please them. "The house of God" and "the ark of the covenant" are both mentioned in Judges.

[8] See next page.   [9] 1 Sam. iv 4 ; cf. above, p. 137.

[10] 1 Sam. ii. 14, 19 ; iii. 19, 21.

[11] 1 Sam. iii. 3 ; cf. Ex. xxvii. 20–21.

[12] 1 Sam. xxi. Dr. Driver objects that these allusions do not prove that the institutions "were observed *with the precise formalities prescribed in P*."—*Introd.* p. 142. How much does one expect in a historical allusion !

with the shewbread. Elkanah goes up yearly to worship,[1] and his sacrifice for his vow is according to the law.[2] In 1 Sam. ii. 22, there is allusion to "the women who did service at the door of the tent of meeting"—the only other mention of these women being in Ex. xxxviii. 8. (P). The genuineness of this important passage, the second half of which, for reasons that may be guessed, is omitted in the LXX (Vat. Cod.), has been disputed, but, it seems to us, without sufficient reason.[3]

Thus far the resemblance of "the house of God" in Shiloh to the tabernacle of the law must be admitted. But objections, on the other hand, are urged, which, it is thought, disprove the identification.[4] It is pointed out that the sanctuary is described, not as a tent, but as a "temple" (*hēkal*), with doors and posts, which implies a permanent structure;[5] that Samuel is represented as sleeping in the room where the ark of God was;[6] that the sons of Eli were within their Levitical rights in demanding uncooked flesh, etc.[7] But there is needed here not a little forcing of the text to make out a case in favour of the critics. "*Everywhere else* in 1 Sam. i.–iii.," says Wellhausen, arguing against the name *ohel moed*, "the sanctuary of Shiloh is called *hēkal*":[8] the "everywhere else" being simply twice. And it does not prove his point. Whatever structures or supports may have grown up about the sanctuary (for safety, stability, protection, convenience) during its century-long stay at Shiloh—and from its age such were to be expected —it was still essentially, as 2 Sam. vii. 6 shows, "a tent and a tabernacle," nor did Israelitish tradition ever know of

When the Chronicler expands, it is taken as a proof of non-historicity. See below, p. 300.

[1] 1 Sam. i. 3, 7. Professor W. R. Smith allows that the yearly feasts were observed (*O.T. in J. C.*, p. 345).

[2] 1 Sam. i. 21, 25 ; cf. Lev. vii. 16 ; Num. xv. 8–10.

[3] The name *ohel moed* is, as we have seen, an old, well-attested name of the tabernacle (cf. Graf, p. 58), and is found again, in both Heb. and LXX, in 1 Kings viii. 4. As regards the women, even on the supposition, which we do not accept, of a post-exilian composition of Ex. xxxviii., it is inconceivable that there should occur *this single mention* of the women at the tabernacle in the Code, if there was not old, well-established tradition behind it.

[4] Cf. in Wellhausen, Kuenen, W. R. Smith, and the critics generally See the very dogmatic statements in *O.T. in J. C.*, pp. 269–70.

[5] 1 Sam. i. 9 ; iii. 3.   [6] 1 Sam. iii. 3.

[7] 1 Sam. ii. 15.   [8] *Hist. of Israel*, p. 41 (italics ours).

any other kind of habitation of Jehovah. The further supposition that Samuel slept literally in the shrine of the ark
is, from the point of view of an Israelite, an outrage on all
probability; neither does the language of the text compel
any such meaning.[1] Samuel and Eli slept in contiguous
chambers of some lodgment connected with the sanctuary,
such as may be presumed to have been provided for the
priests and others engaged in its service. The sin of the sons
of Eli consisted in their greed and violence, and in the appro-
priating of such portions as their "flesh-hooks" laid hold of,
before the fat was burned on the altar, as the law required.[2]
The Levitical dues are presupposed: not contradicted.

What remains to be said on the tabernacle may be briefly
summed up. Ark and tabernacle, as above noted, were
separated during the long period that the former was at
Kirjath - jearim. When David brought the ark to Zion,
the tabernacle, probably then old and frail, and unfitted for
removal, was at Gibeon.[3] Thence it was brought up with
its vessels, and preserved, apparently, as a precious relic, in
Solomon's temple.[4] The supposition that the *ohel moed*
of 1 Kings viii. 4 was not this historic tabernacle, but the
temporary tent set up by David on Zion, is contradicted by
the name,[5] which is not given to that tent, by the mention
of the vessels, and by the unlikelihood that a temporary
tent would have such honour put upon it, while one can
well understand why the old tabernacle should.

V. The Unity of the Sanctuary

We now approach a subject of cardinal importance—
probably the one of most importance—in this discussion:
the unity of the sanctuary, and the conflict alleged to exist
on the *centralisation of the cultus* between Deuteronomy and
the earlier law and practice in Israel. The point of the

---

[1] Delitzsch says: "That he should sleep *beside the ark* would certainly
be a colossal contradiction of the law, but Wellhausen reads this *into* the
text."—Luthardt's *Zeitschrift*, 1880, p. 232. Cf. Wellhausen, p. 130. On
the alleged *priesthood* of Samuel, see below, pp. 189–90.

[2] Lev. iii. 1 ff.; vii. 28 ff.

[3] 1 Kings iii. 4; viii. 4; cf. 1 Chron. xvi. 39, 40; 2 Chron. i. 3
According to 1 Chron. xvi. 39, Zadok ministered at Gibeon.

[4] 1 Kings viii. 4; 2 Chron. v. 5. If this be admitted, then the tabernacle,
as well as the ark, was there for inspection till late times.

[5] Cf. Delitzsch, as above, p. 63.

critical position on this head, briefly, is, that, while in Deut. xii.—placed in or near the age of Josiah—we have the law of a central sanctuary at which alone sacrifices are lawful, in the earlier history we have not only no trace of this idea of a central sanctuary, in which all lawful worship is concentrated, but, in the absolute freedom of worship that prevailed, convincing proof that such a law was neither observed nor known. The older law in Ex. xx. 24, on which the people acted in that earlier time, granted, it is alleged, unrestricted liberty of worship; as Professor W. R. Smith interprets it—"Jehovah promises to meet with His people and bless them at the altars of earth or unhewn stone which stood in all corners of the land, on every spot where Jehovah has set a memorial of His name."[1] The idea of the central sanctuary was, it is contended, the outcome of the great prophetic movement which resulted in the reign of Josiah in the suppression of the *bamoth*, or "high places," till then regarded as lawful. The relation of the Deuteronomic to the Priestly Code—assumed to be still later—on this subject is thus expressed by Wellhausen: "In that book (Deuteronomy) the unity of the cultus is *commanded*; in the Priestly Code it is *presupposed*. . . . In the one case we have. so to speak, only the idea as it exists in the mind of the lawgiver, but making no claim to be realised till a much later date; in the other, the Mosaic idea has acquired also a Mosaic embodiment, with which it entered the world at the very first."[2] The case, however, is not nearly so strong as these statements would imply, as many critical writers are coming themselves to perceive.[3] Reserving, as before, what is to be said on the purely critical aspects, we proceed to look at the subject in its historical relations.

The Priestly Code may be left out of consideration at this stage, for it will scarcely be denied that, if there was a sacrificial system in the wilderness at all, it would be a system centralised in the sanctuary, as the Code represents. The question turns then, really, on the compatibility of the law in Deuteronomy with the enactment in Ex. xx. 24, and

[1] *Prophets of Israel*, p. 109.   [2] *Hist. of Israel*, pp. 35, 37.
[3] This point is emphasised in an interesting lecture by Dr. S. A. Fries, delivered to a Scientific Congress at Stockholm in 1897, entitled *Moderna Vorstellungen der Geschichte Israels* (Modern Representations of the History of Israel). See below, pp. 176, 273.

with the later practice. And the first condition of a satisfactory treatment lies, as the lawyers would say, in a proper
adjustment of the issues.

1. We do well to begin by looking at the precise form
of the *fundamental law* in Ex. xx. 24 itself. The passage
reads: "An altar of earth thou shalt make to Me, and
shalt sacrifice thereon thy burnt offerings, and thy peace
offerings, thy sheep and thine oxen: in every place where I
record My name, I will come to thee and I will bless thee."
The law is general in form, but it must be observed that
there is nothing in it warranting the worship "at the altars
of earth and unhewn stones in all corners of the land,"
which Professor W. R. Smith reads into its terms. It is
addressed to the nation, not to the individual; and it does
not speak of "altars," but only of "an altar." It is not a
law in the least giving unrestricted liberty of worship; its
scope, rather, is carefully limited by the clause, "in every
place where I record My name." [1] It would be unduly
narrowing the force of this law to confine it, with some, to
the *successive* places where the sanctuary was set up during
the wilderness wanderings and in Canaan; it must at least
include all places sanctified to their recipients by special
appearances or revelations of God. This fully explains,
and legitimises, *e.g.*, the cases of Gideon," [2] of Manoah, [3]
of David, [4] of Solomon, [5] of Elijah. [6] Neither is there anything here that conflicts with Deuteronomy. The law in
Deut. xii. gives the general rule of worship at the central
sanctuary, but is not to be understood as denying that
circumstances might arise in which, under proper divine
authority, exceptional sacrifices might be offered. The
clearest proof of this is that Deuteronomy itself gives
directions for the building of an altar on Mount Ebal,
precisely in the manner of Ex. xx. 25. [7]

[1] Professor W. R. Smith, replying to Dr. Wm. H. Green, seems to insist
that these words can only bear the meaning, "in all places" in the sense of
a number of co-existent sanctuaries.—*Prophets*, p. 394.   On this see Note B
on the Force of Ex. xx. 24.

[2] Judg. vi. 25, 26.   [3] Judg. xiii. 16.
[4] 2 Sam. xxiv. 18.   [5] 1 Kings iii. 4, 5.
[6] 1 Kings xviii. 31.

[7] Deut. xxvii. 5, 6.—Van Hoonacker advocates the view that there were
two systems of worship—a private and a public—and supposes that the law
in Exodus refers to the former, and the law in Deuteronomy to the latter.
See his ingenious discussion in his *Le Lieu du Culte dans la Législation*

2. With this, in the next place, must be taken the fact, which the critics too much ignore, that, even in the earliest period, *the rule and ideal in Israel is that of a central sanctuary*, as the legitimate place of worship. It has just been seen that the fundamental law itself speaks of "an altar," not of "altars," and no countenance is given anywhere to a multitude of co-existing altars.[1] It is not questioned that the Priestly Code—the only Code we possess for the wilderness—"presupposes" unity of worship; neither, in the history, is there trace of any other than centralised worship of a lawful kind during the wanderings. The Book of the Covenant—the same which contains the law of the altar—has plainly the same ideal of the unity of the sanctuary. It takes for granted "the house of Jehovah thy God," and requires that three times in the year all males shall present themselves there before Jehovah.[2] The idolatrous shrines in Canaan are to be broken down.[3] It is in keeping with this, that, in prospect of entering Canaan, Deuteronomy relaxes the law requiring the slaying of all oxen, lambs, and goats at the door of the tabernacle,[4] and permits the slaying of animals for food at home.[5] In the Book of Joshua, the incident of the altar *Ed*—the narrative of which, in a way perplexing to the critics, combines peculiarities of P and JE[6]—is a striking testimony to the hold which this idea of the one altar had upon the tribes. We have already seen that the tabernacle at Shiloh was the recognised centre of worship for "all Israel" in the days of

rituelle des Hébreux, and in his *Le Sacerdoce Lévitique* (pp. 5 ff.). Similar views are advocated by Fries, referred to above (p. 174), in his work, *Die Zentralisation des israelitischen Kultus*. The hypothesis is probably not without its elements of truth, and would explain certain anomalies, but we have not felt it necessary to adopt it.

[1] Ex. xx. 24 ; xxi. 14. Cf. Robertson's *Early Religion*, pp. 405-13. "It is remarkable," says Professor Robertson, "that we do not find in all the Old Testament such a divine utterance as 'My altars' ; and only twice does the expression 'Thy altars,' addressed to God, occur. It is found in Elijah's complaint, which refers to Northern Israel, at a time when the legitimate worship at Jerusalem was excluded ; and in Ps. lxxxiv., where it again occurs [on the critical view, post-exilian], no inference can be drawn from it. On the other hand, Hosea says distinctly, 'Ephraim hath multiplied altars to sin' (Hos. viii. 11)" (p. 112).

[2] Ex. xxiii. 14-17.

[3] Ex. xxiii. 24.

[4] Lev. xvii. 1 ff. The object of the law is to prevent promiscuous sacrificing to demons (vers. 5, 8).

[5] Deut. xii. 20. See below, pp. 276, 314.

[6] Josh. xxii. 9-34. On the criticism, cf. Oxf. *Hex.*, Driver, etc.

Eli.[1] In Judges, legitimate sacrifices are offered at the
sanctuary,[2] or before the ark,[3] or where God has "recorded
His name" in a special revelation ;[4] all others are condemned
as transgressions.[5] The period succeeding the captivity of
the ark is considered below.

3. When we turn, next, to Deuteronomy, we discover
another fact of great importance in this connection, viz.,
that there also, as Wellhausen says, the unity of the cultus
is an "idea" which makes "no claim to be realised till a
much later date."[6] The law in Deut. xii., in other words,
is *not given as a law intended to come into perfect operation
from the first.* It has just been seen that the *principle* of
centralisation of worship was involved in the Mosaic system
from the commencement, but the realisation of the idea
was, and in the nature of the case could only be, gradual.
The law of Deuteronomy, in agreement with this, bears on
its face that it was not intended to be put strictly in
force till certain important conditions had been fulfilled—
conditions which, owing to the disobedience of the people,
who, during the time of the Judges, so often put back the
clock of their own history, were not fulfilled till as late as
the days of David and Solomon. The law reads thus:
"When ye go over Jordan, and dwell in the land which
Jehovah your God causeth you to inherit, and He giveth
you rest from all your enemies round about, so that ye
dwell in safety: *then* shall it come to pass that the place
which Jehovah your God shall choose to cause His name to
dwell there," etc.[7] In point of fact, the unsettled state of
things here described lasted till the reign of David.[8]

[1] See above, p. 171. Of. Jer. vii. 12.   [2] Judg. xxi. 19.
[3] Judg. xx. 26, 27 ; xxi. 2-4 (for "house of God" read "Bethel").
[4] Gideon, Manoah, as above, p. 175. Cf. Judg. ii. 1-5. It has been
inferred, and is not improbable, that Gideon's altar in Judg. vi. 24, to
which he gave the name "Jehovah-Shalom," was a monumental altar, like
the altar "Ed" in Josh. xxii. This would explain why he was required next
day to build a new altar beside it (ver. 26).
[5] Judg. viii. 27, xvii. 5, 6, etc. Dr. W. R. Smith appears to assume
that the phrase "before Jehovah" (Judg. xi. 11, etc.) always implies
sacrifice. That, however, is not so. Cf. Gen. xxvii. 7 ; Ex. vi. 12, 30 ;
Deut. iv. 10 ; ix. 25 ; 1 Sam. xxiii. 18. See Graf, *Geschicht. Bücher*, p. 58.
[6] See above, p. 174.   [7] Deut. xii. 10, 11.
[8] 2 Sam. vii. 1. Professor W. R. Smith allows that Deuteronomy "puts
the case as if the introduction of a strictly unified cultus was to be deferred
till the peaceful occupation of Palestine was accomplished."—*O.T. in J. C.*,
p. 272. Where then is the contradiction ?

12

Accordingly, in 1 Kings iii. 2, it is not urged that the law did not exist, or that it was not known, but the excuse given for irregularities is that "there was no house built for the name of Jehovah until these days."[1] This principle alone solves many difficulties, and goes a long way to bring the history and the law into harmony.

4. This leads, finally, to the remark that, in the interpretation of these laws, large allowance needs to be made for the *irregularities* incident to times of political confusion and religious declension. It is not fair to plead, as contradictory of the law, the falling back on local sanctuaries in periods of great national and religious disorganisation, as when the land was in possession of enemies, or when the ark was in captivity, or separated from the tabernacle, or when the kingdom was divided, and the state-worship in the Northern division was idolatrous. In particular, the period following the rejection of Eli and his sons was one of unusual complications, during which Samuel's own person would seem to have been the chief religious centre of the nation.[2] It is here that the critical case finds its strongest support, and there are undoubted difficulties. How could it be otherwise, after "the capture of the ark, the fall of Shiloh, and the extension of the Philistine power into the heart of Mount Ephraim"?[3] We are reminded, however, that even after the ark had been brought back, and settled in the house of Abinadab, Samuel made no attempt to remove it to Nob, but "continued to sacrifice at a variety of shrines"[4] —Bethel, Gilgal, Mizpah, Ramah. It is a sweeping and unwarranted inference to draw from this that "Samuel did not know of a systematic and exclusive system of sacrificial ritual confined to the sanctuary of the ark."[5] Samuel evidently knew something of it as long as Shiloh stood ; for we read of no attempt *then* to go about the shrines

---

[1] Cf. 1 Kings viii. 29 ; ix. 3 ; 2 Chron. vi. 5, 6.

[2] Shiloh had probably fallen. Cf. Jer. vii. 12, xxvi. 6, with subsequent mention of Nob, 1 Sam. xxi.

[3] *O.T. in J. C.*, p. 271.

[4] *Ibid.* p. 272. Professor Smith, as usual, overshoots the mark in his statement that "Eleazar ben Abinadab was consecrated its *priest.*" There is no mention of a "priest" in 1 Sam. vii. 1. Eleazar was sanctified for the custody of the ark. Samuel's apparent neglect of the ark has to be accounted for on *any* theory (see above, p. 164).

[5] *Ibid.* p. 274.

sacrificing.[1] The ark and Shiloh had been rejected; the former had been taken to Kirjath-jearim under judgment of God; Israel felt itself in a manner under bereavement, and "all the house of Israel lamented after Jehovah."[2] The age was truly, as Professor Smith says "is generally argued," "one of religious interregnum";[3] are we, in such circumstances, to judge Samuel by the law of an orderly and settled time? He fell back naturally, as even the law in Deuteronomy permitted him to do, on local sanctuaries until such time as Jehovah would give the people rest. The law had its place; but even under the law, "the letter killeth, but the spirit giveth life;[4] and in no age were prophetically-minded men the slaves of the mere letter of the commandment to the degree that the critics suppose.[5] Samuel acted with a measure of freedom, as his circumstances demanded; and writers who suppose that priests and prophets were perpetually engaged in changing and modifying laws believed to be divine should be the last to challenge his right to do so.

5. When all is said, it is plain from the statement in the Book of Kings that, in the beginning of Solomon's reign, there was a widespread resort of the people to *high places* for worship, and that even the establishment of Solomon's great temple, with its powerful centralising influence, was not effectual to check this tendency. The compiler of Kings looks on worship at "high places" before the temple was founded as irregular, but excusable;[6] after that it is condemned. The history of these "high places" has yet to be written in a fairer spirit than is generally manifested in notices of them. Much obscurity, in reality, rests upon them. In Judges the word does not occur, and the defections described are mostly of the nature of worship at the Canaanitish shrines of Baal and Ashtoreth.[7] The few allusions in Samuel are connected with Samuel's own city

[1] The statement that Samuel regularly sacrificed at all the places mentioned is an importation into the text. The special mention of his building an altar at Ramah (1 Sam. vii. 17) would suggest that he did not. Professor Smith's list of "sanctuaries" needs a good deal of sifting.
[2] 1 Sam. vii. 2.   [3] *O.T. in J.C.*, p. 272.   [4] 2 Cor. iii. 6.
[5] See Note C on Freedom under the Law. Cf. **Num. x.** 16–20; 1 Sam. xv. 22; xxi. 1–6; 2 Chron. xxix. 34; xxx. 17, 19.
[6] 1 Kings iii. 2, 3.
[7] Allusions to Canaanitish "high places" are found in **Lev. xxvi. 30**; Num. xxi. 28; xxii. 41; xxxiii. 52.

of Ramah, and with the residence of the band of prophets at Gibeah:[1] elsewhere in Samuel they are unnoticed. It may be inferred from the toleration accorded to it that the greater part of what worship there was at "high places" prior to the founding of the temple was directed to Jehovah; afterwards, partly through Solomon's own evil example,[2] idolatry found entrance, and rapidly spread. What the "high places" became in the Northern Kingdom, latterly in Judah also, we know from the prophets. It is, however, a perversion of the facts to speak of the prophets as ever sanctioning, or approving of, this style of worship. If it is replied that it is *idolatrous* worship which the prophets so strongly reprobate, not worship at the "high places" as such, it may be pointed out that they never make such a distinction, or use language which would suggest the acceptableness of the *bamoth* worship in any form.[3] That Elijah mourned the breaking down of the altars of Jehovah in Northern Israel is readily explicable from the peculiar circumstances of that kingdom. To Amos and Hosea, Micah and Isaiah, not less than to Jeremiah and Ezekiel, the one legitimate sanctuary is that of Zion at Jerusalem.[4]

The conclusion we reach on this subject of the unity of worship is, that the history is consistent with itself, *provided we accept its own premises*, and do not insist on forcing on it an alien theory of religious development. The reformations of Hezekiah and Josiah then fall into their proper places, without the necessity of assuming the invention of *ad hoc* "programmes."

VI. THE AARONIC PRIESTHOOD AND THE LEVITES

Ark and tabernacle imply a priesthood, and the notices already cited from Joshua, Judges, 1 Samuel, and Deuteronomy, abundantly show that from the days of Moses such

---

[1] 1 Sam. ix., x.   [2] 1 Kings xi. 7, 8.

[3] Dr. W. H. Green says: "The people are never told that they may sacrifice on the high hills and under green trees, or at Bethel and Gilgal and Beersheba, if only they sacrifice to the Lord alone, and in a proper manner. They are never told that God will be pleased with the erection of numerous altars, provided the service upon them is rightly conducted."—*Moses and the Prophets*, p. 157.

[4] Cf. Amos i. 2; Isa. ii. 2; Mic. iv. 2; Hos. iii. 5. See Robertson, *Early Rel.* p. 405.

a priesthood existed, and that it was *Levitical.* But was it *Aaronic*? And was there from early times such a distinction between *priests* and *Levites* as the Priestly Code represents ?

1. It is a fundamental contention of the new school that a *distinctively Aaronic priesthood* was unknown before the exile. Till Ezekiel, in his sketch of the new temple arrangements (chaps. xl.–xlviii.), initiated a distinction between Zadokite priests and other Levites—a theory considered in a later chapter [1]—there was no distinction in principle between priests and Levites : all Levites are *possible* priests. In particular, a high priest of Aaronic descent was unknown. The question of the relation of the priests to other Levites is considered below; we inquire at present whether it is the case that the earlier books give no traces of an Aaronic priesthood. We affirm that they do, and believe that the proof of this can only be set aside by the usual circle method of first *assuming* that the Aaronic priesthood is late, then, on that ground, disallowing the passages which imply it.

Wellhausen has some wonderful constructive history on this subject, on which we need not dwell. The Levites of history, he affirms, have nothing to do with the old tribe of Levi : in the J narrative in Exodus, Aaron was not originally mentioned at all; it is the line of Moses, not of Aaron, that gives rise to the clerical guild.[2] As an instance of the critical procedure, we may take the case of the high priest. It is, as just said, an essential part of the Wellhausen theory that this functionary is a creation of the exile. He is, we are told, still " unknown even to Ezekiel." [3] Unfortunately for the theory, the high priest is expressly mentioned in at least four places in 2 Kings, viz., in chaps. xii. 10, xxii. 4, 8, xxiii. 4 [4]—the last two chapters being those relied on as furnishing one of the main pillars of the critical theory, the finding of " the book of the law " in the reign of

[1] See below, Chap. IX.
[2] *Hist. of Israel*, pp. 142–43. " Aaron," he says, "was not originally present in J, but owed his introduction to the redactor who combined J and E into JE." Precisely the opposite view is taken by Dillmann, *Exod.-Lev.* p. 437. See also Kuenen below.
[3] *Ibid.* pp. 148–49.
[4] It occurs earlier in 2 Sam. xv. 27, if Wellhausen's amended reading of that text is accepted.

Josiah. The texts are sustained by the parallel passages in Chronicles and by the LXX. What is to be done with them? They are simply *struck out* as interpolations, though it is unaccountable why a redactor should have inserted them in just those places, when so many more invited his attention.[1]

If, on the other hand, we let the history speak for itself, we get such notices as these, which are sufficiently unambiguous. Deut. x. 6, attributed by the critics to E,[2] informs us that, after Aaron's death, " Eleazar his son ministered in the priest's office in his stead." [3] Josh. xxiv. 33 carries this a step further by narrating the death of Eleazar, the son of Aaron, and his burial in the hill of Phinehas, his son. This is continued in Judg. xx. 27, 28, where we read that "Phinehas, the son of Eleazar, the son of Aaron, stood before it [the ark] in these days." From some cause unexplained, the high priesthood became transferred from the line of Eleazar to that of Ithamar, and in the opening of 1 Samuel, Eli, of this younger branch,[4] is found in office. For the sins of his sons it is announced to Eli that his house shall be deprived of its pre-eminence.[5] This took place in the reign of Solomon, when Abiathar was deposed,[6] and Zadok, of the older line, obtained the sole high priesthood.[7] Thus far the case is exactly that described in the words of the "man of God" to Eli in 1 Sam. ii. 27, 28: " Thus saith Jehovah, Did I reveal myself unto the house of thy father, when they were in bondage to Pharaoh's house? And did I choose him out of all the tribes of Israel to be

---

[1] Graf does not challenge the earlier mention of the "high priest" (*Geschicht. Bücher*, p. 4, etc.). Delitzsch (*Zeitschrift*, 1880, p. 228); Dillmann (*Num.-Jos.* p. 645); Baudissin (*Dict. of Bible*, iv. p. 73); Van Hoonacker, etc., defend the passages. Kautzsch removes 2 Kings xii. 10 as a gloss, but lets the others stand. See below, p. 306. Cf. Professor H. P. Smith's treatment of the Levites in Samuel, above, p. 163.

[2] Thus Oxf. *Hex.*, Addis, etc.

[3] Van Hoonacker draws attention to the harmony of JE and P in passing by Nadab and Abihu ; see below, p. 354.

[4] Thus 1 Chron. xxiv. 3, but in 1 Sam. ii. 27, 28 also, Eli is assumed to be of the house of Aaron. Wellhausen's idea that in this passage Moses, not Aaron, is intended scarcely deserves notice. Cf. W. R. Smith, *O.T. in J. C.*, p. 268.

[5] 1 Sam. ii. 27-36. [6] 1 Kings ii. 26, 27.

[7] 1 Kings ii. 35. Owing to the political division in the reign of David there was for a time a double priesthood. On Wellhausen's denial of the Aaronite descent of Zadok, see Note D on the Genealogy of Zadok.

My priest, to go up unto Mine altar, to burn incense, to wear an ephod before Me?"[1] In using here the term "high priesthood," we do not forget that it is held that the high priest is an exilian creation. But is that so? It has just been pointed out that the title is repeatedly used in the history of the kings. How, in fact, can we otherwise express the undoubted position of supremacy or dignity held by priests like Eleazar, Phinehas, Eli, Abiathar, Zadok? But there is another point of much interest. If the high priesthood was a creation of the exile, we should expect that the title would be one frequently met with in the Levitical Code—at least more frequently than elsewhere. Yet it occurs there only *three times* altogether— twice in Num. xxxv. (vers. 25, 28), and once in Lev. xxi. 10 —the last a passage which many take to be very old.[2] The term ordinarily used in the Code is simply "the priest."

The priesthood was Aaronic, but was it *exclusively* so; or even exclusively Levitical? This is contested, but without real force, on the ground of certain notices in the historical books, as where the king is represented as taking a lead in religious celebrations, offering sacrifices, blessing the people,[3] etc., or where David's sons and others are spoken of as "priests."[4] A peculiar place is accorded, certainly, to the king, as representative of Jehovah, in the arrangements and conduct of worship,[5] but this as much in Chronicles and Ezekiel[6] as in the Books of Samuel or Kings. Nor is the king permitted to usurp functions strictly sacerdotal.[7] It is not to be supposed that Solomon offered with his own hand the 22,000 oxen and 120,000 sheep mentioned in 1 Kings viii. 63, to the exclusion of the

[1] Kuenen differs from Wellhausen in allowing in his *Religion of Israel* a Levitical and *originally* Aaronic priesthood. "Levi was one of the twelve tribes from the first . . . Moses and Aaron were Levites; Aaron's family discharges the priestly office at the common sanctuary," etc.—ii. p. 302. Baudissin argues for an Aaronic priesthood at least older than Josiah's reform.—*Dict. of Bible*, iv. p. 89.

[2] On this subject see more fully below, Chap. IX. Cf. also Delitzsch, Luthardt's *Zeitschrift*, 1880, p. 228.

[3] David, 2 Sam. vi. 17, 18; Solomon, 1 Kings iii. 4; viii. 62-64.

[4] 2 Sam. viii. 18 (R.V.); xx. 26 (R.V.); 1 Kings iv. 5 (R.V.).

[5] See the admirable remarks on this in Van Hoonacker, *Le Sacerdoce*, pp. 256 ff.

[6] 1 Chron. xv. 27; xvi. 2; 2 Chron. vi. 3, 12 ff.; vii. 4 ff., etc.; Ezek. xliv. 3; xlv. 7, 16, 17, 22, etc.

[7] Cf. the judgment on Uzziah, 2 Chron. xxvi. 16 ff.; cf. 2 Kings xv. 5.

priests mentioned in vers. 3, 6, 10 ; [1] or that David, earlier, slew for himself the numerous offerings of 2 Sam. vi. 17, 18, from which " a portion " was given to the whole multitude (also with his own hand ?). The priesthood of the sons of David, however that difficult passage and related texts are to be understood,[2] was evidently something different from the ordinary service of the altar, and cannot outweigh the very full testimony to the Levitical character of the latter.

2. This brings us to the second question—that of the relations of *priests and Levites.* The subject will come up at an after stage, and we need not do more here than inquire whether the representation of a special order of Aaronic priests, in distinction from other Levites, is really, as alleged, in conflict with Deuteronomy, and with the facts of the earlier history. The general position of critical writers is that the view of the priesthood in the Levitical Code is irreconcilable with the representation in Deuteronomy, and with the earlier practice. In the Code a strong distinction is made between "the sons of Aaron," who are the only lawful priests, and the ordinary Levites, who are servants of the sanctuary. In Deuteronomy, it is held, this distinction has no place. The tribe of Levi as a whole is the priestly tribe. As Professor W. R. Smith puts it : "Deuteronomy knows no Levites who cannot be priests, and no priests who are not Levites. The two ideas are identical." [3] The phraseology in this book, accordingly, is not "sons of Aaron," but "sons of Levi." It speaks of "the priests the Levites," not of "priests and Levites.' This also, it is pointed out, is the phraseology of the older historical books—so far as not revised. The distinction between "priests" and "Levites" is held to be due to a later degradation of priests of the "high places," as sketched by Ezekiel.[4]

---

[1] Wellhausen says that doubtless Solomon with his own hands offered the "first" sacrifice (*Hist. of Israel,* p. 133), on which Van Hoonacker remarks : "If the 21,999 oxen that remained can be said to be offered by Solomon, when in reality they have been offered by others in his name, the first may have been so also ; the text knows nothing of an offering of the first " (p. 259).

[2] Cf. the discussion in Van Hoonacker, pp. 268 ff., and see Note E on David's Sons as Priests. On other questions in the historical books bearing on the priesthood, see pp. 358, 363 ff., 388 below.

[3] *O.T. in J. C.,* p. 360.

[4] See below, Chap. IX. p. 315 ff. The older theory was that Deuteronomy implies an *elevation* of the Levites from their original lower status, and

What is true in this contention is to be frankly acknowledged. The difference in point of view and mode of speech in Deuteronomy must be apparent to every reader; and it may at once be conceded to an able writer on the subject [1] that, if we had only Deuteronomy, we should never be able to arrive at a knowledge of the sharp division of the tribe of Levi into the superior and subordinate orders with which the Levitical law makes us acquainted. But it does not follow that the distinction is not there, and is not presupposed throughout.

(1) We do well, in the first place, to look with some closeness into *the phraseology* on which so much—practically the whole case—is based. When this is done, we discover that the phenomena are not quite so simple as the above statement would suggest. The expression "the priests the Levites," occurring in Deut. xvii. 9, 18, xviii. 1, xxiv. 8, xxvii. 9—*not earlier* in the book,—of itself, it will be allowed, decides nothing: it means simply "the Levitical priests." It is not found, indeed, in the Priestly Code; but as little is the other expression, "priests *and* Levites." That is peculiar to the later books,[2] and even in Chronicles is sometimes interchanged with "the priests the Levites." [3] The Book of Joshua, likewise, has "the priests the Levites": [4] never "priests and Levites." On the other hand, the Priestly Writer occasionally uses "Levites," as in Deuteronomy, to cover *both* priests and Levites: [5] this is the case also in Chronicles.[6] Finally, it is true that "sons of Aaron" is not used in Deuteronomy to describe the priests, though there is the recognition of the Aaronic high priest. But it is very noticeable that, even in the Levitical

---

the late date of the book was argued for on the ground that it must have taken a long time to bring this change about. The newer criticism gives up the premises, but retains the conclusion.

[1] Van Hoonacker, *Le Sacerdoce*, p. 170. The theory of this writer is, that the distinction existed, but in popular usage the name "priests" came to be applied to *all* Levites, whether of the higher or lower grade (cf. Dillmann on Deut. xviii. 1). The theory, while containing suggestive elements, does not seem to us in this form tenable.

[2] Chronicles, Ezra, Nehemiah; once in 1 Kings viii. 4, where the parallel passage in 2 Chron. v. 5 has "the priests the Levites."

[3] 2 Chron. v. 5; xxiii. 18; xxx. 27.

[4] Josh. iii. ff. (or "priests" simply).

[5] *E.g.*, Num. xxxv. 2, 6, 8; Josh. xiv. 4; xxi. 8 (cf. Van Hoonacker).

[6] 1 Chron. xvi. 4, 37; 2 Chron. xxix. 5 ff. In Malachi also (chap. iii. 3) the priests are "the sons of Levi."

Code, "sons of Aaron" is by no means the only, or universal, designation for the priests; there are considerable
sections of the Code in which it either does not occur at
all, or occurs only sparingly.[1] It is, moreover, chiefly in the
laws and narratives of the *earlier* part of the wilderness
sojourn that this usage is found; it is not characteristic of
the later chapters of Numbers. Nor can this change from
a narrower to a more general designation, on the assumption
of the truth of the history, be regarded as strange. At first
the priests, "the sons of Aaron," stood out from the people
with sharp distinctness as alone invested with sacred office.
The case was greatly altered after the separation of the
tribe of Levi,[2] when the designation "sons of Aaron" seems
to have been gradually dropped for another identifying the
priests more directly with their tribe.[3] Priests and Levites
had more in common with each other than either class had
with the general body of the people; and, besides, the
priests *were* Levites. The rise of such a designation as "the
priests the Levites" is therefore quite natural, and the view
in Deuteronomy of the tribe of Levi as, collectively, a
priestly tribe, is entirely in keeping with the situation in
which the discourses are supposed to have been delivered.
To the popular eye, the tribe of Levi stood apart, forming,
as a whole, one sacred body, engaged in ministering in holy
things to God.

(2) It does not surprise us, then, to find in Deuteronomy
the functions of the priestly ministry—even to the "Urim and
Thummim," which was the peculiar prerogative of the high
priest—ascribed to the tribe of Levi as a whole.[4] The question
of real importance is—Does the book contain any indication of
such a distinction as we have nevertheless assumed to exist
between the different orders in this tribe, or does it exclude
such distinction? We believe there *is* evidence of such distinction; the newer critics deny it.[5] The question belongs
more properly to the discussion of Deuteronomy,[6] but, in the

---

[1] For details see Kittel, *Hist. of Hebs.* i. p. 120.
[2] Num. i. 47 ff.; iii. 5 ff.; viii. 5 ff., etc.
[3] After Numbers the phrase occurs only in Josh. **xxi.**, **where discrimination** is necessary in the appointment of the cities.
[4] Deut. x. 8; xxxiii. 8.
[5] Dillmann, Delitzsch, Kittel, etc., Van Hoonacker **also from his own**
point of view, hold that distinctions are *not* **excluded.**
[6] See below, Chap. VIII

interest of the history, we may be permitted thus far to anticipate. We would draw attention first, then, to the fact, that
in Deuteronomy the terms " priest" and " Levite " are, after
all, not quite synonymous. There are " the priests the
Levites," but there are also " Levites" who are not priests.
Even allowing them to be " possible" priests, though we do
not believe this to be the meaning of the book, they have
still to be distinguished from those who, in the sense of the
writer, are *actual* priests. It is a perfectly unwarranted
assumption that, wherever the term Levite is used we
have a synonym for priest. A distinction is already indicated, and the fact of at least certain gradations within
the tribe established, by the statement in chap. x. 6 that
" Aaron died, and Eleazar his son ministered in the priest's
office in his stead." [1] The clearest indication, however, is
in chap. xviii. 1–8, where an obvious distinction is made
between the " priest" serving at the sanctuary (vers. 3–5),
and the " Levite" not thus serving [2] (vers. 6–8); the only intelligible reason for the more general designation being,
either that ordinary non-priestly Levites are meant, or at
least that they are intended to be *included*. It is a reading
into the text what is not there to assert that every
" Levite" going up to the sanctuary is a " possible" priest
in the stricter sense. This rules the meaning to be
attached to the opening sentence: " The priests the Levites,
all the tribe of Levi." [3] The second designation includes
the first: in apposition it cannot be, since, in the writer's
sense, all Levites are not actual priests. To us it seems
most evident that when he speaks of " the priests the
Levites," he has a definite class in view, and by no means
the whole body of the tribe.[4] This view of the passage,

---

[1] Cf. chap. xxxiii. 8. To what again can the separation in chap. x. 8
refer, if not to the setting apart of the sons of Aaron, and afterwards of
the whole tribe of Levi, recorded in the P sections of the history? Critics
suppose an *omitted* narrative of this separation in JE (cf. Driver, *Deut.*
p. 121).

[2] Thus, *e.g.*, Dillmann, *Num.–Jos.*, *in loc.* It is to be remembered that
it is only in the few passages above cited that priests are mentioned at all.

[3] Chap. xviii. 1.

[4] Dr. Driver refers to the frequency of explanatory appositions in
Deuteronomy, and gives examples (*Deut.* p. 214). The case seems rather
analogous to those in which the lawgiver *expands* his original statement by
enlarging additions ; *e.g.*, "Ye shall eat . . . ye and your household "
(chap. xii. 7) ; "Ye shall rejoice . . . ye, and your sons, and your
daughters," etc. etc. (chap. xii. 12) ; cf. chap. xii. 18 ; xv. 11, etc.

we are aware, the critical school meets with a direct negative, assigning as a reason that the terms used in ver. 7 to describe the Levites' services ("to minister in the name of Jehovah," "to stand before Jehovah") are those regularly used of priestly duties. We believe this is far from being really the case; but the question is a little intricate, and had better be discussed apart.[1]

(3) A word may be said before leaving the subject on the difficulty arising from the representations in Deuteronomy of the *dispersed and needy condition* of the Levites. The objection is urged that, instead of being furnished with cities and pasturages, and enjoying an independent income from tithes, as the Priestly Code provides, the Levites appear in this book as homeless and dependent, wandering from place to place, and glad to be invited, with the stranger, the widow, and the fatherless, to share in charitable feasts.[2] Here, in the first place, it must be remarked that the legal provision is not ignored, but is, on the other hand, expressly alluded to in chap. xviii. 1, 2 (cf. chap. x. 9), " And they shall have no inheritance among their brethren; Jehovah is their inheritance, as He hath spoken to them," where the reference seems unmistakable to the law in Num. xviii. 20, 23, 24. Dillmann says: "The corresponding law stands in Num. xviii."[3] But, waiving this, may we not suggest that, if a time is sought when these exhortations to care for the Levite would be suitable, no time is so fit as that when they are supposed to have been delivered, before the tithe-laws had come into regular operation,—when in truth there was little or nothing to tithe,—and when the Levites would be largely dependent on the hospitality of individuals. The Levites were dependent then, and might from very obvious causes

---

[1] See Appendix to Chapter—"Priests and Levites." Cf. also the case of Samuel, considered below, pp. 189–90.

[2] Deut. xii. 12, 19 ; xvi. 11, etc.

[3] *Num.-Jos., in loc.* Dr. Driver argues against this on the ground that in Num. xviii. 20 "the promise is made expressly to the *priests* (Aaron) alone, as distinguished from the Levites (vers. 21–24), whose 'inheritance' is specified separately (ver. 24) ; here it is given to the whole tribe without distinction."—*Deut.* p. 125 (on chap. x. 9). But surely it is obvious that the whole passage in Numbers (xviii. 20–24) goes together, and that the principal part of the "inheritance" of the priests is the tenth of the tithe they are to receive from the Levites (ver. 26). Let the reader compare the passages for himself.

come to be dependent again. Their state would not be greatly bettered in the unsettled times of the conquest.[1] Nothing could be more appropriate in itself, better adapted to create kindly sympathies between Levites and people, or more likely to avert neglect of the tribe by the withholding of their just dues, than the perpetuation of these primitive hospitalities. It is to be remembered that no tribunal existed to enforce payment of the tithes: all depended on the conscientiousness of the individual payer. It is easy to see that an income of this kind was in the highest degree precarious, and that, in times of religious declension, the body of the Levites would be reduced to great straits. The Levites no doubt suffered severely in the days of the Judges, and under bad kings; under good kings, like David, and Solomon, and Hezekiah, the order, we may believe, experienced considerable revivals. At other times it sank in the general corruption, and Levites were content to earn a doubtful livelihood by irregular ministrations at the "high places." There is no evidence we know of that their condition in the later days of the kingdom was so deplorably destitute as the critics represent.

(4) It will be seen later how little can be inferred from the general silence of the history about the Levites;[2] yet that silence, as has already been hinted, is not altogether unbroken.[3] Two instances, at least, of mention occur in 1 Sam. vi. 15, and 2 Sam. xv. 24; perhaps also the presence of Levites may be inferred where Hophni and Phinehas are spoken of as "*with* the ark of Jehovah."[4] A case of special interest is that of the youthful Samuel, who is described as "ministering unto," or "before" Jehovah at Shiloh,[5] though his duties were the subordinate ones of the Levite.[6] The words "ministered before Eli" also show that this was his position.[7] The attempt, on the other hand, sometimes made to prove Samuel to be a *priest*

---

[1] Cf. König, art. "Judges," *Dict. of Bible*, ii. p. 816 : "Further, we see a Levite wandering about, ready to settle down wherever he found office and bread (Judg. xvii. 8 ff. ; xviii. 19 ff. ; xix. 1). This situation of the members of the tribe of Levi was an actual one as long as a number of the Levitical cities were not yet conquered [König accepts the historicity of these], such as Gezer, and those remarks of the Book of Judges would have possessed no probability if they had proceeded from a period when Jeroboam selected priests from among the people at large," etc.

[2] See below, Chap. IX. p. 304.   [3] Cf. p. 163.   [4] 1 Sam. iv. 4.
[5] 1 Sam. ii. 11, 18 ; iii. 1.   [6] 1 Sam. iii. 15.   [7] 1 Sam. iii. 1.

(in contradiction of the law) from the mention of his
"linen ephod" and "little robe," must be regarded as
another instance of forcing the text.[1] It is inexcusable
exaggeration when Professor W. R. Smith writes: "As a
child he ministers before Jehovah, wearing the ephod
which the law confines to the high priest, and not
only this, but the high priestly mantle (*me'il*)."[2] The
high priestly ephod, as every reference to it shows,[3] was
something distinctive, and different from "the linen ephod,"
which was worn by ordinary priests,[4] but not by them
exclusively.[5] The *me'il*, or robe, again, was a long sleeve-
less tunic, "worn," says Gesenius, "by women of rank
(2 Sam. xiii. 18), by men of rank and birth (Job i. 20;
ii. 12), by kings (1 Sam. xv. 27; xviii. 4; xxiv. 4, 11)"[6]
—therefore no peculiar property of the high priest. The
usurpation of high priestly or even of ordinary priestly
functions by Samuel is on a par with his sleeping in the
inner temple beside the sacred ark.

NOTE.—*The Ark*: In connection with the discussions,
pp. 137–38 and 161–65, the author would draw attention
to the searching Essay by Professor Lotz, of Erlangen, *Die
Bundeslade* (1901), which did not fall into his hands till this
chapter was printed. It lends valuable support to the
contentions in the text. See especially the discusssion of
the *names* of the ark (pp. 28 ff.).

[1] Thus Wellhausen, W. R. Smith, etc. Wellhausen's note should be
quoted: "*House of God* is never anything but the house of an image.
Outside the Priestly Code, *ephod* is the image; *ephod bad* (the linen
ephod), the priestly garment."—*Hist. of Israel*, p. 130. Was Abiathar's
ephod then (p. 132) an image?
[2] *O. T. in J. C.*, p. 270.
[3] Cf. Ex. xxviii. 6; 1 Sam. ii. 28; xxiii. 6, 9; xxx. 7.
[4] 1 Sam. xxii. 18. It was not, however, a *prescribed* part of the dress.
[5] 2 Sam. vi. 14   [6] *Lexicon, in loc.*

APPENDIX TO CHAPTER VI

PRIESTS AND LEVITES

DR. DRIVER gives a reason for rejecting the view of the relation of priests and Levites indicated in the text, which, if it were valid, would be fatal; but which, as it stands, seems to us, we confess, an example of that overstraining which plays so large a part in these discussions. He writes: "The terms used in [Deut. xviii.] 7 to describe the Levite services are those used regularly of *priestly* duties. *To minister in the name*, as xviii. 5 (of the priest; cf. xvii. 12; xxi. 5); *to stand before—i.e.*, to wait on (see, *e.g.*, 1 Kings x. 8)—*Jehovah*, as Ezek. xliv. 15; Judg. xx. 28; cf. Deut. xvii. 12; xviii. 5. (The Levites 'stand before'—*i.e.*, wait upon—*the congregation*, Num. xvi. 9; Ezek. xliv. 11*b*. In 2 Chron. xxix. 11, *priests* are present; see **v. 4**)." [1] We should not, of course, presume to differ from Dr. Driver on a question of philology or grammar; but this is a question of palpable fact, and invites examination. All Hebrew scholars, besides, are far from agreeing with Dr. Driver in the above *dicta*. The statement made, we venture to think, needs much qualification. It is not denied that the terms employed are appropriate to priestly duties; the question is whether they are used of these duties "regularly" and *only*. And this it is difficult to admit. The exact phrase "to minister in the name" is, so far as we know, found nowhere else than in vers. 5, 7, of this passage; but the verb itself, "minister" (*shareth*) is used constantly in the law and in Chronicles of *Levitical* as well as of priestly service. [2] The Levites, we read, shall be appointed over the tabernacle of the testimony, "and they shall minister

---

[1] *Introd.* p. 83 (note); cf. W. R. Smith, *O.T. in J.C.*, p. 361.
[2] Num. i. 50; iii. 6, 31; iv. 9, 12, 14; viii. 26; xvi. 9; xviii. 2; 1 Chron. xv. 2; xvi. 4, 37.

to it";[1] aged Levites "shall minister with their brethren in the tent of meeting,"[2] but shall do no service; the Levites "are chosen to carry the ark of God and to minister unto Him for ever";[3] they "minister before the ark of the covenant of Jehovah,"[4] etc. *In fact, the only use of the word "minister" in the Book of Numbers, if we are not mistaken, is with reference to the service of the Levites.*[5] With this may be compared Dr. Driver's own note in his *Deuteronomy*, where the facts are stated more fully, but still, as we think, onesidedly. "*To minister*," he there says, "is a less distinctive term, being used not only of priests, but also of Levites (Num. viii. 26), and other subordinate attendants, as in 1 Sam. ii. 11, 18; iii. 1 (of Samuel)."[6] [We gather from this that Dr. Driver does not adopt Wellhausen's theory that Samuel was a "priest."] But then, what becomes of its peculiar force in Deuteronomy? For Samuel also ministered "to Jehovah"; so in 1 Chron. xv. 2, etc. It does not fare better with the expression "to stand before Jehovah." Apart from the passage quoted, it is used in Deuteronomy *once* of the tribe of Levi,[7] and *once* of the Levitical priest.[8] In the Levitical law *it does not occur at all*—a curious instance of "regularly." On the other hand, in Chronicles, the Levites "stand every morning to thank and praise Jehovah, and likewise at even,"[9] and "priests and Levites" are addressed together as "chosen to stand before Jehovah."[10] In Nehemiah also "priests and Levites" are spoken of together as those who "stood."[11] Can it be claimed that the case is made out?[12]

[1] Num. i. 50. [2] Num. viii. 26.
[3] 1 Chron. xv. 2. [4] 1 Chron. xvi. 4, 37.
[5] The note on the word as found in P in the Oxf. *Hexateuch* is: "Of priests in the sanctuary, or of Levites attending on priests" (i. p. 216).
[6] *Deut.* p. 123. [7] Deut. x. 8.
[8] Deut. xvii. 12. [9] 1 Chron. xxiii. 30.
[10] 2 Chron. xxix. 11; cf. xxxv. 5. Dr. Driver says that here "*priests* are present." The important point is that *Levites* also are present, and that *both* are addressed.
[11] Neh. xii. 44 (Heb.).
[12] In Lev. ix. 5, and a few places in Deuteronomy (iv. 10; xix. 17, etc.), "stand before Jehovah" is used of Israel generally. "To stand before the congregation" (used of the Levites) occurs *once* (Num. xvi. 9; cf. Ezek. xliv. 11).

CHAPTER VII

Difficulties and Perplexities of the Critical Hypothesis: I. The JE Analysis

> " He His fabric of the Heavens
> Hath left to their disputes; perhaps to move
> His laughter at their quaint opinions wide
> Hereafter, when they come to model Heaven
> And calculate the stars; how they will wield
> The mighty frame;—how build, contrive
> To save appearances;—how gird the sphere
> With centrick and eccentrick scribbled o'er,
> Cycle and epicycle, orb in orb."—MILTON.

"To base a determination of age on bare peculiarities of language, especially in things that concern legal relations, in which the form of expression is not arbitrarily employed by the writer, is precarious. When the relationship of certain sections is assumed on perhaps insufficient criteria, and then other sections are added to them because of some similar linguistic phenomena, and from these again further and further conclusions are drawn, one easily runs the risk of moving in a vicious circle."—GRAF.

"The history of critical investigation has shown that far too much weight has often been laid on agreement in the use of the divine names—so much so that it has twice led the critics wrong. It is well therefore to utter a warning against laying an exaggerated stress on this one phenomenon."—KUENEN.

"No intelligent observer, however, will deny that the work of investigation has gone onwards, and not moved in a circle."—DELITZSCH.

CHAPTER VII

DIFFICULTIES AND PERPLEXITIES OF THE CRITICAL HYPOTHESIS: I. THE JE ANALYSIS

THUS far we have been content to proceed on the assumption of the correctness of the ordinary critical analysis of documents in the "Hexateuch," and, without challenging either documents or dates, have endeavoured to show that, even on this basis, the essential facts of the history, and the outstanding features in the Biblical picture of the religion and institutions of Israel, remain unaffected. We now take a further step, and go on to inquire whether the critical theory of documents, as usually presented, is valid, and, if at all, how far. Here we part company with many, of whose help, in defending the truth of supernatural revelation, we have hitherto gladly availed ourselves, but who, we are compelled to think, have unnecessarily hampered themselves, and weakened their contentions, by assent to critical positions which are far from being solidly established. We shall still seek, as far as may be, common ground with these writers, and hope to show that, if we break with them, our doubts are born, not from an obstinate wedding of the mind to obsolete traditions, but from a sincere regard to the facts, as we are constrained to apprehend them.

It is not uncommon to find the course of criticism during the last century represented as purely a work of unbelief, resulting in hopeless error and confusion. That, however, is not altogether our opinion. If it cannot well be denied that, as before stated, what is called "Higher Criticism" was cradled in, and received its characteristic "set" from the older rationalism,[1] and if, unfortunately,

---

[1] That this statement is not too strong may be seen from the names of its founders as given in Cheyne and other writers. Cheyne himself censures the early excesses of criticism. "In the previous age" (before Gesenius), he

this vice of its origin has clung to it, more or less, in all its subsequent developments, it would be unreasonable not to acknowledge that it is also, in large part, the product of a genuinely scientific temper, and of a true perception of phenomena which are *there* in Scripture, and, on any theory, require explanation. Its course, too, has been marked by a real and continuous advance in the apprehension of these phenomena, and, with whatever mingling of error, has tended to an ever closer definition of the problem to be solved. A brief glance at the principal *stadia* in the history of the development will illustrate what we mean.

I. STADIA OF THE CRITICAL DEVELOPMENT

The chief stages in the development of the critical hypothesis have been the following:—

1. The beginning of the critical movement is usually associated with the French physician *Astruc*,[1] who, in his *Conjectures*, in 1753, drew attention to the presence of Elohistic and Jehovistic sections in Genesis, and on this based his theory of the employment of distinct documents in the composition of the book. The fact thus founded on is a highly interesting one, and, once pointed out, cannot be ignored. It is the case that some chapters, and portions of chapters, in Genesis are marked by the use, exclusively or predominatingly, of the divine name "Elohim" (God), and others by a similar use of the divine name "Jehovah" (E.T. LORD). This distinction continues till Ex. vi., when God reveals Himself by His name Jehovah, then (mainly) ceases. A considerable part of Genesis, accordingly, can really, by the use of this criterion, be divided into

says, "there had been an epidemic of arbitrary emendation in the department of textual criticism, and a tendency (at any rate among some 'higher critics' of the Pentateuch and Isaiah) to break up the text into a number of separate pieces, which threatened to open the door to unbounded caprice."—*Founders of Criticism*, p. 63. [What will a future critic say of Dr. Cheyne?] The result is described by Tholuck in his inaugural lecture at Halle in 1821: "For the last twenty or thirty years the opinion has been generally prevalent, that the study of the Old Testament for theologians, as well as the devotional reading of it for the laity, is either entirely profitless, or at least promises little advantage" (*Ibid.* p. 67).

[1] One of the best accounts of Astruc is that by Dr. H. Osgood in *The Presbyterian and Reformed Review* for January 1892. It shows that Astruc's personal character was deeply marred by the vices of French society.

Elohistic and Jehovistic sections.[1] A fact to be placed
alongside of this, though its full bearings do not always
seem to be perceived, is that in the Psalter we have an
arrangement of psalms into Jehovistic and Elohistic groups
by a similar distinction in the use of the divine names.[2]

2. A further step was taken when *Eichhorn* (1779),[3]
to whom is due the name " Higher Criticism," and who
seems to have worked independently of Astruc, pointed out
that the Elohistic and Jehovistic sections in Genesis were
distinguished, not simply by the use of the divine names,
but by certain other literary peculiarities, which furnished
aid in their discrimination. The Elohistic sections in
particular—not all of them, as came afterwards to be seen—
were found to be characterised by a vocabulary and style
of their own, which enabled them, on the whole, to be
readily distinguished. This result also, whatever explanation may be offered of it, has stood the test of time, and
will not, we believe, be overturned. The long lists of words
and phrases customarily adduced as characteristic of the
Elohist (now P), need, indeed, much sifting,[4] but enough
remains to justify the critic in distinguishing a P hand in
Genesis, different from that of JE.[5]

3. It was at this point that *De Wette* struck in with his
thesis (1805–6) that Deuteronomy, shown by him to have
also a style and character of its own, could not have been

[1] As examples of Elohistic sections in this sense, cf. Gen. i.–ii. 3 ; v.;
xvii.; xxiii. ; xxv. 7–17, etc. : in the story of the flood, vi. 9–22 ; vii. 11–
16 ; ix. 1–18, etc. As specimens of Jehovistic sections, cf. Gen. ii. 4–iv.;
xi. 1–9 ; xii.; xiii. (mainly) ; xviii., xix., etc., with the alternate sections
in the flood story.

[2] The Psalter is divided into five Books, each concluding with a doxology
(Pss. xli. 13 ; lxxii. 18, 19 ; lxxxix. 52 ; cvi. 48). In the first three of
these books the psalms are grouped according to the predominant use of
the divine names : Book I. (i.–xli.), *Jehovistic*, ascribed to David ; Book II.
(xlii.–lxxii.), *Elohistic*, ascribed to sons of Korah, Asaph (one psalm), David ;
Book III. (lxxiii.–lxxxix.), *Jehovistic*, ascribed to Asaph, sons of Korah, etc.
The last two books are mainly Jehovistic. See below, pp. 277 ff., on these
groups of psalms, and their significance. For details, cf. W. R. Smith,
O.T. in J. C., pp. 195–96, etc.

[3] Eichhorn was a rationalist of the Paulus type, giving a naturalistic
explanation of the miracles.

[4] See below, pp. 336 ff.

[5] Astruc and Eichhorn did not carry the analysis beyond Genesis, though
Eichhorn suggests such extension (cf. De Wette, *Introd.* ii. p. 150). Both
regarded Moses (wholly or mainly) as the compiler. Their position may
be compared with that of Principal Cave in his *Inspiration of the O.T.*, who,
however, makes Moses also the probable author of both documents.

composed earlier than the reign of Josiah. This he inferred
mainly from the law of the central sanctuary in Deut.
xii., and from the breaches of that law in the older history,
considered in last chapter. Westphal has declared that
"Deuteronomy is the Ariadne's thread in the labyrinth of
the historical problem of the Pentateuch,"[1] and we are not
sure that we are not disposed to agree with him, if in a
sense different from what he intended. Meanwhile, as
was inevitable, the question arose as to whether the
Elohistic and Jehovistic documents did not extend beyond
Genesis into the remaining books of the Pentateuch, and,
further, into Joshua (Bleek, 1822), with which the earlier
books are so closely connected. In this extension, the
criterion of the divine names failed,[2] but the other linguistic
phenomena, and relations with acknowledged J and E
sections, were relied on to establish the distinction. Thus,
mainly under the guidance of Bleek, Ewald (1831), and
Stähelin (1835),[3] the criticism of the "Pentateuch" passed
definitely over into that of the "Hexateuch" — the
Pentateuch *and* Joshua.

4. The next step is connected with *Hupfeld* (1853), and
marks again a distinct advance. Ilgen (1798) had preluded
the discovery, but Hupfeld, with more success, drew
attention to the fact that the assumed Elohistic document
in Genesis was not all of one cast. Certain sections—all,
indeed, up to chap. xx.—had the well-marked characteristics
now attributed to P; but other portions, agreeing in the
use of the name Elohim, were quite dissimilar in style,
and closely resembled the Jehovistic parts—were, in fact,
indistinguishable from the latter, save in the difference of
the divine names.[4] Hupfeld's solution was that we have
here a document from a *third* writer—named by him the
2nd Elohist (E), who agreed with the older in the use of

[1] *Sources du Pent.* ii. p. xxiv. De Wette, with most scholars of that age,
regarded the Elohistic document as the *older*, and partly *on that ground*
argued for the lateness of Deuteronomy (to give time for development).
Modern scholars, *reversing* the relations of age, yet held by De Wette's
conclusion.

[2] Colenso to the last (in published works) broke off the Elohistic narrative at Ex. vi.; Cave, attributing it to Moses (or earlier writer), does the
same—a curious instance of extremes meeting.

[3] Stähelin made important contributions in *Stud. und Krit.*, 1835
and 1838.

[4] Examples are Gen. xx. ; xxi. 6.–xxii.; xxxi.

the name Elohim, but whose style, vocabulary, and mode of representation were akin to, and nearly identical with, those of the Jehovist. This observation, again, in substance corresponds with facts; for it is the case that in the sections in question there is little or nothing to distinguish the Elohist from the Jehovist, beyond the use of the divine names.[1] A natural solution would seem to be that, despite the difference in names, the documents are not really two, but one;[2] but modern critics generally adhere to Hupfeld's distinction of J and E, and evolve a number of other peculiarities which are thought to distinguish the two writers. The theory had its disadvantages, which kept many of the older scholars, e.g., Bleek, from assenting to it; for, while explaining certain stylistic phenomena, it destroyed, in doing so, the previously boasted unity of the Elohistic narrative,[3] and created in the latter great and unaccountable hiatuses: left in fact, as we shall see, only a few fragments and lists for P after Gen. xxiii. to the end of the book![4]

5. The final stage in the development—if that can be termed development which is more properly *revolution*—outstrips in importance all the preceding. Hitherto, with some little regarded exceptions,[5] the universal assumption had been that the Elohistic Writer, or 1st Elohist—was the oldest of all, and his date was variously fixed in the time of the Judges, or in the reigns of Saul or David. The order was assumed to be: 1st Elohist—Jehovist and 2nd Elohist—Deuteronomy. Then came the somersault of *Graf*, who, in his *Historical Books of the Old Testament*, in 1866,

[1] Colenso, who only partially accepted Hupfeld's analysis, says: "The style of the two writers is so very similar ,except in the use of the divine names, that it is impossible to distinguish them by considerations of style alone."—*Pent.* v. p. 59.

[2] Colenso favours this solution for the parts he accepts of E: so Klostermann. Cf. below, p. 218.

[3] Cf. De Wette, *Introd.* ii. p. 77 : "The Elohistic fragments form a whole which can be reduced to a form almost perfect." (See below, pp. 333, 341.) On the other hand, writers like Bleek (more recently Cave), who accept the Elohistic narrative in its integrity, are in this dilemma, that they destroy their own grounds for distinguishing the Elohist from the Jehovist. For it has to be admitted that considerable sections of the Elohistic document are in every respect of style (except the names) indistinguishable from the Jehovistic. Those again who, like Colenso, in parts identify E with J, have to own that the names are not an infallible criterion.

[4] See below, pp. 341 ff. [5] See below, p. 204.

propounded the view,[1] which he owed to Reuss,[2] that the legislation of the middle books of the Pentateuch (the Levitical law) was not earlier, but later, than Deuteronomy —was, in fact, a product of the age of the exile. Graf, however, was not yet of the opinion that all the Elohistic sections of the Pentateuch were late: he accepted the ordinary view that the Elohistic writing was the oldest for the *historical* sections, but contended that the priestly *laws* were a later, and post-exilian, insertion.[3] Kuenen and Riehm, from opposite sides, wrote to show that this was an untenable position. History and laws go together, and either the whole is early, or the whole is late.[4] Graf before his death acknowledged the force of Kuenen's arguments for the late date of the (P) history as well as of the legislation,[5] while not admitting that the P writing constituted an independent document. Owing mainly to the powerful advocacy of Wellhausen,[6] the more thoroughgoing view has prevailed, and, as formerly stated, it is now held to be one of the "settled" results of criticism[7] that the Priestly element is the very latest constituent in the Hexateuch, and is of exilian or post-exilian date. Yet in one respect

[1] See above, p. 160. An earlier work in 1855, *De templo Silonensi*, preluded the idea of his chief work.

[2] Cf. Kuenen, *Hex.* pp. xxxiv-v. Reuss's own work, *L'Histoire Sainte et la Loi*, was published in 1879.

[3] This also was Colenso's position in his published works, after he had come round to Graf's standpoint (*Pent.* Pts. v. and vi.)—*history* early, *laws* late. See below, p. 334.

[4] Kuenen puts it thus: "Must the laws stand with the narratives, or must the narratives fall with the laws? I could not hesitate for a moment in accepting the latter alternative."—*Hex.* p. xxii.

[5] *Ibid.* pp. xxviii, xxx. Professor Robertson properly says: "To say bluntly that the narratives must go with the laws, is no more a process of criticism than to say that the laws must go with the history. It is therefore inaccurate to describe the position of Graf as a conclusion of criticism. It was simply a hypothesis to evade a difficulty in which criticism had landed him."—*Early Rel.* pp. 418-19.

[6] Wellhausen tells us: "I learned through Ritschl that Karl Heinrich Graf placed the law later than the prophets ; and, almost without knowing his reasons for the hypothesis, I was prepared to accept it."—*Hist. of Israel*, p. 3.

[7] Professor W. R. Smith names "Kuenen and Wellhausen as the men whose acumen and research have carried this inquiry to a point where nothing of importance for the historical study of the Old Testament still remains uncertain."—*Rel. of Semites*, p. vii. There can be "no doubt," says a recent able writer, that "all this part of the Hexateuch is, in its present form, post-exilic."—McFadyen, *Mess. of Historians*. See Note A on Self-Confidence of Critics, p. 240.

even this theory, which we shall have occasion to oppose very decidedly, appears to us to mark an advance. In so far as a documentary hypothesis is to be accepted at all—on which after—it is difficult to resist the conviction that P must be regarded as relatively later than JE, for whose narratives, in Genesis at least, it furnishes the "framework,"[1] and that it is not, as former critics held, a separate older work. In agreement with Graf,[2] however, we do not suppose that *at any period* it ever formed a separate, independent writing.

As supplementing this sketch of the chief stadia in the critical development, a glance may be taken at the views which have been held on the *relation of the elements* of the Pentateuch in the course of this long history. These may be roughly divided into the *fragmentary*, the *supplementary*, and the *documentary*.

(1) At an early stage Vater (1805) and others developed the idea that the Pentateuch was made up, not of continuous documents, but of a great number of smaller *fragments*. This view was vigorously contested, especially with respect to the Book of Genesis, by Stähelin, Ewald (1823), Tuch (1838), etc., as well as by the thoroughgoing defenders of the Mosaic authorship, who, till the middle of the century, formed an influential group.[3] The fragmentist view was regarded as overcome ; but it will be seen as we advance that the newer criticism, with its multiplication of documents (P^1 P^2 P^3 etc.), its substitution of "schools" for individual authors, and its minute tesselation of texts, represents largely a return to it.[4]

(2) The theory which superseded the fragmentary was that of an Elohistic groundwork, or fundamental document (*Grundschrift*), *supplemented* at a later time by Jehovistic additions. This was the view of Bleek, and of most of the above-named writers : later representatives of it are Knobel,

---

[1] Cf. Klostermann, *Pentateuch*, p. 10. On P as "framework," see below, pp. 215, 340.

[2] Graf adhered to this till his death, cf. Kuenen, *Hex.* p. xxx. See below, Chap. X.

[3] The best known names in this conservative school are those of Ranke, Drechsler, Hengstenberg, Hävernick, Keil.

[4] For examples, cf. text and notes in Oxford *Hexateuch*, which hardly leaves a paragraph, verse, or even clause untouched.

Schrader, and Colenso.[1] It was a theory which, granting
its initial assumption, had much to recommend it. Its
advocates based on the fact that the Jehovistic narrative,
as it stands, is incomplete, and presupposes the Elohistic:
e.g., it has no command to build the ark (cf. Gen. vii. 1),
and contains no notices of the deaths of the patriarchs.
"It is still more unmistakable," argued Bleek, "that those
Elohistic portions in the first part of our book refer to one
another, presuppose one another, and follow one another
in due course, whilst they take no notice of the Jehovistic
passages lying between them."[2]   Its opponents reply that it
is impossible that the Jehovist could have filled in passages
which, as they hold, are contradictory of the main narrative.[3]
Hupfeld's theory of the 2nd Elohist weakened this view,
and it fell to the ground altogether when the Graf theory
came to prevail, that P (= the Elohist) was not the earliest,
but the latest, of the sources.

(3) The *documentary* hypothesis—earliest of all—afterwards revived by Hupfeld, rose again to favour, and since
Graf's time has generally been held in the form already
described, viz., JE and P as independent documents, which
have been combined with each other, and with Deuteronomy
(D), by a redactor, or series of redactors.   So stated, the
theory seems simple : its enormous difficulties are only revealed when the attempt is made to work it out in detail.
We advance now to the consideration of these difficulties,
with a view to the attainment of a more positive result.

II. DIFFICULTIES OF THE CRITICAL HYPOTHESIS
IN GENERAL

The course of criticism, we have granted, has been in
a very real sense onward, so far as the discovery of
phenomena is concerned.   As the outcome, the critics are
justified in saying that on certain leading points there is
very general agreement in their ranks.   It is agreed that
four main sources are to be distinguished in the Pentateuch
(or Hexateuch)—J E D P—and that these have been com-

---

[1] Colenso maintained his supplementary theory to the close against
Hupfeld and Kuenen.   See below, p. 334.
[2] *Introd.* i. p. 275.
[3] Cf., *e.g.*, Dillmann, *Genesis*, i. pp. 14, 15 ; Kuenen, *Hex.* p. 160.

bined by one or more hands to form the present work. It is also very generally believed (not, however, by Dillmann), that J and E were combined, if not before the time of Deuteronomy (Kittel, Addis, and others think *after*), at least before their final union with that book (D) and with P. Beyond these very general results,[1] however, it is, as will immediately be seen, highly misleading to speak, as is sometimes done, of unanimity. Agreement in main features of the critical division there is, especially with regard to P, — the original premises being granted, there is little alternative,—but whenever the attempt is made to carry the analysis into details, or to establish a consistent theory of the relations of the documents, or of their mode of combination, divergences wide and deep reveal themselves, complications thicken at every step, and inevitable doubt arises as to the soundness of the premises which lead to such perplexity in the results. Two unimpeachable witnesses may be cited at the outset in general corroboration of what is said as to the absence of unanimity. Kautzsch, the author, with Socin, of one of the best typographical analyses of the Book of Genesis, makes this remarkable statement: "In the Pentateuch and the Book of Joshua, it is only with regard to P that something approaching to unanimity has been reached."[2] Kuenen, again, says with special reference to JE: "As the analysis has been carried gradually further, it has become increasingly evident that the critical question is far more difficult and involved than was at first supposed, and the solutions which seemed to have been secured have been in whole or in part brought into question again."[3] These words might be taken as the text of nearly everything that follows.

1. With every allowance for what may be said of progress, inevitable doubt is awakened in regard to the soundness of the critical process by the *conflicts of opinion* which the

---

[1] Westphal reduces the results on which there is agreement to three: "(1) The existence, henceforth established, of four sources in the Pentateuch: the 1st Elohist, or Priestly Code, the 2nd Elohist, the Jehovist, and the Deuteronomist ; (2) the admission of the fact that each of these sources, before its entrance into the composition of our Biblical books, existed as an independent writing ; (3) the unanimity of scholars as to the manner in which it is necessary to reconstruct, at least in their great lines, the four sources indicated."—*Sources du Pent.* ii. p. xxvi. We shall see that even this statement requires considerable modification.

[2] *Lit. of O.T.*, p. 226.   [3] *Hex.* p. 139.

history of criticism itself discovers. It is to be remembered, in discussing this subject, that the J E D P of the critics—so far as not simply symbols for the supposed documents themselves—with their serial duplicates, to be immediately referred to, and the numerous retinue of redactors, are, though spoken of so familiarly, purely hypothetical entities —postulated beings, of whom history or tradition knows nothing.   Moses, Joshua, Samuel, we know, or think we do; but these shadows have left no trace of themselves, save, if it be so, in their work, now taken to pieces again by the critics.   When we desire to know something more of their time or their relations, we are in a region in which, the history of criticism being witness, the agreements are far overborne by the disagreements.   Do we ask when they lived ? the dates assigned to P (the 1st Elohist), we have found, range from the days of Samuel (Bleek, Colenso, older writers generally), through the period of the kings (Riehm, Dillmann, Nöldeke, Schrader, etc.), to the time of the exile, or later (Graf school).   The dates of JE run from the time of the Judges (König, Köhler, etc.) to the tenth, ninth, eighth centuries, with, in the view of Kuenen, " Judæan editions " after. The composition of Deuteronomy is commonly placed in the reign of Josiah, or of Manasseh ; but many able critics (Delitzsch, Oettli, Klostermann, etc.) hold it to be much older, and in kernel Mosaic ; while others divide it up, and put extensive portions later than Josiah.   Do we inquire as to dependence ?   The older view was, as we saw, that J and E are supplementary to P ; the newer theory is that P is later than JE and presupposes them.   J is held by many (Dillmann, Nöldeke, Schrader, Kittel, etc.) to be dependent on E and to have borrowed from him ; Wellhausen, Kuenen, Stade, etc., as confidently reverse the relation, and make E dependent on J ;[1] others treat the documents as practically independent (*e.g.*, Woods).[2] One set of critics (Dillmann, Riehm, etc.) hold that the marks demonstrate E to be about a century older than J ; the prevailing tendency at present is to make J about a century older than E.   Addis says that this question of priority " is

[1] Wellhausen points out that E "has come down to us only in extracts embodied in the Jehovist narrative," and appears to doubt its independence. *Hist. of Israel*, pp. 7, 8.   See below, p. 217.
[2] Art. "Hexateuch " in *Dict. of Bible*.

still one of the most vexed questions in the criticism of the Hexateuch."[1] The interesting point in the discussion is the cogency with which each critic refutes the reasonings of his neighbours, and shows them to be nugatory. All this would matter little, if it were, as is sometimes said, mere variation on the surface, with slight bearing on the soundness of the theory as a whole. But it is far from that. The criteria which determine these judgments are found on inspection to go deep into the substance of the theory, and afford a valuable practical test of the principles by which it is built up.[2]

2. These perplexities are slight, however, in comparison with those arising from another cause now to be mentioned —the excessive *multiplication of sources.* The matter is relatively simple when we have to deal only with a J E D or P, and when the critic honestly abides by these. But, as the analysis proceeds, we find it impossible to stop here. As the old Ptolemaic astronomer discovered that, to explain the irregularities in the visible motions of the heavenly bodies, he had to add epicycles to his original cycles, then fresh epicycles to these, till his chart became a huge maze of complications—and incredibilities; so the critic finds that the application of the same criteria which guided him in the severance of his main documents, necessitates, when pushed further, a continuance of the process, and the splitting up of the documents into yet minuter parts. Hence new divisions, and the gradual resolution of the original JE, etc., into the nebulous series, $J^1J^2J^3$; $E^1E^2E^3$; $P^1P^2P^3P^4$; $R^1R^2R^3$, etc., or equivalents; all of which have now become part of the recognised apparatus of the critical schools.[3] Can we wonder that

[1] *Hex.* i. p. lxxxi.

[2] *E.g.*, Driver says on the opposite views of Dillmann and Wellhausen about J and E: "The difference turns in part upon a different conception of the limits of J. Dillmann's 'J' embraces more than Wellhausen's 'J' . . . Dillmann's date, *c.* 750, is assigned to J largely on the ground of just those passages which form no part of Wellhausen's J."—*Introd.* p. 123. Kittel, again, upholding Dillmann's view, says: "When Wellhausen finds E to be in closer contact than J with the specially prophetic spirit . . . this arises, at any rate in part, from his altogether peculiar analysis of J; an analysis which, again, is based on this character assigned to J by him."—*Hist. of Hebs.* i. p. 80. Again: "Kuenen will not admit any reference [in Amos and Hosea] to E, but only to J; Dillmann cannot see any acquaintance with J, but only with E. I cannot assent to either view."—*Ibid.* p. 83.

[3] Cf. Oxford *Hexateuch*, or any of the text-books. As a popular book,

even a tolerably advanced critic like Dillmann should write: "with a $Q^1Q^2Q^3$ [= P], $J^1J^2J^3$, $E^1E^2E^3$ I can do nothing, and can only see in them a hypothesis of perplexity." [1] Assume such multiples to have existed, does anyone with a modicum of common sense believe it possible for a twentieth century critic to pick their handiwork to pieces again, and assign to each his proper fragment of the whole? These processional Js and Es, however, should not be scoffed at as arbitrary. They are really indispensable parts of a critical stock-in-trade *if the original principles of the theory are to be consistently carried out*. In that respect they serve again as a test of the value of these principles. The critic thinks he observes, for instance, within the limits of the same document, a discrepancy, or a new turn of expression, or a duplicate incident—the denial of a wife, *e.g.*, in Gen. xii. xxvi., both in J,[2] or a seeming intermingling of two stories—in Korah's rebellion, *e.g.*, in Num. xvi. 2–11, P,[3]—or a reference in J (older writer) to E (younger): what is to be done except to assume that there is here a trace of a distinct source, or of a redactor?[4] The hypothesis is as essential to the critic as his epicycle was to the Ptolemaic star-gazer.

3. The matter becomes still more complicated when, finally, the problematical J E D P lose all individuality, and are frankly transformed, as they are by most of the newer writers, into *schools*.[5] When these "schools" are made to extend over a very long period, as from the statements made, and the work attributed to them, we must suppose them to have done, the problem of maintaining for them the identity of character and style with which the investigation started becomes insoluble. Obviously, if the writers are to be regarded as "schools," it will be impossible, as before, to insist on minute criteria of language, often descending to single words, and the finest *nuances* of expression, as infallible means of distinguishing their several

see Bennett's *Genesis*, Introd. pp. 23, 32, 37, 52, etc. Kuenen has a P[4], with redactors (*Hex.* pp. 86 ff.).

[1] Pref. to *Exod.-Lev.*   [2] Cf. Oxford *Hexateuch*, ii. p. 19.

[3] *Ibid.* p. 212. Cf. Dillmann, *in loc.* See below, p. 358.

[4] For a longer example, see Note B on Cornill's Decomposition of J, and compare in full Cornill's *Einleitung*, pp. 52–53.

[5] See Note C on the Views of J and E, etc., as "Schools." See also below on P, Chap. X p. 335.

contributions. It is possible to argue, however unreasonably, that an individual author must be rigidly bound down to one style, one set of phrases, one idea or circle of ideas ; but this will hardly apply to "schools," lasting for centuries, where, within the limits of a general tradition, there must, with difference of minds, inevitably be wide diversities of culture, thought, and speech. We may properly speak, *e.g.*, of an "Anglican," a "Ritschlian," or a "Cobdenite" school, and may mark how in each the influence of dominant ideas stamps a general resemblance on the style and speech of the members, but none the less individual idiosyncrasies will assert themselves in each writer. If, further, the writers are to be regarded as "schools," the question of date assumes a new aspect. How far may or do these "schools" go back? Why must J and E be any longer forced down to the ninth or eighth century?"[1] Why must the priestly narratives be of the same age as the priestly laws? Delitzsch was of opinion that "the literary activity of the Elohistic pen reaches far back to ancient times nearly approaching the time of Moses."[2] Why, on this hypothesis should it not be so?

There is, one cannot help feeling, something essentially mechanical in this idea of "schools" of writers continuously engaged for centuries in patching, revising, tesselating, resetting, altering and embellishing, the work of their predecessors. We are here back, in fact, by another route, and under another name, to the old "fragmentary" hypothesis, thought so long ago to have been exploded.[3] But the striking thing about the labours of these manifold unknowns is that the product shows so little trace of this excessive fragmentariness of its origin. The Pentateuch— pre-eminently the Book of Genesis, but even the legal part[4] —is undeniably a well-planned, massively-compacted work. Apart from the "firmly-knit" character of its story, it is marked by a unity of thought and spirit, is pervaded by

---

[1] Carpenter allows that the question of the date of J (so of the others) has become "increasingly complex" under the influence of this new idea (*Hex.* i. p. 106).

[2] *Genesis*, p. 49.

[3] Carpenter says with reference to this newer theory of "schools": "This was the truth that lay behind the fragment-hypothesis of the older criticism : is it possible to re-state it in more suitable form ?"—*Hex.* i. p. 108.

[4] See below, pp. 294, 325-26.

great ideas, is instinct with a living purpose, as **no other book** is. Its organic character bespeaks for it **a higher origin** than a concourse of literary atoms.[1]

III. SPECIAL PROBLEMS OF JE: PLACE OF ORIGIN AND EXTENT

It is now necessary, in order that the value of the current critical theories may be thoroughly tested, to investigate the analysis and other questions connected with the different documents more in detail; and first we consider *the problems involved in the relations of J and E.* These problems, in our view, all converge ultimately into one—Are the critics right in distinguishing two documents at all? To set this question in its proper light, and reveal more clearly the serious differences that emerge on fundamental points, it will be advisable to look, first, at the views entertained as to the *place of origin* of the assumed documents, and as to their *extent.* Some hint of the range of these differences has already been given.

1. Much light is cast on critical procedure by observing the methods employed to determine *the place of origin* of the documents, with the implications as to their *age.* We saw before that it has become customary to take for granted, though without real proof,[2] that J and E first originated, the one (*which* one is in dispute) in the ninth century, the other about the middle of the eighth century B.C. It is also very generally held, and is confidently stated, that E was a native of the Northern Kingdom, while J, probably, was a native of the Southern, or Judæan Kingdom.[3] The chief reasons given for localising E in Ephraim are his peculiar interest in the sacred places of Northern Israel (Bethel, Shechem, etc.), his exaltation of the house of Joseph, and his preference in the story of Joseph for Ephraim over Judah. How shadowy and assumptive all this is, and how inadequate as a ground of separation of the documents, will be evident from the following considerations :—

(1) In the first place, there are eminent critics (*e.g.,*

---

[1] See further in Chap. X.

[2] See above, p. 73.

[3] Cf. Dillmann, Driver ("*relatively* probable," *Introd.* p. 123), Addis, Carpenter, etc.

Schrader, Reuss, Kuenen, Kautzsch), who *place J also in Northern Israel*, and for precisely the same reason of his supposed interest in Ephraimitic shrines.[1] The two writings, therefore, it may be concluded, cannot really stand far apart in this respect. Kautzsch, *e.g.*, thinks it inconceivable " that a Judahite, at a time when the temple of Solomon was already in existence [note the assumption on date], brought the sanctity of Shechem, Bethel, and Peniel into the prominence they have at Gen. xii. 6, xxviii. 13 ff., and xxxii. 30 ff." [2] Yet the Judæan origin of J is one of the things which Dillmann, among others, regards as " demonstrable with certainty." [3]

(2) In the next place, the whole reasoning proceeds on the assumption that the writings are as late as the ninth or eighth century, and that the *motive* for recording the movements and residences of the patriarchs is to glorify existing sacred places, or exalt one branch of the divided kingdom above the other. The *naïveté* of the narratives might save them from this charge of " tendency," which has really nothing tangible to support it. There is no trace of the divided kingdom,[4] or of partiality for one side or the other, in the patriarchal narratives. The history of Joseph is recorded with fulness and freshness by *both* writers. Gunkel takes strong ground on this point. " There can," he says, " be no talk of a party-tendency in the two collections for the North or for the South Kingdom: they are too faithful." [5] Even Kuenen writes: " It would be incorrect to say that the narratives in Genesis exalt Joseph at the expense of his brothers, and are unfriendly to Judah. This

---

[1] " The data," says Carpenter, " do not appear to be decisive, and each possibility finds eminent advocates. . . . Critical judgment has consequently been much divided."—*Hex.* i. pp. 104–5. Hommel also places J in Northern Israel (*Anc. Heb. Trad.* pp. 289–90).

[2] *Lit. of O.T.*, p. 38. Kittel also thinks it " *impossible* to assert that J originated in Northern Israel " (p. 85). Kautzsch and Kuenen explain recalcitrant phenomena by the hypothesis of a later Judæan redaction (which Kittel rejects, i. p. 85).

[3] *Genesis*, p. 10.

[4] Cf. Gunkel, *Genesis*, p. lx, and see above, p. 111. The older writers justly laid stress on this in evidence of date (*e.g.*, Bleek, *Introd.* pp. 291 ff., 298 ff.). It is curious how little stress, for different reasons, critics are disposed to lay on the one passage which might be regarded as an exception —the reference to the subjection of Edom in Gen. xxvii. 40. De Wette urged this as proof of a late date, but the inference is rejected by Bleek, Kittel (i. p. 88), Kautzsch (*Lit.* p. 39), etc.

[5] *Genesis*, p. lx.

14

would contradict their ever present idea that all the tribes **have** sprung from a single father, and on the strength of this common descent are a single people. . . . Neither J nor E takes sides with any one of the tribes, or specifically for or against Joseph or Judah; for both alike occupy the Israelitish position, in the widest sense of the word."[1]   The real reason why the sojournings of the patriarchs are followed with such interest in J and E is simply that, in the old Israelitish tradition, Hebron, Beersheba, Bethel, Shechem, were *believed to be the real spots* where these patriarchs dwelt, and built their altars.[2]

(3) When, further, we look into the narratives, we *do not find, in fact, that they bear out this idea* of a special favouritism in E for localities in the North, and in J for places in the South.   Addis remarks on J's "large-hearted interest in the myths (?) and sacred places both of Northern Israel and of Judah."[3]   Abraham's home in J is at Hebron, but his first altar is built near Bethel.[4]   Latterly, in both J and E, he lives at Beersheba (in South).[5]   Isaac also, in both sources, lives at Beersheba.   J narrates the vision of Jacob at Bethel (with E),[6] his wrestling with the angel at Peniel,[7] his residence at Shechem (with E and P),[8] etc.   E also has his stories about Bethel, Shechem, and Beersheba, but he records Jacob's residence in "the vale of Hebron" (South),[9] as, earlier, he had shared in the story of the offering of Isaac on Mount Moriah.[10]   As little are we disposed to

---

[1] *Hex.* pp. 230–32.   He thinks he finds significance, however, in the fact that Joseph was "crowned" of his brethren, etc.

[2] "In weighing these accounts," says Kuenen, "for our present purpose, we must remember that the writers were not free to choose whatever spots they liked.   Hebron was Abraham's 'territorial cradle,' and Beersheba Isaac's.   It needs no explanation or justification, therefore, when they make the two patriarchs dwell respectively in these two places"; but, he adds, "we have to give some account of why Abraham is transplanted to Beersheba."—*Hex.* p. 231.   But why? if, as both J and E declare, he actually went there?   The lives of Abraham and Isaac were mainly spent in the South, that of Jacob in the middle of Palestine.

[3] *Hex.* i. p. liv.   [4] Gen. xii. 8.   [5] Gen. xxi. 33 ; xxii. 19.
[6] Gen. xxviii. 10 ff.   [7] Gen. xxxii. 24 ff.   [8] Gen. xxxiv.
[9] Gen xxxvii. 14.   Though it is clear from the context that Jacob's home was not at Shechem (vers. 12, 13), yet simply on the ground that it mentions Hebron, this verse is treated by Kuenen, with others, as an interpolation (*Hex.* pp. 230, 231).   Carpenter says flatly: "Of Hebron, which belonged peculiarly to Judah, no notice is taken."—*Hex.* i. p. 116.
[10] Gen. xxii.

trust the critic's "feeling" for an "Ephraimitic tinge" in E,
when we find, *e.g.*, one authority on this "tinge" (Kautzsch)
declaring that "it [E] no longer conveys the impression
of a triumphant outlook on a glorious future, but rather
that of a retrospect on a bygone history, in which were
many gloomy experiences;"[1] and another (Kittel) assuring
us that "the whole tone of E bears witness to a certain
satisfaction of the national consciousness, and joy over what
has been won."[2]

(4) Finally, if anything were lacking to destroy our
confidence in this theory of tendencies of J and E, it would
be supplied by the *interpretations* that are given of particular
incidents in the narrative. It strains our faith to breaking-
point to be asked to believe that the interest of a prophetic
writer like E, of the days of Amos and Hosea, in Bethel and
Beersheba, arose from the fact that these places were the
then famous centres of (idolatrous) worship (cf. Amos
v. 5; viii. 14; Hos. iv. 15);[3] or that Gen. xxviii. 22 is
intended to explain and sanction the custom of paying
tithes at the calf-shrine at Bethel;[4] or that Hebron was
preferred as Abraham's residence because it was "the
ancient Judæan capital" (Kittel),[5] or had become "the
great *Judaic* sanctuary" (Driver).[6] In the view of one set
of critics, Gen. xxxviii. is a bitter mockery of Judah (J
therefore is Northern);[7] according to another, it is a tribal
history written expressly to *favour* Judah (J therefore is
Southern).[8] Kautzsch is of opinion that "at Ex. xxxii.
1 ff. there is in all probability a Judahite condemnation of
the Ephraimite bull-worship";[9] others see in the narrative
an *Ephraimitic* condemnation of the same practice;[10] Kuenen
thinks it glances at a claim of the Northern priests to a

[1] *Lit. of O.T.*, p. 44. [2] *Hist. of Hebs.* i. p. 88.
[3] Carpenter, *Hex.* i. p. 116 ; cf. Driver, *Introd.* p. 118.
[4] Driver, *ibid.* p. 122 ; Dillmann, Kittel, Bennett, etc. See above, p. 135.
What of *J's* motive in the references to Bethel and Beersheba?
[5] *Hist.* i. p. 83. [6] *Introd.* p. 118.
[7] Thus Reuss, Schrader, Renan, etc.
[8] Thus Kittel (i. p. 83), etc. Cf. Kuenen, *Hex.* p. 232 : Westphal,
Sources, ii. p. 259 ; Carpenter, *Hex.* i. p. 105.
[9] *Lit. of O.T.*, p. 38.
[10] Dillmann thinks a North Israelite could not have framed this protest against Jeroboam's bull-worship (*Exod.-Lev.* p. 332); Kittel differs
(i. p. 89). It should be noticed that Kautzsch, Dillmann, Kittel, etc.,
ascribe the main story in Ex. xxxii. to J ; others, as Westphal, as
confidently give it to E.

descent from Aaron.[1] So *ad libitum*. When one remembers that it is chiefly on the ground of these supposed
" mirrorings " of later events that the narratives are placed
where they are in date,[2] one begins to see the precariousness
of this part of the critical structure. Thus far nothing has
been established as to place or time of origin, or distinct
authorship of the documents.

2. A second problem of much importance in its
bearings on the possibility of a critical distinction of J and
E is that of the *extent* of the supposed documents. The
consideration of Genesis may be reserved. There is agreement that the J narrative in Genesis begins with chap. ii.
3*b*, and, in union with other sources, continues throughout
the book, and into Exodus. E, on the other hand, though
some find traces of its presence earlier,[3] is understood to
enter clearly first in chap. xx. With Exodus iii., the
criterion of the divine names fails, after which it is allowed,
on all hands, that the discrimination is exceedingly difficult,
and often impossible. In the words of Addis, " In other
books of the Hexateuch [after Genesis] the Jahvist and
the Elohist are rather fused than pieced together, and
discrimination between the two documents is often impossible." [4] In their union, however, it is commonly agreed
that the presence of the two documents can be traced, not
only through Exodus and Numbers (in small measure in
Deuteronomy) but through Joshua—that Joshua, in fact,
is an integral part of the total work now called the
" Hexateuch." The validity of this conclusion will occupy
us immediately.

Beyond this rises another question, now keenly exercising
the minds of scholars, viz., whether there must not be

[1] *Hex.* p. 245 ; cf. Van Hoonacker, *Le Sacerdoce*, p. 136. See above,
p. 122.

[2] Cf. Carpenter, *Hex.* i. p. 107 ; Kuenen, *Hex.* p. 226. See above,
p. 74 ; also Gunkel, *Genesis*, p. lxii.

[3] See below, p. 217.

[4] *Hex.* i. p. xxxi. McFadyen says similarly : " After Ex. vi. it is
seldom possible to distinguish with much confidence between the Jehovist
and the Elohist, as they have so much in common."—*Mess. of Historians*,
p. 18.   The impossibility is owned by critics (as Kautzsch and Socin) in
considerable parts of Genesis as well. Strack says generally : " Since J and
E are on the whole (*im Grossen und Ganzen*) similar to one another, it is
often no longer possible to separate what originally belongs to E and what
originally belongs to J."—*Die Bücher Genesis, etc.* (" Handkommentar,"
i., ii.), *Introd.* p. xviii.

recognised a still further continuation of these documents—J and E—into the Books of Judges, Samuel, and even Kings. Such a possibility was early hinted at,[1] but the newer tendency to resolve J and E into "schools" has led to a revival of the idea,[2] and to its adoption by many critical scholars. Cornill and Budde have no doubt about it; Moore adopts it in his Commentary on Judges; Westphal goes so far as to make it a chief ground in his determination of the dates of the documents.[3] E.g., Cornill discerns J in 1 Kings "with perfect certainty";[4] the traces of E, he thinks, are slight after the story of the death of Saul. These conclusions, with good reason, do not commend themselves to other scholars, so that the camp remains here also divided.[5] The hypothesis has a value as showing the precarious grounds on which writers often build their critical "certainties."

Returning to Joshua, we may briefly test the assertion that the J and E documents are continued into this book, and that Joshua forms with the Pentateuch a single larger work. The question of "Pentateuch" or "Hexateuch" need not be discussed at length; we touch on it only as far as relates to our subject. Addis, however, speaks far too strongly when he declares that the unity of Joshua with the other five books "is acknowledged by all who admit the composite character of the Pentateuch."[6] This is by no means the case. Even Cornill says: "Many now speak of a Hexateuch. Joshua, nevertheless, presents an essentially different literary physiognomy from that of the Pentateuch, so that it appears to me more correct to treat the latter by itself, and the Book of Joshua as an appendix to it."[7] There are, in fact, tolerably strong indications of a tendency among recent critics to separate Joshua again from the Pentateuch, and regard it as a more or less

[1] Gramberg (1830); Schrader (1869).

[2] Cf. Westphal on the views of Ed. Meyer (1884) and Bruston (1885) in *Sources du Pent.* ii. pp. 255 ff. Stade thought he discovered traces of E in above works; Böhme traces of J, etc.

[3] *Sources*, ii. p. 256.

[4] *Einleitung*, pp. 117, 121.

[5] Kittel acutely criticised the theory in *Stud. und Krit.* 1891 (pp. 44 ff.); cf. his *Hist.* ii. pp. 16 ff. Kuenen, Kautzsch (*Lit. of O.T.*, pp. 27, 237–39). Driver (*Introd.* pp. 171, 184), König, H. P. Smith (*Samuel*, p. xxii), etc., reject it.

[6] *Hex.* pp. xiv, xxxi.   [7] *Einleit.* p. 86.

independent work.[1] For such a view also there are many
cogent grounds. Cornill gives as one reason that the
sources are quite differently worked up in the Book of
Joshua from what they are elsewhere. In the narrative
portions they are fused together so as to be ordinarily
inseparable. The language, too, presents peculiarities.
Even in the P parts, as will be seen immediately, it is
doubtful if the sections are from the same hand or hands
as in the other books. The book has, also, according to the
critics, been subjected to a Deuteronomic revision,[2] which,
curiously, was not extended (or only slightly) to the earlier
books.[3]

It is beyond doubt, at least, that, in the separation of
the sources in Joshua, the critics continually find themselves involved in inextricable difficulties. With respect
particularly to J and E, it has become not simply a
question of whether J and E can be severed (admittedly
they can not), but *of whether J and E are present in the
book at all.* Wellhausen came to the conclusion that J was
wholly absent,[4] and Steuernagel more recently has affirmed
the same opinion.[5] "The original scope and significance
of E" are admitted by Carpenter to be "hardly less
difficult to determine."[6] The high-water mark of his

[1] Cf. the views of Wellhausen, *Compos. d. Hex.* pp. 116–17 ; Carpenter,
Hex. i. pp. 178–79 ; Bennett, *Primer of Bible,* p. 90 ; cf. his *Joshua*
("Polychrome Bible"), p. 44 : "Perhaps the Joshua sections of JED and
P were separated from the preceding sections before the latter were
combined to form the Pentateuch" (or perhaps never formed part of them).

[2] That is, if "revision" is the proper word, and not rather "invention."
If, *e.g.,* the incident of the reading of the law on Mount Ebal in Josh. viii.
30–35 did not happen, it was simply invention on the basis of Deut. xxvii.
The Deuteronomic reviser is called D² to distinguish him from the author
of Deuteronomy (D¹). He belongs to the D "school," and writes a
similar style.

[3] On supposed Deuteronomic traces in the earlier books, see below,
pp. 254–55.

[4] *Comp. d. Hex.* p. 116. Kittel's view of the matter is: "The comparatively few traces which point at all decisively to J frequently allow of
the assumption that they have no longer precisely the same form as when
they came from the author's pen. E is in almost the same case : of this
source, too, there are only a few remnants in the Book of Joshua."—*Hist.
of Hebs.* i. p. 263.

[5] Carpenter notes that Steuernagel's *Das Buch Josua* invites comment,
"for his results vary very widely from those already set forth. . . . In
regard to J, Steuernagel returns to the view of Wellhausen and Meyer that
it recognised no Joshua," etc.—*Hex.* ii. p. 318. Thus theories chase each
other like clouds in the sky.

[6] *Ibid.* ii. p. 308.

assurance is reached in the statement: "Budde, Kittel, Albers, and Bennett have all concurred in believing that the main elements of J and E *are not disguised beyond recognition*, though their results do not always run side by side."[1] The separation of the P sections in Joshua at first sight seems easier, but in detail the difficulties are nearly as insuperable, and of a kind that set theorising at defiance. "The inquiry" (as to "the relation of the P sections to the rest of the book"), Carpenter admits, "is full of difficulty, and the seemingly conflicting facts have been differently interpreted in different critical schools."[2] The language, as already said, is markedly different. "In chaps. i.-xii., xxiii., xxiv.," says Professor Bennett, "there are only a few short paragraphs and sentences in the style of P, and most of these are rather due to an editor than derived from the Priestly Code."[3] Still more instructive is the fact, pointed out by Professor G. A. Smith, that "in the Book of Joshua P does not occupy the regulative position, nor supply the framework, as it does in the Pentateuch."[4] As Wellhausen puts it: "Without a preceding history of the conquest, these [P] sections are quite in the air: they cannot be taken as telling a continuous story of their own, but presuppose the Jehovistic-Deuteronomic work. . . . We have already shown that the Priestly Code in Joshua is simply the filling up of the Jehovistic-Deuteronomic narrative."[5] As interesting illustrations of the stylistic perplexities, reference may be made to the two important chapters—xxii. and xxiv. The phraseology in chap. xxii. 9–34, "is in the main that of P," says Dr. Driver ("almost a cento of P's phrases," says

---

[1] *Hex.* ii. p. 306 (italics ours).

[2] *Ibid.* p. 315. *E.g.*, "If xvi. 1–3 is rightly assigned to J, a probability is established that it may have contained other geographical descriptions, now perhaps absorbed into P's more detailed survey. But it appears to be beyond the power of any critical method to discover the clues to their separation" (pp. 307–8).

[3] *Primer*, p. 90. The P sections, Carpenter says, "show several curious features, and doubts have consequently been expressed concerning their original character (*e.g.*, by Wellhausen)."—*Hex.* i. p. 178.

[4] Art. "Joshua" in *Dict. of Bible*, ii. p. 784. Similarly Bennett says: "In the Pentateuch P is used as framework; in Joshua JED."—*Book of Joshua* ("Polychrome Bible"), p. 45.

[5] *Hist. of Israel*, pp. 357, 385. As shown later (Chap. X.), Wellhausen regards the "main stock" of the Priestly narrative as ceasing with the death of Moses.

Carpenter), "but the narrative does not display throughout the characteristic style of P, and in some parts of it there occur expressions which are not those of P." He proceeds: "Either a narrative of P has been combined with elements from another source in a manner which makes it difficult to effect a satisfactory analysis, or the whole is the work of a distinct writer, whose phraseology is in part that of P, but not entirely."[1] Wellhausen, on the other hand, thinks it is P's wholly (but not the P of the earlier books). Addis, with Kuenen, assumes that "it is a late production in the school and after the manner of P."[2] Chap. xxiv., in turn, is assigned generally to E; yet, says Dr. Driver, "it might almost be said to be written from a standpoint approaching (in this respect) that of D²."[3] Addis assumes a Deuteronomic revision, and abundant interpolation.[4] What, one is tempted to ask, can such criteria avail?

Not much support, we think it will be felt, is to be got from the Book of Joshua for an original distinction of J and E—if for their existence in that book at all. When it is added that the Samaritans seem from the beginning to have had, in Buhl's words, "outside of the Canon an independent reproduction of the Book of Joshua,"[5] it may be realised that the reasons for affirming a "*Hex*ateuch" are not so conclusive as is generally assumed.

IV. ARE J AND E TWO OR ONE? DIFFICULTIES OF SEPARATION

The decisive grounds for the separation of J and E must be sought for, if anywhere, in the Book of Genesis, where the divine names are still distinguished. It is important

---

[1] *Introd.* pp. 112-13.   [2] *Hex.* ii. p. 473.   [3] *Introd.* p. 115.
[4] *Hex.* i. p. 233. It is a curious observation of Carpenter's that "the Deuteronomic editors of the national histories during the exile were contemporary with the priestly schools of Ezekiel and his successors, and some interchange of phraseology would be only natural" (this to account for occasional appearances of P in D passages). — *Hex.* ii. p. 315. It is interesting to see how the theory of JED and P schools extending into the exile tends to work round to a theory of *contemporary* authorship for much of the matter. But may not the same thing be assumed for *early* co-operation in the production of the book? See below, pp. 375-6.
[5] *Canon of O.T.*, p. 41. On the historicity of Joshua, see **Appendix to chapter.**

for the purpose of our inquiry here to remember how the discrimination of J and E was originally brought about. It will be recalled[1] that, till the time of Hupfeld, E was commonly regarded as an integral part of P—a proof that, notwithstanding their differences, even these documents are not so far apart as many suppose.[2] Then E was separated from P on the ground of its greater literary affinities with J, and, not unnaturally, in view of the difference in the divine names, continued to be regarded as a distinct writing from the latter. Now the question recurs—Is it really distinct? The only actually weighty ground for the distinction is the difference of usage in the names, and that peculiarity must be considered by itself. Apart from this it is our purpose to show that the strongest reasons speak for the *unity* of the documents, while the hypothesis of distinction is loaded with improbabilities which amount, in the sum, well-nigh to impossibilities.

1. In the first place, then, there is no clear proof that E ever *did* exist as a continuous independent document. It has a broken, intermittent character, which excites doubts, even in Wellhausen.[3] Roughly, after Gen. xx.–xxi., where the document is supposed abruptly to enter,[4] we have only fragments till chap. xxxi., then again broken pieces till

[1] See above, p. 196.
[2] Bleek, Cave, Lange, Perowne, etc., retained the older view. An interesting series of equations might be drawn up along this line, based on the axiom that things that are equal to the same thing are equal to one another, weakening somewhat the force of the ordinary documentary theory. If, *e.g.*, E resembles P sufficiently to have been regarded by most critics till Hupfeld, and by many since, as part of P, and E is at the same time practically indistinguishable stylistically from J, an obvious conclusion follows as to the relations of J and P. So in other places approximations may be shown to exist between E and D, D and J, and even between JE and P, D and P. See below, pp. 253 ff.
[3] Wellhausen says: "Not merely is the Elohist in his matter and in his manner of looking at things most closely akin to the Jehovist; his document has come down to us, as Nöldeke was the first to perceive, only in extracts embodied in the Jehovist narrative." And, in a note: "What Kuenen points out is, that certain elements assigned by me to the Elohist are not fragments of a once independent whole, but interpolated and parasitic additions. What effect this demonstration may have on the judgment we form of the Elohist himself is as yet uncertain."—*Hist. of Israel*, pp. 7, 8.
[4] Traces of E are thought by some to be found in chap. xv. (Wellhausen, Dillmann, etc.). Dillmann would attribute to E part of the material in chaps. iv. (17 ff.); vi. (1–4) and xiv.; but he is not generally followed in this. Cf. Kuenen, *Hex.* p. 149.

chaps. xl.–xlii., in the life of Joseph, and a few portions there-after, chiefly in chaps. xlv. and l.[1]

2. Next, doubt, and more than doubt, is awakened by the *thoroughly parallel* character of the narratives. As was shown at an earlier stage,[2] the two supposed documents are similar in character, largely parallel in matter, and, as proved by their complete interfusion in many places, must often have been nearly verbally identical. A few testimonies on this important point may not be out of place.

"In the main," says Wellhausen, "JE is a composition out of these two parallel books of history," adding, "We see how uncommonly similar these two history books must have been."[3]

"The two books," says Addis, "evidently proceeded in parallel lines of narrative, and it is often hard—nay impossible—to say whether a particular section of the Hexateuch belongs to the Jahvist or the Elohist."[4] "Two accounts of Joseph's history, closely parallel on the whole, but discordant in important details (?)[5] have been mingled together."[6]

"It [JE]," says Kautzsch, "must have run in almost unbroken parallelism with the Jahwist in the patriarchal histories, the history of the Exodus, and of the conquest of Canaan."[7]

"In the history of the patriarchs," says Dillmann, "especially in that of Jacob and Joseph, it [E] shows itself most closely related to [J]; so much so that most of its narratives from chap. xxvii. onwards have their perfect parallels in [J]."[8]

After this, it does not surprise us that an able scholar like Klostermann—at one time a supporter of the usual critical hypothesis—was so impressed with the similar character and close relation of these "throughout parallel" narratives as to be led to break with the current theory

[1] Colenso, so far as he accepted Hupfeld's E, did not regard it as independent, but identified it with J. See above, p. 199.

[2] See above, p. 71.

[3] *Comp. d. Hex.* p. 22. It has already been seen that Wellhausen extends this parallel, as regards matter, to P (*Hist. of Israel*, pp. 295, 318). Cf. above, p. 107 ; but specially see below, pp. 344 ff.

[4] *Hex.* p. liii.   [5] See below, p. 237.   [6] *Hex.* p xlix.

[7] *Lit. of O.T.*, p. 43.

[8] *Genesis*, p. 11. In a similar strain Driver, König, Strack, Gunkel, etc.

altogether, and to recast his whole view of the origin of the Pentateuch.[1]

3. Again, the marked *stylistic resemblance* of J and E speaks strongly against their being regarded as separate documents. On this point it may be sufficient at present to quote Dr. Driver. "Indeed," he says, "stylistic criteria alone would not generally suffice to distinguish J and E; though, when the distinction has been effected by other means, slight differences of style appear to disclose themselves."[2] *How* slight they are will be afterwards seen.

4. The force of these considerations is greatly enhanced when we observe the *intimate fusion* and *close interrelations* of the documents, and the impossibility of separating them without *complete disintegration* of the narrative. The facts here, as elsewhere, are not disputed.[3] "The mutual relation of J and E," Kuenen confesses, "is one of the most vexed questions of the criticism of the Pentateuch."[4] "It must," he says again, "be admitted that the resemblance between E and the narratives now united with it is sometimes bewilderingly close, so that when the use of Elohim does not put us on the track, we are almost at a loss for means of carrying the analysis through."[5] "There is much difference of opinion," acknowledges Addis, "on the contents of J and E considered separately: the problem becomes more difficult when we pass beyond Genesis to the later books of the Hexateuch, and to a great extent the problem may prove insoluble."[6] The close interrelation of the several narratives is not less perplexing. This interrelation appears all through—*e.g.*, the very first words of Gen. xx., "And Abraham journeyed *from thence*," connect with the preceding narrative; the difficulties of chap. xxi. 1–7 (birth of Isaac), in which J, E, and P are concerned, can only be got over by the assumption that "all three sources, J, E,

---

[1] Cf. his *Der Pentateuch*, pp. 10, 52–53. On Klostermann, see further below, pp. 227–29, 345.

[2] *Introd.* p. 126 ; cf. p. 13 : "Other phraseological criteria (besides the names) are slight." Cf. Colenso, quoted above, p.199 ; and Hupfeld, below, p. 234. Dr. Driver himself speaks on the duality of the documents with considerable reserve, though "he must own that he has always risen from the study of JE with the conviction that it is *composite*" (p. 116).

[3] The notes to Kautzsch and Socin's analysis of *Genesis* are here very instructive.

[4] *Hex.* p. 64.   [5] *Ibid* p. 144.   [6] *Hex.* p. xxxiv.

and P seem to have contained the account of the birth
of Isaac " [1]—but it is at its maximum in the history of
Joseph.[2] Illustrations will occur as we proceed.[3] The usual
way of dealing with these difficulties is by assuming that
sections in J parallel to E, and sections in E parallel to J,
once existed (so of P), but were omitted in the combined
work. This, if established, would immensely strengthen the
proof of parallelism—would, in fact, practically do away with
the necessity for assuming the existence of two histories; but
the hypothesis, to the extent required, is incapable of proof,
and its assumption only complicates further an already too
complicated problem.[4]

5. Finally, the argument for unity is confirmed by the
violent expedients which are found necessary to make the
opposite hypothesis workable. We have specially in view
here the place given, and the functions ascribed, to that
convenient, but most unsatisfactory, appendage of the critical
theory — the *Redactor*. The behaviour of this remarkable individual—or series of individuals (R[1], R[2], R[3], etc.)—
is one of the most puzzling features in the whole case. At
times he (R) puts his sections side by side, or alternates
them, with little alteration; again he weaves them
together into the most complicated literary webs; yet again
he "works them up" till the separate existence of the
documents is lost in the blend.[5] At one time, as Klostermann says, he shows an almost "demonic art"[6] in combining and relating; at another, an incapacity verging on
imbecility. At one moment he is phenomenally alert in
smoothing out difficulties, correcting mistakes, and inter-
polating harmonistic clauses; at another, he leaves the
most glaring contradictions, in the critics' view, to stand

---

[1] Oxf. *Hex.* ii. p. 29 ; see below, p. 352.

[2] Cf. Addis and Dillmann above.

[3] Cf., *e.g.*, on the analysis of Gen. xxii. and Gen. xxviii. 10. ff., below,
pp. 234–35.

[4] Cf. below, Chap. X. pp. 343, 348–9, 362.

[5] It is customary to speak of the Hebrew writers as if they were
scrupulously careful simply to *reproduce* the material at their disposal—
combining, re-arranging, but not *re-writing*. That, if the critics are right,
can only be accepted with much qualification. P, on Wellhausen's theory,
must have re-written the history. According to Kuenen, the "legends"
have "been worked up in one way by one writer and another by another
. . . so often as to be notably modified, or even completely transformed.—
Hex. p. 38 (on the process in Joshua, cf. p. 158).

[6] *Pentateuch*, p. 36.

side by side. Now he copies J's style, now D's, now P's.[1]
A serviceable, but somewhat unaccountable personage!

V. THE PROBLEM OF THE DIVINE NAMES IN J AND E

The *crux* of the question of the distinction of documents
lies, it will be admitted, in the use of the divine names in
Genesis, and this problem, so far as it concerns J and E—
P stands on a somewhat different basis [2] — must now
seriously engage our attention.

1. The first thing to be done is to *ascertain the facts*,
and here, once more, we believe, it will be found that
the case is not quite so simple as it is ordinarily represented
to be. The broad statement is not to be questioned that
there are certain sections in the narrative attributed to
JE in which the divine name "Jehovah" is preponder-
atingly used, and certain other sections in which the name
"Elohim" (God) is chiefly used. It is this which constitutes
the problem. We must beware, however, of exaggeration
even here. When, *e.g.*, Dr. Driver says that in the
narrative, Gen. xii. 10-20, "the term Jehovah is uniformly
employed," [3] it would not readily occur to the reader that
"uniformly" in this instance means *only once*. The truth
is, as we soon discover, that *no absolute rule about the use of
the names can be laid down.* Even eliminating those
instances in which the "redactor" is invoked to interpolate
and alter, there remains a not inconsiderable number of cases
to show that the presence of the divine names is not an
infallible test. Kuenen himself says—and the admission
is striking—"The history of critical investigation has shown
that far too much weight has often been laid on agreement
in the use of the divine names [it is the pillar of the whole
hypothesis]. . . . It is well, therefore, to utter a warning
against laying an exaggerated stress on this one
phenomenon." [4] There are grounds for this warning.

(1) There can be no doubt whatever that the name
"Elohim" is sometimes found *in J passages*. In the
narrative of the temptation in Gen. iii. (J), *e.g.*, the name

---

[1] Cf. Dillmann, *Genesis*, p. 21 : "The redactor R often writes the language
of A [=P]," etc. See later on "imitations" of D, P, etc.
[2] See below, p. 226. [3] *Introd.* p. 13 ; *Genesis*, p. xi.
[4] *Hex.* p. 61.

"Jehovah" is not put into the mouth of the serpent, but, instead, the name "Elohim":[1] "Yea, hath Elohim said," etc. Similarly, in the story of Hagar's flight (J), the handmaid is made to say: "Thou Elohim seest me."[2] In such cases one can easily see that a principle is involved. In the story of the wrestling at Peniel, again, in Gen. xxxii. (J), we have "Elohim" in vers. 28, 29. In the life of Joseph, Gen. xxxix. is assigned by Dillmann, Kuenen, Kautzsch, and most to J (as against Wellhausen), despite its "linguistic suggestions" of E, and the occurrence of "Elohim" in ver. 9; and Kuenen writes of other passages: "*Elohim* in chaps. xliii. 29, xliv. 16, is no evidence for E, since Joseph speaks and is spoken to as a heathen until chap. xlv."[3]

(2) Examples of the converse case of *the use of Jehovah by E* are not so numerous, but such occasionally occur. Addis, indeed, says roundly: "The Elohist . . . always speaks of Elohim and never of Yahweh, till he relates the theophany in the burning bush."[4] But Dr. Driver states the facts more cautiously and correctly. "E," he says, "prefers *God* (though not exclusively), and *Angel of God*, where J prefers *Jehovah* and *Angel of Jehovah*."[5] *E.g.*, in Gen. xxii. 1–14 (E) "Angel of Jehovah" occurs in ver. 11, and "Jehovah" twice in ver. 14. Similarly, in Gen. xxviii. 17–22 (E), Jacob says: "Then shall Jehovah be my God."[6] When the use of the divine names is taken from the former exclusive ground, and reduced to a "preference," it is obvious that new possibilities are opened. We ask that it be noted further that isolated Elohistic sections occur *after* Ex. iii.,[7] *e.g.*, in Ex. xiii. 17–19, xviii. —a singular fact to be afterwards considered.

(3) We would call attention, lastly, to the lengths which criticism is prepared to go in acknowledging the principle of *discrimination* in the use of the divine names. Kuenen, with his usual candour from his own point of

---

[1] Gen. iii. 1, 3, 5.　　　　[2] Gen. xvi. 13.

[3] *Hex.* pp. 145–46.　　　　[4] *Hex.* i. p. liv. Thus most critics.

[5] *Genesis*, p. xiii. Cf. *Introd.* p. 13.

[6] Ver. 21. A redactor is here brought in, as elsewhere, but unwarrantably. What caprice should lead a redactor to change these particular expressions, when so many others are left untouched?

[7] But note the use of "Jehovah" in this chapter *before* the revelation (vers. 2, 4).

view, allows to this principle considerable scope. "The original distinction between Jahwe and Elohim," he says, "very often accounts for the use of one of these appellations in preference to the other."[1] (Dr. Driver allows it "only in a comparatively small number of instances.")[2] He gives in illustration the following cases. "When the God of Israel is placed over against the gods of the heathen the former is naturally described by the proper name Jahwe (Ex. xii. 12; xv. 11; xviii. 11). When heathens are introduced as speaking, they use the word Elohim (Gen. xli. 39). . . . So, too, the Israelites, when speaking to heathens, often use Elohim, as Joseph does, for instance, to Potiphar's wife, Gen. xxxix. 9; to the butler and baker, Gen. xl. 8; and to Pharaoh, Gen. xli. 16, 25, 28, 32 (but also in vers. 51, 52, which makes us suspect that there may be some other reason for the preference of Elohim); so, too, Abraham to Abimelech, Gen. xx. 13 (where Elohim even takes the plural construction). Where a contrast between the divine and the human is in the mind of the author, Elohim is at anyrate the more suitable word (*e.g.*, Gen. iv. 25; xxxii. 28; Ex. viii. 15; xxxii. 16, etc.)."[3]

2. What now, we go on to inquire, is the *explanation* of these phenomena?

(1) We have already seen the difficulties which attend the critical solution of *distinct sources* in the case of documents so markedly similar and closely related as J and E. There can be no objection, indeed, to the assumption of the use by the writer of Genesis of an older source, or older sources, for the lives of the patriarchs; such, in our opinion, *must* have been there. But such source, or sources, would, if used, underlie *both* J and E sections, while the general similarity of style in the narratives shows that, in any case, older records were not simply copied. It may be further pointed out that the supposition of two or more documents (JEP, etc.), combined by a redactor, does not in reality relieve the difficulty. We have still to ask—On what principle did the redactor work in the selection of his material? What moved him, out of the several (parallel) narratives at his disposal, here to choose J, there to choose E, in another place to choose P, at other times to weave in stray sentences or clauses from this

---

[1] *Hex.* p. 56.   [2] *Introd.* p. 13.   [3] *Hex.* pp. 58–59.

or *that* writing? Did he act from mere caprice? **If he** did not, the difficulty of the names seems only shifted back from the original authors to the compiler.

(2) Shall we then say, sustaining ourselves on such admissions as those of Kuenen above, that the alternation of names in JE narratives in Genesis is due to the fact that these names are always used *discriminatively*? This has been the favourite view of writers of a conservative tendency,[1] and there is assuredly a deep truth underlying it, though we do not think it can be carried through to the full extent that these writers desire. It is the case, and is generally admitted, that there is a difference of meaning in the two names of God,—"*Elohim* and *Jahweh*," as Dr. Driver puts it, "represent the divine nature under different aspects, viz., as the God of nature and the God of revelation respectively,"[2]—and it will also be allowed that to some extent this is the principle governing their selection in particular passages. But is it the principle of distinction throughout?

In this connection it is necessary to consider the important fact, on which the critics rightly lay much stress, that in the case of E the distinction in the use of the divine names ceases (not *wholly,* as we saw, but *generally*) with the revelation in Ex. iii. What does this fact mean? The critical answer is simple : a new name of God—the name Jehovah—is here revealed, and with the revelation of the new name the use of the older name is discontinued. This explanation, however, as a little reflection shows, is not quite so satisfactory as it seems. For, *first*, it is not a distinction between E and J that the one knows of a revelation of God to Moses by His name Jehovah, and the other does not. Both, as we find, are aware of, and describe in nearly the same terms, the commission to Moses. In both Moses was to tell the children of Israel that "Jehovah, the God of [their] fathers" had sent him, Ex. iii. 15 (E); 16 (J); iv. 5 (J). And, *second*, while it is E who records the words of revelation "I AM THAT I AM" (ver. 14), it is not E, but P, who later has the declaration: "I appeared unto Abraham, unto Isaac, and unto Jacob, as El-Shaddai, but by My name Jehovah I was not known to them."[3] There is thus no indication that E regarded

---

[1] *E.g.*, Hengstenberg, Keil, Green, Rupprecht, etc.
[2] *Introd.* p. 13.
[3] Ex. vi. 3.

the revelation to Moses in any other light than **J** did:[1] therefore, no apparent reason why E, any more than J, should draw in his narrative so sharp a distinction between the period before and that after the revelation in Exodus. Nor, in fact, did he; for we have seen that Elohistic sections are found later in the book, and many able critics hold the view that originally the E document had this name Elohim till its close.[2]

The general sense of the revelation to Moses is evidently the same in all the three supposed sources, and this helps us in determining the meaning of the words above quoted from P—"By My name Jehovah I was not known to them." Do these words mean, as most critics aver, that the name Jehovah was up to that time absolutely unknown? Was the revelation merely a question of a new vocable? Or, in consonance with the pregnant Scriptural use of the word "name,"—in harmony also with the declarations of J and E that the God who speaks is "Jehovah, the God of your fathers,"[3]—is the meaning not, as many have contended, that the God who in earlier times had revealed Himself in deeds of power and mercy as El Shaddai, would now reveal Himself, in the deliverance of Israel, in accordance with the grander character and attributes implied in His name Jehovah—the ever-abiding, changeless, covenant-keeping One?[4] For ourselves we have no doubt that, as this is the deeper, so it is the truer view of the revelation; any other we have always felt to be a superficialising of it.[5]

There is, therefore, good ground for laying stress on the distinction of meaning in the divine names. This, probably,

[1] E, in point of fact does, as we saw, occasionally use "Jehovah" in Genesis.

[2] Cf., *e.g.*, Dillmann, *Num.-Jos.* p. 617; Addis, *Hex.* i. p. liv. See below, p. 226.

[3] That the name Jehovah was probably really older, as J, certainly, and probably both J and E, assume, is shown in Note B to Chap. V. above.

[4] The "name" denotes in general the revelation-side of God's being. Jehovah, as we understand it, denotes the God of the Covenant as the One who remains eternally one with Himself in all that He is and does: the *Self-Existent* and therefore the *Self-Consistent* One. Kautzsch takes the name as meaning the "eternal and constant."—*Dict. of Bible* (Extra Vol.), p. 625.

[5] It is interesting to notice that Colenso, who at first tenaciously resisted this view, came round latterly to regard it as admissible—even suggests it as an explanation of how J might use the sacred name in Genesis without a sense of discrepancy with P. "Whereas," he says, "if it means (as some explain it) that it [the name Jehovah] was not fully *understood* or *realised*, the contradiction in terms would disappear altogether," etc.—*Pent.* vi. pp. 582-83.

15

—so far we go with the critics,—is the real reason of the predominating usage in the P parts prior to Ex. vi. The usage in this writing is ruled by the contrast of two stages of revelation, which the writer desires to emphasise. Still we think that, while this explanation of discriminative use is perhaps not *impossible* for JE, and often has real place,[1] it is highly *improbable* that the same author should designedly change the name in so marked a fashion through whole chapters, as is done in this narrative, without more obvious reason than generally presents itself. Only, as formerly remarked, the critics themselves cannot wholly get away from this difficulty. If not the author, then the redactor, must have had some principle to guide him in choosing, now a Jehovistic, now an Elohistic section. He is too skilful a person to have worked at random; the distinction of names in his documents must have been as obvious to him as to us; he is supposed to have often changed the names to make them suit his context; it is difficult, therefore, to think that he had not some principle or theory to guide him.

3. This leads to another, and very important question— Is it so certain that in the case of JE there has been no *change* in the names? The question is not so uncalled for as it may seem. We do not need to fall back on the redactor of the critics to recognise that the Pentateuch has a *history* —that, like other books of the Bible, it has undergone a good deal of revision, and that sometimes this revision has left pretty deep traces upon the text. The differences in the Hebrew, Samaritan, and LXX numbers in Gen. v. and xi. are a familiar example. But in the use of the divine names also suggestive facts present themselves. It has been mentioned above as the conjecture of certain critics that the E document had originally "Elohim" till its close, and was designedly changed to "Jehovah" after Ex. iii. (but why then not wholly?). A plainer example is in Gen. ii.-iii. (J), where the two names are conjoined in the form "Jehovah Elohim" (LORD God). It is generally allowed that this is not the original form of writing,[2] and that the

---

[1] As in Gen. iii. above, p. 222. Cf. also below, pp. 234-35. As analogous, the usage in the prologue and close of the Book of Job may be compared with that in the body of the book.

[2] Gunkel, however, following Budde, actually thinks that we have here also the working together of two stories of Paradise—an Elohistic and a Jehovistic.—*Genesis*, p. 4.

names are intentionally combined to show the identity of the "Elohim" of chap. i. (P) with the "Jehovah" of the subsequent narratives. If we may believe Klostermann, the ancient Hebrews could never have used in speech such a combination as "Jehovah Elohim," and would read here simply "Elohim."[1] The LXX is specially instructive on this point, for it frequently reads "God" simply (chap. ii. 5, 7, 9, 19, 21), where the Hebrew has the double name. So in chap. iv. 1, for "I have gotten a man by the help of Jehovah," the LXX reads "God" (conversely in ver. 25, for "God" in the Hebrew it reads "Lord God"); and in ver. 26, for "call on Jehovah," it has "Lord God." This raises the question, more easily asked than answered—Did this combination of the names stop originally with chap. iii. ? Or if not, how far did it go ? The LXX certainly carried it a good way further than our present text—at least to the end of the story of the flood.[2]

There is, however, yet another class of phenomena bearing closely on our subject—which has, in fact, furnished Klostermann with the suggestion of a possible solution of our problem well deserving of consideration. We refer to the remarkable distribution of the divine names in the *Book of Psalms.* It was before pointed out that in the first three of the five Books into which the Psalter is divided, the psalms are systematically arranged into Jehovistic and Elohistic groups: Book I. is Jehovistic (Davidic); Book II., Elohistic (sons of Korah, Asaph, David); Book III., Jehovistic (sons of Korah, etc.).[3] Here, then, in the Pentateuch and in the Psalter are two sets of phenomena sufficiently similar to suggest the probability of a common cause. What is the explanation in the case of the psalms ? Is it, as Colenso thought, that David wrote Elohistic psalms

[1] *Pentateuch,* p. 37. "Only in the temple, according to Jacob (*Zeit. d. Alttest. Wissenschaft,* 1896, p. 158), was the sacred name JHVH pronounced." —Kirkpatrick, *Psalms,* p. 57.

[2] The compound expressions "Jehovah, God of Shem" (Abraham, etc.), Gen. ix. 26 ; xxiv., etc., also deserve consideration. Is it, besides, certain that the divine names in the oldest script were always written in full, or as words, and not represented by a sign? Dillmann, it may be observed, thinks that, conversely, Elohim in E is frequently changed into Jehovah (*Num.–Jos.* p. 52), a statement which proves rather the uncertainty of his hypothesis than the necessity of the change.

[3] Cf. above, p. 197. For details see W. R. Smith, *loc. cit.* ; Kirkpatrick, *The Psalms,* pp. lv ff., etc.

at one period of his life, and Jehovistic psalms at another? Few critics at the present day would accept this solution; besides, it does not explain the phenomena of the other groups. The real key, it is generally allowed, is furnished in the fact that, in a few cases, the same psalms (or parts of psalms) appear in different groups—in one form Jehovistic, in the other Elohistic. Thus Ps. liii. is an *Elohistic* recension of the *Jehovistic* Ps. xiv.; Ps. lxx. is an *Elohistic* recension of the *Jehovistic* Ps. xl. 13–17 (in the remaining case, Ps. cviii. = Ps. lvii. 7–11, and lx. 5–12, both versions are Elohistic). As the psalmist cannot well be supposed to have written the psalm in both forms, it is clear that in one or other of the versions the name has been designedly changed. This also is the nearly unanimous opinion of modern scholars.[1] Facts show that there was a time, or were times, in the history of Israel, when in certain circles there was a shrinking from the use of the sacred name Jehovah,[2] and when, in speech, the name "Elohim" or "Adonai"[3] was substituted for it. Not only was the name changed in reading, but versions of the psalms apparently were produced for use with the name *written* as it was to be read—that is, with Elohim substituted for Jehovah.[4] Klostermann's suggestion, in brief, is that precisely the same thing happened with the old Jehovistic history-book of Israel, which corresponds with what we call JE. There was an *Elohistic* version of this work in circulation alongside of the original *Jehovistic*—a recension in which the divine name was written "Elohim," at least up to Ex. iii., and possibly all through. When the final editing of the Pentateuch took place, texts of both recensions were employed, and sections taken from one or the other as was thought most suitable.[5] In other words, for the J and E

---

[1] Cf. W. R. Smith, *O.T. in J. C.*, p. 119; Driver, *Introd.* p. 372; Kirkpatrick, *Psalms*, as above, *Library of O.T.*, p. 39; Klostermann, *Pentateuch*, p. 36; König, *Hauptprobleme*, p. 28, etc.

[2] Cf., *e.g.*, *Ecclesiastes*, and the preference for "Elohim" in Chronicles. "The compiler of Chronicles," says Driver, "changes conversely *Jehovah* of his original source into *God*," etc.—*Introd.* p. 21; cf. p. 372.

[3] It is well known that the Jews change "Jehovah" in reading into "Adonai" or "Elohim," and that the vowels of "Jehovah" itself are really those of "Adonai." The name, we have seen, is properly Jahweh.

[4] Cf. Klostermann, as above.

[5] Evidently on this theory the need remains of finding a *reason* for the preference of the divine names as much as ever. This brings us back, as at

documents of the critics, Klostermann substitutes *J and E recensions of one and the same old work*.[1] To him, as to us, the piecing together of independent documents in the manner which the critical theory supposes, appears incredible. If hypothesis is to be employed, this of Klostermann, in its general idea, seems to us as good as any.[2]

VI. LINGUISTIC AND OTHER ALLEGED GROUNDS FOR SEPARATION

It has been shown that the strongest reasons exist, despite the distinction in the divine names, for believing that J and E never had currency as separate documents; it is now to be asked whether these reasons are overborne by the remaining grounds ordinarily alleged to prove that J and E were originally independent. The long lists of marks of distinction adduced by Dillmann and other critics[3] have at first sight an imposing appearance. On closer inspection, however, they reduce themselves to much scantier dimensions. They were, for the most part, not obvious to the earlier critics, and, as proofs of independence, can be shown to be largely illusory. Such, *e.g.*, are all the marks, formerly adverted to, supposed to show a superior interest of E in Ephraimitic localities and in the house of Joseph. It turned out that J displayed at least as warm an interest in Northern places, while E dwells also on Beersheba, the one Southern locality that comes prominently into the part of the history he narrates. Indeed, "the South country" is adduced as one of his favourite phrases.[4] The chief remaining grounds of dis-

least the main reason, to the feeling of a superior appropriateness of one name rather than the other in a given context.

[1] Cf. *Pentateuch*, pp. 10, 11, 27 ff.

[2] We do not gather that Klostermann supposes his Elohistic recension to be necessarily late—the same causes probably operated at earlier periods —or to be inconsistent with a union of JE with P. His own theory is that such a union goes far back (*Pent.* p. 185). The fault of Klostermann's treatment is the excessive scope he allows for variations of the text in course of transmission. The well-marked physiognomy of the JE and P text is an argument against such wide change.

[3] Cf. Dillmann, *Num.-Jos.* pp. 617 ff. ; more moderately, Driver, *Introd.* pp. 118–19. *Genesis*, p. xiii.

[4] E mentions also Hebron (see above, p. 210), and, if his hand is really present, as some suppose, in Gen. xv. he must have had an account of the

tinction are alleged linguistic peculiarities, distinctive modes
of representation, duplicate narratives, etc. Let us look at
these.

1. On the subject of *linguistic peculiarities*, Dr. Driver's
statement was formerly quoted that "the phraseological
criteria" distinguishing J and E are "slight."[1] They *are*
slight, in fact, to a degree of tenuity that often makes the
recital of them appear like trifling. In not a few cases
words are fixed on as characteristic which occur only once
or twice in the whole Pentateuch, or which occur in *both* J
and E, or in contexts where the analysis is doubtful, or
where the reasoning is of the circular order which first
gives a word to J or E, then assigns a passage to that
document *because* the word is present in it. Here are a few
examples :—

E is credited with "what may be called an antiquarian
interest,"[2] on the ground, among other things, that he *once*
uses in Genesis (xxxiii. 19), in narrating a purchase, the
word *Kesitah* (a piece of money)—found elsewhere in the
Bible only in Josh. xxiv. 32 (E ?) and Job xlii. 11.

" Land of the South," above referred to, occurs only three
times in the Pentateuch—in Gen. xx. 1 (E), in Gen. xxiv.
62 (which Delitzsch says cannot be referred to E), and in
Num. xiii. 29 (doubtful); and once in Josh. xv. 19 (J).

The phrase "after these things," said to be a mark of E
(Well.), is found first in Gen. xv. 1 (J)—E's presence in this
context is contested, and the analysis is declared to be at
best "only probable"—then in three passages given to E
(Gen. xxii. 1; xl. 1; xlviii. 1); but also in two J passages
(Gen. xxii. 20; xxxix. 7), and in Josh. xxiv. 29 (possibly P,
as giving an age).

The word *Koh* (in sense of "here") in Gen. xxii. 5,
assigned as a mark of E, is found elsewhere *once* in Genesis
(xxxi. 37 E), in Num. xxiii. 15 (mixed), and besides in
Ex. ii. 12, assigned by Wellhausen to J, and in Num. xi. 31,
given by Kuenen to J.

When we turn to instances which may be judged more
important, we are in hardly better case. One observes that

covenant with Abraham at Mamre. If otherwise, it is not easy to see how
E can be expected to speak of localities which belong to a period before his
own narrative begins.

[1] *Introd.* pp. 13, 126 ; see above, p. 219.   [2] Addis, *Hex.* i. p. lv.

where other writers indulge in the customary "always" and "invariably," Dr. Driver frequently uses the safer word "prefers."[1] The following are a few principal examples, and the extent of the "preference" may be gauged from them :—

"The Jahvist," we are told, "calls a female slave or concubine *Shiphhah*, the Elohist invariably *Amah*."[2] Dr. Driver says in the case of E, "prefers"—and prudently. *Amah* is used by E some half-dozen times in Genesis (xx. 17 ; xxi. 10, 12, 13 ; xxx. 3 ; xxxi. 33), but *Shiphhah* occurs nearly as often in E or in inseparably interwoven contexts (Gen. xx. 14 ; xxix. 24, 29, assigned to P ; xxx. 4, 7, 18).[3] Whether *Amah* is used by E or J in Ex. ii. 5, xx. 10 (Fourth Com.), xxi. (Book of Covenant—repeatedly), depends on the accuracy of the analysis which assigns these parts to E, and on this critics are quite divided.[4] Ex. xxi.–xxiii., *e.g.*, are given by Wellhausen, Westphal, etc., to *J*.

We are told again that "the Jahvist speaks of 'Sinai,' the Elohist of 'Horeb.'" E's usage reduces itself to three passages (Ex. iii. 1 ; xvii. 6 ; xxxiii. 6)—the last two determined mainly by the presence of the word ; J employs Sinai *solely* in chaps. xix. (cf. ver. 1 ; xxiv. 16, P) and xxxiv. 2, 4, in connection with the actual giving of the law.[5] The related expression "mountain of God" seems common (Ex. iii. 1, E ; iv. 27, J ; xxiv. 13 ?).

"The Jahvist," it is said, "calls the aborigines of Palestine 'Canaanites,' the Elohist 'Amorites.'" This, on examination, breaks down entirely. E has no monopoly of "Amorite" (cf. Gen. x. 16 ; xiv. 13 ; xv. 21),[6] and the

---

[1] *Genesis*, p. xiii.

[2] Addis, i. p. lvi. The quotations that follow are also from Addis, pp. lvi, lvii.

[3] It is pure arbitrariness and circular reasoning to change this single word in chap. xx. 14 and xxx. 18, on the ground that "the regular word for women slaves in E is *Amah*," and that "J on the other hand always employs *Shiphhah*" (Oxf. *Hex.* ii. pp. 29, 45)—the very point in dispute. In chap. xxix. 24, 29, the verses are cut out and given to P ; chap. xxx. 4, 7 are similarly cut out and given to J (p. 45).

[4] Ex. ii. 5 is confessedly given to E because "the linguistic conditions in vers. 1 and 5 [*i.e.*, this word] point to E rather than J" (Oxf. *Hex.* ii. p. 81). Jülicher, however, gives the verse to J. The assignment of the Decalogue and the Book of the Covenant are matters of much controversy. Delitzsch remarks on the latter: "Such words as *Amah* . . . are no marks of E in contradistinction to J and D."—*Genesis*, i. p. 32.

[5] Possibly Horeb is a wider designation.

[6] Oxf. *Hex.* itself says: "Otherwise in lists." Cf. Kuenen on Gen. x., *Hex.* pp. 140, 149.

two instances assigned to him in Genesis (xv. 16; xlviii. 22)
are in passages of most doubtful analysis.[1] Similarly with
the few instances of 'Canaanite' in J (Gen. x. 18; xii. 6;
xiii. 7, etc.; cf. xv. 21, "Amorite and Canaanite," given
to R).

Óne other instance must suffice. "The Jahvist calls
Jacob in the latter part of his life 'Israel'; the Elohist
retains the name 'Jacob.'" Dr. Driver more cautiously
says "prefers"; Kuenen says "generally."[2] Here, again,
the case is only made out by tearing asunder the web of what
is evidently a closely-connected narrative, and by liberal
use of the redactor. It will be observed that it is only in
the "latter part" of Jacob's life that this peculiarity is said
to be found. J had recorded the change of name from
Jacob to Israel in chap. xxxii. 24–32,[3] but from some
eccentric motive he is supposed not to commence his use of
"Israel" till xxxv. 21. Yet, as the text stands, "Jacob" is
found in a J narrative later (chap. xxxvii. 34), and "Israel"
in a long series of E passages (Gen. xxxvii. 3; xlv. 27, 28;
xlvi. 1, 2; xlviii. 2, 8, 10, 11, 14, 21). There is no reason
for denying these verses to E *except that this name is found
in them*. The logician could find no better example of the
circulus vitiosus than in the critical treatment of Gen. xlviii
It may be noted that in Exodus J has "the God of Abraham,
of Isaac, and of *Jacob*" (chap. iii. 16), and E in both Genesis
and Exodus has "sons of *Israel*."

2. Connected with these alleged peculiarities of language
are others which turn more on general style, "tone," *mode
of representation* of God, and the like. E has a more
elevated idea of God; J is more vivid and anthropomorphic,
etc. Much depends here on subjective impression,[4] and on
the view taken of the relation sustained by E to J—whether

---

[1] Gen. **xv.** 16 is attributed by Wellhausen, Budde, Kuenen, etc., to
another hand (not to E).

[2] "At present we can only say that in the E sections after Gen. xxxii.
the patriarch is *generally* called 'Jacob,' whereas the J passages *generally*
speak of Israel," but "in our mongrel state of the text numerous exceptions
occur" (*Hex.* p. 145).

[3] If, with some critics, as Dillmann, we assign Gen. xxxii. 24–32 to E,
we have, as Dr. Green points out, "this curious circumstance," that "P
(xxxv. 10) and E (xxxii. 28) record the change of name to Israel, but never
use it; J alone makes use of it, and, according to Dillmann, he does not
record the change at all."—*Genesis*, p. 450.

[4] Cf. the illustration given on p. 211.

earlier or later. Two examples may be selected of these alleged differences, and one or two illustrations given of the analysis of passages resulting from the theory.

We take examples universally accepted. " The God of whom he [E] writes," we read, "appears in dreams, or acts through the ministry of angels."[1] "His angel calls out of heaven."[2] The "dream" criterion is one much insisted on, and for various reasons deserves attention. As the "dream" is a lower form of revelation, and is generally employed in connection with secular personages — Abimelech, Laban, Joseph (dreams of secular pre-eminence), the butler and baker, Pharaoh, etc.—it is not wonderful that it should commonly appear in passages of a prevailingly Elohistic cast. But the attempt to make out this to be a peculiar criterion of E proves, on inspection, to be an exaggeration. The passages adduced in its support, indeed, frequently prove the contrary. Thus, Gen. xv. 1, given by Driver, is on the face of it Jehovistic.[3] Gen. xx. 3, and most of the other instances (Abimelech, Laban, Pharaoh), fall under the above rule of fitness, and in some of the cases are assigned to E simply because a "dream" is recorded. Gen. xxviii. 10-22—Jacob's vision at Bethel (cf. chap. xlvi. 2)—is divided between E and J (arbitrarily, as shown below), but the dream is implied in both. In E, Jacob sleeps and dreams (ver. 12); in J, he awakes (ver. 16). In J also God reveals Himself to Isaac in a night vision (chap. xxvi. 24: cf. E passage above, xlvi. 2). Further, it is not the case that in E God reveals Himself *only* in dreams or by angels, as on the theory He ought to do. God speaks directly with Abraham in chaps. xxi. 12 (contrast with case of Abimelech), xxii. 1; and with Jacob in chap. xxxv. 1. He " appears " to Jacob at Bethel in E, chap. xxxv. 7, just as He does in P (ver. 9). Finally, Wellhausen himself concludes from chap. xxxvii. 19, 20 that the "Jahvist" also must have related Joseph's dreams;[4] and Professor Bennett, who adduces this very criterion of E,[5] follows suit and

---

[1] Addis, i. p. lv; cf. Driver, *Genesis*, pp. xx, xxi; McFadyen, *Mess. of Hist.* ; " In the Elohist He usually appears in a dream " (p. 19).

[2] Driver, *ibid.* p. xxi; cf. Addis, i. p. 36; McFadyen, p. 19, etc.

[3] There is certainly no agreement that chap. xv. 1 is E's. This refutes also the exclusive right of E to a "coming" of God in a dream (Driver)—twice elsewhere in Genesis. Why, it may be asked, if the dream is so peculiar a mark of E, is it not carried into the other books?

[4] *Comp. d. Hex.* p. 54.   [5] *Genesis*, p. 31.

says: "Perhaps J had also an account of Pharaoh's dream." [1]
So falls this hypothesis of "dreams"—itself a dream.

The argument based on the calling of the Angel of God "out of heaven" is not more successful. The expression occurs once in an E passage, in Gen. xxi. 17, then *twice* in chap. xxii. (11, 15), but in both the latter cases in a Jehovistic form, "the Angel of *Jehovah* called out of heaven." Even if the redactor be called in to change the word to "Elohim" in ver. 11, because of the E context, this is inadmissible in the second case, where the context is Jehovistic. There is, in truth, no warrant for changing it in either case. Yet on this infinitesimally slender basis an argument for the distinction of E is reared.

This leads us to say that no stronger proof for the inadmissibility of the partition hypothesis in the case of J and E could be desired than the two passages just referred to—Gen. xxii. 1–19 (the sacrifice of Isaac), and Gen. xxviii. 10–22 (Jacob at Bethel). We would almost be willing to stake the case for the unity of the alleged documents on these narratives alone. Each, on its face, is a single story, which needs both the parts ascribed to E and those ascribed to J to constitute it in its completeness, and for the dividing of which nothing of importance but the variation in the divine names can be pleaded. The E and J portions, on the other hand, are unintelligible, if taken by themselves. Even on the basis of the divine names, the analysis presents great difficulties, and critics are far from agreed in their ideas of it. Thus, in Dr. Driver's scheme, Gen. xxii. 1–14 is given to E, though "Jehovah" occurs in ver. 11 and twice in ver. 14; in Gen. xxviii. 21, "Jehovah" occurs in the E part, and has to be forcibly excised. The unity of the story in both cases is destroyed by the partition. In Gen. xxii. vers. 1–14 are given, as said, to E, vers. 15–18 to J (others give vers. 14–18 to a Jehovistic "redactor"), ver. 19, again, is given to E. But each of these parts is evidently complementary to the others.[2] If we break off

---

[1] *Genesis*, p. 29.

[2] Hupfeld, to whom is due the 2nd Elohist, has a remarkable admission of this. "I cannot conceal the fact," he says, "that the entire narrative seems to me to bear the stamp of the Jehovist; and certainly one would never think of the Elohist, but for the name Elohim, which here (as in part of the history of Joseph) is not supported by the internal phenomena, and embarrasses criticism" (*Quellen*, p. 178). Knobel also says: "Apart from

with E at vers. 13 or 14 (still more, with the older critics, at ver. 10), the sequel of the story is clearly lacking. It is the same with Gen. xxviii. 10–22. E begins with vers. 10–12; vers. 13–16 are given to J; vers. 17, 18 again fall to E; ver. 19 is credited to J; and vers. 20–22 are once more E's.[1] Is such a patchwork credible, especially when "redactors" are needed to help out the complicated process?[2] It is clear that both documents must have had the story, yet neither, it appears, is able to tell it completely. Jacob, as already pointed out, falls asleep in the one document, and awakes in the other. Even as respects the names, it is difficult not to see an appropriateness in their distribution, whether that is supposed due to an original writer, or to a later editor combining Elohistic and Jehovistic recensions. In both narratives the story begins on a lower level and mounts to a higher—the "crisis" in each case being marked by the change of name. Hengstenberg,[3] but also Knobel, Delitzsch, and others,[4] have pointed this out in the case of the sacrifice of Isaac. "Elohim" tempts Abraham, and the name continues to be used till the trial of faith is complete; it then changes — ascends — to "Jehovah" with the new revelation that arrests the sacrifice, and confirms the covenant promise. So in Gen. xxviii. 10 ff., Jacob, leaving his father's house, is practically in a state of spiritual outlawry. As befits this lower level, he receives his revelation in a dream ("angels of Elohim ascending," etc.); but "Jehovah" appears to him above the mystic ladder, and renews the covenant. It was a revelation of grace, wholly undeserved and unexpected, designed to set Jacob on his

Elohim nothing in this narrative reminds us of the Elohist; on the contrary, everything speaks for the Jehovist" (quoted by Green, *Genesis*, p. 483).

[1] There are variations among the critics here as elsewhere, several, *e.g.*, give ver. 10 to J.

[2] Orelli says: "Gen. xxviii. is probably Yahwistic, at least the splitting up of the narrative is in the highest degree arbitrary."—*O.T. Prophecy*, p. 105.

[3] *Gen. of Pent.* i. p. 348.

[4] Knobel, who gives the whole narrative to J, says: "We have to assume that the Jehovist here uses Elohim so long as there is reference to a human sacrifice, and only introduces Jehovah (ver. 11) after setting aside such a sacrifice, which was foreign to the religion of Jehovah" (as above). The change to the divine name, says Delitzsch, "is in its present state significant, the God who commands Abraham to sacrifice Isaac is called '(Ha)-Elohim,' and the divine appearance that forbids the sacrifice, 'the Angel of Jehovah.'"—*Genesis*, ii. pp. 90–91.

feet again, and make a new man of him.   Only the highei
name was suited to such a theophany.

3. One of the strongest of the evidences—because not
depending on single words—relied on to prove the distinction of J and E, and the validity of the documentary
hypothesis generally, is the occurrence of "duplicate"
narratives of the same event ("doublets"), and to this
subject we may now finally refer.   Duplicates, or what are
held to be such, are pointed out in the case of JE and P, as
in the two narratives of creation, Gen. i.–ii. 3 (P), ii. 3 ff.
(J), and the twice naming of Bethel, Gen. xxviii. 19 (J),
xxxv. 15 (P), cf. ver. 7 (E); but also between J and E, as in
the twice naming of Beersheba, Gen. xxi. 31 (E), xxvi. 33
(J), the two flights of Hagar, Gen. xvi. 4–14 (J), xxi. 9–21
(E), and specially in the stories of the denials of their wives
by Abraham and Isaac, Gen. xii. 10–20 (J), xx. (E), xxvi.
6–11 (J).[1]   Similar duplications are thought to be found
in the Mosaic history.   The presence of such differing
and so-called contradictory accounts is held to prove
distinct sources.

On these alleged "duplicate" narratives the following
remarks may first be made *generally*:—

(1) Narratives of the same event may be different in
point of view and detail, without being necessarily, as
is constantly assumed—"contradictory" or "discordant"
(creation, flood, etc.[2]).

(2) Similar acts may be, and frequently are, repeated
under new circumstances.   *E.g.*, in the cases of Bethel and
Beersheba above, the second narrative expressly refers back
to the first (Gen. xxxv. 9, cf. on E below; xxvi. 15, 18).
This close interrelation of the different parts of the narrative
(JEP) is one of the most striking facts about it.

(3) It weakens the argument that "duplications" do not
always occur in *different* documents—as on the theory they
ought to do—but in no inconsiderable number of cases fall
within the limits of the *same* document.   Thus E has a
second visit to Bethel as well as P (Gen. xxxv. 6, 7); J
has two denials of wives — see below; alleged duplicate
accounts of the Korahite rebellion are found in Num. xvi.

---

[1] See a list of duplicates in Kuenen, *Hex.* pp. 38 ff.   De Wette laid great
stress on this argument in his *Introduction.*

[2] See below, pp. 346 ff.

3–10 (P),[1] etc. Criticism is driven here to further disintegrations.

(4) This suggests, lastly, that, even were the similarity of incidents as clear as is alleged, it would not necessarily prove different authorship. The same author might find varying narrations in the traditions or sources from which he drew, and might *himself* reproduce them in his history. Suppose, to take a favourite instance, that the narrator of the life of Joseph found the merchants to whom Joseph was sold described in one of his sources as Ishmaelites and in another as Midianites, is it not as likely that he would himself introduce both names (Gen. xxxvii. 27, 28, 36 ; xxxix. 1), as that a later "redactor" should weave together the varying histories of J and E ?[2] Even this hypothesis is not necessary, for we have independent evidence that "Ishmaelites" was used as a wide term to include "Midianites" (Judg. viii. 24). In Hagar's flights (in second case an expulsion),—one before the birth of Ishmael, the other when he was grown up to be a lad,—it seems plain that tradition had preserved the memory of *two* incidents, connected with different times and occasions, and each natural in its own place.[3]

Without delaying on other instances, we may take, as a test-case, the most striking of all these "doublets"—the denial of their wives by Abraham and Isaac—and subject that, in closing, to a brief analysis. The results will be

[1] Cf., *e.g.*, McFadyen's *Mess. of Hist.* p. 7, where this case is founded on. See below, pp. 358–59.

[2] The critics evolve from the narrative two discrepant histories of Joseph, according to which, in the one case (E), Joseph is, unknown to the brothers, taken out of the pit by passing *Midianites*, and sold to Potiphar, captain of the guard, in Egypt ; in the other (J) he is sold by the brothers (no pit) to a company of *Ishmaelites*, who sell him in turn to an unnamed Egyptian (no Potiphar). The "they" in ver. 28 is referred to the Midianites. In chap. xxxix. 1, indeed, Potiphar is expressly said to have bought him from the Ishmaelites, but this is excised as an interpolation. The whole thing seems to us an exercise of misplaced ingenuity, refuted by the narrative, which hangs together as it is, but not on this theory.

[3] A difficulty is created about the *age* of Ishmael in the second story. The critics adopt the reading of the LXX for chap. xxi. 14, "put the child on her shoulder," and find a discrepancy with the representation of him as a lad of some fourteen years of age (cf. Addis, *Hex.* i. p. 34). But the story itself describes him as a "lad" (vers. 12, 17, 18, 19, 20), and the "mocking" of Isaac (ver. 9) implies some age. Colenso, for once, is not stumbled by the "carrying," and cites a curious Zulu parallel (quoted in Quarry, *Genesis*, p. 456). The LXX reading has no claim to supersede the Hebrew (cf. Delitzsch, *in loc.*). See further below, p. 352.

instructive, as throwing light on critical methods, and as showing how far from simple this matter of "duplicates" really is.

(1) We have first, then, to observe that what we have here to deal with is not *two*, but *three* incidents (not *duplicates*, but *triplicates*)—one denial in Egypt (Gen. xii. Abraham), and two in Gerar (chap. xx. Abraham, xxvi. Isaac). Of these narratives, *two* are classed as Jehovistic (Gen. xii. xxvi.), and *one* is classed as Elohistic (chap. xx.). In strictness, therefore, on the duplication theory, we seem bound to assume for them, not two, but *three* authors; and this, accordingly, is what is now commonly done. It is allowed that "the narrative in chap. xii. shows the general style and language of J,"[1] *but* "it can hardly be supposed that the story of Abram passing off Sarai as his sister at Pharaoh's court, and that of Isaac dealing similarly with Rebekah at Gerar, belonged originally to the same series of traditions."[2] The former story, therefore, must be given to some later representative of the J "school."[3] We have here the critical process of disintegration in a nutshell.

(2) We have next to look at the phenomena of the divine *names*. In Gen. xii. 10–20, Dr. Driver, in words formerly quoted, tells us that "the term *Jehovah* is uniformly employed."[4] In point of fact, it is employed only *once* (ver. 17), and, strikingly enough, it is employed *once* also in the Elohistic narrative (chap. xx. 18) in a similar connection. In the third narrative (Gen. xxvi. 6–11), the divine name does not occur *at all*, though the context is Jehovistic (vers. 2, 12). So uncertain, indeed, are the criteria, that, according to Dillmann,[5] Wellhausen actually at first gave Gen. xii. 10–20 to E (same as in chap. xx.). Now, he gives the section, as above hinted, to a later writer on the ground, for one thing, that Lot is not mentioned as accompanying Abraham to Egypt (Lot's presence, however, is plainly assumed, cf. chap. xiii. 1). As respects the third narrative (Gen. xxvi.), so far from there being disharmony, the opening verse of the chapter contains an express reference to the going down of Abraham to Egypt in the first narrative (Gen. xii. 10); but the whole text of this passage (vers. 1–5)

[1] Carpenter, *Hex.* ii. p. 19.
[2] *Ibid.* i. p. 108.
[3] See Wellhausen, below.
[4] *Genesis*, p. xi.
[5] *Genesis*, ii. p. 17.

is made a patchwork of by the critics.[1] Finally, in chap. xx. it remains to be explained how a Jehovist verse comes to stray into the story of E at ver. 18. It is easy to say "redactor"; but one desires to know what moved a redactor to interpolate into his E context the mention of a fact for which he had no authority, and to employ in doing so a divine name out of keeping with his context.

(3) The facts as they stand may be *summed up* thus. All three scenes are laid in heathen courts. In the first and third stories, the divine name is not used in the body of the narrative (in the third is not used at all); in the first and second, the name "Jehovah" is used towards the close (chaps. xii. 17; xx. 18) in connection with the divine action in inflicting penalty. As two of the narratives are allowed by the more moderate critics (*e.g.*, Dillmann, Driver) to be by the same writer (J), there is no need, on the mere ground of duplication, to assume a different writer for the third story. All three stories may well have belonged to the original tradition. Nor do the conditions require us to treat the stories as simply varying traditions of the *same* incident. There are resemblances, but there are also great differences. From both chaps. xii. and xx. it appears that it was part of Abraham's *settled policy*, when travelling in strange parts, to pass off Sarah, still childless, as his sister (chap. xii. 13; xx. 13: on the half-truth by which this was justified, cf. chap. xx. 12).[2] This of itself implies that the thing was done more than once (cf. "at every place," etc.); if, indeed, chap. xx. 13 is not a direct glancing back to the former narrative. What Abraham was known to have done, Isaac, in similar peril, may well have been tempted to do likewise. In the story about Isaac there is, in fact, as above noticed, a direct reference to his father's earlier visit to Egypt (chap. xxvi. 1).[3]

---

[1] Cf. Oxf. *Hex. in loc.*   [2] See above, p. 109.

[3] It would obviously be easy, on similar lines to the above, to make out a series of "demonstrable" duplicates in, say, British history, as in Spanish wars, Chinese wars, Afghan wars, mad Mullahs, etc. : so in history generally.

APPENDIX TO CHAPTER VII

THE HISTORICITY OF THE BOOK OF JOSHUA

THE historical character of the Book of Joshua is assailed, partly on the ground of discrepancies in the narrative, as in the chapters on the crossing of Jordan (chaps. iii., iv.), where two accounts apparently blend; but chiefly because of an alleged difference in the mode of representation of the conquest. On the so-called discrepancies we have no need to deny the use of separate sources,[1] if these are not held to be contradictory. In the above instance, Köhler remarks that the notices of the two monuments (of twelve stones, one in Jordan, the other at Gilgal), while belonging to distinct sources, do not exclude each other, and are both to be held fast:[2] so in other narratives.

As regards the conquest, it is urged that, according to one representation, that derived from the Deuteronomic redactor and the still later P, the conquest under Joshua was rapid, continuous, and complete; while older notices in separate passages,[3] and in Judg. i., show that it was in reality only achieved gradually, by the efforts of the several tribes, and never completely. There is, however, if the book be taken as a whole, and allowance be made for the generalising tendency peculiar to all summaries, no necessary contradiction in the different representations of the conquest,[4] while the circumstantiality, local knowledge, and evidently full recollection of the narratives, give confidence in the truth of their statements. On the one hand, the uniform assumption in all the JE history, from the

---

[1] Probably not, however, the J and E of the previous books. See above, p. 214.
[2] See his *Bib. Geschichte*, i. pp. 473–74.
[3] *E.g.*, chaps. xiii. 13 ; xv. 13–19, 63 ; xvi. 10 ; xvii. 12 ff. ; xviii. 2 ff.
[4] Cf. König's criticism of Budde in his article on Judges in *Dict. of Bible*, ii. pp. 818–19.

original promise to Abraham of the possession of the land
to the actual conquest, in the Deuteronomic discourses, and
generally in the tradition of the people, is, that the tribes
under Joshua *did* take effective possession of the land; and
this is borne out by the fact that in Judges it is not the
Canaanites chiefly by whom they are molested (an exception
is the temporary oppression by Jabin[1]), but surrounding
and more distant peoples (*e.g.* Chushan-rishathaim, king
of Mesopotamia,[2] Moab,[3] Ammon,[4] Midianites,[5] Philistines[6]).
With this agrees the picture given of the conquest, beginning with the taking of Jericho and Ai, advancing to the
defeat of the confederacy of the kings at Bethhoron, and
destruction of their cities,[7] then to the defeat of the greater
confederacy in the North under Jabin, and conquests there,[8]
afterwards, in more general terms, to further campaigns
in the middle, South, and North of Palestine, till the whole
land has been overrun.[9] The course of conquest is what
might have been expected from the terror described by
Rahab (JE ?),[10] and accords with the retrospect of Joshua
in his last address (E ?).[11] On it the division of the land,
described with so much topographical minuteness, naturally
follows.[12]

On the other hand, the Book of Joshua itself gives many
indications that, notwithstanding these extensive, and, as
respects the main object, decisive conquests, there still
remained much land to be possessed, which the tribes
could only conquer gradually.[13] Much detail work had
to be done in the several territories; and there is no
difficulty in the supposition that, after the first sweeping
wave of conquest, the Canaanites rallied, and regained
possession of many places, *e.g.*, Hebron, from which they
had been temporarily expelled. An instance of this we
have in Jerusalem, which had been taken by the Israelites,

[1] Judg. iv.
[2] Judg. iii. 12 ff.
[5] Judg. vi. 1 ff.
[7] Josh. x.
[9] Josh. xi. 15 ff., xii.
[11] Josh. xxiv. 11, 18.

[3] Judg. iii. 8 ff.
[4] Judg. x. 7 ff.
[6] Judg. xiii. 1 ff.
[8] Josh. xi. 1–14.
[10] Josh. ii. 9 ; cf. ver. 24.

[12] Chaps. xii. ff. On the historicity of this, see below, pp. 379–80, and cf.
König on Judges in *Dict. of Bible*, ii. p. 820. It is noted below (p. 242) that
a division of the land is implied in Judg. i., as Budde himself admits (cf.
König, *loc. cit.*).

[13] Josh. xiii. 1, 2 ; see passages cited on p. 240.

16

and burnt with fire, and the population destroyed,[1] but which the Jebusites regained, and held till the time of David.[2] These facts do not really contradict the other narrative:[3] indeed, it is hard to see how a Deuteronomic redactor could have incorporated them unchanged in his narrative, if he believed they contradicted it. The language in Joshua about the conquest is not more sweeping than that in the Tel el-Amarna tablets about the Khabiri. In the letters of Abdi-Khiba, king of Jerusalem, e.g., to Amenophis IV. of Egypt, we have such expressions as the following: "The cities of my lord, the king, belonging to Elimelech, have fallen away, and the whole territory of the king will be lost. . . . The king has no longer any territory. . . . If no troops come, the territory of my lord, the king, is lost." "Bring plainly before my lord, the king, these words: 'The whole territory of my lord, the king, is going to ruin.'" "The Khabiri are occupying the king's cities. There remains not one prince to my lord, the king: every one is ruined." "The territory of the king has fallen into the hands of the Khabiri."[4]

There is no feature in the conquest better attested than that Joshua was the leader of the tribes in this work, and that they advanced and acted under his single leadership till the first stages of the conquest were completed. This was not a thing done at once, but probably occupied several years. Kittel, who defends in the main the truth of the historical recollections in the narrative, and emphasises this point about Joshua,[5] thinks that a partition of the land (which he finds implied in Judg. i., etc.[6]) must have taken place before the conquest began, and supposes that, after the general crossing of Jordan under Joshua, and capture of

[1] Judg. i. 8 ; cf. Josh. x.

[2] 2 Sam. v. 6–8.

[3] König says: "It is a groundless assertion that the record of Judg. i. 'excludes' the narrative of the Book of Joshua" (p. 820).

[4] See Bennett's *Book of Joshua* ("Polychrome Bible"), p. 55. The Khabiri are supposed by some to have been the Hebrews. See further below, Chap. XI. p. 421.

[5] *Hist. of Hebs.* i. p. 274. He points out that the view of Meyer, Stade, etc., that J did not know Joshua, is impugned by Kuenen, Dillmann, and Budde.

[6] The summary in Judg. i., he says, begins with the question, "Who shall begin the fight ?" and the territory of each tribe is called its "lot"— "two facts which clearly enough presuppose a previous common agreement," etc.—*Ibid.* p. 275.

Jericho, Judah and Simeon separated from the main body to act for themselves in the south.   Joshua was thereafter leader of the Joseph tribes alone.[1]   The view seems artificial, and no improvement on that in the book.   The course of events is, we may believe, correctly represented in Josh. xxiv.

[1] *Hist. of Hebs.* pp. 272–77.

CHAPTER VIII

Difficulties and Perplexities of the Critical Hypothesis: The Question of Deuteronomy

"The Book of Deuteronomy in and for itself teaches nothing new. . . . How could Josiah have been so terrified because the prescriptions of this book had not been observed by the fathers, and the people had thereby incurred the wrath of Jahweh, if he had not been aware that these commands were known to them?"—GRAF.

"I am still certain that the finding of the book of the law in the eighteenth year of Josiah is neither meant, nor is, to be understood of the first appearance of the Book of Deuteronomy, originating about that time." —DELITZSCH.

"Our review of sources has convinced us that it [Deuteronomy] draws from old Mosaic tradition, which in fact in many places goes back demonstrably into the Mosaic time, and *par excellence* to the person of the lawgiver. It goes so far as to incorporate such ordinances as no longer suited the writer's own time, but only suited the time of the conquest and settlement in Canaan."—OETTLI.

"Leaving out of account isolated passages, especially the close, Deuteronomy is a whole proceeding from one and the same hand."—RIEHM.

CHAPTER VIII

DIFFICULTIES AND PERPLEXITIES OF THE CRITICAL HYPOTHESIS: THE QUESTION OF DEUTERONOMY

THE questions we have been engaged in discussing with relation to J and E, while interesting as an object-lesson in criticism, and, in their bearing on dates, important, are secondary in comparison with those which yet await investigation—the age and origin of Deuteronomy and of the so-called Priestly Code. It will be remembered that the Graf-Wellhausen school does not pretend to settle the age and relations of documents or codes by critical considerations alone. Criticism is to be guided, and its conclusions are to be checked, at every step, by history. A parallel, it is alleged, can be traced between the course of the history and the successive stages of the legislation. Up to the time of Josiah, it is held, no trace can be discovered of the existence and operation of any body of laws but that of the Book of the Covenant in Ex. xx.–xxiii. With the finding of "the book of the law" in Josiah's reign,[1] there enters a manifold influence of the spirit and teaching of the Book of Deuteronomy, strongly reflected in the later literature—for instance, in Jeremiah; but no sign is yet shown of the peculiar institutions of the Levitical Code. These first begin to be visible in the sketch of the restored temple and its ordinances in Ezekiel (chaps. xl. ff.), and emerge as a definitely completed system in the law-book which Ezra brought with him from Babylon, and gave to the post-exilian community in Jerusalem.[2] Thenceforth they rule the life of the nation. The ingenuity of the new scheme is undoubted, and the acceptance it has won is sufficient evidence

---

[1] 2 Kings xxii.
[2] Ezra vii.; Neh. viii. For a popular statement of the theory of the three Codes see Professor W. R. Smith's *O. T. in J. C.*, Lects. viii., ix.

of the skill with which it has been expounded and defended.
But is it really tenable? Many reasons—not the least
cogent of them derived from the course of criticism itself—
convince us it is not. We shall deal in this chapter with
the application of the theory to the Book of Deuteronomy.[1]

I. STATE OF THE QUESTION AND GENERAL VIEW

The Book of Deuteronomy, in its main part, consists, it
is well known, after a slight introduction, and with some
connecting notes, of three hortatory discourses purporting
to have been delivered by Moses in the *Arabah*[2] of Moab,
shortly before his death (chaps. i. 6–iv. 40, v.–xxviii.; xxix. 2–
xxx.). To these discourses are appended an account of
certain closing transactions of Moses (chap. xxxi.), the Song
and Blessing of Moses (chaps. xxxii., xxxiii.), and a narrative
of Moses' death on Mount Nebo (chaps. xxxii. 48–52; xxxiv.).
The longest of the discourses (chaps. v.–xxviii.) embraces a rehearsal (chaps. xii. ff.), in the form of popular address, of the
principal laws given by God to Moses at Horeb, as these
were to be observed by the people in their new settlement
in Canaan. There is general agreement that the laws to
which reference is made in this recapitulation are chiefly—
though, as will be seen after, by no means *exclusively*—those
contained in the Book of the Covenant (Ex. xx.–xxiii.);
but they are handled by the speaker, not literally, but
in free reproduction, with rhetorical amplification or
abbreviation, and occasionally modification to suit new
circumstances.

Deuteronomy is the one book of the Pentateuch which
might seem on the face of it to make claim to direct Mosaic
authorship. "Moses," it is declared, after the rehearsal is
completed, "wrote this law."[3] This view of its origin
modern criticism decisively rejects; will hardly allow even

[1] Graf makes the Book of Deuteronomy his starting-point. His work
opens: "The composition of Deuteronomy in the age of Josiah is one of the
most generally accepted results of the historical criticism of the Old Testament, for all who do not simply ignore these results."—*Geschicht. Bücher*,
p. 1; cf. p. 4.

[2] "That is, the deep valley running north and south of the Dead Sea"
(R.V.). Usually (in P) *Arboth*, the steppes or plains of Moab. See an
interesting description in an article on *The Steppes of Moab* by Professor G. B.
Gray in *Expositor*, January 1905.

[3] Deut. xxxi. 9, 24–26; see below, pp. 262 ff.

to be discussed.[1] It was De Wette's achievement in criticism, as we saw, that he relegated Deuteronomy to the age of Josiah; and in this judgment the great majority of critics now follow him, only that a few carry back the composition of the book a reign or two earlier—to the time of Manasseh or of Hezekiah. Views differ as to how the book is to be regarded—whether as a pseudograph ("forgery"), or as a free composition in the name and spirit of Moses without intention to deceive; but it is generally agreed that, in its present form, it is a production of the prophetic age, and has for its leading aim the centralising of worship at the sanctuary at Jerusalem. The reasons given for this view are its prophetic tone and standpoint, its obvious connection with the work of reformation, the irreconcilability of its law of the central sanctuary with the older history, inconsistencies with earlier legislation, etc. A main objection of the older critics was its alleged incompatibility with the Levitical legislation, then believed to be in substance Mosaic:[2] but the newer criticism has taken the ground from this objection by putting the Levitical laws still later than Deuteronomy—in the exile.

What weight is to be allowed to these opinions is considered below. The composition of a book of exhortation or instruction in the form of addresses by Moses—provided this is *only* literary dress, with honest motive in the writer —is not *a priori* to be ruled out as inadmissible, or incompatible with just views of Scripture.[3] The only question is whether Deuteronomy is a book of this character, or, if it is so, in what sense and to what extent it is so, and to what age it belongs. On the other hand, we cannot shut our eyes to certain far-reaching consequences of the acceptance of the critical view. If Deuteronomy is a work of the age of Josiah, then, necessarily, everything in the other Old Testament books which depends on Deuteronomy — the Deuteronomic revisions of Joshua and Judges, the Deutero-

[1] Cf. Graf, above. Wellhausen says : "About the origin of Deuteronomy there is still less dispute ; in all circles where appreciation of scientific results can be looked for at all, it is recognised that it was composed in the same age as that in which it was discovered, and that it was made the rule of Josiah's reformation, which took place about a generation before the destruction of Jerusalem by the Chaldeans."—*Hist. of Israel*, p. 9.

[2] Cf. Bleek, *Introd*. i. pp. 328 ff.

[3] Ecclesiastes, *e.g.*, put into the mouth of Solomon, is generally admitted, even by conservative critics, to be a work of this kind.

nomic allusions and speeches in the Books of Kings,[1]
narratives of facts based on Deuteronomy—*e.g.*, the blessings
and cursings, and writing of the law on stones, at Ebal,[2] all
must be put later than that age. If, again, it be the case
that the Levitical laws are later than Deuteronomy, this
requires the carrying of these down to where the critics
place them — at or near the exile. The very gravity of
some of these conclusions is our warrant for raising the
question — Is the critical view correct? The course of
criticism itself, as just hinted, despite the apparent
unanimity, forces this question upon us. For, as we soon
come to discover, even on the subject of Deuteronomy, the
critical school is rent within itself by divisions which raise
the greatest doubts as to the soundness of the original
premises. The mania for disintegration—the appetite for
which seems to grow with what it feeds on—has been at
work here also. In the Oxford *Hexateuch*, *e.g.*,—so far to
anticipate,—the unity of Deuteronomy with which criticism
started—that even of the Code in chaps. xii.-xxvi.—is lost in
a sort of dissolving view.[3] There are, however, in our judgment, other and far stronger reasons for scepticism than
even these critical vagaries. We hear much of the reasons
for putting the book late, many of them, we shall find, sadly
overstrained; but we hear little or nothing of the enormous
difficulties attaching to the critic's own hypothesis. These
are either ignored completely, or are toned down and
minimised till they are made to appear trifling. We are
content, when the case has been presented, to let the reader
judge on that matter for himself. The time, at all events,
we venture to think, has fully come, when a halt should be
called, and the question should be boldly put for reconsideration—Is the Josianic origin of Deuteronomy a result

---

[1] *E.g.*, Solomon's prayer, 1 Kings viii., or Amaziah's sparing the children
of murderers, 2 Kings xiv. 5, 6.

[2] Josh. viii. 30 ff.

[3] Cf. *Hex.* i. pp. 92–96; ii. p. 246. On the Code it is said: "The
Code and its envelopments, homiletic and narrative, hortatory or retro-
spective, must thus be regarded as the product of a long course of literary
activity to which the various members of a great religious school contributed,
the affinities with the language and thought of Jeremiah [not Jeremiah's
affinities with Deuteronomy] being particularly numerous." To this group,
it is added, "other additions were made from time to time, involving further
dislocations"; to these again final additions when J E D were united
with P (ii. p. 302).

of scientific criticism which the impartial mind is bound
to accept ?

II. UNITY AND STYLE OF DEUTERONOMY

As clearing the way for the discussion of date, a few
words may be said, first, on the subject of *unity* and *style*.

1. No book in the Bible, it may be safely affirmed, bears
on its face a stronger impress of *unity* than the Book of
Deuteronomy. It is not disputed that, in the form in which
we have it, the book shows traces of editorial redaction.
The discourses are put together with introductory and
connecting notes,[1] and the last part of the work, with its
account of Moses' death, and in one or two places what
seem unmistakable indications of JE and P hands,[2] points
clearly to such redaction. This suggests the possibility that
such archæological notices as occur in chap. ii. 10–12, 20–22,
and perhaps slight annotations elsewhere, may come from the
same revisional hand. But these minor, and in general
readily distinguishable, traces of editorial labour only throw
into more commanding relief the general unity of the book
in thought and style. The most ordinary reader cannot
peruse its chapters without perceiving that, as one has said,
" the same vein of thought, the same tone and tenor of
feeling, the same peculiarities of thought and expression,"
characterise it throughout. Accordingly, up to a comparatively recent period—till Graf's time—the unity of Deuteronomy, as respects the discourses, was recognised on nearly
every hand as one of the surest results of criticism.[3]   It

---

[1] These, however, differ little in style from the rest of the work.
[2] Chap. xxxii. 48–52 is generally given to P, and chap. xxxi. 14, 15, 23,
to JE ; both are found in chap. xxxiv.
[3] " By far the greater part," says De Wette, " belong to one author."—
Introd. ii. p. 131.
   " These " (the discourses), says Bleek, " are so homogeneous in their
language and whole character that we may assume as certain—and on this
point there is scarcely a conflicting opinion—they were on the whole composed in the shape in which we now have them, by one and the same
author."—*Introd.* i. p. 320.
   In 1864 Colenso wrote : " There can be no doubt that Deuteronomy is
throughout the work of the same hand, with the exception of the last
chapter . . . the book is complete in itself and exhibits a perfect unity of
style and subject."—*Pent.*, Pop. edit. p. 185.   By 1871, in Pt. vi. of his
large work, he had come to believe that that which admitted of " no doubt '
earlier was wrong, and that the original Deuteronomy began with chap. v.

was not doubted that the book found in the temple and read to Josiah was substantially the Deuteronomy we possess.

This can no longer be affirmed. The fine art of distinction acquired in the dissection of the other Pentateuchal "sources" soon led, as it could not but do—as it would do with any book in existence—to the discovery of abundant reasons for dividing up Deuteronomy also, first, into a number of larger sections of different ages, then into a variety of smaller pieces,[1] till, latterly, as indicated above, the unity tends entirely to disappear in the flux of the labours of a "school." Kuenen, who, in this point, is relatively conservative, extends the length of what he calls "the Deuteronomic period, which began in the year 621[2] B.C., and which called the additions to D^1 into existence," beyond the beginning of the Babylonian captivity.[2] Broadly, however, two *main* opinions on division may be distinguished, in regard to which we are happy in being able to leave it with the critics to answer each other. (1) There is the view of Wellhausen, Cornill, and others, who would limit the original Book of Deuteronomy (its "kernel") to chaps. xii.–xxvi.; but this, as Dr. Driver justly says, "upon grounds which cannot be deemed cogent."[3] Even Kuenen contests the reasons of Wellhausen on this point, and upholds the unity of chaps. v.–xxvi.[4] He gives also chap. xxviii. to the author of these chapters, as against Wellhausen.[5] (2) Kuenen, however, following Graf,[6] here draws a new line, and, "with the majority of recent critics," says Dr. Driver, "declares chaps. i.–iv. to be the work of a different hand."[7] The resemblance of style cannot be denied, but, says Kuenen, "the great similarity of language must be explained as the result of imitation."[8] To Dr. Driver himself there seems "no conclusive reason" for questioning the unity of

---

[1] See Note A on the Breaking up of Deuteronomy.

[2] *Hex.* p. 225.   [3] *Deut.* p. lxv.

[4] *Hex.* pp. 113 ff.   [5] *Ibid.* pp. 126 ff.

[6] Cf. Graf, *Geschicht. Bücher.* pp. 4, 5. It is interesting to notice the reasons given by Graf, as a pioneer in this division. He does not base it on style. He thinks, indeed, that in parts a greater "diffuseness" may be detected, but this "may perhaps seem too subjective." His objective reason is that, through the first four chapters, Deuteronomy is "closely bound with the preceding books," even as "the last four chapters contain the continuation of the historical narrations of those books." This does not suit his hypothesis that the Pentateuch as a whole did not exist in Josiah's day.

[7] *Deut.* p. lxvii ; cf. Kuenen, *Hex.* pp. 117 ff.   [8] *Hex.* p. 117.

chaps. i.–iii. with the body of the work, and he doubts whether "the only reason of any weight" for questioning chap. iv. 1–40 is conclusive either.[1] Oettli, another witness, says on chaps. i.–iv.: "The usage of speech is the same as in chaps. v.–xi."[2]

For ourselves, the broad argument from unity of thought, language, and style throughout the book seems overwhelming against all these attempts at disintegration. Dr. Driver is mainly with us here. He points out how "particular words, and phrases, consisting sometimes of entire clauses, recur with extraordinary frequency, giving a *distinctive colouring* to every part of the work."[3] Almost more important is his statement that "the majority of the expressions noted occur seldom or never besides; others occur only in passages modelled upon the style of Deuteronomy, and representing the same point of view."[4] As respects the opinions of other critics, Dillmann, Westphal, Kittel, Oettli, Delitzsch and others, defend, like Dr. Driver, the general unity of Deuteronomy. Dillmann and Westphal, however, have hypotheses of transpositions, etc., which Dr. Driver, with good reason, rejects as "intrinsically improbable."[5] The unity of Deuteronomy, it may be concluded, is likely to survive the attacks made upon it.

2. An interesting question arises here, with considerable bearings on later discussions—How does the *style* of Deuteronomy stand related to that of the other Pentateuchal books, and to those passages said to be "modelled" on it in other Old Testament writings? There are marked differences between the Deuteronomic and the JE and P styles, but it is important that these should not be exaggerated, and that affinities also should be noted.[6] Delitzsch, in his *Genesis*,

[1] *Deut.* p. lxxii.   [2] *Com. on Deut.* p. 9.
[3] *Deut.* p. lxxvii. Dr. Driver's words on chaps. v.–xxvi., xxviii. are worth quoting: "There is no sufficient reason for doubting that the whole of these chapters formed part of the law-book found by Hilkiah; all are written in the same style, and all breathe the same spirit, the only material difference being that, from the nature of the case, the parenetic phraseology is not so *exclusively* predominant in chaps. xii.–xxvi., xxviii. as it is in chaps. v.–xi. . . . Chaps. v.–xxvi. may thus be concluded, without hesitation, to be the work of a single author; and chap. xxviii. may be included without serious misgivings."—Pp. lxv, lxvii.
[4] *Ibid.* p. lxxxv.
[5] *Ibid.* p. lxxv. Kittel sympathises with Dillmann and Westphal. See his *Hist. of Hebs.* i. pp. 53 ff.
[6] See Note B on Deuteronomic and Priestly Styles.

made an interesting attempt, from comparison of the
Decalogue and Book of the Covenant with Deuteronomy
(which he took to be Mosaic in kernel), to arrive at an idea
of the mode of thought and language of Moses. He found
many Deuteronomic assonances in the above writings, and
concluded that there was "an original Mosaic type," which
he termed "Jehovistic-Deuteronomic."[1] It is at any rate
certain that comparison with the other Pentateuchal books
reveals some curious relations. Of all styles, that of the so-
called P is furthest removed from Deuteronomy; yet in
Lev. xxvi., which is of the P type, the language rises to a
quite Deuteronomic strain of hortatory and admonitory
eloquence. The resemblance is in fact so remarkable that
it is commonly allowed that a close relation of some kind
subsists between Lev. xxvi. and Deuteronomy, whether of
priority or dependence on the part of Leviticus remains yet
to be considered.[2] The affinities of Deuteronomy with JE
are much closer.[3] Such are clearly traceable in the Decalogue and Book of the Covenant,[4] whether we ascribe the
latter, with some critics, to J, or, with others, to E.[5] More
generally, "there are," says Dr. Driver, "certain sections of
JE (in particular, Gen. xxvi. 5; Ex. xiii. 3–16; xv. 26; xix.
3–6; parts of xx. 2–17; xxiii. 20–23; xxxiv. 10–26), in
which the author (or compiler) adopts a parenetic tone, and
where his style displays what may be termed an approxima-
tion to the style of Deuteronomy; and these sections appear
to have been the source from which the author of Deuteronomy adopted some of the expressions currently used by
him."[6] Not, it will be observed, *borrowed* from Deuteronomy,—a proof, surely, of an early Deuteronomic type.

[1] *Genesis*, pp. 29–32.

[2] Cf. Colenso, *Pent.*, Pt. vi. pp. 4 ff.; and see on Law of Holiness below,
Chap. IX. pp. 308 ff. On P phrases in Deuteronomy, see below, p. 277.

[3] Some older critics, as Stähelin, even attributed the composition of
Deuteronomy to the Jehovist. De Wette writes of Deuteronomy: "By
far the greater part belongs to one author, and, as it appears, to the
Jehovistic, of which it has numerous characteristic marks."—*Introd.* ii. p. 131.

[4] Cf. Delitzsch above. Wellhausen—Dillmann also—explains the references by a "back-current" from Deuteronomy. But the Decalogue, whether
provided with "enlargements" or not, must in its present form, as incorporated in the JE history, have been older than Deuteronomy (on critical date
of that book). So with the Book of the Covenant.

[5] See above, p. 231; below, p. 276.

[6] *Deut.* pp. lxxvii–lxxviii; cf. pp. lxxxv–vi. Delitzsch also finds
Deuteronomic traces occasionally in Genesis (*e.g.*, chap. xxvi. 5). Colenso

Still more interesting in this connection are certain passages in Joshua, Judges, and Samuel, described by Dr. Driver as "pre-Deuteronomic" (*i.e.*, pre-Josianic), and "allied to E," yet which have affinities in thought and expression to Deuteronomy.[1] And a last interesting and curious fact, as bearing on the alleged "modelling" on Deuteronomy, is that, if Dr. Driver is correct, the purity of the Deuteronomic revisers' style seems to *diminish* as we recede further in the history from the Mosaic age. It is, he tells us, most "strongly-marked" in Joshua and Judges, hardly appears in Samuel at all, is mingled with other forms of expression in Kings. "It is interesting to note," he observes, "what is on the whole an interesting accumulation of deviations from the original Deuteronomic type, till in, *e.g.*, 2 Kings xvii. it is mingled with phrases derived from the Book of Kings itself, Judges, and Jeremiah."[2] The inference we are disposed to draw from these facts is not quite that of the learned author. They appear to us to point to a much earlier dating and influence of Deuteronomy than he would allow.

III. DIFFICULTIES OF CRITICAL THEORY ON AGE AND ORIGIN

We now approach the central problem of the *age* and *origin* of the book. Was the Book of Deuteronomy, as the critics, with nearly united voice, allege, a production of the age of Josiah, or of one of his immediate predecessors? If not, what were the circumstances of its origin? It is extremely important to observe that for most of the critics this question is already settled before they begin. Deuteronomy is universally allowed to presuppose, and to

finds the hand of the Deuteronomist traceable from Genesis to 2 Kings (*Pent.*, Pt. vi. p. 28). He finally finds 117 Deuteronomic verses in Genesis, 138½ in Exodus, and 156½ in Numbers (Pt. vii. pp. i–vi ; App. pp. 145 ff.). Kuenen points out that Wellhausen approaches the positions of Stähelin and Colenso " when, from time to time, he notes a relationship between JE, *i.e.*, the redactor of the two works J and E, and the Book of Deuteronomy, and even asks whether JE may not have been revised by a deuteronomic redactor."—*Hex.* p. 137.

[1] *Ibid.* p. lxxxvi. Cf. *Introd.* pp. 106, 107, etc. Such passages are parts of Josh. xxiv. 1–26 ; Judg. vi. 7–10 ; x. 6–16 ; 1 Sam. ii. 17–36 ; parts of 1 Sam. vii.–viii. ; x. 11–27, etc.

[2] *Ibid.* p. xcii.

be dependent on, the laws and history contained in JE, and, these writings being brought down by general consent to the ninth or eighth century B.C., a later date for Deuteronomy necessarily follows.[1] We decline to bind ourselves in starting by this or any similar assumption. It may well be that the result of the argument will rather be to push the date of JE farther back, than to make Deuteronomy late. Reasons for the late date are found in the narrative of the finding of "the book of the law" in 2 Kings xxii., in statements of Deuteronomy itself, and in the character of its laws, compared with the earlier code, and with the history.[2] It seems to us, on the other hand, that, under these very heads, insoluble difficulties arise, which really amount to a *disproof* of the critical theory. Reversing the usual procedure, it will be our aim, first, to set forth these difficulties which call for a revisal of the current view, then to weigh the force of the considerations adduced in its support.

1. Investigation naturally begins with the narrative of the *finding of "the book of the law"* in the eighteenth year of the reign of Josiah (B.C. 622), which criticism holds to be the first appearance of Deuteronomy. The story, in brief, is that, during repairs in the temple, Hilkiah the high priest found a book, identified and described by him as "the book of the law." He announced his discovery to Shaphan the scribe, who, after reading the book himself, presented and read it to the king. Josiah was extraordinarily moved by what he heard, confessed the guilt of the "fathers" in not hearkening to the words of this book, sent to inquire of Jehovah at the prophetess Huldah, finally, after the holding of a great assembly, and the renewal of the nation's covenant with God on the basis of the book, instituted and carried through the remarkable "reformation"

[1] "Of course," remarks Dr. Driver, "for those who admit this [viz., that JE is long subsequent to Moses], the post-Mosaic authorship of Deuteronomy follows at once ; for, as was shown above, it is dependent upon, and consequently later than, JE."—*Deut.* p. xlii. Thus one part of the theory rules another.

[2] Dr. Driver again says : "As a work of the Mosaic age, Deuteronomy, I must own, though intelligible, if *it stood perfectly alone,—i.e.*, if the history of Israel had been other than it was,—does not seem to me intelligible, when read in the light shed upon it by other parts of the Old Testament."—*Ibid.* Pref. p. xii. This seems to show that it is the *history* (or view taken of it) which really decides the late date.

connected with his name.[1] There is no reason to doubt that the book which called forth this reformation, embraced, if it did not entirely consist of, the Book of Deuteronomy.[2] The critical theory, in its usual form, is, that the book was composed at or about this time, and was deposited in the temple, with the express design of bringing about just such a result. Is this credible or likely?

(1) Now, if anything is clear on the face of the narrative above summarised, it surely is, that this finding of the book of the law in the temple was regarded by everybody concerned as the *genuine discovery of an old lost book,* and *that* the " book of the law " of Moses. This is evident as well from the terms in which .the book is described (" the book of the law,"[3] " the book of the covenant,"[4] " the law of Moses "[5]), as from the profound impression it produced on king and people, and from the covenant and reformation founded on it. Hilkiah, who announced its discovery in the words, " I have found the book of the law in the house of Jehovah,"[6] the king, who was vehemently distressed " because our fathers have not hearkened to the words of this book,"[7] Huldah the prophetess, who confirmed the threatenings of the book,[8] had no other idea of it. There is not a whisper of doubt regarding its genuineness from any side—from priests at the temple, whose revenues it seriously interfered with, from prophets, on many of whom it bore hardly less severely, from the people, whose mode of life and religious habits it revolutionised, from priests of the high places, whom it deposed, and whose worship it put down as a high crime against Jehovah. The critics

---

[1] 2 Kings xxii., xxiii. ; cf. 2 Chron. xxxiv., xxxv. The credence accorded to this narrative in 2 Kings by the critics contrasts singularly with their free treatment of other parts of the later history of Kings, *e.g.,* the reforms of Hezekiah (2 Kings xviii. 4 ff.) questioned by Wellhausen, Stade, Smend, etc.), and the deliverance from Sennacherib (chap. xix. ; cf. H. P. Smith, *O.T. Hist.* p. 245).

[2] The narrative in Kings generally does not require, though at points it suggests, more (*e.g.,* chap. xxiii. 21) ; the Chronicler's account of the great Passover implies the Mosaic ordinance.

[3] 2 Kings xxii. 8.   [4] Chap. xxiii. 2.   [5] Chap. xxiii. 24, 25.

[6] Chap. xxii. 8.

[7] Chap. xxii. 13 ; cf. Jer. xxxiv. 13 ff. Professor W. R. Smith could persuade himself that " it was of no consequence to him [Josiah] to know the exact date of the authorship of the book "—*O.T. in J. C.* Not its *exact date,* perhaps, but its antiquity !

[8] Chap. xxii. 16.

17

themselves do not dispute, but freely allow, that it was taken for a genuinely Mosaic book, and that it was this fact which gave it its authority. The last thing, we may be certain, that would enter the minds of Josiah or of those associated with him, was that the book which so greatly moved them was one newly composed by prophetic or priestly men of their own circles. This was a point, moreover, on which we may be sure that king and people would not be readily deceived. People at no time are easily deceived where their own interests or privileges are concerned, but in this case there were special difficulties. A new book, after all, does not look like an old one; and if high priest, scribe, king, prophetess, were misled into thinking that they were dealing with an old Mosaic book, when the parchment in their hands was one on which the ink was hardly dry, they must have been simpletons to a degree without parallel in history. On the other hand, assume the book to have been old, mouldy, defaced, and what are we to say of its recent origin? Did its authors, as Oettli asks, disfigure the book to make it look old?[1]

(2) To these objections, there is but one plain answer, if the Josianic origin of the book is to be upheld, and that is an answer which the more influential leaders of the new school do not hesitate to give—the book was a result of *pious fraud*, or of a deliberate intention to deceive. It was a " pseudograph"; in popular speech, a "forgery." This, without any disguise, is the view taken of the matter by Reuss, Graf, Kuenen, Wellhausen, Stade, Cornill, Cheyne, etc.,[2] as by Colenso,[3] and many older critics. Many believing scholars, to their credit, repudiate it, but their scruples are treated by the real masters of the school as the result of timidity and weak compromise. Yet, as Klostermann says, in criticising it, "What a swallowing of

[1] *Deut.* Introd. p. 19.

[2] One of Reuss' propositions (endorsed by Wellhausen) is : "Deuteronomy is the book which the priests *pretended* to have found in the temple in the time of Josiah."—Wellhausen, *Hist. of Israel*, p. 4. For the views of other scholars, see Note C on Deuteronomy as *Fraus Pia*.

[3] Colenso, who thinks it likely that Jeremiah was the *falsarius*, writes : "What it [the inner voice] ordered him to do, he would do without hesitation, as by direct command of God ; and all considerations of morality or immorality would either not be entertained," etc. (*Pent.* Pop. edit. 1864, p. 201 ; cf. pp. 196 ff.).

camels is here!"¹   It is a view which, despite the excuse
attempted to be made for it by talk about the "less strict"
notions of truth in those days,² shocks the moral sense, and
is not for a moment to be entertained of a circle to which
the prophet Jeremiah, with his scathing denunciations of
lying and deceit, and of the "false pen of the scribes" that
"wrought falsely,"³ belonged.   Not that even on this
supposition the difficulty of the transaction is removed.
Hilkiah might be a party with prophets and priests in an
intrigue to palm off a "book of the law" on the unsuspecting
king;⁴ but how should he be able to use such language to
Shaphan as, "I have found *the* book of the law"? or how
should Josiah speak of the disobedience of the "fathers"
to commandments which he must have been aware were not
known to them? Is it not apparent that, though "the
book of the law" had long been neglected, disobeyed, and
allowed to become practically a dead letter, men still knew
of the existence of such a book, and had sufficient idea of
its contents to be able to recognise it when this old temple
copy, which had evidently been left to lie covered with its
dust, one does not know how long, in some recess, was
suddenly brought to light. It is nothing to the point to
urge, in answer, that, had Deuteronomy existed earlier,
there could not have been that long course of flagrant
violation of its precepts which Josiah deplores. The whole
condition of Jerusalem and Judah at this time, as described
in 2 Kings xxiii., was in flagrant violation of far more
fundamental statutes than that of the central sanctuary in
Deuteronomy. Let one read, *e.g.*, the account of the state
of things under Manasseh, or in Josiah's time, alongside
of such a sentence as the following from Dr. Driver:
"Now if there is one thing which (even upon the most
strictly critical premises) is certain about Moses, it is
that he laid the greatest stress upon Jehovah's being
Israel's only God, who tolerated no other God beside Him,
and who claimed to be the only object of the Israelite's

---

¹ *Pent.* p. 97.
² Kuenen, *Rel. of Israel*, ii. p. 19. See Note C.
³ Jer. viii. 8 ; cf. chaps. v. 30, 31, vi. 3-8, etc. See below, p. 294.
⁴ The extreme improbability of Hilkiah being a party to the forgery of
a work which (on the theory) seriously infringed on the privileges of the
Jerusalem priesthood, is pointed out by many writers (W. R. Smith,
Dillmann, Kittel, Driver, etc.).

allegiance." [1] And are there no parallels in history, both
to the condition of neglect into which the book of the law
had fallen, and to the startling effect of the timely rediscovery of a book long forgotten? [2]

(3) In light of these facts, it is not a little singular that
Dr. Driver, in repelling the charge that "if the critical
view of Deuteronomy be correct, the book is a 'forgery,'
the author of which sought to shelter himself under a great
name, and to secure by a fiction recognition or authority
for a number of laws 'invented' by himself" [3]—should not
make it clearer than he does that this opinion—represented
by him as a groundless "objection" of opponents—is, so far
as the pseudographic character of the work is concerned,
precisely and explicitly that of the heads of the school with
which "the critical view" he defends is specially associated.
It is the theory also, we cannot help agreeing, to which we
are logically brought, if it is assumed that Deuteronomy is
really a product of the age of Josiah, in which it was found. [4]
Dr. Driver himself, however, and, as already said, most
believing scholars, separate themselves from this obnoxious
hypothesis of deceit, and, to explain the "discovery" of the
book by Hilkiah, commonly suppose that it belongs to a
somewhat *earlier* period [5]—*e.g.*, to the reign of Manasseh,
or that of Hezekiah, or the age immediately *before* Hezekiah. [6]

---

[1] *Deut.* p. lix.

[2] The general neglect of the Scriptures in the age before the Reformation,
and the effect on Luther's mind and work of the discovery of a complete
copy of the Bible at Erfurt, offer a partial illustration. For a remarkable
instance of the total oblivion of a noted code of laws in the Middle Ages, see
Note D on Oblivion of Charlemagne's Code.

[3] *Deut.* p. lxi. Dr. Driver refers to the plot theory on p. liv. Even as
regards "invention," it may be noticed that this was the view of De Wette,
who first set the ball a-rolling. The book may be proved, De Wette
thought, "to rest entirely on fiction, and indeed so much so that, while the
preceding books amidst myths contained traditional data, here tradition
does not seem in any instance to have supplied any materials."—*Beiträge*,
ii. pp. 385 ff. ; cf. i. p. 268.

[4] Cf. Kittel, *Hist. of Hebrews*, i. pp. 64 ff.

[5] Dr. Driver says that "the narrative of the discovery certainly supports
the view that the book which was found was one which had been lost for
some time, not one which had just been written" (p. liv). His own mind
leans to an origin in the *childhood* of Josiah. But does this answer to the
idea of a book "lost" for some time, and, apart from fraud, what would be
the appearance of such a book?

[6] So Ewald, Bleek, W. R. Smith, Kittel, Kautzsch, etc. (Manasseh);
Delitzsch, Riehm, Westphal, Oettli, König, Klostermann, etc. (Hezekiah or
before).

The moral qualms which lead to these theories are to be respected, but those who adopt them now labour under the disadvantage that, having cut themselves away from the age of Josiah, they have no fixed principle to go by, and, apart from *a priori* assumptions in regard to the course of development, there is no particular reason why they should stop where they do, and not carry the date of Deuteronomy much higher still.   They find themselves exposed also to the attacks of the advocates of the Josiah date, who point out the unsuitability of Deuteronomy to Manasseh's gloomy reign ("the calm and hopeful spirit which the author displays, and the absence even of any covert allusion to the special troubles of Manasseh's reign"[1]); but, above all, urge what Kuenen calls "the great, and in my opinion fatal objection," "that it makes the actual reformation the work of those who had not planned it, but were blind tools in the service of the unknown projector."[2]   It would, indeed, be strange procedure on the part of anyone composing a work in the spirit of Moses, yet not desiring to pass it off as other than his own, to deposit it secretly in the temple, there to lie undiscovered for perhaps a century—finally, in the irony of history, on its coming to light, to be accepted as a work of Moses, and continuously regarded as such by the Jewish and Christian world for over two millenniums!   "Fatal" objections thus seem to lie at the door of all these hypotheses, and we are driven to ask whether some other explanation is not imperative.

(4) It may be added that the critics are seriously at variance on another point, viz., whether the author of Deuteronomy in Josiah's—or an earlier—age is to be sought for among the *prophets* or the *priests*.   It seems a curious question to ask, after starting with the view that Deuteronomy was a "prophetic" programme; yet it is one of no small importance in its bearings on origin, and the reasons against *either* view, on the critical premises, seem extremely strong.   If a prophet, why, unlike the practice of other prophets, did he adopt this device of clothing his message in the form of addresses of Moses,

[1] *Deut.* p. liii.
[2] *Hex.* p. 219.   Kuenen adds: "The *rôle* assigned to D himself is almost equally improbable; for he is made to commit his aspirations to writing, urge their realisation with intense fervour—and leave the result to chance (p. 220).   Cf. Carpenter, *Hex.* i. pp. 96–97.

and whence the strength of his interest in the **sanctuary,**
its worship, and its feasts ?   As Kuenen, who favours **the**
view of the *priestly* origin, points out: " It is obvious from
Deut. xxiv. 8, and still more from chaps. xvii. 18, xxxi. 9,
that the Deuteronomist had relations with the priesthood
of Jerusalem.   In chap. xiv. 3–21 he even incorporates a
priestly *torah* on clean and unclean animals into his book
of law." [1] But then, on the other hand, if a priest,
how account for the remodelling of the older laws **in a**
direction inimical to the prerogatives of the Jerusalem
priesthood ? [2] The last thing one would look for from a
priest would be the concocting of ordinances which **meant**
the sharing of his temple perquisites with all Levites **who**
chose to claim them.   The idea, again, of a *joint* composition
by prophets and priests is not favoured by the conditions of
the age, and is opposed to the unity of style and spirit in
the book.   This apparent conflict of interests, so difficult **to**
harmonise with the time of Josiah, seems to point to **an**
origin far nearer the fountainhead.

2. The next natural branch of inquiry relates to *the testi-*
mony of the book itself as to the circumstances of its own origin.
To the ordinary reader it might seem as if no doubt whatever
could rest on this point.   The book would appear in the
most explicit fashion to claim for itself a Mosaic origin.
Not only are the discourses it contains affirmed to have
been delivered by Moses in the *Arabah* of Moab—this *might*
be accounted for by literary impersonation—but at the close
there are express attestations that Moses *wrote* his law,
and delivered it into the custody of the priests for safe
preservation.   " And Moses wrote this law," we read, " and
delivered it unto the priests, the sons of Levi. . . . When
Moses had made an end of writing the words of this law in
a book, until they were finished, Moses commanded the
Levites, which bare the ark of the covenant of Jehovah,
saying, Take this book of the law, and put it by the side of
the ark," etc. [3]   In view of these declarations, one does not
well know what to make of the remarkable statement of
Dr. Driver that, " though it may appear paradoxical to say

[1] *Hex.* p. 273.   It is to be remembered that Hilkiah was a priest.
[2] Cf. Kautzsch, in criticism of this view, *Lit. of O. T.*, pp. 64–65.
[3] Deut. xxxi. 9, 24–26.   The Song and the Blessing of Moses are also said
to be from Moses—the former to have been written by him (chaps. xxxi. 22,
xxxiii. 1).

so, *Deuteronomy does not claim to be written by Moses.*" [1]
The paradox Dr. Driver defends is, at all events, not one
accepted by the leaders of the critical school, who lay stress
upon the fact that the writer obviously *intended* his book to
be received as genuinely Mosaic, and in that way sought to
gain authority for its teachings.[2] It was undoubtedly as a
genuine work of Moses—subject, of course, to any necessary
revisional processes—that it was received by Josiah and his
contemporaries.

There is, however, the possibility of a mediating view,
which must in justice be taken account of, though it is not one,
it seems to us, which greatly helps the newer critics. First,
we should say, as respects the *scope* of the above testimony,
we entirely agree that the words, "Moses wrote this law,"
cannot, in the connection in which they stand, be fairly
extended, as has sometimes been attempted, to cover the
whole Pentateuch.[3] On the other hand, we see no fitness
or probability in confining them, with Delitzsch[4] and many
others, to the "kernel" of the Mosaic law in chaps. xii.–xxvi.
The word *torah* must be taken here in its widest sense as
covering the hortatory and admonitory parts of the book,
not less than its strictly legal portions.[5] The godly of later
times, who found their souls' nourishment and delight in

[1] *Introd.* p. 89. The fact that the above statements are made in the third
person does not alter their purport. Dillmann's explanation of the notice
of authorship is singularly roundabout and lame. "The statement,"
he says, "is satisfactorily explained by the fact that the writer was convinced
of the antiquity and Mosaic character of the law [represented as] expounded
by Moses, and it was precisely for one who wished to give out the old
Mosaic law in a renewed form that an express statement of the writing down
and preservation of that law was indispensable."—*Num.-Jos.* p. 601.
"Indispensable" to assert that as a fact which existed nowhere but in his
own imagination!

[2] De Wette says : "The author of Deuteronomy, as it appears, would have
us regard his whole book as the work of Moses."—*Introd.* ii. p. 159. Cornill
instances Deuteronomy as "an instructive proof that only under the name
of Moses did a later writer believe himself able to reckon on a hearing as a
religious lawgiver."—*Einleit.* p. 37.

[3] Thus Hengstenberg, Hävernick, etc.

[4] *Genesis*, i. pp. 36–37.

[5] Cf. chap. i. 5 : "began Moses to declare this law." There is little force
in the objection drawn from the command to write the law on plastered
stones on Mount Ebal (Deut. xxvii. 3). The recently discovered Code of
Hammurabi shows what was possible to ancient times in the way of writing
on stones. It is stated by Dr. Green that "the famous Behistun inscription
of Darius in its triple form is twice as long as this entire Code (Chaps. xii.
xxvi.), besides being carved in bold characters on the solid rock, and in a
position difficult of access on the mountain side."—*Moses and Prophets*, p. 53

the "law of Jehovah" (cf. Pss. i., xix. 7 ff., cxix., etc.), had, we may be sure, other material before them than the bare legal precepts of either the Deuteronomic or the Priestly Code.[1] The notice can only fairly be understood as meaning that Moses put in writing, and delivered to the priests, the substance, if not the letter, of what he had just been saying; and such a statement, once and again repeated in the book (cf. in addition to the above, chap. xvii. 18), must, for those who recognise its honesty of intent, always have the greatest weight.   But, this being granted, the question remains whether the words "this law" necessarily apply to the discourses *precisely as we have them, i.e.,* in their present literary form.   Assuming that Moses, as Delitzsch conjectures, "before his departure left behind with the priestly order an autograph *torah* to be preserved and disseminated,"[2] may we not reasonably suppose that, in the book as we possess it, we have, not a literal transcription of that *torah,* but a "free literary reproduction" of its contents, in the form best adapted for general instruction and edification, with occasional developments and modifications suited to the time of its origin ?   So again Delitzsch and not a few others think.   "The Deuteronomian," he says, "has completely appropriated the thoughts and language of Moses, and from a genuine oneness of mind with him reproduces them in the highest intensity of divine inspiration."[3]

There will be little doubt, we think, as to the *admissibility* of this "reproduction" theory, if the circumstances are shown to require it.   It implies no purpose to deceive, and stands on a different footing from theories which, under the name "development," assume the attribution to Moses of ideas, laws, and institutions, not only unknown to him, but, if the critical hypothesis is correct, actually in conflict with his genuine legislation.   Perhaps, also, in a modified degree,

---

[1] See below, pp. 376-77.   [2] *Genesis,* i. p. 35.
[3] *Ibid.* Cf. also art. in Luthardt's *Zeitschrift,* 1880, pp. 503-5. For related views, cf. Oettli, *Deut.* Introd. pp. 16-18 ; Ladd's *Doct. of Sac. Scripture,* i. p. 527-29 ; Robertson, *Early Religion,* etc., pp. 420-25. Dr. Driver approximates to this view. "Deuteronomy," he says, "may be described as the *prophetic reformulation, and adaptation to new needs, of an older legislation.* It is probable that there was a tradition, if not a written record, of a final legislative address delivered by Moses in the steppes of Moab ; the plan followed by the author would rest upon a more obvious motive, if he thus worked upon a traditional basis" (p. lxi). This too much ignores the strong *positive* testimony that Moses *did* write his last discourses.

some recasting in form and language, in the sense of this hypothesis, *must* be admitted, if we suppose—what is very probable—that the script which Moses used was other than the ancient Hebrew, or grant that the discourses were written out rather in substance than in full detail—leaving it to the transcriber or interpreter to fill out, and give the living impression of scene and voice. If this was done (as we believe it must have been) when the remembrance or tradition of Moses and his time was still vivid and reliable, it would give us a book such as we have in Deuteronomy. On the other hand, if so much is admitted about Moses, the question which must always recur regarding this theory, even to the very limited extent indicated, is—*Cui bono?* If, as Delitzsch supposes, the contents of Deuteronomy are *substantially* Mosaic,—if Moses really delivered testamentary discourses, and in some form wrote them down for posterity, —whence the necessity for this literary " double " to re-write and improve them? Why should the form in which Moses spoke and wrote them not be substantially that in which we have them? Shall we suppose that the actual discourses were less grand and sustained in style—less tender, glowing, and eloquent—than those we possess,—that they contained less recitation of God's dealings,[1] less expostulation, exhortation, and affectionate appeal,—or were less impressive in their counsels and warnings? Or that Moses, when he came to write them down—"till they were finished," says the text—was not able to make as noble and powerful a record of them as any inspired man of a later date? We, at least, have a less mean idea of Moses, the man of God, and of his literary capabilities. We have a full and vivid picture of him, and specimens of his style of thought and pleading, in the history; we can judge of his lofty gifts, if the Ode at the Red Sea, or the Song in Deuteronomy,[2] are from his pen; and we may well believe that, of all men living, he was the one most capable of giving worthy literary form to his own addresses.[3] If the book, in substance, is from Moses, very

[1] If so, what dealings? Those in the JE history? It is to be remembered that, wherever we place Deuteronomy, the JE history, in substance at least, stands behind it.

[2] Nothing necessitates us," says Delitzsch, "to deny the Song to Moses."—Luthardt's *Zeitschrift*, 1880, p. 506; cf. *Genesis*, i. p. 45.

[3] "In presence," says Delitzsch, "of the Egyptian and Babylonian-Assyrian written monuments, which likewise contain great connected

cogent reasons must be shown for putting it, even in its literary form, at a much later date.

In reality, however, so far as critics of the newer time are concerned, such a hypothesis as we have been considering is wholly in the air. Possessed of quite other ideas of what *must* have been, these writers will hardly entertain even the possibility, either of Moses having written these discourses, or of his being able to write them. For them the Mosaic age is literally, as Duhm says, "wiped out."[1] Underlying their refusal of Deuteronomy to Moses will generally be found the denial that we know anything definitely at all about Moses, or of his literary capabilities. or that he delivered any testamentary discourses, or that any of the laws or institutions ordinarily attributed to him —even the Ten Commandments—are actually of his age.[2] In that case, Delitzsch's hypothesis, with other mediating views, falls, and we are brought back essentially to the old alternative. The thorough-paced critic will have nothing to say to a hypothetical or traditionary basis for a book admitted to belong in its present shape to the age of the kings.[3] Kuenen will allow no alternative between "authenticity" and "literary fiction."[4]

3. When, finally, from the external attestation, we turn to the *internal character* of the book—and it is here the strength of the critical position is held to lie—we find a series of phenomena which, so far from supporting, throw very great, if not insuperable, obstacles in the way of its ascription to the age of Josiah. On these the minifying end of the critical telescope is persistently turned, while the

oratorical pieces, and represent a form of speech which remained essentially the same during 1000 years, one need not be disturbed by the high antiquity of a written production of Moses."—Luthardt's *Zeitschrift*, 1880, p. 506. See his testimony to Moses as a poet in *Genesis*, i. pp. 44–45.

[1] *Theol. d. Proph.* p. 19. See below, p. 286.

[2] It is not advanced writers alone that fall into this arbitrary style of reasoning. Such a reason, *e.g.*, as that assigned even by a believing critic like Riehm for refusing the Deuteronomic discourses to Moses—"the spiritual apprehension of the law, as seen in the demand for a circumcision of the heart" (*Einleit.* i. pp. 245–46)—belongs to the same *a priori*, subjective system of judging of a past age, which scientific investigation is increasingly discrediting.

[3] "The opinion," said De Wette long ago, "that these latter passages (Deut. xxxi. 9, etc.) refer to a short treatise which has been worked over in Deuteronomy is quite arbitrary."—*Introd.* ii. p. 159.

[4] *Hex.* p. 219.

magnifying end is brought to bear in its full power on any difficulties that seem to tell against an earlier date. We have to remember that the book, on the critical view, was composed with the express design of calling into being such a reformation as that which followed its "discovery" in the reign of Josiah.[1] The proof of its origin in that age is held to be its suitability to the conditions of the time, and the stress it lays on the demand for centralisation of worship. When, however, we open the book itself, we are forcibly struck by the *absence* of clear evidence of any such design on the part of the author, and by the numerous indications of *un*suitability to the age in which it is believed to have been composed. The book and the history, in a word, do not fit each other.

(1) It is extremely doubtful if " centralisation of worship," in the critical acceptation of that phrase, was *the dominant motive* in Josiah's reformation at all. The idea of the un-lawfulness of worship—even of Jehovah—on high places need not have been absent; it had, we believe, been in the background of men's minds ever since the founding of Solomon's temple. But it was not that which so strangely moved Josiah to alarm and action. His reformation from beginning to end was a crusade against the *idolatry* which had everywhere infected Church and state—central sanctuary included,[2]—and the "high places" were put down as part of this stern suppression of *all* idolatrous and heathenish practices. Of a movement for unity of worship as such the narrative gives not a single hint. On the other hand, when we look to Deuteronomy, we find little or nothing that points directly to a consuming zeal against the "high places"—in Josiah's time the crying sin, because the chief centres of idolatry, in Judah. There are warnings against falling into the idolatries and other abominations of the *Canaanites*, when the land should be possessed,[3] and in chaps. vii. 5, 25, xii. 2–4, injunctions to "utterly destroy" the sanctuaries, altars, pillars, Asherahs, and graven images of these former inhabitants. But there is nothing peculiarly

---

[1] " It was not by accident," Kuenen says, " but in accordance with the writer's deliberate purpose, that it became the foundation and norm of Josiah's reformation."—*Hex.* p. 215. Cf. Wellhausen, *Hist. of Israel*, p. 33.

[2] Cf. 2 Kings xxiii. 4, 7, 11, 12, etc.

[3] Cf. especially chap. xviii. 9 ff.

Josianic in this—it is all there already in the older Book of the Covenant.[1] Still further, while Deuteronomy gives prominence to the idea of the centralisation of worship at the sanctuary, it is far from correct to say that this is the dominating idea of the book—the one grand idea which inspires it.[2] It has its place in chap. xii., and recurs in the regulations for feasts, tithing, and priestly duty; but the *preceding* discourses have nothing to say of it, and in the Code it appears with a multitude of other laws, some of them more fundamental than itself. The bulk of the laws in the book, as will appear below, are taken from the Book of the Covenant; others are from a priestly source yet to be investigated.

(2) Here already is a puzzling problem for the critics— to account for the relevancy of this wide range of laws, many of them dealing with seemingly trivial matters, in a book assumed to be specially composed to effect a reformation in *worship*.[3] The irrelevancy of the greater number of the precepts for such a purpose is obvious at a glance. But the incongruity of the Code in structure and contents with the supposed occasion of its origin appears in other respects. The most favourable view of the book is that it is a *corpus* of old laws reproduced in a hortatory setting with special adaptation to the circumstances of a late time. Yet in

[1] Ex. xx. 3 ff.; xxii. 18, 20; xxiii. 13, 24, 32, 33; cf. xxxiv. 14–17. The exception is the sun, moon, and "host of heaven" in Deut. iv. 19, xvii. 3, founded on by Riehm (i. p. 245) and others. But the worship of sun, moon, and other heavenly bodies goes far back beyond Moses, and is alluded to in the Old Testament long before the time of Josiah (Isa. xvii. 8, R.V.; Amos v. 26). Cf. Beth-shemesh in Josh. xv. 10, etc.

[2] Oettli says : "It rests on an unusual onesidedness in the mode of consideration, if, as now mostly happens, the aim of Deuteronomy is restricted to the centralisation of the cultus, and the ordinances of worship connected with this. That is one of its demands, but it is neither the most original nor the weightiest, but only an outcome of its deepening of the thought of the covenant."—*Deut.* Introd. p. 21.

[3] This is in fact made the starting-point by the newer critics for their hypothesis of "gradual accretion." "There is no apparent appropriateness," we read, "so far as the programme of the Deuteronomic reforms is concerned, in the historical retrospect, i. 6–iii. But neither is there, for example, in the laws which regulate birds'-nesting or parapets upon a roof in xxii. 6–8. With what feelings [one may well ask it] could Josiah have listened to these details ? . . . It is plain that the contents of the Code, at least in its later portions, are very miscellaneous."—Carpenter, *Hex.* i. p. 93. But then, instead of recasting the theory of "programmes" which thus has the bottom taken out of it, the law-book of Josiah is reduced practically to chaps. xii.–xix. (p. 95).

point of form everything is thrown back into the age of
Moses.   The standpoint of the speaker is the East of Jordan,[1]
with the prospect of the people's immediately entering
Canaan; Israel is treated *in its unbroken unity as a nation*
("all Israel"), and there is not a hint anywhere of the great
division that, centuries before Josiah's time, had rent the
kingdom into twain, and had ended in the destruction of
one of its branches (Ephraim).   What is even more remarkable, the laws frequently are, not only long obsolete, but of
a character ludicrously out of place in a reforming Code of
the end of the seventh century.   We need not dwell at
length on these anachronisms of the Code, which have been
so often pointed out,[2]—the law, *e.g.*, for the extermination
of the Canaanites,[3] when no Canaanites remained to be
exterminated; the injunction to destroy the Amalekites;[4]
the rules for military service (inapplicable to the later
time),[5] for besieging of foreign cities,[6] for arrangements in
the camp;[7] the warnings against choosing a foreigner for a
king, and causing to return to Egypt,[8] the friendly tone
towards Edom,[9] so strangely in contrast with the hostile
spirit of the prophets;[10] and the like.   These things may
seem as the small dust of the balance to the critic,[11] but
they may not appear so insignificant to others.   Dr.
Driver's answer, that the injunctions against the Canaanites
and Amalekites are repeated from the older legislation, and
"in a recapitulation of Mosaic principles addressed *ex
hypothesi* to the people when they were about to enter
Canaan, would be naturally included,"[12] only corroborates

[1] On the expression "the other side Jordan," see below, p. 281.
[2] Cf. Delitzsch, *Genesis*, p. 38 ; Oettli, *Deut.* Introd. pp. 11, 12, 17 ff.
[3] Chaps. vii. 1, 2, xx. 10–18.
[4] Chap. xxv. 17–19.   Dr. Green speaks of these injunctions as being as
utterly out of date as would be at the present day "a royal proclamation in
Great Britain ordering the expulsion of the Danes."—*Moses and the Prophets*,
p. 63.
[5] Chap. xx. 1–9.   [6] Chap. xx. 9–15, 19, 20.
[7] Chap. xxiii. 2–9.   Imagine these provisions in a Code seven centuries
after Moses.
[8] Chap. xvii. 15–16.   See Note E on the Law of the King.
[9] Chap. xxiii. 7, 8.
[10] Jer. xlix. 17, 18 ; Obadiah ; Joel iii. 19 ; Isa. lxiii. 1–6.
[11] Cf. Kuenen, *Hex.* pp. 218–19.   Kuenen has no difficulty, because he
frankly attributes to the author the design to deceive.
[12] *Deut.* p. lxii.   Dr. Driver's suggestion that the injunctions against the
Canaanites would have an *indirect* value as a protest against heathenish
practices in Judah is without support in the text, which evidently

our point, that they were suitable to the times of Moses, but not to those of Josiah. The difficulty is not touched *why* a writer in that age should go out of his way to include them, when they did not bear on his purpose, and had no relevancy to existing conditions. But even in the matter of reformation of worship, it is important to observe that the laws in Deuteronomy were not of a kind that could be, or were, enforced by Josiah in their integrity. In the Code, *e.g.*, it is ordained that idolaters of every degree, with all who secretly or openly entice to idolatry, are to be unsparingly put to death.[1] Josiah, it is true, slew the priests of the high places of Samaria upon their altars. But he did not attempt any such drastic measures in Judah. He brought up, instead, the priests of the high places to Jerusalem, and allowed them to "eat of the unleavened bread among their brethren."[2] It is one of the most singular instances of the reading of a preconceived theory into a plain text, when, in face of the law ordaining death for all idolatry, these "disestablished priests" of the high places are regarded as the Levites of Deut. xviii. 8, for whom provision is made out of the temple dues.[3] Of course, there is not a syllable hinting at "disestablished priests" of the high places in the provisions of Deuteronomy for the Levites. The latter, besides, were permitted to minister at the sanctuary, while Josiah's priests were not.

IV. CRITICAL REASONS FOR LATE DATING OF THE BOOK: VALIDITY OF THESE

It is now incumbent on us, having indicated the difficulties which seem to us decisive against a late dating of Deuteronomy, to consider the reasons ordinarily adduced in favour of that late dating, or at least of the origin of the book in times long posterior to Moses. We have already seen that, of those who reject the substantially Mosaic

means them to be taken quite seriously, and does not apply to the Amalekites, etc.

[1] Deut. xiii.   [2] 2 Kings xxiii. 9.

[3] Thus Dr. Driver connects—as if it were a matter of course—Deut. xviii. 8 with "Josiah's provision made for the support of the disestablished priests out of the temple dues."—*Deut.* p. xlv. Cf. Wellhausen: "He [the Deuteronomist] provides for the priests of the suppressed sanctuaries," etc.—*Hist. of Israel*, p. 33.

origin of the book, a *few* place the book earlier than Hezekiah, *some* put it in the reign of Manasseh, *most* put it in the reign of Josiah. It may be found that several, at least, of the reasons for this late dating turn, on examination, into arguments for the opposite view.

It cannot be too constantly borne in mind, what was before said, that, with the majority of critics of the Graf-Wellhausen school, the really determining grounds for the late dating of Deuteronomy lie outside the region of properly critical discussion altogether, viz., in the completely altered view taken of the age of Moses, and of the subsequent course of the religious history of Israel. If the accounts we have of Moses and his work are, as Kuenen says, "utterly unhistorical,"—if it is inconceivable that he should have had the elevated conceptions or the prophetic foresight attributed to him in these discourses,—then it needs no further argument to prove that Deuteronomy must be late. The date of Deuteronomy is, in this case, no longer *merely* a literary question, and the critics are not wrong in speaking of it, as they have sometimes done, as the pivot of the Pentateuchal question. It does not, indeed, follow, as we formerly sought to show, that the Mosaic history and religion are subverted, even if a late date is accepted for the present form of the book. But very important conclusions certainly *do* follow, if the book is admitted to be early. If Deuteronomy, in its present form, be even *substantially* Mosaic,—if it conveys to us with fidelity the purport of discourses and laws actually delivered by Moses to the people of Israel before his death,—then we must go a great deal further. For Deuteronomy undeniably rests in some degree on the JE history embodied in our Pentateuch; on the Code of laws which we call the Book of the Covenant, incorporated in that history; as well as on priestly laws from some other source. The effect of the acceptance of an early date for Deuteronomy, therefore, is to throw all these writings back practically into the Mosaic age, whatever the time when they were finally put together. We should like to be more sure than we are that it is not the perception of this fact which is at least one motive in leading the critics to put down Deuteronomy as far as they do, in the age of the kings.

1. It is important, in this connection, to observe how

much is *conceded* by the more moderate advocates of the
critical hypothesis themselves. These concessions are very
considerable—so extensive, in fact, that they really amount,
in our view, to the giving up of a large part of the critical
case for the late dating. We have seen how Delitzsch
postulates written "testamentary discourses" and laws of
Moses; but critics like Oettli and Driver also go a long way
in allowing, in the words of the latter,[1] "a continuous Mosaic
tradition," reaching back to Moses' own time, and "embracing a moral, a ceremonial, and a civil element." When,
particularly, the object is to vindicate Deuteronomy against
the charge of "forgery" and "invention," stress is strongly
laid on the fact that the great bulk of the legislation is old,
and that the few laws which are really new are but "the
logical and consistent development of Mosaic principles."[2]
So far, indeed, is this insistence on the antiquity and
genuinely Mosaic character of the legislation carried—in
striking and favourable contrast with the more radical
tendency to deny *all* legislation to Moses—that one begins
to wonder where the contradictions with earlier law and
practice come in which are to prove indubitably that the
book *cannot* be Mosaic. Thus we are bid remember "that
what is essentially new in Deuteronomy is not the *matter*,
but the *form*."[3] Dillmann is quoted as testifying that
"Deuteronomy is anything but an original law-book."[4]
"The new element in Deuteronomy," it is said, "is not the
laws, but their *parenetic* setting. . . . [The author's] aim
was to win obedience to laws, or truths, which were already
known, but were in danger of being forgotten."[5] "It was
felt to be (in the main) merely the re-affirmation of laws
and usages which had been long familiar to the nation,
though in particular cases they might have fallen into
neglect."[6] Most significant of all is a sentence quoted from
Reuss: "The only real innovation . . . was the absolute
prohibition of worship outside of Jerusalem."[7]

Here at length we seem to come to a definite issue.
The "only real innovation" in Deuteronomy is *the law of
the central sanctuary*. We are not unjustified, therefore, in

---

[1] *Deut.* p. lvii. Cf. Oettli, *Deut.* Introd. pp. 17, 18. Delitzsch may be
quoted again : "The claim of Deuteronomy to a Mosaic origin is justified on
internal grounds."—Luthardt's *Zeitschrift*, 1880, p. 503 ; cf. p. 504.

[2] *Ibid.* p. lvi.   [3] *Ibid.*   [4] *Ibid.*
[5] *Ibid.* p. lxi.   [6] *Ibid.* p. lvi.   [7] *Ibid.*

regarding this as the *fundamental pillar* which upholds the case for the late dating of Deuteronomy. Even this law, moreover, it is conceded, is only "relatively" new; it was a genuine development from Mosaic principles, and focalising of tendencies which had long been in operation.[1] The natural inference one would draw from this is, that it cannot be *really* incompatible with the law in Ex. xx. 24, with its supposed permission of unlimited freedom of worship.[2] The subject was discussed in an earlier chapter, to which it is sufficient here to refer.[3] The conclusion there arrived at was that there is nothing in this Deuteronomic law essentially at variance with the altar-law in Exodus, or with the later religious practice, if allowance is made for times of religious backsliding and neglect, and for the complete disorganisation of an age like Samuel's, when ecclesiastical and every other kind of laws were necessarily in large part in abeyance. One fact which should lead criticism to pause before giving too narrow an interpretation of the law is that, as before noted, in Deuteronomy itself a command is given for the building of an altar for sacrifice on Mount Ebal, in harmony with the law in Exodus.[4] We marked also a tendency in the newer criticism itself to break with the Wellhausen "dogma" of an absolute centralisation of worship in Deuteronomy, and a consequent conflict with the older law in Exodus.[5]

2. If this fundamental prop of the Wellhausen theory gives way, as we are persuaded it does, most of the *other* considerations adduced in favour of the late date of Deuteronomy may fairly be treated as of subordinate importance. They resolve themselves, partly into alleged discrepancies between the Deuteronomic *laws* and those of the Book of the Covenant, and of the Levitical Code; partly into alleged

---

[1] *Deut.* p. lvi.   [2] See above, pp. 173 ff.
[3] Chap. VI. pp. 173 ff.   [4] Deut. xxvii. 5-7.
[5] See above, Chap. VI. pp. 174, 176. Fries, in his *Moderne Vorstellungen der Geschichte Israels*, speaks of this "dogma" as playing well-nigh the same part in the Wellhausen criticism as did formerly "the opposition between Jewish and Pauline Christianity in the school of Baur in the New Testament domain" (p. 15) ; and Van Hoonacker, in his *Le Sacerdoce Lévitique*, says : "The whole historical and critical system of the school of Wellhausen rests in effect on the pretended first promulgation of the principle of the unity of the sanctuary in the seventh century" (p. 14). This writer points out that the unity of the sanctuary is not so much enacted as *presupposed* in Deuteronomy (p. 13).

18

discrepancies with the *history* of the preceding books; and partly into a few *expressions* in the book thought to imply a later date than that of Moses. On none of these classes of objection will it be found necessary to spend much time: a few typical examples may be examined.

(1) The subject of *laws* may be glanced at first. In a previous chapter we endeavoured to show that there is nothing in Deuteronomy necessarily incompatible with the Aaronic priesthood and Levitical arrangements of the middle books of the Pentateuch[1]—arrangements now held, however, by the critical school to be *later* than Deuteronomy; and we shall see as we proceed that, while it was no part of the design of the speaker in these farewell addresses to dwell on details of ritual, chiefly of interest to the priests, yet Levitical regulations are presupposed, and in some instances are referred to, in his recital.[2] As to the Book of the Covenant, it is allowed on all hands that the bulk of its provisions are taken up, and reiterated and enforced in the discourses.[3] In such hortatory recapitulation, where much is left to be understood by the hearer, points of difficulty in comparison with other Codes may be expected to arise; but, considering the number of the laws, the seeming discrepancies must be pronounced very few. In some cases it may be that we do not possess all the elements for a complete solution, but there is no reason to suppose that, if we had them, a solution would not be forthcoming.

A chief example of discrepancy between Deuteronomy and the Priestly Code—*the* chief, perhaps, after that of the priests and Levites[4]—is in the tithe-laws in chaps. xii. 6, 17–19, xiv. 22–29, xxvi. 12–15, which certainly present a different aspect from those in Num. xviii. 21–31.[5] In the latter case the tithe is devoted in fixed proportions to the maintenance of Levites and priests; in the former, it is used by the worshippers for two years out of three in

[1] Cf. Chap. VI. pp. 180 ff.

[2] See below, pp. 311 ff. On the relation of Deuteronomy to the so-called "Law of Holiness," see next chapter.

[3] Lists of comparison of the laws in the Book of the Covenant and in Deuteronomy may be seen in Driver (*Deut.* pp. iv ff.), Westphal, Oettli, or any of the text-books.

[4] See above, pp. 184 ff.

[5] Cf. on the discrepancy, Kuenen, *Hex.* pp. 28, 29; Driver, *Deut.* pp. 168 ff.

feasts at the sanctuary, to which the Levites are invited, and on the third year is given up wholly, at home, to the Levites, orphans, widows, and strangers. Apart, however, from the fact that the Levitical provision seems clearly (indeed, verbally) referred to in chap. xviii. 1, 2,[1] it appears, if better solution does not offer,[2] a not unreasonable explanation that, in accordance with later Jewish practice, the festal tithe of Deuteronomy is different from, and additional to, the ordinary tithe for the maintenance of the Levites (a "second tithe").[3] We may perhaps venture the suggestion that it is really this Deuteronomic tithe which was the old and traditional one, and the Levitical tithe which was the second and additional impost. The tithe devoted to Jehovah probably goes back in pious circles to remotest times (cf. Gen. xiv. 20; xxviii. 22), and then can only be supposed to have been used in a religious feast, or in charity. This was the old and well-understood voluntary tithe; the Levitical had a different object. But if the Deuteronomic tithe creates difficulty, what is to be said of the counter-theory of the critics? Is it really to be credited—for this is the alternative supposition—that a tithe-law for the maintenance of the Levites, unknown in the days of Josiah, first came in with Ezra, yet, though previously unheard of, was unmurmuringly submitted to by everybody as a law given in the wilderness by Moses?[4]

Minor examples of discrepancies, as those which relate to firstlings (chap. xv. 19, 20; cf. Num. xviii. 17, 18), to priestly dues (chap. xviii. 3, 4), to the treatment of bond-

[1] See above, p. 187.
[2] Van Hoonacker has here an ingenious, but, as it seems to us, untenable theory, based on the expression in Deut. xxvi. 12, "the third year, which is the year of tithing," compared with Amos iv. 4, that the Levitical tithe of Num. xviii. was not an annual, but a *triennial* one, and that the yearly festal tithe of Deuteronomy was a secondary and less strict taxing of produce, which only improperly got the name tithe (*Le Sacerdoce*, pp. 384 ff.).
[3] Thus in Tob. i. 7; Josephus, *Antiq.* iv. 8. 22; LXX in Deut. xxvi. 12. The explanation does not remove all difficulties, especially the absence of allusion to the primary tithe. It is to be noticed, however, that the speaker is here evidently alluding to a custom already established, not (as Dr. Driver has it), instituting a second tithe for the first time.
[4] See below, pp. 296, 319. Seeing that in Deuteronomy also the tribe of Levi is set aside for sacred service, and has therefore no inheritance with the other tribes, is it conceivable that no provision should be made for the tribe but these rare feasts at the sanctuary, or every third year? Does chap. xviii. 1, 2 not suggest a different view?

servants (chap. xv. 12; cf. Ex. xxi. 1–6), to the law of carrion (chap. xiv. 21; cf. Lev. xvii. 15), seem capable of reasonable **explanation.**[1] A few modifications on older laws are made in view of the altered circumstances of settlement in Canaan, notably the permission to kill and eat flesh at home (Deut. xii. 15), in room of the wilderness requirement that all slaying for food should be at the door of the tabernacle (cf. Lev. xvii. 3 ff.).

(2) There are alleged, next, certain *historical* discrepancies, some of them, we cannot but think, instructive examples of that *Widerspruchsjägerei*—"hunting for contradictions"— which Delitzsch not unjustly ascribes to the school of Wellhausen.[2] The opponents of the unity of Deuteronomy find numerous inconsistencies in the different parts of the book itself (*e.g.*, between chaps. v.–xi. and xii.–xxvi., or between chaps. i.–iv. and v.–xxvi.); but these the critical *defenders* of the unity find means of satisfactorily explaining.[3] A slight extension of the same skill, we are persuaded, would enable them to dispose as satisfactorily of most of the others. On the general relation to the preceding history, it is agreed on all hands that the retrospects in Deuteronomy presuppose the narratives of JE, and reproduce them with substantial fidelity.[4] The Wellhausen school, in accordance with its principles, denies any similar dependence on the P sections of the history;[5] but this it is difficult to maintain in view of the considerable number of references to particulars, and turns of expression, found only in P. Only in P., *e.g.*, is there mention of Moses and Aaron being debarred from Canaan as a punishment;[6] of " seventy " as the number who went down to Egypt;[7] of " twelve " as the number of the

---

[1] See Note E on Minor Discrepancies in Laws.

[2] Luthardt's *Zeitschrift*, 1880, p. 623.

[3] Cf. Kuenen (against Wellhausen), *Hex.* pp. 113 ff. ; Driver, *Deut.* pp. lxviii ff. etc.

[4] Driver represents the general view in saying that Deuteronomy "is demonstrably dependent upon JE" (p. xix ; cf. p. xv). Some assume a closer dependence on E than on J, but this depends on what is attributed to E, and what to J. Westphal, *e.g.*, as before noticed, gives the Book of the Covenant to J ; Dillmann and Kuenen give it to E. Dillmann, on the other hand, gives the story of the golden calf (Ex. xxxii.) to J ; Westphal and others give it to E.

[5] *Ibid.* p. xvi.

[6] Num. xx. 12 ; xxvii. 13 ff. ; Deut. xxxii. 50 ff. Cf. Deut. i. 37 ; iii. 26 ; iv. 21.

[7] Gen. xlvi. 27 ; Ex. i. 5. Cf. Deut. x. 22.

spies;[1] of the making of the ark of acacia wood.[2] The
words, "Since the day that God created man upon the
earth," in chap. iv. 32, seem a verbal reference to Gen. i. 26,
27 ; and there are numerous phraseological assonances with
P in this fourth chapter,—"belonging usually to P," says
Carpenter,—"suggesting occasional contact with the school
that produced P,"[3]—and later, as "horses and chariots,"
"hard bondage," "stretched-out arm," etc. (only in P).[4] In
no case, however, is there slavish dependence on the letter
of the history.[5] The speaker deals with his materials with
the freedom and intimate knowledge of one who had been a
chief actor in the events he recounts; amplifies, abbreviates
supplies fresh details; groups according to subject rather
than time; passes by swift association to related topics. It
is this which in a few instances gives rise to the appearance
of what the critics are pleased to call "contradictions."
Instead of telling against the genuineness of the book, they
constitute, to our mind, one of the most convincing internal
evidences of its genuineness. For what later composer,
with the JE history before him, would have allowed himself
these freedoms, or have wilfully laid himself open to the
charge of "contradiction" of his sources ?[6]

But what, taken at their utmost, do these "contradictions" amount to ? We shall glance at a few of the chief
cases. It is to be borne in mind that the question here is
not, whether Moses wrote personally the JE or P sections
of the Pentateuch, but whether there is such contradiction
with these as to forbid us ascribing the discourses in
Deuteronomy to Moses as their speaker. We do not
disprove, e.g., the Mosaic character of the discourses by

[1] Num. xiii. 2–10. Cf. Deut. i. 23.   See below, p. 279.
[2] Ex. xxxvii. 1. Cf. Deut. x. 3.   The critical view is that JE also had a
story of the making of the ark.
[3] Hex. ii. p. 254.
[4] Deut. xi. 4 ; xxvi. 6 (cf. Ex. i. 14) ; iv. 34, etc. Cf. Driver, Deut. pp.
xvii, lxxi.
[5] Graf concludes from the freedom of reproduction that the author draws
from oral tradition and not from written sources. Geschicht. Bücher,
p. 13.
[6] Unless, indeed, the reader is prepared to accept for the Deuteronomist
the patronising apology of Colenso : "He treats them [the statements of
the older narrative] often with great freedom, and sometimes in a way which
shows that, though generally familiar with that document, he was not so
thoroughly at home with it as a devout English reader of the Pentateuch
would be."—Pent. Pt. vi. p. 27.

showing, *e.g.*, that the P sections are not directly, or at all, from Moses' pen.

A first instance of discrepancy is, that in Deuteronomy (i. 9 ff.) Moses reminds the people how, with their consent, he appointed judges over them; in Ex. xviii. we are told that this plan was originally suggested to Moses by Jethro. We submit that there is not here the shadow of a real difficulty? Can it be supposed that the composer of the book, whoever he was, imagined that there was any conflict? Yet this is one of two "discrepancies" which Dr. Driver allows "are not absolutely incompatible"[1] with Moses' authorship. The other is, that in Deuteronomy (i. 22, 23) the people *ask* that spies be sent to search the land, while in Num. xiii. 1 (P), Jehovah gives the *order* for the mission. "Not *absolutely* incompatible"!

As an example of a discrepancy held to be *irreconcilable* with Mosaic authorship, we take the passages relating to Jehovah's anger against Moses, and the prohibition to enter Canaan. "In Num. xx. 12 (cf. xxvii. 13 ff.; Deut. xxxii. 50 ff.)," we are told, "Moses is prohibited to enter Canaan on account of his presumption in striking the rock at Kadesh, in the thirty-ninth year of the Exodus; here (Deut. i. 37, 38; iii. 26; iv. 21), the ground of the prohibition is Jehovah's anger with him *on account of the people*, upon an occasion which is plainly fixed by the context for the second year of the Exodus, thirty-seven years previously."[2] We invite the reader to compare carefully the passages, and judge for himself whether there is any real basis for this assertion. In three places in his address, Moses refers to his exclusion from Canaan, and in one of them tells of his pleading with Jehovah (fixed in the fortieth year, chap. iii. 23) to have the sentence reversed. The narrative of this exclusion is given at length in Numbers, with the rebellion of the people that led to it, and the permission to view the land alluded to in Deut. iii. 27 (cf. Num. xxvii. 12, 13). It is surely only the hyper-acute sense of a critic that can see in the words "for your sakes," which evidently refer to the provocation of the people that occasioned the offence of Moses (Num. xx. 2 ff.), a "contradiction" of the statement that he, with Aaron, personally sinned at Meribah (Num. xx. 10); while the assertion that the

[1] *Deut.* p. xxxvii.   [2] *Ibid.* p. xxxv.

Incident is "plainly fixed" in Deut. i. 37 in the second year
of the Exodus is a "plain" misreading of the text. Moses
is speaking in the context of the exclusion of that older
generation from Canaan, and by a natural association he
alludes in passing to how the rebellious spirit of the living
generation had brought a similar sentence of exclusion on
himself. The discourses are full of such rapid transitions,
determined not by chronology, but by the connection of the
thought. Cf., *e.g.*, chap. i. 9, where the discourse turns back
to events a year before the command in ver. 6 ; chap. ii. 1, 2,
where there is a leap over thirty-seven or thirty-eight years ;
chaps. ix.,x.,where x. 1 resumes, with the words "at that time,"
the transactions at Horeb, left far behind in chap. ix. 22 ff.

The mission of the spies, alluded to above, is itself a
fruitful source of "contradictions," occasioned, however,
mainly by the merciless way in which the narrative in
Numbers is torn up.[1] The incident will be examined in
detail in a future chapter ;[2] only the main point, therefore,
need be anticipated here. Deuteronomy, it is said, following JE, knows nothing of Joshua as one of the spies, and
represents the search party, in contrast with P, as proceeding only as far as Eshcol (chap. i. 24, 25). Yet Deuteronomy knows of the choosing of "twelve" spies, "one
of a tribe," as in Num. xiii. 2 (P), where Joshua is included
in the list (ver. 8); and the statement in Deut. i. 38 that
Joshua (as well as Caleb, ver. 36) would enter the land,
connects most naturally with the promise given in Num.
xiv. 30.[3] If the letter in JE is pressed to mean that
Caleb only was to enter the land, it would seem to
exclude Joshua, not only from the number of the spies,
but from Canaan, which cannot be the meaning. In the
JE narrative also it is clearly implied, as will be afterwards

[1] The critical analysis of Num. xiii.–xiv. certainly results in a mass of contradictions (see below, pp. 356 ff.). Addis says of the JE parts : "Attempts
have been made to separate the component documents. . . . But the task
seems to be hopeless, and there is nothing like agreement in results."—
Hex. i. p. 165.

[2] Cf. Chap. X. pp. 356 ff.

[3] Dillmann and Kittel take Joshua to be included among the spies in
the J narrative, but not in the E narrative—a distinction that falls, if JE
are one, and at any rate is an acknowledgment of the inclusion of Joshua
in the combined JE story. Cf. Dillmann, *Num.-Jos.* p. 69, and on
Num. xxvi. 65 ; xxxii. 12, pp. 177, 195 ; Kittel, *Hist. of Hebs.* p. 201.
See below, p. 357.

seen, that the spies, or some of them (for there surely were
several parties; they did not all march in a body), went
through the whole land (Num. xiii. 28, 29).

The last-named instance is one of several involving the
question of the possibility of an acquaintance of Deuteronomy with the P history. The denial of such acquaintance
is founded in part on the mention of Dathan and Abiram,
and the silence about Korah, in chap. xi. 6.[1] Here, it is
concluded, the mention of Korah is omitted because he
had no place in the JE narration. This, however, we
would point out, does not necessarily follow. Apart from
the question of "sources" in Num. xvi., it is evident that,
in the combined uprising there narrated, Dathan and
Abiram represented the general spirit of murmuring in
the congregation (vers. 12–15), while Korah stood for the
Levites, in their aspiration after the privileges of the priesthood (vers. 8–11). This of itself is sufficient reason why Moses,
in his address to the people, should refer only to the former.[2]

A more definite "contradiction"—likewise implicated
with intricate questions of analysis—is in the brief notice
of Aaron's death, and of the journeyings of the people in
chap. x. 6, 7, as compared with the notice in the list of
stations in Num. xxxiii. In Deuteronomy, Aaron is stated
to have died at Moserah, while his death is placed in
Numbers (ver. 38) at Mount Hor; in Deuteronomy, four
stations are mentioned in the journeyings (Bene-Jaakan,
Moserah, Gudgodah, Jotbathah), but in Numbers (vers.
31, 32) the first two are named in inverse order. Moserah,
however, as we discover from comparison, was in the
immediate neighbourhood of Hor, and there is evidence
in the list in Numbers itself that after wandering southwards
to Eziongeber, at the Red Sea, and turning again north-
wards, the people returned in the fortieth year from Kadesh
to the district of Mount Hor, where Aaron died (vers. 35–39;
cf. Num. xx.). The old camping spots would then be
revisited, as stated in Deuteronomy. The mention of
these places may thus be regarded rather as an un-

[1] On this incident, see below, pp. 358–9.

[2] It must be allowed that great suspicion attaches to the clause—" of
Korah, Dathan, and Abiram"—in Num. xvi. 24, 27, in the connection in
which it stands with *mishkan* (dwelling), which everywhere else in these
narratives is the designation of the tabernacle (not of an ordinary tent).
Cf. Strack, *in loc.*

designed corroboration of the accuracy of the list in Numbers.[1]

Finally, a word should perhaps be said on the alleged "contradiction" between the law in Ex. xxi. 12-14, and the Deuteronomic appointment of three cities of refuge (chap. iv. 41-43; cf. xix. 1 ff.). The asylum in the older law, Wellhausen argues, is the altar; now "in order not to abolish the right of asylum along with altars [mark the change to the plural], he [the Deuteronomist] appoints special cities of refuge for the innocent who are pursued by the avenger of blood."[2] It is a little difficult to understand how anyone could hope to persuade the people of Josiah's age that three cities of refuge had been appointed by Moses (three more afterwards) when, *ex hypothesi*, they knew perfectly well that up to their day no such cities existed. The whole objection, however, is largely a creation of the critic's fancy, as shown by the fact that the future appointment of a place of refuge for the manslayer is provided for in the very law of Exodus to which appeal is made (chap. xxi. 13).

3. For the above reasons we cannot allow that a case has been made out on the ground of discrepancies in laws and history for denying the Deuteronomic discourses to the great lawgiver with whose name they are connected. When these are set aside, there remain as proofs of post-Mosaic origin chiefly incidental expressions, as "other side of (or beyond) Jordan," "unto this day," and the like. The first of these expressions—"other side of Jordan"— is much relied on, as showing that the standpoint of the author of the book was the *Western* side of Jordan.[3] If we have not hitherto taken notice of this favourite argument, it is principally because, after the fairest consideration we

---

[1] The supposition that, according to JE, the Israelites stuck immovably like limpets on a rock to Kadesh for thirty-eight years, is against common sense, and can only be made out by tearing the narrative to pieces. Even then, the command to the Israelites in JE, "Turn ye, and get you into the wilderness by the way of the Red Sea" (Num. xiv. 25), implies intervening wanderings, as in Num. xxxiii. In the beginning of the fortieth year (not the third, as Bleek), the Israelites are found again at Kadesh (chap. xx. 1 ; cf. Dillmann, *in loc.*). Criticism rejects the thirty-eight years' wanderings, but in contradiction to *all* the sources, J E D P. Cf. Kittel's remarks, *Hist. of Hebs.* i. pp. 231-32.

[2] *Hist. of Israel*, p. 33 ; cf. W. R. Smith, *O.T. in J. C.*, p. 354.

[3] Cf. Driver, *Deut.* pp. xlii ff.

have been able to give it, it seems to us to have extremely little force. So far as the expression occurs in the framework of the book (*e.g.*, chap. i. 1, 5), it occasions little difficulty, but it may appear to be different when it is found in the discourses themselves. It does occur there, but (as also in the framework) with an application both to the *Eastern* (chap. iii. 8), and, more commonly, to the *Western* (chaps. iii. 20, 25 ; xi. 30), sides of the Jordan.[1] Very generally there is some determinative clause attached, to show which side is meant—" beyond Jordan, toward the sunrising" (chap. iv. 41, 46), " eastward " (ver. 49), " behind the way of the going down of the sun" (chap. xi. 30), etc. It is most natural to conclude that the phrase " beyond Jordan " was a current geographical designation for the Moabite side of the river ; but that, along with this, there went a local usage, determined by the position of the speaker.[2] Far more reasonably may we argue from the minute and serious care of the writer in his geographical and chronological notices in the introduction to the discourses and elsewhere, that he means his book to be taken as a genuine record of the last utterances of the lawgiver.

It may be serviceable at this stage to sum up the conclusions to which the discussions in this chapter have conducted us.

1. The discovery of "the book of the law" in Josiah's day was a genuine discovery, and the book then found was already old.

2. The age of Manasseh was unsuitable for the composition of Deuteronomy, and there is no evidence of its composition in that age. The ideas of Deuteronomy no

---

[1] Num. xxxii. 19 is a remarkable case of the use of the phrase in both senses in a single verse. Dr. Driver explains the passage, not very convincingly, by an " idiom " ; and accounts for Deut. iii. 20, 25 by the assumed position of the speaker, which, he thinks, by a lapse, is forgotten in ver. 8, where the *real* situation is betrayed. We may, however, pretty safely clear the writer of Deuteronomy from the suspicion of such unconscious " betrayals " of his position.

[2] When Dr. Driver says : " It is of course conceivable that this was a habit of the Canaanites, but it can hardly be considered likely that the usage suggested by it passed from them to the Israelites, before the latter had set foot in the land," etc. (p. xliii), he seems to forget that the fathers of the Israelites had lived for at least two centuries in Canaan, and that the traditions and hopes of the people were all bound up with it (cf. their words for " West," etc.).

doubt lay behind Hezekiah's reformation, but there is no evidence of the presence of the book, or of its composition, at or about that time. Had it been newly composed, or then appeared for the first time, we should have expected it to make a sensation, as it did afterwards in the time of Josiah The question also would again arise as to its Mosaic claim, and the acknowledgment of this by Hezekiah and his circle.

3. From Hezekiah upwards till at least the time of the Judges, or the immediately post-Mosaic age, there is no period to which the composition of the book can suitably be referred, nor is there any evidence of its composition in that interval. Traces of its use may be thought to be found in the revision of Joshua, in speeches like those of Solomon (1 Kings viii.), in Amaziah's action (2 Kings xiv. 5, 6), and in allusions in the early prophets.[1] But this we do not at present urge.

4. The book definitely gives itself out as a reproduction of the speeches which Moses delivered in the *Arabah* of Moab before his death, and expressly declares that Moses wrote his addresses ("this law"), and gave the book into custody of the priests.

5. The internal character of the book, in its Mosaic standpoint, its absence of reference to the division of the kingdom, and the archaic and obsolete character of many of its laws, supports the claim to a high antiquity and a Mosaic origin.

6. The supposition that Deuteronomy is "a free reproduction," or elaboration, of written addresses left by Moses, by one who has fully entered into his spirit, and continues his work, while not inadmissible, if the facts are shown to require it, is unnecessary, and, in view of the actual character of the book, not probable. The literary gifts of Moses were amply adequate to the writing of his own discourses in their present form. This is not to deny editorial revision and annotation.

7. There are no conclusive reasons in the character of the laws or of the historical retrospects for denying the authorship of the discourses, in this sense, to Moses.

8. It seems implied in Deut. xxxi. 9, 24–26, that Deuteronomy originally subsisted as a separate book. It may have done so for a longer or shorter period, and separate copies may have continued to circulate, even after its union

[1] See below, pp. 323 ff.

with the other parts of the Pentateuch.[1] It was probably a separate authentic copy which was deposited in the temple, and was found there by Hilkiah.

9. It is *possible,* as some have thought, that the JE Pentateuchal history may originally have contained a brief account of the testamentary discourses of Moses, and of his death (cf. the fragment, chap. xxxi. 14, 15, 23). This would be superseded when Deuteronomy was united with the rest of the Pentateuch.

10. The historical laws and narratives which Deuteronomy presupposes must, in some form, have existed earlier than the present book, if not earlier than the delivery of the discourses. These also, therefore, are pushed back, in essentials, into the Mosaic age. They need not, however, have been then completed, or put together in their present shape; or may only have furnished the basis for our present narratives.

The relation of Deuteronomy to the Priestly Writing has yet to be considered.

NOTE.—*Steuernagel's Theory of Deuteronomy*: A word should perhaps be said on the novel theory of Deuteronomy expounded by C. Steuernagel in his work, *Deuteronomium und Josua* (1900). Discarding, with much else (as the dependence of Deuteronomy on the Book of the Covenant), the view of a division of the Book into hortatory and legal portions, Steuernagel contends for a division, as it were transversely, into sections, distinguished respectively by the use of the singular ("thou," "thy," etc.) and the plural ("ye," "your," etc.) numbers (Sg and Pl). These sections (Pl being itself highly composite) were united in the pre-Josianic period, and subsequently underwent extensive enlargements and redactional changes. It is difficult not to regard this theory as another instance of misplaced ingenuity. The use of singular and plural affords no sufficient ground for distinguishing different authors. The nation addressed as "thou" was also a "ye," and there is a free transition throughout from the one mode of speech to the other, often within the limits of the same verse or paragraph (cf., *e.g.,* Deut. i. 31; iv. 10, 11; 25, 26; 34–36; vi. 1–3; 17, 18; viii. 1, 2; 19, 20; ix. 7; xi. 12, 13, etc.).

[1] See below, p. 376.

CHAPTER IX

Difficulties and Perplexities of the Critical Hypothesis: The Priestly Writing. I. The Code

"Nothing in fact is simpler than the Grafian hypothesis: it needs only the transference of *a single source*—the collection of laws named commonly the *Grundschrift*, by others the Book of Origins, the Writing of the Older Elohist, or of the Annalist, which we would call the *Book of Priestly Law or Religion*—into the post-exilian time, into the period of Ezra and Nehemiah, and at one stroke the 'Mosaic' period is wiped out."—DUHM.

"I have specially drawn attention to the fact that one result of these criticisms must inevitably be that, for all those who are convinced of the substantial truth of the above results, the whole ritualistic system, as a system of divine institution, comes at once to the ground. . . . The whole support of this system is struck away, when it is once ascertained that the Levitical legislation of the Pentateuch is entirely the product of a very late age, a mere figment of the post-captivity priesthood."—COLENSO.

"But, if we place at the head of their whole history [the Hebrew nation's] a great positive act of the will, a legislation by which the natural development is forestalled, and its course prescribed, we account for the rise of that discrepancy [the sense of guilt, consciousness of departure from the known will of God] and the peculiar tone of the national character among the Hebrews."—DE WETTE (against VATKE).

"But again the questioning spirit revives when one is asked to believe that Moses is partly at least a historic figure. Alas! how gladly would one believe it! But where are the historical elements? . . . No one can now be found to doubt that Sargon is a historical personage with mythic accretions. But can one really venture to say the like of Moses?"—CHEYNE.

CHAPTER IX

DIFFICULTIES AND PERPLEXITIES OF THE CRITICAL HYPOTHESIS: THE PRIESTLY WRITING. I. THE CODE

IT was indicated in our sketch of the critical development that the greatest revolution in Pentateuchal criticism up to the present has been the acceptance by the majority of scholars of the Graf-Wellhausen contention that the legislation of the middle books of the Pentateuch, instead of being, as was formerly all but universally supposed, the oldest, is in reality the very youngest of the constituent elements in that composite work—not, as it professes to be, a creation of the work of Moses, but a production of priestly scribes in exilian and post-exilian times. Up to the appearance of Graf's work on *The Historical Books of the Old Testament* in 1866, as was then pointed out, though earlier writers like Von Bohlen, George, and Vatke had advocated the idea, and Reuss, Graf's teacher, had been inculcating it in his class-room at Strassburg,[1] the hypothesis of a post-exilian origin of the law had met with no general acceptance. De Wette repudiated it;[2] Bleek declared it to be "decidedly false to hold with Vater, Von Bohlen, Vatke, and George, that Deuteronomy, with the laws it contains, is older than the foregoing books with their legislation";[3] even Kuenen, in 1861, pronounced its grounds to be "not worthy of refutation."[4] Since the publication of Graf's book, the tide has

[1] On Reuss, see below, p. 288.
[2] *Introd.* ii. p. 143. Similarly Ewald.
[3] *Com. on Deut.*, Introd. p. 107.
[4] See quotation from Kuenen in full in Note A. Nearly the only writer who seems to have had a glimpse into the possibilities of George's view was Hengstenberg, who wrote: "The view maintained by De Wette, that Deuteronomy was the latest of all, the topstone of the mythical structure, which at one time seemed to have won universal acceptance, begins now to yield to the exactly opposite opinion, that Deuteronomy is the most ancient

decisively turned, and the previously rejected theory has now become the dominant (though by no means the universally-accepted) hypothesis among critical scholars.

There are many reasons, apart from the skill and plausibility with which its case has been presented, which account for the fascination of this theory for minds that have already yielded assent to the previous critical developments. It is not without justice, as we shall by and by see, that the claim is made for the Wellhausen hypothesis that it is the logical outcome of the whole critical movement of last century. A chief value of the theory is that, by the very startlingness of its conclusions, it compels a halt, and summons to a reconsideration of the long course by which its results have been reached.

I. Graf-Wellhausen Theory of the Priestly Code

We shall best begin by sketching more fully than has yet been done the Graf-Wellhausen position. The problem relates, as said, to the age and character of that large body of laws found in Exodus, Leviticus, and Numbers, which forms the kernel of the writing described by the critics as the Priestly Code. Whereas formerly this Levitical legislation was held to be at least older than Deuteronomy, and probably in its main parts Mosaic,[1] the newer theory supposes it to be the work of scribes in the exile, or after. It is not, indeed, contended, as we shall find, that everything in the Code was absolutely the creation of that time.[2] There had been, of course, a temple, priesthood, religious institutions, sacrificial ritual, priestly rules and *technique.* Still the law, as elaborated in the exile, was practically a new thing. What belonged to the practice of a previous age was taken up, transformed, had a new meaning put into it, was brought under new leading ideas, was developed and

among all the books of the Pentateuch."—*Gen. of Pent.* **i.** p. 58 (he refers to George's work).

[1] Thus, *e.g.*, Bleek, *Introd.* i. pp. 212 ff.

[2] Cf. Graf, as above, p. 93 ; Kuenen, *Rel. of Israel*, ii. pp. 96, 192. (But see below, p. 291.) Reuss, on this point, does not go so far as some of his successors. He says : " It is self-evident that the existence of a Levitical tradition in relation to ritual, as early as the days of the kings, cannot be denied ; we cannot speak, however, of a written, official, and sacred codex of this kind."—*Geschichte der Heil. Schriften A. T.* i. p. 81 (in Ladd, i. p. 530). See below, pp. 300 ff.

enlarged by new rites and institutions. Above all, in order to clothe it with a Mosaic character, and secure for it the necessary authority, old and new alike were thrown back into the age of Moses and the wilderness, and were represented as originating and being put into force there. This Mosaic dress was a fiction. The elaborate descriptions of the tabernacle and its arrangements, the dispositions of the camp in the wilderness, the accounts of the consecration of Aaron and his sons, of the choice and setting apart of the Levites, of the origin of the passover, etc.—all was a "product of imagination."[1]

The idea of the Code was not wholly original. The first conception and sketch of a Priestly Code was in Ezekiel's vision of the restored temple in the closing chapters of his book.[2] The scheme of the scribes, however, was not that of Ezekiel, but was independently wrought out. A chief feature borrowed from the prophet's programme was the idea of the Levites as a class of temple servants subordinate to the priests. It will be seen below[3] how, in Ezek. xliv., the law is laid down that the priests who had gone astray into idolatry were to be degraded from their priestly office, and made servants in the sanctuary. Only the Zadokites, who had remained faithful, were to retain their priestly dignity. This, according to the theory, is the origin of the class of Levites. The priests thus degraded were, it is contended, the "disestablished priests" of the high places, for whom some sort of provision had to be made. We are called to trace here a development. Deuteronomy had, it is alleged, allowed such "disestablished priests" the full rights of priesthood when they came up to the temple; Ezekiel degrades them to the rank known afterwards as Levites: now the Priests' Code gives them a permanent standing in the sanctuary, and represents them as always having had this secondary position, and as having been originally honourably set apart by Jehovah for His service in the wilderness. The Israelites being thus organised as a hierarchy—"the clergy the skeleton, the high priest the head, and the tabernacle the heart"[4]—liberal provision is

---

[1] Cf. Kuenen, *Rel. of Israel*, ii. pp. 171, etc.
[2] Ezek. xl. etc.   [3] See below, pp. 315 ff.
[4] Wellhausen, *Hist. of Israel*, p. 127. Cf. p. 8: "The Mosaic theocracy, with the tabernacle at its centre, the high priest at its head, the priests and Levites as its organs, the legitimate cultus as its popular function."

made for the sacred body. Tithes, hitherto unknown for such a purpose, are appointed for the support of the priests and Levites, and the priestly revenues are otherwise greatly enlarged. Forty-eight cities, with pasturages,[1] are—only, of course, on paper—set apart for the Levitical order. The sacrificial system, now centralised in the tabernacle, is enlarged, and recast in its provisions. Sin- and trespass-offerings (the sin-offering is held by Wellhausen to appear first in Ezekiel)[2] are introduced; a cycle of feasts is established, with new historical meanings; an annual day of atonement—previously unheard of—is instituted. Sacrifice loses its older joyous character, and becomes an affair of the priesthood — a ritual of atonement, with associations of gloom.[3]

Still better to facilitate the introduction of this novel scheme, a *history* is invented to suit it. In its preparatory part in Genesis, this history goes back to the creation, and is marked in the patriarchal period by the rigid exclusion of all sacrifices;[4] in the Mosaic part, there is the freest indulgence in the invention of incidents, lists, genealogies, numbers, etc. All this, if we accept Wellhausen's view, was, some time before the coming of Ezra to Jerusalem in 458 B.C., put together in Babylon; was afterwards combined with the previously existing JE and D, which knew nothing of such legislation, and indeed in a multitude of ways contradicted it; finally, in 444 B.C., as related in Neh. viii., was produced and read by Ezra to the people, was accepted by them, and became thenceforth the foundation of post-exilic religion. Precisely at this crucial point, however, a serious divergence of opinion reveals itself in the school. According to Wellhausen, it was the *completed Pentateuch*, substantially, that was brought by Ezra to Jerusalem, and read by him to the people;[5] according to perhaps the majority of his followers, it was only the *Priests' Code* that was then made known, and the combination with JE and D

---

[1] The Levitical cities are held by Wellhausen to be a transformation of the old *bamoth* or high places.—*Ibid.* pp. 37–38, 162.

[2] *Ibid.* p. 75.

[3] *Ibid.* p. 81 : "No greater contrast could be conceived than the monotonous seriousness of the so-called Mosaic worship." Delitzsch and others have shown the groundlessness of this allegation.

[4] See above, p. 156.

[5] "Substantially at least Ezra's law-book must be regarded as practically identical with our Pentateuch."—*Ibid.* p. 497. Cf. p. 404.

did not take place till later, after new redactions and developments of the Code.[1] Wellhausen, who retains his opinion, argues convincingly that the narrative (cf. Neh. ix.) clearly requires that the book should be the whole Pentateuch;[2] the others as triumphantly ask how Codes of laws, which *ex hypothesi* were in flat contradiction of each other, could simultaneously be brought forward with any hope of acceptance! We agree that neither set of critics succeeds in answering the others' reasons.

Such, in barest outline, is the nature of the scheme which is to take the place of the "traditional" view of the Mosaic origin of the Levitical legislation. It will, we venture to predict, be to future generations one of the greatest psychological puzzles of history how such a hypothesis, loaded, as we believe it to be, with external and internal incredibilities, should have gained the remarkable ascendency it has over so many able minds. It is a singular tribute to the genius of Wellhausen that he should have been able to secure this wide acceptance for his theory, and to make that appear to his contemporaries as the highest wisdom which nearly all his predecessors scouted as the extreme of folly. His feat is hardly second to that of Ezra himself, who, on this new showing, succeeded in imposing on his generation the belief that a complex system of laws and institutions had been given by Moses, and had been in operation since the days of that lawgiver, though, till the moment of his own promulgation, nothing had been heard of them by anyone present![3]

[1] For a sketch of these supposed developments after 444 B.C., cf. Kuenen, *Hex.* pp. 302 ff. ; Professor W. Robertson Smith, *O.T. in J. C.*, Note F. Professor Smith differs again in thinking that "the Priestly Code has far too many points of contact with the actual situation at Jerusalem, and the actual usage of the second temple [?], to lend plausibility to the view that it was an abstract system evolved in Babylonia, by someone who was remote from the contemporary movement at Jerusalem ; but, on the other hand, its author must have stood . . . outside the petty local entanglements that hampered the Judæan priests" (pp. 448–49). He holds that to conjecture "that Ezra was himself the author of the Priests' Code is to step into a region of purely arbitrary guesswork" (p. 449). Thus the theories eat up each other.

[2] Professor H. P. Smith gets rid of Ezra and the narrative altogether. Cf. below, p. 295.

[3] "They were not," says Kuenen, "laws which had been long in existence, and which were now proclaimed afresh and accepted by the people, after having been forgotten for a while. The priestly ordinances were made known and imposed upon the Jewish nation *now for the first time. As we have*

II. Initial Incredibilities of the Theory

There are, it seems to us, *three huge incredibilities* which attach to this theory of the origin of the Levitical legislation, and to these, at the outset, as illustrative of the difficulties in which the modern criticism involves itself, we would refer.

1. There is no mistaking in this case the serious nature of the *moral* issue. In the case of "the book of the law" brought to light in Josiah's reign, there is at least always open the assumption of a literary artifice which involved no dishonest intention on the part of the writer. Here, on the other hand, there can be no evading of the meaning of the transaction. What we have is the deliberate construction of an elaborate Code of laws with the express design of passing it off upon the people in the name of Moses. It is not a sufficient reply to urge that much in the law was simply the codification of pre-exilian usage. A codification of ancient law—if that were all that was meant—even though it involved some degree of re-editing and expansion, is a process to which no one could reasonably take exception, provided it were proved that it had actually taken place.[1] But though this notion is, as we shall see, a good deal played with, the Wellhausen theory is assuredly not fairly represented, when, with a view to turn the edge of an objection, it is spoken of as mainly a work of "codification." The very essence of the theory, as Kuenen and Wellhausen expound it, is, that in all that gives the Priestly Code its distinctive character, it is something entirely new.[2] There never, *e.g.*, existed such an ark or tabernacle as the Code describes with minute precision. The tabernacle is

seen, no written ritual legislation yet existed in Ezekiel's time," etc.—*Rel of Israel*, ii. p. 231. Cf. Wellhausen, *Hist. of Israel*, p. 408.

[1] Few of the critics of the Wellhausen hypothesis object, within reasonable limits, to a theory of codification, but treat it as a question of evidence. Cf. Robertson's *Early Religion of Israel*, p. 394. It already goes beyond codification when the object is to stamp pre-existing usage with a divine sanction.

[2] According to Wellhausen, the Code was not only not in operation, but "it did not even admit of being carried into effect in the conditions that prevailed previous to the exile."—*Hist. of Israel*, p. 12. "The idea that the Priests' Code was extant before the exile," says Kautzsch, "could only be maintained on the assumption that no man knew of it, not even the spiritual leaders of the people, such as the priests Jeremiah and Ezekiel."—*Lit. of O.T.*, p. 116.

a pure fiction, obtained by halving the dimensions of the temple, and making it portable.[1] There never was a choice of Aaron and his sons to be priests, or a separation of the Levites to be ministers to the priests. There never was a tithe system for the support of priests and Levites; there never were Levitical cities; there never were sin- and trespass-offerings, or a day of atonement, such as the Code prescribes; there never were feasts having the historical origin and reference assigned to them in the law. These institutions were not only not Mosaic, but they never existed at all; and *the constructors of this Code knew it,* for they were themselves the inventors. This cannot be evaded by saying, as is sometimes done, that it was a well-recognised custom to attribute all new legislation to Moses. For first, apart from the singular problem which this raises for the critics who attribute *no* laws to Moses, such a custom simply did not exist;[2] and, second, this is not a case of mere literary convention, but one of serious intention, with a view to gaining a real advantage by the use of the law-giver's authority. The nearest parallel, perhaps, that suggests itself is the promulgation in Europe in the ninth century of our era of the great collection of spurious documents known as the Isidorian Decretals, carrying back the loftiest claims of the mediæval Papacy to apostolic men of the first century. No one hesitates to speak of these spurious decretals, which gained acceptance, and were for long incorporated in the Canon law, by their rightful name of "forgeries."[3] Can we help giving the same designation to the handiwork of these exilian constructors of a pseudo-Mosaic Code?[4] It is futile to speak, in excuse, of the

---

[1] See above, pp. 165 ff.

[2] *E.g.,* Ezekiel did not attribute his laws to Moses; the Chronicler did not attribute the elaborate ordinances in 1 Chron. xxiii. to Moses but to David; Ezra and Nehemiah themselves did not attribute their modified arrangements to Moses. Circumcision was not attributed to Moses, etc. We do not know of any laws being attributed to Moses which were not *believed* to be Mosaic.

[3] Hallam says of these in his *Middle Ages*: "Upon these spurious decretals was built the great fabric of papal supremacy over the different national Churches; a fabric which has stood after its foundation crumbled beneath it; for no one has pretended to deny, for the last two centuries, that the imposture is too palpable for any but the most ignorant ages to credit" (*Student's Hallam*, p. 295).

[4] "Such procedure," says Riehm, "would have to be called a fraud."— *Einleit.* i. p. 217.

different standards of literary honesty in those days. It
is not overstepping the mark to say, as before, that men
like Jeremiah, Ezekiel, and Ezra, were as capable of distinguishing between truth and falsehood, as conscious of
the sin of deceit, as zealous for the honour of God, as
incapable of employing lying lips, or a lying pen, in the
service of Jehovah, as any of our critics to-day.[1] We
simply cannot conceive of these men as entering into such
a conspiracy, or taking part in such a fraud, as the
Wellhausen theory supposes. For it was undeniably as
genuine Mosaic ordinances that it was meant to pass off
these laws upon the people. Let only the effect be imagined
had Ezra interpolated his reading with the occasional explanation that this or that principal ordinance, given forth
by him as a law of Moses in the wilderness, was really a
private concoction of some unknown priest in Babylon—
perchance his own !

2. Besides the moral, there confronts us, in the second
place, a *historical* incredibility. We do not dwell on
the peculiar taste of these exilian scribes, of whose very
existence, it must be remembered, we have not a morsel of
evidence, who, out of their own heads, occupied themselves
with tireless ingenuity in elaborating these details of
tabernacle, encampments, and ceremonial, planning new
laws, festivals, and regulations for imaginary situations—
devising everything with such care, and surrounding it with
so perfect an air of the wilderness, that, as Wellhausen
owns,[2] no trace of the real date by any chance shines
through. Neither do we dwell on the singular unity of
mind which must have pervaded their ranks to enable them
to concert so well-compacted and coherent a scheme as, on
any showing, the Levitical law is.[3] We shall assume that
some peculiarly constituted minds might delight in evolving
these fanciful things, and might even, at a sufficient distance
of time, get their romance by mistake accepted as history.

[1] See above, p. 259. Cf. Jer. viii. 8 ; xiv. 14 ; xxiii. 32 ; Ezek. xiii. 6,
7, 19, etc.

[2] "It tries hard to imitate the costume of the Mosaic period and, with
whatever success, to disguise its own. . . . It guards itself against all
reference to later times and a settled life in Canaan. . . . It keeps itself
carefully and strictly within the limits of the situation in the wilderness."—
Hist. of Israel, p. 9. Riehm says : "Nowhere are any anachronisms found
in the Levitical legislation."—*Einl.* i. p. 217.

[3] Cf. Note B on Unity of the Law.

The thing which needs explanation is, how the scheme, once conceived, should be able to get under weigh as it did, in the actual circumstances of the return from the exile. That problem has only to be faced to show how incredible is the critical solution.

We turn to the account of the production and reading of the law by Ezra in Neh. viii., as before we did to the narrative of the finding of "the book of the law" in 2 Kings, and are there presented with a plain, unvarnished tale, which bears upon its face every mark of truth. We read how the people of Jerusalem, gathered "as one man into the broad place that was before the water-gate," asked Ezra the scribe "to bring the book of the law of Moses, which Jehovah had commanded to Israel."[1] Ezra, who before has been described as "a ready scribe in the law of Moses, which Jehovah, the God of Israel, had given,"[2] and as coming from Babylon with the law of God in his hand,[3] now, at the people's request, produced the book, and from an improvised "pulpit of wood" read its contents to the congregation "from morning till midday," while others who stood by "gave the sense."[4] This was repeated from the first to the last day of the feast of Tabernacles in the seventh month.[5] Everything in the narrative is plain and above board. There is not a hint that anything contained in this "book of the law" was new,[6] though the knowledge of much that it contained had evidently been lost. The entire congregation listen to it with unquestioning faith as "the law of Moses." They hear all its enactments about priests and Levites, its complicated regulations about sacrifices, about sin-offerings,

[1] Neh. viii. 1.   [2] Ezra vii. 6.
[3] Ezra vii. 14.   [4] Neh. viii. 2-8.
[5] Vers. 8, 18. Professor H. P. Smith, unlike Wellhausen and Kuenen, who found upon it, discredits, as before intimated, the whole story, and doubts the very existence of Ezra. His account is worth quoting, as a specimen of a phase of criticism : "During the century after Nehemiah the community in Judah was becoming more rigid in its exclusiveness and in its devotion to the ritual. Ezra is the impersonation of both tendencies. Whether there was a scribe named Ezra is not a matter of great importance. Very likely there was such a scribe to whose name tradition attached itself. First, it transferred the favour of Artaxerxes to him from Nehemiah. Then it made him the hero of the introduction of the law, and finally it attributed to him the abrogation of the mixed marriages. . . . The wish was father to the thought, and the thought gave rise to the story of Ezra. Ezra was the ideal scribe, as Solomon was the ideal king, projected upon the background of an earlier age."—*O.T. Hist.* pp. 396-97.
[6] Cf. Kittel, *Hist. of Hebs.* i. p. 104.

about tithes, but do not raise a question. Nothing, on the
premises of the theory, could be more surprising. Tithes
of corn and oil, not to say of cattle, for the support of the
Levitical order, had never before been heard of,[1] but the
people submit to the burden without dissent. They hear
of a day of atonement, and of the solemn and elaborate
ritual by which it is to be annually observed, but it does
not occur to them that this institution has been unknown
in all the past of their history. The Levites, descendants,
on the theory, of Ezekiel's degraded idolatrous priests—of
whose degradation, however, to this lower rank, history
contains no mention — show no amazement when they
learn for the first time that their tribe was specially set
apart by Jehovah for His service in the wilderness, and had
then a liberal provision made for their wants; that cities
even had been appointed for them to dwell in. Many
of the more learned in the gathering — men versed in
genealogies and priestly traditions—must have been well
aware that the most striking of the ordinances which Ezra was
reading from his roll, were unhistorical inventions, yet they
take it all in. There was, as the Book of Nehemiah itself
clearly shows, a strongly disaffected party, and a religiously
faithless party, in the city,—a faction keenly opposed to
Ezra and Nehemiah,[2]—but no one raises a doubt. Priests
and people, we learn from Malachi, were alike shamefully
remiss in the discharge of their obligations,[3] yet they never
question the genuineness of any article in the Code. The
very Samaritans—the bitterest of the Jews' enemies in this
period—receive not long after the whole law at the hands
of the Jews as the undoubted law of Moses.[4] Is anything
in the "traditional" theory more astounding, or harder to
believe, than all this is?[5] There is another fact. Ezra's

---

[1] Wellhausen says the tithe was introduced by Ezra, *Hist. of Israel*, p. 166.
[2] Cf. Neh. vi. 10–19; viii. etc. W. R. Smith even says: "All the
historical indications point to the priestly aristocracy being the chief
opponents of Ezra."—*O.T. in J. C.*, p. 448. This makes matters still more
inexplicable.
[3] Mal. i. 6–14; iii. 7–15; Neh. xiii. 10 ff. Cf. W. R. Smith, as above,
p. 445.
[4] See below, Chap. X. p. 370, and Note there.
[5] Wellhausen says: "As we are accustomed to infer the date of the composition of Deuteronomy from its publication and introduction by Josiah, so
we must infer the date of the composition of the Priestly Code from its
publication and introduction by Ezra and Nehemiah."—*Hist. of Israel*,

reading of the law was in 444 B.C. But nearly a century earlier, in 536 B.C., at the time of the first return under Zerubbabel, we find no inconsiderable part of the law *already in operation.* Priests and Levites are there; the high priest is there;[1] a complete organisation of worship is there, morning and evening sacrifices are there, set feasts are there, etc.[2] Even if details are challenged, the central facts in this narrative, *e.g.*, the presence of priests and Levites, and of an organisation of worship, cannot be overthrown.[3]

3. There is yet, however, a third incredibility arising from the *unsuitability* of the Code itself. We found the Code of Deuteronomy to be in many respects unsuitable to the age of Josiah. But the unsuitability of Deuteronomy is slight compared with the lack of agreement in the Levitical Code with the state of things in the days of Ezra and Nehemiah. From the point of view of the theory, the Code was designed to be put in force after the return from the exile. The return, therefore, even in the exile, must have been confidently expected. Yet, when the Code is examined, nothing could seem less suitable for its purpose. The whole wilderness framework of the legislation was out of date and place in that late age. The sanctuary is a portable tabernacle, whereas the circumstances of the time demanded a temple. Many of the laws, like that requiring that all sacrifices should be offered at the door of the tabernacle, with the reason for this regulation,[4] were quite out of keeping with the new conditions, had, indeed, no relevancy from the time when the people entered on a settled life in Canaan. Suitable in its place, if it precedes the relaxing rule of Deut. xii. 15, it is unintelligible after. Other parts of the Code had to be dropped or changed, as inapplicable to the post-exilian order of things. There was, *e.g.*, no ark, or priestly Urim or Thummim, in the second

---

p. 408. We contend, on the contrary, that the narrative of this introduction is a conclusive *disproof* of Wellhausen's view of its date.

[1] Cf. Zech. iii. 1.

[2] Ezra iii. 2 ff.

[3] Delitzsch says: "It is a fact as credibly attested as possible that the distinction of ranks of priests and Levites existed already in B.C. 536, and long before B.C. 444 ; and indeed so uncontested, so thoroughly established, so strictly maintained, that it must be dated back beyond the exile, in which it cannot have originated, as one regulated by law and custom in the pre-exilian time."—Luthardt's *Zeitschrift*, 1880, p. 268.

[4] Lev. xvii. 1–4. See below, p. 314.

temple. The tax imposed by Nehemiah was a *third* part of a shekel, instead of the *half*-shekel of the law.[1] The law, in one place, prescribes twenty-five years as the age for the Levites entering on service, and in another place thirty years.[2] We find, however, that, after the return, neither of these laws was adopted, but, in accordance with a rule ascribed in Chronicles to David, the Levites commenced their duties at the age of twenty.[3] A more striking example of unsuitability to contemporary conditions is found in the tithe-laws, declared to be a direct creation of the exile. The Levitical law in Numbers is based on the assumption of a large body of Levites, and a relatively small body of priests. The tithes are to be paid directly to the Levites, who are then required to give a tenth of what they receive to the priests.[4] But these provisions were absolutely unsuitable to the times succeeding the exile, when, as we see from the Book of Ezra, the number of Levites who returned was very small, while the number of priests was large.[5] Instead of ten Levites for every priest, the proportion may have been about twelve or thirteen priests for every Levite. This rendered completely nugatory the arrangements of the Code, and made readjustment inevitable. Wellhausen calls this discrepancy " a trifling circumstance,"[6] but fails to explain why a law should have been promulgated so entirely unsuited to the actual situation. The history, besides, has no mention of the tithing of cattle under Nehemiah as prescribed by the law—only of tithes of field produce.[7] As if to render the contrast more striking, while we have in the Code these rules about tithes, so absolutely unsuitable to the circumstances of the exile, with its numerous priests and handful of Levites, we have, on the other hand, mention in the history of an extensive *personnel* connected with the service of the temple—porters, Nethinim, children of

---

[1] Ex. xxx. 11–16 ; cf. Neh. x. 32.

[2] Num. iv. 23, 30, etc. ; cf. viii. 24. The LXX makes both passages thirty years. This is one of those unessential variations in laws, which, if the ordinary harmonistic explanation is not accepted, viz., that the one law (Num. viii.) refers to the lighter service of the tabernacle itself, the other (Num. iv.) to the harder work of transportation, points to a liberty of varying the strict letter of the law, provided its spirit or principle was adhered to. See above, p. 179.

[3] Ezra iii. 8 ; cf. 1 Chron. xxiii. 24, 27.

[4] Num. xviii. 24–26.   [5] Ezra ii.; viii. 15 ff.

[6] *Hist. of Israel*, p. 167.   [7] Neh. x. 39 ; xiii. 5.

Solomon's servants, singing-men, and singing-women[1]—of which, curiously enough, the law, supposed to be drawn up specially for this community, knows nothing.[2] How is this to be rendered natural or conceivable on the critical assumption of the date of the Code?[3]

III. THE ARGUMENT FROM SILENCE IN ITS BEARINGS ON THE CODE

We pass now from these initial incredibilities to the examination of the *positive* foundations of the critical theory; and here, if we mistake not, the impression produced by the above considerations will be more than confirmed. The argument for the exilian or post-exilian dating of the Priestly Code may be said to have two main branches: (1) the alleged silence of pre-exilian history and literature as to the peculiar institutions of the Code; and (2) the alleged incompatibility of the sanctuary and ritual arrangements of the pre-exilic time—mirrored to us in the history, the prophets, and the Book of Deuteronomy—with the Levitical regulations. We shall under the present head consider the general value of this argument from silence; we shall then inquire whether the silence regarding the laws and institutions of the Priests' Code is as unbroken as is alleged; finally, we shall endeavour to show that the critical theory itself breaks down in its attempt to explain these institutions—this with special reference to the Ezekiel theory of the origin of the distinction of priests and Levites. The "incompatibility" argument has already been in considerable part anticipated, but will be touched upon as far as necessary.

The argument from mere silence then, to begin with that, is proverbially precarious; in a case like the present it is peculiarly so. It is easy to understand why a ritual law, which, all down, must have been largely an affair of the

---

[1] Ezra ii. 41, 55, 58, 65, 70. The members of some of these guilds were probably Levitical (1 Chron. xxiii. ; cf. Delitzsch, *Zeitschrift*, 1880, p. 287), though the name "Levite" was specially appropriated to those directly ministering to the priests. This would increase somewhat the proportion of returning Levites.

[2] Delitzsch, Dillmann (*Num.-Jos.* p. 671), Baudissin ("Priests and Levites" in *Dict. of Bible*, iv. p. 88), etc., urge this point.

[3] For additional instances of unsuitability, cf. Kittel, *Hist. of Hebs.* i. p. 106.

priests, should not frequently obtrude itself upon the **view**: when it does, as in the Books of Chronicles, it is set down as a mark of untrustworthiness. Particularly, the fact that the Levitical laws are, in their original form, adapted to a tabernacle, and to wilderness conditions, precludes the possibility of much reference to them in that form, after the people were settled in Canaan, and after a temple had been built. Assuming the sanctuary and sacrificial ordinances of the Code to have always been in the most perfect operation,—and it is certain that in many periods they were not,—it would still be unreasonable to expect that they should be constantly thrusting their heads into the story, and foolish to argue that, because they did not, therefore they had no existence. We take, however, broader ground, and propose to show, with the help of the critics themselves, that, notwithstanding the silence, a large part of the Code may have been, and indeed actually was, in operation.

1. On the showing of the Wellhausen theory itself, it is not difficult to establish that the argument from mere silence is *far from conclusive.* We fall back here on the admission freely made that everything in the Priestly Code is not new. It is allowed, on the contrary, that *materially* a great part of the Levitical legislation must have been in existence before the exile. Especially, as before in the case of Deuteronomy, when the object is to free the hypothesis from the aspect of fraud, remarkable concessions on this point are frequently made. If, at one time, we are told by Dr. Driver that "the pre-exilic period shows no indications of the legislation of P as being in operation,"[1] at another time we are assured that "in its main stock, the legislation of P was not (as the critical view of it is sometimes represented by its opponents as teaching) 'manufactured' by the priests during the exile; it is based upon *pre-existing temple usage.*"[2] We do not defend the consistency of

[1] *Introd.* p. 136.
[2] *Ibid.* p. 143. See below, p. 312. Similarly the quotations from Kuenen and Wellhausen on pp. 291–92 above, may be compared with the following from Kuenen: "The decrees of the priestly law were not *made* and *invented* during or after the exile, but *drawn up.* Prior to the exile, the priests had already delivered verbally what—with the modifications that had become necessary in the meantime—they afterwards committed to writing."—*Rel. of Israel,* ii. p. 96. "I have already drawn attention to the probability that disconnected priestly ordinances or *torahs* were in circula-

these statements; the one is, in fact, as we shall immediately see, destructive of the other. The tendency in writers of this school is, in reality, to a kind of *see-saw* between these two positions; the one that the Priestly Code was in the main a simple "codification" of pre-exilic usage—a comparatively innocent hypothesis; and the other that the characteristic institutions of the Priestly Code—ark, tabernacle, Aaronic priests, Levites, tithes, Levitical cities, sin-offerings, day of atonement," etc., were, one and all, the free creation of the exilic period—were then, despite Dr. Driver's disclaimer, " manufactured "[1]—and were absolutely unknown earlier. If the latter proposition cannot be maintained, the whole hypothesis goes to earth. Here again we are entitled to say that the critics must really make their choice. They cannot well be allowed at one time to employ arguments which are of no force unless on the assumption that the Levitical law is, as a whole, in matter as well as in form, *new*; and at another, to use arguments based on the contention that the bulk of the legislation is, in practice, *old*.[2]

Let us, however, accept, as we are glad to do, the statement that " the main stock " of the legislation of P is " based upon pre-existing temple usage," and see what follows. The observance of this " main stock " before the exile either appears in the history, or it does not. If it does *not*, what becomes of the argument from silence against the other institutions? If it *does*, what becomes of Wellhausen's statement that "no trace can be found of acquaintance with the Priestly Code, but, on the other hand, very clear indications of ignorance of its contents?"[3] It is nothing to the purpose to reply, as is commonly done, that before the exile there was indeed *praxis* — usage — but no written

tion before the exile, even though a system of priestly legislation was wanting at that time " (p. 192).

[1] We may take in illustration the law of the passover in Exodus, referred to further below, pp. 320-21. Graf treats Ex. xii. 1-28 as a pure creation of the time of the exile, and deduces from the fact of its agreement with the priestly and sacrificial laws of Leviticus, that these must be exilian or post-exilian also (*Geschicht. Bücher*, pp. 34-36). Wellhausen's view is that the law has undergone a transformation which inverts the relation of cause and effect. It was the Israelitish custom of offering the firstlings which gave rise to the story of the slaying of the firstborn in Egypt, not *vice versa*.—*Hist. of Israel*, pp. 88, 100, 102, 352.

[2] Cf. Robertson on Wellhausen, *Early Religion*, etc., pp. 393-94.

[3] *Hist. of Israel*, p. 59.

Priestly Code, or Code of ritual law attributed to Moses.[1]
For (1) *the very ground on which the existence of a written
Code is denied is that there is no proof of the practice* ; and (2)
if the practice is allowed, who is to certify that a written
law, regulating the practice, was not there ? Against the
existence of a written law, we have only Wellhausen's
dogmatic *dictum*, repeated by other critics, that, so long
as the cultus lasted, people would not concern themselves
with reducing it to the form of a Code.[2] It was only when
it had passed away that men thought of reducing it to
writing. That, however, Wellhausen certainly cannot prove,
and his view is not that of older and of a good many
recent scholars.[3] Nor has it probability in itself. Are
written Codes—especially in the light of modern knowledge
—so entirely unknown to antiquity as to warrant anyone in
saying *a priori* that, even where an elaborate ritual is
acknowledged to be in operation, a Code regulating it
cannot have existed ?[4]

2. There is an admitted "pre-existing temple usage,"
constituting "the main stock" of the priestly law; reflection
may next convince us that this "pre-existing usage must
have covered a much larger part of the Levitical Code than
is commonly realised. There existed at least a splendid
temple, with outer and inner divisions; a sacred ark;
temple furniture and utensils; a hereditary priesthood.
The priests would have their sacred vestments, prescribed
duties, ritual lore, their *technique* in the manipulation of
the different kinds of sacrifices, their recognised rules for
the discernment and treatment of leprosy, their rules for
ceremonial purification, their calendar of sacred festivals,
etc. These things *existed* ; assume the laws relating to them

[1] *Ibid.*; cf. Kuenen, as above, p. 96. [2] *Ibid.*

[3] Cf. Bleek, *Introd.* i. pp. 221 ff.; Dillmann, *Exod.-Lev.* Pref. p. viii
(see above, p. 160) ; p. 386.

[4] Analogy and discovery furnish strong grounds for believing that Israel
would have a written law. Kittel says on this point : "Israel came out of,
and always continued to be connected with, a country where external
prescriptions and rules played their part in all ages. As in Egypt, so in
Babylonia and Assyria, rules were laid down for sacrificial worship at an
early period. The Marseilles Table of Offerings has brought the same fact to
light as regards the Phœnicians. Is it to be believed that with all this
scrupulosity on the part of the surrounding priesthoods, a primitive
informalism, of which there is no other example, prevailed in Israel alone
until the days of the restoration ?"—*Hist. of Hebs.* i. p. 113. Cf. Dillmann,
Num.-Jos. p. 647.

to be written down, what ground have we for supposing that they would have differed greatly from the laws preserved to us in Leviticus and Numbers? Yet how little of all this obtrudes itself in the history? Nothing, we have again to point out, is gained by the substitution of *praxis* for written law; for it is not the written law, usually, but the practice, that history takes cognisance of, and, if silence in the history is compatible with the *practice*, it must also be compatible with the existence of any *Code* that regulates it. How far this reaches will appear more clearly if we look at specific instances.

Wellhausen speaks repeatedly of the splendour and elaboration of the pre-exilic cultus. There was a cultus " carried on," he tells us, " with the utmost zeal and splendour " [1]—" splendid sacrifices, presumably offered with all the rules of priestly skill." [2] " Elaborate ritual may have existed in the great sanctuaries at a very early period." [3] He correctly infers " that Amos and Hosea, presupposing as they do a splendid cultus and great sanctuaries, doubtless also knew of a variety of festivals." [4] But he has to add, " they have no occasion to mention any one by name." To the same effect Isaiah is quoted: " Add ye year to year, let the feasts go round." [5] But where shall we look in history for any notice of these feasts? It is allowed that the three feasts of the Book of the Covenant were observed from early times; yet, says Wellhausen, " names are nowhere to be found, and in point of fact it is only the autumn festival that is well attested, and this, it would appear, as the only festival, as *the* feast." [6] Still the critic has no doubt that " even under the older monarchy the previous festivals must also have already existed as well." [7] As particular examples, let the reader take his concordance, and note the exceeding paucity of the allusions in the historical books to such institutions as the sabbath, the new moon, or even the rite of circumcision. How easy, on the strength of this silence, would it be to say in the familiar way: " Joshua, Judges, the Books of Samuel, know nothing of the sabbath!" Drop one or two incidental references, which might easily

[1] *Hist. of Israel*, p. 56.　　　　　　　　　[2] *Ibid.* p. 55.
[3] *Ibid.* p. 54.　　　　　[4] *Ibid.* p. 94.　　　　　[5] *Ibid.*
[6] *Ibid.* It is not the case, however, that no other feasts are named. See below, pp. 321–22.
[7] *Ibid.* p. 96.

not have been there, and the evidence in the history for the above, as for many other institutions, disappears altogether. Does it follow that the sabbath, or a law of the sabbath, had no existence?

3. The test may be applied in another way. It is urged, *e.g.*, that there is no clear reference in pre-exilian literature to the existence of a class of Levites as distinct from the priests. It has already been seen that this is not altogether the case,[1] and, at least, as pointed out, the Levites appear quite distinctly at the return, nearly a century before the Priestly Code was promulgated by Ezra. But what of *post-*exilian literature? Apart from Ezra and Nehemiah, and the Books of Chronicles, how many references to the Levites could be gleaned from exilian and post-exilian writings? The second Isaiah (assuming the critical date), the prophets Haggai, Zechariah, Joel (if he be post-exilian), Malachi,[2] the Psalter—declared to be the song-book of the second temple —*all are silent,* with the possible exception of Ps. cxxxv. 20. The Priests' Code generally finds little reflection in the Psalter. Even in the Priestly Code itself, it is surprising to discover how large a part contains no allusions to the Levites. In Leviticus—the priestly book *par excellence*— with the solitary exception of chap. xxv. 32, 33, they are not so much as named.[3] Equally remarkable is the silence of the *New* Testament on the Levites. One stray allusion in the parable of the Good Samaritan;[4] one in the Fourth Gospel;[5] one in Acts, where Barnabas is described as a Levite[6]—that is all. The Epistle to the Hebrews, even, has nothing to say of them. Priests everywhere, but Levites nowhere. This, surely, is a sufficiently striking object-lesson in silence. Yet it is on the ground of a similar silence to this that we are asked to believe that there was no pre-exilian observance of the day of atonement.[7] Doubtless there is no mention in the history of this yearly day of expiation—any more than there is of the

[1] See above, pp. 163, 189.
[2] The Levites in Malachi are the priests.
[3] Cf. Kittel, *Hist. of Hebs.* i. pp. 120–21. Kittel shows that in large parts of the Priestly Code "there is no contrast between priests and Levites."
[4] Luke x. 32.   [5] John i. 19.   [6] Acts iv. 36.
[7] We are aware that it is argued that its observance is on certain occasions *precluded* by the narrative. But see Delitzsch's article, Luthardt's *Zeitschrift* 1880, pp. 173 ff.

allowed on all sides that there exists a close relation.[1]
What is the nature of that relation? Is it, as the world
has till recently believed, the Levitical Code, with which
as a priest he was necessarily familiar, which furnished
Ezekiel with suggestion and guidance in the framing of his
sketch of a new theocracy, in which older institutions are
freely remodelled and changed?[2] Or is it, as the newer
critics allege, that no written priestly laws as yet existed,
and that Ezekiel's sketch was the first rough draft—
"programme"—on the basis of which exilian scribes
afterwards worked to produce their so-called Mosaic Code.[3]
The latter view is necessary to the Wellhausen hypothesis,[4]
yet it is one against which a powerful note of dissent is
raised by an influential company of scholars, many of them
well-nigh as "advanced" as Wellhausen himself.[5] It is
pointed out, surely with justice, that the vision of Ezekiel
is only conceivable as the product of a mind saturated with
the knowledge of temple law and ritual; that the parallels
with the Priestly Code are not confined to chaps. xl.–xlviii.,
but go through the whole book;[6] that much is simply
alluded to, or left to be understood, which only the Priestly
Code can explain;[7] above all, that the scheme of the
Levitical Code deviates so widely in conception and detail
from that of Ezekiel as to render it unthinkable that its

link between Deuteronomy and the Priestly Code, and it thence follows
that the latter is exilian or post-exilian."—*Ezechiel*, p. 312.

[1] "On one point," says Baudissin, "there can be no doubt, namely this,
that the affinity between the law of Ezekiel and the Priests' Code is so
great that it can be explained only by the dependence of one of these upon
the other."—*Dict. of Bible*, iv. p. 86.

[2] It seems obvious that the vision is a work of prophetic imagination,
and is not intended to be taken as a literal programme for future realisation.
One has only to read the vision of the waters, and the direction for the
division of the land in chap. xlvii. to see that they belong to the region of
the ideal—not of fact.

[3] Cf. Kuenen, *Rel. of Israel*, ii. p. 116.

[4] One of the theses on which, from 1833, Reuss based his lectures was this :
"Ezekiel is earlier than the redaction of the ritual code, and of the laws,
which definitely organised the hierarchy." (Cf. Wellhausen, *Hist.* p. 4.)
See above, p. 200. Since the time of Graf, Delitzsch says, "the Book of
Ezekiel has become the Archimedean point of the Pentateuchal criticism."
—Luthardt's *Zeitschrift*, 1880, p. 279.

[5] Among critics of the theory may be mentioned Delitzsch, Riehm,
Dillmann, Schrader, Nöldeke, Baudissin, Kittel, Oettli, etc.

[6] See below, pp. 308–9.

[7] *E.g.*, the sin- and trespass-offerings, chaps. xl. 39 ; xliv. 29. See
Note C on Ezekiel and Earlier Law and Observance.

authors took the temple-vision of Ezekiel as a pattern.
How, indeed, if they viewed the vision of Ezekiel as a
prophetic revelation, should they presume to ignore or
contradict it so directly as they do?[1] We are aware that
the objection is retorted: how should Ezekiel presume to
alter a divinely-given earlier Code?[2] But the cases are
quite different. Ezekiel is not putting forward a code in
the name of Moses. He is a prophetic man, avowedly
legislating in the Spirit for a transformed land and a
transformed people in the future. Not only, however, does
the prophesying of Ezekiel *presuppose* an older law, but the
references with which his pages are filled to "statutes and
judgments," or "ordinances" of God,[3] which the people had
transgressed (in their "abominations" at the sanctuary
among other things), show explicitly that he had such laws
habitually before him.

2. But the subject admits of being brought to a nearer
determination. There is at least *one important section* of
the Priestly Code which, it is allowed, stands in the closest
possible connection with Ezekiel. We refer to "that
peculiar little collection of laws," as Wellhausen calls it,[4]
embraced in Lev. xvii.–xxvi. (with, according to most,
extensive fragments elsewhere), which modern writers,
following Klostermann, usually name "The Law of
Holiness."[5] The resemblances with Ezekiel here, particu-

[1] "It is," says Delitzsch, "incomprehensible how Ezra and Nehemiah
could dare to publish a law-book whose ordinances contradict those of
Ezekiel on all sides, and which still, in matter and form, shows itself well
acquainted with the latter."—*Zeitschrift*, p. 281. The systematic character
of Ezekiel's law, as compared with the *un*systematic character of the
Levitical Code, shows that it is not the latter which is dependent on the
former, but *vice versa*.

[2] Thus Graf, Kautzsch, etc. Professor Robertson remarks: "Well, on the
critical hypothesis, the Deuteronomic law at least existed as authoritative,
and yet Ezekiel deviates from it."—*Early Religion*, pp. 432–33. Dr. A. B.
Davidson points out: "Inferences from comparison of Ezekiel with the
Law have to be drawn with caution, for it is evident that the prophet
handles with freedom institutions certainly older than his own time."—
Ezekiel, Introd. p. liii.

[3] Ezek. v. 6; xi. 12, and *passim*.

[4] *Hist. of Israel*, p. 51 (cf. pp. 75, 86, 376, 384).

[5] Klostermann gave it this name in 1877 in a searching article since
reprinted in his *Der Pentateuch*, pp. 368 ff. "The principle," says Dr.
Driver, "which determines most conspicuously the character of the entire
section is that of *holiness*—partly ceremonial, partly moral—as a quality
distinguishing Israel, demanded of Israel by Jehovah."—*Introd.* p. 48.
Characteristic of it is the phrase "I am Jehovah."

larly in Lev. xxvi.,[1] are so numerous and striking that no one doubts the reality of some kind of dependence, but opinions have widely differed in critical quarters as to the nature of that dependence. At first it was confidently maintained, as by Graf, Kayser, Colenso (in part), etc., that *Ezekiel himself* must be the author of these sections. " Amidst all the peculiarities," wrote Graf, " by which these passages, and especially chap. xxvi., are distinguished from the other portions of the Pentateuch, there is exhibited so strange an agreement in thought and expression with Ezekiel, that this cannot be accidental, nor can be explained by reference to the sameness of the circle within which Ezekiel and the writer worked, but leads necessarily to the assumption that Ezekiel himself was the writer." [2]   Subsequently, when this theory was effectually disproved, on the basis of a wider induction, by Klostermann, Nöldeke, and Kuenen, the view was adopted that the writer was some one *acquainted with Ezekiel*, who, in Kuenen's words, " imitated him, and worked on in his spirit." [3]   This, however, is too evidently a makeshift, and does violence also to all probability ; for how should an " imitator " be supposed to have picked out just these isolated expressions of Ezekiel, and inserted them into a Code presenting throughout such marked peculiarities ?   " That the Law of Holiness is formed after the model of Ezekiel's speech," says Delitzsch, " is, to unprejudiced literary criticism, a sheer impossibility." [4]   The only view which simply and naturally meets the case is that favoured also by Dr. Driver [5]—viz., that *the prophet was acquainted with and used the law in question*, which, therefore, is older than himself.

---

[1] For lists of parallels cf. Colenso, *Pent.* Pt. vi. pp. 5–10 ; Driver, *Introd.* p. 147 ; Carpenter, *Hex.* i. pp. 147–48, etc.

[2] *Geschicht. Bücher*, p. 81 ; cf. Colenso, as above, chaps. i., ii.

[3] *Hex.* p. 276.   See below, p. 339.

[4] Luthard's *Zeitschrift*, 1880, p. 619.

[5] Dr. Driver says : " His [Ezekiel's] book appears to contain clear evidence that he was acquainted with the Law of Holiness. . . . In each instance he expresses himself in terms agreeing with the Law of Holiness in such a manner as only to be reasonably explained by the supposition that it formed a body of precepts with which he was familiar, and which he regarded as an authoritative basis of moral and religious life." —*Introd.* pp. 145–46 ; cf. p. 149 : " It may further be taken for granted that the laws of H—at least the principal and most characteristic laws—are prior to Ezekiel." So Ryle, *Canon*, pp. 72 ff.   Dillmann says : " Ezekiel lives and moves in the precepts of the Law of Holiness."—*Num.-Jos.* p. 646.

This yields at once certain important conclusions. It demonstrates, in the *first* place, the fallacy of the statement that no priestly written law existed before the exile—for here is at least one important Code of priestly law; and, *second*, it opens up large vistas of possibility as to the extent of this written law, and casts valuable light on the pre-exilian existence of many disputed institutions. Critical ingenuity, indeed, is amply equal to the fresh task of dissecting the Code it has discovered — of distinguishing in it a P[1] and P[2], even an H[1], H[2], H[3], and of relegating to later hands everything which it thinks unsuitable.[1] Thus Baentsch, a recent writer, distinguishes between chaps. xviii.-xx. (H[1]) as post-Deuteronomic, but prior to Ezekiel, and the group later than Ezekiel, chaps. xxi.-xxii. (H[2]), and finally chaps. xvii. and xxvi. (H[3]).[2] On the whole, however, the tendency of critical opinion has been to enlarge the scope of this "Law of Holiness" rather than to contract it [3]—the expansion, when the assumption of late date gives the critic a free hand, assuming sometimes quite remarkable proportions.[4] Even if some degree of redaction is admitted, it remains certain that in these chapters of Leviticus with which Ezekiel shows himself so closely in *rapport*, laws are embedded relating to the most contested points in Israel's religion. This Code is, in fact, in a very real sense, the quintessence of Levitical law. We find in it, to adduce only main instances,

---

[1] Kuenen lays down somewhat naïvely the following canon for identifying the fragments of P[1]: "We may assign to P[1] with high probability (*a*) the sections which obviously are not a part of P[2], with its later amplifications," etc.—*Hex.* p. 277.

[2] *Das Heiligkeitsgesetz*, 1893.

[3] With, again, the usual wide divergence. "Thus," says Carpenter, "Driver ascribes to this document Ex. vi. 6-8; xii. 12; xxxi. 13-14; Lev. x. 9*a*, 10; xi. 44; Num. xv. 37-41, while Addis allows only Lev. xi. 43-45, and Num. xv. 37-41."—*Hex.* i. p. 145. See next note.

[4] The following from Carpenter will illustrate: "Other scholars, again, like Wurster, Cornill, Wildeboer, further propose to include within it a considerable group of Levitical laws more or less cognate in subject and style. . . . Are all these [passages included by Driver] to be regarded as relics of P[h]? In that case it must have contained historical as well as legislative matter on an extensive scale. It must have related the commission to Moses, the death of the firstborn, the establishment of the dwelling, and the dedication of the Levites to Yahweh's service. Even if the latter passages be denied to P[h], the implications of Ex. vi. 6-8 suggest that the document to which it belonged comprised an account of the Exodus, the great religious institutions, and the settlement in the land promised to the forefathers," etc.—*Hex.* p. 145. The vista, indeed, is widening!

the Aaronic priesthood,[1] the high priest,[2] sin- and trespass-offerings,[3] the day of atonement,[4] the three historical feasts,[5] the sabbatic year,[6] the year of jubilee,[7] the Levitical cities,[8] etc.   We shall think twice, and require strong evidence, before surrendering all this, at the bidding of critical theory, to post-exilian hands.

3. Accepting it as established that the Law of Holiness, and other Levitical laws, were known to Ezekiel, we may now carry the argument a considerable way higher, with fresh confirmation of the result already reached.   It is essential to the Wellhausen hypothesis to prove that the Levitical Code is posterior to Ezekiel; it is still more indispensable for its purpose to show that it is later than *Deuteronomy*.   But is this really so?   The assertion is, no doubt, continually made; but on this point, once more, the critical camp is keenly divided, and there appears the clearest evidence that, as the older scholars all but unanimously maintained, the author of Deuteronomy is familiar with, and in his legislation actually embodies or alludes to, many provisions of the Levitical Code.   Here again Dr. Driver will be our witness, though this time, perhaps, against his own intention.   At first sight, indeed, this careful scholar seems altogether against us.   "The pre-exilic period," he tells us, "shows no indications of the legislation of P being in operation. . . . Nor is the legislation of P presupposed in Deuteronomy."[9]   Ere long, however, we discover that here, also, after the critical fashion, we have to distinguish *two* Dr. Drivers (Dr.[1] and Dr.[2], shall we say?)—a first, who contends unqualifiedly that the pre-exilic period "shows *no* indications of the legislation of P," and a second, who admits that it is only "the *completed* Priests' Code" that is unknown before the exile, and that "the contradiction of the pre-exilic literature does not extend to the *whole* of the Priests' Code indiscriminately."[10]   Citation is made of Deut. xiv.

---

[1] Lev. xvii. 2; xxi. 1, 17, 21, etc.   [2] Chap. xxi. 10–15.
[3] Chaps. xix. 21, 22; xxiii. 19.   [4] Chaps. xxiii. 27–32; xxv. 9.
[5] Chap. xxiii.   [6] Chap. xxv. 2–7.   [7] Chap. xxv. 8 ff.
[8] Chap. xxv. 32, 33.   The notice of the cities is the more valuable that it comes in incidentally in connection with a different subject.

[9] *Introd.* pp. 136, 137.   Cf. above, p. 300.

[10] *Ibid.* p. 142 (italics are Dr. D.'s).   As statements so discrepant within a short compass can hardly be supposed to come from the same pen, we are

4–20, but in the remarks that follow there is a slight variation between the first and the revised editions of the
Introduction which deserves attention.   We quote the first
edition, as better representing the facts, and give the revised
form below.[1]   " Here," it is said, "is a long passage virtually
identical in Deuteronomy and Leviticus; and that it is
borrowed by D from P—or at least from a priestly collection of *toroth* — rather than conversely, appears from
certain features of style which connect it with P and not
with Deuteronomy. . . . If so, however, one part of P was in
existence when Deuteronomy was written; and a presumption at once arises that other parts were in existence also.
Now the tenor of Deuteronomy as a whole conflicts with
the supposition that *all* the institutions of the Priests' Code
were in force when D wrote; but the list of passages just
quoted shows that *some* were, and that the terminology
used in connection with them was known to D."[2]   The
"list" referred to gives in parallel columns a long catalogue
of passages of Deuteronomy corresponding " with P (including H)," with note of some peculiarities in the mode of
quotation.[3]   On another page it is said: " In Deuteronomy
the following parallels may be noted," with list again given.[4]
These are significant admissions, and completely dispose of
the unqualified statements first quoted.   Reduced to its
real dimensions, Dr. Driver's argument only is that some
of the *characteristic* institutions of P—*e.g.*, the distinction
of priests and Levites—conflict with the tenor of D;[5] and
even this contention, resting largely on the argument from
silence, cannot be allowed the weight he attaches to it.   As
he himself says: " That many of the distinctive institutions
of P are not alluded to—the day of atonement, the jubilee
year, the Levitical cities, the sin-offering, the system of

driven back, on critical principles, upon the supposition that the work is
really the composition of a Driver "school" whose members vary slightly in
their standpoints—a hypothesis which other indications support.

  [1] The 7th edition reads: "Here is a long passage in great measure
verbally identical in Deuteronomy and Leviticus, and a critical comparison
of the two texts makes it probable that both are divergent recensions of a
common original, which in each case, but specially in Leviticus, has been
modified in accordance with the spirit of the book in which it was incorporated.   It is thus apparent that at least one collection of priestly
toroth, which now forms part of P, was in existence when Deuteronomy was
written," etc. (p. 145).   The rest as above.
  [2] *Ibid.* pp. 137–38 (1st edit.).   [3] *Ibid.* pp. 73–75.
  [4] *Ibid.* p. 144.   [5] *Ibid.* p. 137.

sacrifices prescribed for particular days—is of less importance: the writers of these [historical] books may have
found no occasion to mention them."[1] The argument from
silence applies nearly as much to the parts of the law
which he admits to have existed, as to those which he
thinks did not exist; and as much to *praxis* as to Code.[2]

However the matter may appear to Dr. Driver, it is
certain that to many able critics,[3] looking at the facts from
a different point of view, the evidence seems conclusive
that Deuteronomy *was* acquainted with the laws of P.
"The Deuteronomic legislation," says Riehm positively,
"presupposes acquaintance with the Priestly Code."[4]
Dillmann puts the Priests' Code earlier than Deuteronomy,
and the Law of Holiness, named by him S [= Sinai], in the
main earlier still.[5] He says: "That D not merely knows
priestly laws, but presupposes them as well known, appears
from many passages of his book."[6] "It is just as certain
that D presupposes and has used other laws (S) which now
lie before us in the connection of A [= P]."[7] Oettli says:
"Here certainly such laws as now lie before us only in the
codification of P appear as well known and in validity."[8]
He agrees with Delitzsch and the others quoted that
Deuteronomy shows itself acquainted with the priestly
laws.[9] Baudissin also puts the Law of Holiness before
Deuteronomy.[10] These judgments of leading critics, which
might be largely multiplied, are not based on slight grounds.
The proofs they offer are solid and convincing. We can as
before only give examples, but these will sufficiently indicate
the line of argument.

[1] *Introd.* p. 137. The author, accordingly, falls back on "the different
tone of feeling, and the different *spirit*" of the historical books; and allows
that "it is not so much the institutions in themselves as the system with
which they are associated, and the principles of which in P they are made
more distinctly the expression, which seem to bear the marks of a more
advanced stage of ceremonial observance" (*ibid.* p. 152). Thus the matter
tends to get refined away. Cf. Dr. A. B. Davidson on the argument from
silence, quoted in Note C above.
[2] Dr. Driver makes a point of the difference in the mode of quotation in
Deuteronomy from, or reference to, JE and P respectively (*ibid.* pp. 76, 137).
But his statements need qualification. See Note D on Quotations from JH
and P.
[3] *E.g.* Dillmann, Delitzsch, Riehm, Kittel, Oettli, etc.
[4] *Einleit.* i. p. 218.   [5] *Num.-Jos.* pp. 644–47, 660.
[6] *Ibid.* p. 605.   [7] *Ibid.*   [8] *Deut.*, Introd. p. 14.
[9] *Ibid.* p. 15.   [10] *Dict. of Bible*, iv. p. 82.

Deut. xiv. 4–20 (on clean and unclean animals) is, as Dr. Driver admits, "in great measure verbally identical" with Lev. xi. 4–20.

The permission to kill and eat flesh at home in Deut. xii. 15, 20 ff., presupposes and modifies (in view of the entrance into Canaan, ver. 20) the stringent law in Lev. xvii. 1–3, that all slaying was to be at the tabernacle door;[1] and the reiterated prohibitions of eating the blood (vers. 16, 23–25) rest on the enactments in P on the same subject (Lev. xvii. 23–25; cf. Gen. ix. 4; Lev. iii. 17; vii. 26, 27, etc.).

In Lev. xi. there is a law relating to the eating of things that die of themselves (vers. 39, 40; cf. chap. xvii. 15, 16); in Deut. xiv. 21 there stands a law which, with some modification, presupposes the former. This is marked by the use of the word "carcase" (Heb.). The discrepancy alleged to exist between the laws probably arises from the prospect of altered conditions in Canaan.[2]

"The year of release" in Deut. xv. 1 ff. glances at the Sabbatic year of Lev. xxv. 2 ff.

The law of the Passover in Deut. xvi. 1 ff. presupposes throughout the law in Ex. xii. (P), and modifies it in the important respect that the Passover is to be no longer a domestic festival, but is to be observed at the central sanctuary (vers. 5, 6). This implies the earlier family observance, while it is inconceivable that a law ordaining the home observance should arise *after* Deuteronomy.

The references to uncleanness in Deut. xxiii. 9, 10, imply a knowledge of laws of ceremonial impurity, as in Lev. xv.

Deut. xxiv. 8 expressly affirms the existence of a Mosaic law of leprosy given to the priests (cf. Lev. xiii., xiv.).

Deut. xxii. 30 certainly does not intend to limit the crime of incest to this one case, but, as Delitzsch says,[3] has in view the whole series of enactments in Lev. xviii. 7 ff.

It has before been pointed out that in Deut. xviii. 2 we have a verbal reference to the provision for the Levites in Num. xviii. 20 ff. In the same chapter we have parallels in vers. 10, 11 to Lev. xviii. 21 ff., xix. 26, 31, etc.

---

[1] Kuenen by a peculiar logic will have it that the command in Deuteronomy *excludes* the law in Leviticus; why, Oettli says, is "unerfindlich" (*Deut.* p. 14).

[2] Cf. p. 276 above and Note there.

[3] *Genesis*, i. p. 42. See Delitzsch's whole list, pp. 41–42.

accepting *this* reading of its meaning are to our mind insurmountable.

(1) That the temple service prior to the exile was in a *deplorable condition*—that both *in* and *out of* the temple the priesthood had largely fallen into abominable idolatries—all indications show.[1] Irregularities abounded, and the prophet is sufficient witness that the place which the law gives to the Levites had been mostly usurped by uncircumcised strangers.[2] But the first point evidently which claims notice here is, that this very ministry of the uncircumcised the prophet denounces as an iniquity, a violation of God's covenant, and the setting up by the people of keepers of His charge in His sanctuary for themselves (vers. 7, 8). This ministry, therefore, was not, in his view, a lawful thing, but a breach of law, an abomination like the idolatry itself. What, then, in the prophet's mind, *was* the lawful order? who, prior to the degradation of the idolatrous priests, *were* the lawful keepers of the charge of the sanctuary? Not the priests themselves, for the services in question were subordinate ministries—the very ministries ascribed elsewhere to the Levites (ver. 11; cf. Num. xviii 3, 4). Is not the inference very plain, though the critics generally ignore it, that, in Ezekiel's view, there did already exist a law on this subject, which in practice had been wantonly violated?[3] It can hardly be mistaken that the only properly official classes recognised by the prophet in the service of the temple are Levitical, and that these are distinguished into a higher and a lower class—the keepers of the charge of the house (chap. xl. 45), and the keepers of the charge of the altar (ver. 46). The unfaithful priests are punished by being degraded to the lower rank.[4]

(2) The next point to be borne in mind is, that this programme of Ezekiel was, and remained, *a purely ideal one*. It was probably never intended to have literal realisation; it was at least never actually put in force at the return, or

---

[1] Cf., *e.g.*, Jer. vii., viii.; Ezek. viii.

[2] On the view advocated, *e.g.*, by W. R. Smith, *O.T. in J. C.*, pp. 262-3, that these already are the guards of the sanctuary in the reign of Joash (1 Kings xi.), cf. Van Hoonacker, *Le Sacerdoce Lévitique*, pp. 93 ff.

[3] Cf. Delitzsch, Luthardt's *Zeitschrift*, 1880, pp. 279 ff.; Van Hoonacker, *Le Sacerdoce Lévitique*, pp. 191 ff. The prophet would seem to be familiar with the name "Levites" for the lower order distinctively (Ezek. xlviii. 13— "And answerable to the border of the priests, the Levites shall have," etc.).

[4] See Note E on Levites in Ezekiel.

at any earlier time. The degradation it depicts was never historically carried out; therefore could not affect the state of things subsisting after the exile. Scholars have indeed pleased themselves with pictures of "vehement struggles" (adumbrated in the story of Korah) on the part of Ezekiel's degraded priests to regain their lost privileges;[1] but these "struggles" exist nowhere, so far as we know, but in the critics' own imaginations, for there is no trace in history that any such degradation ever took place. On the other hand, we have seen that the distinction of priests and Levites was already known, and universally recognised, at the time of the return from exile. The Books of Ezra and Nehemiah assume it, but in no sense create it. If, therefore, this distinction was not made by Ezekiel's law directly, as little can it have been called forth by the Priests' Code founded on that law, for the Code did not make its appearance till Ezra's time, long after. It follows, in agreement with what has been said, that it can only be understood as an inheritance from pre-exilian times.

(3) Still more decisive, perhaps, is the fact that the Code, when it did come, by no means corresponded with Ezekiel's picture, on which it is presumed to be based, but in many respects stood *in direct contradiction* with Ezekiel. There is, as already said, nothing in the Code to suggest "disestablished priests," degradation as a punishment, substitution for uncircumcised strangers, or any of the other ideas of Ezek. xliv. On the contrary, the Levites are represented as set apart by Jehovah Himself in the wilderness for His peculiar service, and their position from the first is one of privilege and honour.[2] Again, in the

---

[1] Kautzsch, *e.g.*, says: "Again in the narrative of the revolt of the Korahites, now blended in Num. xvi. with an older account of a political revolt of the Reubenites, we have a clear reflection of the vehement struggles (subsequently buried in deep silence [!]), occasioned by the dislike the non-Zadokites felt to the manner in which they were employed in religious services."—*Lit. of O.T.*, p. 117. It is thus he accounts for the fewness of the Levites at the return.

[2] Kautzsch says: "According to Ezek. xliv. 10 ff., the sentence which reduced the former priests of the high places to the inferior services of the sanctuary was a deserved punishment; according to the Priests' Code the service of the Levites, by virtue of a divine appointment, is an honourable office of which they may be proud" (*ibid.* p. 117). Kautzsch's theory is, that the revolts of the non-Zadokites above referred to compelled the priestly circles "to find another ground for the position of the Levites" (pp. 117–18). Again a pure imagination of the critic.

Code, the priests are not "sons of Zadok" only (a vital point in Ezekiel), but the "sons of Aaron" generally. Ezekiel can be conceived of as having modelled his picture on the basis of the Code by *limiting* the priestly dignity to the Zadokites; the Code can never be explained as a construction from his ideas.

(4) Yet, apparently, this Code, so discrepant with Ezekiel, harmonised with the people's own recollections and traditions, since we find that *they unhesitatingly received it.* This simple fact, that, according to the history, the provisions of the Code were received without questioning by priests, Levites, and people alike, is of itself sufficient to overthrow the theory that the distinction was a new one, due to the initiative of Ezekiel. How possibly *could* such a thing as the critics suppose ever have happened? Had the Zadokites nothing to say about the loss of the exclusive position given them by Ezekiel? Were the Levites content that certain families of their number—the non-Zadokite Aaronites—should have the priestly prerogatives which Ezekiel had denied them, while others had not? If the records do not deceive us, both priests and Levites knew something of their own past. They had many links with that past by genealogies and otherwise. If the Levites or their fathers had been disestablished priests of high places, they must have been perfectly aware of the fact. Yet the Levites assent to have a position given to them which agrees neither with their own recollections, nor with the rights of priesthood alleged to be accorded to them in Deuteronomy, nor with the degradation theory of Ezekiel—which is thus condemned on every side as unhistorical. That such a patent make-believe should have succeeded is on the face of it incredible. Even had priests and Levites been willing to acquiesce in the new mock status, the people on whom the fresh and heavy tithe-burdens fell would not have been likely to do so. The longer, in fact, the theory is pondered, the more untenable it must appear.

2. What applies to the critical explanation of the distinction of priests and Levites applies with not less force to the explanations offered of *other institutions,* whose pre-exilic existence is called in question. We take a few of the more typical instances.

(1) There are the *three great feasts* of the nation—

passover, or unleavened bread, the feast of weeks, and the feast of tabernacles: these are robbed of their historical reference, and declared to be mere agricultural observances, locally observed till the age of Josiah, when Deuteronomy centralised them. The ceremonial character, in particular, stamped on them by the Priestly Code is held to be wholly post-exilian. But no tenable account is given of this sudden rise of agricultural festivals into historical significance, and of their unquestioned acceptance as feasts having this historical meaning, in the age of Ezra. Special assault is made upon the Biblical account of the institution of the passover, and of its association with the Exodus. Yet we have seen that the law in Ex. xii. 3 ff. is unintelligible, as framed for a domestic observance of the passover, unless it is placed before the centralising ordinance in Deuteronomy; while the latter by its use of this name *pesach* (passover),[1] its reference to the month Abib (chap. xvi. 1), and its distinct historical allusions (vers. 3, 6), as clearly presupposes the older law. The three feasts appear from the first, in *all* the Codes, as *national* (not local) feasts;[2] and in every instance, with but one exception, the passover, or feast of unleavened bread, is directly connected with the Exodus. That one exception, strange to say, is the most instructive of all as a refutation of the critical theory. It is the *priestly* law of Lev. xxiii. 4 ff.; yet it alone (1), as said, lacks a reference to the Exodus; (2) contains the regulation about presenting a sheaf of first-fruits which gives the feast any agricultural character it has; while (3) neither in it, nor in the law for passover offerings in Num. xxviii. 16 ff., is mention made even of the paschal lamb.[3] So that we have this curious result, in contradiction of the critical theory, that the historical reference comes in at the *beginning*, and the agricultural at the *end* of the development!

How, now, on the other hand, do the critics explain the name "passover" and the historical reference attached to this feast? Only, it must be replied, by again arbitrarily blotting out the history we have, and indulging in con-

[1] Wellhausen says this word "first occurs in Deuteronomy," a statement, of course, which (1) begs the question as to the date of Ex. xii., and (2) ignores Ex. xxxiv. 25.

[2] Ex. xxiii. 14–19; xxxiv. 18–26; Lev. xxiii.; Deut. xvi. 1–17.

[3] See Note F on Alleged Contradictions in the Passover Laws.

jectures of their own, about which there is no agreement.
Wellhausen, *e.g.*, will have it that the Exodus was, in the
tradition, connected with the demand to be permitted to
observe a spring festival, a chief feature of which was the
offering of firstlings. Cause and effect became inverted,
and instead of the festival being the occasion of the
Exodus, it came to be regarded as occasioned by it. Out
of this grew—*how* we are not told—the story of the slaying
of the firstborn in Egypt. Even so the meaning of the
name "passover" is allowed to be "not clear."[1] As the
history stands, both the passover rite, and the dwelling
in booths which gives the feast of tabernacles its name
(Succoth),[2] find their appropriate explanation; but it is
impossible to conceive how, in the full light of history,
these meanings could come to be imported into them at so
late an age as Ezra's.

The notices of the feasts in the history are, it is allowed,
scant. But they are more numerous than Wellhausen
admits, and, such as they are, unless again we arbitrarily
reject the narratives, they contradict his theory, and are in
keeping with the law. At the head of the series stands
the observance of the passover in Ex. xii., and the
wilderness observance in Num. ix. 4, 5, which gives rise to
a supplementary ordinance. Then comes the observance of
the passover under Joshua at Gilgal in Josh. v. 10, 11.
Passing the yearly feast of Jehovah at Shiloh (tabernacles?
Judg. xxi. 19; 1 Sam. i. 3, 7, 21), we have a general reference
to the three feasts in Solomon's reign (1 Kings ix. 25; cf.
2 Chron. viii. 13), and special allusions to the feast of
tabernacles in 1 Kings viii. 2, 65, 66; xii. 32, 33. Hosea
makes allusion to the dwelling in tents at this feast
(chap. xii. 9). The Chronicler records a great observance
of the passover under Hezekiah in a narrative too detailed
and circumstantial to be the work of invention.[3] Then we
come to the great passover of Josiah, of which it is said
that the like of it had not been held "from the days of the
Judges that judged Israel."[4] The returned exiles under
Zerubbabel observed both the feast of tabernacles and the

---

[1] *Hist. of Israel*, pp. 87–88.   [2] Lev. xxiii. 39–43.
[3] 2 Chron. xxx. The Chronicler may be held to "improve" for homiletic
purposes an existing narrative, but a history like this, without any
foundation for it, would be an absolute fraud.
[4] 2 Kings xxiii. 21–23; cf. 2 Chron. xxxv. 1 ff.

21

passover according to known laws,[1] and the reading of the
law by Ezra was the occasion of another great observance of
the feast of tabernacles, with special reference to the
requirements of Lev. xxiii. Here again it is declared
that such a feast had not been observed "since the days
of Joshua the son of Nun."[2] It is a straining of these
passages in Kings and Nehemiah, and a contradiction of
their own testimony, to make them affirm that there had
been no observance of the feasts named in earlier times;
the allusion is evidently to the enthusiasm, spontaneity,
and scrupulous attention to the law, with which the feasts
were observed—in the latter case with special regard to
the "booths."[3]

(2) As a second example, we may glance at the case
of the *sin- and trespass-offerings*, of which it is alleged that
the first mention is in Ezekiel.[4] Sin- and trespass-offerings
were in their nature occasional, and we might readily be
tempted to suppose that they had fallen largely into disuse
in pre-exilic times. Yet even this would be a rash inference from silence. It is to be observed that Ezekiel writes
of these offerings, not as something new, but as quite
familiar to his readers;[5] they are found also in the Law
of Holiness,[6] which, we have seen, precedes Ezekiel, and is,
from all indications, very old. Nor is it true that no earlier
trace of them exists. Ps. xl. cannot be put later than the
exile, and is probably earlier, yet in it the sin-offering is
spoken of as a customary sacrifice (ver. 6). Isa. liii. 10
declares that the soul of Jehovah's Righteous Servant
is made a "guilt- (trespass-) offering." Kuenen allows that
the "sin-offering" is not unknown to Hosea (chap. iv. 8),
though he fails to find a distinction between the sin- and
the trespass-offering.[7] Yet in 2 Kings xii. 16 a clear
reference is made to "trespass-money" and "sin-money,"
which, as Kuenen again grants, must have had a certain

---

[1] Ezra iii. 4 ; vi. 22.   [2] Neh. viii. 11 ff.

[3] Hos. xii. 9 may suggest that usage has substituted "tents" for
literal "booths."

[4] "Of this kind of sacrifice," says Wellhausen, "not a single trace
occurs in the Old Testament before Ezekiel."—*Hist. of Israel*, p. 73.

[5] Ezek. xl. 39 ; xlii. 13 ; xliii. 19 ; xliv. 29 ; xlvi. 20. Cf. Dr. A. B.
Davidson, *Ezekiel*, Introd. p. liv. Cf. Note C.

[6] Lev. xix. 21, 22 ; xxiii. 19.

[7] *Hex.* p. 210 ; cf. Kittel, *Hist. of Hebs.* i. p. 114. Even in the law
the distinction is not very rigorously kept.

connection with the Levitical offerings.[1] Even if it be
supposed that a custom had grown up of commutation of
the sacrifices by "pecuniary fines," the sacrifices and the
law requiring them are still presupposed. The *idea* of a
trespass-offering was present in some form to the minds
of the Philistines in the time of the Judges:[2] a fact which
shows it to be old. No proper explanation is given of the
when, where, or how, of the introduction of these sacrifices,
on the critical theory.

(3) One of the most daring strokes of the Wellhausen
criticism is the denial of the existence of the *incense-offering*
in pre-exilic times, and, as involved in this, the denial of an
altar of incense, not simply in the supposed imaginary
tabernacle, but even in the Solomonic temple. Wellhausen
goes still further, and, in face of the express statements in
1 Macc. i. 21 ff.; iv. 49, that the golden altar and golden
table were both carried away by Antiochus Epiphanes,
and renewed at the feast of the dedication, casts doubt on
the existence of an altar of incense even in the *second*
temple.[3] The chief ground for these denials is the fact
that, in Exodus, the command for the making of the altar
of incense does not appear where we might expect it, in chaps.
xxv.–xxix., but at the commencement of chap. xxx. How
arbitrary the procedure is, is shown by the clear testimony
of at least *four* passages of the history (1 Kings vi. 20, 22;
vii. 48; ix. 25; cf. 2 Chron. iv. 19) to the construction and
presence of the golden altar in the temple of Solomon.[4]

The critical theory of the tithe-laws, of the Levitical
cities as transformations of the *Bamoth,* and other matters,
have already been referred to.[5]

3. In conducting the above argument, we have laid little
stress on *incidental words or allusions* in either the historical
or the prophetical books which might seem to indicate
acquaintance with the Levitical legislation. These allusions, though not decisive in themselves, are more numerous

[1] *Hex.* p. 211; cf. Delitzsch, Luthardt's *Zeitschrift,* 1880, p. 8.
[2] 1 Sam. vi. 3.   [3] *Hist. of Israel,* pp. 64–67.
[4] Delitzsch admirably shows the groundlessness of Wellhausen's general
reasonings, and particularly of his assertion that "the golden altar in the
sanctuary is originally simply the golden table" (*Hist.* p. 66), in his article
on the subject in *Zeitschrift,* 1880, pp. 113 ff. Ezekiel, whom Wellhausen
cites in his favour, is shown to be really a witness against him.
[5] See above, pp. 275, 290, etc.

than the critics are wont to allow, and, when a pre-exilian
origin of Levitical laws is independently rendered
probable, acquire enhanced importance. Joel, *e.g.*, which
used to be regarded as one of the earliest of the prophetical
books, has many allusions which suggest the ritual code—
the sanctuary and its altar in Zion, priests, blowing of
trumpets, fasts, solemn assemblies, meal and drink-offerings,
etc.[1]—and is now, largely for this very reason, regarded by
the Wellhausen school as post-exilian.[2] Yet we question
if the allusions in Joel are more definite than those of the
earlier prophets, or would, on critical principles, suffice any
more than these, to establish a knowledge of the written
law, which is yet allowed to have been in existence when he
wrote. Not to dwell on Amos (*e.g.*, chap. v. 21, 22), we may
cite such a passage as Isa. i. 13, 14: "Bring no more vain
oblations; incense is an abomination unto Me; new moons
and sabbaths, the calling of assemblies,—I cannot away with
iniquity and the solemn meeting. Your new moons and
your appointed feasts My soul hateth," etc. (cf. ver. 11;
chaps. iv. 5; xxxiii. 20—" the city of our solemnities "). The
vocabulary of this passage—"assembly" (convocation),
"solemn meeting," "appointed feasts," etc.—and the allusions
to festivals and sacrifices, are entirely suggestive of the
Levitical law (cf. Lev. xxiii.; Num. xxviii.; cf. Deut. xvi. 8).
Reference was before made to the allusions in the prophets
to a *cycle* of feasts, of which little or nothing is said in the
history. Thus, Isa. xxix. 1: " Let the feasts come round "; or
Nah. i. 15: " Keep thy feasts, O Judah, perform thy vows."
It cannot be overlooked, further, that the prophets
constantly assume the people to be in possession of " statutes,"
or " statutes and judgments " [3]—*i.e.*, of fixed laws—evidently
of considerable extent, and, we must suppose, written. That

---

[1] Joel i. 9, 13, 14; ii. 1, 15-17, etc.

[2] Duhm, who led the way here, said in his *Theol. der Proph.* (1875)
that at that time scholars almost unanimously put Joel early (p. 71). His
own proofs are mainly a begging of the question of the post-exilian origin of
the Law. He describes Joel as an "epigon," with a great gift for form,
but not much burdened with thoughts. The theory is combated by
Delitzsch, Orelli, Reuss, Professor J. Robertson, Kirkpatrick, and others.
Delitzsch said of it: "The bringing down of Joel into the post-exilic age by
Duhm, Merx, Stade, and others, is one of the most rotten fruits of the
modern criticism."—*O.T. Hist. of Redemption*, p. 113 (E.T.).

[3] Amos ii. 4 (R.V.); Jer. xliv. 10; Ezek. v. 6, xi. 12, etc. Cf. Lev.
xvii.-xxvi., and Deuteronomy (constantly).

such "statutes" were covered by the word *torah* (instruction, law) we see no reason to doubt. Here comes in that much-debated passage, Hos. viii. 12 : "Though I write for him my law in ten thousand precepts (R.V. *marg.*, "wrote for him the ten thousand things of my law"), they are counted as a strange thing."[1] If this does not point to written law of considerable compass, it is difficult to know what form of words would. Smend, at an earlier stage, found, as was before shown,[2] Hosea and Amos impregnated with *Levitismus* (*e.g.*, Hos. ix. 3–5). It may be observed that Hosea has also, in the view of many, unmistakable assonances with Deuteronomy.[3] When to these indications in the prophets we add what was before said of allusions in the historical books to ark, tabernacle, Aaronic priesthood, high priest, ephod, shewbread, etc., and of the evidence which these books afford of a knowledge of festivals, of sacrifices (burnt - offerings, peace - offerings, meal - offerings, drink-offerings, probably sin-offerings as well), of ritual of worship, of laws of purity, of clean and unclean food, of leprosy, of consanguinity, prohibitions of eating blood, etc.—we may begin to feel, with Dillmann, that the allusions in history and prophecy are well-nigh as numerous as we had any right to expect.

Of the law itself, we would only say in closing, in opposition to the purely secular, and often unworthy, views of its origin we have been discussing, that it is pervaded by a spirit of holiness, and, in its aim and structure, is as unique as all the other parts of the Jewish religion.

---

[1] Wellhausen renders this passage : " How many soever my instructions may be, they are counted those of a stranger."—*Hist. of Israel*, p. 57. This leaves out altogether the word of chief importance—"write." Delitzsch thinks that passages like Hos. iv. 6 ; viii. 1 ; Amos ii. 4 ; Isa. i. 11–14 show "that a codex of the Mosaic law was already in existence in the time of the prophets of the eighth century," and says : "with the last passage we may compare Hos. viii. 12, which should be translated, 'were I to write for him the myriads of my law, they would be regarded as strange,' that is, a still more extensive *Torah* would have the same fate as the existing one." Then, after quoting Smend's translation, "I wrote for him myriads of my law," he says : "These words of Hosea certainly indicate, as even Schrader acknowledges, the existence of a divinely obligatory law in the form of a codex."—*Mess. Prophecies* (E.T. 1880), p. 11.

[2] See above, p. 159.

[3] Cf. Hos. ii. 8, xii. 8, xiii. 6, with Deut. vii. 13, viii. 7–20, xi. 14–16 ; Hos. viii. 11, with Deut. xii. ; Hos. xii. 13, with Deut. xviii. 18 ; Hos. iv. 4, with Deut. xvii. 12 ; Hos. viii. 13, ix. 3, with Deut. xxviii. 68 ; Hos. xi. 8, with Deut. xxix. 23 ; Hos. xii. 7, with Deut. xxv. 13–16, etc.

Whatever the formal resemblances, the Levitical law had nothing essentially in common with heathen ritual, but rested on a basis of its own. No heathen religion had a system based on the idea of the holiness of God, and governed by the design of restoring and maintaining fellowship with God, and the peace of conscience of the worshipper, by the grace of atonement. For this was the real nature of the Levitical system. It was designed in all its parts to impress on the mind of the worshipper a sense of the separation which sin had put between him and the holy God, and provided a means by which the people, notwithstanding their sin, could have access to God, and enjoy His favour.[1] There is nothing in this, if the Bible's own view of the course of revelation is accepted, incompatible with its early origin. It is one of the groundless assumptions of the newer theory that the idea of expiation by sacrifice was foreign to the pre-exilian, and earlier Israelitish, mind. One sufficient proof to the contrary is furnished in 1 Sam. iii. 14: "Therefore I have sworn unto the house of Eli, that the iniquity of Eli's house shall not be purged ("atoned for," the Levitical word) with sacrifice nor offering for ever."

VI. Time of Origin of the Levitical Law

To sum up our argument thus far: we have sought to show, on both moral and historical grounds, and by positive proof to the contrary, that the Graf-Wellhausen theory of a post-exilian origin of the Levitical Code cannot be upheld. Its main stronghold is the argument from silence; but that silence is neither so complete as is alleged, nor are the inferences drawn from it warranted. By a similar argument, if Deuteronomy were left out of account, it might be proved that the Book of the Covenant also, as a written Code, was not known before the exile. Yet Deuteronomy shows how erroneous would be such an inference.

If, however, the Priestly Code is not a post-exilian production, when did it originate? Here we pass over unreservedly to the standpoint of Wellhausen as against those *mediating* critics, who, with more or less admission of antiquity in parts, assume the law as a whole to have taken

[1] Cf. Heb. ix., x. On Unity of the Law see above, p. 294.

shape in the hands of the priests about the ninth century
B.C., or between that and the time of Deuteronomy—but
still only as a quasi-private document,—a "programme"
struggling for recognition and very imperfectly attaining
it,—and receiving changes and additions as far down as the
exile. Such, in general statement, is the midway theory
advocated by critics like Nöldeke, Dillmann, Kittel, and
Baudissin, and against it the more compact and internally
consistent hypothesis of Kuenen and Wellhausen bears
down with irresistible force.[1] Such a theory is strong,
indeed, in its proof, as against the Wellhausen contention,
that the Levitical law is older than Deuteronomy, no trace
of whose existence it betrays, while Deuteronomy very
evidently shows traces of *its* influence, but it is weak as
water in arguing for the existence of a Code which embodies
the idea of the unity of the sanctuary a century or two
before Deuteronomy was heard of, while yet holding, with
the De Wette school, that this idea first came to recognition,
or at least to influence, with the publication of Deuteronomy
in the reign of Josiah. Kuenen is fully justified in protest-
ing against this "idea of the passive existence of these laws
for ages before they had any practical influence." [2] A
theory which, like that of the older scholars, carries back
the bulk of the laws to Mosaic or immediately post-Mosaic
times, or, again, a theory which, like Wellhausen's, brings
them all down to times subsequent to Deuteronomy,—
which means, practically, to the exile or after,—
can be understood: there is coherence in it. But this
intermediate theory, which ascribes to the laws an unacknowledged existence—suspends them, as it were, in the
air—in the days of the kings, and supposes them to have
remained inoperative for centuries, is impotent against the
assaults of its energetic opponents.[3] It encounters all the
difficulties of the older theory, arising from the supposed

---

[1] On Nöldeke's views, cf. Wellhausen, *Hist. of Israel,* pp. 46–51 ;
Kuenen, *Hex.* Introd. pp. xxxvi ff. For Nöldeke also the tabernacle is "a
mere creature of the brain." On the theory generally, see Note G on the
Mediating View of the Priestly Code.

[2] As above, p. xxxi.

[3] Wellhausen ridicules those "who in blind faith hold fast, not to the
Church tradition—there would be sense in that—but to a hypothesis which
is but two decades old, viz., De Wette's discovery that Deuteronomy is more
recent than the Priests' Code."— *Geschichte Israels,* p. 173 (1st edit. : the
passage is dropped in *Proleg.*).

silence of the history and conflict with Deuteronomy and has none of its compensating advantages. For the law presents in no sense the aspect of a private priestly programme, struggling, without success, for recognition and acceptance. It rests on very definite principles and ideas, gives itself out in all seriousness as a Code of wilderness legislation (why, it may be asked, should ninth century priests throw their "programme" into this form?), and presents not the slightest trace of hesitation or doubt in its demands. It ascribes its legislation in obvious good faith to Moses, or, more correctly, to God through him. We agree, therefore, that this middle theory of a "trance-like" existence of the Levitical Code in the ninth or eighth century, to the priestly circles of which it owed its origin, cannot stand before the rigorous logic of the newer criticism. It is such theories which give the Wellhausen criticism its "case." We reckon it, indeed, one of the greatest services of the Graf-Wellhausen scheme that it effectually *cuts out* this mediating, but logically helpless view which weakly contests the ground with it, and leaves us fairly face to face with the ultimate alternative—a post-exilian origin of the law, which many reasons show to be untenable, or a real antiquity of the law answerable to its own profession.

It is involved in what has been said that it is the latter alternative which we adopt, and so come back to the older position of a substantially Mosaic origin of the laws. It is not necessarily implied in this that Moses wrote all these laws, or any one of them with his own pen; or that they were all written down at one time; or that they underwent no subsequent changes in drafting or development; or that the collection of them was not a more or less gradual process; or that there may not have been smaller collections, such, *e.g.*, as that lying at the basis of the Law of Holiness—in circulation and use prior to the final collection, or codification, as we now have it. There is much plausibility in Dillmann's conjecture that the Law of Holiness (Lev. xvii.–xxvi.), with its Sinaitic signature (chap. xxvi. 46), its constantly recurring formula, "I am Jehovah your God," and its references to deliverance from the bondage to Egypt, in its original form stood after the Book of the Covenant in Exodus (cf. chap. xxiv. 12), as a summary of the priestly legislation of Sinai.[1]   However this may be—and we lay no stress upon it—there appears no good ground for assuming that the general codification was not completed at a very early date, possibly before the relapse in the time of the Judges, and probably not later than the early days of the monarchy.   There is nothing we can discover which points to a later date; though it does not follow that there may not have been minor modifications and adjustments after.[2]

[1] Dillmann, *Ex.-Lev.* pp. 261, 534.
[2] See further below, pp. 372 ff.

CHAPTER X

Difficulties and Perplexities of the Critical Hypothesis: The Priestly Writing. II. The Document

"A really vivid picture of the manner in which the documents are interwoven cannot be given by merely stating the numbers of the verses. And it is just as impossible to state with each single verse or section whether it is assigned to the document in question by all investigators or by the majority or only by a few. In the Pentateuch and in the Book of Joshua it is only with regard to P that something like unanimity has been reached."
—KAUTZSCH.

"In the present state of Hexateuch criticism the weightiest question is not, how much of the Pentateuch, as it comes to us, has Moses himself written . . . but this is the *chief question*: Does the Priestly Writing contain trustworthy accounts of the time and work of Moses, or is everything narrated in it, as the modern 'science' maintains, only defacement, fiction, yea, 'the merest fiction,' and full of contradictions with the (so-called) alone old tradition offered by J and E? I venture to say that in many cases the alleged contradiction is not present; elsewhere the word of Augustine holds good, *Distingue tempora et concordabit scriptura*; and in yet other places the difficulty is occasioned through glosses of other readers—glosses for which we cannot make the redactor or redactors responsible."—STRACK.

"I suppress my regret that Wellhausen has still not advanced to the point of recognising in the firmly-defined writer Q [=P], whose narrative is composed with regard to JE, and enclasps this element, as taking the place of the inner content lacking to itself, the everywhere sought for and nowhere found R."—KLOSTERMANN.

CHAPTER X

DIFFICULTIES AND PERPLEXITIES OF THE CRITICAL HYPOTHESIS: THE PRIESTLY WRITING. II. THE DOCUMENT

IN nothing are critics of all schools more at one than in the recognition of a writing, partly historical and partly legislative, running through the Pentateuch and Joshua, which, from its linguistic and other traits, has been variously described, in the course of opinion, as the Elohist document, the *Grundschrift* (primary document), the 1st Elohist, the Priestly Writing, the Priests' Code, or simply P.[1] Yet the history of opinion on this Priestly Writing, as on other parts of the documentary theory, has been a slow development, and has been marked by at least four critical stages, the general nature of which has already been indicated.

1. With reference to the *compass* of the writing, it has already been seen that all Elohistic matter, or matter agreeing with the Elohistic in character and style, was originally assigned to this assumed fundamental document. Even here, indeed, it was soon found necessary to make distinctions and multiply parts, but these variations may at present be disregarded. The first critical point was reached when, on the ground of its greater affinity with the Jehovist, Hupfeld removed a considerable part of this Elohistic matter, and set it up as a separate document, thenceforth known as E, or the 2nd Elohist. Previously much stress had been laid on the unity and completeness of the Elohistic document, as giving " a connected narrative of the theocracy " from the creation to the settlement in Canaan.[2] Now,

---

[1] Wellhausen uses the symbol Q (*Quatuor*—Book of the Four Covenants); Dillmann and others use A for this document.
[2] Cf. Bleek, *Introd.* i. p. 290.

however, that the 2nd Elohist was cut out of it extremely little, as will be shown, was left to the older writer in Genesis after chap. xvii., and it was felt to be curious that the 1st Elohist should become so extremely fragmentary just where the new writer came in.

2. In respect to the *age* of the document, we have seen how, originally, the Elohistic document was all but universally recognised as the fundamental part, or *Grundschrift*, of the Pentateuch, while the Jehovist was viewed as supplementary.[1] A change was prepared for here also by Hupfeld's contention that J and E were independent histories. Then came the Graf-Wellhausen upturning, by which the supposed *Grundschrift* was lifted from the beginning of the literary history, and carried down bodily to its close. Graf, however, as was formerly mentioned, did not at first contemplate so great a revolution. He brought the Levitical *laws* down to the exile, but was content to leave the Elohistic *history* in its old place—prior to Deuteronomy. Subsequently, in deference to Kuenen, he renounced that view, and accepted the late date for both.[2] It is carefully to be observed that it was not critical reasons, but a *dogmatic* consideration—the supposed necessity of keeping history and laws together—which led Graf to this *tour de force* as respects the P *history*.

3. A difference next emerged in respect of the *independence* of the document. In putting the Priestly Writing late, Graf felt that the ground was taken from the older view that the *Grundschrift* was an independent document, complete in itself, and he sought to show, as Kuenen states it, "that its narratives not only presuppose those of the Yahwist, but were intended from the first to supplement them, and to constitute a single whole with

---

[1] See above, p. 201.

[2] See above, p. 200. Colenso, in *Pent.* Pt. vi. pp. 579 ff., adhered to, and contended strongly for, Graf's original view of the history: thus also in Pt. vii. Carpenter says that "he finally acquiesced in the modern view."—*Hex.* i. p. 69. If he did, Cheyne does not seem to have known of the change (*Founders of Crit.* p. 203), and Kuenen only says: "He subsequently came to the conclusion that he had been at least to some extent mistaken." —*Hex.* p. 70 (with reference). We are very certain that whether, under pressure of the opinion of others, Colenso changed his view or not, he never refuted his own arguments against the late date. A change of this kind would mean the collapse of the reasoning of a great part of his volumes.

them."[1] In this, as we shall seek to show, Graf proved himself more logical, and took up a sounder position, than Kuenen and Wellhausen, who held to the old assumption that the Priestly Writing originally subsisted by itself.

4. With respect, finally, to the *unity* of the writing, a great change has latterly been brought about (1) by the splitting up of the P document into a P[1], P[2], P[3], etc., and (2) by the abandonment of the idea of a single writer for that of "schools," whose activity extended over a long period.[2] This change also strikes a blow at the idea of the P writing being a complete and independent history, as was at first imagined.

It will already begin to appear that the problem of the Priestly Writing is by no means so simple as it is apt to seem in the neat statements of the text-books. The difficulties inherent in the current view will, we believe, only become clearer on nearer inspection.

I. Is there a Priestly Writing in distinction from JE?

The initial question is as to the *right* to speak of a Priestly Writing,[3] or style of writing, at all in the Pentateuch, in distinction from JE, already considered. Here it is at once to be admitted that the case stands somewhat differently from what it did with JE. It cannot, we think, be reasonably disputed, and only a few critics of the present day, even among the more conservatively disposed,[4] would be prepared to deny, that the sections ordinarily attributed to P have a vocabulary, and a

---

[1] *Hex.* pp. xxx, xxxi. See below, p. 341.

[2] Graf also originally explained in this way the resemblance of the style of the Levitical laws to the P sections in Genesis. Thus on Gen. xvii. : "We can only conclude that this older law of circumcision served as a model in formulating laws during the exile and after it, with an aim at antiquity . . . or that these formulæ were generally at all times usual in certain circles of priestly legislators, from whom the composition of that law proceeded."—*Geschicht. Bücher*, p. 93.

[3] In using this customary designation we by no means commit ourselves to the position that the authors are necessarily *priests*. Colenso vigorously combats the idea that the Elohistic sections in Genesis are *priestly*, cf. *Pent.* Pt. vi. pp. 581 ff. ; App. pp. 126 ff.

[4] Thus the late Principal Cave, as already mentioned, in his *Inspiration of the O.T.*, distinguishes an Elohistic and a Jehovistic writing in Genesis, inclining to attribute both to Moses.

stylistic character, of their own, which render them *in the main* readily distinguishable. The case for the distinction, indeed, is often enormously overdriven. The long lists of words alleged to be peculiar to P admit of great reduction, many of the marks assumed for the document are no sure *criteria*, the skill that distinguishes a P[1], P[2], P[3], P[4] is continually to be distrusted, some of the descriptions of the P style are little better than caricatures.[1] Yet on the whole it is a *distinct* style. It is a style stately and impressive of its own kind; in such a chapter as Gen. i. rising to sublimity, in narrative often exhibiting a grave dignity, as in Gen. xxiii., occasionally, again, as in the story of Gen. xxxiv., not readily distinguishable from that of JE.[2] It is a style, however, less flowing, lively, picturesque, anthropomorphic than that of JE; more formal, circumstantial, precise. We should speak of it in the Book of Genesis as less a *priest-like* than a *lawyer-like* style; the style of a hand trained to work with laws, genealogies, chronologies, to put things in regular and methodical shape, to give unity and exactitude to looser compositions. It is marked by general adherence to the name "Elohim" till the revelation of the name Jehovah in Ex. vi. 2 ff.

We have referred to the *limitations* with which the statements often made as to the vocabulary, and other supposed marks of the P document, are to be received, and, to form a just idea of the writing, these also need to be remembered. In sifting the lists of words and phrases put forth as signs of this document,[3] we are speedily struck with the fact that many of them occur only once or twice

[1] Wellhausen exhausts the vocabulary of contempt in conveying his idea of the pedantry, verboseness, insufferable tediousness, and barrenness of the Priests' Code. "Art-products of pedantry. . . . One would imagine that he was giving specifications to measurers for estimates, or that he was writing for carpet-makers or upholsterers. . . . Of a piece with this tendency is an indescribable pedantry, belonging to the very being of the author of the Priestly Code. . . . Nor is it any sign of originality, rather of senility," etc.—*Hist. of Israel*, pp. 337, 348, 350, 353. Addis considerately grants that the "intolerable pedantry" of the Priestly Writer in Ex. xxxiv.-xl. is due more to "the successors of the Priestly Writer and his school" than to the Priestly Writer himself.—*Hex.* i. p. lxix.

[2] What most critics ascribe to P in this narrative, Colenso gives to J. See further below, p. 352.

[3] The lists may be seen in detail in Dillmann, Driver, Carpenter, Westphal, etc. The reader will do well to note how small a proportion of them is carried on to Joshua.

in the Book of Genesis, or in the whole Pentateuch; that some belong to particular passages from the nature of their subject, and are not general in P, or elsewhere; that some are found also in JE; that other examples are doubtful (JE *or* P); that within the limits of P itself the language varies greatly, and in very few cases are the words uniformly distributed through the sections. This statement may be briefly illustrated. There are few better examples of the words and phrases of P than the following: "After his (their) kind," "be fruitful and multiply," "male and female," "swarm," "establish (give) a covenant" (JE has "cut" = make), "self-same day," "possession," "create," "expire" (A.V. "die," Gen. vi. 17, etc.), "substance," etc. Yet of these, "kind," "swarm," "male and female," occur in Genesis only in the narratives of the creation and flood. "Kind" occurs elsewhere only in the laws of clean and unclean food, Lev. xi. (P) and Deut. xiv. (D); "swarm" in the same laws, but also in Ex. viii. 3 (JE); "male and female" three times in ritual passages in Leviticus "Create" (*bara*) occurs only in Gen. i.–ii. 4; v. 1 (P), and chap. vi. 7 (J), with Deut. iv. 32 (D). "Substance" occurs five times in P passages in Genesis, but also in Gen. xiv. (five times), and chap. xv. 14—which are *not* P; elsewhere twice in Numbers. We are probably not unwarranted in regarding such formulæ as "be fruitful and multiply," "establish My covenant," preserved in Gen. i., ix., xvii., etc., as very old, and belonging to pre-Mosaic tradition of covenant and promise.[1] It is thus evident that many of the alleged marks of P are absent from the greater part of the P writing just as much as from JE;[2] too much stress, therefore, should not be laid on them. The significant thing is that where they *do* occur, and are repeated, it is *mostly*

[1] P varies the formula about multiplying, *e.g.*, in Ex. i. 7; and the JE passages that follow in Ex. i. have clear verbal references to P's language (vers. 9, 10, 12, 20—in Heb.).

[2] We cannot follow the late Dr. Green in his denial of a distinct literary hand in P, but that able scholar is surely justified in pointing out that "only two words or phrases noted as characteristic of P in chap. i. occur again in Genesis after chap. ix.," and that "after the covenant with Abraham (chap. xvii.), which recalls that of Noah (chap. ix.), almost every mark of P in the preceding part of Genesis disappears entirely. Scarcely a word or phrase that is reckoned characteristic of P in chaps. xvii. or xxiii. is found in later chapters of Genesis, except where the transactions of the latter are explicitly referred to, or the promises of the former are repeated."—*Genesis*, p. 553.

in P passages. The wide statements one meets with on this subject need, in fact, constantly to be checked. Mr. Addis, *e.g.*, writes: "He [the Priestly Writer] says 'Paddan-Aram,' not, *like the other writers*, 'Aram of the two rivers.'"[1] Yet this latter designation (Aram - Naharaim) actually occurs only once altogether (Gen. xxiv. 10). "Destroy," sometimes claimed as a P word, occurs, outside the narrative of the flood (Gen. vi. 13, 17 ; ix. 11, 15), only *once* in P (Gen xix. 29), while it is found repeatedly in JE passages. Many of the other criteria of distinction of P from JE are equally insecure, or depend on false assumptions. Wellhausen, *e.g.*, finds in P the idea of "sin, as the root of ruin, explaining it, and capable of being got rid of," in contrast with J, who is marked "by a peculiar sombre earnestness . . . almost bordering on pessimism ; as if mankind were groaning under some terrible weight, the pressure not so much of sin as of creaturehood."[2] Yet P, we are often told, has no knowledge of the fall, while J has. Elsewhere, also, it is P who is represented as gloomy, monotonous, and serious.[3] Kuenen makes it a fault of P that he is "completely dominated by his theory of a graduated progress alike of the history of mankind and of the divine revelation,"[4] as if this were not equally true of JE.[5]

II. Question of the Unity and Independence of the Priestly Writing

When the existence of a P writing, or quality of writing, in the Pentateuch has been ascertained, we are still only at the beginning of our investigation. Is this alleged document a unity ? Had it ever an independent existence ? How is it related to JE ? Of these questions the most fundamental is that which relates to P's existence as an independent document, but it will clear the way for dealing

---

[1] *Hex.* p. lxxiii (italics ours).
[2] *Hist. of Israel*, pp. 314–15. Dillmann, on the other hand, declares of J that "especially of all the three narrators does he show the deepest knowledge of the nature, origin, and growth of sin."—*Genesis*, i. p. 15. Neither P nor E, according to these writers, have any account of the fall.
[3] *Hist. of Israel*, p. 81.   [4] *Hex.* p. 301.
[5] See above, p. 62.

with this to consider briefly, first, the question of its unity and homogeneous character.

1. The old idea of P was that, whatever its date, it was essentially a *connected narrative* from a single pen, though naturally working up older materials. We have seen that the case is fundamentally altered when the individual writer is transformed into a "school." With the assumption of a *series* of priestly writers, belonging to yet wider "circles," the later members of the succession inheriting the vocabulary and methods of the earlier and continuing their work, unity of composition tends to disappear. It is now open to account for resemblance of style by "imitation." As in regard to Deuteronomy we have a D^2, who successfully "imitates" the ideas and style of D^1, with numerous Deuteronomic revisers of historical books later;[1] so we can now speak of a P^2, P^3, etc., who "imitate" the style of P^1, of an author of the Law of Holiness who "imitates" Ezekiel,[2] of a P writer in the Book of Joshua who "imitates" the P of Leviticus,[3] etc. On this new basis it can no longer be urged that similarity of style means necessarily sameness of author, or pleaded that the author who drew up the Levitical laws *must* be identical with the author of the P sections in Genesis. There is no longer anything to preclude the supposition of Delitzsch, formerly referred to, that the literary activity of the Elohistic pen may reach back to times nearly approaching those of Moses;[4] or even the belief, if one is disposed to entertain it, that its earlier models go back *beyond* the time of Moses.[5] The protocol style characteristic of this writing was certainly not the invention of the people of Israel, nor its peculiar property; there are, besides, marked features distinguishing the Elohist in Genesis from the

[1] Cf. Kuenen, as quoted above, p. 252 : "The great similarity [of Deut. i.-iv. to the rest of the book] must be explained as the result of imitation."— *Hex.* i. p. 117. "It hardly seems possible to ascribe the Deuteronomic recension [of Joshua] to a single author; nor is there anything against our supposing several hands to have been at work on the same lines" (p. 131).

[2] See above, p. 309. The explanation, says Kuenen, of the relation between Ezekiel and P^1 is found "in the supposition that P^1 was acquainted with the priest-prophet, imitated him and worked on in his spirit. . . . It follows that in Lev. xxvi., where P^1 coincides with Ezekiel, he is imitating him—sometimes word for word."—*Ibid.* pp. 276, 287.

[3] See above, pp. 214 ff.   [4] *Genesis*, i. p. 48. See above, p. 207.

[5] Gen. xiv. shows traces of this P style, though probably an old independent source.

Levitical writer or writers in the middle books. Colenso, *e.g.*, in support of this distinction, draws attention to the curious fact that " the peculiarities of expression which distinguish the *non*-Elohistic portions of Genesis, — *and which the Elohist never employs,*—appear, almost all of them, in the Levitical laws or in Ezekiel." [1] Colenso himself supposes that the original Elohistic writing ends with Ex. vi. 2–5.[2] What is more to our purpose, Wellhausen, on his part, finds that after Exodus " the independent main stock of the Priestly Code more and more gives way to later additions, and ceases altogether, it appears, at the death of Moses." [3]   He excludes from it the priestly portions of the Book of Joshua.[4]

We do not require to adopt any of these theories to admit that the facts just noticed with regard to the differences of vocabulary and style in different parts of the P writing give probability to the idea, within, however, narrower limits, of a *process* of composition, rather than of a single author. With this strikingly accords the altered relations which the P writer is found to sustain to JE in Genesis, in the middle books of the Pentateuch, and in the Book of Joshua, respectively. In Genesis, as is universally admitted, P furnishes the systematic "framework" into which the remaining narratives are fitted.[5] In the middle books the systematic arrangement disappears. The parts (JE, P) appear as co-ordinate, and are more closely fused together; the narrative in the main follows a simple chronological order ;[6] the laws are interspersed, singly, or in masses, as occasion offers. In Joshua, finally, it is the

[1] *Pent.* Pt. vi. p. 583 (italics his). We should prefer to say, "many of them." Colenso makes large use of this principle of "imitation." According to him, later writers "*affected* the language" of the Elohist (p. 585): "The following [in Lev. xxvi.] appear to be imitations of expressions in Deuteronomy" (App. p. 3) : " We can only conclude that the resemblance in question has arisen from a deliberate attempt of the Levitical writer to imitate the phraseology of the Elohist " (App. p. 126); though he can on occasion rebuke Kuenen for *his* use of it (App. p. 144). Similarly Graf, *Gesch. Bücher,* p. 93.

[2] *Ibid.*, p. 576 ; App. pp. 116 ff. ; cf. Pt. v. pp. 197–211.

[3] *Hist. of Israel*, p. 357.   [4] *Ibid.*   See above, p. 216.

[5] " It actually forms," says Kautzsch, "(at least in Genesis) the framework in which the united whole is fitted."—*Lit. of O.T.*, p. 33. Cf. Driver, *Genesis*, Introd. pp. ii, iii, vi ; Dillmann, *Genesis*, i. p. 16.

[6] This formed the ground on which Principal Cave based his " Journal " theory of the origin of these narratives.—*Inspir. of O.T.*, pp. 230 ff., 239 ff.

JE narrative which furnishes the basis, while the priestly parts appear as supplementary or filling in.[1] The significance of this important fact will appear as we proceed.

2. We come now to the principal question of the *independence* of the Priestly Writing? Was P ever a distinct or self-subsisting document? Here Graf, as we saw, severed himself from his fellow-critics, and surely with good logical reason. For once that (1) the supplementary theory was abandoned, and J was erected into an independent history; (2) E was cut out of the *Grundschrift*, thereby reducing the latter after Gen. xvii. to the smallest dimensions; (3) the unity of the Priestly Writing was piecemeal surrendered; and (4) P was removed down to the exile, long after JE had attained a recognised authority,[2] nearly every tenable ground for maintaining the independence of the document was taken away. The most convincing reasons, however, against the independence are those drawn from the character of the writing itself, and from its relations to JE. This must be looked into with some care.

(1) The *structure* of the writing speaks in the strongest way against the theory of its original independence. Reference has already been made to the claim that P, taken by itself, furnishes us with a connected and nearly complete narrative from the creation to the conquest. Kuenen, speaking for the critics, assures us that the P history in Genesis "has come down to us nearly, but not quite complete";[3] and we are frequently told, as by Colenso, how its narrative "forms a continuous and connected whole almost from beginning to end."[4] It is not easy to understand how, if it was, as we were then equally assured, a "connected whole" in the days of Tuch and Bleek, *before* the excision of the extensive sections now assigned to E, it can be so still, *after* these have been removed. This completeness of the P history, however, is a matter on which the ordinary reader is nearly as competent to judge as the critical scholar, and we can fancy the astonishment with

[1] Wellhausen, *Hist.* pp. 357, 385. See above, p. 215.
[2] Cf. Kautzsch, quoted below.
[3] *Hex.* p. 66.
[4] *Pent.* Pt. vi. p. 582. Cf. Dr. Driver, *Genesis*, p. iv: "If read consecutively, apart from the rest of the narrative, it will be found to form a nearly complete whole."

which, after looking into the matter for himself, such a
reader will regard the above *dicta*. In truth, anything more
fragmentary, broken, incomplete, or generally unsatisfactory
as a connected narrative, it would be difficult to imagine.
As Wellhausen correctly says of it: "As a rule nothing
more is aimed at than to give the mere links and articulations of the narratives. It is as if Q [=P] were the scarlet
thread on which the pearls of JE are hung."[1] Or, as
Kautzsch says, the Priests' Writing gives us the preliminary history "in such extremely scanty outlines as to
be only comprehensible when we think of the detailed
representation in J and E as universally known."[2] Yet at
times its mere thread of history widens out into complete
and detailed narration, as in the story of creation (Gen. i.),
part of the narrative of the flood (chaps. vi.–ix.), the covenant
with Abraham (chap. xvii.), the burial of Sarah (chap. xxiii.),
the story of Dinah (chap. xxxiv.), Jacob's second visit to
Bethel (chap. xxxv. 8–15). Hiatuses abound,[3] as will be seen
more clearly after. From chaps. xi. to xvii. all that is told of
Abraham is comprised in some eight verses, or fragments of
verses; after that, till the death of Sarah (chap. xxiii.) in
some six verses, or parts of verses. The gaps are most conspicuous after the entrance (in chap. xx.) of the 2nd Elohist, to
whom, as above said, is transferred most of what was formerly
assigned to the primary document. Thus, in chap. xxv. 19,
we have the heading, "These are the generations of Isaac,"
but of the life of Isaac thus introduced nothing is given,
after ver. 20, but the concluding sentence of ver. 26 : "And
Isaac was threescore years old when she bare them "
(whom ?), the notice of Esau's marriage, and the sending
away of Jacob (chaps. xxvi. 34, 35; xxvii. 46–xxviii. 9).
Jacob is sent to Paddan-Aram to take a wife, but of his long
residence there, with the exception of two interpolated
verses (chap. xxix. 24, 29), not a syllable is breathed, and we
hear no more of him till he is found returning, rich in goods
and cattle (one verse, chap. xxxi. 18). The patriarch fares,

---

[1] *Hist. of Israel*, p. 332 ; cf. p. 7 : "For the most part the thread of
narrative is extremely thin." For the complete story of P after chap. xii.
see p. 327.

[2] *Lit. of O.T.*, p. 107.

[3] Dillmann thinks the document is preserved nearly complete till chap.
xi. 26, after which great gaps occur.—*Genesis*, pp. 16, 17. It will be seen
below that there are gaps enough in the early part as well.

if possible, still worse in his *later* history. Gen. xxxvii. 2 reads, "These are the generations of Jacob," but there is not a scrap more from P till we reach chap. xli. 46: "And Joseph was thirty years old when he stood before Pharaoh," and the descent into Egypt in chap. xlvi. 6 ff. Joseph's birth had been mentioned (chap. xxxv. 24), but we hear nothing further of him till suddenly he stands before Pharaoh as above.[1] This is certainly an unexampled specimen of a connected and "nearly complete" document! The answer given, as before,[2] by the critics is, that no doubt P had originally brief notices of the events in the lives of Abraham, Isaac, Jacob, Joseph, etc., where these gaps occur, but the "redactor" has *omitted* them to make room for the more copious narrations of JE.[3] This, in the first place, it must again be replied, is pure hypothesis—the buttressing of one critical assumption by another, and does not, besides, as we shall immediately see, meet the difficulties arising from the relations of the narratives. But, assuming it to be true, why still speak of the narrative as we have it as "nearly complete," and how explain the arbitrary procedure of the redactor in sometimes leaving the two narratives side by side, sometimes intimately blending them, sometimes preserving a stray verse like Gen. xix. 29, which simply repeats what has gone before[4]—but here so largely *deleting*?

(2) The alleged independence of the document is further discredited when we consider it *materially—i.e.*, in the relation of its *subject-matter* to that of JE. For here the striking fact which immediately confronts us is, that the parts of the history which are lacking in P are precisely those which are

[1] Colenso saves himself *a little* by borrowing a few connecting passages from JE in the lives of Isaac and Joseph, but these the later critics disallow to the Elohist.

[2] See above, p. 220.

[3] To see how far this "omitting" theory is carried—so also with JE, "mutual mutilations," as Dillmann calls them—one would require to go over the chapters in detail. See some examples in Kuenen, *Hex.* p. 67.

[4] Kuenen extols the "conservatism" of the redactor, who "scrupulously inserts even the minor fragments of P in the places that seem best to fit them, when the more detailed notices of the older documents might have seemed to a less zealous disciple to have rendered them superfluous."—*Ibid.* p. 320. How then explain the deleting? This redactor figures in Kuenen's scheme as R[5], but it is explained that he is really "a collective body headed by the scribe who united the two works, etc. . . . For the most part we shall have to club them together, and may indicate them by the single letter R[5]" (p. 315).

given us in JE. The converse of this is equally true, that the elements which are lacking in JE are supplied by P. Thus, P alone records the making of the ark (Gen. vi. 9–22), and the ages and deaths of the patriarchs. The story of Hagar in Gen. xvi. has neither beginning nor end without P, who alone mentions Ishmael's birth (vers. 15, 16).[1] The elements in the narratives are thus materially united in the closest fashion. But the intimacy of the relation between P and JE admits of yet closer determination. So long as the Jehovist was regarded as a mere supplementer of the Elohist, it was impossible to assume any knowledge of his narrative by the latter. Now, however, that the Priestly Writer is regarded as the later, there is found no difficulty in admitting,—rather, as furnishing a proof of his posteriority, the fact is insisted on,—not only that the Priestly Writer is acquainted with JE, but that his narrative is throughout *parallel* with the other.[2] The effect of this change in the point of view, in its bearings on the relations of the narratives, seems even yet hardly to be fully realised. Not merely, as formerly shown, are J and E in the fullest sense parallel narratives, but P, in turn, is parallel with *them*. "The priestly author," says Kuenen, "builds on JE throughout."[3] "That P[2] and JE run parallel, even in details, is undeniable; and hence it follows that they did not spring up independently of each other. P[2] is either the basis of JE or an excerpt from it."[4] The latter, of course, is the alternative he adopts.[5] Wellhausen, in language before

---

[1] The same assumption is made here about JE as above about P, viz., that in all these cases JE had the relevant narrative in his history, but R has left it out, and, for some reason, substituted P's (see above, p. 343). It is possible that in some instances omissions may have taken place, but they are for the most part as problematical in JE as in P.

[2] Gunkel stands nearly alone in denying that P used JE in Genesis (cf. his *Genesis*, p. lxviii), but he admits that the source of P was one to which JE "was manifoldly related." But why then *not* JE, which P must have known? Dillmann makes P dependent in part on E (his oldest document), and says of its relationship to J : "Certainly the relationship in matter between the two is so great, that of necessity one writing must presuppose the other." He supposes P to be dependent in part on J or J's sources, but J in the main to be dependent on P.—*Num.-Jos.* pp. 656–57. The insecurity of such combinations is evident from the fact that the newer criticism rejects most of them.

[3] *Hex.* p. 299.   [4] *Ibid.* p. 301.

[5] In this sense it is allowed that P is not independent. In an article he wrote in reply to Graf, Kuenen says: "We can deny the *independence* of the priestly passages, and at the same time recognise them as *self-subsisting*,

quoted,[1] lays great stress on the parallelism and material identity of the narratives. "The Priestly Code," he tells us, "runs, as to its historical thread, quite parallel to the Jehovistic history"; and, in a note, "The agreement extends, not only to the thread of the narrative, but also to particulars, and even to expressions."[2] Again: "In the history of the patriarchs also, the outlines of the narrative are the same in Q [=P] and in JE."[3] Here, then, are very practical admissions that the substance—and more than the substance[4]—of the two narratives is the same, and we have seen how closely related and interdependent the narratives are in their present form. P, in Genesis, we have also seen, is really not a complete work, but supplies the frame in which the other narratives are set. Does not the *onus* of proof rest on those who maintain that it was ever intended to be anything else? Is not the hypothesis which the facts of interrelation and mutual dependence suggest rather that of *collaboration* in some form, than of entirely independent origin?[5]

The principal proof, however, that P cannot be regarded as an independent document arises when the P writing is considered *textually*—*i.e.*, in its inseparable textual interweaving with the JE narrative. This is a subject of sufficient importance and intricacy to be considered under a separate heading.

i.e., as fragments of a book which once existed in separate form" (*Theol. Tijd.* Sept. 1870). But did it? Graf's later view on this point may be stated in his own words. He says: "These narratives [of the *Grundschrift*] imply everywhere the connection of the circumstantial J narrative; whereas they themselves, except a few longer sections, appear only as notices more or less abrupt, inserted into the narrative" (in Kuenen, as above).

[1] See Chap. IV. above, p. 107.

[2] *Hist. of Israel*, pp. 295–96. Cf. his illustrations.

[3] *Ibid.* p. 318. Cf. Kautzsch, above, p. 342.

[4] It is interesting to note the additional testimony borne by Kuenen that the Deuteronomic history also consists of recensions of prophetic narratives, "in part of more independent compositions, which, however, still run parallel, in almost every case, with JE, and are dependent on it."— *Hex.* pp. 168–69. The *substantial* agreement of the history in the various sources could hardly be more strongly expressed than in the above quotations.

[5] This is substantially the view taken by Klostermann in his *Der Pentateuch*, pp. 9, 10. See Note A on Klostermann on the Relation of JE and P.

III. TEXTUAL INTERRELATIONS OF THE PRIESTLY WRITING AND JE

The interweaving of P with JE in the actual history of the Pentateuch is so intimate that it is only by the utmost critical violence that the different elements can be rent asunder. To illustrate this fully would carry us much beyond our limits, but, the point being crucial, it is necessary to bestow some little pains on its elucidation. We begin with the patriarchal period and the Book of Genesis; then glance at the Mosaic period. The difficulties of the critical hypothesis will reveal themselves in both.

1. We look, first, at the P and JE narratives in *Genesis.* The general relation of P to JE in this book, as already said, is that of "framework." The following, in order of the book, are examples of the closeness of the textual relations.

(1) With regard to the *beginnings of things,* how constantly is it alleged that "we have two contradictory accounts of the *creation.*"[1] It is certain that the narratives in Gen. i.–ii. 4 and chap. ii. 4 ff. are quite different in character and style, and view the work of creation from different standpoints. But they are not "contradictory"; they are, in fact, bound together in the closest manner as complementary. The second narrative, taken by itself, begins abruptly, with manifest reference to the first: "In the day that Jehovah Elohim made earth and heaven" (ver. 4). It is, in truth, a misnomer to speak of chap. ii. as an account of the "creation" at all, in the same sense as chap. i. It contains no account of the creation of either earth or heaven, or of the general world of vegetation;[2] its interest centres in the making of man and woman, and everything

---

[1] Cf. Addis, *Hex.* i. p. xlviii; Kuenen, *Hex.* p. 38, etc.

[2] Dillmann says here: " We now expect before or after ver. 7, intimation of the bringing forth of the plant world and of the finishing of the construction of the world. But nothing of the kind is found. Such a gap can scarcely have existed originally. It rather seems as if something had been left out by R, either because it appeared a needless repetition alongside of chap. i., or because it seemed too little in accordance with chap. i." (This latter reason should have led to the suppression of much more.)—*Genesis,* p. 116. What appears in the narrative is simply the planting of a garden in Eden as an abode for man (vers. 8, 9).

in the narrative is regarded from that point of view.[1] The very union of the divine names—in chaps. ii., iii.—indicates a designed connection of the two narratives which it is arbitrary to refer to a redactor, instead of to the original composers of the book.[2]

We have next, in P, the bare thread of genealogy in chap. v. (with, however, *universal death*) to conduct us from the creation to the flood, when the earth, which God made "very good" (chap. i. 31) is found, without explanation, "corrupt before God," and "filled with violence"—"for all flesh had corrupted his way upon the earth" (chap. vi. 11, 12). Yet we are asked to believe that P, who is admittedly acquainted with the JE history, "builds" upon it, and produces a narrative "parallel" with it, "knows nothing" of a fall.[3] Much more natural is the supposition that P, who furnishes the "framework" for JE, presupposes the JE narrative which it enshrines, and which in Gen. vi. 5–7 contains precisely similar intimations of the corruption of mankind—proceeding from the fall. Here for once we have Wellhausen as an ally. "In JE," he says, "the flood is well led up to; in Q [= P] we should be inclined to ask in surprise how the earth has come all at once to be so corrupted, after being in the best of order, did we not know it from JE."[4] A fact which shows quite clearly how far P is from being complete, and how necessary JE is to its right understanding.

(2) The story of the *flood* (Gen. vi.–ix.), which comes next, is the classical proof of the distinction of the

[1] On the age and origin of these histories, see Chap. XI. pp. 402 ff.

[2] See above, pp. 226–27. We have here the usual variety of critical theories. Most ascribe the combination to the redactor; Reuss postulates a special document distinct from J and P; Budde and Gunkel suppose a combination of two documents, one using Jehovah, the other Elohim, etc.

[3] Thus, *e.g.*, Carpenter: "He knows no Eden, he relates no temptation, he does not seek to explain the stern conditions of human labour or suffering."—*Hex.* i. p. 122. But a few sentences further on we read: "The reader learns with surprise in chap. vi. 11 that corruption and violence filled the earth." And on p. 132: "If the *toledhoth* sections do not describe the origin of evil and the entry of sin and suffering, they are not indifferent to them, rather does the method of Gen. v. presuppose them, and chap. vi. 13 record their consequences." Which destroys the "knows nothing."

[4] *Hist. of Israel*, p. 310. Wellhausen finds many other indications of dependence of P on JE. *E.g.*, "If in spite of this he (the first man) is called simply Adam (Gen. v. 2), as if that were his proper name, the only way to account for this is to suppose a reminiscence of Gen. ii., iii., etc. (p. 309).

two sources P and J; but we must claim it also **as an**
illustration of the impossibility of separating these elements
in the narrative into two independent histories. The *substance* of the story is allowed to be the same in both. " In
chaps. vii., viii.," Kuenen says, " two almost parallel narratives
are combined into a single whole." [1] Since the discovery
of the Babylonian account of the deluge, it is recognised
that both writers drew from very old sources,[2] and, moreover, that it needs *both* J and P to yield the complete
parallel to the old Chaldean version. P, *e.g.*, in Genesis,
gives the measurements of the ark, but lacks the sending
out of the birds—an essential feature in the Babylonian
story. J has the birds, and also the sacrifice of Noah,
which P, again, wants.[3] In not a few passages the criteria
curiously intermingle, and the services of the redactor have
to be called freely into requisition to disentangle them.
E.g., in chaps. vii. 7–10, 23, viii. 1, 2, where there is clearly
literary fusion of some kind.[4] Above all, the parts of the
narrative fit into each other in a way that makes it impossible to separate them. We have just seen how the
" corruption " of chap. vi. 11, 12 (P) implies the Jehovistic
story of the fall. From the sudden mention of Noah in
chap. vi. 8 the J story passes abruptly to chap. vii. 1 : " And
Jehovah said unto Noah, Come thou and all thy house into
the ark." But it is P who mentions Noah's sons, and
narrates the building of the ark (chap. vi. 6–22). The
Jehovistic clause, " And Jehovah shut him in " (chap. vii. 16),
stands isolated if taken from the P connection in which it
stands. J, as stated, records Noah's sacrifice (chap. viii. 20),
but tells us nothing of his going out of the ark. That is
left for P (vers. 15–19).

It is easy, as before, to *assert* that all these lacking parts

---

[1] *Hex.* p. 67. Cf. Wellhausen, p. 296.

[2] On age, see below, Chap. XI. p. 404.

[3] "Noah offers no sacrifice," says Carpenter.—*Hex.* i. p. 123. But this
is really a proof of the unity of the history, for the sacrifice—an essential
part of the Babylonian story, which P must have known—is found in J.

[4] Kuenen says that in chaps. vii., viii. the narratives " are combined into
a single whole, and consequently the analysis does not always yield very
certain results. We find distinct traces of P in chaps. vii. 6, 7, 8, 9, 11, 13,
14, 15, 16a, 18–21 ; viii. 1, 2a, 2–5, 13–19. But the verses have been
worked over by some later hand. . . . It is evident from these indications
that when the two texts were woven together a certain process of assimila-
tion took place."—*Hex.* p. 67.

of J and P were originally present, but were omitted by the redactor, but it is impossible to prove it, and the hypothesis is superfluous, because the missing parts are there in the other narrative. Besides, what in that case becomes of the "completeness" of the P narrative? If "omission" is postulated to the extent required, the two narratives become simply duplicates, and the ground for the assertion that P "knows nothing" of this or that is destroyed. If there has been replacement of parts, as here and there is not impossible, it may be more simply conceived as the result of one writer collaborating with another, or working upon, and in parts re-writing, the materials furnished him by another, in view of a plan, and with a common aim.

Against this view of the unity of the narrative, it is customary to urge the repetitions and alleged inconsistencies of the several parts. On this it may suffice at present to observe that the P writer does not shun repetitions, even of his own statements, where these serve his purpose,—they are in fact a mark of his style,[1]—and that at least the greater number of the inconsistencies arise from the very evil of the hypothesis we are criticising — the pitting of one part of the narrative against another as if each was complete in itself.[2] The most plausible example in the present case is the alleged discrepancy as to the *duration* of the flood. J's numbers, it is said, yield a much shorter duration for the flood $(40 + 21 = 61$ days) than the year and eleven days assigned to it by P.[3] It is not explained how P, with the J narrative before him, should gratuitously invent numbers hopelessly at variance with

[1] The same applies to J, though not to so great an extent. P repeats freely where emphasis is wanted, where he recapitulates, where he commences a new section, etc. *E.g.*, the birth of Noah's sons and their names are several times repeated (chaps. v. 32, vi. 10, ix. 19, 20, x. 1). The corruption of the earth is thrice affirmed in chap. vi. 11, 12 ; the entrance into the ark is thrice mentioned in one section (chap. vii. 13, 15, 16), etc. J repeats the "repenting" of Jehovah (chap. vi. 6, 7).

[2] *E.g.*, it is not a real contradiction if in one place (Gen. vi. 19, 20) the general rule is laid down that the animals shall enter in pairs ("male and female"), and in another (chap. vii. 2, 3) that *clean* beasts and fowls shall go in by sevens (also "male and female"). Cf. chap. vii. 8, 9, 14. Both statements may have been found in the old sources.

[3] Cf. Dillmann, Driver, etc. Delitzsch concedes the discrepancy, unnecessarily, as we think. The unity of the narrative is upheld by Köhler, *Bib. Geschichte*, i. pp. 58–59.

his authority and with the common tradition. But if the narrative be taken *as a whole* there need be no discrepancy. P's longer period is of itself more in keeping with the magnitude of the catastrophe, even as described by J; and the assumption of the critics that J meant to confine the actual flood within forty days can be shown by the text itself to be unwarrantable. For (1) forty days is expressly given by J as the period when "the rain was upon the earth," *i.e.*, when the cataclysm was in process (chap. vii. 12, 17); and (2) is separated from a second forty days (chap. viii. 6) by the mention of an interval of gradual subsidence of the waters—"the waters returned from off the earth continually" (chap. viii. 2, 3; also J)—which P in the same verse dates at one hundred and fifty days. J's second forty days, therefore, with the three weeks spent in sending out the birds, equate with P's interval of two months between chap. viii. 5 and chap. viii. 13, which covers the same period, and the discrepancy disappears.[1]

In further illustration of the divisive methods employed in this part of the history, it may be mentioned that Wellhausen, Kuenen, Budde, Gunkel, etc., distinguish a J^1 and J^2, and suppose that J^1 (cf. Gen. iv. 16–24) had no knowledge of a flood, which, therefore, it is held, does not belong to the oldest tradition; neither does Gen. xi. 1–9 look back, it is said, to a flood.[2] It is even contended that in Gen. ix. 18–27 the names of the three sons of Noah must have been originally Shem, Japheth, and *Canaan*—this on the ground that in ver. 25 the curse is pronounced on Canaan[3]—a notion which, in its direct defiance of the text, Delitzsch justly cites as "a specimen of what emulation in the art of severing can accomplish."[4]

[1] The critics are not agreed whether J has *two* periods of forty days, or only one; and differ, besides, in many details of the analysis. Kautzsch and Socin, Budde, etc., even give chap. vii. 17*a*—"the flood was forty days upon the earth"—to P, but strike out the forty days. Thus discrepancies are *made.*

[2] Cf. in reply König, *Einleit.* pp. 198–99. If Gen. ix. 18, 19 is allowed to J^1, as by Addis, etc., then the overspreading of the earth from the sons of Noah is directly affirmed. Others give these verses to P.

[3] Kautzsch says positively: "At Gen. ix. 20 ff. the sons of Noah, who still dwell with him in one tent, are called in the original text Shem, Japheth, and Canaan."—*Lit. of O.T.*, p. 38. The "original text" states the precise contrary (vers. 18, 22), only the clauses naming Ham are expunged as interpolations. Dillmann, Delitzsch, König, etc., reject the theory.

[4] *Genesis*, i. p. 291.

(3) The critics have admittedly difficulty in dividing up the *table of nations* in Gen. x. "Such being the relation of the two documents," comments Kuenen, "it is easy to understand that chap. x. (always excepting vers. 8–12) has been included in P by some critics, and excluded from it by others."[1] Tuch, Hupfeld, and Kayser gave the chapter to J; Nöldeke, with most critics of his time, to P (excepting vers. 8–11); most critics now divide it between J and P. But the J part, as usual, begins abruptly at ver. 8; has no heading for the descendants of Ham; omits those of Japheth altogether; and, on the other hand, alone gives the descendants of Mizraim and Canaan, previously mentioned by P (ver. 6). The entire table is needed to restore the unity. An incidental proof of the unity is the fact that it is constructed on the principle of seventy names.

(4) We pass to the history of the *patriarchs*, some points in which have already been touched on. The different parts of this history are again found to be inseparably connected textually. Difficulties begin with the life of Abraham. After many variations of opinion, the critics have settled down to give Gen. xi. 28–30 to J, and ver. 27, 31, and 32 to P; beyond this only chaps. xii. 4*b*, 5, and xiii. 6, 11*b*, 12 are assigned to P in chaps. xii., xiii. But this yields some remarkable results. In chap. xi. 28, the J story begins quite abruptly, without telling us who Terah, Haran, Abram, and Nahor are; *i.e.*, it needs ver. 27 for its explanation. The residence of the family is placed by J in Ur of the Chaldees (elsewhere given as a P mark), and nothing is related of the migration to Haran (cf. P, vers. 31, 32). Yet this migration is apparently assumed in the call to Abraham in Gen. xii. 1.[2] In ver. 6, Abraham is said to have "passed through the land into the place of Sichem," but we are not told *what* land. It is P alone who tells of his departure from Haran, and coming to the land of Canaan (ver. 4*b*, 5). But this very fragment in P assumes the departure from Haran as a thing known (ver. 4*b*), and so needs the first part of the verse, given to J. In other words, the story, as it stands, is a unity; divided, its connection is destroyed.

Gen. xiv.—the Chedorlaomer expedition—is, it is well

[1] *Hex.* p. 67. [2] See above, Chap. IV. p. 108.

known, a literary *crux*; so unlike is it to P, yet so many P marks are found in it.[1] As P is made post-exilian, our critics are under the necessity of putting this chapter still later.[2] On the very different verdict to which archæology points, we shall speak in next chapter.[3] In the Hagar episode, chap. xvi., instructive examples of critical division are furnished. The first half of ver. 1, together with ver. 3, is given to P; then the J part begins without explanation—"And she had an handmaid, an Egyptian, whose name was Hagar." The promise of Ishmael is given in J (ver. 11); it is left for P to record his birth (vers. 16, 17).[4] It is the "dry pedant" P who relates Abraham's touching intercession for Ishmael (chap. xvii. 18); afterwards, however, several chapters later, J, who was silent on the birth, suddenly introduces Ishmael as a grown lad, mocking Isaac (chap. xxi. 9). In chaps. xviii. to xx. the solitary indication of P is the isolated verse, chap. xix. 29, which presupposes the destruction of the cities of the plain—intelligible, perhaps, if regarded as a recapitulatory statement, intended to introduce the succeeding narrative, but utterly superfluous as the insertion of a redactor.[5] Chap. xxi. 1–5 is again a fine specimen of critical dissection. The second half of ver. 1 is given to P, despite the fact that Jehovah occurs in it (similarly in chap. xvii. 1); ver. 2 is likewise split between J and P.

P's narrative, as stated earlier, after the introduction

[1] "Gen. xiv. is admitted on every hand," says Carpenter, "to show many peculiarities. . . . The margins show affinities of style with both J and P. . . . These phenomena would point to a writer acquainted with the linguistic usage of both J and P."—*Hex.* i. pp. 155–56. Addis writes: "The unknown author must have read the Pentateuch much as we have it. His language, as shown above, betrays the influence of P, while his facts are partly drawn from the Jahvist. He must have belonged to Judah, for he exalts the sanctuary of Jerusalem, and its sacred right to tithes"!— *Hex.* ii. p. 212. Cf. Kuenen, *Hex.* p. 324.

[2] Professor Bennett says "the narrative may be partly based on information derived from Babylon, possibly by Jews of the Captivity."—*Genesis*, p. 19.

[3] See below, pp. 410 ff. The revolutionary effects of admitting an early date of composition for this chapter are evident from the above.

[4] See above, p. 344.

[5] Colenso, arguing against Kuenen, says: "Is it credible that after the long circumstantial account of Jehovah's visit to Abraham, and conversation with him, and of Lot's being rescued out of Sodom in chap. xviii. 1–xix. 28, a later writer would think it necessary to insert the perfectly superfluous statement in chap. xix. 29?"—*Pent.* Pt. vi. App. p. 121. Carpenter says: "When the 'overthrow' is mentioned in chap. xix. 29, it is apparently assumed that its cause is known."—*Hex.* i. p. 123. But why then mention it?

of the E writer, becomes largely a blank. **Apart from Gen.** xxiii. and later references to the same (chaps. xlix. 29 ff. l. 12, 13);[1] a few other incidents (chaps. xxvii. 46–xxviii. 9; xxxv. 9–15; cf. xlvii. 6–11; xlviii. 3–7); and some genealogies and lists, it is absolutely confined, assuming that even they belong to it, to such disconnected verses, or parts of verses, as those formerly enumerated—"And Isaac was threescore years when she bare them" (chap. xxv. 26b), Zilpah and Bilhah given as handmaids (chap. xxix. 24, 29), "And all his goods that he had gotten, the cattle of his getting," etc. (chap. xxxi. 18), "And Joseph was thirty years old when he stood before Pharaoh" (chap. xli. 46). Chap. xxxiv.—the story of Dinah—is an exception, for here a P narrative is blended with a JE one, but so intimately, and with such peculiarities of style, that the critics do not well know what to make of it, and are at sixes and sevens in their analysis.[2] A similar perplexity attaches to the list of those descending to Egypt in chaps. xlvi. 8–27. "The general evidence," we are told, "points to a writer familiar with P, but also acquainted with other documents besides."[3] Wellhausen, the Oxford analysts, and others, accordingly, treat the P parts of both chaps. xxxiv. and xlvi. 8–27, as belonging to a later and secondary stratum. Other phenomena in Genesis, *e.g.*, the fact that it is P alone who records the deaths of the patriarchs, have already been noticed.

It is needless to do more than draw attention to the results which thus far stand out clear from our review. They are: (1) that the book, as we have it, is a unity; (2) that the unity is destroyed by breaking it up into separately existing JE and P documents; (3) that the unity is too close to be the work of a redactor piecing together such separate documents; (4) that to secure the unity we do not need to go beyond the book we have, *i.e.*, what P lacks,

[1] Colenso, however, gives chap. l. 12 to J, and bases an argument on it (*Pent.* Pt. vi., App. p. 122).

[2] The Oxford writers say of this chapter : "The linguistic affinities of the first story clearly connects it with J. . . . Equally clearly the various marks in the second story bring it within the scope of P. But it is so different in kind from P's other narratives of the patriarchal age, as to make it highly improbable that it ever belonged to the *Toledhoth*-book . . . as the interlacing is very close the assignment of some passages must be doubtful."—*Hex.* ii. pp. 52–53.

[3] Oxford *Hex.* ii. p. 72: on Gen. xlvi. 8 ff. see below, pp. 366 f.

J supplies, and *vice versa*. In brief, whatever the number
of pens employed, the phenomena would seem to point, not
to late irresponsible redaction, but to singleness of plan, and
co-operation of effort, in the original production.

2. When we pass from the patriarchal to the *Mosaic*
period, though P no longer possesses the marked character
of "framework" which it had in the Book of Genesis, but
appears rather as *co-ordinate* with JE, and even, in the
legislative parts, as an inserted content, we discover that the
union of narratives is not less close than in the earlier book,
and the impossibility of separating them into independent
documents equally great.

(1) Not much is given to P *in Exodus* before chap. vi.,
but what little is given is bound up inseparably with its
JE context. From the mention, *e.g.*, of the increase and
prosperity of the Israelites in Egypt (chap. i. 7), P passes
abruptly to their bondage (vers. 13, 14), and the intervening
verses are required to give the explanation. The language
used in chap. ii. 23–25 (P)—"cry," "heard," "saw," "knew"
(in Heb.)—has its verbal counterpart in chap. iii. 7 (J).[1] In
chap. vi. 2, the narrative of the revelation of the name
begins with the words, "And God spake unto Moses"; but
nothing has yet been said in P of either Moses or Aaron.[2]
The information necessary is supplied by JE. Chap. vi. itself
presents many peculiarities, with traces of J, which are
a perplexity to the critics.[3] Vers. 13–20 of this chapter,
embracing the genealogy, are roundly declared to be a
"later amalgam,"[4] or probably "an insertion by a very late
hand."[5] Then follow in chaps. vii.–xii., the narratives of

---

[1] Colenso, accordingly, with his view of the earlier date of the Elohist,
sees in chap. iii. 7 (and in Deut. xxvi. 7) a "plain allusion" to chap. ii. 23–
25. It should be noticed also that chap. ii. 24 alludes to God's covenant
with *Isaac*, mentioned only by J (Gen. xxvi. 2–5, 24).

[2] To obviate this difficulty many ingenious methods are employed
(assumed omissions, transpositions, etc.), which in other hands would be
described as "harmonistic expedients."

[3] Cf. Oxford *Hexateuch* and Addis, *in loc.*

[4] Oxford *Hex.* ii. p. 87.

[5] Addis, *Hex.* ii. p. 236 ; so Kuenen. Van Hoonacker points out an
interesting harmony between this table and the JE history. In ver. 23
Nadab and Abihu are mentioned as the two eldest sons of Aaron. The
names recur in Ex. xxiv. 9 (JE). Further, P relates how these two were
destroyed for the sin of offering strange fire (Lev. x. 1 ff.). In perfect
harmony with this the line of Aaron is viewed in the historical books as
continued in descent from the remaining sons, Eleazar and Ithamar (ver.
23), and Nadab and Abihu are no more heard of.—*Le Sacerdoce*, pp. 138–39.

the plagues, about which many difficulties are raised. Not reckoning the death of the firstborn, P, it is said, knows only of four of the plagues; JE only of seven. Other differences are pointed out. In P the miracles are wrought by Aaron and his rod; in JE, either without human instrumentality (J), or by the agency of *Moses* and his rod (E).[1] It may readily be shown, however, that these differences are greatly over-driven, where they do not turn round into a new proof of the unity of the narrative. It is the case, as stated, that JE has seven of the plagues, or, including the firstborn, eight; while P has only two peculiar to himself (lice and boils). But it results from the new form of the critical hypothesis that P *cannot* have been ignorant of those recorded in JE; therefore, cannot have intended to ignore or contradict them.[2] Accordingly, where the narratives touch, they are closely interwoven. In the plague of frogs, for instance, J records the threatening (chap. viii. i–4), but P narrates the execution of the threat (vers. 5–7). Without P this part of the story would be a blank. Conversely, J alone narrates the judgment on the firstborn (chap. xii. 29, 30), which is announced in the passover law of P (ver. 12), but is not described by P. This further curious result follows from the critical partition, that, while in P Aaron is appointed to be a prophet to Moses, and to speak for him to Pharaoh (chap. vii. 1, 2), in none of the P sections does either Moses or Aaron ever utter a word. All the speaking is done in JE. As respects the *mode* of working the miracles, it is not the case that P invariably represents Aaron as perform-ing the wonders with his rod; in the plague of boils (one peculiar to P), Moses is the agent (chap. ix. 10), and in the destruction of the firstborn Jehovah Himself executes the judgment (chap. xii. 12). But in JE also, even where the fact is not expressly stated (as in P), we are entitled to assume that the same rule applies to the acting as to the speaking, viz., that Aaron is regarded as the agent of Moses.[3] This, indeed, is the rule laid down in JE itself.

---

[1] This again is made a basis of distinction as between J and E, and fresh inconsistencies are evolved.

[2] On the plagues, cf. Köhler, *Bib. Gesch.* i. pp. 185–86.

[3] It is to be observed that in Ex. iv. 2–5 (JE) Moses receives the sign of the rod changed into a serpent to be, with other wonders, displayed before Pharaoh (vers. 17, 21); but in chap. vii. 8 ff. (P), Aaron performs the wonder

Thus in chap. iv. 30 (J) we read : " Aaron spake all the words which Jehovah had spoken unto Moses, and did the signs in the sight of the people"; and in chap. xi. 10 (E): " And Moses and Aaron did all these wonders before Pharaoh." The two are regularly conjoined throughout the history.[1]

(2) The narratives of the *wilderness journeyings* show even closer interweaving than those of the Exodus ; but we shall content ourselves with two typical instances from the Book of Numbers, viz., the mission of the spies (chaps. xiii., xiv.), and the rebellion of Korah (chap. xvi.). These have already been before us in connection with Deuteronomy;[2] it is desirable now to look at them from the point of view of P. There are evidences, we think, of distinct sources in these narratives, but the histories, as we have them, are nevertheless firmly-compacted and inseparable wholes.

First, as respects the *mission of the spies*, it is admitted that the narratives we have to deal with are substantially parallel, but it is held, as before seen, that they conflict in several important particulars. Thus P makes the spies traverse the whole land, in JE they go only as far as Eshcol, near Hebron ; P includes Joshua with Caleb among the spies, JE knows only of Caleb ; P makes the spies bring up an evil report of the country, but says nothing of the inhabitants, while in JE the explorers describe the land as fruitful, but give terrifying accounts of the inhabitants. But now, to make out these discrepancies, which would hardly occur to the reader of the story as it stands, the narrative has first of all to be torn to shreds.[3] The JE contribution, *e.g.*, begins in the middle of a verse : " And said unto them, Get you up this way by the South " (chap. xiii. 17b); its commencement is supposed to be lost. But the proper commencement is there in P, with his list of the spies, if we will only accept it. Again, the second half of ver. 21 is singled out,[4] and given to P, with the result that JE reads: " So they went up, and they went up by the South " (vers. 21a, 22). But this now is an obvious

[1] Chs. v. 1, 4, 20 ; viii. 5, 12, 25 ; ix. 27 ; x. 3, 8, 16, etc.
[2] See above, pp. 279 ff.
[3] We follow the analysis of the Oxford *Hexateuch*, which agrees in most points with that of Dillmann, Wellhausen, etc.
[4] Or the whole verse according to others.

doublet," and forms the basis of a new division between
and E (but what of the sense of the redactor, who so
united them?). Similarly, the first half of ver. 26 is given
to P, and the second half to JE, though the connection is
close, and the second half has a marked P phrase.[1] The
way is now clear for declaring that JE knows nothing of a
searching of the whole land. Yet it seems very evident to
the unprejudiced reader that, both in the commission to the
searchers (vers. 17–20), and in the report they bring (vers.
27–29), in JE itself, an exploration of the whole country is
implied. We go on to chap. xiv., the first verse in which is
divided up among three writers: "And all the congregation
lifted up their voice" (P), "and cried" (E),[2] "and the people
wept that night" (J). In P, Addis tells us, "no mention
is made of the inhabitants, who are indeed treated as
non-existent" (!)[3]—as if this absurdity was not of itself
sufficient to condemn his scheme. But this, like P's ignorance of the fruitfulness of the land, disproved by Caleb's
words in ver. 7, is only made out by separating vers. 8, 9
from their close connection with ver. 7—reserving for P
only the words in the middle: "only rebel not ye against
Jehovah." Even the allegation that JE knows nothing of
Joshua as one of the spies, seems, apart from its connection
with the list in chap. xiii. 1–6, to break down on examination.
Most critics are now disposed to assign chap. xiv. 30–33 to J,
or a related writer,[4] and in it Caleb and Joshua are united.
It happens also that we have yet another rehearsal of this
mission in Num. xxxii. 7 ff.—a section admittedly based on
JE;[5] and there, too, the names occur in like connection

---

[1] "Unto all the *congregation*"—handed over to a redactor.

[2] The second verb changes to masc. plur. "they cried," from the fem.
sing. of first clause. But thoughts are not always rigidly bound to
grammar.

[3] *Hex.* ii. p. 403.

[4] Cf. Dillmann (*Num.–Jos.* pp. 69, 78; J in contradistinction from E);
Wellhausen (*Compos.* p. 102); Oettli, Kittel, etc. Addis adopts this view
in his vol. ii. p. 403—"probably the Jahvist."

[5] Cf. Dillmann, pp. 193 ff. Wellhausen (*Comp.* pp. 113 ff.) assigns vers.
1–15 to a source which takes a "middle position between J and Q [=P],"
and is most nearly related to the Deuteronomist. Its narrative is given as
parallel to JE. Dillmann, Kittel, and others admit that J (not E) reckoned
Joshua among the spies. Cf. also Köhler, *Bib. Gesch.* i. p. 306. This
Numbers xxxii. is one of the most disconcerting chapters for the divisive
hypothesis. "All attempts hitherto at division of sources," says Dillmann,
"go widely asunder" (p. 193).

and order (ver. 12). The critics, clearly, have still a good deal to do before they break up the unity of this story.

The *Korah Episode* (chap. xvi.), to which we next turn, is perhaps a yet more signal example of the perplexities in which the divisive hypothesis of the critics, when carried out to its issues, involves itself. We start with the assertion—for which there is some basis—that there are traces in the narrative of *two* movements—one, headed by Korah, which aimed at securing for the Levites the rights of the priesthood (vers. 4–11); and the other, headed by Dathan and Abiram, a revolt of the general congregation (laity) against the authority of Moses and Aaron (vers. 13–14). The two movements, supposing them to have existed, were no doubt blended in fact, as they now are in the narrative—hence the inextricable difficulties which attend the attempt to make two independent histories out of them.[1] In the first place, the narrative of P itself presents perplexities from this point of view; for with Korah are united, in vers. 2, 3, as many as two hundred and fifty princes of the congregation, "men of renown," who evidently represent the laity in their uprising against Moses and Aaron;[2] *i.e.*, are in the same cause as Dathan and Abiram.[3] Wellhausen, the Oxford critics, and many more, therefore, find it necessary to resolve this part of the P history into two, and even to deny that, in the original form of the story, Korah was a Levite at all. Dillmann and others defend the unity of P in this place; while Kuenen, like Graf earlier,[4] sees in the Levitical parts rather the late work of a redactor.[5] But the JE narrative

[1] Köhler says: "There are no sufficient grounds for the contention that in the narrative as it lies before us, two quite distinct histories—the history of an uprising of the Levite Korah against the exclusive priesthood of Aaron, and the history of a revolt of the Reubenites, Dathan and Abiram against the supremacy of Moses over Israel—have been blended together."—*Bib. Gesch.* p. 307.

[2] This, *e.g.*, is one of the "contradictions" adduced by McFadyen, in his *Messages of the Historians*, p. 7.

[3] Dathan and Abiram throughout the story decline to face Moses and Aaron (vers. 12 ff.). Their absence at the interview, vers. 3 ff., need, therefore, occasion no surprise.

[4] Graf seems to admit that in the original form of the story Korah, Dathan, and Abiram were united.—*Geschicht. Bücher*, p. 89.

[5] From the Graf-Wellhausen standpoint it is of course impossible to admit that the Korah episode had any foundation in fact, or was earlier than the exile. Hence the theory, referred to in last chapter, that it reflects the conflicts of Ezekiel's degraded priests (Levites) for restoration

is equally recalcitrant, for it, in turn, makes it clear that a *religious* claim entered as well into the *popular* movement of Dathan and Abiram. As the Oxford *Hexateuch* has it: ' Dathan and Abiram defy the authority of Moses on the ground that he has failed to fulfil his promise, and he replies by entreating Yahweh to pay no attention to their offering. The basis of ver. 15 is clearly some religious act, culminating in sacrifice, and having affinity rather with Korah's protest than with the rebellion of Dathan and Abiram."[1] It is necessary, accordingly, to find two narratives here also, as well as in P, and still further complications are involved in working the whole into shape. The simplest solution is that the error lies in the original assumption of independent narratives, and that probably the events took place as they are actually described.[2]

IV. ALLEGED INCONSISTENCIES AND HISTORICAL INCREDIBILITIES OF THE PRIESTLY WRITING

Frequent references have been made in the course of these discussions to the inconsistencies, contradictions, duplicate narratives, incredibilities, and the like, which are said to prove that P is a distinct writing from JE, late in origin, and historically untrustworthy. If our contention is correct, it would be truer to say that it is the assumption that the documents in question are independent, and each complete in itself, which gives rise to most of the appearances of inconsistency and contradiction.

1. It was before indicated that only thus can it be made

to their full priestly dignity. As there pointed out, these post-Ezekiel conflicts of a party of degraded priests have no foundation in history ; are, in fact, a pure creation of the imagination.

[1] *Hex.* ii. p. 212.

[2] As a further illustration of the difficulties involved in the divisive hypothesis, we might have referred to the critical treatment of the story of the bringing of the water from the rock at Meribah (Num. xx. 1 ff.). Of this story, Addis says : " Here we have one of the few (?) instances in which the documents of the 'Oldest Book of Hebrew History' have been inextricably entangled, not, as is often the case, with each other, but with the narrative of the 'Priestly Writer.'"—*Hex.* i. p. 169. It is pointed out that here the writer departs from his usual practice of idealising his heroes, in admitting that Moses and Aaron were guilty of great sin. The reason given is an excellent example of the method. "He does so," we are told, " because the fact that Moses and Aaron did not enter the promised land was too fixed and conspicuous in tradition to be gainsaid, and *it had to be accounted for*."—*Hex.* ii. p. 419.

out, *e.g.*, that P "knows nothing" of a fall, or of sacrifices of the patriarchs,[1] or of incidents derogatory to the patriarchs — his narrative being, as Kuenen says, one "from which every trace of hostility between Abraham and Lot, Isaac and Ishmael, Jacob and Esau, Joseph and his brothers, has been carefully removed."[2] Is it credible, on the principles of the critical hypothesis itself, that P, with the JE history in his hands, and founding upon it, should have supposed his readers unacquainted with the fact that the patriarchs built altars and offered sacrifices, or should have intended to "make sacrifices to the deity begin with the Mosaic age"?[3] One might as well argue that J, on his part, "knows nothing" of the deaths of the patriarchs! Again, if P gives only a "thread"—"the mere links and articulations"—of a narrative, and records practically nothing of the lives of Isaac and Joseph, where is the room for the assertion that he "carefully removes" this, or "avoids" that? Especially when the knowledge of the full patriarchal history is throughout presupposed.[4] If P, *e.g.*, gives us no life of Joseph at all, how can it be alleged that he has removed "every trace of hostility between Joseph and his brothers"?[5] Can inferences be drawn from that which does not exist? On the other hand, as we have sought to show in the narratives of the flood, of the plagues in Egypt, of the spies, of the rebellion of Korah, when the narratives are taken in their completeness, nine-tenths of the allegations of inconsistency and contradiction fall of their own accord.

[1] See above, p. 156; cf. Kautzsch, *Lit. of O.T.*, p. 110; Driver, *Genesis*, p. xxii, etc.

[2] *Hex.* p. 301. Carpenter says: "The extent to which the figures of the primeval history were already surrounded, in view of the Priests' Writing, with a kind of saintly aureole, is seen from the obviously intentional omission of *all* the traits which seem to lower the dignity of the patriarchs." —*Hex.* i. p. 301. Probably, on the same principle, P intends throwing an "aureole" round Sodom and Gomorrah, since, as Carpenter says: "Even when Lot settles in the cities of the 'circle,' the writer refrains from commenting on their characters" (p. 123).

[3] Kuenen, *Hex.* p. 301. Cf. Colenso in reply to Kuenen, quoted above, p. 156.

[4] Carpenter says: "Again and again does the brevity of the narrative imply that the author relies on the previous acquaintance of his readers with the facts."—*Hex.* i. p. 123: cf. above, pp. 344 ff.

[5] Kuenen, as above. It was shown earlier that it is P alone who records the sin of Moses and Aaron that excluded them from Canaan (cf. above, p 276).

2. It is not greatly different with alleged duplicate narratives, some of which, as the stories of the creation and the flood, and the denial of their wives by the patriarchs, have already been dealt with. It was found earlier that several of the alleged duplicates fall within the limits of the same document, as the denials of their wives by Abraham and Isaac in J (Gen. xii. ; xxvi. 6 ff.), and two Korah stories, according to Wellhausen and others, in P (Num. xvi. 2 ff.), and may therefore reasonably be supposed to have belonged to the original tradition. By far the greater number of instances we should deny to be "duplicates" in the proper sense at all—*i.e.*, divergent traditions of the *same* incidents. The redactor (not to say the original authors) can hardly have regarded them as such, or he would have omitted one, or sought to combine them in his usual harmonistic way. We said before, in speaking of JE, that there was no good reason, as it appeared to us, for identifying the flight of Hagar, in Gen. xvi. (J), with her expulsion by Sarah in chap. xxi. (E), or even Abraham's denials of his wife at Egypt (chap. xii. J) and at Gerar (Gen. xx. E).[1] So there is no good reason in the nature of the case for identifying the two revelations at Bethel—one before Jacob's going to Paddan-Aram (Gen. xxviii. 10 ff. JE), the other on his return (chap. xxxv. 9 ff. P) ; or the two revelations to Moses —one at the burning bush in Midian (Ex. iii. 1 ff. JE), the other in Egypt (chap. vi. 2 ff. P), etc. On the contrary, in most of these narratives there are plain indications that the incidents *are* distinct, and that the later implies the earlier. In Gen. xxi., *e.g.*, Ishmael is already born, and old enough to "mock" Isaac; but only in Gen. xvi. 15, 16 (P) is his birth narrated. The second vision in Bethel is connected with the first by the word "again"[2] (Gen. xxxv. 9), and is led up to by the revelations in chaps. xxxi. 13, xxxv 1 (E), summoning Jacob back from Paddan-Aram, and recalling him to Bethel—histories admittedly known to P. Ex. vi. 2 ff. introduces Moses and Aaron abruptly, and the earlier JE history is implied, explaining who Moses was, and how he came to be connected with the children of Israel and

[1] See above, pp. 236 ff.

[2] "The editor," say the Oxford critics, "has inserted the word 'again.'" —*Hex.* ii. p. 55. But why? Since P admittedly knew the earlier stories, what motive could he have for ignoring them, and inventing a new one in a different connection ?

with Pharaoh in Egypt[1]—a history again presumed, on the newer theory, to be known to P.[2] Indeed, on the "omission" or "mutual mutilation" hypothesis of the critics, what right have we to suppose that in all these cases *both* stories were not found in the documents concerned, and that, as in so many other instances of parallel narratives, the suppression of one is not due to the redactor?

3. The "historical incredibilities" freely imputed to the Priestly Writing, as to other parts of the narrative of the Pentateuch, can only here be briefly touched on, though they form the real ground of much of the criticism directed against that work.[3] There is, in truth, in this department, extremely little—hardly anything—with which those who have had to do with the subject have not been familiar since the days of the Deistical controversy, or which was not pressed home with skill and cogency by the earlier sceptical writers of last century, as Von Bohlen, etc. Only in those days it was not called "believing criticism" of the Bible, but destructive attack upon it! In modern times the writer chiefly relied on as having irretrievably shattered the historical credibility of the narratives in the Pentateuch—especially those proceeding from the Priestly Writer—is Bishop Colenso. The arguments of this authority are taken over practically *en bloc* by modern critical scholars, and treated as irrefragable demonstrations that the stories in Genesis, but particularly those of the Mosaic period, are throughout utterly unhistorical.[4] On this subject, while we

[1] Cf. Köhler, *Bib. Gesch.* i. pp. 182–83.

[2] It is in the light of such considerations that we see how revolutionary for the critical theory is the admission that P knew, and supposed his readers to know, these earlier histories. To take one other example from Genesis. "The promise of a son to Sarah," says Dr. Driver, "is twice described."—*Genesis*, p. iii. But how is the matter mended if the author of chap. xvii. knew of chap. xviii.? The promises are really distinct—one to Abraham, the other in hearing of Sarah.

[3] Thus Kuenen: "The representations in the later books of the Pentateuch simply defy the conditions of space and time to which every event is subject, and by which, therefore, every narrative may be tested. The Exodus, the wandering, the passage of the Jordan, and the settlement in Canaan, *as they are described in the Hexateuch*, simply could not have happened."—*Hex.* p. 43.

[4] "With one single exception," says Kuenen, "the twenty chapters of his book (Pt. i.) are devoted to an absolutely pulverising criticism of the data of the *Grundschrift*." He speaks of the difficulties as "massed together and set forth by him with imperturbable *sang froid* and relentless thoroughness."—*Hex.* Introd. pp. xiv–xvii, p. 45. Wellhausen says: "Colenso is properly

have no interest in arguing for a supernatural accuracy in chronological or historical matters in the Biblical narratives beyond what the soundness of his information enabled the sacred writer to attain, yet, as having lived through the Colenso storm, and read pretty fully into the literature it called forth, we desire to dissociate ourselves entirely from these extravagant estimates of the success of the Bishop's destructive work. Colenso's courage, honesty, and loyalty to truth, as he understood it, we shall not seek to dispute. But his work lacked from the commencement the first condition of success,—insight into the meaning, and sympathy with the spirit, of the books he was working with. The distinction between a supernatural and a purely natural history was one to which he allowed no weight—did not seem able even to appreciate; many real difficulties he emphasised, which others, perhaps, had passed over too lightly, but many more were the creation of a mind working in narrow arithmetical grooves, and bent on applying to a historical writing the canons of a rigorous literalism, which would be more justly described as "intolerable pedantry" than the work of the Priestly Writer to which it was applied. His book was keenly scrutinised, and manifoldly replied to, at the time; and those are widely mistaken who, on the strength of the laudations of the critics, persuade themselves that the victory was altogether his. We shall best show this by a rapid glance at his criticism.

(1) It would be unpardonable to resuscitate—were it not that they must be presumed to belong to those demonstrations of contradiction of the "universal laws of time and space" which Kuenen speaks of—the extraordinary computations by which Bishop Colenso proves to his satisfaction that "all the congregation" of Israel could not assemble at the door of the tabernacle, or that the Levitical laws could not be observed in their entirety in the wilderness. Who that has read his book will ever forget his wonderful calculations to show that, even excepting *ex gratia* such as may have been detained by sickness or other necessary causes, "the whole congregation" of nearly 2,000,000, could not

entitled to the credit of having first torn the web asunder."—*Hist. of Israel,* p. 347. Addis says: "One has only to read the first two volumes of Colenso to see what absurdities are involved if we take the Pentateuch as it stands, and treat it as one book. There is no end to the chronological monstrosities which meet us at every turn."—*Hex.* i. p. 1.

have been squeezed into the court of the tabernacle, and standing as closely as possible, in rows of nine, not merely at the *door*, but (another concession) at the *end* of the tabernacle, would have reached—the men alone for nearly 20 miles, all the people for nearly 60 miles! Or his reasoning that the Levitical law required the officiating priest "to carry on his back on foot" the carcase of the bullock of the sin-offering to "a clean place" without the camp—on one reckoning a distance of about $\frac{3}{4}$ of a mile, on another reckoning about 6 miles! Or his proof that the three priests in the wilderness could not have offered—not to say *eaten*—the 90,000 pigeons annually, or 88 per diem apiece, required by the law for the 250 cases of child-birth daily![1] Some least grain of common sense might be conceded to the Priestly Writer, who, whatever his faults, certainly did not mean to palm off upon his readers such crude absurdities as these. Most people will feel that the force of his language is abundantly satisfied by large and representative gatherings of the people at and around the tabernacle on solemn occasions;[2] and will remember that, "according to the story," to use the Bishop's phrase, the priests had a whole tribe of Levites to assist them in their menial duties—though these, as formerly noticed,[3] strangely enough, from the critical point of view, never appear in the laws in Leviticus. If the pigeons were not, as the Bishop says they would not be, obtainable in any large numbers in the wilderness, they would not be there to bring or eat; but the objection overlooks that the sacrificial system had specially in view the future settled habitation of the people (cf. Num. xv. 2 ff.), and that in point of fact, it is represented as having been largely suspended during the years of wandering.[4]

(2) No thoughtful reader will minimise the very real difficulties inhering in the Biblical narratives of the Exodus —the remarkable increase of the children of Israel in

[1] *Pent.* Pt. i. See references and quotations in Note B on Bishop Colenso's Numerical Objections.
[2] Publicly-called meetings of "the inhabitants" of large towns or cities are frequently held in halls of very moderate dimensions. Ecclesiastically, the writer has been present at duly-summoned and formally-minuted meetings of a Church Presbytery of several hundred members, for purposes of ordination, where the members present were accommodated on a railed platform of a few feet square. Colenso could prove it impossible.
[3] See above, p. 304.   [4] Josh. v. 5 ; cf. Amos v. 25.

Egypt,[1] the circumstances of the Exodus itself, the passage of the Red Sea, the care of the people in the wilderness and provision for them, etc. These facts, at the same time, are precisely among the best attested in the history of Israel; and, in dealing with them, justice requires that we treat them from the Bible's own point of view, as events altogether exceptional in the history of that people, and, indeed, of mankind, accomplished by divine help, and, as respects the Exodus, under the highest exaltation of religious and patriotic consciousness of which a nation is capable. Many elements, also, which do not appear upon the surface of the narrative, have to be taken into account, e.g., that the patriarchs who went down to Egypt did so accompanied by extensive households.[2] Colenso, in the work referred to, however, will admit none of these relieving considerations (nor even the "households"), insists on bringing everything to the foot-rule of the most ordinary experience —the birth-rate of London, e.g., or a lower rate,[3]—eliminates wholly the supernatural element, founds upon the Biblical data where these suit his purpose, but rejects other statements which throw light upon the former; very often by his grotesque literalism creates difficulties which are not in the Biblical narrative at all. Thus, e.g., he will have it that "in one single day, the order to start was communicated suddenly, at midnight, to every single family of every town and village, throughout a tract of country as large as Hertfordshire, but ten times as thickly peopled"; that "they then came in from all parts of the land of Goshen to Rameses, bringing with them the sick and infirm, the young and the aged; further, that since receiving the summons, they had sent out to gather in all their flocks and herds, spread over so wide a district, and had driven them also to Rameses; and lastly, that having done all this, since they

[1] It is undesirable, on the other hand, to exaggerate the difficulty. The writer has personal knowledge of a family the heads of which celebrated their golden wedding in 1880. In that 50 years the original couple had multiplied to 69 (there were two deaths). If the reader will reckon the result of a similar rate of increase for 300 or 400 years, the figures may surprise him.

[2] This is no doubt the uniform representation in Genesis, cf., e.g., Gen. xiv. 14; xxvi. 13, 14; xxxii. 4, 5, 10, etc. Colenso clings to the literal seventy souls.

[3] He prefers to take his rate from the slow growth in the lifetimes of Abraham and Isaac.

were roused at midnight, they were started again from Rameses that very same day and marched on to Succoth, not leaving a single sick or infirm person, a single woman in child-birth, or even 'a single hoof' behind them." "This is undoubtedly," he avers, "what the story in the Book of Exodus requires us to believe (Ex. xii. 31–41, 51)."[1] "Incredibility," truly! But the picture is a creation of the objector's own imagination, of a piece with his persistence (in which many modern critics support him) that the passover is represented as taking place on the night of the same day in which the first command to observe it was given. Both objections fall together in view of the fact that the text on which the above assertion is based: "I will pass through the land of Egypt *this night*" (Ex. xii. 12),[2] occurs in a law which expressly ordains that the lamb of the passover is to be chosen on the 10th day of the month, and kept till the 14th (vers. 3, 6); which, therefore, *must* have been given still earlier in the month, perhaps near its beginning.

(3) We do not propose to re-thresh the hundred times threshed straw of Colenso's long catalogue of "incredibilities" —most of them retailed by others—but confine ourselves to two examples, which perhaps will be admitted to be fairly typical.

The *first* is the very old difficulty about Hezron and Hamul, the sons of Pharez, whose names are included in the list of threescore and ten who went down with Jacob to Egypt (Gen. xlvi.). A simple reckoning shows that Pharez, the father of this pair, cannot himself have been more than three or four years old at the time of the descent;[3] his sons, therefore, must have been born, not in Canaan, but in Egypt. Dr. Driver, like Bishop Colenso, finds here "a grave chronological discrepancy between P and JE."[4] Yet the

---

[1] *Pent.* Pt. i. pp. 61–62. The passage is partly from E, partly from P.

[2] In ver. 12 as in ver. 8, etc., the words "this night" refer to the night spoken of, not to the night in which the words are spoken. The Oxford *Hexateuch* translates "that night" (ii. p. 96).

[3] Judah was about forty-three years old at the descent, and as his sons Er and Onan had been married and were dead a year or two before the birth of Pharez (Gen. xxxviii.), the latter cannot have been more than the age stated at the descent.

[4] *Genesis*, p. 365. On the contrary, the reference to Er and Onan in ver. 12 is a clear allusion to the JE story in chap. xxxviii., as also is the place given to Hezron and Hamul in the list. Why *should* P, who knew the JE story, wantonly contradict it?

ordinary solution, viz., that Hezron and Hamul are here introduced (Colenso failed to observe, in a separate clause) as the legal representatives and substitutes of Er and Onan, who are said to have died in the land of Canaan,[1] seems not only perfectly admissible, but even required by the peculiar construction of the passage. The story in Gen. xxxviii., forbidding as it is, adequately explains the ground of this substitution. On genealogies generally it is to be remarked that they are commonly constructed on more or less technical principles, and have to be construed in that light. This table of seventy persons, e.g., is evidently one of heads of families, and includes in its enumeration, not only Jacob himself and his daughter Dinah, but Er and Onan, who died in Canaan (represented by Hezron and Hamul), and Joseph's two sons, who, though expressly mentioned as born in the land of Egypt (ver. 20), are embraced in "the souls that came with Jacob into Egypt."[2]

Our *second* example is one usually regarded as among the most formidable—the number of the (male) firstborn in Israel as compared with the total number of males. The firstborn males are given in Num. iii. 43 as 22,273 (a number whose accuracy is checked by comparison with that of the Levites). Assuming now the total number of males to be 900,000, we have a proportion of one firstborn to 42 males, which is interpreted to mean that "according to the story of the Pentateuch *every mother in Israel* must have had on the average 42 sons!"[3] It may again occur that the Priestly Writer, who had at least a genius for manipulating and systematising figures, could hardly have

---

[1] Reckoning Jacob, *either* Er and Onan, *or* Hezron and Hamul, must be omitted to make the number 33 in ver. 15.

[2] Cf. Delitzsch, *Genesis*, i. pp. 337-40 ; Hengstenberg, *Pent.* ii. pp. 290 ff. Kuenen regards this list as a patchwork put together from Num. xxvi. (*Hex.* p. 68) ; Bennett thinks it "may be an abstract of the chapters in Chronicles" (!), and says "the 66 (in ver. 26) is a correction of an editor" (*Gen.* pp. 378, 382). Dr. Driver also brackets "Jacob and his sons" (ver. 8), and the "threescore-and-six" of ver. 26, and all ver. 27, but "threescore and ten" as additions to the original text (*Genesis*, p. 368). There is no authority for any of these assertions or changes, which create difficulties, and remove none. Even in Dr. Driver's revised text, Er and Onan, who never were in Egypt, and Joseph's two sons, who never were in Canaan, are needed to make up the 70 "that came down with Jacob to Egypt" (vers. 26-27).

[3] *Pent.*, People's edit. p. 49.

been unaware of a discrepancy which has been so obvious to his critics from the beginning; and that the more likely explanation is, that he and his critics are proceeding on different principles in their reckonings. Nor is it hard, perhaps, to see where at least the *main* part of the solution lies; the solution is, in fact, as old as the difficulty itself. In the first place, it must be observed that the firstborn in a family would be as often a daughter as a son; this at once reduces the number of sons to each mother by one half.[1] In the next place, it is on every ground unlikely that persons who were themselves married and heads of families would be reckoned as "firstborns." It is more reasonable to suppose that the reckoning was confined, as it has been expressed, "to the rising generation—those who were still children in the houses of their parents"—and that it did not include all who had *ever been* firstborns in their own generation; fathers, grandfathers, and great-grandfathers, if still alive. That this was the real nature of the reckoning seems established, among other considerations, by the analogy of the firstborns in Egypt, where certainly fathers, grandfathers, and more remote ancestors are not regarded as included in the judgment.[2] This again practically limits the firstborns to those under twenty.[3] These may have formed about a third of the total number, or, if regard be had to the longer ages of these times, may have been nearer a fourth.[4] Instead of 42 sons to each mother, therefore, we are now brought down to nearly 5; and account has still to be taken of cases in which the firstborn of a family was dead, of polygamous marriages, or concubinage, where possibly only *the* firstborn of the house was reckoned,[5] and of a probable diminished rate of marriage in the last years of the oppression, and in prospect of deliverance.

[1] Colenso ingenuously observes that this does not rid us of the difficulty, but only "changes the form of it, for each mother has still 42 children" (*ibid.* p. 50). But, with all respect, the daughters are there in any case, and have to be accounted for.

[2] Pharaoh, *e.g.*, was himself probably a firstborn, but was not slain. On Colenso's view, in most houses there would be more than "one dead" (Ex. xii. 30).

[3] Colenso says that the text does not prescribe any such limit. But the text does not state at all on what principle the reckoning was made.

[4] Cf. Köhler's discussion, *Bib. Gesch.* pp. 288-89.

[5] In a family like Jacob's, *e.g.*, how many "firstborns" would be reckoned; Reuben, whom Jacob calls "my firstborn" (Gen. xlix. 3), or all the firstborns of the several wives? Cf. the law, Deut. xxi. 15, 17.

These are not "harmonistic expedients," but explanations that lie in the nature of the case, and are obviously suggested by the reckoning itself.

The conclusion of our inquiry, therefore, brings us back to the point we started from—strong confidence in the unity of the narrative, and in its essential historical credibility.

V. GENERAL RESULTS: MOSAICITY OF THE PENTATEUCH

To what result—we must now ask—does our whole investigation conduct us on the origin of the Priestly Writing, and the age and composition of the Pentateuch generally. We began by leaving it an open question whether, or how many, separate documents were employed in the compilation of that work, and if so, what were the ages and mutual relations of these documents. To what conclusions have we now been led?

For one thing, it is first to be said, *not* to the conclusion that Moses himself wrote the Pentateuch in the precise shape or extent in which we now possess it; for the work, we think, shows very evident signs of different pens and styles, of editorial redaction, of stages of compilation. As before observed, its composition has a *history*, whether we are able ever to track satisfactorily that history or not. On the other hand, next, very strongly to the view of the unity, essential *Mosaicity*, and relative antiquity of the Pentateuch. The unity which characterises the work has its basis mainly in the history, knit together as that is by the presence of a developing divine purpose; but arises also from the *plan* of the book, which must have been laid down early, by one mind, or different minds working together, while the memory of the great patriarchal traditions was yet fresh, and the impressions of the stupendous deliverance from Egypt, and of the wonderful events connected with, and following it, were yet recent and vivid. In the collation and preparation of the materials for this work—some of them, perhaps, reaching back into pre-Mosaic times—and the laying of the foundations of the existing narratives, to which Moses by his own compositions, according to constant tradition, lent the initial impulse, many hands and minds may have co-operated, and may have continued to co-operate, after the master-mind was removed; but unity of

24

purpose and will gave a corresponding unity to the product of their labours. So far from such a view being obsolete, or disproved by modern criticism, we hold that internal indications, external evidence, and the circumstances of the Mosaic age itself, unite in lending their support to its probability.

1. It is in favour of the view we defend that it is in line with the Bible's own constant *tradition* of the *Mosaicity* of the Pentateuchal books, which the modern hypothesis contradicts at every point. The Biblical evidence on this subject of Mosaic origin is often unduly minimised, but it is really very strong and pervasive. Apart from the assumption of the existence of a "book of the law of Moses" in passages of the historical books,[1] and the implication of its existence in passages where it is not expressly mentioned;[2] apart also from the firm belief of the Jews in the days of our Lord and His apostles—a belief which our Lord Himself shared[3]—there can be no question :—

(1) That all the *three Codes*—the Book of the Covenant, the Deuteronomic discourses, and the Levitical Code—profess to come from Moses, and the first and second profess to have been *written* by him.[4]

(2) That the Deuteronomic discourses imply the existence, in substance and in part in written form, of the *JE history*; and that the P writing, likewise, presupposes the JE history, with which, in its narrative part, it is parallel.[5]

(3) That king Josiah and the Jewish people of his day received *Deuteronomy* as a genuine work of Moses, and that the nation ever after regarded it as his.[6]

(4) That the Jewish people of Ezra's time similarly accepted *the whole Pentateuch* — including the Levitical legislation—as genuinely Mosaic.[7]

(5) That the Samaritans received the Pentateuch at the hands of the Jews as an undoubtedly Mosaic book.[8]

To these firm strands of tradition we may with much confidence attach ourselves, without feeling that

---

[1] Josh. i. 7, 8 ; viii. 30–35 ; xxiv. 26 ; 2 Kings xiv. 6 ; cf. 2 Chron. xxv. 4, etc.

[2] *E.g.*, 1 Kings viii. 4 ff.

[3] See Note C on our Lord's Testimony to Moses.

[4] Cf. above, pp. 99, 152, 262.   [5] Cf. above, pp. 107, etc.

[6] Cf. above, pp. 257 ff.   [7] Ezra vi. 18 ; Neh. xiii. 1 ; cf. Mal. iv. 4.

[8] See Note D on the Samaritan Pentateuch.

"traditionalist," in such a connection, is any term of reproach. As has happened in the case of the New Testament,[1] so, it may be predicted, it will prove also in the case of the Old, that greater respect will yet come to be paid to consentient tradition than it is now the fashion to accord to it.

2. It is not, however, tradition merely which supports the idea of an essential Mosaicity of the Pentateuch. A strict application of *critical methods* leads to the same conclusion. We may sum up here the chief results at which we have arrived.

(1) We have found no good reason for separating the *J and E* of the critics, and regarding them as independent documents; and as little for placing their origin as late as the ninth or eighth century. We attach, as formerly said, no importance to the supposed mirroring of later events in the narratives, on which the argument for a late date is chiefly founded.[2] Gunkel, we saw, can find no trace in the tradition in Genesis, apart from the reference to Edom (chap. xxvii. 40), which looks beyond 900 B.C.;[3] and the bulk of the JE narrative may well go back to Mosaic or immediately post-Mosaic times. The older scholars did not feel the need of bringing it, at latest, below the days of the undivided kingdom, and there is no new evidence.

(2) We have been led, on historical and critical grounds, to reject the theory of the Josianic origin of *Deuteronomy*, and, in accordance with the claim of the book itself, to affirm the genuineness of the Deuteronomic discourses, substantially in the form in which we have them. But Deuteronomy, as repeatedly shown, attests the existence and Mosaic character of the Book of the Covenant,[4] founds upon the JE history, and involves at least the presence of a measure of Levitical legislation.[5]

[1] Cf. Harnack, *Chron. d. Altchrist. Lit.*, p. viii.

[2] See above, pp. 111–12. Kuenen says : " References to historical facts, such as might give a clue to the dates of composition, are extremely rare in the 'prophetic' narratives of the Hexateuch."—*Hex.* p. 237. Still he finds a few, as he thinks, in Edom, the wars of the Syrians, etc. In P there are none such.

[3] *Genesis*, p. lxii. See above on Edom, pp. 112, 209 ; also below, p. 373.

[4] Dillmann puts the Decalogue and Book of the Covenant "in the first days of the possession of the land, at latest in the days of Samuel."—*Num.-Jos.* p. 644. He finds a few traces of later revision.

[5] See above, Chap. VIII.

(3) We have found that there are the strongest critical reasons for denying that the *P writing* (the peculiarities of which are acknowledged) ever subsisted as an independent document, and for regarding it, especially in Genesis, as mainly a "framework" enclosing the contents of JE,[1] though it has also, at certain points, its original, and, in parts, considerable contributions to bring to the history. We found ourselves compelled to reject the post-exilian date assigned to the laws in this writing by the critics; but equally (here in agreement with the Wellhausen school) the mediating view of those who regard the Code as a private document originating in priestly circles under the monarchy.[2] There remains as the only alternative to the post-exilian date the view—which was also that of the older scholars—of the substantially Mosaic origin of the laws.[3] It has been seen that these contain no anachronisms, but keep strictly within the limits of the Mosaic age.[4] If, however, the laws are early, there can be no good reason for doubting the antiquity of the history with which they are connected, for it was simply the assumption of the late date of the laws which led, for consistency's sake, to the putting of the history late.[5] Further, from the close relation subsisting between P and JE in the narratives, we are compelled to assign both, as elements in a composite work, to practically the same age.

3. Taking the *Book of Genesis* by itself, we may confidently affirm that, apart from the few words and phrases commonly adduced, as "The Canaanite was then in the land,"[6] "Before there reigned any king over the children of Israel,"[7] there are no indications which point necessarily beyond the Mosaic age,[8] and even these do not point later than the early days of the kingdom—if they do even this.

---

[1] See earlier in chapter, pp. 340 ff. [2] See above, Chap. IX. pp. 326 ff.
[3] Cf. pp. 328–29 above. [4] See above, p. 294.
[5] See above, pp. 200, 334.
[6] Gen. xii. 6 ; xiii. 7. The proper meaning of these passages seems to us to be that the Canaanites—comparatively recent settlers (cf. Gen. xiv. 5–7 ; Deut. ii. 10–12, 20–23 ; see below, p. 529)—were already in the land when Abraham entered it. No Jew needed to be informed that the Canaanites had not then been dispossessed.
[7] Gen. xxxvi. 31.
[8] Whether as part of the original text, or a reviser's note, the words naturally suggest that when they were written kings were reigning in Israel. The list of Edom's kings, on the other hand, does not necessarily

"The Book of Genesis," says Kuenen himself, in words already quoted, "may here be left out of account, since the picture it contains of the age of the patriarchs gives no unequivocal indications of the period at which it was produced."[1] On the other hand, there are not a few indications in the book, as well as references to it in other books, which imply a high antiquity—*this, also, especially in its Elohistic parts.* There is reason for believing that the narratives of the creation and the flood in the P sections are very old.[2] The Fourth Commandment in Exodus is based, both in chap. xx. 11 and chap. xxxi. 17, on the sabbath-rest of God in Gen. ii. 1–3—a fact doubly significant if, as Graf allows, "the Decalogue in the form in which it appears handed down in Ex. xx. is manifestly older and more original than that in Deut. v."[3] Deut. iv. 32 seems to be a clear reference to the Elohistic account of the creation, with its characteristic word *bara* ("in the day when Elohim created man upon the earth"). The list of the eight kings of Edom in Gen. xxxvi., which stops with Hadar (ver. 39), apparently a person still living, points to a date considerably earlier than Saul or David, when the independence of the kingdom ceased.[4] Colenso, who is our ally here against the post-exilian theory of the P narrative, points out quite a number of other expressions which look back to Genesis.[5] He mentions, *e.g.*, the phrase in Deuteronomy, "Unto them and to *their seed after them*" (chaps. i. 8, iv. 37, x. 15), in which there seems allusion to the re-

carry us beyond the Mosaic age, and can hardly be extended to the time of Saul (see below). Delitzsch says on the passage : "It does not necessarily follow that the writer lived till the time of the Israelite kingdom, though it looks like it."— *Genesis*, ii. p. 247.

[1] *Hex.* p. 42. Cf. above, p. 111. Dr. Driver says on the above allusions : "These are isolated passages, the inferences naturally authorized by which might not impossibly be neutralized by the supposition that they were later additions to the original narrative, and did not consequently determine by themselves the date of the book as a whole."—*Genesis*, p. xv.

[2] See next chapter, pp. 402 ff.

[3] *Geschicht. Bücher*, p. 19 ; cf. Delitzsch, *Genesis*, i. pp. 30–31 ; Colenso, *Pent.* Pt. vi. p. 584 ; App. pp. 124 ff.

[4] Edom was under kings in Moses' time (Num. xx. 14), and it is *possible* that Hadar may be the king then referred to ; at least no stretch of reigns can easily bring Hadar down to the time of Saul. Delitzsch says : "There is nothing against the supposition that Q [=P] is here communicating a document whose original author was a contemporary of Moses, and survived to the entry into the promised land."—*Genesis*, ii. p. 249.

[5] *Pent.* Pt. vi., as above.

curring P formula in Gen. xvii. 8; xxxv. 12; xlviii. 2; cf.
chaps. ix. 19, xvii. 7, 10, 19; the words in Deut. xxix. 13,
"that He may be to thee an Elohim," which seems distinctly
to refer to Gen. xvii. 7, 8, where alone we have such a
promise under solemn covenant; the declaration in Isa. liv. 9
(at least not *post*-exilian), "I have *sworn* that as the *waters*
of Noah should no more go over the earth," etc., which
refers to the P phraseology and covenant in Gen. ix. 11.
The cumulative effect of these allusions, as against the
modern theory, is very great.

4. We have not attempted to go into detailed argument
on the history of the *language*,[1] nor to rebut objections,
more frequently heard earlier than now,[2] on the supposed
ignorance of the Hebrews in the Mosaic age of the art of
writing. The discussion of the language lies beyond our
province; and discovery, as already seen, has thrown such
remarkable light on the existence, and wide diffusion of
writing, in antiquity, specially among the peoples with
whom the Hebrews were brought most closely into contact
(Babylonia, Egypt, Palestine),[3] as to place the possibility
of such literary labours as we have been supposing beyond
reasonable doubt. Few, therefore, now found on the
assumption that writing was unknown, or not practised,
among the early Hebrews;[4] less even is heard of the unlikelihood of an "undisciplined horde" of nomads possess-
ing a knowledge of letters.[5] Every indication shows that
the Hebrews, as they came up out of Egypt, were not a
people of this character, but had a good knowledge of the
arts and ways of civilised life.[6] The Pentateuch, we saw

---

[1] Cf. the *general* argument in Chap. III.

[2] The argument was formerly very often urged, as by Von Bohlen,
Hartmann, etc., and is still *occasionally* met with. Cf. Reuss, *e.g.*, *Geschichte
des A.T.*, p. 96. Even Dillmann thinks it against the Mosaic composition of the books that writing was not *generally* practised in the
beginning of the people's history (*Num.–Jos.* p. 594). Later discoveries
would probably have altered his opinion.

[3] Cf. above, pp. 78 ff.; see further in next chapter.

[4] Kuenen (quoted by Vos) says: "That the Israelites possessed an
alphabet, and knew the art of writing, in the Mosaic age, is not subject
to reasonable doubt, and is now almost universally admitted." Kautzsch,
we have seen (p. 76), allows that Judg. viii. 14. (R.V.) proves that "the
art of writing had been gradually disseminated among the lower people."—
Lit. of O.T., p. 10.

[5] Thus Von Bohlen, etc. Most older scholars, however, *e.g.*, Bleek,
upheld the Mosaic use of writing. So Colenso.

[6] See above, pp. 79, 104, 154.

before, assumes a knowledge of the art of writing;[1] and if such knowledge was possessed by Moses, and those about him, there can be little doubt but that it would be used. There seems, accordingly, no bar in the way of the supposition that in the age of Moses the main features of the language as a vehicle of literary expression were already established, and, in some form of script, the use of writing may go back much earlier.[2] On this point Dr. Driver says: " It is not denied that the patriarchs possessed the art of writing"; but he thinks that the use of documents from the patriarchal age is " a mere hypothesis, for the truth of which no positive grounds can be alleged." [3] Even if it were so, it would be in no worse case than much in the critical view itself, which, if anything in the world ever was, is hypothesis built on hypothesis.[4] The value of a hypothesis is the degree in which it explains facts, and, in the silence of the Book of Genesis,[5] we can only reason from general probabilities. But the probabilities, derived from the state of culture at the time, from the fixed and circumstantial character of the tradition, and from the archæological notices embedded in the book,[6] are, we think, strong, that the Hebrews, even in the patriarchal age, were to some extent acquainted with books and writing. If so, we may believe that at an early period, in Egypt under Joseph, if not before, attempts would be made to set down things in writing.[7]

5. We have used the terms " collaboration" and " cooperation" to express *the kind and manner of the activity* which, in our view, brought the Pentateuchal books into their present shape,[8] less, however, as suggesting a definite theory of origin, than as indicating the labour of original composers, working with a common aim, and towards a common end, in contrast with the idea of late irresponsible redactors, combining, altering, manipulating, enlarging at

[1] See above, pp. 80 ff.
[2] The question of the script used in early Hebrew writing (old Phœnician, cuneiform, Minæan?) is one of great difficulty, on which opinions are much divided. In the view of some the use of the Phœnician alphabet by the Israelites does not go back beyond about 1000 B.C. But this is unlikely. See Note E on Early Hebrew Writing.
[3] *Genesis*, p. xlii.   [4] See Note F on Hypotheses in Criticism.
[5] The silence must not be pressed too far. See above, p. 80.
[6] See above, pp. 78 ff. ; and cf. next chapter.
[7] Cf. Hommel, *Ancient Hebrew Tradition*, pp. 277, 296.
[8] See above, pp. 216, 354.

pleasure. It has been shown how the critical theory itself tends to approximate to this idea of "co-operation" in the production of the Hexateuch,[1] though at the other end of the development. What it puts at the end, we are disposed to transfer to the beginning.

Beyond this we do not feel it possible to go with any degree of confidence. It may very well be—though everything here is more or less conjectural—that, as already hinted, the original JEP history and Code embraced, not simply the Book of the Covenant, but a brief summary of the Levitical ordinances, analogous, as Dillmann thinks, to the so-called Law of Holiness; possibly also, as Delitzsch supposes, a short narrative, in its proper place, of the last discourses of Moses, and of his death.[2] We have seen that Deuteronomy, in its original form, was probably an independent work; the priestly laws, also, would be at first chiefly in the hands of the priests. Later, but still, in our opinion, early—possibly in the times immediately succeeding the conquest, but not later than the days of the undivided kingdom—the original work would be enlarged by union with Deuteronomy, and by incorporation of the larger mass of Levitical material. In some such way, with possible revision by Ezra, or whoever else gave the work its final canonical shape, our Pentateuch may have arisen.

It is difficult, however, to suppose that this large work, assuming its origin to be as early as we have suggested, ever had, in its completeness, any wide circulation, or was frequently copied in its entirety. As in the Christian Church, before the days of printing, it was customary to copy out selected books and portions, as the Psalter, or the Gospels; so, it may reasonably be presumed, the parts of the Pentateuch copied out for general use, and in more common circulation, would ordinarily be those to which we still turn as the more interesting and edifying—the story of the patriarchs and of Moses, the history of the Exodus and the wanderings, the Book of Deuteronomy, short digests of laws, etc. The detailed Levitical Code would be left to the priests, and would be known mainly through the praxis,

---

[1] See Note G on the idea of " Co-operation " in Critical Theory.
[2] See above, p. 284. Similarly, in place of the present detailed descriptions, there may have been shorter accounts of the making of the ark and tabernacle.

or by oral instruction at the sanctuary. The "law of Jehovah," of which we read so much in the Psalter, by which the piety of the godly in Israel was nourished, which enlightened, converted, directed, warned, comforted, cleansed, made fruitful, the souls that delighted in it, was assuredly, as before remarked,[1] something very different from the dry Levitical regulations. The versions of these books in circulation would also have their vicissitudes; would undergo the usual textual corruptions; may have received unauthorised modifications or additions; may have had their Jehovistic and Elohistic recensions. But the sense in pious minds that it was Jehovah's "law"—embodying the "words of His lips"[2]—which they were dealing with would check rash freedoms, and the means of correction would never be wholly lost. God's people had a "Bible" then, and, as it comes to us from their hands, we may cherish the confidence that it has suffered no change which unfits it for being our Bible also.[3]

[1] See above, pp. 263–64.
[2] Ps. xvii. 4; cf. Pss. i., xviii. 21, 22, xix. 7–11, xxv., etc.
[3] The statements made as to the liberties taken with the text of the Hebrew Scriptures in pre-Christian times are often much too sweeping. See Note H on the State of the Hebrew Text.

APPENDIX TO CHAPTER X

THE LATER HISTORICAL BOOKS

IT is not proposed to discuss at length the problems connected with the age, authorship, and credibility of the later historical books of the Old Testament. Incidentally the history in the later books has been defended in the preceding chapters, and will receive further illustration in the chapter on archæology. The Pentateuchal question is, as everyone acknowledges, the fundamental one in Old Testament criticism. If that stone can be dislodged, the critics have shaken the edifice of the Old Testament to its base. If the attack on that foundation is repelled, the succeeding history has not much to fear from assault. It will be sufficient here to indicate the bearings of the results already arrived at on the composition and authority of the later books.

I. We may briefly indicate, first, the bearing of the acceptance of the *critical* theory on the age and value of the books in question.

1. If the *P element* in the Pentateuch is of exilian or post-exilian date, then necessarily all assumed P sections in the Book of Joshua must be post-exilian also, and, on the theory, destitute of historical worth. This condemns, *e.g.*, the whole account of the division of the land in the second half of Joshua.[1] Similarly, all passages or allusions in later books, which imply the existence of P or its institutions must (or may) be held to be late. Everything of this nature, therefore,—tent of meeting, Levites, high priest, etc.,— is usually struck out as interpolation. The Levitical representations in the Books of Chronicles are *a priori* discredited, and put out of court as worthless.

[1] Cf. below, pp. 379–80.

2. In the same way, if *Deuteronomy* is a composition of the age of Josiah, then all Deuteronomic sections, or revisions in the D style, of the historical books, must be later than Deuteronomy, and cannot be taken as genuine history. Large sections of Joshua—the reading of the law on Mount Ebal, *e.g.*, chap. viii. 30 ff.—and of Judges, are thus discredited as the unhistorical work of a D¹ or D², etc.[1] The Books of Kings are a late compilation from a Deuteronomic point of view, and exhibit a revision of the history in a Deuteronomic spirit which amounts, in its effect, to a falsification of it.[2] The mystery is why this Deuteronomic revision has left nearly untouched the Books of Samuel,[3] and, in view of most, the narratives of the Pentateuch.[4]

3. If the *JE narratives* belong at earliest to the ninth or eighth centuries, a presumption is created, in the opinion of the critics, in favour of their legendary character, and all additions or redactions of members of the "school" must be later, and less trustworthy, still. As Deuteronomy rests on the JE histories, the late date of that book is held to be confirmed.

II. The matter presents itself in a very different light when looked at from the *opposite* point of view.

1. If the P sections in the Pentateuch are *not* of postexilian date, but go back to early times, there is no need for putting the P sections in Joshua late; or for expunging the allusions to priesthood and tabernacle in the historical books; or even, on *this* ground, for discrediting the statements of the Books of Chronicles.[5] Delitzsch, *e.g.*, precisely inverting the usual style of argument, finds his conclusion that "the literary activity of the Elohistic pen reaches back to ancient times nearly approaching those of Moses" actually "*confirmed* by the Book of Joshua," with its account of the division of the land. "Modern criticism," he says, "indeed greatly depreciates the historical authority

---

[1] Cf. Wellhausen, *Hist. of Israel*, p. 235.

[2] *Ibid.* pp. 228, 274, 281, etc.

[3] Kautzsch finds a few traces of Deuteronomic revision in Samuel (*Lit. of O.T.*, pp. 95-96, 238); Driver apparently (with Budde) fewer (*Introd.* pp. 173, 183).

[4] "Comparatively infrequent" (Kautzsch, p. 95)

[5] See below, pp. 388-89.

of the priestly narrator in matters relating to the history of the conquest; but the priestly narrator wrote also the main bulk of the account of the division, and this may lay claim to documentary authority. For that this history of the division is based upon written documents may be conjectured from its very nature, while the *sēpher* (book) of the commissioners entrusted with the task of describing the land (chap. xviii. 9), shows that the division of the land was carried out with legal accuracy. . . . It is therefore quite an arbitrary assertion, at least with respect to the history of the division, that the priestly narrator of the Book of Joshua was of more recent times than the Jehovist and the Deuteronomian, and it is certainly possible that the Deuteronomian himself composed and formed the Book of Joshua from Jehovistic and Elohistic models."[1]

2. If *Deuteronomy* is not late, but early, and if the discourses contained in it are in substance really Mosaic, then the reason falls for discrediting the D sections and colouring in Joshua, Judges, and Kings. A good deal, we shall see below,[2] is taken for granted in speaking of "Deuteronomic" revision. In any case, assuming such to be present, it neither, on the view we uphold, argues late date nor unhistorical presentation. There is no longer ground, *e.g.*, for questioning the genuineness in substance of such speeches as Solomon's at the dedication of the temple (1 Kings viii.), or the justice of the condemnation of the toleration of high places; or for regarding these "Deuteronomic" speeches as compositions of an exilian compiler. We do not deny that there may be a measure of freedom in the reproduction of the speeches, but they need not on that account be late, or untrue to the occasion on which they were delivered.

III. The *critical treatment* of the historical books is itself a strong argument for the second of these views rather than the first. Not only does the critical hypothesis imply invention and falsification of history on an unprecedented scale, but it results in a disintegration of the

---

[1] *Genesis*, p. 49. See above, p. 242, and cf. König, art. "Judges," in Hastings' *Dict. of Bible*, who shows that the partition is implied in the "lot" of Judg. i. (ii. p. 820).

[2] See also above, p. 255.

books in a fashion as complicated and bewildering as in the Pentateuch analysis, and often, as the radical disagreement of critics shows, as assumptive and arbitrary.

The Book of Joshua has already been referred to. A few remarks may be made on the others.

In general, it is not denied that the historical books are compilations, for the most part, from older writings, which criticism is quite within its rights in endeavouring to distinguish if it can. It is the fact that the books embody old and authentic material which gives them their value. The narratives incorporated in the Book of Judges, *e.g.*, must in many cases have taken shape not long after the events which they relate,—the Song of Deborah is practically contemporary,[1]—and the sources of the Books of Samuel are, in like manner, very old. There seems no ground for doubting the view, borne out by the notices in the later books, that the prophets themselves—from Samuel on—acted as the sacred "historiographers" of their nation, and that it is to narratives composed by them that we owe the greater part of the material embodied in our canonical writings[2] (hence the name "former prophets" applied to Joshua—2 Kings, excepting Ruth). What is objected to is not a cautious discrimination based on the clear phenomena of the books, but the assumption of the ability to dissect a historic book into its minutest parts, and distribute out the fragments to writers of widely separated ages, with frequently a wholesale impeachment of the integrity of the composers.

1. We take the *Book of Judges* as a first example. In

[1] See above, p. 76. Such allusions, *e.g.*, as those to Jerusalem and Gezer (chap. i. 21, 29), point to a date before the monarchy, though the book as a whole implies that it was compiled when the kingdom was settled (chaps. xvii. 6, xviii. 1, xix. 1, etc.).

[2] Cf. Kirkpatrick, *Divine Library of O.T.*, pp. 13 ff. (so in Introd. to Samuel); Ottley, *Aspects of O.T.*, p. 145, etc. ; of older writers, Bleek, *Introd.* i. pp. 175 ff. ; S. Davidson, *Introd. to O.T.*, ii. pp. 68–69, 682 ff., etc. Ottley says : "There is little reason to doubt that the documents which form the substratum of the Books of Samuel and Kings were official notices of political events, and nearly contemporary narratives, some of which may reasonably be supposed to have been written by prophets like Gad, Nathan, Iddo, and others" (p. 145). See Kirkpatrick's remarks (*Samuel*, p. 10) on the view "that Samuel, Nathan, and Gad were the subjects, not the authors, of the works referred to." In some cases the fact is patent that the work is a history by the person named ; the presumption is it was so in all. Cf. S. Davidson, *Introd.* ii. pp. 68–69 ; Zöckler, *Chronicles* ("Lange"), pp. 17 ff. ; etc.

Kautzsch, who is by no means the extremest of the critics, we have the book parcelled out into a great number of elements. We have H¹, an older stratum of Hero-Stories, constituting the nucleus of the book; H², Hero-Stories from the early kingly period; *ri*, fragments of a list of Judges from the later kingly period; Ri, the first Deuteronomic compiler; N and N¹, pre-Deuteronomic compilers of the narratives in the appendix ("chaps. xx., xxi. originally came from this source, but have been thoroughly revised by a hand related to the Priests' Code"); R, the post-exilic editor or editors of the present book. In addition there are "later glosses" and "passages of doubtful origin" (Jephthah). As showing the minuteness of the analysis, we may give the parts attributed to N¹—"xvii. 2–4, 6, 12 ; xviii. 1*a*, 2*, 7*, 10*b*, 14*, 15*, 18*, 20*, 30." ¹ The asterisks mean worked over by redactors. Does criticism here by its very minuteness not destroy confidence in itself ? ²

It is the Deuteronomic editor of Judges who, we are told, has supplied the introduction and unhistorical "scheme" of the book, representing the alternate declensions and repentances of the people, with their corresponding experiences of oppression and deliverance. This is declared to be doubly unhistorical : (1) As picturing the people as a unity, "acting together, suffering together, repenting together, ruled over as a whole by one judge at a time," whereas "up to that time the Hebrew tribes had no such sense of unity"; ³ and (2) as crediting them with a religious knowledge and ideal of duty they did not possess. 'There is no conception of spiritual worship or moral duty in the book." ⁴ On which representations three things, in reply, may be said :—

(1) Is it perfectly clear—König at least thinks not ⁵—

¹ *Lit. of O.T.*, pp. 234–36.

² See the searching criticism of the analysis and arguments of Budde and others by König in art. "Judges," in *Dict. of Bible*. A good conspectus of the agreements and differences of critical opinion is given in the tables in the introduction to Nowack's Commentary on Judges and Ruth ("Handkommentar"), pp. xxiv ff.

³ Thatcher, *Judges* ("Cent. Bible"), p. 6. So Driver, Moore, Nowack, etc., after Wellhausen, *Compos. d. Hex.* pp. 229–30 ; *Hist. of Israel*, pp. 231, 233–35.

⁴ *Ibid.* p. 23.

⁵ "Judges" in *Dict. of Bible*, ii. pp. 812, 816 ; cf. *Einleit.* pp. 251–54. Moore thinks there is not sufficient ground for identifying this Deuteronomic author of the preface and framework of Judges "with anyone of the

that the introduction and framework are Deuteronomic in the
sense intended ? But whether they are or not, it is still to
be shown that the representation of alternate declension and
deliverance given as the interpretation of the history is false
to the facts. Professor Robertson points out very pertinently
that the summary in Judges gives precisely the same picture
of the people's behaviour as the prophets give after.[1] It is
not the Book of Judges simply, but Israel's whole representation of its history—early and late—that is challenged.

(2) It is at least an exaggeration to say that Israel had
no sense of its unity. There are the best grounds for
believing that Israel, in the initial stages of the conquest,
acted as *one people* under Joshua,[2] and even when the tribes
settled in their various regions, this sense of unity was never
wholly lost.[3] A consciousness of unity is already very
strongly expressed in the Song of Deborah, and in chaps. xx.,
xxi., which for that very reason (as by Thatcher)[4] is made
post-exilian. A critic like König says: "The assertion that
in the time of the Judges 'a common acting on the part of
the twelve tribes of Israel is excluded' (Budde on chaps. xix.-
xxi.) is quite ungrounded. . . . If in the period of the Judges
one could not entertain the notion that a common danger to
Israel could not be warded off by the common action of all
the tribes, one could not have blamed those tribes which
kept aloof in the struggle against the northern Canaanites
(Judg. v. 15-17)."[5] "It is not only in prose," says Dr.
A. B. Davidson, "that this mode of speech prevails, in which
it might be due to later conceptions, and to a point of view
taken after the rise of the kingdom; the same manner of

Deuteronomic writers in Deuteronomy or Joshua, or with the Deuteronomic
author of Kings" (*Judges*, "Internat. Crit. Com." p. xvii). He puts him
later than the sixth century B.C.

[1] *Rel. of Israel*, pp. 116-17 (see above, p. 40). "This summary of
the period might have been written by Hosea himself, or by Amos ; and if
there is any truth in what they say about prophets before them, anyone
from the days of Samuel might have written it" (p. 117).

[2] See above, p. 241 ; cf. König, "Judges," ii. pp. 814, 819.

[3] Cf. the "all Israel" in Eli's time (1 Sam. ii. 14 ; iii. 20 ; see above,
p. 171).

[4] *Judges*, p. 17. On these chapters, see below.

[5] "Judges," in *Dict. of Bible*, ii. p. 816. Cf. pp. 814, 815, 819. On
chaps. xx.-xxi. he says : "The present writer believes that there are more
traces of the unity of ancient Israel than are wont at present to be recognised
by some scholars. . . . Hence the judgment of the present writer is that
not the section chap. xx.-xxi. 14 as a whole, but only single elements in it
(*e.g.*, the round numbers), bear a secondary character" (p. 819).

speaking appears in the Song of Deborah. . . . In spite of actual disintegration, the conception of an Israel forming a unity, the people of Jehovah, appears everywhere."[1]

(3) It is a still greater exaggeration to say that there is "no conception of spiritual worship or moral duty" in the book. Higher religious and moral conceptions, mingling with the ruder elements, are implied,[2] not simply in the recurrent narratives of repentance, and in the lofty strains of the Song of Deborah,[3] but in the admitted fact that the conditions had in them the germ of the "spiritual and ethical worship"[4] to which the people afterwards attained, and in the possibility, even, of such a religious revival as we find under Samuel.[5] We do not envy the reader who can see no evidences of a spiritual faith in the history of a man like Gideon.[6] Is there not through all the history a vein of recognition of obligation to Jehovah, of a law of righteous providential requital,[7] of the heinousness of wanton cruelty[8] and unrestrained licentiousness?[9] The beautiful family history of Ruth also has to be relegated to the region of post-exilian fiction before the utter lack of spiritual religion can be made out.[10]

The alleged P element in Judges is found in redactional notes, but chiefly in the alleged working over of an older narrative (so most think: not Wellhausen) in chaps. xx., xxi.[11] It is this section also (the story of the Levite and his concu-

---

[1] *O.T. Prophecy*, pp. 33, 34. On the local character of the Judges, König says: "If an explanation of the local origin of these Judges is to be sought for, it is most natural to find it in the circumstance that the hero sprang up from the tribe which felt most the weight of the invader's oppression" (p. 815).

[2] Cf. again König, pp. 816, 821.   [3] See above, pp. 130–31.

[4] Thatcher, p. 24.

[5] 1 Sam. vii. That Samuel effected a revival of religion even an extreme scepticism must admit. This throws back light on the repentances under the Judges.

[6] Judg. vi., vii.   [7] *E.g.*, Judg. i. 7; ix. 24, 56.

[8] Judg. ix. 24, etc.

[9] Judg. xix. 23, 24, 30; xx. 6 ff. Cf. König, p. 816.

[10] Cf. König, *Einleitung*, pp. 287 ff. König sees in Ruth an exilian recension of an old writing of the age of the sources of Samuel and Kings. Driver calls it "pre-exilic" (*Introd.* p. 455). Reuss, Oettli, Strack, etc., also reject the exilian and post-exilian dates.

[11] Driver, Moore, Thatcher, etc., divide chap. xix. from chaps. xx., xxi., recognising the homogeneity of chap. xix. with what goes before; Wellhausen apparently treats chap. xix.–xxi. as a whole (*Compos.* pp. 229 ff.), and does not admit duplication in chap. xx. (cf. Budde, *Richt. und Sam.* p. 389; Moore, p. 406).

bine, and of the war with Benjamin, chaps. xix.–xxi. 14) which, in the eyes of the critics, lacks most clearly in credibility,[1] though a historical kernel is sometimes recognised. Besides the unity argument, and linguistic phenomena thought to betray a later age (dependent on the assumption about P),[2] stress is laid on the apparent exaggeration of numbers. Such exaggerations, assuming them to exist, may grow up in far less time than the critics allow, and may be pressed too far.[3] Dr. Driver, in turn, exaggerates when he reads into the text that on the first two days of battle "not one of the 25,000 + 700 of the Benjamites fell."[4] We are hardly dealing here with head by head counts; besides, "fell," "smitten," "destroyed," do not necessarily mean that *every man* was "slain."

There seems to us no convincing ground, apart from the reasonings on D and P, for placing the Book of Judges later than the period of the undivided kingdom. There is no trace of Jerusalem as capital, or of the temple. The expression "until the day of the captivity of the land" in chap. xviii. 30, is naturally the equivalent of "all the time that the house of God was in Shiloh" in ver. 31.[5] It is precarious, at least, to build an argument for a later date on this verse alone.

2. A next example of critical procedure is afforded by

---

[1] "The historical character of chaps. xx., xxi. 1–14," says Moore, "will hardly be seriously maintained: in the whole description of the war there is hardly a semblance of reality" (p. 405).

[2] Cf. König, as above. In treating of the relation to the Pentateuch sources, König alludes to "the impossibility of making true progress in critical science if a number of results are assumed as already proved, and one makes it his main object always to pile up higher storeys on the building of the literary criticism of the Old Testament" (p. 811).

[3] On the use of round numbers, see below, p. 390. The 400,000, as a number for the whole armed force of Israel (chap. xx. 2, 17), is not out of keeping with other enumerations (Ex. xii. 37; 2 Sam. xxiv. 9), though it is certainly improbable and perhaps is not meant, that all took part in the war at Gibeah (cf. chap. xx. 9, 10).

[4] *Introd.* p. 169. Dr. Driver unnecessarily changes the 26,000 of chap. xx. 15 into 25,000, after Cod. A of the LXX. The ordinary LXX text has 23,000, clearly a mistake, and there may be other confusions in the numbers. Cf. Köhler, *Bib. Gesch.* ii. p. 64.

[5] Bleek, who regards the Book of Judges as pre-Deuteronomic, and in substance early, takes this view of the passage. "The context shows clearly that nothing else can be meant by the *terminus ad quem* . . . than the time indicated in ver. 31" (*Introd.* i. p. 384). Bleek, Riehm, König, etc., think that "land" is a corruption for the (in Heb. resembling) word "ark"; Strack puts the book in the flourishing days of the kingdom, and thinks this clause to be a later addition (*Einleit.* p. 66).

25

the *Books of Samuel.* Kautzsch here admits old and valuable sources—a "Saul-Source," a "David-Source," a "Jerusalem-Source," dating from times immediately after Solomon, with, of course, later and less reliable, but still eighth century, narratives, and "redactional additions of various kinds," some of them post-exilian.[1] Dr. Driver also makes the work as a whole "pre-Deuteronomic."[2] A considerably different view is taken by Professor H. P. Smith. In his Commentary on Samuel this critic distinguishes a work which he calls *Sl,* written soon after the death of Solomon, embracing a brief life of Saul, an account of David at the court of Saul and as outlaw, and a history of David's reign.[3] With this was united a second—divergent and theocratic—account, denoted by him *Sm,* which contained narratives of the early life and doings of Samuel, and of the early life, adventures, and part of the reign of David. This he supposes to have originated, with incorporation of older matter, "perhaps in or after the exile."[4] In details also the analysis is far from agreeing. There is tolerable agreement that chaps. ix.–x. 16, xi., xiii. 2–xiv. 46 belong (mainly) to an old "Saul" source, which represents a different type of narrative from that in chaps. vii. 2–17, viii., x. 17–25, xii., xv.; but otherwise there are important differences. Dr. Driver, *e.g.,* connects chaps. i.–iv. 1*a,* as a "somewhat later" introduction, with chaps. iv. 1*b*–vii. 1; and divides this whole section from chaps. vii. 2–17 ("of later origin"), viii., etc.—the "theocratic" story (= *Sm*). But H. P. Smith puts chaps. i.–iii. into his (exilian) *Sm* story, and assigns to *Sm* also, from older sources, the other parts up to chap. vii.[5] Dr. Kautzsch divides still more minutely, and in 2 Samuel makes a separate source (his "Jerusalem-Source") of 2 Sam. vi., ix.–xx., which H. P. Smith, again, includes in his *Sl.*[6] All, however, happily, make this long narrative quite early. The chief point is that H. P. Smith carries down to the exile a long narrative (*Sm*), beginning with 1 Sam. i.–vi., which the others take to be at least not later (apart from redactional touchings) than the eighth century.[7] But then in an Appendix Professor

[1] *Lit. of O.T.*, pp. 236 ff.; cf. pp. 27 ff.
[2] *Introd.* p. 177.
[3] *Samuel*, p. 408.
[4] *Ibid.* p. xx.   [5] *Ibid.* p. xix.   [6] *Ibid.* p. 408.
[7] On the wide differences of the critical schools see in detail Köhler, *Bib. Gesch.* ii. p. 135.

H. P. Smith has to contend against a new writer, Dr. M. Löhr (1898),[1] who discards *Sm* for fragments inserted into *Sl* at different dates.[2]

All this is bewildering enough; but, even with different sources, the attempt to break up the unity of the book, and establish for the different narrators opposite and irreconcilable points of view, is vastly overdone. The "theocratic" view is presumed to be a later gloss upon the history, and the earlier account, which is said to represent Samuel as "the seer of a small town, respected as one who blesses the sacrifices and presides at the local festival, but known only as a clairvoyant, whose information concerning lost or strayed property is reliable,"[3] is accepted as the really historical version. Thus Samuel gets effectively stripped of any false glory a pious imagination has invested him with! It is, however, the imagination of the critic chiefly that is astray. Dr. Driver, who is not extreme here, divides chaps. i.–vii. 1 from what follows expressly on the ground that "hitherto Samuel has appeared only as a prophet; here (chap. vii. ff.) he is represented as a 'judge.'"[4] Yet *all these chapters*, as shown above, Professor H. P. Smith gives to his "theocratic" narrator (*Sm*) — the same who represents Samuel as a "judge." The charge of "partisanship," again, often brought against the "Saul" and "David" sources (*both* mostly included in H. P. Smith's *Sl*) is fittingly dealt with by Dr. Kautzsch. "But the partisanship," he says, "of the one source for Saul and of the other for David, which used to be so frequently asserted, cannot really be proved. . . . After all, it is by no means impossible for both sources to have come from *one* hand."[5]

The Books of Samuel, it appears to us, may well be based on such nearly contemporary narratives as are referred to in 1 Chron. xxix. 29,[6] and the date of their composition *need*

---

[1] A very full comparative survey of modern views is given in parallel columns in Löhr's *Samuel*, pp. xiv–lxv.

[2] *Ibid.* pp. 409 ff. Löhr's work, though advanced in criticism, is more conservative than most in respect of text (cf. pp. vi, xc).

[3] *Ibid.* p. xvi. Kautzsch puts this more moderately (p. 29).

[4] *Introd.* p. 174.

[5] *Lit. of O. T.*, pp. 27–28. Kautzsch, however, still finds the sources "freely inlaid with passages taken from a quite different source [SS., eighth century = part of *Sm*], and with redactional additions." This also, we believe, examination would show to be precarious, and pushed needlessly far.

[6] See above, p. 381.

not be carried much lower than where Ewald puts it, some twenty or thirty years after the death of Solomon.[1]

3. We glance finally, briefly, at the *Books of Chronicles*. These are, it is well known, the veritable *bête noire* of the critics. The Levitical proclivities and representations of this writer—only, however, be it said, in certain parts of his work,[2] for in the greater portion of it the parallelism with the older texts is close—are a constant irritation to them. De Wette made the first vigorous onslaught on the credibility of Chronicles;[3] Graf returned to the charge with new arguments;[4] and Wellhausen, from the standpoint of the post-exilian origin of the law, has elaborated the attack with unsparing scorn and severity.[5] Yet unfairly—and unnecessarily.[6] Let all be granted that can be fairly alleged of the Chronicler's predominant Levitical interest, of his homiletical expansions, as, *e.g.*, in the speech of Abijah (2 Chron. xiii. 4 ff.),[7] of his dropping the veil on the sins of David and Solomon,[8] of his occasional exaggera-

---

[1] Cf. Bleek, *Introd.* i. p. 400. Bleek himself thinks "probably later," but still, on the basis of older records (p. 405), and before the destruction of the kingdom of the Ten Tribes. Kirkpatrick says "there are no cogent reasons for referring the compilation of the Book of Samuel to a late date," and finds the primary authorities for large parts of the history in Samuel and Kings in "the narratives of contemporary prophets" (*The Divine Library of O.T.*, pp. 14, 15; cf. his Introd. to Samuel).

[2] The most notable examples are the account of David's bringing up of the ark, and his subsequent organisation of the Levites (1 Chron. xv. ff.; xxiii.–xxviii.); Solomon's Dedication of the temple (2 Chron. v. 4, 5, 11-14); Abijah's speech (2 Chron. xiii.); the proclamation of Joash (2 Chron. xxiii.); the reformation of Hezekiah (2 Chron. xxix.–xxxi.); and the Passover of Josiah (2 Chron. xxxv.)—nearly all temple matters. See Van Hoonacker below.

[3] In his *Beiträge* (1806).   [4] *Geschicht. Bücher*, Pt. ii.

[5] *Hist. of Israel*, pp. 171 ff.

[6] How far the last word is from having been spoken on the credibility of the Chronicles in relation to Samuel and Kings may be seen from the full and able discussions (with bearing on the sections noted above) in Van Hoonacker's *Le Sacerdoce Lévitique*, pp. 21 ff. Cf. also Klostermann's art. "Chronik" in the new *Realencyklopädie*, iv. pp. 84 ff.

[7] Even Keil admits an element of free reproduction in the speeches (*Chronicles*, pp. 40, 41), whether due to the Chronicler himself or found in his source.

[8] It is to be remembered that the Chronicler does not aim at giving a complete history, but only excerpts bearing on the progress of the theocracy, and throughout assumes that the older history is known (cf. Dillmann, "Chronik," Herzog's *Realencyk.* iii. p. 221). There is nothing, *e.g.*, of the early life of David, there is a leap from the death of Saul to David's proclamation as king of all Israel at Hebron, the Northern Kingdom is disregarded, etc. Wellhausen allows that "the Chronicler indeed knows

tion in numbers—whether his own or a copyist's [1]—the gravamen of the charge against him still lies in the assumption, wholly unfounded, as we believe, that the Levitical system was not in operation before the exile. If it *was*, there is no *a priori* objection to the representations of the Chronicler. On the other hand, the supposition of Wellhausen, that all the Chronicler's elaborate descriptions, lists of names, details of arrangements, are pure inventions of his fancy, is weighted with the heaviest improbabilities, and cannot be reconciled with the integrity of the writer, which some are still anxious to uphold. We find it hard to imagine, for instance, how anyone can read the long and circumstantial account of Hezekiah's great passover,[2] or even the elaborate descriptions of David's sanctuary arrangements,[3] and not feel that the writer is reproducing *bona fide*—if in some places in his own fashion—documentary information that has come down to him.[4] The critics, on the other hand, will allow him no other sources than our existing Books of Samuel and Kings—a view which not only his own references, but many phenomena in his book decidedly contradict [5]—and set down all else to sheer wantonness of invention. The evidence points in a quite different direction—to the use of older sources dealing with these matters from the point of view of the temple,[6] in which case his narratives afford a valuable positive *corroboration* of the results already obtained.

While, therefore, it is freely admitted that Chronicles can only take secondary rank as a historical authority in comparison with Samuel and Kings, we have no reason to

them all well enough, as is clear from incidental expressions in chaps. xi. and xii." (*Hist. of Israel*, pp. 172–73). What then was he to gain from his silence ? He records David's theocratic sin of numbering the people (1 Chron. xxi.), and narrates impartially the sins of Asa, Joash, Amaziah, etc. (not in Kings). See further below.

[1] See below, p. 390.   [2] 2 Chron. xxx.

[3] 1 Chron. xxiii. ff. Cf. on this, Klostermann, *Geschichte d. Volkes Israel*, p. 161.

[4] The *bona fides* of the Chronicler in the use of his sources is upheld by Dillmann, Klostermann, Van Hoonacker, etc. See below.

[5] It is questioned by hardly any that he knew and used the Books of Samuel and Kings, but these were not his only sources.

[6] Till recently, this was the general view. Cf. Bleek, Keil, S. Davidson, Zöckler, Dillmann, etc. It is vigorously upheld by Klostermann (art. cited) and Van Hoonacker, *Le Sacerdoce*, pp. 70 ff. and *passim*.

doubt the perfect good faith of its author,[1] the value of much of his Levitical information, and, in general, the credibility of his book. In special points in which its accuracy has been impugned—as in the captivity of Manasseh in Babylon[2] —discovery has brought to it valuable corroboration. Apart from the numbers, which, taken literally, are indeed in some cases "incredibly large," Zöckler goes so far as to say that "the only nearly certain example of error on his part, arising, apparently, from geographical ignorance, is the explanation of the Tarshish ships of the Red Sea as being designed to trade to Tarshish" (2 Chron. ix. 21; xx. 36).[3] Even in regard to the numbers he says: "If we except this one passage, all else of an erroneous nature in the text is most probably to be reduced to errors in copying, that either existed in his sources, or were introduced into his text."[4] That may be too unqualified also.[5] Possibly, as Keil suggests,[6] such excessive numbers as we have in 2 Chron. xiii. 3, 17, 800,000 fighting men for Israel, 400,000 for Judah, 500,000 of Israel slain, are, if not corrupt, meant to be taken only as round numerical expressions for the whole or half of the respective forces (cf. 2 Sam. xxiv. 9). It is not to be overlooked, moreover, that sometimes it is Chronicles that gives the smaller number (cf., e.g., 1 Chron. xi. 11, with 2 Sam. xxiii. 8; 2 Chron. ix. 25, with 1 Kings iv. 26), and in some cases the numbers are undeniably corrupt.[7]   On the

[1] "It is now recognised," wrote Dillmann (referring to the attacks of De Wette and Graf) "that the Chronicler has worked according to sources, and that there can be no talk in regard to him of intentional fabrications or misrepresentations of the history" ("Chronik," Herzog, iii. p. 223). Cf. the remarks of Prof. Robertson, Poetry and Religion of the Psalms, pp. 92 ff.

[2] "The account," says Dr. S. Davidson, "awakens grave doubts of the fidelity of the Chronist," and he concludes that the narrative is "unhistorical" (Introd. ii. pp. 97-100). See below, p. 427. Also on Shishak, p. 426.

[3] Chronicles, p. 25. Most admit that the Chronicler has here misunderstood his source (cf. 1 Kings x. 22; xxii. 49); at least it is highly improbable that ships made voyages round Africa from the Red Sea to Tarshish (but see in Zöckler, p. 28).

[4] Ibid.

[5] Dillmann, however, may be quoted again: "So far as we can judge from Chronicles itself, we have no reason to suspect the trustworthiness of the sources; a mass of differences between Chronicles and the Books of Kings in names, numbers, expressions, are satisfactorily explained by accidental corruptions of the text, be it in Kings, in Chronicles, or in the books which are their sources" (as above, p. 224).

[6] Chronicles, pp. 350-55.

[7] A curious illustration of the facility of error is afforded by the fact that, in the very act of stating the large number of Jeroboam's army in 2 Chron.

whole there is abundant ground for the moderate and
sensible judgment of an older critic like Bleek : " If we
only possessed this work alone as an historical source for
the times and circumstances treated of in the Chronicles,
the latter would in no way afford us a complete and exact
picture of them ; but, together with the other books, it gives
us very valuable and important additions to the accounts of
the latter, and a crowd of important details, which serve
to make them complete both in general, and in special
points." [1]

xiii. 3, in Smith's *Dict. of Bible*, i. p. 113, the 800,000 is misprinted
300,000.

[1] *Introd.* i. p. 442. The strong words of Klostermann may be cited in
closing this discussion. "Grant," he says, "that the image conceived by
the Chronist and his predecessors, *e.g.*, of the development of the cultus,
totally contradicts that which the modern theology, with ignoring of their
accounts, has sketched on the basis of the extraordinarily sparse, uncon-
nected, and ambiguous casual intimations of some of the older writings and
prophets, and, as standing outside the current of tradition, with the aid
of inventive fancy ; even so, the traditional materials from which the picture
of the former is obtained, are not mere imaginations, and have not been
designedly distorted or changed contrary to their original intention. The
attempts made of late to figure the narrative in Chronicles, *e.g.*, about the
beginning of David's reign, in details, as the result of a calculated selection
and manipulation of passages from the Book of Samuel—apart from the
craft and stupidity which this supposes, especially in one addressing himself
to readers of the Book of Samuel—leave on the mind the impression, not of
a judge, who seeks to secure that an accused person gets his rights, but
of a prosecuting attorney, who sees in every accidental trifle, a new proof of
an already presumed great crime."—"Chronik," in Hauck's *Realencyk.*
iv. p. 97.

CHAPTER XI

Archæology and the Old Testament

"Speak to the earth, and it shall teach thee."—Job.

"There have been made other and even greater discoveries in Assyrian and Babylonian ruins since Botta's far-reaching exploration of the mounds of Khorsabad, but there never has been aroused again such a deep and general interest in the excavation of distant Oriental sites as towards the middle of the last century, when Sargon's palace rose suddenly out of the ground, and furnished the first faithful picture of a great epoch of art which had vanished completely from human sight."—H. V. HILPRECHT.

"The more I investigate Semitic antiquity, the more I am impressed with the utter baselessness of the view of Wellhausen."—FR. HOMMEL.

"The result is sufficiently surprising; Meyer himself does not conceal the fact. The documents preserved in the Books of Ezra and Nehemiah are (substantially) genuine official documents, and the chronology of the Chronicles is correct in every particular."—Prof. A. R. S. KENNEDY, on Ed. Meyer.

"The systematic historical description, the account of the wanderings which is as exact geographically as it is historically, and in which we find a number of small details that would have been valueless and unknown to later writers, and above all else the accurate dating by the sacred lunar periods of an early age, appear to demand as their original basis the existence of written documents contemporaneous with Moses himself."—Dr. DITLEF NIELSON (Danish archæologist).

CHAPTER XI

ARCHÆOLOGY AND THE OLD TESTAMENT

In the Wellhausen school, as we have seen, literary criticism of the Old Testament came under the control of the history of religion and institutions; contemporaneously, however, with the development of this school, a new claimant to be heard has put in its voice in the science of archæology, which bids fair, before long, to control both criticism and history. It is its witness we are now to hear.

I. GENERAL BEARINGS OF MODERN ARCHÆOLOGICAL DISCOVERY

Nothing in the whole course of last century is more remarkable than the recovery of the knowledge of ancient civilisations through the labours of explorers and the successful decipherment of old inscriptions. The early part of the century witnessed the recovery of the key to the ancient Egyptian hieroglyphics, and the middle and close of the century saw the triumph of skill in penetrating to the secret of that equally strange and difficult system of writing —the cuneiform.[1] When in the palace of Assurbanipal at Nineveh, brought to light by Sir Henry Layard,[2] syllabaries and other aids to the knowledge of the language were obtained, rapid progress in the decipherment was assured. Scholars are now struggling with imperfect means to wrest their meaning from the puzzling characters on the Hittite monuments. Excavations in Crete are yielding new surprises, and carrying knowledge back to a

---

[1] For a full and readable account of these decipherments see Vigouroux's *La Bible et les Découvertes Modernes*, i. pp. 115–69 ; cf. Sayce, *Fresh Light from Ancient Monuments*, chap. i. ; Hilprecht's *Explorations*, pp. 23 ff., 629 ff. etc.

[2] See below, p. 399.

civilisation in its bloom in the second millennium before Christ.[1]

Such discovery might conceivably have taken place, and abundant light have been thrown on the arts, language, institutions, and religions of such lost civilisations as those of Babylonia, Assyria, and Egypt, and yet little direct illumination have been shed on the Bible. It must be accounted a wonderful providence of God that, at a time when so much is being said and done to discredit the Old Testament, so marvellous a series of discoveries, bearing directly on matters contained in its pages, should have been made. Few, indeed, who have not given the matter special study, have any idea of how extensive are the points of contact between these explorations and the Bible, and how manifold are the corroborations of Scripture which they afford. In this as in every new study, of course, there has been much to unlearn as well as to learn. Many rash theories and baseless conjectures have been propounded, and not a few supports sought for the Bible have proved to be illusory. But the area of positive knowledge has always been widening, and there is to-day a mass of material available for the illustration and confirmation of Holy Scripture for which we cannot be sufficiently grateful.

Attempts are made, indeed, to minimise this signal contribution of archæology to faith, and to turn its material to uses hostile, rather than helpful, to revealed religion. Already a great change can be perceived in the attitude and tactics of rationalistic critics in relation to these discoveries. Formerly Israel was looked upon as a people belonging to the dim dawn of history, at a period when, except in Egypt, civilisation had hardly begun. It was possible then to argue that the art of writing did not exist among the Hebrews, and that they had not the capacity for the exalted religious ideas which the narratives of their early history imply. Moses could not have given the laws, nor David have written the psalms, which the history ascribes to them. This contention is now rendered impossible by the discovery of the extraordinary light of civilisation which shone in the Tigro-Euphrates valley, and in the valley of the Nile, millenniums before Abraham left Ur of the Chaldees, or Moses led his people out of Egypt. The

[1] See *The Quarterly Review*, Oct. 1904, pp. 374 ff.

transformation of opinion is revolutionary.[1] The entire perspective is altered, and it is felt that Israel is now rather to be regarded as a people on whom the ends of the earth had come in respect of civilisation. The world was already old in the times of Jacob and Moses, and the tendency is now to see in the religious ideas and institutions of Israel an inheritance from Babylonia, and to bring in Babylonian influences at the beginning of Israel's history, rather than at its close. The gain is appreciable in the breaking up of older critical theories, but the attempt to ignore the distinctive features of the Biblical religion, and to resolve the latter into a simple compound of the ideas of other religions,[2] is bound to fail, and is being met with an effective protest from critical scholars themselves.[3]

Unquestionably the most remarkable result that has accrued from the discoveries in Egypt, Babylonia, and Assyria, has been, as just said, the astonishing revolution wrought in our views of the character and literary capabilities of the most ancient civilisations. It had long been known that Egypt was a literary country as early as, and far earlier than, the time of Moses. Now that the books and monuments of that ancient people have been disinterred, and the writing on them made intelligible, our wonder is tenfold increased at the brilliance of their civilisation as far back as the days of their earliest kings.[4] Still more astonishing is

---

[1] The effect has been most marked on archæologists themselves. Sayce, Hommel, Halévy, all formerly advocates of the critical view, have abandoned it. Dr. Driver having stated that Hommel agreed with Wellhausen's analysis of the Pentateuch (*Expos. Times*, Dec. 1896), Hommel replied (to the late Professor Green) that the citation was from an earlier publication, and that he no longer held these views, but was increasingly impressed with "the utter baselessness" of the view of Wellhausen. It has been the same with Professor Sayce. Halévy, at a meeting of the International Congress at Paris in 1897, made a strong defence of the essential truth of the Mosaic history, as against the Wellhausen school, with which he had been identified.

[2] Thus Fried. Delitzsch, *Babel und Bibel*; Winckler, etc.

[3] Cf. Budde, *Das Alte Testament und Die Ausgrabungen* (against Winckler); Gunkel, *Israel und Babylonien* (against Fried. Delitzsch); and the abundant literature called forth in the "Babel and Bible" controversy (see below, p. 409).

[4] See below, p. 418. The oldest known MS. in existence (dating from twelfth dynasty) is that of the "Precepts of Ptah-hotep," a classical Egyptian work of the fifth dynasty (c. 3000 B.C.). Ptah-hotep lived under King Assa, was himself of royal descent (Brugsch thinks "the son of the king"), and was very old when he wrote, but he appeals to the ancients. Brugsch, *Hist. of Egypt*, i. pp. 92 ff.; Renouf, *Religion of Egypt*, pp. 75, 100, etc.

the light cast by the monuments on the condition of ancient Babylonia. Here, in the Hammurabi age—which is that of Abraham—and long before, we find ourselves in the midst of cities, books, and libraries; of letters, arts, and laws, in a high state of development; of a people among whom not only a knowledge of letters existed, but a taste for books and reading was widely diffused[1]—in short of a highly advanced and capable literary people. Babylonia had by this time its dynasties of great kings, some of whom were distinguished as founders of libraries and patrons of letters. Sargon I., *e.g.*, whose date is usually put at 3800 B.C., founded a famous library at Accad. The French excavator De Sarzec brought to light a few years since (1893–5) the remains of a great library (30,000 tablets) at Tello, in S. Babylonia, which already existed in the reign of Gudea, about 2700 B.C.[2] More recently the Pennsylvania explorers have disinterred the temple library at Nippur, the ancient Calneh. Not only so, but in excavating the foundations of the temple, they came on the abundant remains of an older civilisation, which, from the depth at which the relics were found—25 to 35 feet below the pavement of Sargon I. and Naram-Sin—must, it is thought, be as old as 6000 or 7000 years B.C.[3] Even if less time should suffice, their antiquity is still immensely remote.

It is beyond our province to enter minutely into what may be called the romance of the rediscovery of ancient Nineveh and Babylon; but one illustration may bring out how from the first light has been shed on the Bible by exploration. In 1843, Emil Botta, French Consul in the district, struck into the mounds of Khorsabad, a little to the north of Nineveh, and soon, to his own surprise, was standing in the midst of an immense palace, which proved to be that of Sargon, the conqueror of Samaria. This was a remarkable discovery. In Isa. xx. 1, we read that "Sargon, king of

[1] It has been argued that reading and writing were probably confined to the upper and official classes. The extent and variety of the literature, the fact of published laws, and the use of writing in business (banking accounts, etc.), above all, the lesson and exercise books of young pupils, point to a different conclusion; cf. Hilprecht, *Explorations*, p. 405 : "found them to be the school exercises of a Babylonian child living in the fifth pre-Christian millennium" (at Nippur); pp. 525 ff.

[2] Some of these tablets are older than 4000 B.C.; cf. Hilprecht, *Explorations*, p. 249.

[3] Cf. Hilprecht, pp. 391 ff., 542 ff.; Peters, *Nippur*, ii. pp. 246 ff.

Assyria, sent his Tartan (or commander-in-chief) to besiege Ashdod." But who was Sargon ? This is the only place in which his name occurs in Scripture, or in all literature. Ancient writers knew nothing of him. He was a mystery : some did not hesitate to deny that he ever existed. Yet the first important discovery made was the palace of this very Sargon.[1] It contained his name and portrait; its walls were covered with his sculptures and inscriptions. Sargon, after being forgotten for twenty-five centuries, is now again one of the best known kings of Assyria. He was the father of Sennacherib. His annals recount the siege of Ashdod mentioned in Isaiah. This first discovery was followed by others not less brilliant. In 1847 Mr. Layard began work at the mounds of Nimroud and Kouyunjik—the site of Nineveh itself. At the former place he unearthed four large palaces, and at the latter, the palace of Sennacherib, rebuilt by his grandson Assurbanipal, in the *débris* of which were found the remains of the richly-stored library already referred to.[2]

II. BABYLONIAN LEGENDS AND THE EARLY CHAPTERS OF GENESIS

Beginning with the *origins*, a first question we naturally ask is—Do the early chapters of Genesis really preserve for us the oldest traditions of our race ? There are two reasons entitling us to look with some confidence for an answer to this question to Babylonia. The first is, that in Babylonia we are already far back into the times to which these traditions relate; and the second is, that these traditions themselves point to Babylonia as their seat and centre. Eden was in Babylonia, as shown by its rivers Euphrates and Tigris; the land of Nod, to which Cain and his posterity betook themselves, was to the east of Babylonia;[3] the ark was built in Babylonia, and it was on one of the mountains N. or N.E. of Babylonia that it ultimately rested; from the plain of Shinar (Sumir) in Babylonia was the earth repeopled. If, therefore, the oldest traditions of

[1] Cf. George Smith, *Assyrian Discoveries*, pp. 2 ff. ; Hilprecht, *Explorations*, pp. 76, 84 ff.
[2] *Assyrian Discoveries*, pp. 4, 101, 144 ff., 418, 452; Hilprecht, pp. 104 ff.
[3] Gen. iv. 16.

the race lingered anywhere, it should be in Babylonia. And now that we have in our hands the records of that ancient people, dating back to very early times, it is possible to compare the Bible traditions with them, and see how far they correspond. It may be claimed that the tablets and inscriptions which have been deciphered *do* show that the first chapters of Genesis are indeed what we have assumed them to be—a record of the very oldest traditions of our race. We shall look first at the facts, then at the explanation.

1. Though out of chronological order, we may begin with a statement in that old and much-discussed chapter in Genesis—*the account in chap. x. of the divisions of men* after the flood. This " table of nations," as it is called, we look on as one of the oldest and most precious documents of its kind in existence.[1] In vers. 8–12 of this chapter we read : " Cush begat Nimrod : he began to be a mighty one in the earth. . . . And the beginning of his kingdom was Babel, and Erech, and Accad, and Calneh, in the land of Shinar. Out of that land he went forth into Assyria [or, went forth Asshur] and builded Nineveh, and Rehoboth-Ir, and Calah, and Resen between Nineveh and Calah : the same is the great city." The very names of these cities take us back into the midst of the ancient Babylonia unearthed by exploration. But more particularly, the passage makes three statements of the first importance. It affirms (1) that Babel and the other cities named existed before Nineveh ; (2) that Assyria was colonised from Babylonia ; and (3) that the founder of Babylonian civilisation was not a Semite, but a Cushite—a descendant of Ham.[2] Each of these statements, till the time of the Assyrian discoveries, was confidently disputed. The received tradition put Nineveh before Babylon,[3] and the Babylonians, like the Assyrians, were held to be Semites. The monuments, however, confirm the Bible in all three points.[4] It is no longer

---

[1] Kautzsch says : "The so-called table of nations remains, according to all results of monumental exploration, an ethnographic original document of the first rank, which nothing can replace."—*Die Bleibende Bedeutung des Alttestaments*, p. 17. On critical questions, see above, p. 351.
[2] Cf. G. Rawlinson, *Hist. Illustrations of the O.T.*, pp. 29 ff.
[3] The authority for this was the fable of Semiramis in Ctesias, reported by Diodorus Siculus (ii. 1-20).
[4] Cf. Schrader, *Cun. Inscripts.* i. p. 76, on Gen. x. 10 : "This coincides

questioned that the Babylonian kingdoms were the older [1]
—the antiquity ascribed to some of their cities (*e.g.*, to
Nippur = Calneh) is almost fabulous. It is no longer
doubted that Assyrian civilisation was derived from
Babylonia.[2] Strangest of all, it is now known (for though
there are rival theories, we state correctly the prevailing
view),[3] that the founders of the Babylonian civilisation, the
inventors of its alphabet, laws, arts, the founders of its
libraries, were not Semites, but people of a different
stock—Turanian or Hamitic (the Accadians).[4]

Another instance may be given from this chapter. In
ver. 22 Elam is mentioned as the oldest son of Shem. But
the Elam of history was not Semitic, but Aryan. On the
ground of its language even Hommel wrote recently : "The
Elam mentioned here as one of the sons of Shem cannot

with all that we otherwise know respecting the relation of Assyria to
Babylonia," etc.

[1] The first Babylonian *dynasty*, that to which Hammurabi belonged,
began about 2200 B.C. (some date it a century or two earlier), but the *city*
of Babel is of unknown antiquity. A recent writer says : " The oldest
history of Babylon is still unknown. . . . It is certain that Sargon
(3800 B.C.) raised Babylon to a leading position. From this time Babylon
forms with Borsippa a double city." — Jeremias, *Das A. T. im Lichte des
alten. Orients.* p. 160. The antiquity of Erech, Accad, Calneh, is very
great. Inscriptions of kings of Erech, Lagash, and other places, were
found at Nippur of a date as early as 4000 B.C. (Peters, *Nippur,* ii.
p. 160).

[2] The Assyrian Nineveh (for there seems to have been a Babylonian city
of the same name) is likewise old. An inscription of Dungi, the second
king of Ur (*c.* 2700 B.C.), has been found in it (Jeremias, p. 165). Cf.
McCurdy, *History, Prophecy, and the Monuments,* i. p. 63 : " Before the
union [of Babylonian kingdoms] was effected, emigrants from among those
Babylonians settled along the Middle Tigris, founded the city of Asshur,
and later still the group of cities known to history as Nineveh."

[3] See for counter view, art. " Accad," in *Dict. of Bible,* i. p. 21, with
qualifying editorial note.

[4] Gunkel says : " But the centre of the Orient is Babylonia : there from
an unthought-of antiquity has flourished an amazingly high culture, which
already about 3000 B.C. stands in full bloom : this culture originates from a
non-Semitic people, whom we name Sumerian, and is then taken over and
carried forward by Semitic emigrants." — *Israel und Babylonien,* p. 6.
(Continental scholars generally speak of " Sumerian," English writers of
" Accadian.")

Pinches says : " During the period immediately preceding that of the
dynasty of Babylon there is a gap in the list of kings, which fresh excavations alone can fill up. Before this gap, the records, so far as we know
them, are in the Akkadian language. After this gap they are in the
Semitic-Babylonian tongue."—*O.T. in Light of Hist. Records,* etc., p. 152.
See now, however, Jeremias on the discoveries at Lagash and Nippur
(p. 2).

26

possibly be identical with Elam proper."[1] The work of exploration of the French expedition at Susa, the capital of Elam, has, however, resulted in the remarkable discovery of a civilisation older than any yet known in this region. More striking still, it is found that the inscriptions on the oldest bricks are written in cuneiform characters, and not in the language of later Elam, but either in Semitic Babylonian, or in Accadian. Thus Elam is proved to be, after all, "the son of Shem."[2]

A still wider result from these explorations, in their bearings on our subject, is the growing conviction that "the plain of Shinar" (chap. xi.), or Southern Babylonia, was really the centre of distribution of the families of mankind. Babylonian civilisation is carried back by the discoveries at Nippur to a period so much earlier than that of any other known civilisation, that the inference seems irresistible that it is the source from which these other civilisations are derived. It has been seen that this is true of Assyria. It is beginning to be assumed by leading Egyptologists that the same is true of Egypt.[3] Learned books have been written to show that it is true of China.[4] Probably it will be found to be true of Crete, etc. The Biblical account of these matters, in short, is found to rest on far older and more accurate information than that possessed by any scholars prior to the new discoveries.

2. The stories of the *Creation* and the *Flood* in Genesis have been so often compared with the corresponding Babylonian legends that it is hardly necessary to bestow much space upon them. Among the tablets found in Assurbanipal's palace were some which proved on examination to contain

---

[1] *Ancient Heb. Tradition*, p. 294.

[2] Dr. Driver says in his *Genesis, in loc.* : " It is true inscriptions recently discovered seem to have shown that in very early times Elam was peopled by Semites . . . but the fact is not one which the writer of this verse is likely to have known " (p. 128). The curious fact is, however, that he *did* know it, while modern scholars did not. Is it not more likely that Dr. Driver's theory of the writer's age, and of the extent of his knowledge, is wrong ?

For further illustration, see Note A on Ethnological Relations in Gen. x.

[3] Cf. art. "Egypt," in *Dict. of Bible* i. p. 656 ; Budge, *Hist. of Egypt*, i. pp. 39–43 ; Sayce, *Early Israel*, p. 155 ; Nicol, *Recent Archæology and the Bible*, pp. 92, 319 ; art. in New York *Independent* (1897) on discoveries and views of De Sarzec, Mauss, etc.

[4] See an interesting article in *Quarterly Review*, July, 1882 ; Boscawen, *Chambers's Journal*, July 1896 ; C. J. Ball, in Pinches, p. 121.

an account of creation, resembling in certain of its features
the narrative in Gen. i. The contrasts, indeed, are much
more apparent than the likeness.[1] The Babylonian story is
debased throughout by polytheism — begins, in fact, by
recounting the birth of the great gods from the chaotic
ocean. This is followed by a long mythological description,
abounding in repetition, of the war of Merodach (god of
light) with Tiamat (the primeval ocean), the conflict issuing
in the woman being cut in two, and heaven being formed
of one half, and earth of the other. The order of the
creative works, however, seems to bear some resemblance to
that in Gen. i. The fifth tablet narrates the appointing of
the constellations, and another fragment the making of the
animals. A trace of an older conception may, perhaps, be
discerned in the fact that in the latter (if it really belongs
to the same series, which is doubtful) the work of creation
is ascribed, not to Merodach, but to "all the gods" together,
thus :

> " When all the gods had made (the world),
> Had created the heavens, had formed (the earth),
> Had brought forth living creatures into being,
> The cattle of the field, the (beasts) of the field, and
> The creeping things (of the field)."[2]

Inscriptions show that both Babylonians and Assyrians
had a species of seventh-day sabbath. The word *sabattu*
itself occurs, and is defined as " a day of rest for the heart." [3]
It differed, however, from the Jewish sabbath, in that the
reckoning began afresh each month—7th, 14th, 21st, 28th,—
while the Jewish went on consecutively. On it ordinary
works were prohibited, at least to king and high officials.[4]

---

[1] These are acknowledged by nearly every writer. Gunkel says : " Anyone who compares this ancient Babylonian myth with Gen. i. will perceive
at first hardly anything else than the infinite distance between them ; there,
the heathen gods, inflamed against each other in wild warfare, here the One,
who speaks and it is done."—*Israel und Babylonien*, p. 24 ; cf. *Genesis*, pp.
113, 118 ; Oettli, *Der Kampf um Bibel und Babel*, pp. 9 ff. There is
another ancient Babylonian legend of creation which has greater affinity to
the Jehovistic account in Genesis (chap. ii.). Cf. Pinches, as above, pp.
39 ff. etc.

[2] King, *Bab. Religion*, p. 81.

[3] It seems forced, despite parallels, to explain this as a day when the *gods*
rested from anger, *i.e.*, a day of propitiation (Jastrow, Driver, etc.).

[4] Difficulties arise from the fact that the word *sabattu* is not expressly
applied to the seventh days, and that the prohibitions of work mention
only king, augur, physician. There seems little doubt, however, that

Abundant material exists for the illustration of the narrative of Paradise. On the other hand, no clear account of the fall of man has yet been recovered. But that the Babylonians had some story resembling that in Gen. iii. is rendered probable by the representation on an ancient seal in which a man and a woman are depicted as seated on either side of a tree, and reaching out their hands to pluck the fruit, while behind the woman a serpent rears itself, and appears to whisper in her ear. Scholars are divided in opinion as to the identification;[1] but to most people the picture will seem to speak for itself.

No doubt, at least, can rest on the parallelism between the Biblical and the Babylonian stories of the *Deluge*. The Babylonian story, inserted as an episode in a longer epic poem, must be older than the latter; we may safely place it as early as 3000 B.C. Though defaced, like the creation story, by a gross polytheism,[2] it presents in its general structure, and in many of its details, a striking resemblance to the account in Genesis. It relates, in brief, how the Babylonian Noah[3] was commanded to build a ship for

the above-mentioned days, with some others, fall under the category of "sabbaths," and possibly the prohibition of work is intended to be general. Cf. Gunkel, *Genesis*, pp. 106 ff. ; *Israel und Bab.* pp. 27, 28 ; Jeremias, as above, pp. 86 ff. ; Driver, *Genesis*, p. 34, and art. "Sabbath" in *Dict. of Bible*, iv. p. 319 ; Schrader, Sayce, etc. Gunkel says : "Name and institution of the sabbath are quite surely of Babylonian origin" (p. 108). The narrative in Exodus assumes the sabbath to be already known to the Israelites (Ex. xvi. 22-30) ; and in Gen. ii. 3 ; Ex. xx. 11, its appointment is traced back to the creation. [See Note at end of Chapter.]

[1] The male figure is horned, which some take to be a sign of divinity ; but this is questioned. Cf. Pinches, as above, p. 79. Schrader, Budde, Kittel, Gunkel, Jeremias, Driver, etc., declare the interpretation doubtful. G. Smith, Sayce, F. Delitzsch, and many others, uphold it.

[2] The contrast is again emphasised by Gunkel, as by other writers. Gunkel says : "The polytheism which obtrudes itself in the Babylonian tradition in the strongest way has in the Israelitish wholly disappeared. 'The gods of the Babylonian story are genuinely heathenish in their lying and sanction of lying, in their greed at the sacrifice, in their actions, in their caprice, in their dealings with men, and in the alternation of their humours. How far removed from this is the God who permits a judgment to come on men in His righteousness, who must justify Himself to man's conscience !' (Holzinger). The last point is specially very important ; of the profound knowledge of sin with which the Hebrew bows before God there is not a trace in the Babylonian story."—*Genesis*, p. 66.

[3] The name is variously given as Par-napishtim, Pir-napistim, Ut-napishtim, or in its Greek form Xisuthros. The last is a form of the name Atra-hasis (= very clever), also given to the hero. The full account may be seen in Sayce (*Higher Criticism*, and *Early Israel*) ; Pinches, as above ; Driver's *Genesis*, pp. 104-6, etc.

the saving of himself and of the seed of life of every sort; how, when the ship was built and smeared with bitumen, he took into it his household and the animals (the sun-god Samas commands: "Enter into thy ship, and close thy door"); how the flood came and destroyed mankind; how the ship rested on the mountain Nizir (E. of Tigris); how after seven days he sent forth in succession a dove, a *swallow*, and a raven, the last of which did not return; how he then sent forth the animals, and offered a sacrifice, to which the gods "gathered like flies"; how the bow was set in the heaven (?), etc. The hero is ultimately, like Enoch, translated to the abode of the gods without dying. It was before mentioned that the parallel with the Babylonian story requires for its completeness *both* the Elohistic and the Jehovistic narratives in Genesis—a fact with important bearings on the critical analysis.[1]

3. There can be no dispute, therefore, as to the close relationship of the old Babylonian traditions with the early narratives in Genesis,[2] the question which remains is, How are these similarities to be explained?

(1) The favourite hypothesis in critical circles up to the present is that of *borrowing* on the part of the Israelites from the Babylonians; and, as the Babylonians are undeniably the older people, this view may seem to have much to commend it. The Biblical writers, it is thought, or, before them, the nation, adopted the legends in question, purifying them, perhaps gradually, from polytheistic elements, and making them the vehicles of the purer ideas of their own religion. Then the further question arises—At what period did this borrowing take place? and here we encounter wide divergences of opinion. In accordance with the date they assign to the Priestly Writing, the tendency in the Wellhausen school is to represent it as taking place in the exile, or later.[3] To this view, however, an increasing band of scholars, largely influenced by archæology, raise objections which seem in-

[1] See above, p. 348.

[2] Cheyne says that " a particular critical theory, viz., that the narrative in Gen. i. is the product of the reflection of a late priestly writer, is no doubt refuted." (He refers to Wellhausen, *Hist. of Israel*, p. 298.)—Oxford *Hexateuch*, i. p. 165.

[3] Gunkel says: "It suits the peculiar tendency of modern Old Testament science to place this borrowing, assuming it conceded, as late as possible."—*Genesis*, p. 117.

superable.[1] How extremely improbable that any Israelite,
of the time of the exile, should dream of taking over these
grossly polytheistic stories from a heathen people, and of
placing them, in purified form, in the forefront of his Book
of the Law![2] The purification itself, assuming it to have
taken place, is not so easy a task as is supposed, and can
only be thought of as a long process.[3] The same objection,
nearly, applies to the borrowing of the Babylonian myths
in the age of Ahaz, or in the reign of Solomon. A new vista
of possibility, however, opens itself with the Tel el-Amarna
discoveries—on which more below—which show Canaan
to have been, in the fifteenth century B.C., penetrated with
Babylonian influences and culture. May we not assume
that the Israelites borrowed these legends, with other
elements of their civilisation, from the Canaanites, after
they had come into possession of the land?[4] To anyone
who retains the least faith in the Biblical picture of the
Mosaic age, or of the relations of the Israelites and
Canaanites after the conquest, the improbability of such
borrowing will appear as great as in the exilian theory.
This is the difficulty of the "process"—how is it to get a
start? For at some point the legends must have been
taken over in their grossly polytheistic form: nay, must
long have retained that form in the bosom of Jehovah-
worshipping Israel.[5] Is this likely, or is there any proof

[1] Thus Schrader, Gunkel, Winckler, Zimmern, Oettli, Kittel, etc.

[2] Cf. Gunkel, *Genesis*, p. 117.

[3] *Ibid.* p. 118 : "The two recensions (of the creation story) are so
immensely different, that we must necessarily assume a long history and a
great length of time for the mythological so entirely to vanish and the
Babylonian to become so completely Israelitised." Kittel says : "There can
be no question that such a rejection or complete transformation of mythological ideas would involve a far more pregnant and original act of genius
than that involved in their first conception."—*Bib. Excavs.* p. 45. Cf. Driver,
Authority and Archæology, p. 15 : "It is incredible that the monotheistic
author of Gen. i., at whatever date he lived, could have borrowed any detail,
however slight, from the crassly polytheistic epic of the conflict of Marduk
and Tiamat : the Babylonian myth must have been for long years transplanted into Israel, it must there have been gradually divested of its
polytheistic features," etc.

[4] This is the view favoured by Gunkel (*Genesis*, pp. 68, 118), Sayce,
Winckler, etc.

[5] Dr. Driver truly says that this view "is consistent only with a critical
theory of the authorship of the Pentateuch, not with the traditional view,"
for that Moses, who "set his face sternly and consistently against all intercourse with the Canaanites, and all compromises with polytheism, should
have gone to Canaan for his cosmogony, is in the last degree improbable"

of it ? There is one other possibility—that the Hebrews brought these traditions with them in their original migration from Ur of the Chaldees.[1] But once this is admitted, we come in sight of an alternative hypothesis, on which something will immediately be said.

An objection urged to this view of the antiquity of the Biblical traditions is the absence of all allusions to them in the pre-exilian writings. " With regard both to the Creation and to the Deluge stories," says Dr. Cheyne, " if they were in circulation in early pre-exilic times, it is difficult to understand the absence of any direct allusion to them in the undoubted pre-exilic writings."[2] This is once more the argument from silence, so often shown to be inconclusive.[3] But the argument in this case proves too much : the silence, besides, is not so complete as the objection represents. The Deluge is part of the Jehovistic story, which most critics place in the ninth or eighth century B.C. It is referred to also, as before shown,[4] in Isa. liv. 9, in a way which implies pre-exilian knowledge. The creation narrative, again, forms the basis of the Fourth Commandment in Ex. xx. 11 ; seems alluded to in Deut. iv. 32 ; and is the foundation of Pss. viii. and civ. To put all these references and psalms late *because* Gen. i. is assumed to be post-exilian, is to beg the question.

(2) We do not say that the hypothesis of the borrowing of Babylonian myths, and of their purification by the spirit

---

(*Authority and Archæology*, p. 16). But putting traditional views aside, does Dr. Driver think that the Mosaic religion at *any* time sanctioned intercourse with the Canaanites or "compromises with polytheism"? If not, what becomes of his own view that "the cosmogony of Gen. i. presupposes a long period of naturalisation in Israel, during which the old legend was stripped of its pagan deformities" (p. 17). How was the naturalisation of the pagan myth effected?

[1] This is the view of Schrader and others. (See below). "I am led," says this scholar, "to the obvious conclusion that the Hebrews were acquainted with this [flood] legend at a much earlier period, and that it is far from impossible that they acquired a knowledge of these and the other primitive myths now under investigation as far back as in the time of their primitive settlements in Babylonia, and that they carried these stories with them from Ur of the Chaldees."—*Cuneiform Inscriptions*, i. p. 54.

[2] Oxf. *Hexateuch*, p. 166 : so F. Delitzsch and others.

[3] Gunkel says : "That the legend of the flood is mentioned so late in the part of the literature preserved to us proves nothing at all."—*Genesis*, p. 67.

[4] See above, p. 374.

of revelation in Israel, in such wise that they become the vehicles of higher teaching, is abstractly inadmissible; but we do not think it is the conclusion which most naturally follows from the comparison of the Biblical and Babylonian stories. The former, it is allowed, possess a character of sobriety, monotheistic elevation, and purity of religious and ethical conception, altogether absent from the latter; the contrasts vastly overbear the resemblances; and it is hard to understand how, from legends so debased, and foreign to the whole genius of the Israelitish religion, could arise the noble products of a purer faith which we have in our Bible.[1] The differences are so great as to lead many scholars to seek the explanation of the resemblance along another line altogether—in a relation of *cognateness*, rather than one of *derivation*.[2] On this view, the Biblical stories are not late and purified versions of the Babylonian, but represent an independent related version, going back to a common origin with the Babylonian, but preserving their monotheistic character in the line of revelation, when the others had long sunk under the corrupting influences of polytheism. Or, if purification is to be spoken of, it is purification on the basis of an older and less debased tradition. Such a view harmonises with the Bible's own postulate that the light of a true knowledge of God has never been wholly extinguished among men, and that from the first there has been a line of pious worshippers, a seed of blessing and promise, on the earth.

(3) In the discussions which have arisen on the connection of Israel with Babylonia, it is not surprising that attention should latterly have become focussed on the question of how far the old Babylonian religion, among its other elements, included a monotheistic strain, and whether it is from this source that Israel derived its monotheistic conception. This is the question peculiarly agitated in what—from the title of the lecture of Fried. Delitzsch which inaugurated it

---

[1] "These differences," says Kittel, "show that we are on entirely different ground, and that even in instances where the words may be the same, another and altogether different spirit breathes in them. We are in a sphere differing *toto cœlo* from that of Babylon—it is quite a different world; there it is the sphere of a heathen nature-worship, with all its concomitants, here it is that of a revealed and monotheistic religion."—*Bib. Excavs.* p. 42.

[2] Thus Dillmann, Kittel, Hommel, Oettli, etc. See their views in Note B on the Cognateness of Babylonian and Hebrew Traditions.

—has been called the "Babel and Bible" controversy.[1] The truth, it seems to us, lies midway between those who affirm, and those who deny, a monotheistic substratum in the Babylonian religion.[2] That Israel borrowed its idea of the one God from this source is another matter. The name JA'U — corresponding with Yahweh — may or may not be found, as alleged, on tablets of the Hammurabi age. Reading and meaning of the inscriptions are still under discussion.[3] But this, though interesting in its bearings on the age of the name, proves nothing as to its Babylonian origin. F. Delitzsch himself does not take it to be a *native* Babylonian name of God.[4]

III. THE ABRAHAMIC AGE—THE CHEDORLAOMER EXPEDITION

Archæology throws new and valuable light upon the patriarchal age. The patriarchs themselves, whom it was proposed to resolve into tribal personifications, are found to bear personal names with which their age was perfectly familiar. A name Abe-ramu, almost the same as Abraham, appears on a contract-tablet of the second reign before Hammurabi.[5] Other contract-tablets of that age exhibit

[1] Fried. Delitzsch in this lecture argues that Israel owes its monotheistic conception, and the name Yahweh, to Babylonia.—*Babel und Bibel*, pp. 59 ff.

[2] See above, p. 128. Winckler does not inexactly express the matter when he says: "The character of the Babylonian religion reveals itself at the first glance. It is a star-religion—moon, sun, and stars play in it the chief *rôle*. But it would be to mistake its essence to suppose that in the doctrine the heavenly bodies were the Godhead itself. The stars are rather in the Babylonian doctrine only the chiefest revelation of the divine Power ; that revelation in which its rule and designs can be most clearly observed. For the rest, all being, all that is visible or invisible, is in the same way an emanation or part of the divine essence. There are many, nay numberless gods ; but they are only revelation-forms of the one great divine might," etc.—*Die Babylon. Kultur*, p. 19 (slightly abridged).

[3] F. Delitzsch, Hommel, Sayce, Pinches, etc., uphold the reading ; König (*Bibel und Babel*, pp. 45 ff.) contests it ; Jeremias (*Das A.T. im Lichte des Alt. Orients*, p. 211) agrees with Hommel. Zimmern, and most others, as Budde, Gunkel, Oettli, Kittel, either reject the reading, or regard it as extremely questionable.

[4] Driver also says : "The names [viz., those containing this element] are not Babylonian, and must therefore have belonged to foreigners—whether Canaanites, or ancestors of the Hebrews."—*Genesis*, p. xlix.

[5] Cf. Pinches, *O.T. in Light of Hist. Records*, p. 148. Abu-ramu (Abram) was the name of an Assyrian official in the reign of Esarhaddon (*ibid.*). It may be noticed that "the field of Abram" has been deciphered on a monument of Shishak (Pal. Explor. *Quart. Statement*, Jan. 1905, p. 7).

the names Jacob and Jacob-el.[1] The names Jacob-el and Joseph-el appear on a monument of Thothmes III. of Egypt (about 1500 B.C.) as place-names in Palestine. In other ways the whole period has been lifted up into new and commanding importance. It is generally accepted that the Hammurabi of the inscriptions is no other than the Amraphel of Gen. xiv. 1; and the discovery of the Code of this able ruler has given his name an *éclat* it can never again lose.[2] The discovery was made at Susa in Jan. 1902, and the Code itself, the most complete and finished of any in antiquity, shows the height of civilisation to which the Babylonia of Abraham's day had attained.[3] The discovery bears directly on the possibility of such codes of law as we find attributed to Moses in the Pentateuch—*e.g.*, the Code in the Book of the Covenant,—and particular provisions prove the minute fidelity with which the patriarchal history reflects the customs of that early time. Such, as formerly shown,[4] is the law providing that the childless wife may give her maid to be a concubine; and directing what is to be done should the woman afterwards have a dispute with her mistress because she has borne children![5]

One of the most striking instances of the confirmation of the historical accuracy of the patriarchal narratives is that connected with the expedition of Chedorlaomer in Gen. xiv. The events recorded in this chapter are very remote, going back, most probably, to about 2100 B.C.[6] The

[1] Johns, *Deeds and Documents*, pp. 164, 167. Kittel says: "We now know that in ancient times Jacob was an ordinary personal name, and nothing more."—*Bab. Excavs.* p. 31.

[2] Cf. art. by C. W. H. Johns on "Code of Hammurabi" in *Dict. of Bible* (Extra Vol.); or his *Oldest Code of Laws in the World*. Gunkel says: "And this law was codified about 2200 B.C.; it originates from a time one thousand years before there was any people of Israel. It is removed from Moses as far as we are from Charlemagne!"—*Israel und Bab.* p. 7 (the interval was probably less—see below).

[3] Sayce goes so far as to say that the Babylonia of the age of Abraham "was a more highly educated country than the England of George III."—*Monument Facts*, p. 35.

[4] See above, p. 115.   [5] Cf. *Code*, arts. 145, 146, etc.

[6] On the uncertainties of the chronology, see Hommel, *Ancient Heb. Trad.* pp. 120 ff. Two data are important. An inscription of Assurbanipal states that the conquest of Babylonia by the Elamites happened one thousand six hundred and thirty-five years before his own conquest of Elam, or in 2280 B.C. How long the Elamitic rule lasted we cannot tell, but Chedorlaomer was the last representative of it. More definitely, Nabonidus states that Burnaburias restored the temple of the sun at Larsa seven hundred years after Hammu-

historical relations also are intricate, and in part singular.
They are such as floating tradition could neither have invented nor preserved. It is implied in the story that a
king of Elam, Chedorlaomer (a strange name), at that time
held sovereignty over Babylonia; that, with the vassal
kings, whose names are given, he made an expedition against
Palestine; that a second expedition was undertaken fourteen
years later to crush rebellion. The chapter further tells
how Lot was carried away prisoner, and how Abraham
organised a pursuit, and rescued him. The historical
character of this narrative was widely discredited—as by
Nöldeke.[1] How could a late Israelitish writer possibly
know of such events ? How could such an expedition take
place ? How could such a rescue be effected ? The story
was declared to be a complete fiction. Strange as it is,
however, it has now, as respects its historical framework,
been singularly confirmed. It has been established by
indubitable evidence that Babylonia was at this time under
Elamitic suzerainty; we have even the name and date (c.
2280 B.C.) of the king who overran it. It was found, further,
that the known names of the kings of this Elamitic dynasty
began with the word "Kudur," meaning "servant"—thus
Kudur-Nankhundi, Kudur-Mabug. It was discovered that
there was an Elamitic goddess named "Lagamar," so that
Kudur-Lagamar (Chedorlaomer) was a name of genuine
Elamitic formation. It was found that these kings claimed
sovereignty over "Martu" (the west), or Palestine. It was
ascertained that Kudur-Mabug had a son—Eri-aku (also
called Rim-sin), king of Larsa: there can be little doubt, the
Arioch of Ellasar of this chapter. Amraphel was identified
with Hammurabi.[2] Finally, it was announced that the

rabi. The date of the king referred to (cf. Hommel, art. "Babylonia,"
Dict. of Bible, i. p. 224) is about 1400 B.C., which yields 2100 B.C. for
Hammurabi, the Amraphel of this expedition.

[1] Wellhausen speaks of faith in the historicity of this narrative as having
received its "deathblow" from Nöldeke, and pronounces Nöldeke's
criticism to be "unshaken and unanswerable" (Compos. d. Hex. pp. 311–12).
On earlier attacks on the historicity, see Dillmann, Genesis, ii. pp. 32–33,
and Delitzsch, Genesis, i. pp. 396–98.

[2] For details, reference may be made to Schrader, i. pp. 120 ff. ; and
specially ii. pp. 296 ff.; and to the works of Sayce, Hommel, Pinches,
Driver, Gunkel, Kittel, Jeremias, etc. Gunkel says : "A narrative which
knows how to speak of so many very ancient names and relations makes first
the impression of the highest antiquity. For very ancient also, so far as we
can see, are all the following names (in vers. 1 ff.) : they are almost entirely

name of Chedorlaomer himself had been found on a late inscription. The identification is questioned, and we need not press it; but it is significant that three leading specialists, Dr. Pinches (the discoverer), Professor Hommel, and Professor Sayce, still express themselves satisfied of the correctness of the reading.[1] In any case, it seems abundantly made out that the author of this chapter is not romancing, but writes with a clear knowledge of the historical conditions of the times to which his narrative relates. For the rest, the Tel el-Amarna tablets testify to Uru-Salim as an ancient Canaanitish name for Jerusalem, and even Gunkel is disposed to accept Melchizedek as an historical person.[2]

All this, it is now to be owned, makes not the slightest impression on most of the critics. Even Dr. Driver can write: "*Monumental* evidence that the narrative is historical is at present entirely lacking."[3] It does not matter that the historical setting of the story — even in the points that were formerly challenged—is proved to be surprisingly correct; it is held sufficient to reply that there has not been found on the monuments any direct mention of Abraham and his rescue of Lot. As if this had ever been claimed, or was a reasonable thing to expect. What *is* claimed is, that the writer of this chapter is proved to have his feet on firm historical ground in these remote times; that he knows what he is writing about, and is not romancing; and that, when we find his narrative trustworthy in a multitude of difficult points where we *can* test it, we are entitled to give him credit for like fidelity in the parts we cannot test. This would seem to be the common-sense way of looking at the matter; yet the critics prefer to believe that the chapter is an "unhistorical Midrash" of the time of the exile, or later,

names of peoples and cities which in the time of Israel had long absolutely disappeared, and which the author needs to explain by glosses to his contemporaries."—*Genesis*, p. 256. He combats the post-exilian origin of the story (p. 263).

[1] See their respective works. Professor Sayce, in a personal communication, June 10, 1902, says: "Hommel, Pinches, and myself still adhere to the reading of the name of Chedorlaomer in a tablet discovered by Mr. Pinches."

[2] *Genesis*, pp. 261-62; cf. Jeremias, *ut supra*, p. 218.

[3] *Genesis*, p. 172. Dr. Driver will only go so far as to concede that "the outline of the narrative may still be historical." Cf. also *Authority and Archæology*, pp. 44, 45.

drawn up by someone who had chanced to fall in with a fragment of old Babylonian history, and pleased himself by weaving into it these traditions or fables of Abraham and Lot![1] How interesting the combination of accurate archæologist and romancing fabulist which this theory presents!— a theory for which, we are justified in affirming, there is *no evidence whatever*, and which is opposed to every consideration of probability. One feels, in reading the narrative, that it is of a piece throughout in its archaic character, and must be taken as a whole, or left as a whole.[2] As Hommel well remarks: " Even assuming Gen. xiv. to be nothing more than a very late narrative of a Midrash character, belonging to post-exilic times, how came its author to introduce into it a whole host of ancient phrases and names, to which he himself is obliged to add explanatory glosses, in order that they may be better understood ? . . . Are we to assume that he did this intentionally in order to invest his story with an air of greater antiquity ? In that case, all we can say is, that no similar example of literary *finesse* can be found throughout the whole of the Old Testament."[3] It need not be added that many critics of more positive tendency put much greater value on the narrative, and ably defend its historicity.[4]

IV. JOSEPH IN EGYPT

With Abraham first, and afterwards with Joseph, the patriarchal history quits Canaan, and transports us into the midst of Egypt. Abraham went down to Egypt to escape famine, and was there received with honour by the reigning Pharaoh;[5] but it is with the history of Joseph that we pass definitely into the full blaze of Egyptian civilisation. On the remarkable fidelity of the Egyptian

[1] See Note C on the Alleged Midrash character of Gen. xiv.

[2] Kuenen, who holds the chapter to be a post-exilian Midrash, still allows that "the story is in its proper place, for it presupposes Lot's separation from Abram, and his settlement in Sodom."—*Hex.* p. 143 (cf. p. 324).

[3] *Ancient Heb. Trad.* pp. 163–64.

[4] See the defence of the historicity in Dillmann, *Genesis*, ii. pp. 32–33. Delitzsch, i. pp. 396–98 ; Kittel, *Hist. of Hebrews*, i. pp. 175 ff. (with concession of revisions). So König, Klostermann, etc. Cf. also Tomkins. *Abraham and His Age* (1897), chap. xiii.

[5] Gen. xii. On the Egyptian relations, cf. Tomkins, as above.

colouring of the narrative of this part of Genesis nearly all scholars may be said to be agreed.[1] The colouring is so fresh and vivid, the portraiture of manners so exact, the allusions to customs and institutions are so minute, that it would be endless to dwell on them. We have the slave-market; Potiphar's house, with its Egyptian arrangements; the prison; Pharaoh's butler and baker, the latter with his baskets of confectionery; Pharaoh's dreams, so Egyptian in their character; Joseph as prime minister, buying and selling corn; the divining-cup, the chariots, the waggons sent to Jacob; we have Egyptian names, sitting at meals, shaving the beard, embalming the body, sacred scribes, priests, physicians, other state functionaries; in short, we find ourselves veritably on the banks of the Nile, with Egyptian social and court life in full movement around us.

It is perhaps more to the purpose to remark that it is precisely the points in the history of Joseph which were formerly challenged which have received clearest illustration and confirmation from the monuments. Thus it was denied by Von Bohlen and others, on the authority of Herodotus, that the vine was cultivated in Egypt; it was denied that flesh was an article of diet among the upper classes of the Egyptians; the free manners of the women were alleged to conflict with Oriental privacy; the elevation of a young Hebrew to the position of prime minister was thought to savour of romance; the presents of Pharaoh to Abraham were objected to because they included sheep and oxen, which were objects of hatred in Egypt, and did not include horses, which, in Joseph's day, were common. These objections have disappeared with fuller knowledge, but serve to show the impossibility of anyone in a later age composing a narrative of this kind without falling into serious errors. The monuments, it is well known, show the process of wine-making in all its stages;[2] they reveal that, in the words of Rawlinson, "animal food was the principal diet of the upper

[1] The proof on this subject is so abundant that we must refer to the books for details. Some of the chief are, Ebers, *Aegypten und Die Bücher Moses*, i. pp. 295 ff., and art. "Joseph" in Smith's *Dict. of Bible*, i. (1893); Driver, art. "Joseph," in *Dict. of Bible*, ii., and in *Authority and Archæol. and Genesis*; Tomkins, *Life and Times of Joseph* (1891); Vigouroux, *La Bible et les Découvertes Modernes*, ii. ; Rawlinson's *Historical Illustrations*, pp. 38 ff.; Sayce, *Higher Criticism*, pp. 207 ff.

[2] Cf. Ebers, Smith's *D. of B*. i. p. 1795.

classes ";[1] they illustrate the freedom allowed to women; they furnish representations of sheep and oxen; while the absence of horses in Abraham's time proves to be a mark of truth in the narrative, for horses seem to have been unknown in the twelfth and earlier dynasties, and were first introduced under the Hyksos. There, in Joseph's time, accordingly, they appear.[2] In the story of Saneha, of the twelfth dynasty, we have a close parallel to the exaltation of Joseph;[3] while on the tombs of Beni-Hassan, of the same dynasty, we have a picture of the reception of a company of Amu, or Semites, so remarkably resembling the case of Jacob and his household, that at first it was thought to be a representation of that patriarch's descent into Egypt.[4] Reference cannot be omitted to the Egyptian story, "The Tale of the Two Brothers," which embodies an account of the temptation of one of these brothers by the wife of the other, so strikingly (in parts almost verbally) parallel to the temptation of Joseph by his mistress, that the two can hardly be independent. As the Egyptian tale belongs to the nineteenth dynasty[5]—many centuries after Joseph—the story of Joseph may be presumed to be the original.[6]

A picture, so full and faithful, of Egyptian life and manners could only, one would think, take its origin on Egyptian soil. It is not a sufficient reply to say, with Dr. Driver, that Egypt was not far distant from Canaan, and that the intercourse between the countries during the monarchy made it easy for a Hebrew writer to gain a knowledge of Egyptian customs and institutions.[7] The hypothesis, in the first place, is gratuitous, for there is no reason to suppose that the narrative of Joseph's life, with its Egyptian characteristics, was not a possession of Israel from the beginning;[8] and next, it is inadequate, for it is

[1] *Hist. Illusts.* p. 50. Cf. on these points Wilkinson's *Ancient Egyptians, passim.*

[2] Gen. xlvii. 17 ; cf. Maspero, *Egypt and Assyria,* pp. 81, 82.

[3] Cf. Canon Cook, essay at end of *Speaker's Com.* on Exodus, p. 446.

[4] *Ibid.* Cf. Ebers, *D. of B.* i. p. 1793.

[5] See the story in Sayce's *Higher Criticism,* pp. 209-11. It was written for Seti II., the successor of Meneptah, of the nineteenth dynasty.

[6] Cf. Ebers, as above, p. 1795.   [7] *Genesis,* pp. l, li.

[8] The influence of critical theory is well seen in Dr. Driver's (still reasonably conservative) treatment of the history of Joseph. It cannot be said, he allows, that there are serious historical improbabilities in the *substance* of the history ; but the matter, he says, assumes a different aspect "when account is taken (1) of the fact that the narratives about Joseph are plainly not the

contrary to analogy that a writer of one country should be able so to transpose himself into the midst of a foreign— even if a neighbouring—civilisation, as to produce a picture so marvellously true to its life and conditions. Are we to understand that the problematical J or E undertook a special tour to Egypt—as the modern novelist might do— in order to acquaint himself by personal study with the customs and antiquities of that nation? Or did the *two* writers do so? Even so, we have only to think of a Frenchman, *e.g.*, attempting to depict British or American life or manners; or of an Englishman or American writing minutely about Paris; or of a Londoner trying to describe Scottish characters and institutions, to see how imperfect such a picture would necessarily be. We do not attach much importance to the objections that the narrative does not give the *personal* name of Joseph's Pharaoh, and that the types of names which appear in it—Potiphera, Zaphenath-paneah, Asenath—do not become frequent till the later dynasties (twenty-second, twenty-sixth).[1] It may strike us, indeed, as peculiar that, in the lives of Joseph and Moses, the proper names of the Pharaohs are not given; still, comparison proves that the title "Pharaoh" (simply) was that commonly employed by Hebrew writers for the king of Egypt, even when the personal name was quite well known;[2] while the very occurrence of the other names

work of a contemporary, but were in all probability only committed to writing 700–800 years afterwards ; and (2) of the further curious fact that 'Joseph' (like many of the other patriarchal names) is also a *tribal* name," etc. "The first of these facts," he declares, "at once destroys all guarantee that we possess in the Joseph-narratives a literal record of the facts."—*Dict. of Bible*, ii. p. 771. May not the character of the narratives rather be a proof that Dr. Driver's dating, which has no sure basis, is wrong ? See above, pp. 77–78. It was pointed out earlier, also, that Joseph does *not*, strictly, give his name to a tribe (p. 89).

Kittel's treatment shows likewise the biassing effect of theory. There is, *e.g.*, not a grain of foundation for such statements as "when he [Joseph] emigrated into Egypt his tribesmen were certainly with him," etc.—*Hist. of Hebs.* i. p. 187.

In a striking communication to the *Expository Times*, September 1899, Professor Sayce argues strongly that the history is substantially a work of the Mosaic age, based on an Egyptian original, though written in Palestine.

[1] Driver, *Genesis*, p. li ; *Dict. of Bible*, ii. p. 775 ; cf. Ebers, as above, p. 1798.

[2] *E.g.*, 1 Kings ix. 16, 24 ; xi. 1, 18, 21 (cf. **xi.** 40) ; 2 Kings xviii. 21 ; Isa. xix. 11 ; xxx. 2, 3 ; Jer. xliii. (cf. xliv. 30) ; xlvi. 17 ; xlvii. 1 ; Ezek. xxxi. 2, 18 ; xxxii. 2, etc. Cf. Assyrian usage in Schrader, i. pp. 140, 162 ; ii. p. 88.

shows how easy it would have been for the narrator to decorate his story with names of kings and places, had he wished to do so. The alleged lateness of particular names rests, again, on the argument from silence, which may be upset at any moment,[1] and fails to take account of the fact that the Hyksos period, to which Joseph belonged, is well-nigh a monumental blank. It is doubtful, besides, whether all the names have been rightly interpreted.[2]

V. THE MOSAIC PERIOD—THREE GREAT DISCOVERIES

We come now to the Mosaic period, but, to make the bearings of recent discoveries on this period intelligible, it is necessary, first, to say a few words on the general course of Egyptian history and on the more important of these discoveries.

Three great periods are commonly distinguished in the history of Egypt—the Old, the Middle, and the New Empires. The Old Empire embraces the first eleven dynasties of Manetho; the Middle Empire extends from the twelfth dynasty to the seventeenth;[3] the New Empire runs from the eighteenth dynasty to the thirtieth, after which (340 B.C.) Egypt loses its independence.

Of the *Old Empire*, the fourth and fifth dynasties have left their memorials in the great Pyramids; but of the first three dynasties nothing was known till recently from the monuments but the names of kings; the period from the seventh to the tenth dynasties was (and remains) hardly less obscure. The founder of the first dynasty bore the name of Menes; but scholars were disposed to regard this king, and the first dynasties generally, as mythical. Maspero, in his *Dawn of Civilisation*, treats Menes as purely mythical, and gives an elaborate explanation of how the myth arose.[4]

[1] Cf. Sayce, *Higher Crit.* pp. 212–13; Tomkins, *Joseph*, pp. 183–85. There is an example of a name of the Potiphera type in the eighteenth dynasty (Tomkins, p. 185; Driver, p. 345, and *Dict. of Bible*, ii. p. 775), and it cannot be believed that it stood alone. "Those of the type of Asenath are found now and then earlier" (Driver, *Dict.* p. 775).

[2] This is true both of Zaphenath-paneah and of Asenath. The latter is explained as Nes-Neit, "belonging to Neith"; but Brugsch wrote: "The name of his wife Asnat is pure Egyptian, and almost confined to the Old and Middle Empire."—*Hist. of Egypt*, i. p. 265.

[3] Some begin the Middle Empire with Dynasty XI.

[4] *Dawn of Civilisation*, pp. 233–34. Menes, according to Maspero,

As lately as 1894, Professor Flinders Petrie could write: "The first three dynasties are a blank, so far as monumental statements are concerned; they are as purely on a literary basis as the kings of Rome or the primeval kings of Ireland. . . . We cannot regard these dynasties as anything but a series of statements made by a state chronographer, about 3000 years after date, concerning a period of which he had no contemporary material."[1] The judgment thus passed on the early dynasties has been suddenly reversed, largely by the brilliant explorations of Professor Petrie himself. The actual tombs of Menes and his successors have been discovered, with many valuable objects belonging to them, and the first two dynasties have been clearly proved to be historical. Civilisation, and the hieroglyphic system of writing, are carried back into pre-dynastic times.[2] The result is a striking object-lesson—one of many in recent years—on the unreliableness of what the discoverer calls "the criticism of myths."[3]

In the *Middle Empire*, the period from the thirteenth dynasty to the seventeenth is again one of confusion and uncertainty. This was the time when Egypt was ruled by the Hyksos, or Shepherd Kings, under one of whom Joseph was taken down to Egypt,[4] soon to be followed by Jacob with his household. With the overthrow of the Shepherd

"owes his existence to a popular attempt at etymology" (p. 234). Even Dr. Birch wrote that Menes "must be placed among those founders of monarchies whose personal existence a severe and enlightened criticism doubts or denies."—*Egypt*, p. 25.

[1] *Hist. of Egypt*, i. pp. 16, 19.

[2] On the nature and bearings of "pre-dynastic" discoveries, see Budge, *Hist of Egypt*, i. chap. i.

[3] In an address to the Egyptian Exploration Fund, Nov. 6th, 1901, Professor Petrie is reported to have said : "The continuous order of seventeen kings had been established, and the very foundations of Egyptian history had been settled in a manner which had hitherto seemed beyond hope. . . . The criticism of myths had told them that Mena, the founder of the Egyptian monarchy, was but a form of Manu, the lawgiver of India, and of Minos, the hero of Crete, and to hope for tangible monuments of his time was but seeing castles in cloudland. Now the long line of a dozen kings back to Mena was clear before them ; they had seen and handled the gold, the crystal, the ivory with his name and engravings. . . . No such complete materialisation of history had been obtained at one stroke from any other country or age." See further Note D on the Resurrection of Myths.

[4] Joseph's elevation is traditionally connected with Apophis (Apepi). With the view of the chronology indicated below, we are disposed to place it under Apepi I. (c. 1880 B.C.), not Apepi II.

Kings came the founding of the eighteenth dynasty under Aahmes, and the beginning of the *New Empire*. Under the eighteenth and nineteenth dynasties we reach, perhaps, the period of greatest splendour in Egypt. It is a period of the greatest interest to the Biblical student, for it is under one or other of these dynasties, undoubtedly, that we are to seek for the Israelitish oppression, and for the Exodus. The prevailing opinion among scholars has been that the Pharaoh of the oppression was the great ruler Rameses II., and that the Pharaoh of the Exodus was his son Meneptah, or one of his immediate successors. Much may be said for this identification. Especially does it seem to be indicated by the mention in Ex. i. 11 of the building of the store cities Pithom and Raamses, both of which are directly connected, the one (Pi-tum, discovered by M. Naville in 1883 [1]) by its bricks, the other by its name, with Rameses II.[2] Yet three great discoveries in recent times have again thrown more than doubt on the identification.

1. First in order was the astonishing discovery, in 1881, of *the mummies of the Pharaohs* themselves. In a gallery given off from a pit, 35 feet deep, in a mountain gorge a few miles from Thebes, some thirty-nine mummies were found, which proved on inspection to include amongst them the most renowned kings and queens of Egypt from the seventeenth to the twenty-first dynasties. "At the first report of the discovery," wrote one, "the boldest held his breath, so astounding is the list, which includes almost every name most renowned in the annals of Egypt." The list embraced Aahmes, founder of the eighteenth dynasty; Thothmes III., and other kings of the same dynasty; Rameses I., Seti I., and Rameses II., of the nineteenth dynasty.[3]

[1] Cf. his *Store City of Pithom and the Route of the Exodus* (1885).

[2] On the historicity of these notices, cf. Kittel, *Hist. of Hebs.* i. pp. 254–56. He shows the difficulties of the supposition that the Hebrew writer "obtained information respecting the building of Pithom and Raamses by means of scholarly investigation, and then attached to this the national tradition of the Israelites" (p. 255). It will naturally occur that a writer who could name these cities could also have named the Pharaoh had he chosen. The problems about the city Raamses, however, are not yet satisfactorily solved. See Note E on the Identification of Raamses.

[3] Our notice is based on contemporary reports. A popular account is given of this and of Naville's discovery in *The Pharaohs of the Bondage and the Exodus*, by Chas. S. Robinson, D.D., New York (1887). See also Nicol, *Recent Archæology and the Bible*, pp. 16, ff.

A subsequent discovery of the tomb of Amenophis II., in 1898, added seven other mummies to the list. One of these, taken at first for that of Amenophis II., was found later to be the mummy of Meneptah, the supposed Pharaoh of the Exodus.[1] To whatever period the Exodus is assigned, it is beyond reasonable doubt that we have in our possession the actual mummy of the Pharaoh who oppressed the Israelites, and from whose face Moses fled.

2. This first discovery was eclipsed, in 1887, by a second, still more extensive in its bearings. This was the discovery, already repeatedly referred to, at *Tel el-Amarna* (a place on the eastern bank of the Nile, 180 miles south of Cairo), of *a mass of inscribed tablets,* some three hundred in number, forming part, as it proved, of the official correspondence of two of the later kings of the eighteenth dynasty —Amenophis III. and Amenophis IV.[2] This latter king (*c.* 1380 B.C.), otherwise called Khu-n-aten, was a "heretic king." He sought to introduce, and compulsorily to enforce, a new worship—that of the solar disk (Aten). The opposition he encountered led him to leave Thebes, and found this new capital, whither he removed the court records of his father and himself. The remarkable thing about the correspondence is that the tablets are written, not in Egyptian hieroglyphic, but in Babylonian cuneiform—a fact of the utmost importance as showing that the Babylonian language was at that time not only widely known, but was the medium of official communication between Egypt and other countries, as French is to-day in Europe. The letters reveal the wide political relations of Egypt, and are particularly valuable for the light they throw on the state of culture in Palestine, and on the events transpiring in that country, about 1400 B.C. They include, as will be afterwards seen,[3] many letters from the king of Jerusalem and other rulers in Canaan.

3. The third discovery is still more recent, and bears on

[1] Cf. Nicol, as above, p. 320. The correction was announced by Professor Sayce in 1900.

[2] Good accounts of this discovery may be seen in Sayce's *Higher Criticism,* pp. 47 ff.; Bennett's *Book of Joshua,* pp. 48 ff.; Pinches, *O.T. in Light of Hist. Records,* chap. viii., etc. The most valuable complete translation is Winckler's (1896).

[3] See below, p. 424. Next in importance to the letters of the king of Jerusalem, in their bearings on the Khabiri (below, p. 424), is the long series of Rib-Addi of Gebal (Winckler, pp. 124 ff.).

the question often asked—Is there *any mention of Israel* on the Egyptian monuments? Identifications with the Hebrews have been repeatedly sought, as, *e.g.*, in the *aperiu* mentioned in some of the inscriptions;[1] but it was not till 1896 that the name "Israel" was actually found by Professor Flinders Petrie on a stela of Meneptah, believed, as above said, to be the Pharaoh of the Exodus. The inscription on the monument, however, it was soon found, created more difficulties than it removed. It recounted the victories of Meneptah over various peoples in and about Palestine, and apparently included Israel in the list. "Israel is spoiled," it reads, "it hath no seed."[2] But if Israel was in Palestine in the time of Meneptah—and there seems independent evidence that at least Asher,[3] and perhaps Judah,[4] was—it is clear that Meneptah cannot, in consistency with Bible history, be the Pharaoh of the Exodus. This at once raised a new question—Is the usual assumption that Rameses II. was the oppressor, and that the Exodus took place under Meneptah, or later, a correct one? The question is one which it is now necessary to consider.[5]

[1] The objection to this identification is that *aperiu* are still found, in both noble and servile positions, at dates much later than the Exodus. Thus there is mention of 2083 *aperiu* as settlers in noble positions in Heliopolis in the reign of Rameses III., and 800 *aperiu* are employed in slave labour in the reign of Rameses IV. (cf. Cook, who accepts the identification of Chabas, *Speaker's Com.* Exodus, p. 466 ; Sayce, *Fresh Light*, p. 71 ; Hommel, *Anc. Heb. Trad.* p. 259 ; Driver, *Auth. and Arch.* p. 56). Or did some colony of Israelites remain in Egypt ? (Ebers, *Durch Gosen*, p. 521). Cook regards the *aperiu* of Rameses III. as also "captives" —"prisoners of war."

[2] There are considerable variations in the translation given, but generally the meaning is the same.

[3] Thus W. Max Müller, *Asien und Europa*, p. 236 ; cf. Hommel, *Anc. Heb. Trad.* p. 228.

[4] Thus Jastrow, who finds "men of Judah," on the Tel el-Amarna tablets (*Jour. of Bib. Lit.* 1893). There is another inscription of the reign of Meneptah which speaks of Goshen as "abandoned since the time of the ancestors." Naville infers from this that it was not inhabited ("The Route of the Exodus," *Trans. of Vict. Institute*, vol. xxvi. 1892–93).

[5] For a fuller discussion of the Egyptian traditions and other ancient notices in light of Professor Petrie's discovery, see art. by the author in *Expositor*, April 1897, "Israel in Egypt and the Exodus."

VI. ISRAEL AND THE EXODUS

There have always been scholars who doubted the current theory of the date of the Exodus,[1] but, while the majority, probably, still adhere to the old date, the effect of Professor Petrie's discovery has been to lead many to revise their previous opinions,[2] and to create hesitation in the minds of more. An almost insuperable difficulty in the way of the Rameses-Meneptah theory is the *chronological.* The steady tendency in Egyptian study has been to lower the dates of the Pharaohs of the nineteenth dynasty. Professor Flinders Petrie, *e.g.,* puts the accession of Meneptah as late as 1208 B.C., and the Exodus in 1200 B.C.[3] This, however, leaves little more than 200 years for the interval between the Exodus and the building of Solomon's temple (*c.* 975 B.C.)[4]—a period into which it is impossible to crush the wanderings and conquest, the times of the Judges, and the reigns of Saul and David. At the other end, the period from Abraham (*c.* 2100 B.C.) to the Exodus is far too long, about 900 years—some make it longer. Even if the date of Rameses II. is raised by half a century, the difficulty is only very partially removed. If, on the other hand, we take a date which the Bible itself gives us for the Exodus, viz., 480 years before the building of the temple,[5] as approximately correct, we are taken back to about 1450 B.C., just at the close of the reign of the powerful ruler Thothmes III., of the eighteenth dynasty.[6] This date corresponds also with the interval from Abraham. On this view, the Exodus would fall in the first years of the reign of Amenophis II.,

[1] Cf. the interesting Essay of Canon Cook, *Speaker's Com.* Exodus, pp. 454–55; also Köhler, *Bib. Gesch.* i. pp. 237–45.

[2] Professor Petrie himself, Sayce, Driver, Kittel, etc., adhere to the ordinary view; but leading Continental scholars, as Steindorff, Zimmern, Hommel. etc., with W. Max Müller, Colonel Conder, and others, incline to, or adopt, an earlier date. Hommel, who took the ordinary view in his *Anc. Heb. Trad.*, gives the reasons for his change in *Expository Times*, February 1899.

[3] *Hist. of Egypt*, i. pp. 250–51.

[4] This is the date approximately fixed by the Assyrian synchronisms.

[5] 1 Kings vi. 1. The LXX has 440 years. This is found, however, in none of the remaining versions. The number 480 is found in Aquila, Symmachus, Peshitta, etc. (cf. Köhler, *Bib. Gesch.* i. p. 242; ii. pp. 36, 39).

[6] The years of his sole reign are given by Petrie, after Mähler, as 1481–1449 B.C.—*Hist. of Egypt*, ii. pp. 155–57.

son of Thothmes III., in whose reign Professor Hommel now also places it.

It is next to be observed that, on the supposition of this earlier date, *the conditions are in every way as suitable* as on the Rameses theory—perhaps more suitable. The argument in favour of Rameses II. from the store cities loses much of its force when we find that, as might be shown by examples, it was a habit of this monarch to appropriate the work and monuments of his predecessors, and give his name to them.[1] On the other hypothesis, the oppressor becomes the great ruler, conqueror, and builder, Thothmes III., whose character, length of reign (fifty-four years), and oppression of his subjects, entirely corresponds with the description in Exodus.[2] To his reign belongs the well-known picture of the brick-making by captives, so often used to illustrate the bondage of the Israelites. If the new hypothesis is correct, it need not be a mere illustration, but may be a picture of the bondage itself. As in Exodus, over the slaves stand overseers with their rods, and the words are put into their mouths, "Be not idle."[3] There is another curious agreement. Thothmes III. was preceded by Thothmes II., and he by Thothmes I., whose daughter Hatasu (Hashop) was one of the most remarkable women in Egyptian history. She was associated with her father in the government; she married her brother Thothmes II., and shared his throne; she was regent in the minority of Thothmes III. It is at least a singular coincidence that, on the theory we are expounding, Moses must have been born just about the time this "bold and clever" princess[4] was rising into power. The temptation is great to connect her with the "Pharaoh's daughter" of the story in Exodus.[5]

One other coincidence of much importance remains to be noticed. This takes us back to the Tel el-Amarna tablets.

[1] The "Cleopatra's Needle" on the Thames Embankment, London, was originally an obelisk of Thothmes III.; Pi-Ramessu was the rebuilding of an older city; this seems to have been the case also with Pithom. In this case the use of the name Raamses would seem to show that the *narrative* at least is as late as Rameses II. But it must still be doubtful whether the Raamses of Ex. i. 11 is a city built by this king. See Note E.

[2] Ex. v.

[3] Cf. Brugsch, *Hist. of Egypt*, i. pp. 375–76; see Brugsch on the whole reign.

[4] *Ibid.* p. 296; cf. her history in Petrie, *Hist. of Egypt*, ii. pp. 79–96.

[5] Cf. Ex. ii. 5 ff.

These, as was stated, include many letters from Palestine, and reveal an extraordinary state of things in that country. The land, especially in the south, was overrun by a people called the Khabiri, who had come up, apparently, from Seir, and were carrying all before them. The tone of all the letters that mention them, as Colonel Conder says, "is a despairing cry for help to Egypt, but none of them record that any help was sent, though eagerly expected. They relate no victories over the Khabiri."[1] Specially piteous are the lamentations of Abdi-Khiba, king of Jerusalem. "The Khabiri have devastated all the king's territory"— "The Khabiri are occupying the king's cities"—"There remains not one prince to my lord, the king; every one is ruined"—"If no troops come, the whole territory of my lord, the king, will be lost."[2] This is the reign of Amenophis IV. (c. 1380 B.C.), which is seen ending in defeat and disaster. If, however, the Exodus is placed where the new hypothesis suggests, or possibly a reign later, under Thothmes IV. (the Thummosis of Manetho), their invasion synchronises very closely with the conquest of Canaan by the Israelites, and many leading scholars, accordingly, now seriously propose an identification of these Khabiri with the Hebrews.[3] The subject is still under discussion, but it is easy to see how interesting are the possibilities it opens up.

VII. EMPIRE OF THE HITTITES—PERIOD OF THE KINGS

It remains to indicate in the briefest survey the light cast by archæology on the relations of Israel to the great powers with which, in so many ways, it was brought into contact, after the settlement in Canaan.

1. And first may be mentioned the remarkable corroborations of Scripture in its references to the existence and

---

[1] *Bible and the East*, pp. 40, 41, 106–7.

[2] Cf. in Winckler, letters 179–85 (pp. 303–15). The letters are also given by Sayce in *Early Israel*, App. pp. 287 ff. The descriptions in the letters meet the objection that the conquest could not have taken place at this time, because Canaan was subject to Egypt. If the Khabiri could in this way overrun Palestine, certainly the Israelites could do so.

[3] Zimmern, Winckler, etc., favour this identification ; Hommel now accepts it. One of the best defences of it is by H. Billet in the *Deutsch-Evangel. Blätter*, No. 7. Professor Hommel wrote the author in February 1899 : "I see in them the first onset (*Vorstoss*) of the twelve tribes." See also Benzinger, in Hilprecht's *Explorations*, p. 620.

power of *the Hittites.* In the Books of Joshua and Kings are found various references which imply the existence of a great and formidable Hittite empire or confederacy north of Palestine, and this long after, as well as before, the Israelites had obtained possession of Canaan. Thus, in Joshua i. 4: "From the wilderness and this Lebanon, even unto the great river, the river Euphrates, all the land of the Hittites." In 1 Kings x. 28, 29, we are told of chariots and horses being brought from Egypt for "all the kings of the Hittites." Still later, in 2 Kings vii. 6, we read of a flight of the Syrians occasioned by the belief that the king of Israel had hired against them "the kings of the Hittites and the kings of the Egyptians."[1] As, however, no ancient writer knew anything about such a power, these Scriptural allusions to them were, as usual, treated as unhistorical, or as mere rhetorical flourishes. "The unhistorical tone," wrote Mr. Francis W. Newman in his *Hebrew Monarchy,* "is far too manifest to allow of our easy belief in it" (the flight of the Syrians), adding that the reference to the Hittites "does not exhibit the writer's acquaintance with the times in a very favourable light."[2] Now, it will hardly be disputed that the statements of Scripture on this subject are confirmed to the letter.[3] Alike from Egyptian and from Assyrian inscriptions we learn that this Hittite people were for nearly 1000 years a great ruling power in Syria and Western Asia, extending their influence eastwards as far as the Euphrates. They had, in short, an empire hardly less great than Egypt and Assyria themselves. The kings of the eighteenth and nineteenth dynasties in Egypt conducted extensive campaigns against them, the events of which constitute a considerable part of their annals.[4] But beyond this their own abundant monuments, inscribed with a hieroglyphic which scholars are still busy attempting to decipher, now discover to us what manner of people they were, and testify to the wide range of their supremacy. It

---

[1] Cf. Judg. i. 26, "unto the land of the Hittites."

[2] *Heb. Monarchy,* pp. 184–85.

[3] Cf. the works of Sayce (*Fresh Light, Higher Criticism, Early Israel,* etc.); Wright, *Empire of the Hittites*; Driver, *Authority and Archæology,* pp. 83–87 ; Jensen, in Hilprecht's *Explorations,* pp. 755 ff.

[4] Cf. the treaty of Rameses II. with the Hittites in Brugsch ; also in Sayce, *Early Israel,* pp. 297 ff. The Hittites are prominent also in the Tel el-Amarna tablets. Cf. Pinches, as above, pp. 306 ff.

is already known that the Hittite language was not a Semitic, but an Aryan, tongue, and Jensen has thrown out the conjecture that the Hittites of the monuments were the ancestors of the modern Armenians.[1] It seems evident that the Biblical books in which these references to the Hittites occur must have been written when the power of that people was yet in the ascendant, else the writers would have blundered in regard to them like others.

2. Space would fail to tell of the long series of discoveries minutely illustrating and corroborating the narratives of the historical books of the Old Testament in *the period of the kings*. It is a striking fact that there is hardly a single point of contact with foreign powers in this period which does not receive illustration from the monuments; while the Assyrian synchronisms and notices in the Eponym Canon[2] afford valuable aid in rectifying the Bible chronology. Only to glance at outstanding instances— the walls of the Hall of Karnak give Shishak's own boastful account of his invasion of Israel and Judah in the time of Rehoboam;[3] Mesha, king of Moab, set up his stone at Dibon to commemorate the freeing of his country from the yoke of Israel;[4] the Bible informs us that Ahab at the end of his life made a covenant with Benhadad of Syria,[5] and, on the Assyrian side, we have a notice of Ahab as present with Benhadad at the battle of Karkar, 854 B.C., when the Syrians were defeated by Shalmaneser II.; this apparently brought Israel under tribute to Assyria, and Jehu's servants are next pictured on Shalmaneser's black obelisk as bearing tribute to that monarch; the relations of Israel and Judah with Tiglath-pileser, or Pul (shown by the lists of kings to be the same person) are circumstantially confirmed;

[1] Jensen, as above, p. 777.

[2] A list of the rotation and succession of officers (analogous to the archons of Athens and the consuls of Rome). Cf. article by the author on " Assyrian and Hebrew Chronology " in the *Presbyterian Review*, January 1899.

[3] 2 Chron. xii. This is one of the narratives in Chronicles *not* found in Kings, and proves the use of special and authentic sources.

[4] 2 Kings i. 1 ; iii. 4 ff. The inscription may be seen in full (original and translation, with notes) in Driver's *Samuel*, pp. lxxxv ff. ; and Bennett's art. "Moab" in *Dict. of Bible*, iii. pp. 403 ff. Dr. Driver is clearly mistaken in making the revolt to be already "completed in the middle of the reign of Ahab," and finding therein a discrepancy with Scripture. Mesha's "forty years" from Omri reach down to Jehoram's time, as in 2 Kings. Possibly *he* is the son of Omri intended. Omri's own reign was a short one.

[5] 1 Kings xx. 34 ; xxii. 1.

Menahem, Pekah, and Hoshea appear in this monarch's inscriptions as on the Bible page;[1] Hoshea's rebellion, and the carrying away of the people by Sargon, after the fall of Samaria, are described;[2] Sargon's own palace was, as formerly mentioned, one of the first Ninevite discoveries;[3] Sennacherib's version of his expedition against Hezekiah, his siege of Lachish, and the other events of his reign, may be read from his own annals;[4] his murder by his son, and the accession of Esarhaddon, are duly recorded;[5] Tirhakah appears as "king of Egypt and Ethiopia."[6]

The captivity of Manasseh, his repentance, and his restoration to his kingdom, are, like the invasion of Shishak, recorded only in Chronicles.[7] The narrative has very generally been pronounced unhistorical on the double ground, apart from the silence of the Book of Kings, that we have no mention of the supremacy of the Assyrians at this time in Western Asia, and that the king is declared to have been carried to Babylon, not to Nineveh. Both objections, as Schrader shows, "lose their force in presence of the inscriptions."[8] Manasseh's name occurs in the list of tributaries of both Esarhaddon and Assurbanipal ("Manasseh, king of Judah");[9] and, as kings of Babylon, the sovereigns sometimes held their court in that city.[10] The release of Manasseh has a parallel in the case of Pharaoh-Necho. He was brought to Nineveh, as Manasseh was to Babylon, "in iron chains," yet Assurbanipal, a little later, allowed him to return to Egypt and resume his power.[11] Schrader sums up the results of a careful examination by saying "that there is no reason to cast any suspicion on the statement of the Chronicler, and that what he relates can be satisfactorily

[1] 2 Kings xv.   [2] 2 Kings xvii. 1-6.
[3] See above, p. 398.
[4] 2 Kings xviii. 13 ff. Sennacherib, as was to be expected, is silent about the disaster to his army, which yet is needed to account for the raising of the siege.
[5] 2 Kings xix. 37.
[6] 2 Kings. xix. 9. Cf. Schrader, *Cun. Inscriptions*, ii. p. 10.
[7] 2 Chron. xxxiii. 11-13.
[8] *Cun. Inscripts.* ii. pp. 54 ff.
[9] Cf. Pinches, as above, pp. 386-88.
[10] Schrader, p. 55 ; Sayce, *Higher Crit.* pp. 458-60. Even H. P. Smith concedes : "The mention of Babylon which formerly made a difficulty does so no longer, because we know that Ashurbanipal spent a great deal of time in that city."—*O. T. Hist.* p. 258.
[11] Sayce, as above, p. 461.

accounted for from the circumstances that existed in the year 647 B.C."[1]

VIII. The Book of Daniel

There is something approaching to a consensus of opinion among critical scholars that the Book of Daniel, as it lies before us, is a production of the Maccabæan age; only that, while a majority will have it to be composed wholly in that age, others, like Delitzsch and Orelli,[2] think that it rests on a basis of genuine history and prophecy, and is at most revised, and adapted to the circumstances of the Maccabæan age, as a book of comfort to the confessors and martyrs in their persecution.[3] Without entering into the critical question, we would point out that the sweeping statements often made as to the unhistorical character of the book need to be received with great caution. With the progress of monumental discovery, the objections that have been heaped up against it tend, not to increase, but to disappear. The startling evidence, *e.g.*, that has come to light of the early date and wide diffusion of a high Greek civilisation, and of the continuous intercourse of the Greeks with other countries from remote times,[4] renders nugatory any objection based on the alleged names of Greek instruments in the account of Nebuchadnezzar's music. Readers

---

[1] *Cun. Inscripts.* ii. p. 59 ; cf. Sayce, *Early Israel*, pp. xvii ff.

[2] Cf. Delitzsch, *Mess. Prophecies* (1891), pp. 298 ff. ; Orelli, *O.T. Prophecy*, pp. 454 ff.

[3] The view in question is stated thus by Orelli : "Neither of the narratives of Dan. i.–vi., nor of the visions vii.–xii., can we allow that they owe their origin to the Maccabæan age. As to the former, we are of opinion that they contain history handed down from the time of the exile, and were merely compiled by a late author, who to all appearance, especially according to linguistic indications, belonged to the Maccabæan age. We come to a similar conclusion in respect to the apocalyptic visions. . . . We think that even here traditional visions of the real Daniel, renowned for his prophetic keenness of sight (Ezek. xxviii. 3) form the real kernel, but that these visions were not merely collected and redacted by an author living under Antiochus, but also set by illustrative explanations in intimate relation to the oppression of that age."—*Prophecy*, pp. 455–56. See further below, p. 458.

[4] Active intercourse existed between Greece and Egypt, Canaan, and other lands, from the Tel el-Amarna times, and even earlier. The pottery found at Mycenæ is said to belong to the age of the eighteenth and nineteenth dynasties of Egypt ; conversely, Flinders Petrie found Mycenæan pottery at Tel el-Amarna. The tablets already mention *Yivana* or Javan. Cf. Sayce, *Higher Criticism*, pp. 18–20 ; Kittel, *Bib. Excavs.* pp. 14–18, etc.

of Professor Flinders Petrie's *Ten Years' Digging in Egypt*
may think they find, in connection with the discoveries at
Tahpahnes,[1] what seems a sufficient answer to that objection.
The picture of Nebuchadnezzar, again, given in the book, is
in fullest accord with the idea of him obtained from his own
inscriptions and works. It must at least be allowed that
discovery has proved the historical reality of one personage
whom criticism had persisted in regarding as mythical, viz.,
Belshazzar. Belshazzar appears in Daniel as "king of the
Chaldeans,"[2] but his name is not found in any ancient
historian. The last king of Babylon was called Nabonidus,
and no room seemed left for another. It is now discovered,
however, from inscriptions and contract tablets, that
Nabonidus had a son who bore this name Belshazzar, and
who, to judge from the prominent place he has in the
inscriptions, was in some way associated with his father in
the government.[3] This would explain Belshazzar's promise
to make Daniel the *third* ruler in the kingdom, or, as some
understand it, one of "a board of three."[4] It would seem,
further, from the Babylonian account, that "the king's son
died" on the night in which the city was finally captured.[5]
In other respects discrepancies are alleged to exist between
the account of the taking of the city in the inscriptions of
Cyrus and the statements in Daniel. We are confident that
most of these will disappear with more accurate reading and
interpretation. In the Babylonian account the city is
described as taken "without fighting." It is, however,
carefully to be noted that in the Chronicle a considerable
interval elapses between the first peaceful entrance into the

[1] *Ten Years' Digging*, pp. 54 ff.: "Here then was a ready source for the
introduction of Greek words and names into Hebrew, long before the
Alexandrine age; and even before the fall of Jerusalem the Greek names of
musical instruments and other words may have been heard in the courts of
Solomon's temple" (p. 54). Cf. Professor Petrie's *Tanis*, Pt. ii. pp. 49, 50
(4th Mem. of Pal. Explor. Fund). Dr. Cheyne takes Professor Petrie to
task for accounting in this way for the Greek names of instruments in Daniel
(*Origin of Psalter*, p. 10).

[2] Dan. v. 30.

[3] Cf. Pinches, p. 414. According to Dr. Pinches, Belshazzar was "the
real ruler," but not so officially. Professor R. D. Wilson, of Princeton, who
has made a special study of the royal titles of this period, claims that the
bearing of the title "king" by Belshazzar is in harmony with the usage of
the time. See Note F on Belshazzar and Babylon.

[4] Dan. v. 7.

[5] Cf. the "Babylonian Chronicle," given in Pinches, pp. 415–16; Driver,
Daniel, p. xxix–xxx; Sayce, *Higher Crit.* pp. 502–3.

city and its final fall. The first entrance is made in the month Tammuz (July), but the completion of the capture, and the death of Belshazzar, do not take place till Marcheswan (November)—four months later.[1] The probabilities are that Nabonidus commanded the forces in the field, while Belshazzar held the city within. Nabonidus was defeated, and taken captive in Babylon, and, as we read it, the outer part of the city fell into the hands of Gobryas, the general of Cyrus, and his soldiers. The inner part, however, held out for some months, when Cyrus, in some unknown way, became master of it.[2] Belshazzar was slain on the night of its capture—again in agreement with Daniel. Not improbably, also, the Gobryas of the inscriptions, whom, we are told, Cyrus made governor, and who "appointed governors in Babylonia," is the long-sought-for "Darius the Mede," who "received the kingdom," and reigned for two years.[3]

NOTE.—*The Sabbath* : The strongest reason for doubting that the Babylonian Sabbath was a day of general rest (cf. pp. 403-4) is furnished by Professor R. D. Wilson, in an art. on "Babylon and Israel" in *The Princeton Theol. Review* for April 1903. Dr. Wilson shows, on the basis of a large induction, that contracts were freely drawn up on the Sabbaths as on other days. Cf. also König's *Die Babel-Bibel-Frage*, p. 22.

[1] See the Babylonian Chronicle, as above.
[2] Cf. Pinches, p. 418 ; Driver, *Daniel*, p. xxxi. In a very important note (*Higher Crit.* p. 522) Sayce shows that contracts in Babylon continued to be dated by the year of "Nabonidus king of Babylon" after the capture in July up to November. These are noted as drawn up in "the city of the king's palace, Babylon," while one dated in December "in the accession year of Cyrus" is simply inscribed "Babylon."
[3] Gobryas had already been described as "governor of Gutium." The remarks of Prof. R. D. Wilson on the use of the title "king" apply to Darius also. See, on whole subject, the valuable note of Köhler in *Bib. Gesch.* iii. pp. 535-41.

CHAPTER XII

Psalms and Prophets: The Progressiveness of Revelation

"How varied and how splendid the wealth which this treasury [the Psalter] contains, it is difficult to describe in words. . . . This Book, not unreasonably, I am wont to style an anatomy of all parts of the soul, for no one will discover in himself a single feeling whereof the image is not reflected in this mirror."—CALVIN.

"After busying myself with the Old Testament in its original text for over forty-eight years, I can bear witness with fullest truth, that whatever cleaves to the Old Testament of imperfection, yea, perhaps, of offence, in a word, of 'the form of a servant,' has from year to year for me ever the more shrivelled up into nothingness, with an ever deepening penetration into the overmastering phenomenon of prophecy."—KAUTZSCH.

"Kuenen has designated his investigation of prophecy strictly impartial; but it is not to be mistaken that his arrangement is controlled by the motive of reducing faith in a divine inspiration of the prophets to absurdity."—GIESEBRECHT.

"When I come to such psalms wherein David curseth his enemies, oh! then let me bring my soul down to a lower note, for these words were made only to fit David's mouth."—THOMAS FULLER.

"It is evident, then, that a progressive revelation—if the idea of such a revelation is once admitted—must be judged by its end and not by its beginning. . . . According to any rule of judging in such cases, the morality of a progressive dispensation is not the morality with which it starts, but that with which it concludes. The test is not the commencement, but the result."—MOZLEY.

CHAPTER XII

PSALMS AND PROPHETS: THE PROGRESSIVENESS OF REVELATION

IF the history is the body of the Old Testament religion, the psalms and prophets may be said to be its soul. It is not our purpose in this concluding chapter to enter upon a full discussion of either the Psalter or prophecy. It will be enough to confine attention to two problems in regard to these—first, the place of the psalms in the history of revelation, and specially their connection with David;[1] and second, the place and function of the predictive element in prophecy, with certain canons of interpretation which arise out of the consideration of that subject. Our discussion may then close with some reflections on the progressiveness of revelation, in its bearings on what are called the "moral difficulties" of the Old Testament.

PART I

DAVID AND THE PSALTER

In one point of view, the spiritual teaching of the Psalter—its power of help and inspiration—is independent of any views we may form as to the place and time of its origin. The psalms by which our faith and hope are nourished are the same, whoever were their authors, or in whatever age they were composed. They deal with relations of the soul to God which are above time, or are the same in all time; and if, instead of being largely pre-exilian, as has been commonly supposed, all of them were proved to be post-exilian, they would not lose a jot of their

[1] On the structure of the Psalter, see above, pp. 197, 227.

essential spiritual value. Yet the question of the age of
the psalms is, in another respect, far from being one to
which we can afford to be indifferent. The psalms are
lamps brightly illuminating the religious conditions of the
age in which they had their origin: and if any of them
belong to the pre-exilian age, their aid is of the first
importance in determining the real character of the religion
of that age. It is this, in fact, which makes it necessary for
the newer criticism to put the psalms down into the post-
exilian period. Their earlier existence will not harmonise
with the views put forth as to the stages of the religious
development. If even eight or ten of the psalms be allowed
to David, it is not too much to say that the critical
hypothesis of Kuenen and Wellhausen — at least their
theory of the religion—is blown into the air. It is part of
our problem, therefore, to inquire what the truth is in this
matter.[1]

1. Theory of the Post-exilian Origin of the Psalter

It has now become almost a dogma in the Wellhausen
school that the Psalter is wholly, or with minute and
doubtful exception, post-exilian in origin. Wellhausen lays
it down that, "as the Psalter belongs to the Hagiographa,
and is the hymn-book of the Church of the second temple . . .
the question is not whether it contains any post-exilian
psalms, but whether it contains any that are pre-exilian."[2]
This question he answers for himself in the negative. The
psalms, he says, are "altogether the fruit" of the post-
exilian period.[3] Reuss had preceded him in this judgment;
and Stade, Duhm, Cheyne, and the greater number of this

[1] Delitzsch observes: "Schultz, in his *Alttest. Theol.* (2nd edit. 1878),
acknowledges at least ten psalms as Davidic. The consequences which follow
for the reconstruction of the history of Israel from the recognition, whether
it be of ten or more genuine Davidic psalms, are so important, that the
endeavour of some recent writers to bring down all the psalms to the time
after the exile is comprehensible as an attempt to paralyse these consequences."—*Com. on Psalms*, i. p. 11. With his later change of critical
standpoint, Schultz gave up even the ten psalms, and concluded "that
perhaps only Ps. xviii. can be ascribed to David with anything like absolute
certainty."—*O.T. Theol.* i. p. 64. We shall see, however, that much lies
even in the admission of Ps. xviii.; it, too, accordingly, is now generally
denied to David. See below, p. 446.

[2] Wellhausen's Bleek, *Einleit.*, (1876), p. 507; Psalms ("Poly. Bib."),
p. 163.   [3] *Hist. of Israel*, p. 501.

school, echo the opinion.[1] A more moderate position is taken by Dr. Driver, who allows that several of the psalms —especially those which allude to the king—may be presumed to be pre-exilian; but thinks that "very few of the psalms are earlier than the eighth century B.C."[2] Wellhausen's opinion of the psalms, it may be observed, is not a high one. In one of his latest works he says: "There is nothing analogous to the psalms in pre-exilian times. They are prayers of quite another kind from those known to antiquity: they rest on the despair of Jeremiah and the confidence of the Great Anonymous" (Isa. xl. ff.). And in a note: "They certainly are only to the smallest extent original; are for the most part imitations, which illustrate the saying about much writing: often they are not real prayers at all, but sermons, and even narratives in the form of prayers. One sees how prayer becomes an art and species of literature."[3]

On this theory we remark:

1. This dictum, that the psalms are all, or mostly, of post-exilian date, neither is, nor can be, proved. There are, no one doubts, post-exilian psalms;[4] it is an open question whether there are not a few Maccabæan psalms.[5] Calvin admitted the possibility of such, and, till recently, opinion was divided on the subject—to some extent is so still—generally, however, with a leaning to denial.[6] But only an

[1] For the history of opinion on the psalms, see Robertson, *Poetry and Religion of the Psalms*, pp. 40 ff. ; Kirkpatrick, *The Psalms*, pp. xxxvii ff. ; Baethgen, Cheyne, etc. Reuss says we have "no decisive proofs" of psalms of the period of the kingdom (*Geschicht. d. Heil. Schriften*, p. 366 ; cf. p. 197). Duhm denies that a single psalm is pre-exilian. The discussions of W. R. Smith (*O.T. in J. C.*, 1st edit. pp. 197 ff.) and of Driver (*Introd.* pp. 373 ff.) are unfavourable to the positive ascription of any psalms to David : in his 2nd edit. W. R. Smith discards Davidic psalms altogether, and makes the whole Psalter, with slight exception (p. 220), post-exilian (cf. pp. 218–25).

[2] *Introd.* p. 384.

[3] *Israel. und Jüd. Geschichte* (1897), p. 197.

[4] Such, *e.g.*, manifestly (exilian or post-exilian) are Pss. cii., cxxiv., cxxvi., cxxxvii., and others in the 4th and 5th Books of the Psalter.

[5] The most striking of the psalms claimed for this period are Pss. xliv., lxxiv., lxxix.

[6] Hitzig and Olshausen were the main advocates of Maccabæan psalms : Gesenius, Hupfeld, Ewald, Bleek, Dillmann, etc., refused to acknowledge them : so Hengstenberg, Hävernick, Keil (cf. Delitzsch, *Psalms*, i. p. 15) : Delitzsch admits the possibility. Bleek (*Introd.* ii. p. 239) and Dillmann (*Jahr. d. deutsch. Theol.* iii. pp. 460–62) hold that there is no good ground for placing any psalm later than Nehemiah's age. Of more recent writers, Duhm, Baethgen (*Psalmen*, p. xxviii), Kirkpatrick, etc., reject Maccabæan

anti-traditional bias, combined with assumptions as to the line of development of Israel's religion, can claim to regard it as established that all, or even the bulk of, the psalms are post-exilian compositions. Grant all that is said of the untrustworthiness of the titles, and of the difficulty of proving that a single psalm is from the pen of David—a point to which we shall return later,—the assumption of Davidic psalms has at least behind it a firmly-fixed Jewish tradition, dating from times when the Canon was still in process of formation: the assertion that none—or hardly any—of the psalms are pre-exilian has neither documentary nor traditional support, and is not borne out by considerations of internal probability. As a question of evidence, everything that is urged as to the impossibility of proving that David wrote any of the psalms can be retorted with equal force against the unsupported assertion that the psalms in question are post-exilian.

2. In judging of the assertions frequently made as to the marvellous literary productivity of the post-exilian age, it is important to bear in mind that the greater part of that period is *an absolute blank* to our knowledge. This is hardly always realised as it should be. We speak of the "connection" of the Old and New Testaments, but it is really not in our power, up to the time of the Maccabees, to write a history of the period after the return at all. There is "a great gap" from Nehemiah to Antiochus Epiphanes, *i.e.*, from 400 B.C. to 175 B.C., which even Josephus can fill up with only a few legendary notices.[1] Of the century between Artaxerxes Longimanus (465–325 B.C.), Josephus chronicles nothing, and his history is in great confusion otherwise. What we do know is that, from the time of Ezra, the nation set before itself as its religious ideal the strict and conscientious observance of the law of Moses. Hence the development of the order of the scribes, and the legalistic stamp on the piety of later Judaism. When the curtain lifts again in the time of Antiochus Epiphanes, we

---

psalms. See the grounds clearly stated in Kirkpatrick, *Psalms*, pp. xliv ff. Professor W. R. Smith reasons against Maccabæan psalms in *Books I.–III.* of the Psalter (*O.T. in J. C.*, pp. 207, 437 ff.), but finds some in later Books (p. 211).

[1] Cf. Schürer, *Hist. of Jewish People*, i. p. 86. Professor W. R. Smith says: "It must be admitted that we know but little of the history after the time of Nehemi   "

find ourselves in a new atmosphere of Hellenism, and the
three parties of historical note—the Pharisees, the Sadducees,
and the Essenes—are, in germ at least, already in existence.[1]
This age of stiffening legalism, of priestly ascendency, of
scribism, of cessation of the prophetic spirit, is not that to
which we should naturally look for the creation of such a
book as our present Psalter. Our very ignorance about it,
no doubt, makes the period a convenient receptacle for all
sorts of critical hypotheses;[2] but it cannot be too strongly
borne in remembrance that these hypotheses rest, for the
most part, on unverifiable conjecture. When, *e.g.*, Professor
Bennett says: "The exilic, Persian, and Greek periods were
specially rich in psalms,"[3] he makes a statement which he
no doubt believes to be true, but for which there is no
historical evidence. When, again, Professor Cheyne writes
of "the time when the temple with its music was reorganised
and the Psalter re-edited by Simon,"[4] he must be aware,
indeed elsewhere admits,[5] that history knows nothing of
such transactions. They are simply imaginations of his
own, transformed into facts.

3. It must appear strange, surely, that an age assumed
to be one of such extraordinary literary activity should
have left, among its numerous products, *no record of itself*.
Ezra and Nehemiah wrote of their own times; the Chronicler
recalled and glorified the past; but not a pen, apparently,
was found, after Nehemiah, to record contemporary events.
Does this look like a golden age of psalmody? That the
return from captivity should give rise to a group of psalms,
celebrating that great event, is only what might be expected.
But the post-exilian psalms, for the most part, are easily
recognised, and they constitute a relatively small portion of
the Psalter. The great majority of the psalms—especially
those in the earlier books—have nothing peculiarly post-
exilian about them. They are written in pure and vigorous

[1] Josephus mentions the three parties as in existence in the time of
Jonathan the Maccabee, about 150 B.C. (*Ant.* xiii. 5. 9). The Pharisees are
no doubt correctly identified with the Assidæans (Chasidim) of 1 Macc. ii.
42; vii. 12 ff. Cf. Schürer, *Hist. of Jewish People* (Div. ii.), ii. pp. 26 ff.

[2] In one of the last conversations the writer had with the late A. B.
Davidson, he commented in his pungent way on the use made of this blank
period. "A free coup," he said, using the Scotch phrase applied to places
granted for the free emptying of rubbish.

[3] *Primer*, p. 100.

[4] *Origin of Psalter* p. 458.   [5] *Ibid.* p. 11.

Hebrew.[1] They are personal and spiritual in tone, touching the deepest and most universal chords in religious experience. They show no traces of post-exilian legalism, or of the ideas of the Priestly Code. On the other hand, many of the psalms suit admirably the conditions of an earlier time, where they do not contain features which necessitate or at least are most naturally explained by, a pre-exilian date. Such, especially, is the not inconsiderable series of psalms that make mention of the "king,"[2] which cannot be brought down to a post-exilian time without extreme forcing. Such, to our mind, are those that contain allusions to the "tabernacle" (tent),[3] to the ark and cherubim,[4] to the temple as a centre of national worship,[5] to conquests of surrounding peoples,[6] and the like. In a few of the later psalms we find such expressions used of Jehovah as "among the gods," "above the gods," "God of gods," "before the gods,"[7] which is not what, on the newer theory, we naturally look for from the strict monotheism of post-exilian times. Alternatively, will the critics grant us that the use of such expressions does not imply, as is sometimes argued for pre-exilian times, that monotheism is not yet reached?

4. This raises the larger question of the general history of *psalmody* and of the *connection of psalmody with David*. We touch briefly on psalm-collection after,[8] and meanwhile look only at the indications of pre-exilian psalmody, and at the Davidic tradition. Lyric poetry, as Delitzsch reminds us,[9] is of very early date in Israel. When, in addition, one

---

[1] Some psalms, as Ps. cxxxix., bear marks of lateness, but most are written, as Reuss admits, in good, pure, classical Hebrew. Cf. Robertson, *Psalms*, p. 64.

[2] Such are Pss. ii., xviii., xx., xxi., xxviii., xxxiii., xlv., lxi., lxiii., lxxii., ci., cx. Dr. Cheyne's attempt to explain these psalms from the Maccabæan or Greek age (Judas, Simon, Ptolemy Philadelphus), is justly characterised by Baethgen as "a complete failure." Cf. his *Psalmen*, pp. xxiv–xxv.

[3] See below, p. 447.

[4] Pss. lxxx. 1; xcix. 1; cxxxii. 8. As there was no ark in the second temple, it seems most natural (though "cherubim" *might* refer to the heavenly temple) to regard these psalms as pre-exilian. Cf. Delitzsch and Perowne, *in loc*.

[5] *E.g.*, Pss. xlvi., xlviii., lxxxiv.   [6] *E.g.*, Ps. lx. 6 ff.

[7] Pss. lxxxvi. 8; cxxxv. 5; cxxxvi. 2; cxxxviii. 1. The "liturgical" character of these psalms does not necessarily prove them "post-exilian," but some of them appear made up from earlier passages, and may reasonably be regarded on that account as late.

[8] See below, p. 448.   [9] *Psalms*, i. p. 9.

remembers the deep religious foundations on which the life of Israel as a nation rested, the signal manifestations of God's presence and power in its history,[1] and the powerful workings of His Spirit in individuals and in the community in other directions, it is *a priori* to be expected that sacred hymnody would not be lacking in the public and private worship of pre-exilian times. That religious song and music did exist under the old temple seems abundantly attested by the place given to "singers" in the narratives of the return,[2] and by what is said of their functions,[3] and is further directly evidenced by the taunt addressed to the exiles at Babylon by their captors to sing to them "the songs of Zion"—"Jehovah's songs."[4] Express reference is made to the praises of the first temple in Isa. lxiv. 11: "Our holy and beautiful house, where our fathers praised Thee" (cf. chap. xxx. 29). In regard to particular psalms, Professor W. R. Smith allows that Ps. viii. is the foundation of Job's question in chap. vii. 17, 18 ;[5] and there is what seems to be a clear quotation of Ps. i.—by no means one of the earliest of the psalms, and apparently the preface to a collection of Davidic psalms—in Jer. xvii. 8.[6] It has been seen that many other psalms—*e.g.*, those relating to the king—can only be put in pre-exilian times: even Prof. W. R. Smith admits this of Pss. xx., xxi.[7] Pre-exilian psalmody is thus established; and that a firm and constant tradition traced back the beginnings of this psalm-composition to David—"the sweet psalmist of Israel"[8]—is not less evident from the ascription of so large a body of psalms to David by their titles,[9] and from the fact that in Chronicles the

---

[1] This argument is admirably worked out in detail by Professor Robertson in his *Poetry and Religion of the Psalms*, chaps. vii., viii.

[2] Ezra ii. 41, 65 ; vii. 7, 24 ; Neh. x. 28, 29.

[3] Ezra iii. 10, 11 ; Neh. xi. 22, 23 ; xii. 45–47.

[4] Ps. cxxxvii. 3, 4. [5] *O.T. in J. C.*, p. 220.

[6] See below, p. 450. The alternative suppositions that the psalm is based on this passage in Jeremiah, or that both have a common source, have little probability. "It is the custom of Jeremiah," says Delitzsch, "to reproduce predictions of his predecessors, and more especially expressions found in the psalms, in the flow of his own discourse, and to transform their style into his own."—*Psalms*, i. Cf. Perowne, i. p. 106; Kirkpatrick, p. 1 ; Baethgen, p. 1. See also Ezek. xlvii. 12.

[7] As above. [8] 2 Sam. xxiii. i.

[9] The whole of Book I. of the Psalter is ascribed to David, with the exception of Pss. i. and ii. (preparatory), x. (part of ix.), and xxxiii. ("the first book, therefore, is a formal collection of psalms ascribed to David."—W. R.

whole organisation of the service of song and music in the
sanctuary is traced back to him.[1] It is futile, as was
formerly seen, to dismiss such statements as mere inventions
of the Chronicler.[2] That writer must be presumed to be
drawing in good faith from older sources, and to be express-
ing what, at the time when these sources were composed,
was well-established belief. Such consentient tradition
ought not to be lightly set aside. Instead of rejecting it
on the ground that many of the titles in the psalms are
conjectural and untrustworthy—which admittedly is the
case—we shall act more wisely in using it as a clue for our
guidance where facts do not show that it is clearly at fault.
Before proceeding further, we shall look at what is to be
said in favour of, and what in opposition to, this view that
David is the author of many of the psalms.

II. THE HISTORICAL POSITION OF DAVID AS PSALMIST

In opposition to the Biblical tradition, the position
taken up by the critics is, that the historical David is not
an individual to whom compositions like the psalms can
with propriety be attributed:[3] and, generally, that the
psalms imply a stage of religious development far in advance
of that of the Davidic age.[4] We do not go back on the
question of the religious development, further than to remind
the reader that, till lately, critical experts felt no difficulty
on this point, but would here ask whether the accounts we
have of David are such as to negative his authorship of
many of the psalms. We assume that the accounts we have
rest on good prophetic narratives, when the memory of
David's personality and reign was still fresh, and when his
virtues and failings were recorded with equal fidelity.[5]

Smith, p. 197); eighteen psalms in Book II. ("so again, in the 2nd Book,
the psalms ascribed to David . . . form a connected group," *ibid.*); one in
Book IV; and several in Book V.—seventy-three in all.

[1] Cf. 1 Chron. xxiii. 5; xxv. etc.

[2] See above, p. 390; and cf. the remarks of Professor Robertson, *Psalms*,
pp. 92 ff.

[3] Thus Reuss, Wellhausen, Cheyne, W. R. Smith, more mildly Driver,
etc. See Note A on The Critical Estimate of David.

[4] Cf. Cheyne, *Origin of Psalter*, pp. 192 ff.

[5] See above, p. 381. Cf. Robertson, *Psalms*, p. 343. See his whole chap.
xiii. on "David the Psalmist": also Perowne, *Psalms*, Introd. chap. i.
"David and the Lyric Poetry of the Hebrews"; and Margoliouth, *Lines of
Defence of the Biblical Revelation*, pp. 194 ff.

1. We begin with a brief survey of David's career.

(1) It will not be denied that, in the history, David's character *as a young man* is as free from blemish as anyone could wish. He is chosen by Samuel above the other sons of Jesse on the ground that "man looketh on the outward appearance, but Jehovah looketh on the heart."[1] Saul's servants attest regarding him that "he is cunning in playing, and a mighty man of valour, and a man of war, and prudent in speech, and a comely person, and Jehovah is with him."[2] His character comes out at its best in his encounter with Goliath.[3] Here we see the whole man revealed—his dauntlessness, his faith in God, his unerring skill with the sling, his quiet modesty and decision of character, the energy that slumbered behind. The women who came out to meet him with chants and music only echoed the universal feeling that in this stripling lay the makings of the kingliest man in Israel.[4]

(2) In his life *at the court of Saul*, David's character is equally admirable. As a popular hero he had no rival; he was fast friend to Jonathan; he was set over the men of war; he ate at the king's table, and soon became Saul's son-in-law. But honours like these did not make his brain whirl, or his feet slide. His record at court is a strictly honourable one. He "went out whithersoever Saul sent him, and behaved himself wisely; and Saul set him over the men of war, and it was good in the sight of all the people, and also in the sight of Saul's servants."[5] Another record about him is—and this is after the tide of favour had turned, and he had become the object of Saul's deadly jealousy: "And David behaved himself wisely in all his ways, and Jehovah was with him. And when Saul saw that he behaved himself very wisely, he stood in awe of him. But all Israel and Judah loved David; for he went out and came in before them."[6] David's position, we see from the narrative, soon became a very difficult one. Jonathan was with him, but Saul had become his bitter enemy. His life was sought, both openly and by plot and intrigue, and, with the change in the king's mood, envious, rancorous tongues would not be wanting to shoot their shafts at him. But, amidst all, as David showed no vanity or pride in the day of

[1] 1 Sam. xvi. 7.   [2] Sam. xvi. 18.   [3] 1 Sam. xvii.
[4] 1 Sam. xviii. 7.   [5] 1 Sam. xviii. 5.   [6] 1 Sam. xviii. 14-16.

next care was to bring up the ark of God, and reorganise the worship of Jehovah at Zion.[1] Powerful confederations having been formed to crush his rising power, he called out his forces, and struck a succession of blows, which not only delivered him from the danger, but made him overlord of the whole country from the river of Egypt to the Euphrates.[2] He had even in contemplation the building of a temple; but this the divine voice forbade, while rewarding his intention with the promise that his seed should sit upon his throne for ever.[3]

Such were some of David's services to his age; surveying them impartially, we cannot wonder that his memory should be embalmed with lively gratitude in the minds of the Israelites as that of their first great and god-like king. Over against these services are to be placed the blots on his private life and reign: his polygamy—no sin, however, by the then existing code—his over-indulgence to his children, some acts of severity in war, but, above all, the one great, black crime of his adultery with Bathsheba and the murder of her husband Uriah.[4] Nothing can palliate this crime; yet even here, while condemning David, it is necessary to try to be just. For a Pharaoh, a Nebuchadnezzar, a Xerxes, or other Oriental monarch to covet the wife of a subject, and give orders for the death of her husband, would have seemed to most ancient historians a venial enough fault, and they would probably not have occupied half a dozen lines with the relation.[5] It is the Biblical history itself, by the bold relief into which it throws this shameful incident,—by its impartiality in narrating, in denouncing, and in declaring the punishment of this sin of David,—which makes it bulk so largely in our minds, and inspires us with such just horror in regard to it. But it is not to be forgotten that the same book which tells us of

---

[1] 2 Sam. vi.   [2] 2 Sam. viii.
[3] 2 Sam. vii.   [4] 2 Sam. xi.
[5] Cf. the remarks of Margoliouth in his *Lines of Defence of the Biblical Revelation*, pp. 209–10. He says : " If the worst act of David's life, the painful story of Bathsheba, be considered, the underlying character which David exhibits is much better than that displayed by most men in any age. Max Duncker remarks that the crime which caused David so much penitence and contrition was one of which, probably, no other Oriental monarch would have thought anything, and, if there be any truth in history, it would have occasioned few scruples to most defenders of the faith." See the whole passage.

and many considerations speak to the contrary. We touch only on single points.

1. At the lower end, the Books of Maccabees presuppose the Psalter. The first Book (about 100 B.C.) quotes freely Ps. lxxix. 2, 3 as from Scripture (1 Macc. vii. 17); and the second Book speaks of the writings in the third division of the Canon loosely as "the works of David," showing that the psalms then held a leading place in this division (cf. Luke xxiv. 44).

2. The Psalter was admittedly complete, and divided into its five books, at the time of the Septuagint translation, which, it is allowed, cannot be placed lower than the second half of the second century B.C. (before 130 B.C.), and may possibly be a good deal earlier.[1] It is evident that the Psalter must already have been recognised as part of the Canon for a considerable time in order to its being included in this translation. An important testimony to the antiquity of many of the psalms is afforded by the fact that certain of the musical and liturgical headings—e.g., the common one, "For the Chief Musician"[2]—are unintelligible to the Greek translators.

3. We have indubitable evidence in the Prologue to the Greek translation of the work of Jesus, the son of Sirach (Ecclesiasticus), made by his grandson, 132 B.C., that the Canon in its three divisions was substantially completed, not only in the translator's own time, but in that of his grandfather, the author of the book (about 200 B.C.), and the work itself gives internal evidence of the use of the psalms. This is borne out by the recovery of portions of the Hebrew text.[3]

[1] The LXX translation of the law was made about the middle of the third century B.C., but there is no clear evidence as to when the work was completed by the translation of the Hagiographa. The language of the grandson of the son of Sirach, however, implies that a translation already existed in his day, and other facts support this conclusion. Ehrt, in his work on the subject (quoted by Robertson, *Psalms*, p. 87), believes that the *original* work of Ben Sirach implies the use of the LXX version of the psalms.

[2] This heading is prefixed to fifty-five psalms, of which fifty-two are found in Books I.–III., and three only in Book V. (elsewhere only in Hab. iii. 19). It is misunderstood by the translators, and had evidently long passed out of use.

[3] The grandson refers in his Prologue to "the law, and the prophecies, and *the rest of the books*" (*i.e.*, a definite number), and speaks of his grandfather's acquaintance with the same. This is a strong point with those who argue against Maccabæan psalms (*e.g.*, Riehm, Baethgen, Kirkpatrick). A corroboration of the statement is afforded by the recovery of portions of the

29

4. The Books of Chronicles (not later than about 330 B.C.) know the Psalter, and, as before seen,[1] carry back psalmody and the musical arrangements of the sanctuary to the time of David. In 1 Chron. xvi. 7–36 is given a long psalm as illustrative of the kind of praise offered at the bringing up of the ark to Zion. This piece is found on inspection to be composed of passages from Pss. cv., xcvi., and cvi., and concludes with the doxology at the end of Ps. cvi. which marks the close of Book IV. of the Psalter.[2] The inference is natural that the division into books was already made in the time of the Chronicler.

5. The Book of Jonah, which Professor Robertson places provisionally in the fifth century B.C., and which, in any case, is earlier than the close of the prophetic Canon, contains a prayer of Jonah (chap. ii. 2–10), admittedly based on passages from different parts of the Psalter.[3] This implies some collection of these psalms.

6. It was shown that Jeremiah (chap. xvii. 8) unmistakably quotes from Ps. i., which is generally acknowledged to be an introduction to the first collection of Davidic psalms (cf. Ezek. xlvii. 12).[4] This collection, therefore, is presumably earlier. Further, the formula of thanksgiving in Jer. xxxiii. 11, "Give thanks to Jehovah of hosts, for Jehovah is good: for His mercy endureth for ever," is found only in psalms included in Books IV. and V. of the Psalter.

7. It was seen likewise that the musical arrangements of the second temple were an inheritance from the period before the exile.[5] It is reasonable to suppose that the liturgical use of the psalms was so also.

The conclusion is not overstrained that the basis of the Psalter was already laid before the exile—how much earlier it is impossible to tell, but the Davidic collections may go

original text of Ecclesiasticus. Dr. Schechter holds that the allusions to the psalms in the work extend over "all the books and groups of the psalms." "The impression produced . . . is that of reading the work of a post-canonical author, who already knew his Bible, and was continually quoting it " (in Kirkpatrick, *Psalms*, p. xlviii).

[1] See above, p. 440.

[2] Professor W. R. Smith argues that the doxology is an original part of the psalm, and does not carry with it the inference that the Psalter was already formed. He thinks that doxologies were appended only to the first three books (p. 196), but admits that "the majority of modern scholars are against him in this opinion " (p. 194).

[3] Cf. Robertson, pp. 103 ff.   [4] See above, p. 439.

[5] See above, p. 439.

back a long way—and that the psalms, especially in the earlier books, may fairly be used as evidence of the type of piety in godly circles in Israel from the days of David downwards. The witness they bear in no wise agrees with the Wellhausen representation.

PART II

THE PREDICTIVE ELEMENT IN PROPHECY

Hebrew prophecy will be acknowledged by most to be a perfectly unique phenomenon in the history of religions. Whatever the etymology of the name (*Nabi*),[1] the prophet himself stands clearly out as one who is conscious of receiving a message directly from Jehovah, which he is commissioned to impart to men.[2] In its beginnings prophecy goes as far back as revelation,[3] but the founder of the prophetic order in the stricter sense is Samuel.[4] We may pass over the development of prophecy in the intervening period—over even the great figures of Elijah and Elisha, who are, however, acting rather than teaching prophets,—and come at once to the full bloom of prophecy in the age of the writing prophets. Here, plainly, the nature of prophecy can be studied to best advantage.

It is not denied that genuine prophecy presupposed in the person exercising the prophetic function a special natural endowment, or that it was psychologically conditioned. Its natural basis was a species of genius, which we are still not slow to recognise in those who possess it, enabling them to see deep into the heart of things, where others only behold the surface, and to speak the word necessary for guidance, where others grope and stumble (cf. Ps. lxxiv. 9). While, however, this gift of "geniality," of insight, of divining intuition,

[1] Gesenius, Kuenen, Oehler, etc., derive the word from a root meaning "to bubble"; others explain differently.

[2] Augustine calls the prophet *enunciator verborum dei hominibus*.

[3] All the great revelation-figures (Abraham, Jacob, Moses) are represented as prophesying, and Abraham and Moses are designated prophets. In Mosaic times, cf. the interesting episode of Eldad and Medad and the seventy elders in Num. xi. 24–29. Under the Judges Deborah was a prophetess. Cf. A. B. Davidson, *O.T. Prophecy*, pp. 17 ff.

[4] 1 Sam. iii. 19–21; ix. 9. To Samuel belongs, apparently, the institution of the prophetic guilds.

belongs to the prophetic endowment, it is far from constituting the whole of it.[1] The genuine prophet is conscious of being laid hold of by the Spirit of God as other men are not; of receiving a message from Jehovah which he knows is not the product of his own thoughts, but recognises as God's word coming to him; which is imparted to him with perfect clearness and overpowering certainty; and which brings with it the call and constraint to deliver it to those for whom it is meant. The claim of the prophets to speak the word of God was sustained by the godliness of their character,[2] by the self-attesting power of their message, as a word instinct with spirit and life, and fitted to the time and need for which it was spoken, by its coherence with previous revelation, and, finally, by the sure fulfilment of their word, so far as it was predictive.[3] This brings us to the special topic we are to consider—the predictive element in prophecy.

I. SUPERNATURAL PREDICTION AN ELEMENT IN PROPHECY

It was certainly an error of the older apologetic to place the essence of prophecy, as was often done, in prediction. The prophet was in the first instance a man speaking to his own time. His message was called forth by, and had its adaptation to, some real and urgent need of his own age: it was the word of God to that people, time, and occasion. It needs, therefore, in order to be properly understood, to be put in its historical setting, and interpreted through

[1] Apart from more naturalistic writers, this is the view favoured by Giesebrecht in his *Die Berufgabung der Alttest. Propheten*, pp. 32–36, 72–77, etc. (cf. Preface). Prediction (which in special cases is admitted) is explained "out of a natural faculty with which God has endowed the prophet" (p. 73)—a "gift of *Ahnungsvermögens*" (pp. 74, 76, 77, etc.). But Giesebrecht goes on to ascribe so much to the "supernatural" action of God's Spirit in heightening and directing this natural faculty for the ends of revelation (pp. 77, 87, 97, etc.), that his view comes to differ little *in principle* from that indicated above. See below, p. 456.

[2] Giesebrecht says: "Kuenen himself concedes to the prophets a surpassing piety and moral earnestness. Intentional deception is in the nature of the case completely excluded. The high state of their intelligences, and the stage of clearest religious knowledge and finest moral judgment attained by them excites Kuenen's admiration. Is it credible that these men were self-deceived?"—As above, p. 16.

[3] On the supernatural element in prophecy, see the works on prophecy by A. B. Davidson, Riehm, Delitzsch, Orelli, etc., and Oehler, *Theol. of O.T.*, ii. pp. 313 ff. Cf. also the striking remarks of Kautzsch in his *Das Bleibende Bedeutung des A.T.*, pp. 29 ff.

that. It must be put to the account of modern criticism that it has done much to foster this better way of regarding prophecy, and has in consequence greatly vivified the study of the prophetic writings, and promoted a better understanding of their meaning.

On the other hand, the modern view, in its desire to assimilate prophecy as much as possible to the utterances of natural human genius, does palpable violence to scriptural teaching in denying, or making light of, this element of prediction. Not, indeed, that, up to a certain point, prediction is altogether denied. The prophets, it is allowed, had a peculiar—some would perhaps concede supernatural— insight into the character of God and the laws of His moral government, and, in the strength of their assurance of the divine righteousness, did not hesitate to draw what seemed to them the necessary deductions,[1] announcing chastisement and ruin as the result of national transgression, and proclaiming the certainty of the ultimate triumph of God's kingdom.[2] And, beyond question, they did this. But it is just as certain, if we are to do justice to the full nature of Biblical prophecy, that we must recognise a great deal more. The prophets do more than simply give forecasts of the general course of God's providence which, as deductions of their own mind, might easily be, and it is contended very frequently were, mistaken. How much more they did give can only be seen by looking at the prophecies themselves.

It was, in truth, in a sense inevitable that prediction

[1] Kuenen, as shown in our first chapter, and with him most of the moderns (Wellhausen, Stade, Duhm, etc.), deny the supernatural character of prophecy altogether (*Prophets and Prophecy*, pp. 4, 94–5, 227, etc. See above, pp. 12, 13). Kuenen denies even the truth of the prophetic conception of the divine righteousness, and the predictions based thereon. "While paying homage to the *earnestness* of the prophet's conception of Jahveh, we must positively deny its *truth*. . . . The prophetical prediction of the future now presents itself to us as the necessarily incorrect conclusion drawn from premises which themselves were only half correct" (pp. 354, 359).

[2] Ewald represents perhaps the high-water mark of this way of regarding prophecy. "What the prophet can," he says, "with perfect right, announce as the word of his God, is in its contents nothing but the application of some general divine truth to a given moral condition, or a clear contemplation as to the confusions or unevennesses of moral life before him, springing out of the clear light of the Spirit. What belongs to it falls within the province of the purer, *i.e.*, the divine Spirit; and if a prophet knows anything more, and can give answers to other questions, this is something accidental."—*Die Propheten*, i. p. 12 (E.T. p. 19).

should enter into such prophecy as we have in Scripture.
The prophet spoke, indeed, to his own time, but his message
had of necessity an aspect of warning and promise for the
future. It contained a declaration of what God would do
in the event of disobedience or obedience. Its cogency
depended on such announcements as it gave being reliable.
Prophecy was occupied, moreover, not simply with the
immediate temporal consequences of the nation's conduct.
Its supreme interest was in the kingdom of God, and its
eye was ever directed to the ultimate triumph of that
kingdom. Whatever promises it gave, or hopes it held
out, had all reference to that ultimate consummation. It
could not, therefore, in the nature of the case, ignore the
future.[1] It had statements to make regarding it, growing
out of the peculiar exigencies of the time, which would
have had little worth had they been simply forecasts of the
prophet's own mind. Their whole value depended on their
having on them the seal of true divine revelation. This
is the simple and complete answer to those who meet the
contention that Biblical prophecy contains prediction by
saying that such a view puts prophecy on a level with
"soothsaying." This is in no wise the case. Prediction
is never introduced as a mere wonder, or on its own
account, but always in connection with, and with a direct
bearing upon, the kingdom of God.[2] Soothsaying, on the
contrary, has no moral root, and subserves no wider moral
purpose; but is the result of a mere curious prying into
the future, and involves the use of superstitious, and
generally irrational means, to attain that end. Its chief
value is the testimony it bears to the inextinguishable

---

[1] Cf. Dr. A. B. Davidson, *O.T. Prophecy*, p. 294 : "It is now a commonplace that prophecy did not, even in the main, consist of prediction. The
commonplace is true, if predictions of mere contingent occurrences of a private
nature are meant. Prophecy was occupied with the destinies of the kingdom of God. But the essence of prophecy is prediction—prediction not
only of the far distant consummation and glory of the kingdom, but also
of the nearer steps necessary to this, the downfall of the State, and the
instruments who shall accomplish it." Cf. pp. 89, 96–98, etc. : *Theol. of O.T.*,
p. 177.

[2] Cf. Kautzsch, *Das Bleibende Bedeutung*, p. 31. The distinguishing
mark, he says, by which Hebrew prophecy is raised high as heaven above
all those heathen phenomena is : "*This* prophecy stands in the service of a
divine plan of salvation, and indeed in a service from which it cannot with-
draw itself." It is the more singular that Kautzsch should speak slightingly of prediction (p. 30).

craving of men's hearts for some kind of revelation of God and the future.[1]

II. Reality of Supernatural Prediction

Many are the straits to which rationalism is reduced, as Kuenen's large volume testifies,[2] in its attempt to eliminate the predictive element from prophecy. So deeply inwoven, however, is prediction into the texture of Scripture, that try as the critics may, they cannot altogether get rid of this unwelcome proof of the presence of the supernatural. We vividly recall the impression made upon our mind by the first reading of the book so often referred to in these pages—Wellhausen's *History of Israel*. The book is an attempt to give a thoroughly rationalising account of Israel's history, but the effect it produced was to make us feel as never before the impossibility of every such natural explanation. The supernatural was constantly thrusting in its head, notwithstanding all the critic's attempts to keep it out. Was it, *e.g.*, the Exodus from Egypt? The people were led by Moses round by the Red Sea, but by a singular coincidence—a marvellous piece of good fortune—the sea dried just in time to let them through. "His design," we are told, "was aided in a wholly unlooked-for way, by a marvellous occurrence quite beyond his control, and which no sagacity could possibly have foreseen."[3] Was it the deliverance of Jerusalem from Sennacherib? Isaiah alone of all the people retained his confidence in God's help, and gave Hezekiah in the name of Jehovah the most explicit assurance that the city would not be taken—that the enemy would not shoot an arrow into it, nor bring up a shield against it.[4] He predicted this in words of scornful exultation, and staked his prophetic reputation on the result. "And thus," says Wellhausen, "it proved in the issue. By a still unexplained catastrophe, the main army of

---

[1] In part, as Deut. xvii. 10 ff. shows, prophecy was given to satisfy the need for which an illegitimate satisfaction was sought in heathen mantic. On the contrast with heathen and other forms of prediction, cf. Orelli, *Prophecy*, p. 23 ; Kautzsch, as above, pp. 30, 31.

[2] Cf. the severe criticism of Kuenen's work in Giesebrecht, pp. 3–6.

[3] *Hist. of Israel*, p. 432. Others, as before shown, dispose of the miracle by denying the fact.

[4] Isa. xxxvii. 26–36.

Sennacherib was annihilated on the frontier between
Egypt and Palestine, and Jerusalem was freed from
danger."[1]   Is it the prediction of the downfall and
captivity of Israel by Amos? This prophet, Wellhausen
admits, "prophesied as close at hand the downfall of the
kingdom, which just at that moment was rejoicing most in
the consciousness of power, and the deportation of the
people to a far-off northern land."[2] We have but to
contrast this uniform tone of certainty of the Hebrew
prophets with the language, *e.g.*, of a John Bright during
the progress of the American civil war, to see how great is
the difference between prophecy and political perception,
even when the latter is quickened by the most intense
consciousness of the righteousness of a cause. "What the
revolt is to accomplish," said Mr. Bright, " is still hidden
from our sight; and I will abstain now, as I have always
done, from predicting what is to come. I know what I hope
for—what I shall rejoice in—but I know nothing of future
events which will enable me to express a confident opinion."[3]

These instances would be remarkable enough if they
stood alone; the disconcerting thing for the newer theory of
prophecy is that they do not stand alone. The Bible is full
of cases of the same kind. This can be maintained notwithstanding all theories of the critics as to the dates of the
books. It was when kings and nobles were lying on beds of
ivory, and indulging in every species of dissipation and
amusement, that Amos, as just mentioned, wrote: "Therefore will I cause you to go into captivity beyond Damascus,
saith Jehovah, whose name is the God of hosts."[4] It was
a century and more before the captivity of Judah that
Micah foretold: "Therefore shall Zion for your sake be
ploughed as a field, and Jerusalem shall become heaps. . . .

---

[1] *Hist. of Israel*, p. 483. Kuenen admits the oracle to be indubitably
genuine, but attempts to undermine the fulfilment (pp. 229 ff.). Professor
H. P. Smith has more than doubts about both oracle and history.

[2] *Ibid.* p. 470. Giesebrecht says: "They [the predictions] have often
for their content occurrences of which at the time of the prophet no one
could have any idea: so Amos, in a peaceful, nay, seemingly illustrious
time, predicts the Assyrian campaign, till then unheard of" (p. 73). This
writer, as before stated, finds the explanation of these predictions (which
were not *always* fulfilled) in the divine quickening of a natural faculty of
divination or presentiment, of which sporadic examples are found elsewhere
(pp. 73–76).

[3] Speech, June 30, 1863.   [4] Amos v. 27.

Be in pain, and labour to bring forth, O daughter of Zion, like a woman in travail; for now shalt thou go forth out of the city, and shalt dwell in the field, and shalt come even unto Babylon"—even this is not all, but—"there shalt thou be delivered; there shall Jehovah redeem thee from the hand of thine enemies."[1] Jeremiah's prophecies belong to the last years of the kingdom of Judah, but it is impossible to erase from them the prediction of the seventy years of captivity—fulfilled to a year from the date of the first deportation (606–536 B.C.).[2] "This whole land shall be a desolation, and an astonishment, and these nations shall serve the king of Babylon seventy years. And it shall come to pass, when seventy years are accomplished, that I will punish the king of Babylon, and that nation, saith Jehovah, for their iniquity, and the land of the Chaldeans; and I will make it desolate for ever."[3] The second portion of Isaiah is assigned to the exile; but it is not in the second portion, but in the first, a hundred and twenty years before the exile (contemporary with Micah), that we find this remarkable prediction of the captivity: "Then said I, Lord, how long? And He answered, Until cities be waste without inhabitant, and houses without man, and the land become utterly waste, and Jehovah have removed men far away. . . . And if there be yet a tenth in it, it shall again be eaten up: as a terebinth, and as an oak, whose stock remaineth, when they are felled: so the holy seed is the stock thereof."[4] And again, when Hezekiah had showed his treasures to the messengers of the king of Babylon: "Behold the days come, that all that is in thine house, and that which thy fathers have laid up in store until this day, shall be carried into Babylon: nothing shall be left, saith Jehovah."[5] Even accepting the view that the second part of

[1] Mic. iii. 12; iv. 10. There seems no ground, except the prophecy itself, for challenging the genuineness of these passages. Cf. Davidson, *O.T. Prophecy*, p. 264; Orelli, *Minor Prophets*, p. 206. See below, p. 464.

[2] There would be no objection to taking the number as a round number, but, reckoning from the initial deportation under Jehoiakim in 606 B.C. (cf. 2 Kings xxiv. 1; 2 Chron. xxxvi. 6 ff.; Dan. i. 1 ff.), it seems to be exact.

[3] Jer. xxv. 11, 12.

[4] Isa. vi. 11–13. Cf. the R.V. margin of ver. 18: "But yet in it shall be a tenth, and it shall return, and shall be eaten up." See the remarks of Professor G. A. Smith, *Isaiah*, i. pp. 403–4.

[5] Isa. xxxix. 5–7. These passages show that too much weight must not be laid on Isaiah's supposed belief in the inviolability of Zion.

Isaiah (chaps. xl.–lxvi.) is post-exilian—though we think this
extremely doubtful at least for portions of it [1]—we do not
thereby get rid of prediction.   Cyrus may already, as the
phrase is, have been "above the horizon" when the prophet
wrote, pursuing his conquests in the north; but the most
brilliant part of his career was yet to come.   Mighty Babylon
had not yet fallen,[2] nor had Israel been restored.   But it is
these things which form the burden of the prophecy.   We
cannot, moreover, but be struck by the fact that it is precisely in this second part of Isaiah that the fulfilment of
prophecy is insisted on as the clearest proof that Jehovah is
the true and only God.[3]   Daniel is a book keenly assailed by
the critics, and undoubtedly presents difficulties on the view
that it was written in its present form in Daniel's own age.[4]
Yet, on any theory of date, one cannot but feel that it is
only by forced and unnatural shifts—such as would not be
tolerated for a moment in the "traditional" apologist—that
an interpretation of the "four empires" can be got which
does not include the Roman,[5] or that makes the "seventy
weeks," or four hundred and ninety years, of Daniel, end
in the age of Antiochus Epiphanes (171–164 B.C.).[6]   On the
other hand, it is the case that, reckoning from the decree of
Artaxerxes and the mission of Ezra (458 B.C.), the sixty-nine
weeks that were to elapse till "the anointed one (Messiah)
the prince" (Dan. ix. 26), run out in 29 A.D., the year of
Christ's entrance on His public ministry.   If to these be

[1] The question of the authorship of this second part of Isaiah is one
which, as Professor G. A. Smith truly says, "can be looked at calmly.   It
touches no dogma of the Christian faith."—*Isaiah*, i. p. 402.   The question,
however, becomes more complicated when the second part also is broken up,
and it is recognised that there are at least some sections of the latter which
cannot, with any plausibility, be placed in the exile (*e.g.*, chaps. lvii., lviii.,
lxv. etc.).   See Note B on the Unity of Second Isaiah.

[2] Isa. xiii., *e.g.*, is a limelight prophetic picture of that catastrophe, but
it is not suggested that it was written after the event.

[3] Isa. xli. 21–23, 26–28 ; xliii. 9–12 ; xliv. 7, 8, 25–28 ; xlv. 11, 19, 21 ;
xlvi. 9 ; xlviii. 3–7, 14–16.   Cf. A. B. Davidson, *O.T. Prophecy*, pp.
97, 294.

[4] See above, p. 428.   The chief difficulty is the extremely detailed
character of the prediction in chap. xi., which, on so large a scale, is out
of harmony with the analogy of prophecy elsewhere, and may point to later
redaction.

[5] Dan. ii. 31 ff. ; vii. 1 ff.

[6] Dan. ix. 24 ff.   On the divergent views on these prophecies, cf. Driver,
Daniel, pp. 94 ff. ; 143 ff.; Pusey, *Daniel*, pp. 91 ff., 171, 197–217.   See
Note C on the Prophecies of Daniel.

added the prophecies about the nations, which fill so large a space in the books — the prophecy of Nahum against Nineveh, *e.g.*, or the prophecies against Egypt, Babylon, Tyre, and other surrounding kingdoms[1] — above all, the predictions respecting the captivities and future of the Jewish nation, their scattering through all lands, yet preservation as a distinct people, with promises of latter-day restoration[2] and blessing—we have a mass of prediction, not soothsaying, but all of it standing in strictest subordination to the ends of the kingdom of God, which, taken together, is absolutely unique, and wholly inexplicable except under supernatural conditions. The element of prediction is not less conspicuously present in the New Testament. Many of the parables, announcements, and discourses of Jesus are predictive—we instance only the great discourse on the destruction of Jerusalem and the last things;[3] prediction is interwoven with the narrative of the Acts[4] and with the Epistles;[5] the Apocalypse is a book of prediction in symbolic form.[6] If everything of the nature of predictive prophecy is expunged from the Bible, it will astonish us to find how much has gone with it.

Allusion was made in an earlier chapter[7] to what is distinctively known as Messianic prophecy, and, in connection therewith, to the firm assurance which the prophets entertained that their religion—the religion of Jehovah— would become the religion of the whole earth. This faith they held fast when everything was against them—when their own nation, with which the promises were bound up, was sinking in ruin, or was in exile. Yet this unprecedented thing has been fulfilled, so far, at least, that Israel's religion, in its New Testament form, has now become the religion of all the great civilised and progressive nations of the world, and is spreading itself ever more widely in heathen

---

[1] Kuenen and others contest the fulfilment of some of these predictions. See Note D in Kuenen on Unfulfilled Prophecies.

[2] It will be seen below (p. 464) that nothing can now be inferred as to the precise form in which these prophecies will be fulfilled. See a discussion of the subject in Dr. A. B. Davidson's *O.T. Prophecy*, pp. 468 ff.

[3] Matt. xxiv. Dr. Davidson says: "So far as we see, prediction was actually an element in the activity of most of the prophets, even in that of the prophet of Nazareth "—*O.T. Prophecy*, p. 89.

[4] *E.g.*, Acts xi. 27-30 ; xxi. 10, 11 ; xxvii. 10, 21, 22.

[5] *E.g.*, Rom. xi. 23, 24 ; 2 Thess. ii. 1-10.

[6] Rev. i. 1-3.   [7] Cf. above, p. 34.

lands. On Messianic prophecy in the stricter sense it is
worth while quoting some striking sentences from Professor
R. Flint. After remarking on the "marvellous unity, self-
consistency, and comprehensiveness" of the Old Testament,
and pointing out that "it is at the same time a system
which is not self-contained, but one of which all the parts
contribute, each in its place, to raise, sustain, and guide
faith in the coming of a mysterious and mighty Saviour—a
perfect Prophet, perfect Priest, and perfect King, such as
Christ alone of all men can be supposed to have been,"
Professor Flint goes on to say: "This broad general fact—
this vast and strange correlation of correspondence—cannot
be in the least affected by questions of the 'higher criticism' as to the authorship, time of origination, and mode
of composition of the various books of the Old Testament.
. . . Answer all these questions in the way which the
boldest and most rationalistic criticism of Germany or
Holland ventures to suggest; accept in every properly
critical question the conclusions of the most advanced
critical schools, and what will follow? Merely this, that
those who do so will have, in various respects, to alter their
views as to the manner and method in which the ideal of
the Messiah's Person, work, and kingdom was, point by
point, line by line, evolved and elaborated. There will not,
however, be a single Messianic word or sentence, not a
single line or feature the fewer in the Old Testament." [1]

III. HUMAN CONDITIONING OF PROPHECY—CANONS OF INTERPRETATION

Prophecy, if it has its origin in God, has, nevertheless,
its human side. It comes to us through the mind, faculties,
speech, of particular individuals, living at a particular time,
and variously conditioned by a particular experience.
Keeping this human or psychological side of prophecy in
view, we can readily explain a difference which the atten-
tive reader must observe between predictions of events
belonging to the prophet's immediate future,—not giving
this phrase too restricted a sense,—and predictions that
stretch beyond this limit, and relate to events yet remote

---

[1] St. Giles Lecture (Edinburgh) on "Christianity in Relation to other
Religions." Cf. Dr. Pat. Fairbairn, *Prophecy*, pp. 229 ff.

and indefinable. Predictions of the former class might be, and often were, quite definite and precise. Thus Isaiah predicted the destruction of Sennacherib's army; announced to Hezekiah that God had added to his life fifteen years.[1] Jeremiah predicted the capture of Jerusalem by the Chaldeans, the fates of Jehoiakim and Zedekiah, the seventy years' captivity.[2] But it is different as the event recedes into the future, loses its point of connection with the historic present, above all, belongs to an order of things, higher and more spiritual, for which the existing conditions offer no sufficient analogy. Vision of the future is not magically effected; the future is presented as an evolution from the historically existing; and, where that connection fails, prediction must necessarily take on a more general and ideal character. While, therefore, prediction of the immediate future is relatively definite, the vision of events more remote—especially of those belonging to the consummation of God's kingdom—becomes more general in form, and greater freedom is allowed in shaping it in symbol and metaphor. The *idea* becomes the main thing; the particular *form* of the idea—the clothing of imagery or detail it receives—is less essential. There is even here, no doubt, great difference of degree. Under the guidance of the divine Spirit, prophecy is sometimes quite startling in the individuality and definiteness of its prediction of even remote events.[3] The general principle, however, is undeniably as we have stated it, and from it three things follow which are of great importance as canons in the right interpretation of prophecy of the future.

1. It follows from what has been said that, in the prediction of distant events to which existing conditions no longer apply, there is no alternative but that these should be presented *in the forms of the present.* This is a principle

[1] Isa. xxxviii. 5.
[2] Jer. xxii. 18, 19; xxv.; xxxviii. 14 ff. etc. Cf. the instances in Acts above cited.
[3] We cannot reckon it as accidental, *e.g.*, that O.T. prophecy pointed so definitely to Bethlehem as the place of the Messiah's birth (Mic. v. 2), or to the peculiarity of His birth from a woman (Isa. vii. 14; Mic. v. 3). Cf. Davidson, *O.T. Prophecy*, pp. 359, 362; Dr. Pat. Fairbairn, *Prophecy*, pp. 230–31. Dr. Davidson says: "When we consider that Christianity is the issue of the prior Old Testament period, it is not improbable, it is rather to be expected, that hints should have been given even of its greatest mysteries" (p. 359).

which runs through all prophecy where the future state of the kingdom of God is concerned. It would have served no end, and is, under ordinary conditions, psychologically inconceivable, that the prophet should have been lifted out of all the forms of his existing consciousness, and transported into conditions utterly strange and inapprehensible by him. Such a revelation would, in any case, have been incommunicable to others.[1] We have, in the earthly condition, the same difficulty in picturing to ourselves the conditions of a heavenly state. But, just as supersensible realities cannot be conceived or spoken of by us except under forms of symbol or figure drawn from earthly relations, so prophecy of the future, or of a better dispensation, must necessarily picture that future, or those new conditions, in forms drawn from the present.[2] The kingdom of God, *e.g.*, in the Messianic age, is still figured as a theocracy with Jerusalem as a centre; the nations come up to it to worship; the enemies of the kingdom of God are figured under the old names—Egypt, Babylon, Edom, etc.; the converted nations are these same powers.[3] How far the prophet himself was able to distinguish the symbol from the idea is a secondary question. In some cases, at least, the idea is clearly seen breaking through the symbol, and transcending it.[4]

2. A second principle of interpretation relates to the element of *time* in prophecy. Here the fact to be remembered is, that the one thing immovably certain to the prophet—that with which he starts—is not the way by which the goal of the kingdom of God is to be reached, but

---

[1] Cf. Paul's experience in 2 Cor. xii. 1-4. It is wrong to view the prophetic consciousness as ordinarily a state of ecstasy.

[2] Excellent remarks on this subject will be found in the work above noted, Dr. Pat. Fairbairn's *Prophecy*, pp. 154 ff., 160 ff.

[3] Dr. A. B. Davidson, therefore, puts the matter too sharply when he says : "Such terms in the prophets are always to be taken in their literal, natural sense" (p. 167). His own words furnish the necessary correction. "No doubt, they occasionally broke through the atmosphere of their own dispensation, and soared into regions higher and purer" (p. 167 ; cf. p. 391). "When he says that Egypt shall be a desolation and the like, he means that the enemies of God's kingdom shall certainly then, or ere then, be all quite destroyed," etc. (pp. 180, 187).

[4] *E.g.*, such statements as Isa. ii. 2 : "The mountain of Jehovah's house shall be established in the top of the mountains," etc., are plainly poetic and figurative ; and the description of the flowing waters in Ezekiel's vision of the temple (chap. xlvii.) can hardly be intended to be taken literally.

the goal itself. Whatever might betide in the interval, there is no dubiety about *that*; God's purpose shall be fulfilled, His kingdom shall triumph, righteousness shall be supreme, and shall fill the earth. Whatever opposes itself to God's kingdom and resists it shall be shattered. However proud and powerful wickedness may be, there is "a day of Jehovah" coming—a judgment-day, when God's righteousness shall be vindicated. On the other hand, the steps by which this consummation is to be reached are only gradually unfolded, as the course of providence prepares the way for the discovery of them. Hence arises the feature so common in prophecy, that the consummation, or some phase of it, is the immediate background of the series of events in which the prophet is himself involved: of the Assyrian invasion, of the return from exile, of the Maccabæan deliverance, of the destruction of Jerusalem.[1] That is the one event which in prophetic perspective is always near; for which all events are preparing; to which they are hastening on. Hence the fact that in prophetic vision extending into the distant future so little place is given the element of time. There are exceptions to this rule—sometimes time-measures, as Jeremiah's seventy years, or Daniel's seventy weeks, are very definite. But ordinarily time is a quite secondary element. Events are grasped in their ideal relations, in their implication with one another as conducing to the final result, and not in their empirical succession. Prophecy is not, as Butler described it, history written beforehand, but the seizing of the inner meaning and the greater stadia of things, and the presenting of future developments in such graphic and pictorial forms as will best impress the imagination and move the heart.

3. The third principle is that there is a *conditional* element in prophecy. Expressed or implied, this element is ever present, and ought not to be overlooked in the interpretation of prophecy. The most explicit utterance of this principle is found in Jeremiah: "At what instant I [Jehovah] shall speak concerning a nation, and concerning a kingdom, to pluck up and to break down and to destroy it; if that nation, concerning which I have spoken, turn from their evil, I will repent of the evil that I thought to do unto

---

[1] The same applies to, and in part explains, **New Testament representations** of the *Parousia* (see below).

them. And at what instant I shall speak concerning a
nation, and concerning a kingdom, to build and to plant it;
if it do evil in my sight that it obey not my voice, then I
will repent of the good wherewith I said that I would benefit
them."[1] This obviously has an important bearing on the
time and manner of fulfilment. Often, as in the case of
Jonah's preaching to Nineveh, the object of the prophecy
is to *avert* fulfilment. A striking instance is given in the
Book of Jeremiah itself of how fulfilment of Micah's
prophecy against Jerusalem was delayed because of
Hezekiah's repentance.[2] Jesus, too, said of Jerusalem:
"How often would I have gathered thy children together
. . . and ye would not! Behold, your house is left unto
you desolate."[3] Human repentance may thus avert predicted judgment; human intercession may delay or modify
it; human fidelity will hasten, as, on the other hand, human
unfaithfulness will retard, accomplishment of promise. The
glowing predictions of the prophets as to what God would
do for Israel—even those which were never literally fulfilled
—were not illusions. They held up truly what God was
wishful to do for Israel, and would have done, had the conditions, on their part, been present. It does not follow that
a day of fulfilment will not come, but when it arrives, it
will be under new conditions, and in a new form.[4] In a
deeply important sense the same applies to the New
Testament hope of the Lord's Coming. There is a human
conditioning even here. When the Church prays, "Thy
kingdom come," it implicitly acknowledges that it has a
certain responsibility for the hastening or retarding of
that coming. Had the Church been more faithful—or
were it more faithful now—the consummation would be

[1] Jer. xviii. 7-10.   [2] Jer. xxvi. 17-19.
[3] Matt. xxiii. 37, 38.
[4] Delitzsch has some remarks on this point in connection with Ezekiel's
prophecies. "The condition," he says, "remained unfulfilled, and so with
it also the prophecy. For the grace of God does not work magically, and
prophecy is no fate. It is with the promises as it is with the aims of God's
grace: they are too often shattered on the resistance of man; as, on the
other hand, also, His threatenings are taken back if the threatened anticipate their fulfilment by repentance; for the free will of the creature is no
mere show, and history no play of marionettes. The fulfilment of many
prophecies moves from the appointed time into the future, and remains in
reserve for that: the fulfilment of others is overtaken by the advancing
history of salvation, and for that reason becomes impossible, at least in the
externality of their content."—Luthardt's *Zeitschrift*, 1880, pp. 280-81.

nearer; we might not still be asking, " Where is the promise of His Coming ? "[1]

PART III

THE PROGRESSIVENESS OF REVELATION—MORAL DIFFICULTIES

It would be unfitting to close this discussion of the problems of the Old Testament without a glance at the question of the *progressiveness of revelation*, in its bearings on those " moral difficulties " which are a chief stumbling-block to many in considering the claims of the revelation. That revelation is progressive—has its less developed and more developed stages—has been assumed throughout, and is generally admitted. But the precise mode of application of this principle of progressiveness to the solution of the ethical difficulties is not always clearly apprehended, and needs careful statement.

I. NATURE AND ORIGIN OF THE MORAL DIFFICULTIES

There would be no difficulty, possibly, in connection with the progressiveness of revelation, if the progress in question were simply one of development in moral *knowledge*—of growth from a more or less childlike consciousness of moral truths to a stage of greater maturity. The matter becomes more complicated when we observe that it is also in part the growth of a higher out of a lower morality, and that the lower stages involve much which to the enlightened conscience at the higher stage is positively evil. It is here that ethical difficulties emerge. When we go back to the earlier stages of Old Testament revelation—or even to the Old Testament as a whole—we find, co-existing with the knowledge and worship of the true God, with a high sense of the general obligations of righteousness, and with what we must recognise as great nobility of religious character, many things which perplex and stagger us. We find defects in the idea of duty, as measured by a later standard, the non-recognition of principles of conduct which to us are

[1] 2 Pet. iii. 4.

self-evident, institutions and usages which the enlightened
Christian conscience would not tolerate, things regarded as
permissible or right which we as emphatically pronounce
wrong. For instance, there is in the Old Testament slavery
and polygamy, there is blood-revenge, there is a low standard
—not in the law, indeed, but in individuals—of sexual
morality, there is the cursing of enemies, there is mercilessness in warfare, in the case of the Canaanites there is the
extermination of whole populations. It is possible, no
doubt, to set all this in an exaggerated and distorted light,
and this, as we shall see, is sometimes done. The "moral
difficulties" are no new discovery. They were worked for
all they were worth a century and a half ago in the
Deistical controversy, and many sensible and temperate
replies then appeared to the attacks on the Old Testament
based on them.[1] Little can be said now which was not said,
with far keener edge, by a Chubb, a Morgan, or a Bolingbroke.
But when every allowance for exaggeration or animus is
made, we cannot but recognise that a very real problem
remains.

The difficulty even here, it is next to be observed, is not
so much that such lower stages of morality should exist, and
should need to be overcome—that is only to be expected
—as that the defects in idea and practice cleave to the
organs of revelation themselves,—that these share in, and
give expression to, the same views as their contemporaries,
—that they do this sometimes when speaking in the name
of God,—nay, that God Himself is represented by them as
implicated in, and as sanctioning, these lower forms of
morality. Thus Abraham receives from God a command to
sacrifice his son Isaac; Deborah, a prophetess, pronounces
Jael blessed for her treacherous murder of Sisera; the Mosaic
legislation provides for slavery, polygamy, and divorce; the
command to exterminate the Canaanites is represented as
coming directly from God, and the Israelites are even re-
proved for not executing it with sufficient thoroughness;[2]
David, or whoever was the writer, invokes curses on his
enemies, and prays for their destruction. It is, in these and
other cases, the apparent implication of *God* in the lower

---

[1] Leland's *View of the Deistical Writers,* and *Divine Authority of the Old
and New Testament* (in reply to Morgan), may still be usefully consulted.
[2] Judg. ii. 1-3.

morality, or seeming immorality, which causes the difficulty. The morality of man may and must progress; the morality prescribed by God should, we naturally think, be one and the same throughout. How, on the assumption of the reality of the revelation, can we vindicate the divine action ?

II. ERRONEOUS OR INADEQUATE SOLUTIONS

In facing this problem, our first duty is to beware of solutions which are not really, or only very partially, such. It is, for example, no solution simply to use this word "*progressiveness*," as if that of itself removed the difficulty. It is true that revelation must be progressive; but it may be felt that what applies to the taught need not apply to the teacher—that *God* should not be implicated in any form of sanction of what is wrong.

Again, we do not solve the problem by *denying that these lower forms of morality were*, for that age and stage of development, *really wrong*, or did involve elements of evil. Evolution may be invoked to show that there are numerous intermediate grades between no morality and the highest morality; that society *must* pass through such and such stages of growth; that the moral ideal is only gradually developed, and that, till it *is* developed, such practices as slavery, polygamy, unchastity, mercilessness in war, etc., are not really sinful; that there can be no wrong, therefore, in recognising and sanctioning them. This, like the whole evolutionary conception of a necessary development of humanity through evil, is a dangerous line of defence; is, moreover, repugnant to the genuine Christian point of view. Jesus did not, *e.g.*, regard the Mosaic law of divorce as *per se* right even for the Jews. It was given them, He said, for the hardness of their hearts, and He referred them back to the purer primitive idea of marriage.[1]   Slavery, from the Christian standpoint, is a contradiction of the true idea of man, as God made him, and meant him to exist;[2] is, therefore, something inherently wrong, under whatever circumstances, or at whatever stage in the history of mankind, it occurs.

[1] Matt. xix. 3–9.
[2] Gen. i. 26, 27 ; and see the ground of the prohibition of shedding man's blood, Gen. ix. 6.

Shall we betake ourselves, then, to what may be called *the critical solution*—viz., the denying outright that God had any implication in the matter, and the ascribing of those laws and statements in the Bible which impute such participation in evil to God to the mistaken notions of the Biblical writers themselves? Either the narratives are held to be legends, or they are supposed to reflect only the ideas of the writers; in any case, the attribution of the laws and commands which create offence to Jehovah as their Author has no foundation in reality. What the leaders of Israel—a Moses, a Joshua, a Samuel—or the writers of their histories, ascribed to God of a nature which we think wrong, came really from their own imperfect thoughts and feelings, and God had nothing to do with it. Thus God is thought to be exonerated from participation in everything that offends the moral sense. Such a view may plausibly be held to be a necessary corollary from the admission of growth in religion and moral ideas. For how, it may be asked, can a writer *avoid* colouring his narrative in accordance with the idea of God he himself possesses, representing Jehovah as sanctioning or approving of those things which he *thinks* He must approve of, and as condemning those things which he —the author—reprobates? The writer's own standard of religion and morality would seem to be the inevitable measure of the representations in his history.

This method of treatment no doubt frees God from responsibility for anything in the record which appears objectionable,—Origen of old attained the same end by "allegorising" all such passages,—but the solution has the disadvantage that it is a cutting of the knot, not a loosing of it, for it denies the chief factor in the problem—the reality of the revelation. Neither do we, even in this way, really get rid of the difficulty. We may relieve the earlier history of laws and commands of God which offend us; but it is only to roll the burden upon the shoulders of prophets in an age when the higher morality is presumed to be developed. The strongest injunctions, *e.g.*, to destroy the Canaanites are found in the Book of Deuteronomy—on the theory of the critics, a prophetic work of the seventh century B.C., and the most drastic accounts of the carrying out of these injunctions are those put to the account of the Deuteronomic revision of the Book of Joshua, the date of

which is still later. It is not the early Hebrews only, therefore, who hold these imperfect views of God; but the prophets
themselves, who are assumed to represent the more advanced
stage of religion and morality, and to be the peculiar
exponents of the higher Old Testament revelation, share in
them, and put their *imprimatur* upon them. God's Spirit
in the prophets, if not in the history, still seems implicated
in what is wrong.

Difficulties exist; but it is a pity to add to them, as is
occasionally done, by unnecessarily lowering the character,
and limiting the scope, of early Old Testament morality,
even if it be with the aim of magnifying the divine
leading in Israel in the evolving of higher conceptions.
Here again comes in the tendency to exaggeration, as when
it is affirmed that early Israel had no sense of personal right
or responsibility, no feeling of humanity or mercy for those
outside its own circle, no compunctions about falsehood and
fraud, etc. It could easily be shown that, despite all marks
of a lower stage, the moral standard among the Hebrews
maintained its unique, and, in ancient times, unapproached,
distinction.[1] It is unfair, *e.g.*, to say with a recent writer,
that " the Hebrews were bound by moral obligation and the
sanction of religion in their dealings with one another, but
were entirely free of these in their dealings with foreigners,"
and that " in the latter case they were governed purely by
considerations of expediency."[2] This is not borne out by
the instances quoted, and is disproved by the recognition of
common principles of justice and morality by which *all*
men are judged. Where universal principles of moral
conduct are recognised, there arises of necessity the sense
of mutual obligation; and such are found, not only in Israel,
but in all ancient nations.[3] It is the postulate of the whole
Biblical view of history that the world is under moral government, and that individuals, communities, and nations,
everywhere, are judged and punished for wickedness. What
else is the moral of the narratives of the flood, of the
destruction of Sodom and Gomorrah, of the judgment on the
Canaanites? It was for their vices that the Canaanites were

[1] See below, pp. 470, 475.
[2] Professor G. B. Gray, *The Divine Discipline of Israel*, p. 48.
[3] The ethical codes of Egypt and Babylonia show that common principles
of right were always recognised; that, in fact, the world has always had a
great deal more moral light than it well knew how to make use of.

destroyed.[1] The history is full of instances which show the
recognition of principles of general obligation. Is it
credible, *e.g.*, in view of his own words (Gen. xxxix. 9),
that Joseph in Egypt was guided in his conduct in his
master's house, or towards his master's wife, by no higher
principle than "expediency"? It was on grounds of common
right that the people of Israel protested against their harsh
treatment by Pharaoh.[2] Even Jephthah invokes Jehovah,
as the Judge, to judge between Israel and Ammon.[3] It is
quite true that the Old Testament had not attained to Christ's
wide sense of the word "neighbour," and that the command
to love all, even enemies,[4] would have sounded strangely in
the ears of the ancient Israelite. But short of love there is
justice, and there is no reason for believing that duties falling
under that head were not recognised as applicable to Gentiles
as well as to Jews.[5] Too much, we would add, ought not
to be made of the imperfect conduct, or moral lapses, of
individuals, or even of the prevailing practice of a time, as
indicative of the religious and moral standard; else it would
go hard with ourselves under a higher and purer dispensation.[6] The conduct of Judah[7] and Samson,[8] *e.g.*, cannot be
held to determine the estimate of sexual relations in Israel.
In letter, and even more in spirit, the Mosaic law stands for
a high ideal of sexual morality.[9] Of this we have the

---

[1] Gen. xv. 16; Lev. xviii. 24 ff.; Deut. xii. 29 ff. Cf. Bruce, *Chief End
of Revelation*, pp. 139–40.
[2] Ex. v. 15 ff.   Judg. xi. 27.
[4] Matt. v. 43–45; Luke x. 29–37.
[5] If the Jews (unwarrantably) interpreted the precept "Thou shalt
love thy neighbour" as entitling him to "hate his *enemy*," and if deceit and
stratagem were regarded as lawful towards enemies in war (are they not
held to be so still?), it does not follow that foreigners, simply as such, were
viewed as outside the pale of moral obligations. The Old Testament nowhere
inculcates, like Plato, "a pure and heart-felt hatred of the foreign nature"
(in his *Menexenus*), or makes it, as Seeley says of ancient nations, "almost
as much a duty to hate foreigners as to love fellow-citizens" (*Ecce Homo*,
chap. xiv.). Israel has, indeed, from the first, an aspect of *blessing* to
mankind.
[6] Are there no moral scandals, profanity, fraud, cursing of enemies,
prayers for their destruction, etc., among ourselves?
[7] Gen. xxxviii.   [8] Judg. xvi.
[9] The Mosaic law, which, it is to be remembered, is a code of jurisprudence, not of private ethics, surrounds female virtue with safeguards,
and is stern in the punishment of violations of it (*e.g.*, Ex. xxi. 7 ff.; xxii.
16, 17; Deut. xxii. 13–30); is delicate in its provision for the treatment of
even captive women (Deut. xxi. 10–14); brands, as an abomination, the
prostitution of women at the sanctuary (Deut. xxiii. 17)—therefore, in

purest expression in the teachings of the prophets,[1] who here, as elsewhere, do not claim to be introducing anything new.

III. GENERAL LAWS OF PROGRESSIVE REVELATION

We shall perhaps get nearer the truth in this matter, and conserve what is of value in the above explanations, if, beginning at the other end, we assume the reality of revelation, and ask how, and under what limitations, revelation *could* enter into such a history as man's. We shall not assume that the development is normal; on the contrary, we shall allow it to be in many ways evil; we shall take for granted that slavery, polygamy, cruelty, etc., are wrong, and that this must have been God's judgment on them then as it is now. How then explain the apparent tolerance and sanction of such evils ?

The full treatment of this subject would involve the careful consideration of God's *general relation to the evil of the world*. The truth is here again illustrated that there is no difficulty in theology which does not emerge equally in philosophy; or, as Butler pointed out, that there is no difficulty in revelation which has not its counterpart in God's ordinary providence. From the abstract or *doctrinaire* point of view, it may seem a strange thing that God should uphold, or have anything to do with, a world that has evil in it at all; should permit, and be patient of, that evil; should allow it to develop, and overrule it for His own purposes; should seem, by His silence and seeming indifference, to connive at the crimes and iniquities of which so large a part of the history of mankind is made up. The sword of the Israelite is, after all, only a more acute form of the problem that meets us in the providential employment, in even more horrible forms,[2] of the sword of the Assyrian,

principle, all such conduct. "To play the harlot" is an expression of shame everywhere in Scripture. Cf. Gen. xxxiv. 7, 31 ; xxxviii. 24 ; Deut. xxii. 21, etc.

[1] Hosea iv. may serve as example; cf. specially vers. 2, 10–14. The sin is literal as well as spiritual.

[2] One has only to look at the accounts and pictures on the Assyrian monuments of the barbarities and tortures inflicted by conquerors on their prisoners—the beheadings, impalings, flayings, blindings, mutilations, etc. —to see how terrible a thing war ordinarily was in these times. Such extremes of cruelty are not a feature of Jewish warfare. The cases in

the Chaldean, or Roman, to inflict the judgment threatened of God on Israel itself.[1]   Yet only a little reflection is needed to show that, if the world is to be upheld, governed, and judged, at all, it is only in some such way that even the Holiest can govern and judge it.   As Paul says, in repelling the objection that God is unrighteous in taking vengeance for sins which He has overruled for His own glory: "God forbid; for then how shall God judge the world?"[2]   Let us see how this bears on the progressiveness of revelation.[3]

1. One thing plain is, that, at whatever point revelation begins, *it must take man up at the stage at which it finds him.* It must take him up at his existing stage of knowledge and culture, and with his existing social usages and ethical ideas. Just as it was remarked above of the prophet, that it is psychologically inconceivable that he should be lifted out of all the forms of his existing consciousness, and transported into conditions for which no analogy was found in the contents of that consciousness; so it must be said of historical revelation, that it could not at a stroke annihilate existing conditions, and create a world of new ones.   Revelation must begin somewhere, and must work patiently in accordance with the laws of historical development;[4] must lay hold on what is better to counterwork and gradually overcome what is worse; must be content to implant principles, and bear patiently with much remaining evil, till the good has time to grow, and to give rise to a new order of things that will supplant the old.   This is the true side of the law of evolution, and it applies in grace, as well as in nature.   We see this law in operation even under Christianity.   There is not a word in Christ's teaching, *e.g.*, any more than there is in Paul's, directly denouncing slavery, or instigating to a revolt against it.   Yet nothing

which torture was inflicted (as in David's treatment of the Moabites, 2 Sam. xii. 31) are happily rare.

[1] This is the line of argument chiefly used in a once popular book, Henry Rogers' *Eclipse of Faith.*

[2] Rom. iii. 6.

[3] We proceed on the same lines essentially as Mozley, Hessey, Bruce, etc. See references below.

[4] This does not mean that in revelation the lowest type comes first.   On the contrary, in each new dispensation a start is made, and the foundation of the new era laid, with a typical personality (Abraham, Moses, both still relative to their age); in the case of Christianity with an absolute type of God-manhood.   Cf. Martensen, *Dogmatics*, pp. 249 ff.; Dorner, *Person of Christ*, v. pp. 195, 198.

is plainer than that slavery is opposed to the fundamental ideas and principles of Christ's religion, and that in proportion as these prevail it is bound to be abolished. We speak of the imperfections of the Old Testament; but we should remember how far, as already hinted, society is even yet from being able to conduct its business on the ideal principles of Christ's religion.[1] We have, *e.g.*, to tolerate and regulate houses for the sale of intoxicants; we use oaths, which Christ says " come of evil ";[2] we sanction, and occasionally even glorify, war, which is as frightful a contradiction of Christ's principles as it is possible to conceive. We do not dispute that war—defensive war—is sometimes a necessity; but this only illustrates what we mean, that there is a distinction between principles and the possibility of giving them complete effect at once. Christ condemns war in no other way than He condemns slavery, *i.e.*, the fundamental principles of His religion contradict it; but it needs time to educate the public conscience to the point of abhorring it as it should, and finally of replacing it by more rational methods of settling international disputes.

2. Given this as a first principle, that revelation, wherever it begins, must take up man as it finds him, a second will easily be deduced, viz., that revelation can be held responsible only for *the new element which it introduces*—not for the basis on which it works, or for everything in the state of mind, or limited outlook, of the recipient, with which it happens to be associated. Revelation does one thing at once—implants a truth, constitutes a relation, establishes a principle, which may have a whole rich content implicit in it, but it cannot convey to the recipient from the first a full, all-round apprehension of everything which that principle involves. On the contrary, such applications must necessarily have adaptation to the stage of morality or of social institutions then existing, and it is only gradually that the principle can be clearly disengaged from its temporary form. In the reception of revelation, therefore, two elements have constantly to be distinguished —the one, the form of consciousness, or state of view and moral feeling, into which the revelation is introduced; this

---

[1] The unfortunate thing about society is that it does not always *try to* realise Christ's ideals.

[2] Or " of the evil one," Matt. v. 37.

may be relatively low and undeveloped; the other, the **new** element of revelation itself, which is the positive and germinal factor, and represents the real stage in the advance. There need be no dubiety, or lack of clearness or positiveness, in this new element; it is a pure, original point of knowledge or insight, but its authority extends only to itself, and cannot be employed to sanction every other element associated with it in the same consciousness. For example, the days of the Judges are acknowledged to have been in many ways rude and barbarous; we have seen that the Bible itself declares this. It is no argument, therefore, against the reality of revelation in that age that the Spirit of God came on men—as on Jephthah—whose modes of speech and action (as in his ideas of God, or his vow about his daughter)[1] show many traces of the rudeness of the times. So again, Deborah was a real prophetess, *i.e.*, she possessed from God's Spirit the qualification necessary for judging and rallying by her word the tribes of Israel.[2] But her song of victory, with its panegyric of Jael, shows that, with all her inspired exaltation, she yet stood on the ground of her age in her judgment of deeds which a purer stage of enlightenment would condemn.[3] The same principle applies to certain of the imprecations, and the frequent prayers for the destruction of enemies, in the psalms—on which more is said below. It is the course of revelation which alone can correct these defects of its earlier stages, and, by revelation growing out of revelation, enable the world and the Church to transcend the lower stages altogether.

3. A third principle follows. As, in virtue of the foregoing, revelation can be held responsible only for the new element it introduces, and not for the basis on which it works, or for everything in the state of mind of its recipients, so, conversely, it is the function of revelation *to lay hold on whatever better elements there may be in that state of mind*, in order, by their means, to overcome the imperfections, and create something higher. This is the *educational* function in revelation, which can only reach its end by working with such means as the imperfect state affords towards the production of a more perfect. An illustration of the principle

---

[1] See above, pp. 131, 140.   [2] Judg. iv. 4-6.
[3] Perhaps a complete view of the circumstances would mitigate even our judgment of Jael's action (cf. Mozley, *Ruling Ideas*, pp. 142 ff.).

in question is found in the command to Abraham to sacrifice
Isaac. In so far as this command supposes as its background
the heathen custom of the sacrifice of children, it falls under
the two former principles that revelation takes up a man at
the stage at which it finds him, and is not responsible for
the basis on which it works; but in so far as it uses this basis
to elicit a singular proof of Abraham's faith, and actually
to put the stamp of divine condemnation on human sacrifice
in Israel, it falls under the third, or educative, principle.
For even in this most hateful form of heathen sacrifice, as
has often been pointed out, there was a nobler element
present. This nobler element was the idea of the surrender
of the dearest and best to God, and it was God's will to
elicit and conserve this spiritual fruit, while rejecting as
abhorrent the form in which it was embodied.[1] So the
usage of blood-revenge is one of the rudest methods of justice
in a tribal state of society; yet, by limiting and regulating
this usage by the law of the cities of refuge, its worst effects
were checked, and the way was prepared for its ultimately
dying out altogether. The legislation on marriage and
divorce put salutary restrictions on polygamy, and the wanton
putting away of a wife, and, after the exile especially, mono-
gamy, though not universal, seems to have become the rule.[2]
The same principle applies in some degree even to what
jars upon us most—the apparent sanction given to the spirit
of revenge, or, as it may be better put, the restricted range
of the spirit of mercy. There is here, as elsewhere on this
subject, great need for careful and balanced statement. It
is perfectly certain that the Mosaic religion, taken as a
whole, inculcated mercy with a decision and earnestness
that no other religion before Christianity ever showed;[3] it
is equally certain that hatred and revengefulness, as private

[1] On the sacrifice of Isaac, see Stanley, *Jewish Church*, i. pp. 40 ff.;
Mozley, *Ruling Ideas*, Lect. II.; Bruce, *Chief End of Revelation*, pp. 93 ff.;
Ottley, *Aspects of O.T.*, pp. 177–78; Driver, *Genesis*, pp. 221–22, etc.

[2] Cf. Smith's *Dict. of Bible*, art. "Marriage," vol. ii. p. 246. The
contrast is apparent in Mohammedanism, in which polygamy continues to
flourish.

[3] It is not too much to say that the spirit of tenderness and mercy pervades
the laws of Israel (not to speak of the writings of the prophets) in a way to
which no other ancient code affords any parallel. The poor, the widow,
the fatherless, the stranger, the homeless, the distressed, are Jehovah's
special care, and His law is full of provisions for them. Cf., *e.g.*, Ex. xxii.
21–27; xxiii. 9–12; Deut. xv. 7 ff.; xxiv. 14–22, etc.

passions, are constantly condemned.[1] But where **enmity to** God, or antagonism to His cause, was concerned, the stage at which we find ourselves in the Old Testament is one of un- compromising hostility.[2] It is the principle of justice, in all its stern severity, not yet that of mercy, that rules ; [3] and little distinction is made between the transgressor and his sin. The judgment falls unsparingly on the wrong-doer, and, in the tribal stage of society, on all that are his.[4] This principle is applied, in the case of presumptuous or public transgression, as relentlessly *within* Israel, and *upon* Israel,[5] as it is *without* Israel.   The destruction of the Canaanites is the most extensive, as it is the most awful, application of it, but it is no more than an application.[6]   And even this stage, with its inevitable defects, was one that had to be gone through—as no one has shown more strikingly than Professor Seeley, in his *Ecce Homo*,[7]—if the higher result was to be attained.

In general, then, we perceive that revelation, without parting with anything of its reality or authority, is, in the truest sense, an organic process—a growing from less to more, with adaptation at every point to the stage of develop- ment of its recipients—a light shining often in a *dark* place, but still shining more and more unto the perfect day.   Its higher stages criticise, if we may so speak, its lower ; shed off temporary elements ; disengage principles from the imperfect forms in which they are embodied, and give them more perfect expression ; yet unfailingly conserve, and take up into the new form, every element of permanent value in

[1] See the remarkable precepts bearing on the treatment of an enemy, Ex. xxiii. 4, 5 (cf. Deut. xxii. 1, 4).   Cf. also Ps. vii. 4, with David's treatment of Saul (above, p. 443).

[2] Ps. cxxxix. 21, 22 well expresses the spirit : "Do not I hate them, O Jehovah, that hate Thee ? . . . I hate them with perfect hatred ; I count them mine enemies."   It is in this sense we are to understand most or all of the imprecatory psalms.

[3] Cf., *e.g.*, Deut. xiii.; xvii. 2–7.

[4] *E.g.*, Achan (Josh. vii. 10 ff.) ; Korah (Num. xvi. 24 ff.).   Cf. Mozley, pp. 115 ff.

[5] It is not to be forgotten, on the other side, that this sternness applied only to presumptuous transgressions (cf. Num. xv. 30–31), special theocratic sins, and offences against the criminal law, and that the religion is through- out pervaded with divine mercy and forgiveness (Ex. xxxiv. 6, 7).

[6] Cf. the authors named above : Stanley, i. pp. 217–22 ; Mozley, Lect. IV.; Bruce, pp. 137–44 ; and see Note D on Destruction of the Canaanites.

[7] Cf. his chapters xix. ("The Law of Mercy ") and xxi. ("The Law of Resentment ").

the old. Prophecy does not let fall one element that was of permanent value in the law; Christianity conserves every jot and tittle of the spiritual content of both law and prophets.[1]

The Close

Progressive revelation culminates in Christ. Here, as we began, so we end. In Christ the long development of Old Testament religion—Abrahamic promise, Mosaic covenant, Levitical sacrifice, Davidic kingship, prophetic hopes, Messianic ideals, strain of psalmist, redemptive purpose—finds its fulfilment and point of repose. His Person clasps Old and New Testaments into one. To understand the Old Testament aright we must look to this goal to which all its roads lead. *Respice finem.* On the other hand, if faith has firm grasp of Christ as risen and exalted, this will put all the Old Testament in a new light for us. It is this connection of Old Testament with New, of law with Gospel, of prophecy with Christ, which gives the critical problems we have been studying their keenest interest. The tendency of late has been to make too light of this connection. The storm of criticism which, in the last decades, assailed the Old Testament, was fondly thought by many to leave intact the New Testament. What mattered it about Abraham and Moses, so long as Jesus and His Gospel remained? That delusion is passing away. The fact is becoming apparent to the dullest which has long been evident to unbiassed observers, that much of the radical criticism of the Old Testament proceeded on principles, and was conducted by methods, which had only to be applied with like thoroughness to the New Testament to work like havoc. The fundamental ideas of God and His revelation which underlay that criticism could not, as we set out by affirming, lead up to a doctrine of the Incarnation, but only to a negation of it. The conceptions of Christ and Christianity which have been its tacit presuppositions from the days of Eichhorn, De Wette, and Vatke, to those of Kuenen and Wellhausen, are *toto cœlo* different from those of the believing Church, and could not in time but work themselves out to their logical conclusions. This, accordingly, is what we see actually happening. The principles of a rationalistic

[1] Matt. v. 17, 18.

criticism, having once gained recognition and approval in the
region of the Old Testament, are now being transferred and
applied with increasing boldness and vigour to the New,
with the result that it is rapidly coming to be assumed that
only a Christ from whom all supernatural traits are stripped
off can be accepted as historical by the "modern" mind. Not
only do critics like Wellhausen and Gunkel, who, advancing
from the Old Testament, have entered the New Testament
field,[1] take this ground, but a multitude of works on New
Testament subjects, recently issued and enjoying a considerable popularity in their own tongues and in translations,[2]
have the same as their underlying postulate. A grave peril,
growing out of a long train of conditions in the spirit of the
age, has thus arisen, which cannot be too early or too reso-
lutely faced. This at least is the conviction under which
the present book has been written. If it leads any who
have perhaps yielded too ready or indiscriminating an assent
to the positions of the modern critical movement to examine
more carefully the foundations of the theory of the Old
Testament to which they have given their adherence, its
end will be fulfilled.

[1] Wellhausen translates and critically comments on *Matthew* and *Mark*.
He simply leaves out the first and second chapters of Matthew, and begins
with the third chapter, without a word of explanation. Gunkel entitles his
production, *Zum Religionsgeschichtlichen Verstandniss des Neuen Testaments*.
He seeks to show that the evangelical narratives of the virgin-birth and
infancy of Jesus, of His temptation, transfiguration, resurrection, etc., borrow
from foreign religions (through Judaism).

[2] We have in view writers like Réville, Wernle, Wrede, Oscar Holtzmann,
Percy Gardner, and many more. See in Chapter I. p. 7.

NOTES TO CHAPTERS

NOTE TO CHAPTER I

———

NOTE A.—P. 3

THE JEWISH CANON

DR. DRIVER begins his notice of the Canon (*Introd.* p. ii) with
the son of Sirach; we would prefer to begin lower down, with
the New Testament and Josephus. The New Testament speaks
of a well-known collection of "Scriptures," believed to be
divinely inspired, and follows the usual division into "the
law of Moses, and the prophets, and (from its chief part) the
psalms" (Luke xxiv. 44). The passage in Josephus, which in
his *first* edition Dr. Driver does not mention, is as follows:
"For we have not myriads of discordant and conflicting books,
but twenty-two only, comprising the record of all time, and justly
accredited as divine. Of these, five are books of Moses, which
embrace the laws and the traditions of the origin of mankind,
until his own death, a period of almost 3000 years. From the
death of Moses till the reign of Artaxerxes (465–425 B.C.), the
prophets who followed Moses narrated the events of their time in
thirteen books. The remaining four books consist of hymns to God,
and maxims of conduct for men. From Artaxerxes to our own
age, the history has been written in detail, but it is not esteemed
worthy of the same credit, on account of the exact succession of
the prophets having been no longer maintained" (*Contra Apion*,
i. 8; Driver, p. ix; see Note H, p. 527 below).

This is an important testimony to the belief of the Jews in
the first century A.D. as to the number of the sacred books, their
divine inspiration, and the time, approximately, when the Canon
was completed. The four books which in Josephus's arrangement constitute the third division are the Psalms, Proverbs,
Ecclesiastes, and Canticles. Daniel, in this distribution, falls
among the thirteen prophets. The division into twenty-two books
(with slight variation of enumeration) is one followed in the Church

31

by Origen and Melito of Sardis (both of whom received it from Jews), and by Jerome, who, however, knew of and mentions the Rabbinical division into twenty-four books. The Jewish Palestinian division is into the three parts—five books of the Law; eight of the Prophets, subdivided into "former prophets" (Joshua, Judges, Samuel, Kings), and "latter prophets" (Isaiah, Jeremiah, Ezekiel, and the Twelve Minor Prophets as one book); and eleven Hagiographa (Chronicles, Psalms, etc.)—twenty-four in all. Daniel in this case (as Jerome also testifies) was included among the Hagiographa. The twenty-two of Josephus is harmonised with the twenty-four of the other reckoning by taking Ruth with Samuel, and Lamentations with Jeremiah. Melito reckons Ruth, but omits Esther.

It is clear that Josephus regards the Canon as closing about the reign of Artaxerxes, after which, he says, there was not an exact succession of prophets (the same idea of the cessation of prophecy is expressed in 1 Macc. iv. 46, ix. 27, xiv. 41, and elsewhere), and he represents this as the traditional belief of his time. The same tradition in a more confused form is met with in the spurious letter prefixed to 2 Macc. : "The same things were also reported in the public archives and in the records relating to Nehemiah; and how, founding a library, he gathered together the things concerning the kings and prophets, and the (writings) of David, and letters of kings about sacred gifts." When we proceed to test this tradition, we do not find it wholly unworthy of credence.

The law was plainly of canonical authority in the days of Ezra (see pp. 295 ff.) ; how far it is older is discussed in Chap. IX. There is nothing against the collection of prophets in the time of Nehemiah; though earlier collections may well have existed, analogous to the collections of Paul's Epistles in the early Church. The third part of the Canon was more elastic; whether it remained open to receive contributions of a later date than, say, the fourth century, depends on the view we take of Macca-bæan psalms and of the age of Daniel (see Chap. XII.). But the repeated assertion that the spirit of prophecy had departed is a strong proof that books believed to be new were *not* admitted. The treatment of the work of the son of Sirach (see p. 449) is evidence of this. This author is acquainted with a threefold division of the sacred books, but puts his own work on a quite different level from them; and his book, though highly esteemed, was not received into the Canon. The impression given is, that the collection of law, prophets, and other sacred books was already old—a fact borne out by the LXX translation (see p. 449). It is not an argument against this that Esther and Ecclesiastes were subjects of discussion in the schools, any more than the existence of "disputed books" in the time of Eusebius (fourth century A.D.) disproves that the Canon of the New Testament was already practically fixed in the second century.

On the facts, see, along with Driver, the works of Buhl and Ryle on the O.T. Canon, and the article "O.T. Canon" in *Dict. of Bible*, by Woods (vol. iii.).

NOTES TO CHAPTER II

NOTE A.—P. 31

THE BIBLE AND OTHER SACRED BOOKS

A FEW words of personal testimony may be quoted from Professor Monier Williams on the comparison of the Scriptures with the Sacred Books of the East :—

"When I began investigating Hinduism and Buddhism, I found many beautiful gems ; nay, I met with bright coruscations of true light flashing here and there amid the surrounding darkness. As I prosecuted my researches into these non-Christian systems, I began to foster a fancy that they had been unjustly treated. I began to observe and trace out curious coincidences and comparisons with our own sacred book of the East. I began, in short, to be a believer in what is called the evolution and growth of religious thought. 'These imperfect systems,' I said to myself, 'are interesting efforts of the human mind struggling upwards towards Christianity. Nay, it is probable, that they were all intended to lead up to the one true religion, and that Christianity is, after all, merely the climax, the complement, the fulfilment of them all.'

"Now there is a delightful fascination about such a theory, and, what is more, there are really elements of truth in it. But I am glad of this opportunity of stating publicly that I am persuaded I was misled by its attractiveness, and that its main idea is quite erroneous. . . . We welcome these books. We ask every missionary to study their contents, and thankfully lay hold of whatsoever things are true and of good report in them. But we warn him that there can be no greater mistake than to force these non-Christian Bibles into conformity with some scientific theory of development, and then point to the Christian's holy Bible as the crowning product of religious evolution. So far from this, these non-Christian Bibles are all

484

developments in the wrong direction. They all begin with some flashes of true light, and end in utter darkness. Pile them, if you will, on the left side of your study table, but place your own holy Bible on the right side—all by itself, all alone—and with a wide gap between."—Quoted by Joseph Cook in *God in the Bible* (Boston Lectures), p. 16.

Cf. Carlyle's judgment on the Koran in his *Heroes*, Lect. II. "The Hero as Prophet"; Max Müller on the Hindu Brahmanas, in *Sanscrit Literat.* pp. 389 ff.

NOTE B.—P. 45

MYTHOLOGY AND HISTORY IN THE OLD TESTAMENT

REVELATION is historical, and it is a serious disservice to religion to depreciate the historical element in revelation, or to represent it as immaterial to faith whether the history in the Old Testament is true or legendary. Budde himself says: "God reveals Himself not through words, but through deeds, not in speech, but in action" (*Das Alte Test. und die Ausgrabungen*, 2nd ed., Pref. p. 9). But if the ground is taken from the only facts we have, what remains to yield the revelation? Is it not left in the air? The peculiar combination witnessed in the Anglican Church of acceptance of the results of the Wellhausen criticism with zeal for every jot and tittle of a high patristic orthodoxy—of a method which turns the bulk of the Old Testament history into legend and invention, with stout defence of the historicity of the Gospel narratives of the Virgin Birth, the Transfiguration, and the Resurrection—is one, we are convinced, foredoomed to failure. One side or the other must give way. God, Ottley says truly, "interposes" in miracle (*Aspects of O.T.*, p. 115; cf. pp. 61 ff., 107 ff.). But if the actual miracles are taken away by the narratives being regarded as late and legendary, what better are we? Ottley refers, p. 108, to the "admirable remarks" on O.T. miracle of Schultz, who had no place in his scheme for miracle in the proper sense at all.

It is again a mistake to represent it as a matter of indifference for the right understanding of revelation what theory we adopt of its origins and course of development. What does it matter how the thing came to be, it is said, if we have the result? But in everything else it is recognised that a thing is only known when its real history is known. No scientist would ever allow that one account of origins is as good as another. It is a first principle of science that we can only understand a phenomenon rightly when we accurately understand its antecedents and genesis. It is this which gives its importance to the idea of evolution. Why, among Biblical critics themselves, the stress laid on getting behind the so-called "legends" to the real course of the development, if not because it is felt that it is only when legend is displaced by fact that we have the true key to the nature of the religion? But if the critic's understanding of the history turns out to be a *mis*understanding, that equally will be a fatal obstacle to a right comprehension of the result.

Even legend, however, is not mythology, and, despite recent attempts to revive a mythological interpretation of personages and incidents in the Old Testament (see below, p. 488), there is very general agreement that the Old Testament religion is non-mythological. This absence of mythology is another marked feature of contrast with other religions. We may, if we please, speak of a tradition like that of Eden as "mythical," as others may discuss whether it contains symbol or allegory. But "myth" in this case must be distinguished from mythology proper, *i.e.*, such weaving of stories about the gods in their relations to each other and to the world as are found in other religions, and have generally their origin in nature-phenomena (*e.g.*, sun-myths, dawn-myths, myths of growth and reproduction, etc.). From this element, as most scholars recognise, the Biblical religion seems entirely free. See the remarks of Professor Robertson, *Early Religion of Israel*, pp. 188–9, 299. Professor Robertson quotes from an interesting article by Mr. Andrew Lang in *The New Review*, Aug. 1889; and also quotes Stade, *Geschichte*, i. pp. 438–9. Gunkel may also be referred to, *Genesis*, pp. 113 ff. He thinks traces of an original mythological basis are to be discovered, but contends for the absence of mythology in the proper religion of Israel. (On his theory, see below, p. 494.)

NOTE C.—P. 50

INSPIRATION AND THE MATERIALS OF THE RECORD

INSPIRATION does not create the materials of its record, but works with those it has received. It reveals itself in the insight it shows into them, and in the use it makes of them. An interesting illustration of this truth is furnished in a note of the old commentator, Matthew Henry, on 1 Chron. viii. 1–32. "As to the difficulties," he says, "that occur in this and the foregoing genealogies we need not perplex ourselves. I presume Ezra took them as he found them *in the books of the kings of Israel and Judah* (chap. ix. 1), according as they were given in by the several tribes, each observing what method they thought fit. Hence some *ascend*, others *descend*; some have *numbers* affixed, others *places*; some have historical remarks intermixed, others have not; some are shorter, others longer; some agree with other records, others differ; some, it is likely, were torn, erased, and blotted, others more legible. Those of Dan and Reuben were entirely lost. This holy man wrote as he was moved of the Holy Ghost; but there was no necessity for the making up of the defects, no, nor for the rectifying of the mistakes of these genealogies by inspiration. It was sufficient that he copied them out as they came to hand, or so much of them as was requisite to the present purpose, which was the directing of the returned captives to settle as nearly as they could with those of their own family, and in the places of their former residence."

NOTE TO CHAPTER III

NOTE A.—P. 59

CRITICAL EXTRAVAGANCES

In the *Nineteenth Century* for December 1902, Canon Cheyne
commends to English readers the speculations of the latest school
of Biblical critics, according to which the Jewish literature is
largely a borrowed mythology. According to Dr. H. Winckler,
who represents this school, not only are Abraham, Isaac, and
Jacob legendary heroes, whose histories are derived from astronomical myths, but something similar must be said of Saul, David,
and Solomon. David, he holds, is a solar hero; his red hair is
the image of the rays of the sun; and, if Saul and Jonathan
correspond to the constellation Gemini, David is the legendary
reflection of Leo, while Goliath corresponds to Orion. The
Canon chides the English "sobriety" and "moderation" which
rejects these fantasies!

Winckler's views are expounded in his new edition of
Schrader's work, *The Cuneiform Inscriptions and the Old
Testament* (1902); and are trenchantly dealt with by Budde in
his printed address, *Das Alte Testament und die Ausgrabungen*
(1903). The real originator of the theory is E. Stucken, in
his work *Astralmythen der Hebräer, Babylonier und Ägypter*
(vols. i. Abraham, 1896; ii. Lot, 1897; iii. Jacob, 1901;
iv. Esau, 1901). Abraham is the Moon-god, Lot the Sun,
Sarah is Ishtar, etc.

This "limitless Panbabylonianism," as Budde calls it, has
many modern developments. An instance is afforded in
Wildeboer's recent Commentary on Esther. The Book of Esther,
it appears, goes back for its basis to Babylonia and Elam.
Wildeboer gives the credit of the "solution" of the problem to
Jensen, who thus explains: "Esther reminds us of Ishtar;
Mordecai of Marduk. Esther is the cousin of Mordecai, as Ishtar

probably of Marduk.   For the latter is a son of Ia, while Ishtar
is a daughter of Anu.   But Anu, Bil, and Ia are presumably
viewed as brothers. . . . Haman reminds us of Humman (Homman),
the national god of the Elamites ; Vasti of Masti or Vasti of
the Elamite inscriptions—the name of a divinity with the
attribute Zana. . . . The history that underlies the story of
Esther must have dealt with a defeat of the Elamites or of an
Elamite king.   So much appears certain"!   (Cf. *Expository
Times*, August 1898.)

In other directions, as in Canon Cheyne's own speculations
on "Jerahmeel" in *Encyclop. Biblica* and *Critica Biblica*, the
same tendency to extravagance displays itself.   Commenting on
the theory, Professor J. Robertson says : " The ' last word ' of this
criticism is Jerahmeel, which, being interpreted, means ' God pity '
us !" (Address, 16th April 1902).   A last example may be taken
from Siegfried's work on Ecclesiastes (Qoheleth), giving us the
latest theory of that portion of Scripture.   The sagacity of the
critic has split the book up into its diverse elements.   First, there
is the primitive author of the book, Q^1, a Jew whose faith has
suffered shipwreck.   He is improved on by Q^2, an Epicurean
Sadducee, who glorifies eating and drinking.   Another glossator,
Q^3, resented the depreciation of wisdom, and added a number of
passages which are enumerated.   Still sharper opposition to the
denial of divine providence called forth Q^4, one of the early
Pharisees.   This is not all, for there is yet a number of others,
who are conveniently slumped under Q^5.   As to dates, Q^1 may
have written shortly before 200 B.C. ; Q^2, Q^3, Q^4, Q^5 at various
times down to 100 B.C.   The fact that one finds all this retailed
with due gravity by author and learned reviewers suggests the
question whether the sense of humour is not becoming extinct—
at least in the department of criticism.

NOTES TO CHAPTER IV

NOTE A—P. 91

KÖNIG ON THE PERSONIFICATION THEORY

A FEW sentences from König's discussion in his *Neueste Prinzipien* may not be out of place. "Parallels," he says, "have again been sought in features of the Greek and of the Israelitish tradition (Seinecke, Cornill). Specially it has been recalled that Greek tradition attributed to Lycurgus two sons, Eunomus and Eucosmus, *i.e.*, Law and Order. . . . But is this a sufficient basis for the conclusion that Ishmael and Isaac have in like manner been ascribed to Abraham? What a difference there is between the two pairs of names! The Greek pair, Eunomus and Eucosmus clearly represent personifications of ideas and of the results achieved by the great lawgiver. . . . The two names Ishmael and Isaac cannot be referred to any such design. . . . How, if in the two names Ishmael and Isaac such personifications lie before us, could all the particular traits be derived which are related with respect to Ishmael and Isaac? Were there also families in Sparta that claimed descent from Eunomus and Eucosmus?

"It is further argued that the Hellenes traced their origin to a tribal ancestor Hellen, who had two sons, Æolus and Dorus, and two grandsons, Achæus and Ion. I willingly concede that 'it will occur to no one to see in the bearers of these names individual persons.' . . . [But] to draw a parallel between these Greek names and the tribal fathers of Israel is a very hazardous operation. Have we any such histories of Hellen and the other four names as Genesis contains about the tribal fathers of Israel?" (pp. 42, 43).

One might remark also on the vague and fluctuating notices of the supposititious Eunomus and Eucosmus. Eunomus, *e.g.*, is generally given as the *father* of Lycurgus.

NOTE B.—P. 100

THE COVENANT WITH ISRAEL

KAUTZSCH has valuable remarks on this subject in his art. in "The Religion of Israel" in *Dict. of Bible* (Extra Vol. p. 631). He says:

"In all the Pentateuchal sources, without exception, there is a uniform tradition to the effect that the central place amongst the incidents at Sinai is occupied by the concluding of a *berith*, commonly rendered Covenant. . . . Is all this now to be set down as fiction, a carrying back of much later theological conceptions and terminology, to a time for which no real tradition was any longer extant? This is a view to which the present writer cannot assent, having regard to either external or internal evidence."

After summarising historical evidence, he proceeds: "Would all this be conceivable, if the proclamation of Jahweh as the God of Israel—the founding of the Jahweh religion—had taken place, so to speak, fortuitously, by the incidental passing of the name 'Jahweh' from mouth to mouth? Instead of any theory of this kind, we get the strongest impression that the further development of the religion of Israel during the period of the Judges and of the monarchy was the result of some occurrence of a fundamental kind of whose solemnity and binding force and character the whole nation retained a lively recollection. And this occurrence can have been nothing but the solemn proclaiming of the God *who had manifested Himself in wondrous ways as the Helper and Deliverer of the people* upon a definite occasion, and in the binding of the people to do His will, and to worship Him alone. Every one of the numerous allusions (whether in the Pentateuchal sources, the Prophets, or the Psalms) to the mighty acts of Jahweh at the Exodus, how with a strong hand and a stretched out arm He brought the hosts of Israel out of the house of bondage, held back the waves of the Red Sea from Israel, but plunged the chariots and horsemen of Pharaoh into the waters,—every one of these allusions is at the same time an allusion to the days of Sinai, when for the first time these mighty acts of Jahweh were brought to the consciousness of the people in their true greatness, and extolled accordingly, and made the occasion of a solemn confession of Jahweh as the God of Israel, and the solemn binding of the people to do His will." Cf. also Giesebrecht on *Die Geschichtlichkeit des Sinaibundes*.

NOTE C.—P. 104

THEORIES OF THE EXODUS

THIS is how Von Bohlen disposes of the Exodus: "Here [in Egypt], during the four following centuries, which the popular traditions pass over with a prudent silence, the Hebrew family increased into so powerful a nation, that they entered the field as conquerors, and succeeded at length in establishing themselves among the native tribes of Palestine" (*Genesis*, i. p. 16).

Kuenen accords to Manetho's story of the expulsion of the lepers a credence he is unwilling to give to the narrative in Exodus, and thinks that the Israelites got help from the Hyksos. "The Book of Exodus does not mention the aid given by the Hyksos. . . . But a few slight touches furnish us with proof that the Israelites were supported by the nomadic tribes of Arabia, that is to say by the Hyksos. . . . We may surely take it for granted that the Israelites themselves were not passive spectators of the struggle [between Jahweh and the gods of Egypt]; that a conspiracy was formed among them; that others besides Moses and Aaron played a part in it. But with regard to all this the Book of Exodus is silent or confines itself to a few hints" (*Rel. of Israel*, i. pp. 120–21, 124). Of the Red Sea deliverance: "What actually took place there we do not know. It is undoubtedly founded on fact. But it is very difficult to distinguish the actual circumstances of the occurrence from poetical embellishments. We will not risk the attempt." (*Ibid.* p. 126).

Stade allows no value to the history in Exodus, and denies that Israel as a people came up out of Egypt. But something, he grants, must have given occasion to the story. "It is very possible that a part of those Hebrew tribes which afterwards coalesced into the people of Israel, passing into Egypt, lived there, and fell under bondage to the Egyptians. With the aid of the related nomadic tribes inhabiting the Sinaitic peninsula outside the kingdom of Egypt, they may have fought their way to freedom under Moses" (*Geschichte*, 1887, pp. 129–30). In the 1881 edition of his *Geschichte*, Stade is even more emphatic. "If any Hebrew clan," he says, "once dwelt in Egypt, no one knows its name" (p. 129).

Colenso adopts Kuenen's theories as "very probably the basis upon which the Scripture story of the Exodus has been founded." "No doubt," he says, "the Israelites on their march to Canaan experienced formidable difficulties, perhaps in crossing an arm of the Red Sea, and certainly in their passage through the wilderness—the reminiscences of which may have been handed down from age to age, and given rise to some of the miraculous stories in the narrative, while others are merely the result of the natural growth of legendary matter, or are due to the inventive genius of the writer or writers" (*Pent.* vi. p. 601).

Budde accepts the Exodus by the help of God as an incontestable truth, on the strength of Israel's own self-consciousness. "All that can be considered doubtful is whether it was the whole people of Israel that fell under the Egyptian bondage, or Joseph alone (that is to say, the tribes of Ephraim and Manasseh, including Benjamin)" (*Rel. of Israel,* p. 10). No light is thrown on the *how* of the deliverance which, in the tradition, naturally "bears the stamp of miracle" (p. 13).

See summary of Wellhausen's views in Bennett's art. "Moses" in *Dict. of Bible,* iii. p. 445.

NOTE D.—P. 106

PATRIARCHAL CHRONOLOGY

ESPECIAL exception is taken by Dr. Driver to the patriarchal chronology "as it stands." One example may be given. In an article in the *Contemporary Review* (lvii. p. 221), he instances as a chronological impossibility in the life of Isaac that, "according to the chronology of the Book of Genesis, he [Isaac] must have been lying on his deathbed for eighty years." This, however, supposes that Isaac, at the blessing of Jacob and Esau (Gen. xxvii.) was only a hundred years old, and not, as ordinarily assumed, and as the remaining data combine to show, a hundred and thirty-nine (cf. Gen. xli. 46; xlv. 6; xlvii. 9, etc.). Neither was he on his "deathbed" all this while. The objection is an old one (Von Bohlen, etc.), and has frequently been replied to. On any hypothesis, if Isaac did not die till after Jacob's return from Mesopotamia (Gen. xxxv.), a long period must have elapsed between the blessing and his death.

If the patriarchs were real persons, their lives span the interval between the age of Hammurabi and the time of the descent into Egypt; with four hundred and thirty years added, we get the interval from Abraham to the Exodus (see p. 422). The lives of Abraham, Isaac, and Jacob, must therefore have been as long as the narrative represents. This cannot be pronounced "impossible," since, even in modern times, instances of extreme longevity, though rare, are still found. It would be wrong, however, to transpose our modern conditions into times to which, probably, they did not apply. In Egypt, according to the authorities, a hundred and ten years was regarded as the number of a perfect life (cf. Ebers, art. "Joseph" in Smith's *Dict. of Bible*, i., 2nd ed. (1893) p. 1804; Vigouroux, *La Bible et les Découvertes Modernes*, ii. p. 182; Tomkins, *Life and Times of Joseph*, pp. 78, 135, etc.). According to some, the venerable moralist Ptah-hotep, of the fifth dynasty (see below, p. 397), claims to be already that age when he wrote his book (Birch, *Egypt*, p. 50; Tomkins, p. 135, etc.). This was the age of Joseph at his death (Gen. l. 26).

On some striking modern instances of longevity, see Tomkins, *Joseph*, pp. 77–8, and the list might readily be extended. Cf. also Reusch, *Nature and the Bible*, ii. p. 249.

NOTE E.—P. 112

GUNKEL'S THEORY OF PATRIARCHAL HISTORY

GUNKEL'S own theory of the patriarchal history, it must be allowed, is not less arbitrary and untenable than any which he criticises. The "legends" which, according to him, compose the Book of Genesis, he holds to be no peculiar product of Israel, but to be derived in the main from Babylonian and Canaanitish sources. They originated separately, he thinks, were long sung or recited, and were finally written down singly; only gradually they coalesced, and became gathered round leading personages as we find them. The theory might be described as an explanation of the patriarchal history on the ancient principle of a fortuitous concourse of atoms. To the analysis of verses he adds analysis of personalities. The different names of God—Elohim, El-Shaddai, Jahweh—denote originally different gods. Jacob and Israel are different legendary persons. Noah is composed out of three originally distinct figures; Cain originally out of three, etc. Still the stories, he holds, are very old; the legend-formation was completed by the latter days of the Judges (*c.* 1200 B.C.). See his *Die Sagen der Genesis* (Introd. to Commentary), *passim.* What one fails to find is any explanation of how the monotheism which is recognised as present in Genesis came to be developed out of these casually coalescing legends, or any perception of the deeper ideas in the Genesis narratives, or of their organic relation with the rest of Scripture. In this respect Gunkel stands behind many of those whom he criticises. On the other hand, with all his Babylonian leanings, he writes vigorously in his *Israel und*

Babylonien on behalf of the independence of the religious conceptions of Israel, as against Fried. Delitzsch and others of that tendency.

NOTE F.—P. 114

THE NAME JEHOVAH IN THE PATRIARCHAL AGE

It seems to us, apart from doubtful Babylonian speculations (see above, p. 409), that there are preponderating reasons for regarding Jehovah (Yahweh) as really a very old personal name of God in the patriarchal families. The J writer uses it freely, but is far from putting it indiscriminately into the mouths of the characters of his story. In Gen. iii., *e.g.*, "Elohim" is employed in conversation. In Gen. ix. 26, we have the compound form, "Jehovah, Elohim of Shem" (cf. Gen. xiv. 22; and the similar forms in chap. xxiv. 3, 7, 12, 27, etc.). In Gen. xv. 2, 8, Abraham addresses God as "Adonai Jehovah," and in his intercession for Sodom as "Adonai" (chap. xviii. 27, 31, 32). In the middle chapters (xxiv.–xxxiv.) "Jehovah" occurs frequently in connection with Laban, Isaac, Rebekah, Jacob, Rachel, etc. From chap. xxxv. to the end of the book it practically disappears in speech (an instance in Jacob's blessing, chap. xlix. 18). It may have become disused in Egypt. See further on the antiquity of this divine name, p. 497 below; and on the usage of the name, chap. vii. pp. 221 ff.

NOTES TO CHAPTER V

NOTE A.—P. 128

EARLY IDEAS OF GOD

MAN'S earliest ideas of God were not, as is commonly assumed, his poorest.   There is really no proof that man's religious history began with fetishism, ghost-worship, totemism, or any of the other superstitions with which "primitive religion" is usually identified.   Fetishism is admitted by the best anthropologists to be a "degeneration" of religion, and an abundance of anthropological testimony could be adduced against the sufficiency of each of the other theories in turn.   No savage tribes are found who do not seem to have higher ideas of God along with their superstitions (cf. A. Lang's *Making of Religion*).   Man does not creep up from fetishism, through polytheism, to monotheism, but polytheism represents rather the refraction of an original undifferentiated sense, or consciousness, or perception, of the divine (cf. Rom. i. 19–23).

In historical religions, accordingly, the general law, enunciated by Principal Fairbairn, holds good: "the younger the polytheism, the fewer its gods" (*Studies in Phil. of Rel.* p. 22).   In the oldest religions, without exception, along with the polytheism, we find a monotheistic background.

The oldest texts in Egypt express a monotheistic belief (cf. Renouf, *Rel. of Egypt*, pp. 90–91 ; Budge, *Egyptian Religion*, chap. i.).

The Babylonian religion, it is coming to be generally admitted, had a monotheistic strain (cf. Winckler, above, p. 409).   The discovery of the Code of Hammurabi (cf. above, p. 410) has strengthened that belief.   "The position of Ilu as supreme God, at least in the ideas of Hammurabi," writes C. H. W. Johns, " is certain, despite recent *dicta* that there is no trace of a supreme El in Babylonia " (*Expos. Times*, March 1903, p. 258).

Zoroastrianism was formally dualistic, but in the elevation of its idea of Ahura-Mazda it approached, if it did not actually attain, a form of practical monotheism (cf. *Expos. Times*, Jan. 1905, pp. 185 ff.).

Vedism had few gods, while later Hinduism has an incalculable number. Behind the Vedic polytheism there stands the name for God common to all branches of the Aryan family (Deva = Zeus = Deus), and the proper name of one God (Dyaus Pitar = Zeus Pater).

China from the oldest times knew and reverenced Shang-ti, the Supreme God, or Tien, Heaven (cf. Legge, *Religions of China*).

The monotheistic strain in Greece and Rome was never lost, and comes out in the early simpler forms of belief and worship, in the mysteries, in the dramatists and sages, in later Stoical and Platonic teaching.

Behind the Arabian idolatry of Mohammed's time was the conception of Allah (cf. Hommel, *Anc. Heb. Trad.* p. 292; cf. pp. 82, 88).

The idea that the conception of one God was too lofty for the Israelites to have attained it, even through revelation, must therefore be abandoned as untenable. In Hommel's words: "It becomes clearer every day that the Semites—and more particularly the Western Semites—had from the beginning a much purer conception of the Deity than was possessed by any of the other races of antiquity, such as the Sumerians or Aryans" (*Ibid.* pp. 292, 308–10).

NOTE B.—P. 129

ANTIQUITY OF THE NAME JEHOVAH

THE following are a few indications of opinions of critics as to a pre-Mosaic use of the name Jehovah (Yahweh).

Kuenen says: "Moses can hardly be supposed to have *invented* the name 'Yahweh'; in all probability it was already in use, among however limited a circle" (*Rel. of Israel*, i. pp. 279–80).

Wellhausen says: "Jehovah is to be regarded as having been originally a family or tribal god (?), either of the family to which Moses belonged, or of the tribe of Joseph " (*Hist. of Israel*, p. 433).

Schultz says: "It is in itself more likely that such a name was not *invented*, but simply *found* by Moses" (*O.T. Theol.* ii. p. 137).

32

Driver says : "The total absence of proper names compounded with Yahweh in the patriarchal period makes it probable that, though not absolutely new in Moses' time, it was still current previously only in a limited circle, — possibly, as has been suggested, in the family of Moses" (*Genesis*, p. xix; cf. pp. xlvii and xlix, and references).

Many now trace the name back as far as Babylonia. Cf. Driver, p. xlix, and see above, p. 409. The one thing *not* proved is that it ever denoted in Israel a merely tribal god.

NOTE C.—P. 139

PROFESSOR W. R. SMITH'S THEORY OF SACRIFICE

THIS ingenious scholar develops his theory of the totem-origin of sacrifice in his *Religion of the Semites* (cf. especially pp. 247, 257, 262–4, 266–7, 269, 271, 277). The theory resembles some others in connecting the sacrifice with the idea of food for the gods (pp. 207, 218), but it works from a different basis, and gives the act of sacrifice a different interpretation. (1) The god, in this theory, is conceived of as an animal, from whom the clan derives its descent (p. 425). (2) The primitive mind, it is assumed, does not distinguish accurately between gods, men, and animals. The god, the members of the clan, and the animals of the sacred species, are all viewed as of one blood or stock, or as embraced in the bond of kinship (p. 269). (3) The form in which kinship is declared, and the bond of fellowship sealed, is a *feast* (pp. 247, 257). (4) The peculiarity of the *religious* feast, however, is that in it an animal is sacrificed (p. 262). As Dr. Smith says: "A religious banquet implies a victim . . . the slaughter of a victim must have been in early times the only thing that brought the clan together for a sacred meal" (p. 262). Conversely : "Every slaughter was a clan sacrifice, *i.e.*, a domestic animal was not slain except to procure the material for a public meal of kinsmen" (p. 263). (5) The last point is, that the fact that the slaughter of such an animal was sanctioned for a religious feast implies that it was a sacred, or totem, animal, and itself belonged to the circle of kinship.

It is difficult to criticise a theory which rests so much on hypothetical construction, and seems opposed to all the real evidence we possess as to the Semitic ideas of the gods, and their relation to their worshippers. It will need much stronger evidence to convince us that the Semite peoples generally passed

through a totem stage, and that the God of Israel was originally
a totem-deity, of animal form, whose blood the tribes of Israel
were supposed to share. It is anything but proved that the
early Semites knew nothing, as this theory asserts, of domestic,
but only of clan life; that they knew nothing of individual and
domestic sacrifices (Abel, Noah, Abraham); that gods, animals,
and men, were at first all held to be of common kinship; that
"unclean animals" were totem animals, *i.e.*, those whose life was
sacred, with many more assumptions.

But, to keep to the one point of sacrifice, it is pertinent to
ask—Where is the proof that the animals sacrificed had this
character of totems? (1) They were not "unclean" animals;
on the contrary, only "clean" animals were permitted.
(2) The victims were not confined to one class or species of
animals, as on the totem-theory seems necessary. Sheep, goats,
calves, bulls, pigeons, were all used as sacrifice; but plainly all
could not be totems. Besides, how came many distinct tribes to
have one totem? (3) Why should the totem-animal, of all
creatures, be sacrificed? Ought not the principle of kinship to
have protected it? How should the god, or clansmen, be supposed
to find satisfaction in feeding on the flesh of one of their own
stock? The closer the bond of kinship is drawn, the greater
becomes the difficulty. (4) As explaining sacrifice in Israel, the
theory takes no account of those ideas on which the ritual of
sacrifice rests in this religion, which are as unique as everything
else about it. It gives no help to the explaining of the expiatory
or propitiatory aspect of the Jewish sacrifices, in which the
peculiar virtue of these sacrifices was believed to consist. The
theory seems to us to be baseless in itself, and to break down
whenever tests from evidence can be applied to it.

NOTE D.—P. 141

SACRIFICE OF CHILDREN IN CANAAN

THE recent excavations at Gezer in Palestine afford the most
interesting illustrations yet obtained of the sacrifice of children
in Canaan. The site of Gezer was identified in 1871, and excavations were commenced by the Palestinian Exploration Fund
in 1902, under the charge of Professor Macalister, of Cambridge.
The result has been that seven ancient cities have been unearthed,
one below the other till the last foundations have been reached.
The city, as historical notices also prove, is one of the most

ancient in Canaan. Its earliest inhabitants were cave-dwellers of the neolithic age. After them came the Semitic Amorites, about 2500 B.C., scarabs of the eleventh dynasty of Egypt being found among the remains. These were dispossessed about 1700 B.C. by a second Semitic race — the Canaanites of the Tel el-Amarna letters and of the Old Testament. The Israelites conquered Gezer under Joshua, but could not keep it, and remained there mingled with the Canaanites till the time of Solomon (Josh. xvi. 10). About 950 B.C. the city was conquered and burnt by the king of Egypt, and presented to Solomon's wife (1 Kings ix. 16). It was rebuilt by Solomon (ver. 17).

The excavations bring to light painful testimony of the custom of sacrifice of children. In the Amorite period (2500–1700 B.C.), the ground beneath the "high place" of the city was found to be filled with large earthen jars containing the bones of newborn infants. They were evidently "firstborns" who had been sacrificed to Astarte. Similar jars containing the remains of infants were found beneath the walls of houses. The sacrifice in this case was to secure good luck when a new building was erected. This illustrates the statement in 1 Kings xvi. 34 about the action of Hiel the Bethelite at his refounding of Jericho. The contrast in the religion of Israel is seen in the fact that firstborns were to be dedicated to Jehovah (Ex. xxii. 29). The practices above noted continue during the Canaanite period, though lamps and bowls begin to be used as a substitute for human sacrifice. After the Israelitish occupation of Canaan the traces of infant sacrifice still further decline, though, as a Canaanitish city, Gezer is still marked by this abomination. Latterly the lamp and bowl deposits take its place. There is nothing whatever in all this to implicate the Israelitish religion in sacrifice of children. (See publications of the Palestinian Exploration Fund, and an interesting article by Professor Lewis Bayles Paton, Ph.D.. Hartford, Director of the American School of Oriental Research in Palestine, in the *Homiletic Review*, Dec. 1904.)

NOTE E.—P. 143

H. P. SMITH ON THE BRAZEN SERPENT

THE remarks of this author on Hezekiah's destruction of the brazen serpent of Moses (2 Kings xviii. 4) deserve quotation as an illustration of critical methods :—

"The clause *which Moses made* refers to a well-known narra-

tive in the account of the wilderness wandering. Here we read
that the people were bitten by serpents. Moses is therefore
commanded to make a copper serpent, and raise it upon a pole.
Whoever is bitten and looks at the serpent is healed. It must
be clear that we have here a survival from the primitive totemism
of Israel. . . .

"Why Moses should have made such an image for a people
notoriously prone to idolatry is a question that need not be
discussed. How such an image, if made by Moses, came into the
temple is also difficult to conceive. We are tempted, therefore,
to suppose the words *which Moses made* a later addition to the
narrative and not the expression of Hezekiah's belief or of the
belief of his contemporaries. In that case we must treat the
Nehushtan as a veritable idol of the house of Israel, which had
been worshipped in the temple from the time of its erection.
Serpent-worship is so widespread that we should be surprised
not to find traces of it in Israel. We know of a Serpent's Stone
near Jerusalem which was the site of a sanctuary (1 Kings i. 9),
and this sanctuary was dedicated to Yahweh. This parallel
makes us conclude that the copper serpent of the temple was also
a symbol of Yahweh. If this be so, it may be attributed to Moses,
though in a different way from that taken by the Hebrew author;
for Yahweh was introduced to Israel by Moses. Probably the
serpent was thought to be a congenial symbol of the god of the
lightning—and that in the desert days Yahweh was the god of
the lightning, or of the thunderstorm, seems well made out."—
Hist. of O.T. pp. 239–40. One does not know whether to
marvel most at the logic of this passage, or at the *grounds* of the
reasoning.

NOTE F.—P. 144

DILLMANN ON IMAGE-WORSHIP

THE following statement from Dr. Dillmann (*Exod.–Lev.* pp.
208–9) may be compared with those of Kautzsch and others
about image-worship in Israel:—

"It cannot with good reason be maintained that such a
prohibition involving the idea of the possibility of making any
representation of God, as well as His invisibility and spirituality,
is too advanced for Moses' time, and his stage of knowledge, and
therefore cannot have been given by him, but must have been
just introduced into the Decalogue at a much later date. Apart
from Ex. xxxii., where the narrative attributes to Moses a clear

perception of the unlawfulness of an image of Jehovah, it is certain, in the first place, that in the traditions of their fathers a cultus without images is ascribed to the patriarchs; and, secondly, that in the post-Mosaic period, it was a recognised principle, at least at the central sanctuary of the entire people, and at the temple of Solomon, that no representation was to be made of Jehovah. The worship of the image of Jehovah at Sinai (Ex. xxxii.), in the time of the judges, and in the kingdom of the ten tribes, does not prove that the prohibition of images was unknown, but only that it was very difficult to secure its proper recognition by the mass of the people, especially of the northern tribes, who were more Canaanitishly disposed. Or rather, it was for centuries an object of contention between the stricter and more lax party,—the latter holding that it forbade only the images of false gods, the former that it likewise forbade any image of Jehovah. Prophets such as Amos and Hosea, who contended against the images of the calves, at Bethel and at Dan, never announced the principle that no representation can be made of Jehovah as anything new, but simply presupposed it as known. However far we go back in the post-Mosaic history, we find it already existing, at least as practically carried into effect at the central sanctuary; from whom then can it have proceeded but from the legislator, Moses himself?"

NOTES TO CHAPTER VI

NOTE A.—P. 153

OBJECTIONS TO MOSAIC ORIGIN OF DECALOGUE

THE following is a brief summary of objections to the Decalogue from Addis (*Docs. of Hex.* i. pp. 139–40):—

"It must have arisen long after the Israelites had passed from a nomad to a settled life. . . . The sabbath implies the settled life of agriculture. . . . Moreover, if the second 'word' be an integral part of the whole, the Decalogue must have arisen after the worship of Yahweh in the form of an ox was considered unlawful. To this mode of worship neither Elijah nor Elisha seems to have made any objection [?], and it is very doubtful whether any protest was made against it before the reiterated and energetic protest of Hosea. We may then conjecture that the Decalogue arose in the eighth, or perhaps the seventh century before Christ."

See in reply to this representation the statement by Dillmann in previous note, p. 501.

NOTE B.—P. 175

THE FORCE OF EXODUS XX. 24

As stated in the text, Professor W. R. Smith seems to insist, in opposition to Dr. W. H. Green, that Ex. xx. 24 can only bear the meaning "in all places," in the sense of a number of co-existent sanctuaries (*Prophets*, p. 394). To this Professor Green replies :—

"The collective use of the noun in such a construction is not denied. But attention is called to the significant circumstance that where the conception is that of a coexisting plurality, 'all the places' is expressed in Hebrew by the plural noun (*e.g.*, Deut. xii. 2; 1 Sam. vii. 16; xxx. 31; Ezra i. 4; Jer. viii. 3; xxiv. 9; xxix. 14; xl. 12; xlv. 5; Ezek. xxxiv. 12); while in the other two passages in which the phrase is used with a singular noun, the reference is not to places viewed jointly, but regarded successively (Gen. xx. 13; Deut. xi. 24). The words are used in a different sense, Gen. xviii. 26 " (*Moses and Prophets*, p. 311).

NOTE C.—P. 179

FREEDOM UNDER THE LAW

IT is a mistake to regard the Law as a rigid, inflexible system, which admitted of no modification of development in details to suit circumstances (thus W. R. Smith represents "the traditional view," *O.T. in J. C.*, pp. 227–8). The law was made for man, not man for the law, and the spirit at all times, in the eyes of God, was above the letter (1 Sam. xv. 22). The psalmist most devoted to the law "walked at liberty" under it (Ps. cxix. 45). There was *within* the law abundant scope for development, and the letter of the law itself could, where necessary, give place to the spirit. Thus, the law for the age of service for the Levites was modified (if the same *kind* of service was intended) from thirty years to twenty-five (Num. iv. 23, 30, 35; viii. 24); and David again modified it to twenty (1 Chron. xxiii. 24, 27). In Num. ix. 6–12 a second passover was allowed for those who were unclean or absent at the proper time. The shewbread at Nob (1 Sam. xxi. 1–6) was, as Christ points out (Matt. xii. 3–7), given under necessity to David and his men, though it was not lawful for any but priests to eat of it. In the observance of Hezekiah's passover we have repeated infractions of the letter of the law— noted, too, in Chronicles (2 Chron. xxix. 34; xxx. 17, 19).

NOTE D.—P. 182

THE GENEALOGY OF ZADOK

ON the genealogy of Zadok see 1 Chron. vi. 8, 53; xxiv. 3; xxvii. 17. Wellhausen denies to Zadok, however, an Aaronic, not to say Levitical descent (*Hist. of Israel*, pp. 126–43). His

counter-theory is that Zadok was no Aaronite, but that, after the
setting aside of the house of Eli, there came in a new hereditary
priesthood at Jerusalem—"at first parvenus and afterwards the
most legitimate of the legitimate," and that the derivation of
Zadok from Aaron in 1 Chronicles is a fiction aiming at the
legitimising of the newcomers. This construction Delitzsch
characterises as "a manufacture of history (*Geschichtsmacherei*)
which builds houses on deceitful fancies" (Luthardt's *Zeitschrift*,
1880, p. 284). Cf. Kittel, *Hist. of Hebs.* i. p. 124; ii. p. 182;
Van Hoonacker, *Sacerdoce Lévitique*, pp. 166 ff.

NOTE E.—P. 184

DAVID'S SONS AS PRIESTS

THE meaning of the term "priest" in the three passages cited is
obscure. Delitzsch says: "Only crass self-deception can understand it of sacrificing priests, who have been mentioned just
before" (Luthardt's *Zeitschrift*, 1880, p. 63). The common
view that "priest" is used here in some secondary or honorary
sense of royal officials (Ewald, Delitzsch, Klostermann, Baudissin,
Movers, etc.; R.V. *marg.*), is supported by the parallel
passage, 1 Chron. xviii. 17, which need not be set down to the
motive of recognising none but Aaronic priests, but must
represent a general way of understanding the expression, and
by the LXX. Dr. Driver, however, positively rejects such
explanation (*Notes on Samuel*, pp. 219-20, 293-4; so the
Wellhausen school generally); and there are certainly difficulties
in *proving* this exceptional use. It is a case in which, as Van
Hoonacker argues, there is some ground (at least as regards
David's sons) for suspecting the text. Inspection will show that
the four passages, 2 Sam. viii. 16-18; xx. 23-26; 1 Kings iv.
2-6; 1 Chron. xviii. 15-18, are closely related: represent, in
fact, the same list, with some changes of names under Solomon.
But it is also evident that there is some confusion and corruption
in the copying. The order is not always the same: "Ahimelech
the son of Abiathar" in 2 Sam. viii. 17 (and 1 Chron.) stands
for "Abiathar the son of Ahimelech"; and ver. 18, in which the
words 'David's sons" occur, is in other respects admittedly corrupt
(it reads, "Benaiah the son of Jehoiada, *and* the Cherethites
and the Pelethites"). There is nothing about "David's sons"
in the corresponding passage in chap. xx., but instead, "And Ira

also the Jairite was priest unto David" (cf. "Zabud the son of
Nathan was priest" in I Kings iv. 5). In the transpositions
of the text, words or names may have dropped out or got
changed, or "David's sons" may be a corruption of other words
altogether. This, of course, cannot be proved either.

NOTE A.—P. 200

DELITZSCH speaks somewhere of "the omnipotence which resides in the ink of a German scholar"; and nothing strikes one more in the recent literature of criticism than the unbounded confidence with which the most disputable statements are made. Our pages are full of illustrations. The peremptoriness of Wellhausen is proverbial. *E.g.*, the Levitical cities are "*demonstrably* a metamorphosis of the old *Bamoth* (high places)" (*Hist. of Israel*, p. 37). "'House of God' is never anything but the house of an image" (p. 130). The trick of style is one easily learned, and has infected not a little of our own critical writing. It is not clear, however, why this peremptory tone should be affected in cases where the critics manifestly disagree among themselves. We may take one example from so useful a book as Ryle's *Canon of the Old Testament*. The author begins with the general statement: "Analysis of the Pentateuch *has shown conclusively* that numerous collections of Israelite laws were made at different times," etc. (p. 22). After mention of the Decalogue and Book of the Covenant: "Another ancient, and very distinct collection of laws is incorporated in the section which has been called by scholars 'The Law of Holiness' (Lev. xvii.–xxvi.). . . . It is a fact, *which no scholars have ventured to dispute*, that these chapters contain extensive excerpts from a collection of laws whose general character must have closely resembled the Book of the Covenant, differing only from it in subject-matter so far as it is occupied more generally with ceremonial than with civil regulations" (pp. 25–6). "Ezekiel shows *unmistakable* signs of acquaintance with a collection of Priestly Laws that we *can certainly* identify" (p. 72). We agree (see pp. 308 ff.); but leading critical scholars do energetically dispute both these propositions.

The "Law of Holiness" is *not* by them generally put before
Ezekiel. Dr. G. B. Gray, *e.g.*, says, on his side, as confidently:
"Lev. xix. 2 belongs to a code (known as the 'Law of Holiness')
drawn up in the early part of the sixth century B.C." (*Divine
Discipline of Israel*, p. 41). Further: "Modern Criticism has
probably *shown incontrovertibly* [if incontrovertibly, why probably?] that the period of the final literary codification of the
Priestly Laws can hardly be placed before the era of the exile.
It teaches, however, *no less emphatically* that *the Priestly Laws
themselves have been gradually developed from previously existing
collections of regulations affecting ritual and worship*" (p. 27;
italics in last case author's). If this be so, then Kuenen
and Wellhausen must be excluded from "modern criticism,"
for both "emphatically" deny that *any* written collections of
Priestly Laws existed before the exile, and affirm the contrary.
E.g., "as we have seen, no ritual legislation yet existed in
Ezekiel's time," etc. (Kuenen, *Rel. of Israel*, ii. p. 231; cf.
Wellhausen, *Hist. of Israel*, p. 480). Besides, as shown in
Chap. IX., if this is allowed, the "incontrovertibly" disappears,
for the one grand reason for putting the laws in the exile is
that they were *new*.

NOTE B.—P. 206

CORNILL'S DECOMPOSITION OF J

THE following indicates the process by which Cornill reached the
conclusion that the unity of the J document must be given up:—
"The first incentives proceeded from the Biblical primitive
history; in this both Schrader and Wellhausen marked contradictions which made it impossible to maintain the literary
unity. Gen. iv. 16[b] stands in sharp contrast with the immediately preceding vers. 11–16[a], since in these the ceasing
of that which in chap. iii. 17 is a curse for all mankind, is
threatened as a punishment to Cain; the unquestionably parallel
passages, chaps. iv. 7 and iii. 16, iv. 15 and iv. 24, do not give
the impression of a free reproduction by the same writer, but
rather of imitation; the same author cannot have written chap.
iv. 26 who already in chap. iv. 1 permitted himself to use without hesitation the name Jahve; chap. xi. 1–9 is irreconcilable
with chap. ix. 19, where that appears as a self-evident natural
process which in the other passage is apprehended as the result
of a special punitive interposition of Jahve; the Noah of chap.
ix. 20–27, the father of the three sons, Shem, Japheth, and

Canaan, *i.e.*, the racial ancestor of three specific peoples, is not the Noah of chap. ix. 18–19, who, through the three sons, Shem, Ham, and Japheth, is the ancestor of the whole of mankind after the flood. And this brings us to the weightiest and most deep-going distinction in the primitive history; we have in it still clear traces of a tradition which knows nothing of the flood, which derives the three groups of the whole of humanity from the sons of Lamech, chap. iv. 20–22, which traces back all "Nephilim," still existing in historical times, Num. xiii. 33, to the marriages of the sons of God with the daughters of men. Since all the passages cited are undoubtedly Jahvistic, while no trace is found of E, which appears, rather, to have had no primitive history, there remains no alternative but to surrender the homogeneity of J" (*Einleitung*, p. 52).

NOTE C.—P. 206

THE VIEW OF J AND E AS "SCHOOLS"

WE append a few utterances of recent writers on this subject:—

Budde says: "J and E are throughout not to me persons, but extensive schools of writers, running their course alongside of each other" (*Judges*, p. xiv).

Gunkel says: "J and E are not individual writers, nor yet redactors of old single documents, but rather schools of narrators" (*Genesis*, p. lviii).

Dr. Cheyne says: "The Yahwists were, in fact, perhaps a school of writers" (*Founders of Criticism*, p. 30).

Dr. Driver says that P "seems, as a whole, to have been the work of a school of writers rather than of an individual" (*Genesis*, p. xvi), and no doubt would apply the same to J and E.

Kautzsch says: "A close examination of its (J's) contents showed long ago that here also we have to do with various strata, and therefore with the work of a Jahwistic school" (*Lit. of O.T.*, p. 37; similarly of E, p. 45).

McFadyen says: "More properly they (J and E) were the work of a school, and represent a literary and religious activity that ranges over a considerable period. . . . The priestly document . . . is, like the prophetic documents, not the work of a single author, but of a school, and represents a movement" (*Messages of the Proph. and Priestly Historians*, pp. 22, 224).

The Oxford *Hexateuch*, i. p. x, tabular Contents, says: "J represents a school rather than a single author."

NOTES TO CHAPTER VIII

NOTE A.—P. 252

THE BREAKING UP OF DEUTERONOMY

AN example is furnished in a recent work, *The Book of the Covenant in Moab : A Critical Inquiry into the Original Form of Deuteronomy*, by John Cullen, M.A., D.Sc. (1903), which, however, the author admits "differs radically from that which has come to be regarded almost as a tradition of criticism." We cannot see, however, that his theory differs much *in principle* from some of the other modern attempts. He splits up the book into a greater number of parts than the more cautious critics have done, and seeks to assign to each its place in the total composition. The original appearance of the book he holds, with the critics, to have been in the reign of Josiah. He makes the book *begin* with chap. xxix. 1–4. He leaves out chaps. i.–iv. 9, and transfers chap. v. 2 to a position introductory to chap. iv. 10 ff. This original Deuteronomy extended (with omissions) to chap. xi. 28, but had as its conclusion chap. xxviii. 1–45 (omitting vers. 2–9); chap. xxx. 11–20 : Ex. xxiv. 4–8 (!), and Deut. xxxii. 45, 46. The Decalogue in chap. v. is excised as unsuitable to the context, and is relegated to a "Decalogue Edition," which appeared some time before the exile. The Decalogue in Ex. xx. is still later. Successive developments follow through the addition of "Law Code," a "First Combined Edition," a "Second or Decalogue Edition," a "Third or Minatory Edition," an "Exilic Redaction," "Post-Exilic Additions," and a "P Redaction." If the able author is seriously persuaded that any book under heaven was ever made by such a process, we feel, with all respect, that there is hardly any common ground for argument.

Oettli is a comparatively conservative writer, who defends the unity of the main body of Deuteronomy, but even he is badly

bitten when he comes to the closing chapters. The following is
his analysis of chaps. xxvii.–xxxiv. (*Deut.* p. 12):—

xxvii. 1–3, Dt. ; 4, R. ; 5–7ᵃ, JE ; 7ᵇ, 8, R ; 9–13, Dt. ; 14–
26, R ; xxviii. 1–68, Dt. (with reserve as to enlargements) ;
xxviii. 69–xxx. 20, Dt. (with redactional changes and transpositions) ; xxxi. 1–13, Dt. ; 14, 15, JE ; 16–22, introduction to
Moses' Song out of JE ; 23, JE ; 24–29, Dt. ; 30, R ; xxxii. 1–
44, from JE ; 45–47, Dt. ; 48–52, P ; xxxiii. from JE ; xxxiv.
1 P, Dt. JE ; 2–4, JE ; 5?, 6, Dt. ; 7, P, JE ; 8, 9, P ; 10–12
Dt.

There are elements of truth in this analysis, but it is assuredly
greatly overdone.

NOTE B.—P. 253

DEUTERONOMIC AND PRIESTLY STYLES

IN a note to the first edition of his *O.T. in J. C.* (p. 433),
Professor W. R. Smith cites as "a good example of the fundamental difference in legal style between the Levitical law and
the Deuteronomic Code," the laws about the cities of refuge
in Num. xxxv. and Deut. xix. The case is worth considering as
"a good example" also of the tendency to overdrive argument.
Allowance in any case must be made for the difference between
a careful original statement of a law, and a later general rehearsal
of its substance in the rounded style of free, popular discourse.
But what are the specific differences ? "In Deuteronomy the
word 'refuge' does not occur, and the cities are always described
by a periphrasis." But the Deuteronomist simply says : "Thou
shalt separate three cities for thee in the midst of thy land (chap.
xix. 2) ; "thou shalt separate three cities for thee " (ver. 7) ;
"then shalt thou add three cities more for thee" (ver. 9) ; and
there is no periphrasis. The phrase "that every manslayer may
flee thither " (ver. 3), "the manslayer which shall flee thither "
(ver. 4), is derived verbally from Num. xxxv. 11, 15. "In
Numbers the phrase for ' accidentally ' is *bish'gaga*, in Deut. *bib'li
da'at*." Admitted, but the words convey the same idea, and
are only used twice altogether—in Num. xxxv. 11, 15 and in
Deut. iv. 42, xix. 4. "The judges in the one are 'the congregation,' in the other ' the elders of his city.'" But Deuteronomy
says nothing about "judges," and "the elders," who are once
referred to in chap. xix. 12, plainly act in the name of the
congregation. "The verb for *hate* is different." Rather, "the

verb for *hate* " does not occur at all in Num. xxxv., but the noun
derived from it does (ver. 20), and is translated "hatred," while
in vers. 21, 22, a different term, translated "enmity," is employed,
which expresses nearly the same sense. Had these words
appeared, one in Numbers, the other in Deuteronomy, instead of
standing in consecutive verses of one chapter, they would doubtless have been quoted as further evidence of diversity. So "one
account says again and again 'to kill any person,' the other 'to
kill his neighbour'"—a difference surely not incompatible with
identity even of authorship. "Neighbour" is found repeatedly,
alternating with another word, in Lev. xix. (vers. 13, 16, 18; xx.
10—P), and "to kill a person" occurs in Deut. xxvii. 25. (Cf. the
Heb. idiom in the law itself, Deut. xix. 6, 11.) "The detailed
description of the difference between murder and accidental
homicide is entirely different· in language and detail." But in
Deuteronomy there is no "detailed description" of the kind referred
to. There *is* in Num. xxxv. 16–24; but Deuteronomy confines
itself to one simple illustration from concrete life, admirably
adapted, it will be admitted, to the speaker's popular purpose
(chap. xix. 5). The statement in Deuteronomy, it is evident,
presupposes the earlier law, and is incomplete without it, occupying only about a dozen verses, as compared with over twenty
in Numbers, while even of the dozen, three are occupied
with a new provision for the number of the cities being ultimately raised to nine (vers. 8–10). When, further, Dr. Smith
points out that "Num. xxxv. 11–34 contains 19 nouns and
verbs which occur also in Deut. xix. 2–13, and 45 which do
not occur in the parallel passage; while the law, as given in
Deuteronomy, has 50 such words not in the law of Numbers,"
he applies a numerical test which, considering the different
character of the two passages, is quite misleading. We have
before us the text of Mr. Gladstone's Home Rule Bill, and his
speeches made in introducing it to the House of Commons; but
what havoc a similar enumeration would make of his title to the
authorship of the Bill! It is not contended that Moses with
his own pen necessarily wrote out all these laws, any more than
that Mr. Gladstone drafted his own Bill.

We have not, in these remarks, taken any notice of Josh. xx.
3–6, where the language of Num. xxxv. and of Deut. xix. is
blended. The Deuteronomic expressions are lacking in the
LXX (Vat.), and it is possible they may be a later gloss.

NOTE C.—P. 258

DEUTERONOMY AS *FRAUS PIA*

ONE of Reuss's propositions, endorsed by Wellhausen, is: "Deuteronomy is the book which the priests *pretended* to have found in the temple in the time of Josiah" (Wellhausen, *Hist. of Israel*, p. 4).

Kuenen says: "It is certain that an author of the seventh century B.C.—following in the footsteps of others, *e.g.*, of the writer of the Book of the Covenant—has made Moses himself proclaim that which, in his opinion, it was expedient to the real interests of the Mosaic party to announce and introduce. . . . Men used to perpetrate such fictions as these without any qualms of conscience. . . . If Hilkiah *found* the book in the temple, it was put there by the adherents of the Mosaic tendency. Or else Hilkiah himself was of their number, and in that case he pretended that he had found the book of the law. . . . It is true, this deception is more unjustifiable still than the introduction of Moses as speaking. But we must reflect here also that the ideas of those times were not the same as ours, but considerably less strict" (*Rel. of Israel*, ii. pp. 18–19). We fancy that the ideas of the author of Deuteronomy and of Jeremiah will compare favourably in "strictness" with those of the writer of the above section.

Cornill says: "We must recognise the fact that we have here a pseudograph, and that this was known to the persons interested. . . . The excuse for them must be that they saw no other means of carrying through their work, planned in the spirit of Moses and for the honour of Jahve" (*Einleitung*, pp. 37–8).

Colenso, as seen above (p. 258), thinks Jeremiah may have been the *falsarius*. "It is obvious," he says, "that very few beside the writer may have been privy to the scheme,—perhaps only the priest Hilkiah, and possibly Huldah, and one or two others" (*Pent.* Pop. edit. p. 198).

Dr. Cheyne, after toying with, and half-adopting this hypothesis in his *Jeremiah*, in "Men of the Bible" series (pp. 76 ff.: "What he—Hilkiah—practised, however, was not deceit, not *delusion*, but rather *illusion*" p. 77), goes wholly over to it in his *Founders of Criticism* (pp. 267 ff.). "How is it that Hilkiah, Shaphan, and Huldah display such imperturbability? The easiest supposition is that these three persons (to whom we must add Ahikam, Achbor, and Asaiah) had agreed together, unknown to the king, on their course of action" (p. 267). "I quite enter

33

into the dislike of reverent Bible-readers for the theory of ' pious fraud.' I think that dislike an exaggerated one. No student of Oriental life and history could be surprised at a pious fraud originating among priests. But I do not adopt that theory to account for 2 Kings xxii." [this is simple casuistry] (p. 271). Hilkiah's conduct in imposing the book on Josiah is justified. "Such conduct as that of Hilkiah is, I maintain, worthy of an inspired teacher and statesman in that age and under those circumstances. It is also not without a distant resemblance to the course of Divine Providence, so far as this can be scanned by our weak faculties. Indeed, if we reject the theory of ' needful illusion' we are thrown upon a sea of perplexity. Was there no book [Dr. Cheyne's own] on Jeremiah bringing home the need of this theory to the Christian conscience, to which Dr. Driver could have referred?" (p. 272). Our ideas in these days are "more strict"!

NOTE D.—P. 260

OBLIVION OF CHARLEMAGNE'S CODE

DR. CHEYNE refers in his *Jeremiah* (p. 76), in illustration of 2 Kings xxii., to an instance of successful forgery in the history of England given in Maine's *Ancient Law* (p. 82). Dr. Green, on the other hand, cites from Sir James Stephen an apposite case of the loss of knowledge of a whole Code—that of Charlemagne. "When the barbarism of the domestic government," says this authority, "had thus succeeded the barbarism of the government of the State, one of the most remarkable results of that political change was the disappearance of the laws and institutions by which Charlemagne had endeavoured to elevate and civilise his subjects. Before the close of the century in which he died the whole body of his laws had fallen into utter disuse throughout the whole extent of his Gallic dominions. They who have studied the charters, laws, and chronicles of the later Carlovingian princes most diligently are unanimous in declaring that they indicate either an absolute ignorance, or an entire forgetfulness of the legislation of Charlemagne" (*Lects. on Hist. of France*, p. 94; Green, *Higher Criticism*, p. 156).

NOTE E.—P. 269

THE LAW OF THE KING IN DEUT. XVII. 14 FF.

DR. DRIVER and many critics allow the law of the king in this chapter to be at least in kernel old. Delitzsch says: "The prohibition to make a foreigner king is comprehensible in the mouth of Moses, but without motive or object in so late an age as Josiah's, and generally during the period of the undivided and divided kingdoms" (*Genesis*, p. 38). He discusses the subject more fully in Luthardt's *Zeitschrift*, 1880, pp. 564–5. We can find, he says, "a suitable Mosaic basis for this law. It is on the face of it improbable that a leader and lawgiver coming out of a monarchical country should not have foreseen that the people would wish to have a king. . . . The thought in ver. 16 that the passion for horses would lead to a return of the people to Egypt has hitherto found no satisfactory explanation from the circumstances of the time of the kings—this warning and threatening bear still undeniably the character of a time in which the renewal of the newly lost relation to the kingdom of the Pharaohs was a pressing alarm." The law, it is thought, is sketched in terms borrowed from the court of Solomon. It is rather to be inferred that the description of Solomon's court in the Book of Kings (1 Kings x. 26–29; xi. 1–4) is given in terms partly borrowed from this law. The familiarity of the author of Kings with Deuteronomy is undoubted, and he draws up his account of Solomon's luxury and splendour, particularly of his multiplication of wives, in such terms as will impress the mind by its contrast with this law.

NOTE F.—P. 276

MINOR DISCREPANCIES IN LAWS

MINOR examples of discrepancies are those in the laws relating to firstlings (Deut. xv. 19, 20; cf. Num. xviii. 17, 18), priestly dues (chap. xviii. 3, 4), the law of bondservants (chap. xv. 12 ff.; cf. Ex. xxi. 1–6), the law of carrion (chap. xiv. 21; cf. Lev. xvii. 15), etc. Reasonable explanations have been offered of most of these difficulties, though a few points may remain unclear. In the case of the firstlings, Deuteronomy assumes the feast on the flesh at the sanctuary, without denying that the usual portions went to the priest; Numbers lays stress on the latter, and perhaps means no more than that the sacrifices came under the law of the peace offerings (cf. Van Hoonacker, *Le Sacerdoce*, pp. 405–6). Even if the priests received the whole in the first instance, it may be presumed that, as in peace offerings generally, the offerer had a share given back to him.   In chap. xviii. 3, 4, the dues specified are probably additional to those in Numbers. " A pitiful livelihood truly," as Hengstenberg says (*Pent.* ii. p. 335), if this were all! But the regular income is presupposed. (See pp. 188, 275.)   The mention of the Hebrewess in the law of bond-service (chap. xv. 12) is not a contradiction of the older law; while the case of the bondmaid betrothed to her master or master's son in Ex. xxi. 7 ff. is special, and is not touched on in Deuteronomy. The modification in the law of carrion (chap. xiv. 21) has probably in view the conditions of settled life in Canaan (cf. Bissell, *Pent.* p. 176), but still is not to be understood as dispensing with the purifications of Lev. xvii. 15, even for the stranger.   Generally, it may occur that it is hardly conceivable that the author of Deuteronomy should alter or contradict old laws for no apparent reason.

NOTES TO CHAPTER IX

NOTE A.—P. 287

KUENEN'S EARLY VIEWS OF THE POST-EXILIAN THEORY

IN 1861 (five years before the publication of Graf's work), Kuenen thus expressed himself on the views of Von Bohlen, George, and Vatke, who held, like Graf, that the legislation of Deuteronomy was earlier than that of the middle books of the Pentateuch :—

"He [George] assumes that the historical elements of the Pentateuch are the oldest, that Deuteronomy was written during the reign of Josiah, whilst the greater part of the laws in Exodus–Numbers did not exist until after the exile. His arguments are partly external, partly internal, *i.e.*, derived from a comparison of the two legislations. (1) Jeremiah, who knows Deuteronomy and makes frequent use of it, shows no acquaintance with the laws in Exodus–Numbers, as appears from chap. vii. 21–23, where he appeals to Deut. vii. 6, xiv. 2, xxvi. 18, but ignores the whole sacrificial Thora. But Jeremiah could, as Hosea, Isaiah, and other prophets before him, exalt the moral commands of the law far above its ceremonial prescriptions, and consider the former as the real basis of the covenant with Jahveh, without the implication that a ceremonial code did not yet exist in his time; he could even pronounce his conviction that the laws concerning burnt offering and sacrifice are later than the moral commands, and still it would not follow from this that Exodus–Numbers were committed to writing later than Deuteronomy. (2) Internal evidence. The priority of Deuteronomy is argued on the ground of several strange assertions, *which are not worthy of refutation;* to wit, that, before the Babylonish captivity, there was no distinction between priests and Levites, high priest and priests; that the Mosaic tabernacle never existed; that the spirit and tendency of Deuteronomy

indicate an earlier period than those of Leviticus. Deut. xxxi.
14 is considered wholly arbitrary as a later addition; xviii. 2,
xxiv. 8, are left out of view. The view of George in this form as
presented by him has been almost universally rejected" (quoted
by G. Vos in *Pentateuchal Codes*, pp. 173–4). Vos draws from
the quotation some very pertinent morals.

NOTE B.—P. 294

THE UNITY OF THE LAW

THE unique character, and essential unity of idea and spirit of
the Mosaic law, are abundantly testified to by critical writers.
The following are examples :—

Ewald writes thus of the sacred seasons: "You behold a
structure simple, lofty, perfect. All proceeds as it were from one
spirit, and represents one idea, and is carried into effect by what
resembles counters exactly matched strung upon one cord. . . .
Whoever has a thorough knowledge of these festivals, will be
persuaded that they have not arisen by slow degrees from the
blind impulse of external nature, nor from the history of the
people, but are the product of a lofty genius" (quoted at length
by Green, *Feasts*, pp. 50–1, from *Zeitschrift für die Kunde des
Morgenlandes*, iii. pp. 411, 434).

Riehm says: "Most of the laws of the middle books of the
Pentateuch form essentially a homogeneous whole. They do not
indeed all come from one hand, and have not been written at one
and the same time. . . . However, they are all ruled by the
same principles and ideas, have the same setting, the like form
of representation, and the same mode of expression. A multitude
of definite terms appear again and again. In manifold ways also
the laws refer to one another. Apart from isolated subordinate
differences, they agree with one another, and so supplement each
other as to give the impression of a single whole, worked out
with marvellous consistency in its details " (*Einleitung*, i. p. 202).

Schultz. who holds that "certainly it was only a later age
that created in detail the several institutions," yet says: "Everything is of a piece, from the most trifling commandment regarding outward cleanliness, up to the fundamental thoughts of
the moral law. Civic virtue is indissolubly linked to piety. . . .
The whole is woven into a splendid unity, into the thought that
this people should represent the kingdom of God on earth, and

realise in its national life the main features of the divine order of things" (*O.T. Theology*, i. p. 138).

Kautzsch, after referring to the various strata which he thinks can be distinguished in the Priestly Law, says: "But as regards the spirit which pervades them, and the fundamental assumptions from which they start, *all* the parts bear so homogeneous a stamp that we have contented ourselves in the 'Survey' with the common designation P, *i.e.*, Priests' Writing" (*Lit. of O.T.*, p. 107).

NOTE C.—P. 307

EZEKIEL AND EARLIER LAWS

Cf. RYLE's observations in earlier Note, pp. 507–8 (*Canon of O.T.*, pp. 72 ff.). The following sentences from Dr. A. B. Davidson's Introduction to his *Ezekiel* ("Cambridge Bible") may be compared with the text:—

"Inferences from comparison of Ezekiel with the Law have to be drawn with caution, for it is evident that the prophet handles with freedom institutions certainly older than his own time. The feast of weeks (Ex. xxiii. 16; xxxiv. 22) forms no element in his calendar; the law of the offering of the firstlings of the flock is dispensed with by him; there is no gilding in his temple, and no wine in his sacrificial oblations. His reconstruction of the courts of the temple is altogether new; and so is his provision in the 'oblation' of land for the maintenance of priests, Levites, and prince. . . . It is evident that the ritual in his book had long been a matter of consuetudinary law. He is familiar not only with burnt, peace, and meat offerings, but with sin and trespass offerings (xlv. 17). All these are spoken of as things customary and well understood (xiii. 13, xliv. 29–31); even the *praxis* of the trespass offerings is so much a thing familiar that no rules are laid down in regard to it (xlvi. 20). The sin and trespass offerings are little if at all alluded to in the ancient extra-ritual literature, but the argument from silence is a precarious one, for Ezekiel himself, when not precise, uses the comprehensive phraseology 'burnt-offerings and peace-offerings' (xliii. 27). The people's dues to the priests are also so much customary that no rules are needful to regulate them (xliv. 30). Ezekiel is no more a 'legislator' than he is the founder of the temple" (pp. liii–liv).

NOTE D.—P. 313

QUOTATIONS IN DEUTERONOMY FROM JE AND P

DR. DRIVER makes a strong point of the difference in the mode of the references in Deuteronomy to JE and to P respectively (*Introd.* pp. 76, 137), but his statements need qualification. Dillmann, with others, points out that it does not belong to the task of Deuteronomy to dwell on the priestly laws as it does on those of the Book of the Covenant, and shows that by no means all the laws in the latter (hardly anything of Ex. xxi.–xxii. 14) are taken up into Deuteronomy, and what is repeated is for the most part not verbally repeated, but is modified and expanded (*Num.–Jos.* p. 603).

NOTE E.—P. 317

LEVITES IN EZEKIEL

IT is to be conceded that, while Ezekiel uses "Levites" as apparently a well-known term for the ministers of the second order (chap. xlviii. 13), the only "Levites" that come specifically into his picture are the degraded priests (chap. xl. 45). This agrees with the scope of his representation, and is most naturally explained by supposing that the Levites had been practically ousted from the temple by the uncircumcised strangers, and the degraded priests are viewed as taking their place. It is likely also that, in the general declension, the Levites themselves had very largely broken the bounds of their order, and had arrogated to themselves priestly functions at the high places and elsewhere. They had become by usage and common designation priests also (cf. Dillmann, *Exod.–Lev.* p. 461; Van Hoonacker, *Le Sacerdoce*, pp. 194–5).

NOTE F.—P. 320

ALLEGED CONTRADICTIONS IN THE PASSOVER LAWS

THE assertion of Nowack, W. R. Smith, Driver, and others, that in Deuteronomy (xvi. 2) the choice in the passover is not limited to a *lamb*, as in P, but might be a bullock or a sheep (cf. Driver, *Deut.* p. 191), confuses the passover sacrifice in the strict sense

with the feast that follows.   This is not a device of "harmonists,"
but a plain dictate of common sense in comparing the laws.
Kuenen sees no contradiction with the lamb in Deuteronomy
(*Rel. of Israel*, ii. p. 93).   Even in Lev. xxiii. 4 ff., and Num.
xxviii. 16 ff. (P), no mention is made of the lamb.   Does P,
therefore, not know of it?   The freewill offerings are recognised
in Lev. xxiii. 4–8, Num. xxix. 39; cf. 2 Chron. xxxv. 7–9.
The "passover" in the stricter sense is alluded to in Deut. xvi.
5–7, as in Ex. xxiii. 18, xxxiv. 25.   Neither can a discrepancy
be made out of the word used in Deut. xvi. 7 for the cooking of
the lamb, as though it necessarily meant to "seethe" or "boil,"
2 Chron. xxxv. 13 is a decisive proof to the contrary.   The word
is there used in *both* senses—to roast with fire, and to seethe in
pots.

NOTE G.—P. 327

THE MEDIATING VIEW OF THE PRIESTLY CODE

THE following will indicate the general standpoint of the
mediating critics.   Dillmann says: "The priestly writing was
and remained at first a private document, without royal or public
sanction, and for the most part propagated only in priestly circles"
(*Num.-Jos.* p. 666).   Kittel says: "The whole character of P
proves it to have been originally not a public ecclesiastical law,
but—though not merely a private document—a programme known
at first to the priests alone, and struggling long for recognition
till favouring circumstances helped it to obtain this" (*Hist. of
Hebs.* i. p. 102).   Baudissin says: "The employment of Levites
for this office [in the sanctuary] appears to be a matter of pure
theory on the part of the legislation, whose system elsewhere also
is based in large measure upon ideal construction" (*Dict. of Bible*,
iv. pp. 88–9).   "The tabernacle, *i.e* the antedated single temple"
(p. 89).

NOTES TO CHAPTER X

NOTE A.—P. 345

KLOSTERMANN ON THE RELATION OF JE AND P

THE view indicated in the text is substantially that taken by Klostermann in his *Der Pentateuch*, pp. 9, 10, etc. Klostermann takes it to be one of the most conspicuous proofs of the good taste and feeling for the natural in Wellhausen that he has come to see that the narrative of Q [= P], as criticism separates it out, has no independent subsistence, and is only to be explained by reference to the Jehovistic narration, and that the part of Q left out by R [the redactor], and compensated for by an element from JE, is parallel to the latter, and presumably not much different from it. He regrets that Wellhausen has not advanced to the point of recognising in this sharply-defined Q, whose narrative is framed with reference to JE, and enclasps this element as its inner content, the everywhere sought for but nowhere found redactor himself.

NOTE B.—P. 364

COLENSO'S NUMERICAL OBJECTIONS

THE following are a few specimens of the kind of reasoning extolled by Kuenen and others as irrefragable. The instances are those alluded to in the text :—

First, on the assembling at the tabernacle : the width of the tabernacle being 10 cubits or 18 ft., then, "allowing 2 ft. in width for each full-grown man, 9 men could just have stood in front of it . . . allowing 18 inches between each rank of 9 men," they would have reached "for a distance of more than 100,000 ft.—in fact nearly 20 *miles*! or if we reckon the old men, women, and children, for a distance of more than 60 *miles*" (*Pent.*, People's edit. pp. 30–31. Cf. Pt. i. p. 33).

On the priest's duties: "In fact, we have to imagine the priest having himself to carry, *on his back on foot,* from St. Paul's to the outskirts of the metropolis, 'the skin, and flesh, and head, and legs, and inwards, and dung,' even the whole bullock" (*Pent.* Pt. i. p. 40). This absurd assertion is slightly toned down in the People's edition (p. 33), though still with a clinging to the idea that the priest did all the menial duties himself.

On the sacrifices after childbirth in the wilderness: "Looking at the directions in Lev. i., iv., we can scarcely allow less than 5 *minutes* for each sacrifice; so that these sacrifices alone [250 burnt offerings and 250 sin offerings *per diem*], if offered separately, would have taken 2,500 minutes, or nearly 42 hours, and could not have been offered in a single day of 12 hours, though each of the 3 priests had been employed in the one sole incessant labour of offering them, without a moment's rest or intermission" (*Pent.* Pt. i. pp. 123–4). The truth is, that, supposing the whole 500 pigeons to have been obtainable, and to have been punctiliously offered, the whole work could have been done in a couple of hours! As, however, we read that the rite of circumcision was suspended in the wilderness (Josh. v. 5)—a statement which, at all events, is part of "the story"—it follows that the sacrifices in question, which are prescribed to be offered 33 days after circumcision, were not offered at all!

NOTE C.—P. 370

CHRIST'S TESTIMONY TO THE OLD TESTAMENT

WE have not in this argument sought unduly to press our Lord's testimony, for we allow that His words may fairly be in part explained by His acceptance of current views of authorship, which it was no part of His mission to pronounce upon. We do not, by quoting Homer or Shakespeare under these names, pronounce a judgment on the literary questions involved in the ascription of certain poems or plays to these persons as their authors. Our Lord naturally referred to the books He was citing as "Moses" or "David," or "Isaiah," and no more thought of giving an authoritative judgment on the history or mode of origin of these books, than He had it in view to settle questions of modern science as to the motions of the heavenly bodies, the age of the earth, or the evolution of species. But it remains the fact that our Lord *did* constantly assume the *Mosaicity* of the books of the law He quoted; based on the reality of the revelation they contained; knew in the strength of His divine and human consciousness that God's word was conveyed to men through them; had even, if the narrative of the Transfiguration is to be believed, supersensible communion with Moses and Elias themselves. While refusing to be "a judge and a divider" in questions of merely literary interest, He would, we may believe, have pronounced a very emphatic judgment on some of the modern theories of Scripture, had these been brought before Him.

NOTE D.—P. 370

THE SAMARITAN PENTATEUCH

THE Samaritan Pentateuch, written in old Hebrew characters, after being long lost to view, was brought to light again in the beginning of the seventeenth century, since which time other MSS. have been acquired. Various views have been taken of its origin; but that which has most probability, and seems now generally accepted, connects it with the expulsion by Nehemiah (chap. xiii. 28 ff.) of one of the sons of Joiada, son of Eliashib, the high priest, because he had allied himself in marriage with Sanballat, the Horonite. Josephus (*Ant.* xi. 7. 8) confuses the chronology of this incident, and connects it with the founding of the temple on Mount Gerizim, which he places a hundred years later, in the time of Alexander the Great. The value of the Samaritan text was at first greatly exaggerated; latterly, especially since the exhaustive examination of Gesenius, it has lost nearly all credit in comparison with the Hebrew. Only four readings were thought by Gesenius to be preferable to the Hebrew (Gen. iv. 8; xxii. 13; xlix. 14; xiv. 14), and even these are now rejected by most. On age and origin, see the discussions in Hengstenberg, *Pentateuch*, i. pp. 69 ff.; a lucid examination in Bleek, *Introd.* i. pp. 366 ff.; Ryle, *O.T. Canon*, pp. 91 ff.; and on the question of text, and generally, the valuable article by Em. Deutsch in Smith's *Dict. of Bible*, iii pp. 1106 ff.; Bleek, ii. pp. 371, 391 ff.; W. R. Smith, *O.T. in J. C.*, pp. 61–62, etc.

NOTE E.—P. 375

EARLY HEBREW WRITING

THE square Hebrew character (gradually introduced after the exile) was preceded by the Phœnician, the origin and early history of which is obscure. The oldest known example of this writing is Mesha's inscription on the Moabite Stone (c. 850); the oldest example in Hebrew is the Siloam inscription (reign of Hezekiah). (Cf. Driver on "Early History of the Hebrew Alphabet" in *Text of Samuel*, pp. 11 ff.) A few old seals (perhaps eighth century) have inscriptions in this character, and jar-handles found at Gezer (after Solomon) bear the words "To the king, Hebron" (or other place). It is thought by some that the use of this character by the Hebrews, or in Canaan generally, probably does not date much before 1000 B.C. Previous to that time, it is supposed, the script in use was the cuneiform. The Tel el-Amarna letters (c. 1400) are written in cuneiform, and cuneiform tablets have been discovered at Gezer and Lachish. Professor Paton, Director of the American School of Oriental Research in Palestine, says : "There is no archæological evidence that the ancient Babylonian cuneiform was displaced by the so-called Phœnician character before this date " (*Hom. Rev.*, Dec. 1904, p. 426; so Conder, *The First Bible*, p. 75). This, however, is an inference from our ignorance, and seems unlikely. The character on Mesha's Stone must have been long in use, and could not be unknown to the Hebrews. Something depends on the origin of the Phœnician character itself. Doubt is now cast on its derivation from Egypt (Taylor's theory), and connections are being sought with early Minæan (S. Arabic), Hittite, and other characters. Much is conjectural, but evidence seems accumulating that an old closely-related alphabet was in use in very early times and was probably known to the Israelites (cf. Hommel, *Ancient Heb. Trad.* pp. 77 ff., 276–7 ; Sayce, *Higher Crit.* pp. 39–44). Further discoveries are no doubt yet in store for the explorer. In pre-Mosaic times the Babylonian cuneiform and Egyptian hieroglyphic (while in Egypt) were the likeliest scripts to be used, and cuneiform tablet-writing probably in some measure continued after the settlement in Canaan. We may assume that an alphabetic character was in use in Israel from the dawn of literature. On connection of early Hebrew with old Arabic, cf. Margoliouth, art. "Language of O.T.," in Hastings' *Dict. of Bible*, iii. pp. 26 ff.

NOTE F.—P. 375

HYPOTHESES IN CRITICISM

WHEN it is urged that the assumption of early documentary sources in Israel is a "mere hypothesis," we have to ask—What is the current critical view itself but a congeries of hypotheses, many of them of the most doubtful character? What, *e.g.*, but hypothesis—if not *mere* hypothesis—are the assumed J and E writers, or schools of writers, of the ninth, eighth, and seventh centuries B.C. and later; or the prolific P school of writers in the exile; or the numerous hypothetical redactors and interpolators of the text; or the Judæan and Ephraimitic localisation of J and E, etc.? What but hypotheses are such statements, with which critical writings abound, as that "the narrative of Abraham and Amraphel in Gen. xiv. may be partly based on information derived from Babylon, possibly by Jews of the captivity"; or, "we may naturally suppose that the stories [connected with the Israelitish sanctuaries] were preserved at these places, and that the authors of the Primitive and Elohistic documents derived them from the priests, just as Herodotus gathered information from the priests in Egypt and Babylon"; or that "it is probable that the Israelites might borrow or adopt traditions of their other neighbours, *e.g.*, the Phœnicians, Philistines, Ammon, Moab, and Edom"; or that the stories in Genesis may represent those "told long ago round the camp-fires of the wandering tribes by mothers to their children, and repeated by maidens at the well, by the guests at rustic merry-makings, and in the evening gatherings of the peasants when the day's work was done" (Bennett, *Genesis*, pp. 18–21). We would only ask—Do such casually collected stories yield the *kind* of history we have in the Book of Genesis? Why may we not in turn "suppose," with far greater probability, that we have here carefully transmitted traditions of real persons and events, and that these began to be written down in very early times—*e.g.*, in Egypt under Joseph? There are as many and good grounds for the one class of statements as for the other.

NOTE G.—P. 376

THE IDEA OF "CO-OPERATION" IN CRITICAL THEORY

IT deserves remark how the critical theory itself approximates to the idea of "co-operation" in its view of the production of the Levitical laws, and other parts of the Pentateuch, in the exile and after it, by "schools" of writers working more or less contemporaneously. Plainly the more its Js and Ps and Rs are brought down into exilian and post-exilian times, the nearer it comes to a view of joint-production by minds animated by the same spirit, and governed by one set of ideas (cf. p. 375). Dillmann comes even nearer in his view of the "simultaneous working up of the documents of the Pentateuch," by a single redactor (*Genesis*, i. pp. 18–21). "It seems," he says, "if one takes Genesis into consideration by itself, that a simultaneous working together of the three documents is not excluded, but rather recommended" (p. 21). Principal Cave also has interestingly shown how the radical hypothesis of Vernes, and others of the extremer school, works round to a practical contemporaneousness of authorship (*Inspiration of O.T.*, pp. 173–5).

NOTE H.—P. 377

STATE OF THE HEBREW TEXT

THAT there is corruption in the Hebrew text, all existing MSS. of which are understood to go back to a single archetype (possibly of the first century A.D. ; cf. Driver, *Text of Samuel*, pp. xxxvii ff. ; Swete, *Introd. to O.T. Greek*, p. 319), every scholar is aware, and criticism is justified in applying its best skill, with the aid of versions, etc., to remove its defects.   But the statements made as to the freedoms taken with the text in earlier times are sometimes greatly exaggerated. (Cf. W. R. Smith, *O.T. in J. C.*, pp. 90 ff. ; above all, Cheyne.)   Josephus and Philo testify to the jealous care with which the Scriptures, specially the law of Moses, was regarded, and their testimony carries us back a good way beyond their own day. "So long a period having now elapsed," says the former, "no one has dared either to add or to take away from them, or to change anything" (*C. Apion*, i. 8); and the latter testifies, "they change not even a word of the things written by him [Moses]" (in Euseb. *Prep. Evang.* viii. 6).

But, apart from versions, often helpful, but requiring to be used with caution, we have interesting internal evidence as to the general fidelity with which the text has been preserved, and the degree of corruption or change it has sustained. The purity and beauty of style of the JE narratives in Genesis sufficiently prove that they cannot be seriously corrupted. Specially, however, may appeal be made to the numerous parallel passages, of different types, which furnish us with direct means of comparison. Allowing for obvious mistakes, intentional changes, and, in the case of Chronicles, occasional paraphrase and supplement, we have a large basis of identical matter, showing with what accurate care the text must have been preserved through long periods. We may refer to Ex. xxv.–xxxi., with the parallel recitals of execution of the work in chaps. xxxv.–xxxix. ; the forty or more sections in Chronicles parallel to others in Samuel and Kings (e.g., 1 Sam. xxxi. with 1 Chron. x. 1–12; 2 Sam. vii. with 1 Chron. xvii. ; 1 Kings x. with 2 Chron. ix. 1–12); parallels in Psalms, as Ps. xiv. with Ps. liii. ; Ps. xviii. with 2 Sam. xxii. ; Ps. cv. 1–15 and xcvi., with 1 Chron. xvi. 8–33, etc. When the length of time and difficulties of transcription are considered, the wonder is, in the words of Dr. Driver, "that the text of the Old Testament is as relatively free from corruption as appears to be the case" (*Notes on Text of Samuel*, p. xxxviii). Cf. remarks in Bleek, *Introd.* ii. pp. 391 ff.

As to versions, if there have been times when there has been undervaluation of these, probably the present tendency is to overvaluation of them, especially of the LXX (on which see Swete's *Introduction*), in comparison with the Massoretic text. König has some remarks on this in his art. "Judges" in *Dict. of Bible* (ii. p. 809). In concluding on the condition of the text in Judges, he says (with special reference to Mez on the Bible of Josephus) : "Still this investigation has confirmed the present writer's view that the traditional Massoretic text is the relatively best source from which to ascertain the words of the Old Testament. This judgment is also entirely substantiated by the investigation into the text of Samuel, which Löhr has carried out in the *Kurzgef. Exeg. Handb.* on Samuel, 1898, pp. lxix ff." Cf. his "Introduction," pp. 114–6. (On the Samaritan Pentateuch, see above, p. 524.)

NOTES TO CHAPTER XI

NOTE A.—P. 402

ETHNOLOGICAL RELATIONS IN GEN. X

In addition to the notices in the text, a few words may be said on the ethnological relations of the Canaanites, as indicated in Gen. x. 6, 13–15 ff. All ancient writers trace the Canaanites, including the Phœnicians, to an original seat on the borders of the Persian Gulf. Thence they found their way westward and northward into Palestine. Interesting questions that arise are : (1) When did this emigration (or these emigrations) take place? (2) How are the Canaanites to be classed ethnographically? (1) Biblical and extra-Biblical notices lead us to regard the Phœnician settlements as the oldest (cf. Gen. x. 15: "Canaan begat Sidon his firstborn") Herodotus puts the founding of Tyre about 2300 years before his own time (ii. 14), or about 2750 B.C., and he is probably not much too early. A new note of time is furnished by the excavations at Gezer (see above, p. 500), which show that Gezer was taken possession of in an immigration of Canaanites about 2500 B.C. Probably the settlements in the south were still later. This brings us to a time not much earlier than the Elamitic invasion of Gen. xiv. All the Biblical notices show that before this Palestine was peopled with other tribes, many of whose names are given, and the conquest of whom was not completed till long after (Gen. xiv. 5, 6 ; Deut. ii. 10–12, 20–23). (2) The second question is as to the ethnographical connection. The Phœnicians and the Canaanites generally spoke a Semitic language. This is usually supposed to imply that they were of Semitic origin. The Bible, on the other hand, classes them as Hamites (Gen. ix. 18, 22 ; x. 6). Canaan is said to be the brother of Cush, Mizraim, and Phut (Gen. x. 6). It is interesting to find that recent scholars, on independent grounds, seem to endorse this relationship.

34

Flinders Petrie, *e.g.*, in his *History of Egypt*, derives the dynastic Egyptians from the same region as the Canaanites, *i.e.*, from the neighbourhood of the Persian Gulf. Thence they worked round by Pun or Punt (akin to Ethiopia), at the south end of the Red Sea, into the Nile valley, while another contingent pressed northward into the Delta to Caphtor on the Mediterranean coast, and thence colonised Philistia and Phœnicia. "We see," says Dr. Petrie, "the sense of the kinship stated in the tenth chapter of Genesis between Mizraim (Egypt), Caphtorim (Keft-ur = greater Phœnicia on the Delta coast), and Philistim (or the Phœnicians in Syria)" (*Hist.* i. pp. 12–15). It would be more correct to say that Gen. x. 14 stops the movement with the Philistines (cf. Deut. ii. 23; Jer. xlvii. 4; Amos ix. 7), and connects the Phœnicians (Sidon, ver. 15) with the Canaanite branch, perhaps in a separate immigration by a separate route. The question of language presents less difficulty when it is remembered that the Canaanites came from the Babylonian region, and that the whole west from an early period was saturated with Babylonian influences. They may easily have brought with them a Semitic speech.

NOTE B.—P. 408

COGNATENESS OF BABYLONIAN AND HEBREW TRADITIONS

THE relation of the traditions may be compared with that of cognate branches of the same family of languages, *e.g.*, Latin and Greek.

Kittel says of the conceptions of the Creation and the Flood: "They had long been known to Israel, for the simple reason that they had existed as an immemorial heritage in the East, and the Israelites had imported the substance of them from their ancient home. Everything tends to show that this material, whether found in Babylon or in Israel, is very ancient, and the simplest explanation of its subsequently distinctive forms in both countries is to be found in the assumption that both go back to a common original. . . . The Biblical conception of the universe, which constitutes a part of our faith, and in so far as it does so, is for us not a Babylonian conception, but extremely ancient knowledge, partly the result of experience, partly revealed by God and preserved among His people" (*Bab. Excavs. and the Bible*, pp. 48–50).

Hommel says that with the recognition of the monotheism of Abraham—the "Friend of God," who migrated from the confines of Babylonia in Palestine, "we are put in possession of a new light on *Primitive Biblical History.* . . . I now no longer hesitate to say that the monotheistic concept of the Biblical text, and specially of the 'Priestly Code' (Gen. i.), must, compared with the Babylonian version, be regarded as the original" (*Anc. Heb. Trad.* pp. 308 -10).

"In this," says Oettli, "the possibility is conceded that the Babylonian myth goes back upon a purer original form, and first in the course of centuries became developed into the fantastically variegated form in which we now possess it."—(*Der Kampf um Bibel und Babel*, p. 16).

NOTE C.—P. 413

ALLEGED "MIDRASH" CHARACTER OF GEN. XIV

WELLHAUSEN holds this chapter to be one of the very latest (post-exilian) insertions into the Book of Genesis, and absolutely without historical worth. He refuses even to acknowledge, with Nöldeke, the excellence in style of the narration (*Compos. d. Hex.* pp. 311–3).

Kuenen thinks that in this chapter the redactor "has given us a fragment of a post-exilian version of Abram's life, a *Midrash*, such as the Chronicler had among his sources" (*Hex.* p. 324). He allows, however, that "the story is in its proper place, for it presupposes Lot's separation from Abram, and his settlement in Sodom" (p. 143).

Kautzsch says of this "remarkable" chapter "that it seems to have been taken from a Midrash of the patriarchal history," and regards it as an addition of the last redactor (*Lit. of O.T.*, p. 119).

Cheyne declares his agreement with Wellhausen, Stade, Meyer, Kautzsch, in the view that it is "a post-exilian Midrash" (Oxf. *Hex.* i. p. 168). E. Meyer, quoted by him, thought that the Jew who inserted it "had obtained in Babylon minute information as to the early history of the land" (*Gesch. des Alterthums*, i. p. 166).

Addis asks: "To what does this proof amount? Simply to this, that the writer had acquired some slight knowledge of Babylonian history, as, doubtless, many a Jew in exile did" (*Docs. of Hex.* ii. p. 212).

H. P. Smith speaks of the "desperate attempts" which "have been made of late years to rescue the historicity of this chapter, on the ground of Babylonian literature" (*O.T. Hist.* p. 37).

Yet the "Midrash" thus confidently assumed is nothing but a fiction evolved from the critical imagination. Is it likely that a Jew in Babylon would be found devoting himself to the deciphering of Assyrian cuneiform inscriptions? And where is the proof of his "slight" knowledge?

NOTE D.—P. 418

THE RESURRECTION OF MYTHS

THE effect of discovery has been a wonderful resuscitation of the credit of stories and traditions long regarded as myths. We refer in the text to the discoveries affecting Menes and the early Egyptian dynasties. It has been the same elsewhere. "The spade of Dr. Schliemann and his followers have again brought to light the buried empire of Agamemnon. Our knowledge of the culture and power of the princes of Mycenæ and Tiryns in the heroic age of Greece is no longer dependent on the questionable memory of tradition" (Sayce, *Higher Crit.* p. 18). "I well remember," says Professor Kittel, "in my student days how the scorn of the whole body of the learned, and the ridicule even of the comic papers, was poured on him (Dr. Schliemann) when he came forward to announce his discovery of Priam's city, his palace, and his treasures. For in these days it was an article of belief with scholars that our knowledge of the history of ancient Greece practically began with Herodotus and the time of the Persian wars" (*Babyl. Excavs.* p. 74).

The remarks of the same author on the Cretan excavations are full of interest in this connection. He tells of "a learned friend who was on his way back to Crete, and who had seen there the excavations undertaken by Evans, and was able to boast that he had sat upon the throne and in the palace of King Minos, a monarch well remembered by us all at school, and universally regarded by us as the mere product of a myth" (p. 15). In a note, he adds: "Minos has frequently been regarded as a Cretan god, also a personification of Zeus, or again of the Phœnician domination, and of Baal-Melkart or of Moon-worship, or even as a Sun-god," etc.

Again: "Much that we previously held, and seemed justified in holding, as mythical, is now coming into the light of history; and, side by side with the already mentioned Minos, we have now, through the latest discovered Assyrian inscriptions, come to accept the historical existence of King Midas of Phrygia, of whom we previously knew nothing but the story of his ass's ears, but who is now recognised as an actual and worthy ruler of the eighth century before Christ" (p. 16).   He shows how Midas "continues at the present time to be described as an ancient divinity of the Northern Greeks and Phrygians, more exactly as a 'blessing-scattering nature-god' . . . in the form of an animal. . . . To this ancient demon of vegetable life," etc.

NOTE E.—P. 419

THE IDENTIFICATION OF RAMESES AND PITHOM

THE problems about the city Raamses (Rameses) in Ex. i. 11, are not yet satisfactorily solved. There would seem, in fact, to have been *two* cities of this name — one, of which we have Egyptian accounts, the city of Zoan or Tanis, of the Hyksos, in the Delta, which Rameses II. rebuilt, and called by his name; the other in the neighbourhood of Pithom, in Goshen (cf. Driver, *Authority and Archæology*, p. 55).   Sayce at first (with Brugsch, etc.) identified Rameses with Tanis (*Fresh Light*, p. 65), then distinguished two cities (*Higher Criticism*, p. 239), now again appears to identify the Biblical Raamses with the Egyptian Pi-Ramessu, but disconnects the latter from Tanis ("Raamses" in *Dict. of Bible*, iv. pp. 188–9; *Monument Facts*, p. 90); so Pinches (*O.T. in Light of Hist. Records*, p. 305).   Brugsch, also, after the discovery of Pithom, gave up his earlier view of the site of Rameses.   It still seems to us more probable that the "store city" is to be distinguished from the gay and splendid Pi-Ramessu.   On the possible greater antiquity of the name, see the valuable note in Canon Cook, *Speaker's Com.*, "Exodus," p. 486.

The situation of Pithom is settled by M. Naville's discovery, and inscriptions of Rameses II. show the connection of that Pharaoh with it.   M. Naville, at the same time, "never had the good fortune to find the king's name stamped on any of the bricks" (Report, July 1883).   The evidence, however, is very abundant that Rameses II. habitually erased the names of his predecessors, and substituted his own (cf. Cook, as above, p. 465). Pollard, in his *Land of the Monuments*, gives a striking instance from this very district.   "A large sphinx in black marble is also very interesting, as the name of the king in whose reign it was carved, and whose portrait it most probably bears, has been erased. It belonged, unquestionably, to the period of the Hyksos, or the

Shepherd kings. . . . The only name found on it at present is that of Rameses the Great, who reigned about 1400 B.C. (?). It was—most unfortunately for the records of Egyptian history—the practice of this monarch to cut his name on almost every object that presented itself. This would have been pardonable enough had he allowed all previous names and titles to remain; but he seems to have desired to obliterate all records but those of his own ancestors" (p. 18). In certain inscriptions, however, he effaces even the name of his father (Seti I.), and substitutes his own.

NOTE F.—P. 429

BELSHAZZAR AND BABYLON

VALUABLE confirmatory light is thrown on the Biblical statements about Belshazzar in a full and interesting communication received from Professor R. D. Wilson, of Princeton, after the text of this chapter was printed. Professor Wilson shows that the Aramaic word for "king" is the equivalent of the Assyrio-Babylonian words, *sarru, malku, pahatu, bel pahate,* and *hazannu.* Each of the bearers of these titles would also be a "ruler," and the last three would be called "magnates of the king" (cf. Dan. v. 1.). "Any one of these Assyrian words might be rendered into Hebrew also by 'king.'" He shows how this will explain the title "king" in the cases of both Belshazzar and Darius the Mede. As to Belshazzar's position in Babylon, he remarks, in agreement with the view taken in the text: "From the above account of the course of events it is clear that for the national party that was opposed to Cyrus, the son of the king, *i.e.,* Belshazzar, must have been *de facto* king of the part of Babylon which had not yet surrendered, from the latter part of the fourth month, when his father, or predecessor, Nabonidus, was captured, until the eighth month, when the son of the king was killed in an attack made upon him in the place where he was making his last stand, by Gobryas, the governor of Gutium." Professor Wilson is disposed to identify Gobryas with "Darius the Mede," and furnishes interesting facts on his history, titles, the use of the word "provinces," etc. When published in full, Professor Wilson's researches will be of the greatest value. See his articles on "Royal Titles" in *The Princeton Theological Review,* 1904 (April, July), 1905 (January, April).

NOTES TO CHAPTER XII

NOTE A.—P. 440

CRITICAL ESTIMATE OF DAVID

In the critical view David is not a character to whom psalms can suitably be attributed. Reuss, Kuenen, Wellhausen, Stade, W. R. Smith, Cheyne, etc., agree in this; more mildly Driver.

Thus, *e.g.*, Wellhausen (on Chronicles): "See what Chronicles has made out of David! The founder of the kingdom has become the founder of the temple and of the public worship, the king and hero at the head of his companions has become the singer and master of ceremonies at the head of a swarm of priests and Levites; his clearly-cut figure has become a feeble holy picture, seen through a cloud of incense," etc. (*Hist. of Israel*, p. 182).

In the first edition of his *O.T. in J. C.*, Professor W. R. Smith wrote: "It may appear doubtful whether the oldest story of his life set forth David as a psalmist at all. It is very curious that the Book of Amos (vi. 5) represents David as the chosen model of the dilettanti nobles of Ephraim, who lay stretched on beds of ivory, anointed with the choicest perfumes, and mingling music with their cups in the familiar manner of Oriental luxury" (p. 205). In the second edition, the passage is slightly modified, and more prominence is given to the connection of David with the *music* of the sanctuary—still, however, conceived of as "borrowed from the joyous songs of the vintage," and so as giving "the pattern alike for the melodies of the sanctuary and for the worldly airs of the nobles of Samaria" (pp. 223-4).

Professor H. P. Smith says: "Later times made David a saint after their own ideal, a nursing father of the Old Testament Church, an organiser of the Levitical system, and the author of the Psalter. It is this picture of David which has made the

most difficulty for modern apologists, and which it is impossible
to reconcile with the one we have just considered " (*O.T. Hist.*
p. 155).

Cf. Cheyne, *Origin of Psalter*, pp. 192–4, 211; *Aids to the
Devout Study of Criticism*, pp. 16 ff.

NOTE B.—P. 458

THE UNITY OF SECOND ISAIAH

It would take us too far afield at this stage to discuss the
complicated problems involved in the unity of Isaiah, nor is this
necessary for our purpose. There seems, however, increasing
reason for distrusting the post-exilian origin of at least certain
chapters of the second portion of the book. We have referred as
examples to chaps. lvii., lviii., lxv. The theory that these and
similar chapters are *post*-exilian is not in harmony with the
idolatry and other sins charged upon the people, and with the marks
of Palestinian origin (chap. lvii.). But then the unity of ideas and
style comes in as a reason against separating these chapters too
widely from others, and suggests that, even on critical principles,
a greater portion of Isa. xl.–lxvi. may be pre-exilian than it has of
late been customary to allow. It is certain, at anyrate, that the
dictum of Dr. A. B. Davidson no longer holds good without
qualification : "The chapters Isa. xl.–lxvi. are all pitched in the
tone of the exile" (*O.T. Prophecy*, p. 260). Cf. the discussions
of Cheyne on Isaiah (in *Com.* and in Introduction, 1895), and
Professor G. A. Smith, art. "Isaiah" in *Dict. of Bible*, ii. pp.
493 ff.

NOTE C.—P. 458

THE PROPHECIES OF DANIEL

It is indispensable to the critical view to make the prophecies in
Daniel terminate in the reign of Antiochus Epiphanes, but to
effect this the most violent expedients have to be adopted. This
is specially the case with the prophecies of the four empires
(chaps. ii., vii.), and of the seventy weeks. Dr. Driver says of
the latter : "When it is asked, which of the two interpretations
labours under the most serious objection, it can hardly be denied

that it is the traditional one " (*Daniel,* p. 150). To our mind, *nothing* could exceed the violence to the text on the critical view.

1. It is agreed that the four empires in Nebuchadnezzar's dream in chap. ii. are identical with the four kingdoms symbolised by the four beasts in chap. vii. Further, two of these empires correspond with the ram and he-goat in chap. viii., interpreted of the Medo-Persian and Greek kingdoms. But what *are* the four empires ? The traditional view took them to be the Babylonian, the Medo-Persian, the Grecian, and the Roman. On this view, implied in Josephus (*Ant.* x. 10. 4; 11. 7), and seemingly in Matt. xxiv. 15, the description of the fourth empire—the Roman —is strikingly exact. If, however, on the ground that prophecy cannot reach so far, the Roman empire is omitted, how are the four empires to be made out ? Theories are legion, but everyone seems forced and unnatural, and each refutes the others. Probably the view most favoured is that which makes the Median into a separate kingdom. The order then is — Babylonian, Median, Persian, Greek. But the resort is a desperate one, for, as the critics admit, there never existed a separate Median kingdom, and the Book of Daniel throughout views the Medo-Persian kingdom as one (chaps. vi. 8, 12, 15 ; viii. 20). To make out the theory, a separate kingdom has to be erected out of the two years' reign of the obscure "Darius the Mede," who exercised at best a delegated authority (chap. v. 31 ; ix. 1). If anyone can seriously believe that this brief reign answers to the description of the fierce, devouring bear of Dan. vii. 5—one of the "four great beasts from the sea" (ver. 3)—argument is at an end. The fourth kingdom, on this theory, is the Grecian. We have the Grecian kingdom clearly portrayed in chap. viii. 5 ff., 21 ff., and again the picture of the four horns of the he-goat, succeeding the one great horn, and of the "little horn" (Antiochus) growing out of one of these, is marvellously exact. But the fourth kingdom of the earlier visions, though it also has a "little horn" (growing out of *ten,* chap. vii. 8, 24), of which Antiochus may be viewed as the Old Testament prefiguration, bears little resemblance to the picture of the Grecian—in many respects is entirely diverse from it,—while the third kingdom, symbolised by the leopard, with its four wings and four heads (chap. vii. 6), answers precisely to the latter.

2. The seventy weeks in Dan. ix. present a still more difficult problem—one, indeed, impossible of solution on the assumption that the 490 years which they represent are to run out about 164 B.C. or earlier. It may be assumed as self-evident that the writer means the $7 + 62 + 1$ weeks of his prophecy to make up

the total 70, and that the reckoning cannot begin earlier, though
it may do so later, than the decree of Cyrus in 536 B.C. But
the critical theory has to resort to such makeshifts as making the
7 years at the beginning synchronise with the first part of the
62, and dating the reckoning from Jeremiah's prophecy of the
70 years (606 B.C.), or from later prophecies in 587 B.C. *This*
is "the commandment to restore and build Jerusalem." But
even so the reckoning will not square with the history, and a
serious error in computation has to be assumed. The "Anointed
One" of ver. 25 is different from the "Anointed One" of ver.
26, etc. Much simpler, if predictive prophecy is admitted, is
the view which regards the reckoning as commencing with the
commission of Artaxerxes to Ezra (457 B.C.), which inaugurated
the work of restoration, and was confirmed and extended by the
permission to Nehemiah to build, 13 years later (444 B.C.). What
else than Messianic can be the promises of ver. 24, to which the
seventy weeks are viewed as extending?

On the conflicting views, see at length Pusey's *Daniel*, Lects.
II., III., IV., and Driver's *Daniel*, pp. 94 ff., 143 ff.

NOTE D.—P. 458

KUENEN ON UNFULFILLED PROPHECIES

THE ablest assault on the fulfilment of the prophecies is in the
work mentioned—Kuenen's *Prophets and Prophecy in Israel*.
Giesebrecht, who himself, however, allows that some prophecies
are unfulfilled, subjects Kuenen and his follower Oort to a
severe criticism in his *Die Berufsgabung der Alttest. Propheten* (pp.
1-6), and describes Kuenen's work as a "tendency" production.
In this there is little doubt that he is correct. It might be
shown that the objections taken to the fulfilment of the
prophecies rest (1) on the ignoring of a large mass of clear
and striking fulfilments; (2) in part on the misreading of the
prediction; (3) on claiming that a prophecy is not fulfilled
unless it is fulfilled in its completeness *at once*; (4) on over-
looking the lack of perspective in distant prophecy, and the
conditional element in prophecy, with other peculiarities indicated
in the text. It is interesting that this work of Kuenen's was
ultimately recalled in its English form by Dr. John Muir, who
had been chiefly instrumental in its production, and contributed
a preface to it.

NOTE E.—P. 459

THE DESTRUCTION OF THE CANAANITES

On this subject the words of the late liberal-minded Dr. A. B. Bruce are worth reproducing :—

" Before adverse judgment is pronounced, it is necessary to bear in mind all the Scripture says on the subject. The Scripture representation is to the effect that while God has destined the descendants of Abraham to inherit the land of Canaan, yet He delayed the fulfilment of the promise for this reason, among others, that the old inhabitants might not be dispossessed or destroyed before their wickedness had reached such a pitch that their destruction would be felt to be a just doom. . . . That story in the nineteenth chapter of Genesis explains what is meant by the iniquity of the Amorite. . . . Here is no partiality of a merely national God befriending His worshippers at the expense of others, without regard to justice ; here, rather, is a Power making for righteousness and against iniquity ; yea, a Power acting with a beneficent regard to the good of humanity, burying a putrefying carcase out of sight lest it should taint the air" (*Chief End of Revelation*, pp. 139–41).

Ottley, who quotes part of the above, adds : " After all, the Canaanites were put under the ban, ' not for false belief, but for vile actions' (Westcott), a significant circumstance which plainly implies that in the execution of His righteous purpose Almighty God is guided by one supreme aim, namely, the elevation of human character" (*Aspects of O.T.*, p. 179).

On the general subject of the development of morality, including this particular point, in addition to the authorities already cited, the remarks of Dr. G. T. Ladd, *Doct. of Sac. Scrip.* i. chap. vi., and of Dr. C. A. Briggs, *Introd. to Study of Holy Scrip.*, pp. 641–45, may be compared. The latter writer, however, is all too indiscriminating. Such exaggerations as, *e.g.*, that "there is an entire absence of censure of the sin of falsehood until after the exile," and that even the prophets "seem to know nothing of the sin of speaking lies as such" (p. 308), are beyond the range of comment (cf. above, p. 469). Equally groundless is the assertion that Jephthah's sacrifice of his daughter, and the offering up of children by fire, were acceptable to God—"the training was true and faithful for the time" (p. 642). No "traditional" apologetics is so shocking as this. Not thus is the revelation in which Dr. Briggs believes to be defended.

INDEXES

INDEXES

I

Books and Editions chiefly Referred to

(Unless where otherwise specified, references are to the editions here noted. Where English translations of foreign books exist, references are usually to these.)

ADDIS, W. E. :—
The Documents of the Hexateuch translated and arranged in Chronological Order, with Introduction and Notes, vol. i. 1892; vol. ii. 1898.

BAETHGEN, F. :—
Beiträge zur Semitischen Religionsgeschichte. Der Gott Israel's und Die Götter Der Heiden, 1888.
Die Psalmen, in Nowack's "Handkommentar," 1892.

BAUDISSIN, W. W. Graf. :—
Die Geschichte des Alttest. Priesterthums untersucht, 1889.
Art. "Priests and Levites" in Dict. of Bible (iv.).

BENNETT, W. H. :—
A Primer of the Bible, 1897.
The Book of Joshua, in "Polychrome Bible," 1899.
Genesis, in "Century Bible."
Arts "Moab," "Moses," etc., in Dict. of Bible.

BLEEK, F. :—
An Introduction to the Old Testament, 2nd edit. 1865. E.T., 2 vols. Bohn's Lib., 1875.

BRUCE, A. B. :—
The Chief End of Revelation, 1881.

BRUGSCH, H. K. :—
History of Egypt under the Pharaohs, E.T., 2 vols. 1879.

BUDDE, KARL :—
Religion of Israel to the Exile, 1899.
Das Alte Testament und die Ausgrabungen, 2nd edit. 1903.

BUDGE, E. A. WALLIS :—
A History of Egypt, vols. i., ii. 1902 (8 vols. in all), in "Books on Egypt and Chaldæa."
Egyptian Religion, in do., 2nd edit. 1900.

BUHL, F. :—
Canon and Text of the Old Testament, E.T., 1892.

CARPENTER, J. E. :—
See below, Oxford Hexateuch.

CAVE, A. :—
The Inspiration of the Old Testament Inductively Considered (Congregational Union Lectures), 1888.

CHEYNE, T. K. :—
Founders of Old Testament Criticism, 1893.
The Origin and Religious Contents of the Psalter (Bampton Lectures, 1889), 1891.

Arts. in *Encyc. Biblica* ; *Isaiah* in "Polychrome Bible"; numerous other works.

COLENSO, J. W.:—
The Pentateuch and Book of Joshua Critically Examined, Parts i.-vii. 1862-79.
Same, People's Edition, **Pts. i.-v.** abridged, 1 vol. 1871.

CONDER, C. R.:—
The Bible and the East, 1896, and *The First Bible*, 1902.

CORNILL, C. H.:—
Einleitung in das Alte Testament, 1891.
History of the People of Israel, 1898.

DAVIDSON, A. B.:—
Old Testament Prophecy, **1903.**
The Theology of the Old Testament, in "Inter. Theol. Lib.," 1904.
Biblical and Literary Essays, 1902.
The Book of the Prophet Ezekiel, in "Cambridge Bible" Series, 1892.
Arts. in *Expositor*, and arts. "Angel," "God," "Prophecy," etc., in *Dict. of Bible*.

DE WETTE, W. M. L.:—
Beiträge zur Einleitung in das Alte Testament, 2 vols. 1806-7.
Introduction to the Old Testament, 1817, 3rd edit. E.T. (1843), Bost., 1858.

DELITZSCH, F.:—
New Commentary on Genesis, 2 vols. E.T. 1888.
Biblical Commentary on the Psalms, 4th edit. revised. E.T., 3 vols. 1887-89.
Messianic Prophecies (Lectures), E.T., 1880.
Messianic Prophecies in Historical Succession, E.T., 1891.
Arts. "Pentateuch-kritische Studien," in Luthardt's *Zeitschrift für kirchliche Wissenschaft*, 1880, etc.

DELITZSCH, FRIED.:—
Babel and Bible: a Lecture on the Significance of Assyriological Research for Religion, E.T., 1902 (a large literature growing out of this).

DILLMANN, A.:—'
Commentaries **on the** "Hexateuch," *Die Genesis*, **4th** edit. 1882 ; *Exodus und Leviticus* (on basis of Knobel), 1880 ; *Numeri, Deuteronomium und Josua*, 1886.
Genesis Critically and Exegetically Expounded, E.T. of above, 2 vols. 1897.
Handbuch der Alttestamentlichen Theologie, 1895.
Art. "Chronik" in Herzog's *Realencyc.* (iii.).

DRIVER, S. R.:—
An Introduction to the Literature of the Old Testament, in "Inter. Theol. Lib.," 7th edit. 1898 (1st edit. 1891).
The Book of Genesis, with Introduction and Notes, 1904.
A Critical and Exegetical Commentary on Deuteronomy, in "Inter. Crit. Com." 3rd edit. 1902.
The Book of Daniel, with Introduction and Notes, in "Cambridge Bible" Series, 1900.
Notes on the Hebrew Text of the Books of Samuel, with Introduction, 1890.
Other works, and arts. "Joseph," etc., in *Dict. of Bible*.

DUHM, B.:—
Die Theologie der Propheten, **1875.**

EBERS, G. M.:—
Aegypten und die Bücher Moses, vol. i. 1868.
Art. "Joseph" in Smith's *Dict. of Bible* (2nd edit.).

EWALD, G. H. A.:—
History of Israel, 3rd edit. E.T., 8 vols. vol. i. 1867.
Prophets of the Old Testament, 2nd edit. E.T., 5 vols. vol. i. 1875.

FRIPP, E. T.:—
The Composition of the Book of Genesis, with English Text and Analysis, 1892.

GIESEBRECHT, F.:—
Die Berufsgabung der Alttestamentlichen Propheten, 1897.

II

SCRIPTURE PASSAGES REFERRED TO

(Verses are in parentheses: contiguous verses are sometimes grouped.)

GENESIS.

i.-ii. **(3)**; 197, 227, 236, 337, 342, 346, 403, 406–7.

ii.-iii. 226–7, 347.

ii. (4)-iv. 197, 212, 346, 403–4.

i. 277, 467 (26–7); 347 (31).

ii. 227 (5–21).

iii. 221, 495; 37 (15); 508 (16, 17); 125 (22).

iv. 114, 227 (1); 156 (3, 4); 508 (7); 524 (8); 133 (4, 16); 508 (11–26); 350 (16–24); 399 (16, 17); 223, 227 (25–6).

v. 197, 226, 347; 337 (1); 349 (32).

vi.-ix. 342, 347; vii., viii. 348.

vi. 217 (1–4); 337 (7); 197, 347–8 (5–22); 338 (13, 17).

vii. 112 (2, 8); 197 (11–16); **348–9–50 (1–23).**

viii. 348–50 (1–20); 41, 112, **156** (20, 21).

ix. 337; 197 (1–18); 314 (4); 338, **374** (11, 15); 349, 374 (19, 20); **227**, 495 (26); 350, 508, 529 (18–27).

x. 128, 351; 349 (1); 91 (6, 13 ff.); 351, 400 (6–12); 529–30 (6–15); 231 (16); 232 (18).

xi. 226, 402; 197, 350, 508 **(1–9)**; 351 (27–32); 108 (31).

xii. 197, 239, 361, 413; 33, 37 (3); 108, 351 (4–6); 136, 209, 232, 370 (6); 210 (8); 221, 236, 238 (10–20); 238–9, 351 (13, 17).

xiii. 109, 197; 238 (1); 351 (6, 11, 12); 232, 370 (7); 136 (18).

xiv. 107–8–9, 217, 337, 339, 351, **413**, 531; 370 (5–7); 136, 231 *(13)*; 365 (14); 275 (20).

GENESIS—continued.

xv. 217; 230, 233 (1); 495 (2, 8); 337 (14); 232, 470 (16); 231 (21).

xvi. 344; 352 (1–17); 236 (4–14); 93 (11, 12); 343, 361 (15, 16).

xvii., xviii. 362.

xviii.-xx. 352.

xvii. 107, 197, 337, 341–2; 44, 114, 352 (1); 373 (8–19); 352 (18).

xviii. 362; 136 (1); 130 (14); 37, 86 (18, 19); 41, 44, 125 (25); 504 (26); 31, 32, 495 (27).

xix. 113 (1, 15); 338, 343, 352 (29); 115 (30); 105 (31 ff.).

xx. 197, 212, 217, 219, 236, 238–9, 342, 361; 230 (1); 233 (3); 109, 223, 504 (13); 231 (14, 17); 238–9 (18).

xxi. 197, 217, 361; 219, 252 (1–7); 231, 236–7 (9–21); 233 (12); 113, 234 (17); 124 (22); **136** (25, 30 ff.); 210 (33).

xxii. 140, 210, 220; 233 (1); **113**, 230, 233 (1–20); 524 (13); 37 (18); 210 (19).

xxiii. 109, 197, 336–7, 342, 353.

xxiv.-xxxiv. 495.

xxiv. 227, 353; 495 (3–27); 125 (3); 108 (4, 7, 10); 338 (10); 136 (16); 230 (62).

xxv. 108 (7–10); 197 (7–17); **236** (9); 342 (19, 20, 26).

xxvi. 238; 239 (1); 236, 238 (2–12); 254 (5); 361 (6 ff.); 136, 238 (15, 18, 19); 233 (24); 124 (27, 28); 236 (33); 342 (34, 35).

xxvii. 71, 493; 177 (7); 209 (10 ff.); 93, 209, 370 (40); **108** (43); **342, 353 (46 ff.).**

INDEXES

555

NAHUM.

i. 324 (15).

HABAKKUK.

iii. 449 (19).

ZEPHANIAH.

ii. 34 (11).

HAGGAI.

ii. 34 (6, 7).

ZECHARIAH.

iii. 297 (1); 34 (8).   vi. 34 (12).

MALACHI.

i. 296 (6–14).
iii. 185 (1); 296 (7–15).
iv. 98, 370 (4).

MATTHEW.

v. 3, 38, 477 (17, 18); 470 (43–5).
xv. 3 (3, 6).   xix. 467 (3–9).
xxi. 3 (42).
xxii. 3 (29, 31, 32); 99 (40).
xxiii. 464 (37–8).
xxiv. 459; 536 (15).

LUKE.

i. 77 (1).   iv. 35 (18).
x. 470 (29–37); 304 (32).
xxiv. 3 (24, 27); 3, 449, 481 (44).

JOHN.

i. 304 (19).   x. 3 (35).
xiv. 49 (26).   xx. 49, 51 (31).

ACTS.

iv. 304 (36).   vii. 79 (22).
ix. 459 (27–30).   xxi. 459 (10, 11).

ACTS—continued.

xxvi. 103 (26).
xxvii. 459 (10, 21, 22).

ROMANS.

i. 3 (2).   iii. 472 (6).   v. 457 (20).
xi. 459 (23–4).   xv. 49 (4).

1 CORINTHIANS.

x. 123 (20, 21).   xiii. 140 (3).

2 CORINTHIANS.

iii. 3 (14); 179 (6).   xii. 462 (1–4).

EPHESIANS.

iii. 36 (3, 9).

COLOSSIANS.

i. 36 (26).

2 THESSALONIANS.

ii. 459 (1–10).

HEBREWS.

ix., x. 326.   ix. 35, 305 (7 ff.).
x. 35 (1).   xi. 110 (17–19).

2 TIMOTHY.

iii. 3, 49 (15–17).

1 PETER.

ii. 35 (6).

2 PETER.

i. 3 (21).   iii. 465 (4).

1 JOHN.

v. 51 (20).

REVELATION.

i. 459 (1–3).   ii. 35 (7).
xix. 33 (10).   xxii. 35 (2).

III

NAMES AND SUBJECTS

(Dotted line indicates that intervening pages are included in references.)

WITHDRAWAL BY LIBRARIAN